DE CONTROVERSIIS
CHRISTIANAE FIDEI
ADVERSUS HUIUS TEMPORIS
HAERETICOS

ON THE CONTROVERSIES OF
THE CHRISTIAN FAITH
AGAINST THE HERETICS
OF THIS TIME

ST. ROBERT BELLARMINE
OF THE SOCIETY OF JESUS
DOCTOR OF THE CHURCH

TRANSLATED FROM
THE ORIGINAL LATIN BY

RYAN GRANT

MEDIATRIX PRESS

DE CONTROVERSIIS
TOMUS VI

ON THE SACRAMENTS IN GENERAL
in Two Books

&

ON BAPTISM AND CONFIRMATION

ST. ROBERT BELLARMINE, S.J.

Translated by Ryan Grant

Edited by Frances Thomas

MEDIATRIX PRESS

MMXXI

ISBN: 978-1-953746-81-8

On The Sacraments in General, Baptism and Confirmation is translated from:
Disputationes de Controversiis de Fide Christianae: Adversus Hujus Temporis Haereticos, Prague, 1721, Tomus 3.

© Ryan Grant, 2021
All rights reserved. No reproductions of any part of this work may be made in electronic or physical format except for review in journals, blogs, or classroom use. No part of this work may be placed on archive.org.

Mediatrix Press
607 E 6th Ave.
Post Falls, ID 83854
www.mediatrixpress.com

TABLE OF CONTENTS

Translator's Preface   xiii

ON THE SACRAMENTS IN GENERAL: BOOK I

CHAPTER I
On Errors   3

CHAPTER II
On the Lies and Calumnies of Our Adversaries   6

CHAPTER III
The Lies of Melanchthon   11

CHAPTER IV
The Lies of Calvin   13

CHAPTER V
The Lies of Chemnitz   16

CHAPTER VI
The Lies of Tilman Hesch   19

CHAPTER VII
Whether the Word Sacrament Must be Used   21

CHAPTER VIII
On the Etymology, and Notion of Mysterium and Sacramentum   27

CHAPTER IX
What Is Required to Constitute a Sacrament of the New Law   31

CHAPTER X
Is a Sacrament Able to be Properly Defined?   37

CHAPTER XI
What is the definition of a Sacrament?   40

CHAPTER XII
Whether the Definition of a Sacrament Univocally Agrees with the Sacraments of the Old and New Law.   42

CHAPTER XIII
The Objections of Chemnitz Are Answered   46

CHAPTER XIV
The Definition of the Lutherans Is Refuted   48

CHAPTER XV
The Definitions of the Anabaptists and the Zwinglians Are Refuted   59

CHAPTER XVI
The Definition of Calvin   63

CHAPTER XVII
The Arguments of Our Adversaries Are Refuted   69

CHAPTER XVIII
The Sacraments Are Composed of Things and Words, Namely Matter and Form   75

CHAPTER XIX
The Word with which the Element Makes the Sacrament Is not Proper to a Sermon, but a Consecration   82

CHAPTER XX
Objections Are Answered   93

CHAPTER XXI
The Things and Words of the Sacraments Were Determined in Such a Way That One May Not Add, Subtract or Take Anything Away   100

CHAPTER XXII
On the End and Necessity of the Sacraments   106

CHAPTER XXIII
Christ Alone Is the Author of the Sacraments   113

CHAPTER XXIV
The Ordinary Minister of the Sacraments Is Not Any Baptized Man You Like   116

CHAPTER XXV
The Arguments of Luther Are Answered   123

CHAPTER XXVI
Faith Is Not Required, or the Goodness of the Minister, for the Sacraments to Be Efficacious   129

CHAPTER XXVII
The Intention to Do What the Church Does is Required   137

CHAPTER XXVIII
The Arguments Are Answered   145

BOOK II

CHAPTER I
What Is the State of the Question on the Efficacy of the Sacraments?   155

CHAPTER II
The Teaching of the Heretics on the Efficacy of the Sacraments   164

CHAPTER III
That the Sacraments Confer Grace Ex Opere Operato Is Proven from the
Scriptures   168

CHAPTER IV
The Second Class of Testimonies: The Prophecies of the Prophets   174

CHAPTER V
The Third Class of Arguments: From Councils   178

CHAPTER VI
The Fourth Class of Testimonies: From the Greek Fathers   179

CHAPTER VII
The Same Is Proven from the Latin Fathers   181

CHAPTER VIII
The Sixth Class of Arguments: From Reason   186

CHAPTER IX
Objections Taken from the Scriptures Are Answered   191

CHAPTER X
Objections Taken from the Fathers Are Answered   194

CHAPTER XI
The Objections Taken from Reason Are Answered   198

CHAPTER XII
The Controversy on the Difference between the Sacraments of the Old
Law and the New is Explained   209

CHAPTER XIII
The Teachings of Catholics Are Explained   212

CHAPTER XIV
It Is Proven That No Sacrament of the Law of Nature or of the Written Law Justified Ex Opere Operato   215

CHAPTER XV
The Same Is Proven from the Fathers   221

CHAPTER XVI
The Same Is Proven from Arguments That Have Their Foundation in the Scriptures   225

CHAPTER XVII
We Answer the Objections   228

CHAPTER XVIII
On the Character   240

CHAPTER XIX
The Teaching of Catholics in Regard to the Character   242

CHAPTER XX
The Character Is Proven from the Scriptures   246

CHAPTER XXI
The Character Is Proven from the Fathers   249

CHAPTER XXII
The Character Is Shown from Argumentation   252

CHAPTER XXIII
What the Heretics Suppose about the Number of the Sacraments   259

CHAPTER XXIV
Catholic Truth on the Number of the Seven Sacraments Is Proven from Scripture and the Fathers   263

CHAPTER XXV
That There Are Seven Sacraments Is Proven from Later Councils and Doctors   271

CHAPTER XXVI
The Same Is Proven from Congruous Argumentation   273

CHAPTER XXVII
Objections Are Answered   275

CHAPTER XXVIII
On the Order and Comparison of the Sacraments of the New Law among
Themselves   282

CHAPTER XXIX
On the Name, Definition, and Partition of Ceremonies   285

CHAPTER XXX
On the State of the Case   288

CHAPTER XXXI
The Truth Is Explained and Defended   291

CHAPTER XXXII
The Objections Against Ceremonies Are Answered   302

ON BAPTISM BOOK I

CHAPTER I
On the Name, Definition, and Partition of Baptism.   315

CHAPTER II
On the Matter of Baptism   317

CHAPTER III
On the Form of Baptism   319

CHAPTER IV
On the Necessity and Institution of Baptism   324

CHAPTER V
On the Time in Which Baptism Began to be Necessary   333

CHAPTER VI
On Baptism of Blood and Desire   337

CHAPTER VII
On the Minister of Baptism   345

CHAPTER VIII
On the Baptism of Infants, against the Anabaptists   354

CHAPTER IX
The Objections of the Anabaptists Are Answered   360

CHAPTER X
What Our Adversaries Suppose in Regard to the Faith Which Is Required
in the Baptism of Children   370

CHAPTER XI
It is Declared What Faith Is Required in the Baptism of Infants, and the
Errors of Our Adversaries Are Refuted   374

CHAPTER XII
What Are the True, or False Effects of Baptism   381

CHAPTER XIII
That Baptism Truly Takes Away Sin   382

CHAPTER XIV
That Baptism Does Not Make Men Impeccable   387

CHAPTER XV
Men Are Not Freed from Keeping the Law of God by Baptism   391

CHAPTER XVI
Through Baptism Men Are Not Freed from Obligation to Ecclesiastical
Law   395

CHAPTER XVII
All Vows Are Not Invalidated by Baptism   398

CHAPTER XVIII
Sins Which Are Committed after Baptism Cannot Be Forgiven by the Sole
Memory of Baptism   400

CHAPTER XIX
The Errors in Regard to the Baptism of John   408

CHAPTER XX
The Baptism of John Was Not the Same Sacrament as the Baptism of
Christ   411

CHAPTER XXI
The Baptism of John Did Not Have the Same Force and Efficacy Which
the Baptism of Christ Had   414

CHAPTER XXII
That after the Baptism of John It Was Necessary to Receive the Baptism of Christ   420

CHAPTER XXIII
Objections Are Answered   424

CHAPTER XXIV
On the Ceremonies of Baptism   429

CHAPTER XXV
There are Twelve Ceremonies Before Baptism   431

CHAPTER XXVI
On the Ceremonies Which Accompany Baptism   435

CHAPTER XXVII
On the Ceremonies Which Follow Baptism   437

ON CONFIRMATION, BOOK II

CHAPTER I
On the Errors and Lies in Regard to the Sacrament of Confirmation   439

CHAPTER II
The Sacrament of Confirmation is Proven from Scripture   445

CHAPTER III
The Truth Is Proven from the Testimonies of the Supreme Pontiffs   451

CHAPTER IV
The Truth Is Proven from the Testimonies of Councils   453

CHAPTER V
The Truth Is Proven from the Testimonies of the Greek Fathers   454

CHAPTER VI
The Truth Is Proven from the Testimonies of the Latin Fathers   457

CHAPTER VII
The Answers Which Our Adversaries Give to the Testimonies of the Fathers Are Rebutted, Which Are Also Their Arguments against the Truth   461

CHAPTER VIII
On the Matter of the Sacrament of Confirmation   468

CHAPTER IX
The Objections against the Matter of Confirmation Are Answered   475

CHAPTER X
On the Form of the Sacrament of Confirmation   482

CHAPTER XI
On the Effect of This Sacrament   486

CHAPTER XII
On the Minister of this Sacrament   488

CHAPTER XIII
On the Ceremonies of Confirmation   494

DEDICATIO

Omnibus benefactoribus laboris S. Roberti Bellarmini votum esse, et praesertim Jesse Bonderman, praesidio ejus remoto, hic liber fieri non posset.

Dedicated to all the benefactors of the St. Robert Bellarmine Project, and most especially Jesse Bonderman, without whose assistance this work would not be possible.

TRANSLATOR'S PREFACE

St. Robert Bellarmine's treatises on the Sacraments continue the same apologetic work against early Protestantism as his treatises on the Papacy and the Church. The early Protestant reformers had not only attacked the nature and structure of the Church, and Purgatory, but also the Sacraments themselves. Luther, in his work *On the Babylonian Captivity*, argues that the true Sacraments of the Church are merely Baptism, Eucharist, and Penance (later he changed his mind about Penance), and these were held in captivity to the false Sacraments of the Catholic Church. Luther, his followers, and other Protestants would also attack even the Catholic understanding of Baptism and the Eucharist, and beyond that the notion of a Sacrament itself. Consequently, Bellarmine arranges the treatise on the Sacraments first on the Sacraments in General, to discuss the notion of a Sacrament, that Sacraments confer grace, that there are seven, etc. Then he proceeds to his disputation on the other Sacraments in order.

Since we have given fuller prefaces in those works, we need only add few remarks here. In the treatises on the Papacy and the Church, St. Robert rarely brings in the work of the Scholastics, since the Protestants generally rejected them. In this case, however, as Bellarmine shows, they often misuse the Scholastics or pervert their teaching, and thus Bellarmine felt the need to defend it. Thus, there will be more discussions of scholastic distinctions than in other works, and whenever complicated Latin technical terms appear, we have generally left them unless they have a standard English equivalent, and explained them in a footnote.

We also feel the need to advert the reader to the fact that often times St. Robert will review the opinions of the Protestants at length *before* giving the refutation itself, sometimes a chapter later. Thus, we have added after so many paragraphs which author said what to assist the reader in keeping track of the propositions and refutations.

Additionally, it is beyond our resources at present to go through all the citations of the Fathers and engage in text criticism. Thus, authors such as Pseudo-Dionysius are in this work simple "Dionysius the Areopagate," as it is in the original. Again, if we have noted in other volumes that this or that work is not held to belong to the father whom it is attributed, we have not repeated it. As for Scripture, Bellarmine's text was the vulgate, and one which he had memorized from youth. All translations of Scripture are our own, not that of the Douay, since at times the Douay translators understand a different sense to this or that verse from the sense which Bellarmine understands. Yet, we have endeavored to remain close to the customary rendering in English.

Lastly, the plan of the work follows the canons and decrees of the Council of Trent, so as to defend that Council from the attacks of early Protestants, particularly Calvin, in his work *The Antidote to the Council of Trent*, and Martin Chemnitz in his work *The Examination of the Council of Trent*. All translations come from the Latin editions of those works, and in the case of Chemnitz, the page numbers cited in the work follow the first Latin edition. The same is true of the works of Luther, Zwingli, and others.

I would like to thank, first of all, Mrs. Frances Thomas, who graciously engaged the editing of the work. I need to especially thank Fr. Ripperger, who reviewed my translation of scholastic terms for accuracy. I need to thank Isaac Miller for a small, but no less necessary part contribution, that is rendering the Hebrew for me, and correcting it from the 1721 original print with the correct vowels. Although we are aware that there is an academic standard for how Hebrew is transliterated, we have chosen to transliterate according to pronunciation for the sake of the lay reader.

I would also like to thank Tim Greenwood of Keeping North Coffee in Athol, Idaho, who supplied the necessary ingredients to carry out this work, and again, Mr. Jeff Whitman of Selkirk Abbey Brewery in Post Falls, Idaho, who supplied the necessary ingredients to celebrate its completion. Above all, I would like to thank my wife, whose patient support has made this work possible.

Furthermore, I need to give a special thank you to everyone who has donated to the Bellarmine project on the Mediatrix Press website. These donations, both great and small, have made possible our continuing work to make translations of Bellarmine or others into English.

Post Falls, ID
2021

THE FIRST GENERAL CONTROVERSY

ON THE SACRAMENTS IN GENERAL
Book I

Which Is On the Nature and Causes of the Sacraments

There is a two-part disputation on the Sacraments. First, in general on all things. Then, it must be considered apart on individual things. And the general disputation will have two introductions: one on the errors in regard to the Sacraments; the other on the lies and calumnies of more recent heretics. Then, it will contain six principal controversies: 1) On the name and meaning of a sacrament; 2) On the nature and definition; 3) On the causes, both intrinsic and extrinsic; 4) On the effects, i.e., grace and the character; 5) On the number; 6) On the ceremonies.

Many men have written on this subject, but among the heretics I have particularly seen: Luther, in his work *On the Babylonian Captivity*, and in *The Assertion of the Articles*; Melanchthon in *de Locis* and in the *Apologia for the Augsburg Confession*; John Calvin in the *Institutes*, 4, 14 *seqq.*; Martin Chemnitz in the second volume of his *Examination of the Council of Trent*.

From our side, apart from the Scholastics commenting on book IV of the *Sentences*: Thomas Waldens in Tom. 2; William of Paris in *De Sacramentis*; John Eck in his *Homilies on the Sacraments*; John Fisher in the *Refutatione Articulorum Lutheri*; Cardinal Hosius in the *Confessione Polonica*; Ruyard Tapper in *Explicatione Articulorum Lovaniensium*; Jodocus Tiletanus in *Refutatione Examinis Chemnitii*; William Alanus in his book *de Sacramentis in Genere*; William Lindanus in *Panoplia*, book 4; Pedro del Soto *de Institut. Sacerdotum*.

CHAPTER I
On Errors

THE ANCIENT errors on the Sacraments can be recalled to four headings:

1) Certain men tried to abolish all of the sacraments: they were Archontici, whom Epiphanius calls to mind (*Panarion*, haeresi 40), as well as Theodoret (lib. 1 *On the Fables of the Heretics*, on the Archonticos, and also the Ascodritros, or the Ascodruptias as he calls them). These arose from Peter the Anchorite, a Syrian, and they detested Baptism and the Eucharist, as Epiphanius witnesses. Still, (as Theodoret adds) they constituted all other sensible and bodily signs, and only in recognition of that which is true redemption.

In this regard, the error of the Fraticelli, or the Beguins also pertained, who despised the ecclesiastical sacraments, as Pope John XXII witnesses (*Extrav. Sancta Romana, de religiosis domibus*).

Next from there, the Pauliciani pertain to it, who, as Euthymius witnesses (*Panoplia*, 2 part, tit. 21) abolished all the matter of the sacraments; water, wine, bread, oil, and only used certain words of the sacraments, e.g. they said Baptism is these words, "I am the living water."

2) The second heresy is of those who did not go so far as to detest all of the sacraments, nor abolished them, but deprived them of their virtue and efficacy. These were the Messaliani, who are also called Euchita, from the Greek word for oration. Several write on this heresy: Epiphanius (*Pan.* Haer. 80); Augustine (*haeres* 57); and Theodoret (*de fabulis haeret.* 4); but more profusely, and from their books their decrepit errors, John of Damascus in *de haeres.*, where he witnesses, the dogma of the Messalianorum is that sins are not cleansed by the divine sacraments, but only by prayers, which are rightly founded on them. Therefore, without Baptism, Eucharist, or priesthood they professed absolution, that men can justify themselves by their own prayers, even if they also admitted those Sacraments.

Guido, in his *Summa*, attributed nearly the same heresy to the Armenians, and certain more recent heretics like the Cathars. Accordingly, he says that they deny the Sacraments of the New Law confer grace.

3) The third heresy was of those who abolished some sacraments. Many rejected Baptism, such as those of whom Tertullian calls Gajanus in the beginning of his book on Baptism; likewise the Manicheans, as Augustine witnesses (*haeres.* 46), and the Seleuciani (*ibid*, 59), and others, whom we will discuss later.

Again, certain men rejected the Sacrament of Confirmation, such as Novatian, as Theodoret witnesses (*de Fabulis haeret.* 3).

Others said the Eucharist is not a sacrament. For, Peter of Cluny (*Contra Petrobusianos*) writes that one of the error of the Petrobusians was that the body of Christ, was confected from bread only once, namely on the night on which the Lord was betrayed; and thereafter, it did not nor could not be done again. Euthymius also writes in the *Panoplia* (part. 2 tit. 23), one of the errors of the Bogomils was that the Eucharist is nothing other than the *Our Father*.

Others abolished the Sacrament of Penance, such as Novatian, as Epiphanius (*Pan.* Haeres. 69), and Augustine (*haeres. 38*). Others said the Sacrament of Order is altogether nothing, such as certain followers of Taudemus, as he relates, who supplied the Chronicle of Sigebert, in the year of Christ 1124.

Others detested Extreme Unction, such as the Albigensians, by St. Antoninus' testimony (*Summa Theologicae*, 4 part. tit. 11 c. 8 §5), and later the Flagellantes, as Bernard of Lutzenburg notes in his catalogue of heretics.

Then others abolished Matrimony, such as the Encratiae, as Augustine witnesses (*haeres. 33*), and the Manicheans (*ibid.* 46), and several others.

4) The fourth heresy is of those who did not go so far as to abolish certain Sacraments, but still did not rightly understand or administer them. Among these, were the followers of a certain Marcus, an ancient heretic, who said Baptism must be conferred not in the name of the Trinity, but in the name of the unknown Father; in truth the mother of all; in Jesus, who descended; in the unity and redemption and communion of powers, as Theodoret relates (*de fabulis haereticorum*, 1). Likewise, the Marcionites, who baptized men in the second and third [of these], as Epiphanius relates (*loc. cit.*, haer. 42).

So also many erred in regard to the Eucharist, wishing it to be a Sacrament, but one that does not contain the true body of the Lord, such as certain men who of old were near in time to the Apostles, as Ignatius relates in his epistle to the people of Smyrna, as well as Theodoret (*Dialogue* 3). Thereafter Berengarius held the same thing, as Lanfranc witnesses in his book against Berengarius; later John Wycliffe, as the Council of Constance attests (sess. 8).

Other men erred in regard to Penance, even if they did not abolish it, such as the Audiani, who heard confessions and absolved sins, but did not enjoin a penance, as Theodoret relates (*de fabulis haereticorum*, lib. 4).

Certain men erred in regard to Orders, who also conferred it upon women, such as the Pepuzitae, as Epiphanius witnesses in *haeres*. 49.

These are said generally on the errors of the ancients. We see similar things in our age. For in the first place, there are not lacking those who scorn all sensible and bodily Sacraments; who certainly could be called new Archonici; Frederick Staphylus relates this on the Swenckfeldians, in his book on the *Concord of the disciples of Luther*, and David Chytraeus in the preface of his *Commentary on the Apocalypse*.

Chapter I: On Errors

The other Lutherans, and all Calvinists, although they do not abolish all the Sacraments, they in fact deprive them of their power and efficacy, as formerly the Messialiani did. The former attributed all of these things to oration, the latter to faith, to the extent that the Sacraments are plainly nothing other than empty signs, and those are altogether not necessary. Luther writes in this way in his assertion of the first article, "The heretical, but customary opinion is that the Sacraments of the New Law give grace to those men who do not place an obstacle [to it]. For Scripture says the just man lives by his faith, it does not say he lives by the sacraments." Neither he nor any of the heretics of this time that I know of, dissent from this opinion.

Again, in these times there are not lacking those who abolish some of the Sacraments, although not all of them. For the Swenckfeldians remove all the Sacraments but two, as they receive Baptism and Eucharist; they reject two, Confirmation and Extreme Unction; they receive Matrimony, but not as a sacrament; they dispute among themselves on Penance and Ordination, as we will explain later.

Lastly, there are not lacking those who receive certain Sacraments but mixed with errors, for the Anabaptists receive the Sacrament of Baptism, but for adults, not for infants. Zwinglians receive the Sacrament of the Eucharist, but deny it is the body of Christ. Luther does not deny the Sacrament of Absolution, but does not require or admit either a full confession, or any satisfaction. Nor does he acknowledge a true minister of this Sacrament, as is clear from the *Assertion of the Articles*, articles 5-10. Lastly, they all admit the ordination of ministers, but do not acknowledge a true ministry, nor the true rite of this Sacrament.

So we see all four classes of the heretics, which disturbed the Catholic Church at different times for 1500 years, united together as one in our century against the same Church. But the Catholic triumphed over the ancients under the banner of a certain general. It will also, without a doubt, triumph over the new, seeing that it has same leader, who cannot lose his strength, and he promised with a certain witness he was always going to assist the Church.

CHAPTER II

On the Lies and Calumnies of Our Adversaries

NECESSARILY, we are going to annotate all of the particular lies of the enemies of the Church, because this avails much to tear down their authority, as Luther himself witnesses, who wrote in this way in a book against Hieronymous Emser, "If I should be discovered to have lied, deceived, and crassly in this way, then my whole doctrine, honor and faith, as well as trustworthiness would utterly come to an end; everyone would hold me as a rogue, and an infamous rascal, as they should." Then also, Luther was not ashamed to attribute this very vice to Catholics with an impudent lie, for he writes in this way in his book *Against Cochlaeus*, "But I, plainly, attribute this to the divine counsels, that the Popes and papists have almost no patrons except those who hand down their authority with surprising ignorance, or impudent lies, lest anyone would be more deceived by the Roman abomination. ... Certainly, the lot of the Pope must be deplored, because so many descend into combat protected by their lies." Such words are most suitably applied to Luther himself. As Cochlaeus witnesses (*Actis Lutheri Anni 23*), almost all of the Catholics who wrote against Luther convicted him of many lies. One of whom, named Dietembergius gathered over eighty lies from two books of Luther. Next, in no matter do they harm the Church more than when they persuade the people with many lies that we believe and teach other than what we really believe and teach. Hence, it is a very useful business to detect their lies. Therefore, we will merely annotate some of the more absurd lies on the Sacraments.

1) Luther, in his work *On the Babylonian Captivity*, in his chapter on the Eucharist, lies *firstly* when he says, "I do not devote attention to the Council of Constance, which that ignorant flatterer adduces for his what he has dreamed up. If its authority were valid, why would not Basel also be valid, which had established the opposite, that it was lawful for the Bohemians to take communion under both species?" Now truly, the argument that Constance and Basel oppose each other in regard to Communion under one species is an impudent lie. The Councils of Constance (sess. 13), and Basel (sess. 30), altogether decreed the same thing, namely that the laity are not held by divine law to take the Sacrament under both species, hence the law, or custom of the Church must be preserved. It is not opposed to such decrees that the Council of Basel conceded to the Bohemians the use of each species, provided that they would affirm it was conceded to them by the Church, not that they were held to do so by *divine law*.

Chapter II: The Lies and Calumnies of the Heretics

2) In the same book, he lies *secondly* when he repeats three or four times that St. Thomas is the author of that opinion, which all Catholics hold, that the substance of bread and wine is not in the Sacrament of the altar, but only the accidents, which is a very crass lie. For Innocent III, in chapter 1 of the Lateran Council (that I might pass over more ancient testimonies), defined this very thing in 1215, when St. Thomas was not even born.

3) *Thirdly* he lies in the same book (c. 2 on Baptism), when, speaking about the Scholastics, he says, "These impious men assert that a man ought not be certain on the remission of sins, or the grace of the sacrament, by which impiety they drive the whole world mad." Even Luther himself witnesses that this is a lie, for a little earlier the same man most truly speaks in this way, "Still, they all admit the Sacraments are efficacious signs of grace." Therefore, we do not command men to be uncertain about the grace of the Sacrament when we say they are efficacious signs. We do bid them to be uncertain about *their own disposition*, and hence, concerning the attainment of grace, but this is not to be uncertain about the grace of the Sacraments, since the efficacy of the Sacrament does not depend upon my disposition, but upon the *divine institution*. In the same way that a man who shuts his eyes cannot see the sun, and still, is not on that account uncertain of the efficacy of the sun to bring light. Nor can the Lutherans deny this, for Luther, in his book against the rebaptizers, which he published in 1528, speaks in this way, "Baptism was not founded upon the faith of the one baptizing or the baptized, because both are uncertain in regard to faith, or at least it consists in danger and temptation." In his sermon on Baptism, given in 1535, he says, "That Baptism would be certain for us, God did not found it upon our faith, since it can be uncertain and false, but upon his word and institution." Consequently, we do not disagree with the Lutherans (as Luther lies) that we are uncertain about the grace of the Sacrament while they are not uncertain. Rather, we are uncertain about *the attainment of grace, on account of our indisposition*, while they are not uncertain, by a marvelous temerity, when they affirm without faith that the Sacraments are of no benefit, and at the same time admit that a man is easily deceived when he thinks that he believes, and still really does not believe.

4) The *fourth* lie of Luther (*ibid.*, 2,34) is when he says, "Despise the Master of the Sentences with all of his commentators, who only deal with matter and form of the sacraments, i.e., only their dead and deadly letter when they write best. The rest, the spirit, the life and the use, i.e., the truth of the divine promise and our faith, they completely refrain from mentioning." It is clearly a lie, for St. Peter Lombard disputes many things on the faith of the recipients of the Sacraments, as well as on the right use (4, dist. 4 & 9), and also the Scholastics who comment on that same place. Francis Stancar wrote more truly on the Master of the Sentences, when he

says, "I judge one Peter Lombard to be worth more than a hundred Luthers, two hundred Melanchthons, three hundred Bullingers, four hundred Peter Martyrs, and five hundred Calvins, all of whom, were they to be ground up in a mortar, would not express an ounce of true theology, especially in the article on the Trinity, the Incarnation, the Mediator and the Sacraments."

5) He lies *fifthly* when he speaks this way (*ibid.*), "And hence, they are impelled only to attribute to the Sacraments of the New Law that they established these things to benefit even those who are in mortal sin; nor is faith or grace required, rather, it suffices that a man has not placed an obstacle, i.e., an actual purpose to sin again. ... They say it even benefits the impious and unbelievers, provided they do not place an obstacle, as if incredulity itself were not the most obstinate and inimical obstacle of grace." Not only Luther himself, but his sons and followers repeat this as often as they can. Not only true Lutherans, but even Calvin uses the same words in the *Antidotum*, sess. 7 can. 5 & 6), and they attribute three things to us:

a) One, that we say the Sacraments benefit those who are in mortal sin, which indeed is very true provided the sinners willed to do penance, for Baptism and Absolution were instituted for this purpose, to remit sins. It is certainly a wonder that the Lutherans would attribute this to us as an error, when they themselves would have it that all the Sacraments have the promise of reconciliation, and remission of sins; but we will say more about this matter later. If they speak about impenitent sinners, it is a pure lie to say that Catholics teach the Sacraments benefit sinners; for all Catholics require penance as a disposition to receive grace.

b) Next, they attribute to us that we say grace is not required for this purpose, that the Sacraments would benefit us, which is certainly a manifest lie. If through grace they understand the favor of God, as they ordinarily understand it, all Catholics say justification from sins is given in the Sacraments by the grace of God and the merit of Christ, not on account of the merits of the accidents. Yet, if through grace they understand an inherent quality, whereby we are formally justified, then we affirm this is not required before the reception of some of the Sacraments, such as Baptism, and Penance, which they are also compelled to affirm, who would have it that the Sacraments have the promise of the remission of sins; nevertheless, we say this very thing is infused in the very reception of the Sacrament; hence, it is a mere calumny and lie that Catholics do not require grace for the Sacraments to give benefits.

c) They attribute to us that we say faith is not required, because we do not hold unbelief as an obstacle impeding the Sacrament, in which they also clearly lie. Truly, they are either speaking on the substance of the Sacrament or the fruit of the Sacrament; if on the substance, neither we nor they require faith. All Catholics teach with St. Augustine (*de Baptismo*, 4, 12) that Baptism is true which the heretics receive without true faith.

Chapter II: The Lies and Calumnies of the Heretics

Luther also teaches the same thing in his homilies on Baptism, as well as in his book *Against the Rebaptizers*; even Calvin teaches it (*Instit.* 4, 14 §16). Nevertheless, if we are talking about the fruit of the Sacrament, it is false that Catholics do not hold unbelief as an obstacle. All Catholics necessarily require actual faith in adults, and without this they say no man is justified. See Lombard (4 dist. 4) and St. Thomas (III q. 68 art. 8), and likewise, Canon Law, which Luther burned (*De consecrate.*, dist. 4, for many canons).

The occasion of this fraud was that Catholics do not require that *special* faith in the Sacraments which our adversaries suppose is alone the true justifying faith. Still, to pass over the fact that this is not true faith but a *temerarious* opinion, if the notion that we do not require faith in the Sacraments could truly be attributed to us simply because we do not require that special faith, we could also attribute to our adversaries that they do not require faith in the Sacraments, since they do not require that faith, which we alone teach is the true faith.

Moreover, if we were to argue in all honesty, the questions must be distinguished. It is one thing to ask whether true faith is required in the Sacraments, but another whether *a certain* faith is true. And indeed, we agree in the first question, but disagree in the second.

Again, there is no question regarding infants. This is because for infants, since they have sinned by the will of another and are habitually turned from God, it is enough if they would believe by the will of another, and are converted habitually through the infusion of faith, hope, and charity. This is why Melanchthon (in *Locis*, published in 1541, on the *Use of the Sacraments*) says in regard to adults, it must be understood that they must believe in act.

6) Luther lies *sixthly* in *The Assertion of the Articles*, article 1, where he makes Scotus the author of that opinion, that the Sacraments confer grace to a man who does not place an obstacle, which opinion he calls heretical. But that he is lying is clearly seen in the fact that Innocent III taught the same thing (cap. *Majores, de Baptismo et ejus effectu*), a long time before Scotus was even born. Also St. Augustine (*Epist. 23 ad Bonifacium*) had said that Baptism benefits infants, even if they do not believe in act, for he speaks in this way, "A man who does not believe this, and does not believe it can happen, is certainly an infidel, even if he has the Sacrament of faith; by far it is better that the infant who, even if he does not yet have faith in thought, still does not oppose an obstacle of contrary thought to it, whereby, he faithfully perceives his Sacrament."

7) *Seventhly*, he lies in the same place, when he says that the Scotists do not require faith in the use of the Sacrament, nor a good purpose, or a good motion of heart. John Fisher refuted this lie from the very words of Scotus, who in 4, dist. 4, q. 2, clearly teaches that faith is required, as well as contrition, or at least attrition. See also quest. 5, in the beginning, and in the response *ad ultimum*, likewise in distinction 17, q. 1.

8) His *eighth* lie is in his last *Homily on Baptism*, where he says, "To this point it was the wind of impiety, that they attributed to salt and consecrated water the great power, and at length, the energy of the venerable Sacrament of Baptism, against the word and command." Here, there are two lies:

a) One, that we consecrate salt and water against the command and word of God, for no word or command exists whereby it is forbidden. Why does Luther himself teach the contrary? For in *On the Babylonian Captivity* (on Extreme Unction), he so says, "Therefore, I do not condemn this, our Sacrament of Extreme Unction, but I firmly deny that this is what is prescribed by James the Apostle, since neither the form nor the use nor the virtue, nor its end agrees with ours; nevertheless, we will number it among those Sacraments which we have constituted, such as salt and consecrated water, and aspersion, nor can we deny that any created thing you like may be sanctified by the word of God and prayer, which the Apostle Paul teaches us."

b) The other lie is that we attribute the same force to Holy Water and Baptism; for no Catholic ever taught that; otherwise, we would not have seven Sacraments, but many more. These few from Luther will suffice.

CHAPTER III

The Lies of Melanchthon

FIRSTLY, in the *Augsburg Confession* itself, art. 13, he condemns the Scholastics because they taught faith is not required in the use of the Sacraments. But he explains his mind more profusely and clearly in the *Apologia* of the same article, where he speaks in this way, "Here we must condemn the whole people of the Scholastic doctors, who teach that the Sacraments confer grace *ex opere operato* to one not placing an obstacle, using them without a good motion. This is simply a Jewish opinion, to think that we are justified through ceremonies, without a good motion of the heart, i.e., without faith; and still this impious and superstitious opinion is taught with great authority in the Papist kingdom."

This lie is by far more impudent than the lies of Luther, for Luther does not accuse all the Scholastics, but only the Scotists; Melanchthon, however, condemns "the whole people of the Scholastics." Nay more, he even condemns the whole "Popish kingdom." Moreover, it is a clear lie that is so manifest that it does not need proof. As we said above, all the Scholastics, with Lombard (4 dist. 4) require *actual* faith, which there cannot be without a motion of the heart; and the very same Melanchthon in his *Apologia* for the article on Penance, says that Catholics require contrition, or attrition. And what is contrition or attrition, but a movement of the heart?

2) *Secondly*, also in the *Augsburg Confession* itself, in the article on the Mass, they say, "Our Churches are falsely accused of abolishing the Mass; for we retain the mass and celebrate it with supreme reverence."

We can prove this is a lie from the articles of Smalchald, which are not of lesser authority among Lutherans than the Confession itself; wherefore, they are placed together with it in the book of *Concord*. Therefore, in these articles, we so read, "Moreover, that tail of the dragon [the Mass] gives birth to a multiplicity of abominations, and idolatries. ... The Mass must duly be abrogated." So, if the Mass, as the tail of the dragon, must be abrogated, why do they not abrogate it? Or, if they abrogated it, why would they ask why they are accused of abolishing the Mass? Perhaps, they will say that they abolished the Papist Mass, but retain the Christian, namely the distribution and reception of the Sacrament; for Melanchthon calls this the Mass in the *Apologia*. Now, we do not accuse the Lutherans of abolishing that Mass, namely Communion, but *the true* Mass, i.e., the oblation and the whole canon. Therefore, if through the Mass they understand Communion, it is a lie that they are accused; but if they understand the oblation, it is a

trifle about *ex opere operato* is not only false but is in opposition to the nature of the Sacraments, which God instituted, in order that believers, who are devoid of all good and needy, would bring nothing but beggary. Hence, it follows that in receiving them they do nothing which deserves praise, and that in this action (which in their respect is merely passive), no work can be ascribed to them." By this lie, Calvin witnesses either his ignorance or his malice; for the theologians do not use the term *ex opere operato* for any meritorious work of a man who receives or administers the Sacrament, as Calvin says; for we call that *ex opere operantis*. Moreover, we will speak more about the term *ex opere operato* in Book II, c. 3. It is sufficient to note in this place that to be *ex opere operato* does not depend upon the goodness of the minister, but upon merit.

4) The *fourth* lie (*ibid.*, 17 §43) is where he says in regard to the Sacrament of the Eucharist, that the first to begin using unleavened bread was the Roman Pope Alexander, "The first delighted by unleavened bread, though, by what reasoning I do not see except to drag a new spectacle before the eyes of the people than to establish minds in right religion." This lie is clearly opposed to the Gospel. Matthew (26:17), Mark (14:12), and Luke (22:7) say the Lord's supper was on the day of unleavened bread, hence it was not Pope Alexander, but Christ who was the first to use unleavened bread in the Sacrament.

5) The *fifth* lie (*ibid.*, 19 §12) is where he says, "The fathers, while they speak properly, never recall more than two Sacraments." St. Cyprian (that I might pass over the others) refutes this lie in *Epist.* (2, 1). He would have it that not only Baptism and Eucharist, but even Confirmation is properly a Sacrament, for he speaks this way on Confirmation, "Then, fully sanctified, they can become sons of God if they are born from each Sacrament." St. Augustine (*Contra Litteras Petiliani*, 2, 105) says, "The Sacrament of Chrism is most sacred in the class of visible signs, just as Baptism itself."

6) The *sixth* (*ibid.*) is where Calvin adds on Confirmation itself, "The Fathers speak on the imposition of hands, but do they call it a Sacrament? Augustine clearly affirms it is nothing other than a prayer." The same authors (*loc. cit.*) refute this.

7) The *seventh* (*ibid*. 19, §34), is where he speaks in this way, "Everyone professes matrimony was instituted by God, but in the way it was granted as a Sacrament, no man seems to have done even to the times of Gregory." Yet, St. Augustine, who was almost 200 years older than St. Gregory, (*De Bono Conjugali*, 18) says, "In our marriages the holiness of the Sacrament avails more than the fecundity of the womb." And in *de Nuptiis et Concupiscentia* (1,10), he enumerates Matrimony among the Sacraments three times, as in other places (*passim*).

8) The *eighth* lie is in his *Antidote to the Council* (sess. 7, can. 13), where he says, "All pious men lament, or at least groan, that in Baptism more is made about the chrism, candle, taste of salt, and at length spit than the

Chapter IV: The Lies of Calvin

bath of water in which the completion of Baptism consists." He repeats the same thing in his book on the formula to administer the Sacraments. Here, Calvin endeavors to surpass Luther in lying. For he (as we annotated above in the last lie) only says we make these ceremonies equal to Baptism, but Calvin says we attribute more importance to ceremonies. Truly, Catholics do not hold these ceremonies as more important or equal to Baptism, to such an extent that they call them *preparations* for Baptism; likewise, the ceremonies are *accidental*, if they are conferred with the washing itself, in which the substance of Baptism consists. Lastly, all Catholics affirm that a simple Baptism without the candle, without salt, without oil, and other things suffice for justification; moreover, these ceremonies do not suffice. See Lombard and the other Doctors on the *Sentences* 4, dist. 6.

CHAPTER V

The Lies of Chemnitz

MARTIN Chemnitz repeats many things from the lies of Luther and Calvin, and he adds many of his own. Since it would take too long to relate them all, I will take note of a few of them from the beginning of the second part of his *Examination of the Council of Trent*, where he argues on the Sacraments in general.

1) *Firstly*, in the *Examination* published in 1566, in 8, p. 14, he lies in this way, "If by Matrimony, which Pope Syricius defined that to live according to the flesh cannot please God, how, I ask, through Matrimony does the justice of faith begin, or will be increased, or restored according to their description of a Sacrament placed in the decree?" This lie is taken up from the *First Epistle of Syricius* (7), where that holy Pope meant to show that priests ought to restrain themselves from a wife, he took up for his argument those words of Romans 8:8, "Those who are of the flesh cannot please God." Hence, Chemnitz adduces that Matrimony, in Syricius' mind, is nothing other than life according to the flesh, which cannot please God.

But Chemnitz should have noticed that Syricius does not speak on just and legitimate wedlock, but on the wedlock *of priests*, which is illegitimate, and wedlock in name only. In the same epistle (c. 4), he had already said that legitimate weddings are blessed by priests; and certainly, he did not mean to say that life according to the flesh was blessed by the Church, which cannot please God. Therefore, legitimate spouses can so live that they would please God, and they are said not to be in the flesh, but in the spirit, if they legitimately use their legitimate wife. But priests, to whom marriages are forbidden, cannot marry, or have use of a wife, lest they would displease God and live according to the flesh; and this is what Syricius most truly writes.

2) *Secondly*, he lies (*ibid.*, p. 39) when speaking about the Sacraments of Order and Matrimony, "Although Abbot Richard disputes whether *gratia gratum faciens*[1] is conferred through those rites, nevertheless, the rest acknowledge this cannot stand." This is a most impudent lie, since nearly all theologians say the same thing which Richard says. In this place the testimony of St. Thomas will suffice (III q. 65, a. 1) who teaches and proves

---

1 Translator's note: *Gratia gratum faciens* is a technical term which literally means "grace making one pleasing [to God]," and hence means sanctifying grace. See St. Thomas, III q. 110, a. 5, in the body of the article.

Chapter V: The Lies of Chemnitz

there are seven Sacraments of the New Law, and in response to the last he says, "In each Sacrament the grace of the New Law is infused."

3) The *third* lie is on page 40, where asking why holy water, a blessed rose, a blessed sword and similar things are not Sacraments, he says, "One or another of the Scholastics make some answer, but still they neither obtain it themselves, nor satisfy their readers, except that the ingenuity of Gabriel Biel is proved, who says holy water is not a Sacrament because it lacks a divine institution."

Here there are two lies. *a*) The first is that the Scholastics labored much to show why water, and a rose, and similar things, when they are blessed in the Church are not Sacraments. But the Scholastics treated it so lightly that many do not even touch upon it, as something known per se, while others only explained it in passing. For none of these is an efficacious sign of justifying grace, which is particular in all the Sacraments.

b) The second lie is that Gabriel Biel ingeniously professed that nothing prevents holy water from being a Sacrament except divine institution. This is plainly a lie, because Gabriel (4 dist. 1 q. 1 art. 1) where he argues on the matter, though he says holy water was not instituted by God, but by the Church, and therefore it is not a Sacrament, he does not assert that nothing else is lacking but divine institution; nay more, he clearly points out that many other things are lacking. For, he does not dispute in that place properly on holy water, but explains the definition of a Sacrament. Next, because he had said that divine institution was required for the Sacraments, thence he deduces from the definition that holy water, bathing and all natural signs are excluded. Moreover, just as it is not lawful to gather from this disputation of his that nothing prevents a bath from being a Sacrament except for divine institution, so it is not lawful to gather that nothing is lacking for holy water to be a Sacrament apart from divine institution.

4) *Fourthly*, on pp. 94 & 95, there are as many lies as there are words, "Certain men, such as Alexander of Hales, Thomas, Durandus, etc., felt that a certain supernatural virtue is conferred by word in the external elements of the Sacraments." It would seem that he has not read these authors, in fact, Durandus teaches the contrary, and opposes St. Thomas in 4 dist. 1 q. 4.

5) *Fifthly*, he lies (*ibid.*) when he says, "Moreover, they add to show neither they nor others understand what they say, the *ens incompletum* (the force provided in the Sacraments), which is per se not in some of the ten predicates." Now, that Chemnitz does not understand what the Scholastics said can be easily believed. But that the Scholastics did not understand motion, that many call this the force provided in the Sacraments, that it is an *ens incompletum* (incomplete being), which per se is in no predicate, is a manifest lie. For there is no one with even a modest experience of Physics, or even Logic alone, who does not know that motion is an *ens incompletum*, and does not pertain to any predicate.

6) *Sixthly*, he lies (*ibid.*) when he says that Cyprian supposed the Baptism which was conferred by heretics and wicked ministers was useless. For Cyprian everywhere distinguished bad Catholic ministers from heretics, and affirmed the wicked usefully baptize, while heretics did not. Therefore, Chemnitz badly joins from the opinion of Cyprian the very things that Cyprian himself separated. See Augustine, explaining the opinion of Cyprian (*de Baptismo* 4, 10 & 6, 12), and Cyprian himself (*Epistles to Jubajanus, Pompeius, Stephen and Quirinus*).

7) *Seventhly*, he lies (p. 95) when he says, "But that opinion, which holds grace is essentially contained in the very elements of the Sacraments, just as medicine in a vial, so also is the power of the Sacraments is either an essence or a quality adhering to the corporal elements of the Sacraments: even among the Scholastic writers, this was not proven to all, such as Bonaventure, Richard, etc." Here, Chemnitz puts his ignorance and rashness on display when he rebukes what he does not understand. For, in the first place, he confuses grace with the virtue of the Sacraments, when they are very different things. Grace is the effect of the Sacrament, while the virtue is that through which the Sacrament operates. For this reason, no Catholic denies that grace is contained in the Sacraments, whereas all admit that physical power. Next, no Catholic says grace essentially, i.e., the very essence of grace, adheres in the Sacraments like medicine in a vial; for we all affirm grace adheres in the *soul*, not in the Sacraments. Still, they posit, as we said above, that in the Sacrament, as in a vessel, by taking up the metaphor of a vessel, in the way in which weapons are called the vessels of death, because in them death is contained like an effect in its cause.

8) The *eighth* lie (*ibid.*), is when he says, "There were also those who constituted the power of the Sacraments in the work itself, whereby the Sacraments are either celebrated or received, to the extent that the Sacraments were said to confer grace from the dignity and merit of the work, which it exercises, or the celebrant, or the recipient." This lie is also a witness to Chemnitz's ignorance, although it is not his own, rather he took it up from Calvin (See above in the *third* lie of Calvin). There are a great many others in Chemnitz, but these have only been plucked from the beginning of the book.

CHAPTER VI

The Lies of Tilman Hesch

TILMAN Hesch, who calls himself the bishop of Sambia, wrote a book on six hundred errors of the Popes; that book does not have one grain of salt, for he gathers errors so inconsiderately that they are either pure lies, or the contradictory heresies among all Lutherans.

We will merely, for the sake of example, dissipate *Locus 15*, which is on the Sacraments. The *third* error which he notes is taken from the Roman Catechism in these words, "The virtue, which flows from the passion of Christ, i.e., grace, which he merited for us on the altar of the cross, should flow down to us through the Sacraments, like through a certain bowel movement." Here he perverts the words of the Roman Catechism; accordingly, from "channel" [*alveus*], which is the term used in the Catechism, he made it a bowel movement [*alvum*], to make the teaching of the Catechism foul and ridiculous. Next, the teaching of the Catechism cannot be condemned, lest all the Lutherans would also be condemned. Take the contradictory opinion, which, without a doubt, will be this: Christ on the cross did not merit grace for us, or if he merited it, it still does not flow down to us through the Sacraments as if through a channel. But certainly, all Lutherans condemn this opinion, nay more, by all means they hold that grace from the passion of Christ is offered and applied to us through words and Sacraments. He doesn't relate that they do not call it a channel, for they name it an instrumental cause which is greater than a channel by far. See Chemnitz in 2 part. *Examinis*, p. 87, and Calvin in *Antidoto Concilii*, sess. 7 can. 4.

The *fifth* "error" that Tilman cites that the Sacraments of the Old Law did not impress a character, which is a spiritual sign. Take, therefore, the opposite, namely, the Sacraments of the Old Law impressed a spiritual character, and can you find even one Lutheran that would approve of it? For the Lutherans do not ever give more importance to the Sacraments of the Old Law over the New, although they often equate them; and still, with a supreme consensus they deny the Sacraments of the New Law impress a character. Even Hesch himself denies this (*ibid*. in 7 err.).

The *ninth* error that he cites is that an interior good motion is not required in the one receiving the Sacrament. From there, Hesch attributes the error to Gabriel Biel (4 sent. Dist. 1 q. 3), but the words of Gabriel, which he cites, uncover the fraud. For Gabriel does not say an interior motion is not required, since he clearly requires faith and penance, along with all the other doctors; rather, he says with Scotus that an interior motion is not required which is meritorious of grace *de congruo* or *de condigno*. For Scotus and Gabriel, and many others teach, such interior motions are meritorious *de congruo justificationis*; but they add that if ever these motions were not so perfect that they would merit *de congruo*, nevertheless, it would suffice with the Sacrament for justification.

The *tenth* error is that the Sacraments of the Old Law do not confer grace, either *ex opere operato,* or *ex opere operantis,* or by the manner of merit, even if they are done in faith and charity. Now, take up the contrary proposition, and say the Sacraments of the Old Law confer grace *ex opere operato,* or *ex opere operantis,* or by the manner of merit, and now the whole thing is heretical to all Lutherans. For they all condemn what we say in regard to *ex opere operato* and much more, what we say in regard to *ex opere operantis.* That the Sacraments confer grace *ex opere operantis*, is to confer grace from the dignity and merit of the work, but they acknowledge no work as worthy or meritorious rather, they would have it that all are mortal sins, and especially the same Hesch in the same book (*tit. De Justificatione, de lege, de operibus*).

The *thirteenth* error is taken from the Council of Trent, sess. 7, can. 13, where he says, "they teach without external Papist rites, neither the truth, nor the dignity, nor the efficacy of the Sacraments exist." But this is a most impudent imposture, since the Council taught nothing of the sort. These are the words of the Council, which Hesch posits in the same place, so that he should not only be, but be held as a deceiver, "If anyone says the received and approved rites of the Church customarily applied in the solemn administration of the Sacraments may be either scorned or omitted at the pleasure of the ministers without sin, or can be changed into other new ones by any pastor of the Church, *anathema sit.*

THE FIRST CONTROVERSY

On the Word Sacrament

CHAPTER VII

Whether the Word Sacrament Must be Used

On the word *Sacrament* there are two controversies of the heretics, both among themselves and with us. One, whether this name may be used; the second, what this word *Sacrament* properly means.

In regard to the first question, Martin Luther in the beginning of his new preaching seemed to shudder not a little at this name. For, in his book *On the Babylonian Captivity*, which he published in 1520, in his chapter on Matrimony he says, "Not one place in Sacred Scripture has the word *Sacrament*, in that meaning which we use, but in a contrary meaning. For everywhere it means not a sign of a sacred thing, but a sacred, secret, and hidden thing." Then, in his book *De Abroganda Missa*, which he published in 1521, he says, "A pious and faithful conscience should duly and rightly weep, lest he would call this a sacrifice or believe it to be so, because it is most certain with God and in the Scriptures it is not called a sacrifice. The only thing he should call a sacrifice, is what God for certain calls a sacrifice. What could be a more insane temerity than to put the mouth into heaven in this way, that you would call this a sacrifice and cult of God, which he does not call a sacrifice, and the worship of God?" When Luther affirms the word *Sacrament* is not in Scripture in the sense in which the Church uses the Sacraments, and at the same time affirms it is insane boldness to use terms which God himself does not use in Scripture to signify the things of God, then certainly we gather that the use of this term did not please him.

Moreover, Melanchthon followed Luther in *Locis Communibus*, published in 1521 and 1522. The chapter in which he argues on the Sacraments he titles "On Signs," and in the middle of that chapter he says, "what others call the Sacraments, we call signs." Moreover, such was the lust of these men to make all things new, that they preferred the Greek term, altogether unheard of by the Latins, σφραγίδας (i.e., a seal) in place of Sacrament.

Likewise, Andrew Carlstadt, in his book *On Images and the Sacraments*, professedly followed the same Luther in treating against the word Sacrament.

Hence Zwingli, the father of the Sacramentarians, in his book *de Vera et Falsa Religione*, published in 1525, says he refuses to make much trouble on account of the term; nevertheless, he clearly rebukes it. So he holds in his chapter on the Sacraments, "This term, Sacrament, I especially wish had never been received by the Germans."

So also Calvin (*Instit.* 4, 14 §13) says that he does not contest the word Sacrament, and still, does not obscurely rebuke it, when speaking in this way, "It is abundantly proven that the Fathers, who introduced the name of Sacraments, scarcely regarded what the use of this word was among Latin writers, but embellished it with this new meaning for their convenience, whereby they simply designate sacred signs."

Moreover, when Luther saw that Carlstadt and Zwingli, with whom he had great disagreement, shuddered at the term Sacrament, he changed his mind on the spot and began to approve the word Sacrament. So, he writes in his book *Against the Heavenly Prophets* (part. 2), "Carlstadt says Christ and the Apostles did not call the supper a Sacrament; He would rather have a name from the Bible; God imposes names upon his creatures, but we who are men should not introduce names for divine things. ... Well then, soul-slayer, you and the spirit of sin, we indeed affirm God did not call it a Sacrament, nor did he command it be called a Sacrament, but tell us on the other hand, where he forbade it to be called a Sacrament? Therefore, who gave you the power to forbid what God does not forbid? Is he not a true soul-slayer, who puts himself in place of God over us, and removes our liberty?" He then asserts and proves that it is lawful to use this name, nay more, it is fitting to use it. All of these things are no more opposed to Carlstadt and Zwingli, than against Luther himself, from whom they learned, as we have shown.

Moreover, when Luther changed his mind, so did the rest of the Lutherans. For, in the *Augsburg Confession*, they receive the word Sacrament, and Melanchthon, in *Loci Comm.* published in 1536, titles the chapter *de Sacramentis*, which before he had titled *de Signis*. Brenz also, in the Württemberg Confession (cap. *de Sacramentis*), retains the same name, and at length Chemnitz, in the second part of his *Examination*, not far from the beginning, says that the term is ἄγραφον, i.e., unwritten in Scripture, and nevertheless that it must be retained and preserved. Therefore, the controversy only remains with the Sacramentarians, and the earlier opinion of Luther.

Yet, we can easily prove this term must be taken up and preserved.

1) The *first* argument is that it is found in the Scriptures. Two things must be noted, however, before we explain this argument.

a) It is certainly in the Scriptures but it was not written by the Prophets and Apostles in Latin, rather in either Hebrew or Greek; hence, we do not

Chapter VII: The Term Sacrament

need to prove that the Latin word *Sacramentum* is in the Scriptures, but the Greek word which corresponds to it, namely, μυστήεριον. *Mysterium* for the Greeks is altogether the same word which *Sacramentum* is in Latin. And there is no difference in this; for our adversaries *Sacramentum* and *Mysterium* are the same word, and so, they say each term is ἄγραφον in our meaning.

b) Secondly, the word Sacrament can be proven one way among Catholics and another way among the heretics. For among Catholics, who affirm that Matrimony is a Sacrament properly speaking, we prove the word Sacrament is in the Scriptures, not only *in genere*, but also *in specie*, i.e., to mean those seven things which we properly call Sacraments. For the Apostle says in Ephesians 5:31-32, "For this cause shall a man leave his father and mother, and shall cleave to his wife, and they shall be two in one flesh. This is a great Sacrament [or *Mysterium* as it is in the Greek]; but I speak in Christ and in the church." Here, the Apostle, as the Council of Trent witnesses (sess. 24) calls Matrimony a Sacrament properly speaking, or the union of a man and a woman; for this union is a sign of a sacred and hidden thing, i.e., the union of Christ with the Church. Nor is it opposed that Paul seems to speak on the marriage of Adam and Eve, which certainly was not a Sacrament of the New Law. For Paul, even if he brings the words of Adam, nevertheless, he accommodates them to the wedlock of his time, for what Adam said suits every marriage, namely, "They shall be two in one flesh." Wherefore, Paul does not say this *was* a great Sacrament, but this *is* a great Sacrament, namely, after Christ added the promise of grace to it.

Yet, among the heretics who do not admit Matrimony is a Sacrament properly speaking, we cannot prove from the Scriptures the word Sacrament, as it is the specific and proper term of our Sacraments. For in Scripture, Baptism, Eucharist, Penance, Order or even Confirmation or Extreme Unction, are never called *Mysterium* or *Sacramentum*. Nevertheless, we can show from the Scriptures the word "Sacrament," as it is a *generic and common* name, is certainly sufficient for our seven Sacraments and certain other things namely, to mean a sign of a sacred or secret thing, so we can use that name even from the testimony of the Scriptures. For the generic name truly suits the thing, although it does not agree with that alone.

Therefore, we will show against Luther that name is found in the Scriptures from the prophet Daniel (2:27), where he often calls the statue of Nabuchodonosor a *Mysterium*, or *Sacramentum*, because it was a sign of a hidden thing, i.e., the succession of the four kingdoms and the reign of Christ after them, from which we gather the Hebrew word רָז *razi*, and the Aramaic רָזָא *raza*, not only mean a secret thing, such as in Isaiah 24:16, "My secret to myself," but also *a sign of a secret thing*, even in this passage of Daniel, although in this passage I will not deny that sometimes it means a secret thing, since sometimes the Scripture calls the forgotten dream itself a *Mysterium*, and hence hidden and secret, and sometimes the very meaning of the statue which had appeared in a dream.

We prove the same thing from Apocalypse 17:5 and 7. "And on her forehead a name was written: A mystery [*sacramentum*] ... I will tell you the mystery of the woman." Hence, we have that woman, in the form of a harlot, whom John saw, was a certain *Sacramentum*, i.e., a sign of a hidden thing, namely the Roman Empire, or Antichrist, as we have explained elsewhere. Not the hidden thing itself, but *the woman*, whom he saw, is called a *Mysterium*, and *Sacramentum*, on account of the signification which it contains, as is clear from the name written on the forehead.

Likewise, it is proven from that of 2 Thess. 2:7, "For the mystery of iniquity is already at work." Here, the Apostle calls the mystery of iniquity the persecutions of the primitive Church aroused by the emperors and heretics, because they signified the persecutions that would be aroused by Antichrist in the last days. For Chrysostom, Theophylactus, Ambrose and nearly all others explain the passage in this way.

Next, the same is most efficaciously proven from Ephesians 5:32, "This is a great sacrament." Even if Erasmus, and Calvin contend that the mystery that Paul speaks of is not the union of man and woman, but Christ and the Church, from the fact that the Apostle adds, "but I speak in Christ and in the Church," they are still clearly deceived. Paul does not attribute the word Sacrament to Christ and the Church, but *to the union of man and woman*, which is clear from the relative pronoun *this* [*hoc*]. It refers to what had already been said, namely, "they will be two in one flesh," and also, because the whole argument of the Apostle would be ruined, namely that men ought to love their wives, but he proves it, because that "the two will be in one flesh" is a great Sacrament in Christ and the Church. If this mystery is in the union of Christ and the Church and did not pertain at all to marriage, what I ask, does Paul prove? See the commentary of Jerome, Chrysostom, Oecumenius, and other Fathers on this passage. Thus, the sensible and external union of the man and woman is a Sacrament, i.e., *a sign of a sacred spiritual and hidden thing*, i.e., the union of Christ and the Church. Moreover, Chemnitz was persuaded by these testimonies, and affirmed the term Sacrament as it is generic was written although it was not written as a specific term.

Therefore, it is false what Luther says, that a Sacrament in all of Scripture means a secret thing, but never the sign of a sacred secret thing. What he adds in the same place is no less false, that Catholics, wherever they find the word "Sacrament" in scripture make a sign from it, for we do not say everywhere the word of "Sacrament" means a sign, but only *in certain passages*, whereas in other passages it means a secret thing, such as in Tobit 12:7, "For it is good to hide the secret [*Sacramentum*] of the king," and Ephesians 1:9, "To make known to us the mystery [*sacramentum*] of his will." And in Timothy 3:1, he calls the incarnation the great Sacrament of piety. Nor were the Scholastics ignorant of this, rather more they all

Chapter VII: The Term Sacrament

point out with Lombard these are different receptions of *Sacramentum* according to the Scriptures. See in 4, dist. 1 and St. Thomas, III q. 60, art. 1.

If *Sacramentum* derives from *sacrando* and *initiando* (which pleases Zwingli, as we will discuss later), the Hebrew term in the Old Testament Scripture corresponding to our Latin term is מִלּוּא (*milva*), or מִלּוּאָה (*miluah*), i.e., a rite of consecration (Exodus 28:20; Leviticus 8:22, and other places).

2) The *second* argument is taken from the Fathers. The most ancient Fathers use this term to signify Baptism, Eucharist, and other sacred symbols of that kind. Tertullian, the most ancient of the Latins, in his book *De Praescriptionibus* (cap. 16), says, "The devil imitated the very matter of the divine Sacraments in the mysteries of idols; he baptized and he signed certain of his soldiers on the forehead, etc." (See also *in Marcion* 1). St. Cyprian (*epist.* 2, 1 on Baptism on Confirmation), says, "If they are born in both Sacraments." To Caecilius (*epist.* 2, 3), he says, "By which Sacrament our people are shown to be united." And to Magnus (*Epist.* 4, 7), "The contagion of sin is not in the salutary Sacrament in the way that the filth of skin and body are washed in a carnal and worldly bath." Others use the same term (Lactantius 4, 17; Hilary *on Psalm 121*; Jerome *on Ezekiel* 44 & *Malach.* 1; Augustine *Epistl.* 118 & *Doct. Chr.* 2,3; and at length all later writers).

We gather from the teachings of the Fathers that this term is most ancient, and hence must be retained even if it is not found in the Scriptures. In the same way, we retain many other names which are not in the Scriptures, such as: Trinity, consubstantial person, etc. The freedom to confect new terminology in the Church is most perilous, since little by little new things will descend from new terms, seeing that everyone will be allowed to fashion names in divine matters. For this reason, St. Paul forbids profane novelties of speech in 1 Timothy 6:20, as well as St. Augustine in *City of God* (10, 23), "The philosophers speak with free terminology, and in very difficult matters they are not afraid to give offense to religious ears; but we are bound to speak according to a certain rule, lest freedom of speech beget impiety of opinion about the matters themselves of which we speak."

Again, we gather, both from the Scriptures and the Fathers we have cited, that Chemnitz says false and contradictory things on this term. For on p. 28 he argues, "First, Augustine almost began to extend the term 'Sacrament' in this matter, and took it up more broadly than antiquity had done. And in his *Epistle* 5 to Marcellinus speaking on signs, he says, 'When such things pertain to divine matters, they are called Sacraments.' Thus, for Augustine, for something to be called a Sacrament, it is enough for it to be a sign of some divine or sacred thing." It is false that Augustine was the first to extend this term to sacred signs other than Baptism and Eucharist. It is clear from all the Scriptures that have been cited, as well as from Tertullian, Cyprian, and Lactantius (*loc. cit.*) and besides, it is clear from Chemnitz himself, who a little earlier (*ibid.*, p. 22) said, "The union of man and woman in wedlock is the Sacrament of the union of Christ and the Church, according to Ephesians 5:32. ... The Fathers call Sacraments all the figures and allegories signifying something. Tertullian (*Contra Marcionem* 5), when he speaks about the two sons of Abraham, names the Sacraments of figures and allegories of the Sacraments. Against the Jews he names the Sacrament of wood, disputing on the axe of Elisha and on the wood of Adam." Did anyone notice how consistent he is when he makes Augustine the author of this thing, which is found in Tertullian and other ancient Fathers, as well in the Apostle Paul himself?

Lastly, the fact that all vernacular languages in the Latin Church retain this term, namely Italian, French, Spanish, German and others, is an argument that this term Sacrament was always held as venerable in the Church. But this is enough for the first question.

CHAPTER VIII

On the Etymology, and Notion of Mysterium and Sacramentum

SINCE it is certain that the Hebrew and Greek terms were earlier than the Latin *Sacramentum*, and the Latin Fathers meant to express nothing else by the word "Sacrament" than what the Hebrews and Greeks expressed through their terms. First, we will speak about the Hebrew, and then on the Greek, and lastly on the Latin terms.

Hebrew has three terms whereby they customarily mean the Sacraments. 1) *First*, all of the ceremonies, among which the Sacraments are numbered, they call קִים (*chukkim*), or חֻקָּה (*chukah*), as is clear from Exodus 28:43 and elsewhere, but this term does not so much mean a ceremony itself, as it means the ceremonial law. For חָקַק (*chakak*) means to establish, and מְחוֹקֵק (*mechokek*), a legislator. This is why in the New Testament the ceremonies of the Jews are called laws, such as in Matthew 11:13, "The law and the Prophets even to John," i.e., those figures of ceremonies and prophecies of the Prophets, even to John. In Gal. 5:3, "I testify again to every man circumcising himself, that he is a debtor to do the whole law," i.e., those who admit circumcision, should by the same law, admit all the ceremonies.

2) Another term is מִלּוּא (*millua*), מִלֻּאִים (*milluim*), and מִלּוּאָה (*miluah*), which means consecration or initiation, and is found in Exodus 28:20, and Leviticus 8:22, where it is a question on the consecration of a priest. This term, however, is deduced from the verb מָלְא (*mela*), which means "to fulfill" and "to complete," because the recipient of the Sacrament is completed, so that he is suitable to carry out a sacred function.

3) The *third* term is רָז (*raz*), and רָזָא (*raza*), which is more in use in Aramaic than in Hebrew. For this reason, the Jews have not yet discovered its true root, but as we said above, it is gathered clearly enough from Daniel 2:28 that this term means both a secret thing itself and also a sign of a secret thing.

Moreover, Clement of Alexandria, when explaining the etymology of *mysterium* in his oration *ad Gentes*, which Eusebius also mentions (*De Praeparatione Evangelica*, 2, 5), says μυστήριον derives from μύσος, which is "crime," and means "wickedness." Domingo del Soto finds fault with this etymology in 4 dist. 1 q. 1 art. 1, that μῖσος, with the change of one iota, means crime and hatred, but μυστήρειον is written with an upsilon (υ). Still, it is not useful for a Latin to contend with very grave authors, as well as the Greeks, on the etymology of a Greek term. For, even if μῖσος is "hatred," nevertheless, μύσος properly means "wickedness." Hence, Clement, deduced μυστήριον from μύσου not from μίσου, although some Latin codices of Eusebius do this on account of an error of copyists. Besides, Clement did not mean to explain the proper and germane etymology in that place, but makes his purpose a certain less proper etymology, though very apt to mock the sacred rites of the Gentiles, which he also did. Therefore, seeing that he meant to mock those sacred rites, he said they should either be called μυστήερια ἀπὸ τοῦ μύσους, which is that they are wicked and must be cursed, or they should be called μυστήρεια, like μυθήρια (i.e., legendary).

Others deduce μυστήριον from the verb μύω, which is "I close," and στόμα, which is "mouth," in other words, the Mysteries should be honored in silence. Otherwise, from μύσειν and τηρεῖν, i.e., "to hide" and "to preserve," because sacred things should be preserved secretly.

It can also fittingly be deduced from μυέω μυήσω, which is "I begin," or "I imbue with sacred things," from where μύστης is an overseer of sacred rites who initiates others.

Moreover, there are three meanings of this term. The *first*, and most particular, is that *Mysterium* is said to be those ceremonies whereby men are initiated in sacred rites. For this reason, Cicero (*de Legibus*, 2) calls them "beginnings" [*initia*], and St. Ambrose wrote a book on these, *On those who are initiated in the Mysteries*. And this meaning corresponds to the etymology which we placed from the verb μυέω, and to this term in this meaning the Hebrew term מִלּוּאָה (*milluah*) corresponds, that is "a consecration." Because the mysteries were celebrated by the Gentiles at night, and it was fitting for them to be secret, from there the term was born.

The *second* meaning is that everything which is hidden and secret is called *Mysterium*, hence, that of the Apostle in 1 Cor. 13:2, "And should I know all mysteries, etc.," Matthew 13:11, "To you it has been given to know the *mysteries* of the kingdom of God," and the Hebrew word רָז (*raz*) corresponds in the prior meaning, or even סוֹד *sod*, i.e., secret, which they use more frequently.

The *third* meaning is begotten from the second, whereby *Mysterium* is said to be every outward sign of a secret and hidden thing by which meaning all the figures of the Old Testament are said to be mysteries, and even the parables and similitudes which are found either in the Gospel or in the Apocalypse, such as the testimonies that were brought above show. And רָז (*raz*) corresponds to this the term in the second meaning.

The etymology of *Sacramentum* has been well-known for a long time. It is said to be derived from *Sacer*, but there are many meanings. The *first*, is that *Sacramentum* is called the pledge placed by those litigating in a sacred place. Varro (*de Lingua Latina* 5,180), writes that it was the custom among the Romans that when two were litigating, one who affirmed and

Chapter VIII: Mysterium and Sacramentum

the other who denied, they would deposit 500 bronze coins in a sacred place before the priest; when the suit was finished, the one who conquered received his deposit back, while the one who was conquered lost it, and yielded his deposit in money as a penalty for unjust litigation. Therefore, what was deposited was called *Sacramenta*, because it was preserved in a sacred place. This meaning pleased Zwingli above all others (*de Vera et Falsa religione*, c. de Sacramentis), who says "A Sacrament is nothing other than an initiation and a pledge. Just as those who entered into litigation deposited a certain weight of money, so they initiated in Sacraments, they bound and pledged themselves."

The *second* sense is that *Sacramentum* is the same as an oath, which cannot be made except through some sacred thing, since everyone who swears invokes God himself as a witness. Moreover, this is a frequent reception in civil and Canon law, and is found in both Gentile and Christian authors. This sense pleased Calvin (*Inst.* 4, 14 §13). Nevertheless, in this way a Sacrament is not so much an oath whereby a man binds himself to God, as one in which God binds himself to man. For this reason, Nicholas Selnecker (*Pedagogiae*, 2 par. Cap. *de Sacramentis*) says that μυστήρειον comes from μύω, which is "I close," because the Sacraments close and bind the divine promises like seals of God.

The *third* meaning is that *Sacramentum* is the same thing as *Mysterium*, and hence it means those three things which we said were meant by the term *Mysterium*, namely, a secret thing and a sign of secret things, and a thing consecrating as well as initiating.

All of these senses agree with our Sacraments, though what we have named in the last place is the most proper. For that *first* of Varro, and that of Zwingli is not foreign to our Sacraments. For truly, by the Sacraments we bind and pledge ourselves to God; still this sense is not found in the Scriptures, nor is it so proper that it would agree with our Sacraments alone. For there are many other things besides the Sacraments whereby we pledge ourselves to God, such as all vows.

The *second* sense of Calvin also squares with our Sacraments. For in the Sacraments, as we are bound by God to his service, so also he binds himself to our protection in a certain measure. But this is not found in the Scriptures, nor is it proper for our Sacraments, since even without the Sacraments, God customarily binds himself by a simple promise.

The *third* and *fourth* sense, whereby some sacred, hidden thing or a sign of a sacred and secret thing is said to be a Sacrament is found in the Scriptures, as we have already shown, and agrees with our Sacraments. For all of our Sacraments are Sacred things, not only because they are of God, and are hidden, since they are known only among the faithful, but also should not be easily revealed to others, as Dionysius teaches (*de Eccles. Hierarc.*, 1) and Cyril (*In Julianum*, 7), and at length, the other Fathers (*passim*). Lastly, they signify a sacred and hidden thing, namely grace. But these senses are not proper to our Sacraments, since there are a great many other sacred and hidden signs, and those which signify sacred and hidden things, such as nearly all the figures of the Old Testament.

Therefore, the *fifth* sense, whereby a Sacrament means an initiating ceremony and consecrates a man to God, or (which is nearly the same thing) a sign of a sacred thing, not anything you like, but of a sacred thing consecrating and initiating a man, is most proper. For in the first place, it agrees only with the Sacraments, as we will show more profusely later on.

Next, it clearly corresponds to the etymology of *Mysterium* and *Sacramentum*; for *Mysterium* is deduced from μυέω, which is beginning [*initio*], and *Sacramentum* is rightly deduced from consecration. For this reason, St. Augustine (*City of God*, 15, 26) says, "Thence, the Sacraments flow, whereby believers are initiated." There he says they are initiated in the Sacraments of the New Law. And in *Epistle* 23, he says the Sacraments of the New Law consecrate men to God. And Tertullian (*de Praescriptionibus*), meaning to show the extent that the devil labored to imitate God, says, "He imbued, and he promised certain men, who also believed, and were his faithful, the expiation of crimes from washing, and so initiated Mithra." There he addresses the initiating Sacrament of Baptism. And St. Ambrose (*de Mysteriis*), where he treats on the Sacraments of Baptism and Eucharist. Likewise, Lombard (4 dist. 1) and with him a great many doctors, say *Sacramentum* is so called from *sacrandum*. St. Thomas (1. 2 q. 102 art. 5) says, "The Sacraments are properly called those things which are applied to the worshipers of God to a certain consecration, through which they are reckoned in a certain measure to the worship of God."

Lastly, the Sacraments of the Old Law were never called secret in the Scripture of the Old Testament, or the sign of a sacred thing, i.e., סוֹד (*sod*), or רָז (*raz*), rather, they were always called consecrations and initiations, i.e., מִלֻּאִים (*miluim*), or ceremonies, i.e., חֻקִּים (*chukkim*).

THE SECOND CONTROVERSY

On the Definition of a Sacrament

CHAPTER IX

What Is Required to Constitute a Sacrament of the New Law

We have spoken on the term, now we are going to treat on the thing itself. There will be three parts of the disputation on the nature of a Sacrament. Firstly, we will have to explain what is required from the common teaching of all Catholics to constitute a Sacrament of the New Law. Then, we are going to treat on the formal and technical definition of a Sacrament. Lastly, we will examine and refute the various teachings of the heretics, as well as depravations in regard to the nature and definition of the Sacrament.

So, to the *first*, Catholic doctors, although they disagree on certain philosophical and minute matters, such as whether the Sacrament is one per se, or whether it is an *ens rationis*, etc., nevertheless, they wonderfully agree on the Theological argument, while the heretics marvelously disagree among themselves, as we will demonstrate shortly.

Therefore, these things are necessarily required to constitute a Sacrament of the New Law:

1) *First*, that it be a *sign*. A sign, moreover, is defined by St. Augustine (*Doct. Christ.* 2, 1) in this way, "A thing which, apart from the impression it makes upon the senses, causes something else to come into the mind of itself." For this reason, a sign should be some knowable thing; likewise, it should lead into the knowledge of another thing. And because this second, namely to lead into the knowledge of another thing, is chiefly in the sin, as the same Augustine teaches (*ibid.*, 1, 1), therefore, a sign is fitting insofar as it is a sign, more imperfectly than that thing which signifies and greater than that which represents the very thing. This is why a man is not called a sign of his image, although from cognition of a man images are often understood; but on the contrary, the image is said to be a sign of man. Moreover, that a Sacrament is a certain sign is clear from Scripture, since in Genesis 17:11, circumcision is called a sign of the Covenant; in Romans 6:4, Baptism is called a sign of burial and resurrection; in 1 Cor. 11:26, the Eucharist is called the sign of the passion and death of Christ; in Ephes. 5:32, Matrimony is said to be a sign of the union of Christ and the Church. Then

from the Fathers, Dionysius (*Eccl. Hier.* Cap. 1) and other Greek Fathers call the Sacraments σύμβολα, that is, "signs," and St. Augustine, sometimes calls them "little signs" (*de Catc. Rud.*, c. 26), at other times "visible words" (*Contra Faust.* 19, 16).

2) The *second* is, that this is a *sensible* sign; for there are certain invisible signs, such as the character impressed upon the soul. But the visible Sacraments, or the sensible signs, should be absolutely certain. William of Ockham (4 dist. 1) is almost the only the only one who upheld that the Sacraments are sensible signs but does not think it is in regard to essence, because God could institute a Sacrament in a spiritual thing, as if he would set up mental prayer or meditation on the passion of Christ to confer grace *ex opere operato*. But Ockham is deceived, because that prayer or meditation would indeed have the effect of a Sacrament, but would not be a Sacrament. For a Sacrament is intrinsically and essentially a ceremony of religion; moreover, a ceremony is an extrinsic act. For this reason, the Fathers (*passim*) teach that the Sacraments are certain vestiges and guides to spiritual and invisible things, as is clear from Dionysius and Augustine (*loc. cit.*), as well as Chrysostom (*homil.* 83 *in Matth.*).

3) The *third*, is that this sign is *voluntary*, or given, not natural. For certain signs are natural which do not depend on a new institution, but signify by their nature, such as smoke, a sign of burning, and smell, a sign of a thing presenting a smell, and dawn, a sign of the nearby sun; other signs are by the will of the one instituting it, such as names, all words, the banners of soldiers, and all insignia of households. Moreover, St. Augustine teaches the Sacraments are signs of the second kind (*Doct. Christ.* 2, 3 and 3, 9), nor does anyone contradict him. The matter speaks plainly for itself.

4) The *fourth* is that this sign should have with the thing which it signifies some *analogy* and *similitude*. For three kinds of signs are found. Certain ones have such a similitude with the thing signified, that without any institution they signify it naturally, in the way that an image of Christ is a sign of Christ and a footprint pressed in the sand is a sign of a foot.

Certain other kinds have no similitude with the thing signified, and so the whole things depend upon the institution; in this way, words are signs of things, and the sound of a bell a sign to hold an assembly.

At length, certain signs stand in a middle way. For they have some analogy with the thing, but are so indeterminate, and vague that they are more suited to give a signification than to signify in act, unless they were determined by someone; in this way an image of a man not made to the similitude of some particular man signifies nobody in particular, and still it can signify anyone you like if it were determined by a name ascribed to someone, or by adding a garment, or by another sign of a particular man.

All the Sacraments are of this third kind. For they do not signify in act per se, except that they are determined, and nevertheless they are suited to signify if they are determined. It will become clear by reviewing each

Chapter IX: Sacraments of the New Law

one. Outward washing imposes the similitude of internal washing, hence it is suited to that internal washing, if it is applied to a thing. The same in regard to Extreme Unction, the nourishment of the Lord's body, and the same can be said regarding the other Sacraments.

The Sacrament of Penance alone, since it essentially consists only of words, does not seem to have a natural analogy with the thing signified, but has one none the less. For the words, "Ego te absolvo," are the Sacrament insofar as they signify from human institution, i.e., insofar as they are words; but insofar as they are like a certain thing instituted by God to signify and effect justification from sins. Moreover, outward absolution has an analogy which is pronounced by mouth, with internal justification, which God effects. Therefore, absolution signified by words is a Sacrament, not that it is signified by words, but *as it signifies internal absolution itself.*

For this reason, St. Augustine (*epist. 23 ad Bonifacium*) says, "If the Sacraments were not to have a certain similitude to those things, for which they are Sacraments, they would not be Sacraments at all." The Greek Fathers also call the Sacraments ἀντίτυπα, a word that means a thing so similar to another thing, that when it seems to vie with the form, say if an image was depicted so well, it's as if it expresses a living thing, then it doesn't seem like an image, but the thing itself. St. Gregory Nazianzen receives it in this way (2 *Orat. De Pascha*), where he calls the Paschal night, on account of the countless multitude of burning candles with which it was illuminated, the antitype of the heavenly firmament, where infinite lights of stars are seen. So even before Gregory, St. Peter (1 Peter 3:21) calls Baptism our antitype in respect to the ark of Noah, which our translation rightly renders *similis forma* (like a form). Therefore, since the Fathers call the Sacraments ἀντίτυπα of these things, of which they are sacraments, they mean it is nothing other to them than that the Sacraments have a particular similitude with these things of which they are Sacraments.

5) The *fifth* is that this sign represents something *sacred*, not profane. For the Sacraments are ceremonies of religion, for which reason to violate them is unanimously held to be a sacrilege. It is also clear from the very name, as *Sacramentum* derives from *sacrum* (sacred). Next, St. Augustine (*Epist. Ad Marcellinum*) says signs which pertain to divine things are termed *Sacramenta*.

Moreover, that sacred thing, which signifies Sacraments of the New Law, is threefold: *a*) justifying grace, which is shown as the present; *b*) the passion of Christ, which is the cause of grace, and remembered as past; and *c*) eternal life, which is the effect of grace, prefigured as the future. St. Thomas teaches this way (III q. 60 art. 3) as well as all other doctors. On Baptism and Eucharist, the matter is well known. For in Romans 6:3, Paul shows that Baptism is a memorial of the passion when he says, "All we who have been baptized in Christ Jesus have been baptized in his death"; and in verse 7 on the grace of justification, "For he that is dead has been justified from sin"; and in verse 4, "For we are buried together with him by Baptism into death; that as Christ is risen from the dead by the glory of the Father, so we also may waLk. in newness of life"; and 5, "For if we have been planted together in the likeness of his death, we shall be also in the likeness of his resurrection." For equal reasoning on the Eucharist, Luke 22:19, "Do this in my commemoration," i.e., in memory of the passion, for as Paul explains in 1 Cor. 11:26, "As often as we eat this bread ... we announce the death of the Lord." Likewise, on grace, in John 6:58, "Who eats me, he also will live on account of me." On glory in verse 52, "If anyone will eat from this bread, will live forever." So for this reason the Church sings, "O sacred banquet, in which Christ is received, and the memory of his passion renewed; the mind is filled with grace, and we are given a pledge of future glory" (Magnificat for 2nd Vespers of Corpus Christi).

Concerning the other Sacraments it is not as well known, nevertheless it is certain, at least implicitly, to signify all these things, since when they all signify grace, consequently they also signify the beginning and end of the same grace.

Furthermore, we must note in this place, that which is particularly and essentially signified by a Sacrament of the New Law, is only *justifying grace*. For, as we will say below, the Sacraments of the New Law effect what they signify, but they do not effect the passion of Christ, nor eternal life, but only justification; for they presuppose the passion, and they promise eternal life; but they properly produce justification.

Besides, the Sacraments, as we will say below, were instituted to sanctify. But in what we are properly and formally sanctified, is grace: the passion of Christ and eternal life are extrinsic.

Next, the Sacraments properly signify that thing which is expressed by words; however, for the most part, only justification is expressed in the words of the Sacraments. For it means: I wash you, I confirm you, I absolve you, etc. Nor is it opposed that the words of the Eucharist, namely *This is my body*, do not seem to sound out sanctification, but the Lord's body itself. For they signify that thing, as food for souls and spiritual refreshment of mind, which takes place by an internal grace.

And also in this chapter many sacred signs are excluded from the notion of a Sacrament, such as all created things which are signs of the power and wisdom of God, for "The heavens announce God's glory" (Psalm 18[19]:1). Likewise, all sacred images of Christ and the Saints, Scripture, the Sign of the Cross, and other things of this sort, which are indeed sacred signs and of sacred things, but they do not properly signify grace sanctifying souls.

6) The *sixth* is that this sign not only signifies sanctification, but also signifies in such a way that then it is done, *while the Sacrament is administered*. All theologians agree that the Sacraments of the New Law signify sanctification which then takes place, for the words themselves show it, I absolve you, I wash you, etc., and hence, many sacred signs

Chapter IX: Sacraments of the New Law

signifying sanctification are excluded from the notion of a Sacrament. For example, the manna which pleased the Israelites, signified the spiritual refreshment and sweetness which the Eucharist offers; nevertheless, it was not a Sacrament, but a figure of a Sacrament because it signified that refreshment as *future*, not as to be given then. So also, the dove which appeared above Christ in Baptism, was a sign of the sanctity and innocence of Christ, but not of something that then just began or increased; he was already full of grace at the time of the Incarnation.

7) The *seventh*, is in which even all agree, that the Sacraments of the New Law not only signify the sanctification, which then took place, but even what takes place by the force of the Sacrament itself, in such a way that the Sacrament is the instrumental cause of sanctification; this is going to be proved later against the heretics. Hence, the fiery tongues are excluded from the notion of a Sacrament, which appeared over the Apostles on Pentecost; for they signified the most ardent charity, which was so infused upon the Apostles together with wisdom, and distinctly divine eloquence, but they were not a Sacrament, because charity was not infused in them by the force of those tongues. The question only remains, whether grace given by the force of the Sacrament is proper for a Sacrament of the New Law, whether it would suit the Sacraments in general. But we will take up an argument on this later; now it is sufficient enough that all the Doctors agree that the Sacraments of the New Law have this.

However, here we must note that when we said it is in regard to the notion of a Sacrament to signify and effect sanctification, it is understood not on an act, but on the *natural aptitude*. For it can happen that while an infant is baptized, there is no man who would think what the Sacrament signifies, moreover, then it will signify nothing in act, except that of itself it will be suited to signify. It can also happen that the effect of the Sacrament is impeded. For when someone approaches Baptism, or the other Sacraments, with a mind to continue in sin, he is certainly not sanctified in act; still, the Sacrament truly sanctifies, nay more, it can also be said to effect sanctification, because *of itself* it signifies and effects that, whereas it is *per accidens* from the indisposition of the one receiving that the effect would not follow.

8) *Eighth*, and last, is that it pertains to the notion of a Sacrament that a ceremony of religion is *appointed*, and also *solemn* which consecrates a man to God. St. Thomas teaches in this way (I IIæ q. 102 art. 5) and it can easily be proven. For, as St. Augustine teaches (*Contra Faustum* 19, 11; *de Baptismo* 4,22), without the Sacraments there can be no religion; hence, religion would endure as long as the Sacraments endure. This is why in Exodus 12:14 and elsewhere, the Sacraments of that time are said to be preserved by a rite, i.e., they are never going to have an end except in the coming of the Christ, when the Old Testament itself was going to come to an end. So also in 1 Cor. 11:26 Paul speaks on the Eucharist, "As often

as you will eat this bread and drink this chalice, you will announce the death of the Lord, until he comes," i.e., this rite will endure, in which we commemorate the death of the Lord, until the world itself should come to an end, and the Lord would come to judge it. Therefore, the Sacraments are not signs extended for a short period of time, but unique, durable, and solemn ceremonies.

And also, here we understand why the word of Christ to the sinful woman was not a Sacrament, "Your sins are forgiven you" (Luke 7:48), and when he breathed upon the Apostles (John 20:48). For Christ did these things once, but he did not institute a ceremony from it in the Church, and perhaps did not apply the words and the breathing as instruments to sanctification, but only expressed through a bare sign what he willed; perhaps he also applied these, as instruments, as otherwise mud to illumine the blind man, and the imposition of hands to cure the sick, but (as I said) he applied it then because it pleased him to do so, who can use anything you like to do anything, but thence did not institute a ceremony, hence not a Sacrament. Therefore, these are what pertains to the notion of a Sacrament of the New Law.

CHAPTER X

Is a Sacrament Able to Be Properly Defined?

SINCE we have so constituted the matter, we must argue on the formal and technical definition of a Sacrament, and three things must briefly be treated: 1) whether a Sacrament can properly be defined; 2) secondly, which is properly the definition of a Sacrament; 3) whether this would only suit our Sacraments, or every Sacrament in general.

Therefore, the *first* question is whether a Sacrament can truly and properly be defined, or only described in a certain rough manner. The reason for the difficulty is that a Sacrament is a certain thing that has been gathered *per accidens*, since it is constituted from things and words, or it is an *ens rationis*, if it were to be considered formally as a signifying sign by the arbitrary institution. Moreover, only an *ens realis* can be properly defined, as well as those things which are one per se.

Moreover, there are three teachings of the doctors: 1) Some think a Sacrament cannot properly be defined, due to causes we have already spoken about. (Ockham, Major, and Richard commenting in 4 dist. 1. 2) Others would have it that a Sacrament is indeed an *ens rationis*, still it is one per se, hence it can be defined at least imperfectly as Scotus (dist. 1 q. 2) and del Soto (dist. 1 q. 1 art. 2) say. Even if there are many things in the Sacraments, which they signify, nevertheless the signification is one arising from different things, just as one is the figure of a house, although there are many which come together to make a house. 3) Lastly, others would have it that a Sacrament can properly be defined (Martin Ledesma tr. *De Sacramentis in Genere*, q. 1 art. 2).

Briefly, to say what I think, the Sacraments can be considered in two ways. In one way, physically; in the other, morally; inasmuch as a man may in one way be considered as a physical being, and in the other as a political being.

Now, according to the physical consideration, which is not proper for this place, and does it pertain much to Theology, by far I find the first opinion to be the most probable. *a) Firstly*, because not only does the signification, but even the *very sensible thing* pertains to the notion and essence of a Sacrament, which is a certain substance, and with the adjoined signification, it constitutes *a thing per accidens*. For, if the essence of a Sacrament consisted in the signification alone, the thing itself would be nothing sensible, except for the subject of the Sacrament. The Church by far teaches us otherwise, since in the Council of Florence, and in the writings of all the Doctors, it affirms the Sacraments consist of things and words, and the former is the matter, while the latter is the form. How would that which is called the matter and form of a Sacrament not pertain to the essence of a Sacrament?

b) Secondly, a Sacrament, as Sacrament, not only signifies, but also *sanctifies*, as all Catholics teach on the Sacraments of the New Law. But to signify, and to sanctify, are things of different predications, namely of relation and action; therefore, they cannot make one thing per se.

Add that those who posit a certain real and physical quality are necessarily compelled to compose Sacraments as *ens realis* and *ens in ratione*. For the signification of a Sacrament, since it depends upon voluntary institution, cannot be an *ens rationis*. How can one thing, per se, be that to the essence of which an *ens realis* and *ens rationis* pertain?

But if we were to consider a Sacrament *morally*, as it truly ought to be considered by a theologian, it is an *ens reale* and by its mode, one, and also in that manner it can be defined. For among the moral philosophers, kingdom, city, and family are defined, and from all these the passions are proven, although all of them are beings through aggregation, if they would be considered physically; so also theologians define the Church, a Council, a Sacrament, and other things of that sort, although they cannot be defined physically.

Moreover, a Sacrament morally, is one because it is one medium, or instrument to justify men. Even if water and words act and signify, they are very different things in themselves. Nevertheless, as they make one instrument of justification, they are one, and also this one thing is said to be composed from the genus and difference, and again, from the matter and form, on account of the similitude of composite Metaphysics and Physics which it has. For, in composite Metaphysics there are two predicates, one more universal and imperfect, the other less common and more perfect; so also, a Sacrament has two predicates, one more common and less perfect, namely, it is a sign. Every Sacrament is a sign, but not every sign is a Sacrament. The second is less common and more perfect, namely sanctifying instrumentally and through the manner of a ceremony; that agrees with the Sacraments alone. Hence, a sign is on the one hand a genus, sanctifying, on the other, a difference. For equal reasoning, such as in composite Physics, there are two parts, neither of which predicated on the whole, and one is indeterminate, the other determining, the former is the matter, the latter is said to be the form. So also, in the Sacraments, there are things like matter; and words like form; because the thing itself. Water, for the sake of example, is indifferent of itself to signify or even effect many things, but it is determined by words to signify and effect one thing. This is why Augustine (*Tract. 80 in Joan.*) says, "The word is added to the element and this becomes a Sacrament."

So, it is not necessary to discuss this too meticulously, whether the

Chapter X: Can A Sacrament Be Defined?

whole notion and all the properties of the genus and difference, matter and form suit the parts of the Sacrament, because (as we said), a theologian must consider the Sacraments *morally*, not physically.

CHAPTER XI

What Is the Definition of a Sacrament?

THE *second* difficulty is: By what words should the definition of a Sacrament be conceived? There are many definitions among theologians, which we are going to propose and explain briefly. One is: *A sign of a sacred thing.* The other is a little more explicit: *An invisible form of visible grace.*

These definitions are gathered from Augustine, who writes in this way (*City of God* 10,5), "The visible sacrifice is a Sacrament of invisible grace," i.e., *it is a sacred sign,* and they are common among Catholics, as is clear from Hugh of St. Victor (1 part. 9, c. 2), Bernard (*serm. De Coena Domini*), St. Thomas (III q. 60 art. 1 & 2), and Thomas Waldens (t. 2 c. 20). Moreover, if these definitions are accepted, as they sound words absolutely, they are imperfect. There are a great many signs of sacred things or invisible grace than there are Sacraments, but if these were received *as they sound according to the sense and intention of the Church and the Doctors,* they are good and legitimate. Accordingly, by sign, they understand a sensible sign, instituted, practical, bearing a similitude of the thing signified; through that sacred thing they understand justifying grace. Although (if Hugh rightly advises, *loc. cit.*), the one who first said a Sacrament is a sign of a sacred thing does not seem to have meant to define the very thing accurately, as much as he meant to explain *the interpretation of the name.*

Moreover, those who argue too much in favor of defending this definition do not act rightly, especially since St. Augustine (*loc. cit.*) speaks about a Sacrament with such a full meaning that it would also include a sacrifice.

The *third* definition is of Hugh (*loc. cit.*), who defines it this way, "A Sacrament is a corporal or material element, proposed sensibly and externally, giving a representation from a similitude, and signifying from its institution, and from sanctification containing some invisible and spiritual grace." Here, two things must be noted. Firstly, by the term "element," we should not take up an element in the way it is received when we speak of the four elements of the world, rather, something *distinguished by a word,* according to that of Augustine, "The word approaches the element, and a Sacrament is made." Moreover, Hugh and certain others call an element the matter of all the Sacraments, because in the first Sacrament, i.e., in Baptism, the matter is the true element of water; so, from the matter of the first Sacrament, they meant to name the matter of all the Sacraments. So also, seeing that the material element is most suited to signify, since it is an imperfect body, and by its nature ordered to a mixed composite, for that reason, Aristotle also called matter the first element.

Chapter XI: Definition of a Sacrament

Secondly, we must note that when Hugh says a Sacrament has the force to confer grace from sanctification, he does not, as Chemnitz incorrectly reads him (p. 94), understand by sanctification some blessing or preceding consecration such as that whereby water is blessed (seeing that without this blessing the Sacrament of Baptism can still be conferred); rather, he understands *the word of God*, which is like a form bringing the Sacrament about. By these words, an element is said to be sanctified, because through it a Sacrament is effected. Moreover, this definition, even if it could be embraced with fewer words, still, it is enough to completely embrace the whole nature of a Sacrament.

The *fourth* definition is of Peter Lombard (4 dist. 1) where he says, "A Sacrament is an invisible form of visible grace, bearing the image of the same grace and the existing cause." Such a definition, which pertains to the sense, is no different than the first. For it seems in this definition that the explanation of the sign is missing, naturally whether or not it is from the institution; but this is manifestly gathered from that particle, *existing cause*. No sensible sign can be the cause of grace, nor infallibly signify it unless it is from the institution of God, as is known.

The *fifth* definition is of the Catechism of the Council of Trent, "A Sacrament is a thing subjected to the senses, which, by the institution of God has the force not only to signify holiness and justice, but also to effect it." Such a definition is very beautiful, since it is also brief and still embraces all of those eight headings which we said pertain to the nature of a Sacrament. *Firstly*, that a Sacrament is a sign is clear from the particle "to signify." *Secondly*, that it is sensible, from "subjected to the senses." *Thirdly*, that it is voluntary, from, "by the institution of God." *Fourthly*, that it is in regard to a sacred thing, from, "of holiness and justice." *Fifthly* and *sixthly*, because of sanctity, which then came about by the force of the Sacrament itself, from, "has force." *Seventhly*, because it is a solemn ceremony, from that it is gathered that it is said to be a thing subjected to the senses, instituted to sanctify. *Eighthly*, that bears a similitude of the thing signified, it is not expressly held in this definition, but can be gathered from the particle, "to signify," and from, "by the institution of God." For God, who sweetly disposes all things, never instituted one thing to signify another thing, except when it has some analogy. There is another definition found in the works of Gratian (1 qu. 1 can. *Multi saecularium*), "A Sacrament is that through which, under a covering of visible things, divine power works salvation more secretly." Gratian attributes this definition to St. Gregory; St. Thomas (in 4 dist. 1, q. 1) attributes it to Augustine. But it is of neither; rather, it is of Isidore (*Sex. Tymologiarum*, c. 18) unless perhaps Isidore received that from some book of Augustine or Gregory unknown to us. Whatever the case about that, why do we labor much, when it is certain enough to have been brought forward by Isidore, to explain the meaning of the name, not to accurately define the thing itself?

CHAPTER XII

Whether the Definition of a Sacrament Univocally Agrees with the Sacraments of the Old and New Law

Now, the *third* and last question follows: Do the definitions posited square with a Sacrament in general, or only with the Sacraments of the New Law? There are two opinions of the theologians. The *first* is of Lombard (4, dist. 1), and St. Thomas and St. Bonaventure commenting on the same place, as well as others, who teach that no definition univocally suits the Sacraments of the New and Old Law, but all properly, and perfectly suit the Sacraments of the New Law; to be sure however, the same analogously and imperfectly suit the Sacraments of the Old Law.

The foundation of this opinion is that the cited authors suppose, by the notion of a Sacrament, even in general, that it is not only to signify, but also to effect sanctification; and again, they suppose the Sacraments of the Old Law do not effect true sanctification, but only a certain legal sanctification, which is a figure of true sanctification, which only the Sacraments of the New Law effect. From these two they rightly conclude a Sacrament can be spoken of analogously in regard to the Sacraments of the Old and New Law, just as sanctification itself, the purpose for which they were instituted to signify and cause, is spoken of analogously in regard to the true sanctification of the soul, and the typical and legal sanctification.

The *second* opinion is of St. Thomas (III q. 60 art. 1&2, for it clear he changed his opinion), as well as Domingo del Soto, and Martin Ledesma (dist. 1 q. 1 art. 1&2), who teach that definition, *a sign of a sacred thing*, agrees univocally with the Sacraments of the New Law and of the Old, hence it is the definition of a Sacrament in general.

Their foundation is that they suppose the notion of a Sacrament in general does not require that it be a cause of sanctification, but only that it would signify it. Hence, they add, the Sacraments of the Old Law were the truest signs of the truest sanctification, namely, because they signified that the grace justifying us will be given through Christ. Furthermore, they rightly conclude from these, that the Sacraments of the Old Law univocally agree with ours in general, although they are distinguished in particular, because ours effect sanctification, while the old did not. Both opinions partly satisfy, and partly do not; consequently, I posit the following propositions.

1) The *first* proposition: *It is not enough for the notion of a Sacrament in general to signify something, but it is also required that it effect sanctity or sanctification, nay more, it is more proper for a Sacrament to sanctify*

Chapter XII: Does the Definition Suit Old and New? 43

than signify. This is on behalf of the first opinion. It is proved *a) firstly*, because (as we said above) in the Old Testament the Sacraments are rarely said to give a sign, but they are very frequently said to consecrate and sanctify, or to initiate, as is clear from Exodus 28:41 and Lev. 8:11. Also in the New Testament, Baptism is called the laver of regeneration (Tit. 3:5), and certainly to regenerate effects more than to signify.

b) Secondly, from etymology, all the terms similar to "Sacrament" signify an *action*, not a sign, as is clear from the clothing, shoe, impediment, ornament, firmament, foundation, and the other types of this sort of form; thus, Sacrament gets its name from consecrating (*sacrandum*), not from signifying (*significando*).

c) Thirdly, the whole reason why the second opinion holds that a Sacrament in general is nothing other than a sign is the definition, "A Sacrament is a sign of a sacred thing." There, it is not attributed to a Sacrament to effect a sacred thing, but only to *signify* it. We have already shown that definition is not perfect, since Augustine himself, who was its author, impugned it, seeing he meant it also to suit a sacrifice.

2) The *second* proposition: *The Sacraments of the Old Law are not Sacraments because they signify justifying grace, but because they signify and effect legal sanctity*. This is also on behalf of the first opinion against the second. It is proven *a)* first from the preceding conclusion. If it is required more for a Sacrament in general to sanctify than to signify, certainly the Old Sacraments, if they were Sacraments in any way, not only signified, but also effected.

b) Secondly, because to signify grace which will be given to others is not of a Sacrament, inasmuch as it is a Sacrament, but inasmuch as it is a *figure* and a *type of a future thing*. For a Sacrament, as Sacrament, designates order to that which is begun by the Sacrament, not to other things, as St. Thomas rightly teaches (I IIæ q. 101 art. 4, and q. 102 art. 5); moreover, the figure designates order to future things. And it is confirmed, because to signify grace given to other things was not proper to the Old Sacraments, but even to sacrifices, and other observances of the Jews, as St. Augustine shows (*Contra Faustum*, 19, 8-11). Not only that, but even the bronze serpent signifies the healing from sins, which Christ had brought (John 3:14); the sweet manna, the Eucharist; and the crossing of the Red Sea, Baptism (1 Cor. 10:1), and still neither the serpent, the manna, nor the ark, were Sacraments of the Old Testament or the New.

3) The *third* proposition: *A Sacrament is the univocal genus in regard to Sacraments of the Old and New Law, hence the Old Sacraments were simply and absolutely Sacraments*. This is for the second opinion against the first. It is proved *a) firstly*, because a Sacrament in general requires nothing else except a signifying and efficient ceremony of some consecration or sanctification, but it does not require that the sanctification is through grace cleansing the soul from sins, for that special sanctification constituted a certain species

of the Sacrament, not the genus itself absolutely. Moreover, Sacraments of the Old Law were truly signifying and effecting a certain consecration. Through circumcision the Jews were initiated and consecrated to God, that they would be his particular people; through priestly anointing the sons of Aaron were truly consecrated to God to exercise the priesthood, and the same thing can also be said on other Sacraments of this sort (see more on this in St. Thomas, *loc. cit.* q. 102 art. 5). Consequently, these were truly and properly Sacraments.

b) Secondly, there can be no religion without Sacraments, as St. Augustine teaches (*Contra Faustum* 19, 11). In the Old Testament there was a true Church, a true religion, a true sacrifice; why not also true Sacraments?

Nor is it opposed that all of these things came to pass among the Jews in figure (1 Cor. 10:11), and hence, the sacrifices, Sacraments, all the rites, were certain types of our sacrifice, our Sacraments, and our rites. From there it seems to be gathered there were not sacrifices and Sacraments except through analogy to our own. This, I say, does not oppose us; accordingly, the Jewish Sacraments were figures of our Sacraments, not only figures, but even *things per se*. Therefore, circumcision was not merely a figure of Baptism, but was also, per se, a ceremony instituted to initiate men of that time and join them to the people of God. This is why it was more imperfectly a Sacrament than Baptism is; still, absolutely and properly, it was a Sacrament. An ox is a more imperfect animal than a man, and still an ox is absolutely and properly an animal; so also, the Aaronic ordination was not only a figure of our ordination, but also per se a ceremony consecrating men to offer sacrifices. Now, the sacrifices themselves were not only a figure of our sacrifice, but also per se sacrifices, instituted to show worship to God as the supreme beginning and end of all things. Lastly, the Jewish people itself was a figure of the Christian people (1 Cor. 10:6). Nevertheless, who could be uncertain as to whether or not it was also a certain people per se?

Therefore, Jewish things should not be compared with ours, like a painted image with a living man, where there is no image except of another thing, but as little sons are compared with grown men, as the Apostle does (Galatians 4:1-2). The Son is the image of the Father, and still he is also a man per se, just as struggles and puerile exercises are compared with the exercises of men. For, there are puerile contests as certain images of greater contests; still, they have also their delight and utility suitable to that time.

4) The *fourth* proposition: *The definition, "a sign of a sacred thing," univocally suits all the Sacraments, both the old and new*. This favors the second opinion against the first. We must note, however, that definition can be explained in three ways.

a) Firstly, to understand a practical sign through a sign, justifying grace through a sacred sign. In this way, the definition only properly suits the Sacraments of the New Law, the Old, however, only *secundum quid*, and analogically, because there were practical signs of legal cleanliness, which

Chapter XII: Does the Definition Suit Old and New? 45

is not justifying grace except through a type, in the way an image of a man is called a man. That exposition, however, is not according to the mind of St. Augustine, as we said above.

b) Secondly, it can be explained in this way. A practical sign is understood from a sign, and a consecration in general from a sacred thing, not from the descent to internal or legal justification, and in this way the definition is univocally suitable to all the Sacraments. This exposition is not according to the mind of St. Augustine, for he does not speak on the practical sign, as St. Thomas rightly adverts.

c) Thirdly, it can be explained in this way, that through a sign we understand a bare sign, while through a sacred sign, justifying grace; in this way the definition is univocally suitable to all the Sacraments, and we say this in conclusion, following St. Thomas. Moreover, that definition, as we advised above, is not perfect, since it is also suitable to sacrifice, as Augustine witnesses (*loc. cit.*).

Hence, the other definitions (i.e., of Hugh, Lombard, and the Roman Catechism), are not suitable for anything but the Sacraments of the New Law; nevertheless, they can easily be accommodated to a Sacrament in general if, in place of *invisible grace*, or *justice*, one were to place *some consecration*, in this way: A Sacrament is a thing subjected to the senses which, by the institution of God, has the force of any consecration you like, both to signify and to effect.

CHAPTER XIII

The Objections of Chemnitz Are Answered

Now, from the foregoing, we will easily be able to answer the calumnies of Chemnitz. In his *Examination of the Council of Trent* (2 par. c. On the Number of the Sacraments), he attacks all the definitions which we brought forward, with the exception of the Roman Catechism, which he does not mention; besides, he adds two definitions, one of Scotus, the other of William of Ockham, with which he also finds fault.

1) In the *first*, on page 38, he complains of the definition of Isidore, "How will Matrimony be a Sacrament according to this definition?" *I respond:* This definition is most suitable to Matrimony, seeing that under the covering of visible things, i.e., the union of husband and wife, invisible grace is signified, through which God is joined with the soul, whether he infuses justice or increases what has been infused. Nor is what the Apostle says opposed to these things: Matrimony is a sign of the union of Christ with the Church; accordingly, the same Sacrament can be a sign of many things.

2) *Secondly*, he complains about the definition of Hugh of St. Victory, that a Sacrament is not rightly called a corporeal element, seeing that according to Catholics, the Sacrament of the Eucharist is not some substance, but only the accidents of bread and wine. *I respond:* The very substance of bread and wine is not an element, properly so called, i.e., a simple body, rather, a mixed element. As we showed above, Hugh called an element some sensible thing which is applied to carry out the Sacraments.

3) *Thirdly*, he complains of the definition of Peter Lombard in his *Sentences*, because he does not rightly hold that a Sacrament is a visible form. In Matrimony, Catholics hold that the matter is the expression of the words of consent; but words are neither visible things nor can be called an element, according to Hugh, if an element is distinguished against a word, according to, "the word is added to the element and this becomes a Sacrament."

I respond: There are not lacking many Catholics who hold that in the Sacrament of Matrimony, the persons themselves contracting are the matter, while the words are only the form; hence, they assign a visible matter which can also be called an element. See Peter Paludanus (4 dist. 1 q. 4). Yet, if words alone were in the Sacrament of Matrimony, still, the argument of Chemnitz would prove nothing. For the words can also be called an element insofar as they hold the place of matter; when we argue

Chapter XIII: The Objections of Chemnitz Refuted

on the Sacraments, we say that element, which is indeterminate of itself, is also determined by certain words, as it were, by the form. We no less assert that words may be said to be visible, since what is visible may be accommodated to all sensible things, and the sense of sight itself is usually transferred to every sense. As Augustine teaches (*Confess.* 10, 35), we rightly say see how it looks, how it smells, how it tastes, how hard it is, how good it sounds, but we do not say conversely, listen to how it sees, taste how it shines, smell how it glitters, touch how it shines.

4) *Fourthly*, he complains of the same two definitions, that we do not rightly hold a Sacrament is a sign of invisible grace, if through grace we understand *gratia gratum faciens*. Even if Richard argues on Matrimony and Ordination, as a grace of this sort is given in the other Sacraments, Chemnitz says, "Nevertheless, the rest acknowledge this cannot stand." This is an impudent lie, as we showed in chapter 2.

5) *Fifthly*, he complains of the definition of Scotus and Ockham, but unduly, seeing that they contain nothing false. Rather, in their opinions they only disagree with the words, not the common definition.

6) *Sixthly*, he opposes all definitions together, "If a Sacrament is a sign efficaciously signifying the gratuitous effect of God, how will the blessing of monks, holy water, blessed roses, a blessed sword, an Agnus Dei, the blessing of plants, fields, images, royal anointing, consecration of a church, cemetery, altar, and so much else, not be Sacraments? That happens in certain consecrations, and they are composed to have spiritual effects." But all of these can easily be refuted from a twofold heading. *a*) Firstly, neither the blessing of monks nor the other things enumerated signify or effect justifying grace, but certain other effects, such as the blotting out of venial sins and protection against demons, which are the particular effects that holy water has, *b*) Second, because they do not *infallibly* have these very effects, seeing as they do not have force from divine institution, but from the prayers of the Church.

CHAPTER XIV

The Definition of the Lutherans Is Refuted

WE now come to examine and refute the definitions of our adversaries. In this matter they are at variance, which is a manifest sign that they have departed from the truth which is one. Certainly Chemnitz, who otherwise attempts to conceal or reconcile their differences (in 2 part. *Exam.* c. On the Efficacy of the Sacraments p. 96), enumerates five different opinions of the Lutherans, apart from his own which is the sixth.

Therefore, the first opinion is of Luther from the last chapter of his book *The Babylonian Captivity*, where he says a Sacrament is properly a promise connected to an outward sign. The Lutherans commonly receive this, but explain it a little more. The *Apologia for the Augsburg Confession* (art. 13) says, "A Sacrament is a rite which has the command of God, and to which a promise of grace is added." Peter Martyr holds similar things, although the Calvinists hold otherwise in their commentaries on Romans 4, 1 Cor. 10 and 11, as well as in their Italian explanation of the Creed, art. 9 and 10. But Martin Chemnitz most accurately tries to explain everything which pertains to the nature of a Sacrament.

Now, since both in his *Apologia* and in *de Locis*, Melanchthon prefaces that he gives an interpretation of the name, and the words of his definition are often different, it will be more useful to propose and explain the things which Chemnitz teaches pertain to the nature of a Sacrament. Firstly, he would have it that a Sacrament should be an external material, or a corporal and visible element, or sign, which is handled with an external rite.

Secondly, it is required that the sign should have an express command, or divine institution.

Thirdly, that command must be in the New Testament, which is the same thing Melanchthon teaches (*Locis*, c. de Sacramentis) where he says a Sacrament is a ceremony instituted in the Gospel.

Fourthly, he requires that a Sacrament not be a temporary ceremony, but something which will endure even to the end of the world.

Fifthly, he calls it a promise in regard to grace and the effect or fruit of the Sacrament is required.

Sixthly, he says the promise should be connected to a sign, and robed by it, as if by divine ordination.

Seventhly, he adds that promise should not be in regard to any gift of God, but on the reconciliation of the sinner and the remission of sin; Luther also insists on that part (*Babyl.*), as well as Melanchthon (*de Locis*, c. De

Chapter XIV: The Lutheran Definition Is Refuted

numero Sacramentorum).

Eighthly, he requires that a promise, which is otherwise general, be applied through the Sacrament and bound in specific individuals who use the Sacraments with faith. Luther (as well as Melanchthon and Chemnitz himself) more clearly explains this phrase under the heading of the efficacy of the Sacrament; for they would have it that the Sacraments are infallible testimonies of the grace of God, instituted for this purpose, to arouse and nourish faith according to that mode in which they customarily do miracles. This is why Melanchthon, in *Locis* published in 1522, compares the Sacraments to miracles whereby God once confirmed faith; in the *Apologia*, art. 13, he says a Sacrament is an infallible testimony, as if God would promise that he meant to forgive from heaven with a new miracle. Luther, in his book *Against Cochlaeus*, says, "By Baptism, or an external sign, Peter means faith which saves is called forth and exercised." And in *Babylonian Captivity* (c. de Baptismo), he compares the Sacraments with the fleece of Gideon, with the rainbow which Noah received as a sign, and with the sign which Isaiah offered to King Ahaz (Isaiah 7:11). In the *Augsburg Confession* itself (art. 13) they say, "The Sacraments were instituted to be signs and testimonies of the will of God toward us, to rouse and strengthen faith, proposed in these who use them." Chemnitz (*loc. cit.*, p. 102), says the word and Sacrament show where faith should seek and discover Christ the mediator, and on pp. 101 and 105, says the Sacraments are seals of the promise. Therefore, this is their opinion.

Chemnitz devised this definition to show only Baptism and Eucharist are Sacraments properly speaking, but he has not yet obtained what he desired. We can easily prove that definition does not even suit these two Sacraments, and is absolutely bad.

1) Therefore, the *first* phrase either receives a visible and tractable element for any sensible thing you like, as Catholics receive it, so that even priestly absolution will be a Sacrament properly speaking, as absolution is a sensible thing which is perceived with the ears; or it receives (as it really receives) a visible and tractable element for a specific thing, which is perceived by the sense of sight and touch. Then he concocts a definition for himself without any testimony of Scripture, for Scripture holds nothing as a Sacrament unless it is a visible and palpable thing.

Chemnitz does not prove this phrase in any way except from the fact that Baptism and Eucharist, which are true Sacraments, are visible and tractable signs. Such argumentation assumes that it has been proven, and that from the very definition the same Chemnitz later tries to prove, Baptism and Eucharist are the only Sacraments; or if he does not assume this, he proves nothing. Just as it is a *non sequitur* to say: A man and a bird have two feet, therefore every animal has two feet, so also it is a *non sequitur* to say Baptism and Eucharist are visible and tractable signs, therefore every Sacrament is a visible and tractable sign. It is enough, therefore, in regard to the nature of the Sacrament, insofar as it is a sensible sign, that it be perceived in *some* sense; nor should the sense of hearing be excluded, seeing that the most excellent signs of all are those which are perceived by this sense, as Augustine teaches (*Doct. Christ.* 2, 3).

2) The *second* phrase, which requires an express command, or divine institution, either requires that the command be expressed in the Scriptures or it is enough if it were certain God had given this command, even if we do not expressly find it in this way in Scripture. If this second were sufficient, we admit that phrase, but then we will prove all seven Sacraments. Although it was not written that God commanded or instituted the Sacrament of Confirmation, nevertheless, because we read in Acts 8:18 that through the imposition of hands of the Apostles the Holy Spirit was given to the baptized as an ordinary practice, we certainly gather it was instituted by God; for no created power can effect that through the imposition of hands the Holy Spirit would be given to men. We can prove the same thing in regard to the other Sacraments, especially seeing it agrees with ancient tradition and the declaration of the Church.

If on the contrary, Chemnitz would have it (as he shows he really does) that an express command of God is required in Scripture, then the phrase is false. For *per accidens* it is in regard to a command or divine institution which is written or unwritten. Otherwise, Baptism and Eucharist, which Christ and the Apostles gave, would not be true Sacraments before the Gospels were written. Accordingly, it is certain the Gospel was not written when Christ was baptizing (John 3:22), nor when he gave the Eucharist to his disciples (Matthew 26:26), nor even when St. Peter commanded three thousand men to be baptized (Acts 2:41), in which time the Sacrament of the Eucharist became frequent, as St. Luke points out (*ibid*).

3) The *third* phrase, that this institution would be in the New Testament, is absolutely true. Nevertheless, it destroys the opinion of our adversaries, since by their common consensus, they teach against the common consensus of the Catholic Church, that the Baptism of John had the same force and efficacy as the Baptism of Christ; hence, Christ did not so much institute the Sacrament of Baptism, as he approved what had already been instituted by John. Calvin teaches this way (*Instit.* 4, 14 §7), as do Chemnitz (*Exam.* 2 par., cap. *On the Baptism of John*) and Melanchthon (*Locis*, c. de *Baptismo Joannis et Apostolorum*).

Certainly, if the matter so stood, then the Sacrament of Baptism was not instituted in the New Testament, for the author and prince of the New Testament is Christ, as St. Paul says in Hebrews 9:15, on account of what is said in Isaiah 9:6: "Father of the coming age." Consequently, if the Baptism which we use began with John, who came before Christ, and he followed his precursor and herald, then this Sacrament would not have been instituted in the New Testament, but in the Old.

The fourth phrase, that a Sacrament should be a perpetual ceremony,

Chapter XIV: The Lutheran Definition Is Refuted 51

i.e., to endure as long as religion itself endures. I do not take any issue with it since we taught the same thing above. Nevertheless, let Chemnitz see what he would answer Luther, who in his work *On the Babylonian Captivity* (chapter on Baptism) numbers among the Sacraments the dew falling on the fleece of Gideon and the shadow falling back in the garden of Ahaz.

5) The fifth phrase, that the promise of grace is necessarily required for a Sacrament, may be understood in two ways: *a)* in one way, on the promise of grace which is the effect of the Sacrament, so that it is the same thing, the promise of grace in the Sacraments, and the institution of the Sacrament, as the efficacious sign or instrument of justification; *b)* in the second way, on the promise of preceding grace which is signified in the Sacrament, as a seal. Just as it is one thing to promise some seal is efficacious to publish a book, and on the other, to promise a hundred gold pieces and a contract to mark it with a seal; so also, it is one thing to promise grace with words, and then confirm this promise by an external sign, and another to promise a Sacrament will be an efficacious instrument to justify. Hence, Chemnitz confuses these two. In this fifth phrase, he says the promise is required in regard to grace, or the fruit of the Sacrament. There, he seems to speak on the promise of efficacy of the Sacrament; still later, where he says with the other Lutherans that the Sacrament is the seal of the promise, he speaks about the preceding promise, on which, without a doubt, all the Lutherans speak.

Indeed, the promise in regard to the efficacy of the Sacrament is found in the word of God according to Catholics, inasmuch as it regards all the Sacraments, but not according to our adversaries. Catholics recognize even traditions for the word of God, but our adversaries, who receive the Scriptures alone, will not easily show that promise on grace and the fruit of the Sacrament in all the Sacraments. An example for us is the Eucharist, which for our adversaries is also a Sacrament properly speaking. There are many conspicuous promises in John 6:59, such as "he that eats this bread will live forever." But our adversaries do not admit that it is a question of the Eucharist in this sixth chapter of John. Luther says (*loc. cit.* c. On the Eucharist), "First, the whole chapter 6 of John must be excluded, since not even a syllable speaks on the Sacrament." Calvin teaches the same thing, as well as the other heretics of this time in their commentaries of this passage. By excluding the chapter, they will never discover the promise. In Matthew 26:26, Mark 14:22, Luke 22:19, where the institution of the Sacrament is found, there is no promise, for it only has these words, "This is my body, which is given for you," and "This is my blood, etc., which will be shed for you and for many in remission of sins." Where a promise from the handing over of the body and the effusion of blood is not related to the Sacrament, but to *the sacrifice*, which he was offering to God in the Supper, and later was going to offer on the cross. For the Lord does not say that his body is given to the Apostles in remission of sins, but it is given *for them*, namely to God, in remission of sins; and similarly he does not say his blood is offered as drink for the Apostles, but it is shed *for them* in remission of sins.

The preceding promise, however, which is marked in the Sacrament like a seal is not necessary, nor found in all the Sacraments; hence, the definition of our adversaries for this part is false. In Baptism, which is a Sacrament, by the consensus of all, a promise of this sort is not easily discovered.

Luther (*Visitatio Saxonica*) and Melanchthon (*Locis* c. de Baptismo) assert that promise in Mark 16:16, "He who believes and is baptized will be saved," but this is not a preceding promise, rather, it is an *explanation of the efficacy of the Sacrament*. Besides, Our Lord said those words after the resurrection, but the Sacrament of Baptism was also instituted before the passion of Christ, and began to be introduced into habit, as is clear from John 3:22 and 4:1.

Perhaps they will say another promise is found in John 3:5 in the words "unless a man be born again from water and the Holy Spirit, he cannot enter into the kingdom of God." This is not so much a promise, as a threat, from which necessity and the virtue of Baptism is certainly gathered, but not some preceding promise which is marked in Baptism. Furthermore, the Baptism of John which our adversaries suppose had the force of our Baptism existed before these words.

A certain promise of the Eucharist is found (as Luther notes in *Visitatio Saxonica*), preceding the sign. In Luke 22:19 and 1 Cor. 11:24 we have the Eucharist is the sign of the Lord's body, given for us, and his blood shed for us. We do not have, in this passage, that the Eucharist is a sign that witnesses and confirms the promise, such as they require, as is clear from the last phrase, but merely a *commemorative* sign. Thus, the Lord says, "Do this in my commemoration."

6) The sixth phrase, that a promise should be connected to a sign by divine ordination, is false. For a word, which is connected by divine ordination like it was clothed with a sign, so that from there it becomes a Sacrament, is never promissory, but *assertory* or *deprecatory*. When water is sprinkled in Baptism, it is not said, "He that believes and is baptized will be saved," which our adversaries call a promise. Rather, it is said, "I baptize you in the name of the Father, and of the Son, and of the Holy Spirit" (Matt. 28:19); such words are not promissory. The Lord, when he first confected the Eucharist and gave it, did not say, "He who eats this bread will live forever," or something else of this sort. Rather, he says, "Take, and eat, this is my body." Now, in the Sacraments of Confirmation and Extreme Unction, we use a deprecatory word, because the Acts of the Apostles (8:15) and James (5:14) teach us. In the Sacrament of Order it is a command, "Receive the power," in the rest, assertory.

If our adversaries preach the word before they administer the

Chapter XIV: The Lutheran Definition Is Refuted

Sacrament, and announce the remission of sins, and then employ the seal of the Sacraments, as Calvin prescribes (*On the Formula for the Administration of the Sacraments*), they do it from their own source, not (as Chemnitz requires) from divine ordination. No divine ordination exists whereby we are commanded not to give the Eucharist, or Baptism, except after preaching. For neither the Lord (Matt. 26), nor Paul (1 Cor. 11), where they hand down the rite of administering the Eucharist, teach that preaching must precede it; and certainly, in the Baptism of infants, preaching would be applied in vain.

7) The seventh phrase, that the promise should be in regard to the remission of sins, is also false, and indeed Chemnitz added this phrase to exclude Ordination from the number of Sacraments, properly speaking. Since the outward sign is found in the Scriptures, whereby Ordination is conferred, namely the imposition of hands and also the conferral of grace when the Apostle says (1 Tim. 4:14), "Do not neglect the grace that is in you, which was given you by prophecy, with the imposition of the hands of the priesthood," Chemnitz did not think Ordination could be excluded from the Sacraments properly speaking, unless he were to add "the grace" ought to be the remission of sins. Now, if that phrase were true, it would also exclude the Eucharist from the Sacraments properly speaking, since the Eucharist was not instituted properly to remit sins, but *to nourish and increase charity*. Therefore, it is given under the species of bread and wine, which nourishes the living, but does not rouse the dead. And St. Paul (1 Cor. 11:28) bids that men prove themselves, namely whether they are without sin, before they approach that table, "He that eats and drinks unworthily, eats judgment upon himself."

8) The eighth phrase, that the Sacrament marks the form of a seal and the form of a miracle, as well as confirms the promise of grace to rouse and nourish justifying faith, is equally false and will be diligently refuted, both because it is obvious, and also because Calvin places it in his definition.

a) Firstly, if the Sacraments confirm the promises of God in the form of a miracle, or a seal, they would be better known and more efficacious to persuade faith than the very words of God; but this is false, so the phrase is false. The proposition is proved both because one would be applied to confirm another in vain, unless it is better known and stronger than it, and also because this is the force of a seal and miracle. For the royal seal is better known and stronger than the letters of the king; for everyone knows to discern the seal, not everyone discerns the letters, and the seal without letters has authority, the letters without a seal do not. So also, a miracle is better known and more efficacious than preaching. For everyone sees a blind man given his sight, or a man raised from the dead, and they understand that it is a supernatural and divine work, hence, they are moved to believe that which is confirmed by such a testimony; not everyone, however, who hears preaching immediately understands it is the word of God.

There we must note, by the miracles which are done to confirm faith, divine authority is not confirmed, as if the miracle were more to be believed than God speaking; everyone knows God cannot lie, and nothing is greater than divine authority, but the authority *of those proposing* the faith is confirmed. We are moved more to believe what has truly been revealed by God, which the preacher proposes, if we see miracles than if we rest upon the sole authority of the one proposing it. This is why in Mark 16:20, we read, "Going forth they preached everywhere, the Lord working withal, and confirming the word with signs that followed." There you see, God confirmed with signs, not his authority, but the authority of those *preaching the word*.

The assumption of the argument has already been proven, that it is false that the Sacraments are more known and efficacious than the word of God itself. For firstly, nothing can be devised better and more efficacious than the word of God. Secondly, experience teaches that it is easier to understand if something is said by word than signified by a nod. What are the Sacraments, however, if they are compared with words, except a type of *nod*? For equal reasoning, experience teaches that words persuade more than silent signs, provided they are not miracles. For this reason, Luther himself affirms that the words of the promise are much more efficacious than the Sacraments, which are silent sermons, "The word itself, which by far prevails over a visible sin, still justifies no one of itself except the believer" (*Contra Joannem Cochlaeum*).

Calvin answers (*Inst.* 4, 14 §3) that the Sacraments do not confirm promises on the side of God, but on our side, because although they are from God, they should be most certain, but that we receive them on account of the weakness of our faith, they are not received so certainly unless they are confirmed by the testimony of the Sacraments.

Now, this is easily rejected. The fact is, the promises of God require confirmation on our side, so either it will happen that we do not know what the promises of God are and we learn it from the Sacraments, or that although we know both those are the promises of God, and these the Sacraments, still, we believe the Sacraments more than promises. The latter has already been refuted. We do not believe, rather we also *know* by the most evident reason, that God cannot lie, hence nothing is more certain than the promises of God, and our adversaries cannot deny it. The former can equally be refuted; accordingly it is false that we learn the promises of God from the Sacraments, since on the contrary, we learn the Sacraments from the word of God. Moreover, if the royal seal were unknown and could only be gathered from the letters upon which it has been attached, it would plainly be superfluous. Either men believe the letters are the king's, without the seal, or they do not; if they believe, why make the seal? If they do not believe, certainly they do not believe the royal seal; therefore, it confers nothing. For equal reasoning, since the Sacraments are not known

Chapter XIV: The Lutheran Definition Is Refuted 55

to be the seals of God, except because Scripture says this, if it is believed by word without the Sacraments, what are the Sacraments? If it is not believed, certainly the Sacraments are not believed to be Sacraments; hence nothing is worked.

Calvin answers this argument (*Inst.* 4, 14 §5) that in charters the seal is also of no avail without letters, which is obvious if they hang from a charter upon which nothing has been written; and still, when it is attached to a written charter, they avail much to confirm it. He also adds that it is hardly marvelous if the promises are confirmed by the Sacraments, since now and then one promise is confirmed by another.

This response, however, does not refute the argument. That I might begin from the second example, a promise confirms a promise because one does not depend upon the other. The Angel of Luke 1:36 confirmed the promise of the conception of the Virgin, from the promise of a conception which had already taken place in an old and sterile woman. Those two miraculous works do not depend upon each other hence, one, which had already taken place, had great force to confirm the other which had not yet come about. But the Sacraments, as we have said, simply depend upon the word. Moreover, what Calvin says pertaining to the similitude of a seal and a charter is altogether nothing. A seal attached to an unwritten paper really confirms nothing, but in this way, it does not depend upon the letters or it is nothing. Nay more, we understand from this how ineptly our adversaries call the Sacraments seals, since they have an altogether contrary propriety. For a charter with a seal has its authority without the letters of the charter, but letters do not have authority without a seal; on the other hand, in the word and the Sacraments, the word of God even without the Sacraments has an infallible authority, the Sacraments without the word have none. This is why the word should rather more be called the seal of the Sacrament, than the Sacrament the seal of God.

Perhaps they will say: Be that as it may, the Sacraments do not confirm the promises by the custom of a miracle or a seal; nevertheless, they help and at least confirm in that mode in which the external action helps and confirms the prayer of those teaching. For it cannot be denied that the action itself confers something to explain and persuade, as well as the movement of the hands, and the eyes, although prayer holds the first parts. So, there will be Sacraments, like a certain action of God, which together with the word, move more to faith than the word alone.

I respond: Not even that can be conceded. For the action among men helps prayer because human prayer is imperfect, just as all things are created, and even because an action does not have its force from the word, but of itself. Moreover, the pagans believed the oracles of Apollo, which they thought could not be false although they were published in words alone, more than the speech and action of any orator you like. So, seeing that the words of God are per se of supreme authority, and the Sacraments have all their force from words, they can add nothing to the word itself.

Still it is true what Catholics say, that God willed to give his grace through sensible signs, to instruct men through them and lead them to understand spiritual things. It is one thing to teach spiritual things through similitudes of corporal things, and another to confirm the firmest thing through another less firm.

The *second* argument: The essence and nature of the Sacraments cannot be gathered better from any place than from the words of the one who instituted them. In the Holy Scriptures, which are the words of God, the author of the Sacraments, they are never called testimonies of promises, rather, they are everywhere described as instruments of justification. In John 3:3, we are told to be born again through Baptism and similarly in Eph. 5:26, the Apostle says, "The Church sanctified and cleansed by the laver of water in the word of life"; and Tit. 3:5, the Apostle calls Baptism the "laver of regeneration and renewal." So also, on the Eucharist, it is said in John 6:59, "He that eats this bread will live forever," and we can prove the same from other things. Moreover, these sentences cannot be explained in this way, except absurdly, that when the Sacraments regenerate, cleanse, give eternal life, it is nothing other than to give testimony of the divine promises. Who would advance that, who so says: Baptism regenerates, i.e., gives testimony of the divine will? Or, I baptize you, i.e., I give witness? And this is the most efficacious argument against the Lutherans. Luther, whom the rest gladly follow in this matter, in his book against Cochlaeus, says, "In sacred matters, the most emphatic and robust place is to argue from negative authority." So, let them advance a passage where the Sacraments are called testimonies of promises, or certainly let them affirm, most emphatically and robustly that we have the argument.

Customarily they advance only three passages, which seem to have some substance. One is Gen. 17:11: where circumcision is called the sign of the covenant. The other is Romans 4:11: where circumcision is called the seal of the justice of faith. The third is 1 Pet. 3:21: where Peter says Baptism saves, not of the flesh in regard to the condition of filth, but the examination of a good conscience, or (as they add) the stipulation or agreement with God. In these places a promise is not named, or a testimony, nor do these passages bear on the matter, as we will show later in the response of the arguments.

The *third* argument: If the Sacraments were merely testimonies of the promise, and grace, they are either redundant, or certainly hardly necessary, for we have other testimonies that are by far more efficacious; accordingly, good works are better testimonies of securing justice than the washing of water, or the reception of the Eucharist. For many impious men are baptized with an insincere heart, and take the Eucharist, who are then worse and more hateful to God than they were before. "For our glory is this, the testimony of our conscience." (2 Cor. 1:12); "Labor the more, that

Chapter XIV: The Lutheran Definition Is Refuted 57

by good works you may make sure your calling and election." (2 Pet. 1:10); "He that does justice, is just ... Whoever is born of God does not commit sin" (1 John 3:7, 9).

The *fourth* argument: If the Sacraments were only testimonies of promise instituted to arouse faith, infants, and the insane, whom it is certain not only do not believe, but cannot believe in act, would be baptized in vain. But all Lutherans favor the Baptism of children against the Anabaptists; therefore, the same Lutherans do not truly hand down what a Sacrament is. This argument compelled Luther, (*Contra Cochlaeum*) and the other Lutherans to assert that infants believe in act when they are baptized; still, that is absurd, as St. Augustine (*Epist. 57 ad Dardanum*) wrote that they do injury to human senses who say this. We see infants weep at the touch of the water, recoil, and struggle as often as they can, which certainly if they had the use of reason and were to do so, not only would they not be cleansed from original sin, but they would also add their own actual sin.

The *fifth* argument: If the Sacraments were testimonies of grace, which are conferred on someone in particular, they would be repeatedly false, namely, since the Sacrament is administered to a man, who feigns himself to believe, when he really does not. Hence, it is not lawful to baptize anyone, lest we would compel God as a false witness, for we do not know with any certainty whether someone truly believes or pretends that he believes.

Perhaps they will say the Sacrament is not absolutely a testimony of grace, but if someone receives the Sacrament, he believes the promise.

Yet, on the other hand, I will prove the testimony is absolute and not conditioned. Firstly, Luther, in his assertion of the first article, says that a man who does not believe the word of the minister saying "I baptize," or, "I absolve you," makes God, whose words those are, a liar; but if the words are understood with a condition, if the other would believe, they would not be false, nor would God become a liar.

Secondly, if the words were conditioned, the justifying faith of the Lutherans would come to ruin. Seeing that they would have it that a man should believe absolutely, without any hesitation that he is just; therefore, God absolutely testifies that he is just, for a man should not believe unless God witnesses it. Besides, faith should be certain; therefore, it should not depend upon a condition, namely if a man would believe. According to Luther, no man is of himself certain whether he believes; so Luther writes in his work against the Rebaptizers, published in 1528, "Baptism must not be founded upon the faith of the one baptizing, or of the one baptized, because both are uncertain in regard to faith ... So it happens, and customarily comes about in regard to faith, that one who thinks he believes, often is found altogether to believe nothing, and on the other hand, one who thinks he believes nothing, especially believes everything."

Thirdly, our adversaries speak on this matter in such a way, that they seem to believe the testimony of God in the Sacraments is absolute.

For Melanchthon speaks in this way (*Locis*, c. de Baptismo), "I," says the minister, "by divine command, baptize you in place of Christ, i.e., I give witness in this sign that your sins are washed away, and you are reconciled to the true God, etc.," where he makes no mention of the condition. That is enough on the definition of the Lutherans.

CHAPTER XV

The Definitions of the Anabaptists and the Zwinglians Are Refuted

THE next opinion on the nature of the Sacrament is of certain men, whom Luther and Calvin everywhere call fanatics. They teach: The Sacraments are nothing other than certain signs instituted to pick out the Christian people from the Jews and pagans, just as the toga was once a sign among the Romans, whereby they were discerned from the Greeks, and now how different forms and colors of garments distinguish different kinds of monks. Luther considers Andrew Carlstadt the author of this opinion, in his sermon on the words of the supper, "This is my body." This Carlstadt was once among the first disciples and friends of Luther, which is why in his second writing against the King of England he calls him his Absalom and Judas; just as Absalom was a rebel against his Father, and Judas a traitor to his teacher, so Carlstadt was a rebel and treacherous.

In the beginning, Melanchthon did not shudder from this opinion, as is clear from *De Locis* that he published in 1522, where he thinks this sentence is probable in the chapter on *Signs*, "The purpose of those who compare these signs with symbols, even military tokens, is probable, because they are only known by the things whereby they are recognized, to which the divine promises pertain," although he later opposed it in the *Apologia for the Augsburg Confession* (art. 13), and in the later edition of *Loci Comm.*

Here it must be noted that the two first opinions which Chemnitz enumerates, *a)* that the Sacraments are signs whereby Christians are distinguished from non-Christians and *b)* that they are certain symbols of Christian society, as Melanchthon rightly remarks make one opinion for they only acknowledge two Sacraments, Baptism and the Supper. And they make Baptism a symbol whereby we are discerned from non-Christians, but the Supper is a symbol of Christian society among us.

This opinion is partly true and also partly false. Even if the Sacraments were to have that use, to distinguish true religion from certain false ones, still, this is not the only, or particular use of our Sacraments. *Firstly*, we never read in the Scriptures that Baptism, Eucharist, or the other Sacraments were instituted to distinguish the Christian people from others; we frequently, however, read there that the end for which they were instituted was to justify men. In Mark 16:16 we read, "He who believes and is baptized will be saved." It did not say that he will be discerned from others, but he will be saved. In Acts 2:38, we read, "Do penance and be baptized, every one of you in the name of Jesus Christ, for the remission of your sins, and you shall receive the gift of the Holy Spirit." In Acts 22:16, "Be baptized and wash away your sins, invoking his name." Additionally, the passages cited above which teach the same thing, namely, the Sacraments were instituted to justify.

Secondly, other signs are better to distinguish the people of God from other peoples, such as the confession of faith, which suits true Catholics alone, seeing that Baptism is common with heretics; mutual charity also, which is in Catholics alone, seeing that all the Sacraments are common with schismatics. This is why the Lord, in John 13:35, did not say, "In this all will know that you are my disciples" if you have Baptism or Eucharist, but if you love one another.

Thirdly, all the Sacraments have their force from the passion of Christ, as a sign of which, blood and water flowed from the pierced side of the Lord (John 19:34), for water signified Baptism as the Fathers teach (Ambrose *in Luc.* 10, 105; Chrysostom.; Cyril; Theophylactus *in John* 19; Leo *epist.* 4, 6; Damascene 4, 10; Jerome *epist.* 83 *ad Oceanum*). Also, Augustine teaches the same thing in another place (*loc. cit.* tr. 15) and proves it from the words of Paul in Eph. 5:25-26, "Christ loved the Church and delivered himself up for it to sanctify it, cleansing it by the laver of water in the word of life." Furthermore, in *City of God* (15, 26) he proves the same from other testimonies. Now certainly, if they should merely distinguish, in the way togas distinguish, then the passion of Christ was not needed, rather human good will would be enough.

Lastly, that opinion is by far absent from the sense and words of all the Fathers, of whom, in the name of one let us hear Augustine (*Q.* 84 *in Levit.*), "Without the sanctification of invisible grace, what is the benefit of visible Sacraments?" Again (*Contra Faustum* 19, 11), "The power of the Sacraments avails very much, and scorn for them makes impious men; nay more, it is impiously scorned, without which piety cannot be brought about."

The *third* definition is of the Anabaptists, who teach the Sacraments are nothing other than allegories, and like certain signs of good works and life, as well as spiritual morals. They would have it that men are baptized to show that Christians ought to withstand adversity, and death itself for Christ. Melanchthon relates this error, (*Loc. Com.*, c. *de Sacramentis*) as well as Brenz (*hom.* 25 on Luke 3), and Chemnitz (*loc. cit.* 2 part., p. 96).

This opinion can be refuted without hardly any effort. Even if the Sacraments have this advantage for others, to remind men of good works and virtues (for certainly it cannot be denied that immersing in water in Baptism, and coming out again, reminds one of death, whereby we should be dead to sin; or again the resurrection, whereby we should rise again to new life. Even the Apostle calls a thing of this sort to mind in Romans 6:3. Or again the Eucharist reminds us of the peace and friendship which we should have among us, "For we are one body, who partake of the one bread

Chapter XV: Anabaptists and Zwinglians Refuted

[1 Cor. 10:17], nevertheless, it is not this alone, nor the particular use of the Sacraments; hence, the essence and nature of the Sacrament is not placed in it.

This is proved by the same argumentation which we have used against Carlstadt. Firstly, because Scripture says the Sacraments were instituted to justify as in 1 Cor. 6:11, "You have been washed, you are sanctified." And Ephes. 5:26, "Cleansing it by the laver of water in the word of life." Secondly, if they should only be allegories, it would not have been necessary that they flow from the side of Christ; the good will of men would have sufficed. Thirdly, there is no lack of more useful and efficacious admonitions to live well, such as exhortations and the examples of Christ and the Saints. Fourthly, add that if that opinion were true, the Sacraments would not be signs of anything except *future things*. They are, however, also signs of past and present things, for the Eucharist represents the death of Christ (1 Cor. 11:26), and according to Acts 22:16, Baptism signifies the internal washing which is completed at the time when we are baptized on the outside, "Be baptized and wash away your sins."

The *fourth* definition is of others who would have it that the Sacraments are signs of grace which is not received then, but which has already been received. Zwingli (*True and False religion,* c. On the Sacraments) and Chemnitz (*loc. cit.*, p. 96) relate and refute this without the name of the author, though it can easily be refuted, because the Scripture teaches with clear words that the Sacraments cause graces *in the present* (Acts 22:16, "Wash away your sins.").

The *fifth* definition is of Zwingli and his followers, save for Peter Martyr, as we said above. Zwingli (*On True and False Religion,* c. On the Sacraments) after he refuted the opinion of Catholics and Lutherans, opened his mind and teaches that the Sacraments are nothing other than a certain initiation and pledge, whereby men obligate themselves to Christ, and give their name to his army. From there, he deduces that the Sacraments are not properly testimonies of justice to a man who receives the Sacraments, as the Lutherans said, but they are public testimonies of the whole Church on the obligation and fidelity which a man owes to Christ, to whom he consecrated himself. Martin Bucer follows the same teaching in his commentaries on Matt. 3. In the preface of the second edition of the same commentaries, he adds, "But if men who are baptized are predestined, and the Sacrament is not only a sign which they give their name to Christ, and are received in the external Church, but also advances a certain consolation; but if they are not predestined, then the Sacrament is a bare sign, which they receive in the external Church, but not from God." For this reason, he also deduces that when infants are not predestined, Baptism is of no benefit, rather they perish, even if they are baptized.

This opinion is similar to the ones above, for he advances some part of the truth (nor can it be denied that we are initiated through the Sacraments, and give our name to Christ, as well as publicly witness that we are members of the Church), but he errs in that, he does not acknowledge another more sublime end of the institution of the Sacraments, and hence, he does not rightly explain the nature of the Sacrament. This is proven *firstly*: from the opinion of Zwingli that Christ does nothing, but a only man witnesses that he is faithful. However, in John 1:33, it is said, "He [Christ] it is that baptizes," and in Ephesians 5:26, "Cleansing it, etc."

Secondly, because Zwingli requires that before men receive the Sacraments they should be justified, and inwardly joined with Christ, they merely witness and profess outwardly through the Sacraments that they want to be a soldier for Christ, and joined to the external Church. Yet, the Scriptures witness the Sacraments were instituted to sanctify and cleanse a man inwardly. The Apostle shows this when he says "Cleansing it by the laver of water in the word of life" (Eph. 5:26). In respect to that passage, St. Augustine (*Tr. In Joan.* 80) wrote, "How is it that water has this power to touch a body, and wash the heart?" Likewise, in John 3:5 and Tit. 3:5, Baptism is called the laver of regeneration and renewal. From such passages we hold that a man is reborn through Baptism, because it pertains to the *inward* man, and does not only witness outwardly that he is faithful. On this point, the Scriptures already cited pertain against other errors (cf. Acts 2:38, 22:16, and 1 Cor. 6:11).

Thirdly, this same thing is proved, for the Apostle clearly says in Romans 6:3 that Baptism signifies the death and resurrection of Christ; and 1 Cor. 11:24 says the Eucharist was instituted in memory of the Lord's passion. Therefore, the Sacraments do not signify that a man is only initiated to God or *joined with the Church*.

CHAPTER XVI

The Definition of Calvin

THE last definition is also the teaching of John Calvin, who says the simple and proper definition of a Sacrament is contained with these words, "A Sacrament is an external symbol, whereby the Lord pledges the promises of his benevolence to our consciences, to sustain the weakness of our faith; and we in turn, witness our piety toward him, in his presence as well as that of the angels" (*Inst.* 4, 14 §1).

Moreover, it must be observed, the teaching of Calvin seems to have been composed from the teachings of Luther and Zwingli. When he says a "symbol pledging promises to sustain the weakness of faith," is taken from Luther; what he adds at the end, that in the same symbol we witness our piety toward God among men, has been taken from Zwingli. Nevertheless, Calvin disagrees very much with both in the matter. When he acknowledges with Zwingli, that in the Sacrament we witness our piety among men, still, he rejects that this is the only, or primary purpose of the Sacrament, and bitterly opposes it (*Ibid.* 14 §5 -14), on behalf of the opinion of Luther, and answers all the arguments which Zwingli and Bucer make against Luther, although he names none of them. For equal reasoning, although he affirms with Luther that the Sacrament is a testimony of grace and remission of sins, still he by far understands it otherwise than Luther does. He always speaks about grace, which is given to men at the time they receive the Sacraments, but Calvin speaks about the grace of predestination, and hence would have it, that the Sacraments are testimonies of predestination, instituted to nourish faith, whereby a man believes for certain that he is predestined; from which it follows what Bucer says, the Sacraments are not true signs, nor of any benefit to predestination.

The foundation of this whole affair is that Calvin thinks (as he profusely treats in *Inst.* 3, 2) true faith once held can never be lost; hence it follows that true faith, without which the Sacraments do not avail, is proper predestination, nor can it be had in any way by those who are not predestined. For this reason, in his *Antidote to the Council* (sess. 6 cap. 5), he says that Baptism is given to infants because they are already reckoned members of the Church, since they are adopted by God as sons, namely, through the grace of predestination, and again (*ibid.*, sess. 7 can. 7 on Baptism) he says the Sacrament renders us certain on the perpetual grace of adoption. Very clearly, in his book on the consensus among the people of Zurich and Geneva, on the matter of the Sacrament, Calvin says, "We teach in earnest that God does not indiscriminately exercise his force in everyone who receives the Sacraments; rather, only in the elect. To the extent that he does not illuminate anyone in regard to faith, except for those whom he had preordained to life; in this way, he effects by the secret virtue of his spirit, that the elect would partake of what the Sacraments offer."

Now that these matters have been explained this definition must be refuted: the whole is vicious, as will become clear if we review every word. 1) The first word is "outward symbol," which is absolutely true, but not in that sense whereby Calvin receives it. He understands it as a bare symbol (i.e., a symbol which only signifies but does not work anything), for in the whole definition he does not place any effects of this symbol, except to seal the promises of God and give witness to our piety. Nor is it opposed that Calvin says in the *Antidote to the Council of Trent* (sess. 7 can. 5) that the Sacraments are instruments of justification, for he understands them to be instruments because they excite or nourish faith, and not through some efficacy, but merely objectively. Theodore Beza most clearly explains this (*de Summa rei Sacramentariae* q. 2) when he speaks in this way, "From where is that efficacy of the Sacraments? It is wholly from the operation of the Holy Spirit, but not from signs, except inasmuch as the inward senses are moved by those outward objects." By such reasoning, the signs which hang on doors of inns may certainly also be called instruments of a dining room, because they move a man to think the table has been prepared in that house, etc.

The Scriptures, however, teach (*passim*) that the Sacraments are certain things that *operate*, namely, which cleanse, wash, sanctify, justify, and regenerate (John 3:5, 1 Cor. 6:11: Eph. 5:26, Tit. 3:5, Acts 22:16). Furthermore, the Scriptures never say that the Sacraments are testimonies of the promises of God and our piety, or certainly, they do not say this as expressly as that which we assert, namely that they are *causes of justification*.

2) The next word is, "of his benevolence toward us."[2] That word is rightly placed in the definition of a Sacrament by a double meaning firstly, because it follows from this word that the Sacrament is always a sign of a past thing, or better, an eternal one. He cannot deny this because for benevolence, he understands the grace of predestination; besides, he clearly concedes it in the *Antidote* (sess. 6 c. 5), "Their salvation does not have a beginning from Baptism, rather, what has already been signed in Baptism was founded in the word. ... For, unless previously the promise of life would pertain to them, anyone who would give Baptism to them would profane it." Therefore, he conceded that the Sacrament is a seal of a past thing, namely of God's benevolence. This is not opposed with what he says in the Antidote (sess. 7 can. 4 & 5), that the Sacraments are instruments

---

[2] Translator's note: Bellarmine's exposition follows the order of the Latin words, which is at variance with the order of the English translation at the beginning of the Chapter.

Chapter XVI: Calvin's Definition

of justification. He would have it that the Sacraments, inasmuch as they sustain and nourish faith, confirm or increase justification (for faith is that which justifies among them), nevertheless, he would not have it that the Sacrament is a seal of this justification which is held through faith, but of the grace of predestination. He also does not hold that the Sacrament brings the first justification, but only an increase, and confirmation, which he also teaches in his *Small Catechism*. The first justification is held by faith, conceived from the preaching that preceded it.

But this whole thing is very clearly opposed to the Scriptures, which attribute to the Sacraments the force of bringing the first justification. What else is it to regenerate, which is attributed to Baptism (John 3:5, Tit. 3:5), which makes a man dead in sin but alive in the life of grace? We will speak of this more profusely later in its proper place.

Next, that promise of the grace of predestination is not rightly posited in the definition of a Sacrament, both because God would often be made to testify falsely, and because no man could baptize another without sin. One profanes Baptism (as Calvin says in the *Antidote*, sess. 6 c. 5), who confers it upon a man to whom the promise does not pertain; he compels God to witness what is false, namely that he loves the man, whom he really does not love. But no man can be certain about another man, whether he has been predestined or not, therefore, either no one should baptize any man, or he acts rashly and faithlessly when he exposes Baptism to the danger of profanation.

Bucer answers this argument, that ministers do not have the intention to baptize anyone but the predestined (*Commentary on Matthew*, preface).

He does not satisfy his purpose. In the first place, he excuses the minister, but not *God*, except perhaps God also at some time baptizes without the intention to baptize, which is ridiculous. Next, from the opinion of the Lutherans and all Calvinists: The Sacraments do not depend upon the intention of the minister. Luther writes (*On the Babylonian Captivity*, on Baptism) that Baptism is true and ratified even if the minister does not intend to baptize, but to pretend. Calvin does not disagree (*Antidote*, sess. 7 can. 11).

Calvin answers otherwise (*Inst.* 4, 15 §16 & 17). Clearly God, on his side, truly supplies the promise and the seal of the promise to all who are baptized, whether they receive it or not; hence God is always truthful. He does not even say that the ministers sin if they confer Baptism on men who profess to believe, if they are adults or sons of faithful parents, for Calvin believes the sons of faithful parents are holy, from the promise of God in Genesis 17:17, "I will be your God, and of your seed." The reason why the ministers do not sin, is that they have a probable reason whereby they gather those whom they baptize are predestined and holy.

But this solution does not satisfy. In the first place, if anyone supplies Baptism to a man to whom he knows the divine promises do not pertain, he profanes Baptism, as Calvin himself says, because he bears a false witness. Why would God himself not profane Baptism and bear false witnesses when he supplies it to a man whom he knows he did not predestine? God does not act on the one hand, and the minister on the other, rather, it is *one thing* that they do; for God acts through the minister, as is clear from John 1:33, "It is he who baptizes in the Holy Spirit."

Moreover, he does not only supply the Sacrament, but he also *supplies* the testimony of benevolence, seeing that the same Calvin speaks in this way in his *Small Catechism*, "The Sacrament is the witness of divine benevolence toward us." So, God supplies the seal of benevolence to one who is baptized, even if he does not believe, for without faith the fruit and the *res Sacramenti* cannot be received. Nevertheless, a true Sacrament is received, as Calvin also teaches in the *Institutes* (4, 15 §16) where he acknowledges, against the Anabaptists, that a true Sacrament is given and received among Catholics, where he does not think there is any true faith. Therefore, if God really supplies the seal and testimony of benevolence to a man whom he does not love, how does he not lie and profane the Sacrament?

Besides, it is proven that the minister would sin. Even if he had a probable reason to believe that the man who professes faith is predestined, nevertheless, he does not have *certitude*. It may happen that he lies when he says that he believes; it could also happen (as Calvin affirms in *Inst.* 3, 2 §10) that he thinks he believes and still really does not. To witness something in the name of God, however, *the truest certitude* is required; probable opinion does not suffice. It is clear in a similar thing, namely an oath; it is not lawful to use an oath, i.e., the testimony of God in some matter, which we suppose is true, rather, only in a business which we are absolutely certain is true. Moreover, a greater certitude by far should still be required in the Sacrament, according to our adversaries, than in our oath, seeing that a Sacrament is like an oath of God. The oath of God differs from our oath, however, since when a man swears, he is the one who asserts something, although he invokes God as a witness. For this reason, our oath can be false without any injury to God, just as if someone swore that he knew for certain, and was still deceived in the very matter, then God does not give testimony, nor does the man who cited God as a witness to falsity sin, because he believed he was altogether certain. For example, if perhaps a man sees someone killed by someone who was very similar to another man, whom he had never seen. Nevertheless, in the Sacraments, according to our adversaries, God himself affirms, and in a certain measure, swears that the man who receives the Sacrament is of the elect, and just. Moreover, God cannot be deceived by any error, so he would sin most gravely, who confers the Sacrament on a man whom he does not know for certain is just and among the elect, because he compels God to lie.

Next, even if the minister would know for certain he who professes

Chapter XVI: Calvin's Definition

faith, or is the son of a faithful man, is just and elect, still, what will he do if an infant is offered to him to be baptized who is the son of a Turk or a Jew, and the parents, although they are infidels, gladly suffer him to be baptized and remain among Christians? If the minister will baptize him, he profanes Baptism, since he has no sign whereby he understands he is predestined, but if he will not baptize, he acts contrary to the use of the whole Church.

Perhaps someone will object on Calvin's behalf, that Catholics have the same problem, since even they supply the Sacraments to those whom they do not know whether they are disposed, and nevertheless, affirm they are divinely instituted signs of divine grace.

I respond: Catholics do not suffer any problems in this regard, for they say the Sacraments are efficacious causes of grace, *unless an obstacle were to be placed in the way*; at the same time they show the infusion of the same grace, *as far as it is on the side of the Sacrament itself.* Lastly, the same Sacraments are signs of the effect which grace does, *wherever it is present.* As the water of Baptism washes the body, so the grace of the Savior washes the soul; that is perpetual and infallible, and it does not depend upon the disposition. The disposition helps one to receive grace, rather, because grace, wherever it is, washes the filth of the soul if it should discover any; it is intrinsic and inseparable to it.

3) The third word in the definition of Calvin was "promises." Certainly, we treated on the promise of the remission of sins in the refutation of the definition of the Lutherans; but Calvin speaks on the promise of benevolent predestination, which can be refuted more easily by far. For no promise of this sort exists in the whole Scripture; all the promises include some condition, such as faith, or penance, or another virtue, and in all these the condition of perseverance.

Hence, all the testimonies which they advance can clearly be refuted. The primary one is that of Gen. 17:7, "Therefore I will be your God, and the God of your seed after you." Yet this also requires the condition of faith and perseverance, for "The seed of Abraham" (as Paul explains in Romans 4:13 and 9:8), "are not sons of the flesh, but faith," i.e., those who imitate Abraham in faith, they are his seed, with whom the agreement of God intercedes. Certainly, as anyone begins to be the seed of Abraham, when he begins to believe, in this way he ceases to be if he would cease to believe. Who could persuade himself for certain that he never departed from the faith, especially when especially when faith and perseverance in faith are gifts of God?

4) The fourth word is "to our consciences," which can be joined with "to sustain the weakness of faith." These words are not rightly placed in the definition of a Sacrament, as the Baptism of children witnesses, which is the truest Sacrament, even with Calvin, and still, there is no conscience in infants, nor actual faith for which the Sacrament is necessary to sustain. Rightly, if the promise is like a diploma, and the Sacrament like a seal,

conscience will be like the paper or the wax. So, how can a charter be written or sealed when there is no paper? Hence, what the Lutherans say, that children believe in act while they are baptized, has already been refuted above; nor does Calvin dare to affirm it, even if he did not wish to reject it, as is clear from the *Institutes* (4, 16, §19).

Calvin answers that the Baptism of infants is worked in the consciences of infants, as soon as they begin to have the use of it, even if it had already been conferred; for later they remember that they received baptism, and nourish and sustain their faith by that sign (*ibid.*, 4, 1, §20 & 21). He says the same thing about those who are baptized as Catholics and later become Calvinists (4, 15, §17). In any event, we rightly prove that the Calvinists do not act rightly when they baptize infants, for it would by far be more useful to baptize them as adults, when they are capable of faith. We have no knowledge of the Baptism which we receive in infancy except from the relation of others; hence, we have no certitude except upon human trust, which can deceive. Next, even if we were absolutely certain, nevertheless things that are seen move more than what is heard; this is why it would be better for an adult to be baptized than an infant if the purpose is to nourish faith. But to nourish faith is the primary end and use of Baptism in Calvin's definition, therefore it is wrong for them to baptize infants.

They cannot answer that infants are baptized lest they might perish before they become adolescents, and in that way die without the grace of God, for Calvin teaches that predestined infants are saved even without Baptism, while those who are not predestined perish, even with Baptism.

Therefore, nothing can be said except infants are baptized only for the reason that they are admitted into the external Church, or profess that they are members of the external Church. This still does not answer the argument. According to Calvin's opinion (*Inst.* 4, 14 §5 *seq.*), the principal end of the Sacraments is to seal the promises so as to nourish faith; the less principal end is to profess that they are a member of the external Church. Moreover, the less principal end should not impede the greater principal end; so infants should not be baptized among the Calvinists, seeing that among them in the Baptism of infants, on account of the less principal end, the greater principal end is impeded.

5) The fifth word is "seals" and we said many things on that word in refutation of the opinion of Luther; and on the rest of the words of Calvin's definition we spoke in refutation of the opinion of Zwingli. Lastly, it only remains that we refute their arguments.

CHAPTER XVII

The Arguments of Our Adversaries Are Refuted

The arguments which not only the Lutherans but even the Calvinists use to show the Sacraments are seals of promises, are these: 1) For the *first* passage, Calvin, in the *Institutes* (4, 14 §5), advances the words of the Apostle in Romans 4:11: where he calls Circumcision σφραγίδα, i.e., the seal of his covenant, by faith in which Abraham was already justified.

I respond: a) Firstly, the things that are said on Circumcision alone cannot rightly be derived for all the Sacraments. We argue rightly from a kind to a species, and not vice versa.

b) Secondly, the Apostle does not mention a promise, or agreement, when he speaks on the seal of Circumcision; he calls it *the seal of justice of faith*, not the seal of the promise and pact. Moreover, it is called the seal of justice of faith for one of two reasons: *one*, because (as Origen writes on this passage) Circumcision sealed and closed the justice of faith which was revealed in its time, that is to say the Circumcision of heart (the true justification which Christ had brought) was signified secretly, and hence veiled under a figure and type of that carnal Circumcision. In the *other* (as Chrysostom, Theophylactus, and others teach) the seal is called the justice of faith because it was given to Abraham in a sign and testimony of justice, which he acquired for himself through faith.

c) Thirdly, I say: this was a privilege of *Abraham alone*, and could not be transferred to others, as though Circumcision (as the heretics would have it) would be a witness of that justice in everyone that had it. The privilege was Abraham's, as he was the father of all the faithful, both of the uncircumcised and the circumcised and because he was the father of the uncircumcised faithful, because he had faith, even while he was uncircumcised, as is clear from Genesis 12:3, and from this passage of Paul, "He received, first of all the sign of Circumcision, that in this way he would also be the father of all the circumcised." Because he rightly had this privilege of justice, which he had acquired through faith, therefore, the sign of Circumcision was to him a seal of the justice of faith. Hence, for the rest of the Jews, Circumcision was a certain sign, namely that they were sons of Abraham, but it was not for them the seal *of the justice of faith*, just as not all the Jews are fathers of many nations.

That this is true is clear *firstly* because Paul joins these two together when he says, "And he received the sign of Circumcision, a seal of the justice of faith, to be the father of all believers" (Rom. 4:11). Therefore, all the circumcised did not have the seal of the justice of faith, since they are not all fathers of all believers.

Secondly, because Paul distinguishes the sign from the seal when he says, "He received the sign of Circumcision, the seal of the justice of faith," for sign, in Greek is σημεῖον, which properly expresses a seal. Moreover, this is why he distinguishes these terms, otherwise he would show that Circumcision is always and to all a certain sign, when it is not for all, rather, it was the seal of justice *for Abraham alone.*

Thirdly, Scripture, although it speaks very often about Circumcision, still never calls it a seal except in this place, where it is a question of Abraham; which is a manifest argument that Circumcision was a seal for Abraham alone. Certainly, when Paul asks in Romans 3:1, "What use is Circumcision?" and answers in verse 2, "Much every way," according to our adversaries he should have posited in the first place this primary utility, that it is a seal of the divine promise, but he did not even mention it.

2) Calvin (*ibid.* §6), takes the *second* argument from Genesis 9:13, where the heavenly rainbow is called the sign of the covenant between God and Noah, and from Gen. 17:11: where Circumcision is called the sign of the covenant between God and Abraham and his posterity. If the rainbow and Circumcision were seals confirming the agreement and promise of God, why can the same thing not be said on Baptism and the Eucharist? He confirms his argument from the fact that among men it is also customary that agreements are ratified by an external sign, such as a slaughtered pig,[3] or giving the right hand, which were signs of nothing other than the words of the agreement that preceded.

I respond: The rainbow and Circumcision were signs of the covenant, but to *help memory*, not to confirm faith; in the same we also taught above that Baptism and Eucharist are commemorative signs of the passion and death of the Lord. Moreover, there is a great difference between a commemorative sign and a confirmative one. A commemorative sign can be that which is presented to the eyes, even if its whole efficacy depends upon a promise, but a confirmative sign cannot be anything if it altogether depends upon a promise. Moreover, it is clear that the only commemorative signs were the rainbow and Circumcision. In this way they depended upon the word of God, that if anyone would not believe the word of God, or not believe it is the word of God, he would also not believe those signs, and vice versa, if anyone would believe the word, he would not need these signs.

Add that St. John Chrysostom explains these passages in this way: In his *Homily 39 on Genesis*, on Circumcision he says, "After he gave a perpetual memorial to them, he began the sign of Circumcision with them."

---

3 Translator's note: In the Aeneid (8.641), a sow was slaughtered to effect a treaty. Moreover, the standard etymology of *foedus, foederis* (n.), the Latin word for treaty, and in the Vulgate "covenant," comes from the practice of a foul (*foeda*) slaughter of some sort of animal as a pledge of trust.

Chapter XVII: Arguments of the Heretics Refuted

Later, he says the sign of Circumcision was not given by God for men to believe him, but was demanded of men by God, because God did not trust men, "When we do not have faith in someone, we take care to receive a sign of a pledge from them in its place. Similarly, the Lord, knowing the inconstancy of all minds, willed to seek this sign from them." Moreover, on the sign of the rainbow, he says in *Homily 28 on Genesis*, "What do you say, O Blessed Prophet? 'I will remember my Covenant, i.e., my pact, promise'; not because he needs to remember, but that we, looking to that sign, will suspect nothing hard, but immediately remember the divine promise, and we shall be strengthened and trust."

Now, somebody will raise the objection that the same Chrysostom says in that sermon, "If my word does not suffice, behold, I give a sign, etc.," where it seems he meant the rainbow was a confirmative sign. This objection will be refuted a little later.

I respond to the confirmation from human custom, that there is a great difference between the agreements of God, and of men. From men, because we do not see his mind and we are afraid lest perhaps he might deceive us, or forget his agreement, we seek an outward sign that we might convict him thereby if he will deny or forget it; yet we are quite certain God cannot deceive or forget.

3) Luther takes up the *third* argument (*Bab. Capt.* c. on Baptism), from marvelous signs with which God customarily confirms his promises; such a sign was in the dew, in the fleece given to Gideon (Judg. 6:37), and in the shadow of the receding sun-dial of Hezekiah (4 King 20:11).

Now this, and similar things are not relevant. Miracles, because they do not depend upon a word, but have force *of themselves*, seeing that they are works above nature, are rightly applied to prove God exists, who promised, or that God really promised something, but the Sacraments have no force without the word (as we said above). Moreover, we understand from where Chrysostom thought the Rainbow was not only a memorial sign, but also a confirmative one. He thought the rainbow was a thing established by a new miracle, speaking in this way, "Although the flood of waters was great, in this way, looking up at it, we should not fear it, but trust in the miracle." Still, because it is more probable that the Rainbow was a natural thing, therefore, we said the sign was only memorial.

4) The Lutherans take up the *fourth* argument from the words of 1 Peter 3:21, "Now, Baptism being of the like form, now it saves you also; not the putting away of the filth of the flesh, but the examination of a good conscience towards God." Luther, in his commentary on this passage, takes the Greek word ἐπερώτημα, which our translators render "examination," and would have that it means agreement, and explains it in this way, "Baptism saves us, not insofar as it washes the body, but insofar as it shows the agreement which the soul has with God, while it receives his promises by faith." From which it follows that Baptism is a seal of the promise. Calvin

explains it in nearly the same way, although he would have it that the term ἐπερώτημα does not mean an agreement, but a response and a testimony.

I respond: This present passage is very obscure, nevertheless, it brings no assistance to the cause of our adversaries. Oecumenius, in his commentary on this passage, seems to understand through *examination*, a pledge of good conscience, i.e., men who, by God's inspiration, conceive a good desire, and they pursue an immaculate life, and everywhere seek it, and inquire after it. Whereby, when they hear that their souls will be cleansed through Baptism, they run to Baptism as soon as they can to cleanse their filth; by this reasoning, Baptism is a pledge of a good conscience.

This exposition does not favor the heretics, as is clear; nevertheless, it does not seem to be according to the mind of St. Peter. By far, St. Peter attributes more to Baptism than being a pledge of good conscience, when he says we are saved through Baptism.

There is another exposition of Lyranus, Gagnaeus, and John of Louvain, who for examination of a good conscience, understand the examinations and responses which are made before Baptism. The priest asks the Catechumen, "Do you believe in God?" and the latter responds, "I believe." "Do you renounce Satan and all his pomps?" "I do renounce them," etc. Baptism is beneficial for anyone who responds to these questions with a good conscience, but otherwise to those who do not.

This also does not favor the heretics, but it does not seem literal, nor is it of Ambrose, Basil, and Augustine, as John of Louvain supposes, for St. Peter makes the antithesis when he says "not the putting away of the filth of the flesh, but the examination of a good conscience." Without a doubt, this will be the formal antithesis: not the washing of the filth of the flesh, but the washing of the filth of *the mind*. By such an antithesis our Baptism is distinguished from the Baptism of the Jews, which was merely exterior. Hence, that part of this antithesis (namely, the washing of the filth of the mind) was not expressed by St. Peter in his own words, but in figures, as everyone concedes. Therefore, it is fitting for it to have to been expressed by the cause, or the effect; if through the effect, then their exposition has no place. For that examination, and response, on which they argue, or even faith and charity which are detected through those examinations and responses, precede Baptism, and hence the washing of the mind, which Baptism does; therefore, they are not the effects of that washing. Moreover, it is necessary that they say the washing is described through the cause, and hence that examination which precedes Baptism is the cause of that washing, but this cannot be said. Otherwise, the Sacrament would have efficacy *ex opere operantis*, not *ex opere operato*; justification would be attributed to the preceding faith and love of the recipient of Baptism, not to the sacramental washing itself; and there would not be any difference between our Baptism and the Jewish, since the Jewish Baptism, although it did not justify *ex opere operato*, nevertheless, could justify from the faith

Chapter XVII: Arguments of the Heretics Refuted

and love of the one receiving it, just as any meritorious work.

Perhaps they will say the examination, or preceding faith, is not the efficient cause of internal washing, but the disposition. On the contrary, that is rightly said, but it does not square with the words of the Apostle, for he attributes a greater efficacy to this examination of a good conscience than to the external washing, which is still an instrument of justification.

There is another exposition, which I think is of the saints (Augustine, *Tr. 80 in Joan., Serm. 30 de verb. Dom.*; and Basil, *On the Holy Spirit* c. 15), that the washing of the mind is clearly expressed by St. Peter, which through the antithesis is opposed to the washing of the flesh, not through a cause, as the preceding opinion would have it, but *through the effect*. It is a very common figure of a metonym, whereby through the effect we understand the cause. Peter calls the internal washing the examination, or response of a good conscience toward God, because from that cleansing peace arises, as well as rest of conscience, and hence, the response of a good conscience, and even the examination with God, because he dares with trust to approach God and examine, i.e., speak with him, and ask him on his own behalf, as well as on behalf of others.

I add secondly that this passage does not favor our adversaries, but us even if the word ἐπερώτημα means testimony or a pact. In the first place, St. Peter does not speak about testimony, or a pact of God, but *of our conscience*, for they ought to prove the Sacrament is the seal of testimony or the pact of God. There is a great difference between testimony, or the pact of God, which they would have it is shown by the Sacrament, and testimony, or the pact of our conscience. For that is the written word of God, which precedes the use of the Sacrament, and the fruit, i.e., justification; however, the testimony of our conscience follows justification, and hence the use and fruit of the Sacrament.

Secondly, St. Peter does not say that a pact, or testimony is shown in Baptism. Rather, he says souls are saved and justification is effected, from which the testimony of a good conscience arises. This much is proven from that phrase, "being of a like form." The Apostle means in that mode we are saved through the waters of Baptism, in the way that those who were in the Ark of Noah were saved in the waters of the flood. Hence, the waters of the flood did not save the ark of Noah by testifying or sealing promises, but really by elevating the ark on high, lest it would be overturned with the rest of the buildings of this world. So in this way, Baptism also saves us, not by sealing or testifying, but really by justifying the soul; from where, as we said, the testimony, or examination of a good conscience toward God follows.

5) The *fifth* argument can favor our adversaries, namely the testimony of the holy Fathers, who do not rarely call the Sacraments seals.

I respond: By far, the Fathers speak with a different signification in regard to the seals of the Sacraments than the heretics would make, for the Fathers never call the Sacraments seals of the promise of God, as the heretics suppose; rather, some of them speak on seals in three ways. *a)* Firstly, they call the seals Sacraments because they sign the faithful, and like certain marks, separate them from others, who are not of the flock, or from the army of the Lord. Basil receives the term in this way in his exhortation on Baptism; likewise Jerome in *Eph.* 4, Augustine in *Contra Faustum* 19, 11, and others (*pass.*). So also, Gregory Nazianzen in his oration on Baptism, not far from the beginning, where he says that Baptism is called a seal because in this way it conserves the baptized man, as a royal mark conserves the things it has signed. No man dares to touch what bears the seal of some great king.

b) Secondly, they call the Sacraments seals, because they shut a sacred thing within themselves, i.e., invisible grace. That which is closed is usually sealed, according to that of Apocalypse 5:1, "The book sealed with seven seals." Also, by this signification Augustine calls the Sacraments sacred seals (*de Cath. Rud.*, 26), as well as the Scholastics, the seal of Confession. Gregory Nazianzen speaks in nearly the same way (*Orat. de Baptismo*), when he calls Baptism a seal, because it seals and closes many mysteries which are uncovered in the faithful alone, "Moreover, you will learn within what also has been hidden within your selves, you will have what has been closed, sealed, and retained by Baptism."

c) They call Baptism a seal, or a sign of faith because Baptism is a public approbation and witness of the faith of the man who is baptized. Tertullian uses this term in that way (*de Poen.*), where he says that catechumens are proved for a while, whether they believe, and at length after it is certain that they truly and firmly believe, Baptism is given to them in a seal and approbation of faith. Basil uses this same term in this way (*Contra Eunom.* 3) where he says first of all it behooves one to believe, and then at length to receive Baptism as the seal of faith. In his book on the Holy Spirit (c. 12), he calls Baptism the seal of faith, because he that is baptized witnesses that he believes in that sign.

Lastly, Baptism is also called the seal of faith because it perfects and absolves the faithful man in a certain measure, in the way the Fathers call dying for Christ *the seal of martyrdom*, as Eusebius relates (*Hist.* 5, 3). The confession of martyrs, and their suffering for Christ, does not have perfect praise while the danger of inconstancy and change is present; but then, at length when it is perfect, they are thought to be fortified and sealed with a certain seal when they are consummated with a precious death. That is enough on the definition.

THE THIRD CONTROVERSY

On the Causes of the Sacrament

CHAPTER XVIII

The Sacraments Are Composed of Things and Words, Namely Matter and Form

WE are going to dispute on the causes of the Sacrament. First we will speak on the intrinsic causes, then on the extrinsic causes and on three intrinsic questions: *First*, whether the Sacraments are constituted from things, such as matter, and words, such as form. *Second*, what are these things, and those words. *Thirdly*, whether these things and words are determined in such a way that nothing can be changed in them.

1) The first question: whether the Sacraments are constituted from things and words, like matter and form. Although it is disputed among Catholics, it is not so much due to actual disagreement, as it is to explain matters; nevertheless, it is a very useful question, or even necessary, on account of the calumnies of the heretics, who from this doctrine of Catholics, whereby we require things and words in the Sacraments, try to show that there are many Sacraments from these, which we hold for Sacraments. Therefore, there are different opinions of the Doctors.

The first is of certain more recent doctors, who held that properly in the Sacraments, matter and form are not things and words, but a sensible thing is the matter, whether it is a thing or a word, or both; while the signification is the form. Moreover, it is commonly said a thing in the Sacrament is the matter, the word is the form, they would explain it on the Sacrament taken materially. Domingo del Soto teaches this (4 dist. 1 q. 1 art. 1 & 2), and it seems that Cajetan says the same thing (3 part. q. 60 art. 6), except that Cajetan affirms the signification of a Sacrament is one and simple, resulting from the sensible composition of things and words, which del Soto does not say.

The second opinion is of others, who teach that the Sacrament itself, and not only its material part, is constituted from things as matter and form. St. Thomas argues in this way (III q. 60 art. 6, ad secundum), as well as the old theologians in common.

Again, certain men think that not all the Sacraments are constituted from things and words, but only certain ones. Durandus (4 dist. 1 q. 3) and

Adrian (q. 2, *de Baptismo*) speak this way.

Others teach that all the Sacraments of the New Law are constituted from things and words. Alexander of Hales teaches this (4 part. summae q. 8 memb. 3 art. 1 & 3) as well as the common opinions of Theologians (4 dist. 1 or 3).

Then others would have it that all the Sacraments are constituted from things and words, if the things and words are received broadly for these signs which are true things and true words, or certainly they manage in their place; but if they are received rigorously, then not all the Sacraments are constituted from things and words. Domingo del Soto teaches in that way (4 dist. 1 q. 1 art. 6) as well as certain other more recent ones, but these opinions can be reconciled for the most part.

Therefore, the *first* proposition: *It is probable that the Sacraments of the Old Law did not have things and words, but only things.* This is the view of St. Thomas (III q. 60 art. 6 ad ultimum). The reason is, because in the Scripture of the Old Testament, where the particular rites of the Sacraments are prescribed, there is no mention of words, as is clear from Gen. 17:10 *et seq.*, where the rite of Circumcision is prescribed; in Exodus 12:3 *seq.*, where the right of the Paschal Lamb is prescribed; and Leviticus 8:2 *seq.*, where the rite of Ordination is prescribed. Besides, reason seems to demand that the new Sacraments instituted by Christ himself should be clearer signs than the Old, which Moses instituted as a minister of God.

The objection could be made that in Leviticus 4:20, where the sacrifices are prescribed for sin (which were also Sacraments of the Old Law and they correspond to our Sacrament of Penance, as St. Thomas teaches in I IIae q. 102 art. 1), it is also prescribed that the priest will pray for those on whose behalf the sacrifice is offered. But the response can be made that the prayer of the priest was not concerning the essence of the sacrifice for sin, but only should be added in use, or in the administration of that Sacrament *to more easily obtain it*. That which is gathered from it, which, as we find in the same place, in the sacrifice for sin, no prayer of the priest is applied, but only in the sacrifice for the sin of others in regard to the people. Moreover, that which is found in Num. 5:19 on the prescribed words in the Ceremonies of Zelotypia do not bear on the matter, for that ceremony was not a Sacrament, since it was not instituted to sanctify, but to discover and punish adultery.

The *second* proposition: *In all the Sacraments of the New Law things such as matter and words such as form are found.* This proposition, at least in regard to its manner of speech, cannot be denied. It is expressly held in the Council of Florence, in the *Instruction of the Armenians*, which was made with the approval of the same Council, as we read in the same place. Besides, we find expressly in the Scriptures that things and words are in four of the Sacraments: Matthew 28:19, "Baptizing them in the name of the Father, and of the Son, and of the Holy Spirit"; in the Eucharist in

Chapter XVIII: Matter and Form

Matthew 26:26, where bread and a word are posited, "This is my body"; In Confirmation in Acts 8:15, 17, where there is an imposition of hands and a prayer made, which is with words; In Extreme Unction, James 5:14-15, where anointing and a prayer is placed. Therefore, it is believable that the other Sacraments are also constituted of things and words, although they are not so expressly found in the Scriptures. Likewise, it is the common teaching of the old Theologians, save for one, Durandus, or a few other exceptions, whose manner of speech must be corrected, although *in re* they do not disagree much from the rest.

The *third* proposition: *Not only is there some material thing in the Sacrament, but the whole Sacrament itself is rightly said to be constituted from things, such as matter, and words, such as form.* This is in some manner against Cajetan and del Soto, although they say that is also true in some way.

So we must note, the Sacrament is not properly composed of some physical thing, nor an artificial one, but it has a certain similitude to both. Indeed, if it were compared with an artificial composition, then without a doubt its form is partly a meaning and partly an operative virtue; but the things themselves are matter, and the words, in which the meaning resides, are also the operative virtue. In an artificial composition the whole substance is called a material, but the form is in a certain measure an accident. In this way, as a sign the Sacrament formally designates a signification, as a cause it designates the operative force. All the rest pertains to the matter or the subject. And by receiving Sacraments in this way, Cajetan and del Soto speak rightly.

Nevertheless, the Sacrament can also be considered as similar to a physical composite. For, as matter precedes in a physical composite, the form is added. So also, in a Sacrament, the word is added to the element. Likewise, as in a physical composite the matter is indeterminate, but it restricts the form, so in the Sacrament, the word determines the want of distinction of the element. Lastly, as in a physical composite, the matter is imperfect, but the form is perfect, and gives being to the thing; thus, in a Sacrament, the words are more perfect than the things since they are much more clear and excellent signs.

In this way, the whole word with its signification is the form, and the whole element with its signification is the matter. That fact is proven firstly, because the Council of Florence speaks in this way, as well as all of the older theologians. They say: A Sacrament is constituted from a thing and a word, just as from matter and form. But by a remote signification, there is no union from the thing and word, for, there is no other union of things and words except inasmuch as the indeterminate signification of a thing were to be determined through the signification of the word. Therefore, the Council and the Theologians do not mean that only the subject of the signification is constituted from things and words, but the whole Sacrament itself also, formally as a sign.

Next, the composite is from a sensible thing and the signification, it is not a composition from the matter and form, as essential parts, but it is the composition from the subject and the accident. The Council and the Theologians, however, say the Sacraments are constituted from matter and form, not from subject and accident; often, they also add the matter or form of the Sacraments cannot be changed by the Church, because they are of the essence, or substance.

Secondly, it is proven by reason, for the signification of the Sacrament is not one simple signification, as Cajetan teaches, rather two partial ones, from which one entire is composed. Thus, the very signification from the matter and form can be said to be constituted; hence, the whole Sacrament is composed from the matter and form, as from essential parts.

The antecedent is proved in two ways. a) Firstly, before the union of the element and the word takes place, both have their own signification; but from the union no signification is lost, for the word cannot take away the signification of the element, which is natural, but only determine it. For example, since water can naturally signify any cleansing you like, it will be determined by the word to signify cleansing *from sins*. In this way, both significations remain, but are joined together so that from the two parts one whole and total thing comes about.

b) Secondly, both the word and the element in the Sacraments signify something, as everyone teaches, and as is clear from St. Thomas (III q. 60 art. 6 ad 1 & 2), but the word does not communicate its signification to the element, nor the element to the word; thus they are two, not one. The assumption is proven because the signification of the element is natural, as St. Thomas says (*ibid*), but the signification of the word is voluntary. So, the signification of the element is not communicated to the word, because it would then be a natural signification, not a willed signification of the word, while on the other hand, the signification of the word is not communicated to the element, because then the signification of the element would be merely voluntary, and in no way natural.

4) The *fourth* proposition: *As the Sacraments are constituted from things and words, it is not necessary that things would not be words, and words not things, but rather, it is enough if one thing were exercised in place of a thing, and another in place of a word.* This proposition reconciles the last three opinions, for as Ledesma rightly advises (q. 1 art. 6) it is not a question between Durandus and others except in name only.

The proposition is proved, for in the Sacrament of Penance it can happen that there are no other signs apart from the words. From the common consensus of the Theologians, in the Sacrament of Penance the form is absolution, the remote matter is the sins, and the proximate matter is acts of repentance, i.e., contrition, confession and satisfaction, insofar as produced by an external sign. It can happen, however, that someone may

Chapter XVIII: Matter and Form

not have anything but sins consigned to word, and then the remote matter will be the words alone. It can also happen, that he may not show signs of contrition, confession, and satisfaction except in words. For that is not concerning the essence of the Sacrament, that the penitent would weep, sigh, genuflect, etc., rather, if only he would say his sins by word, and that he is contrite and wishes to make satisfaction, he can be absolved. This is why the matter there will not then be proximate matter, except words. Nevertheless, things and words are truly said to exist in that Sacrament, because the sign consigned to the word, not as it is a word, but as it is *a sin*, is the matter of the confession; a sin however is not formally a word, but a very distinct thing from the notion of a word. So also confession is not properly the matter of the Sacrament, as a certain prayer, but as an *action of the penitent*. As St. Thomas elegantly teaches (4 dist. 14 q. 1 art. 1) it is unique in this Sacrament that the action of the one receiving it is part of the essence of the Sacrament. As among bodily medications, they are altogether certain extrinsic things, such as a bandage, which is applied to sick people, and does not require their action, as part of the medication; certain others are partly extrinsic, partly intrinsic, such as potions which require walking as part of the medication, so also certain Sacraments are applied on all sides, and conferred by a minister, such a Baptism, Eucharist, etc., but the Sacrament of Penance is partly applied by a minister through absolution and partly requires the action of the sick man himself, namely confession, etc.

Now we can show the same thing in regard to the form, for in the Sacrament of Matrimony, in the consensus of all, in place of words a nod or letter suffices, provided the consent of both parties is expressed. This is what Pope Nicholas says (28, quaest. Can. *Sufficiat*), as well as Pope Alexander (cap. *Cum locum, de Sponsalibus et Matrimoniis*), that consent alone effects Matrimony. It is not received in a way as if interior consent would suffice without external consent; accordingly, the same Pope Alexander (cap. *Licet, de Sponsa Duorum*), teaches it is necessary that the consent be expressed in customary words. Therefore, the particle, *consent alone is said to effect Matrimony*, does not exclude a sin in which consent is expressed, but excludes *the consent of parents, the solemnity*, and other things which do not concern the essence of Matrimony.

5) The *fifth* proposition: *It is not necessary that in every Sacrament the things and words are so joined that they are essential parts of the same thing*. In this place we must note that the Sacrament has a certain similitude with natural things which are constituted of matter and form; still, it is not really a natural composite, and for that reason, does not require all the properties of matter and form, rather it is enough if some are found.

This proposition is proven by the Sacrament of the Eucharist. Accordingly, in the Eucharist, by the consent of all, things are discovered for the matter, i.e., bread and wine, and for the form: *This is my body; this is my blood.* Nevertheless, these things and the words are never so joined that the matter and form are in natural things, for either the Sacrament of the Eucharist is only the very thing consecrated, i.e., the species of bread and wine, as they contain the body and blood of Christ, or even the consecration, or the reception, as some would have it, can be called Sacraments. If the consecration were called a Sacrament, then we have words, but we do not have a thing, from which the Sacrament is composed, for the whole consecration consists in these words. The bread and wine do not come together as part of a consecration, but as a subject, in regard to what the priest does, and in which the action of the one consecrating is taken up. Yet, when the Sacrament is called the very matter consecrated, or the reception, then we have a thing, but we do not have words from which a Sacrament is composed. The words, in respect to the thing consecrated, are not the essential part, but the productive principle, for the essential part remains with the very thing. Moreover, the words do not remain with the thing consecrated, nay more, then it first begins to be a consecrated thing when the words have finished. For this reason, the Council of Florence, in its *Instruction to the Armenians*, does not say the words of the Eucharist are the form of the Sacrament, but the form *of the consecration*, from which we understand when the same Council teaches that in every Sacrament there are things for the matter and words for the form. This should not be understood so properly that we would understand it in a true natural composite.[4]

The same thing can be shown from the Sacrament of Confession. As we said, not only are words the matter in that Sacrament because they act in place of things, but it can also happen that in one day confession would happen, and on another day absolution be given, and hence, the matter and form are not together at the same time; this state of affairs is never found in a truly physical composite. For this reason, both the Council of Florence, in its *Instruction to the Armenians*, and the Council of Trent (sess. 14 can. 4) say in the Sacrament of Confession, acts of penance are *like* matter; but they did not dare to say absolutely it is the matter.

From all of which, we very clearly gather the matter and form in the

---

4 Recognitio I: In book 1 c. 18, § This proposition is proved. *He said the words of consecration of the Eucharist from the Council of Florence are not the form of the Sacrament, but the form of the consecration*: in which place I did not relate the words, but the sense of the Council; nor did I mean to deny those words: *Hoc est Corpus meum* can be called the form of the Sacrament of the Eucharist, but I only wished to advise that these words are not the form, whereby the Sacrament is constituted, but from which it is confected, and through this matter and form are not so properly in the Sacrament of the Eucharist, as in a physical composite. The words of the Council are these, "The words of the Savior are the form of this Sacrament, whereby he confects this Sacrament," where you see the words of the Lord are called the form of the Sacrament, because through it the Sacrament is confected.

Chapter XVIII: Matter and Form

Sacrament must be received *broadly*, and hence all of what is usually objected against it is answered.

CHAPTER XIX

The Word with which the Element Makes the Sacrament Is not Proper to a Sermon, but a Consecration

We have said things and words are required in the Sacraments, in which we agree with our adversaries. No doubt remains on the matter, namely the fact that in the Sacraments something must be applied such as a sensible sign seeing that they affirm with us that water must be applied in Baptism; bread and wine in the Eucharist. It does not make much difference concerning the matter of other Sacraments because our adversaries do not hold these as Sacraments.

Here I add one thing: Brenz (*Württemberg Confession*, c. *On Baptism*) ridiculously excludes chrism from the use of the Sacrament because he says it pertains to the elements of the world and was in use among the Jews in the ceremonies of the Old Testament. If this argumentation would avail in any way, it would also be fitting to exclude water. Water pertains more to the elements of the world than oil, since it is one of the four elements of the world, while oil is not numbered among them, rather, among the mixtures. Also, in the ceremonies of the Jews, washings with water were by far more frequent than anointings of oil.

Now we will pass over all these things, which we will speak of more in another place, and focus on the very serious question on the *word* which, when joined with a thing, makes the Sacrament. For all Catholics teach the word of the Sacrament is made up of a few specific words prescribed by God, which must be pronounced over the matter by the minister, such as in Baptism, the words, "I baptize you in the name of the Father, and of the Son, and of the Holy Spirit"; and in the Eucharist, "This is my body," and on the rest to the same manner.

John Calvin, however, contends in the *Institutes* (4, 14 §4) the Sacramental word is nothing other than a sermon, for he speaks in this way, "This is what they commonly say, the Sacrament consists in a word and an external sign. We should understand the word, not whispered without sense and faith, with only a noise like a magical incantation that has the force of consecrating the element; rather, let the aforesaid make us understand what a visible sign actually means. Therefore, under the tyrannical practice of the Pope, there was no want of profanation of the great mysteries; for they think it is enough if the priest murmurs the formula of consecration, while astounding the people without understanding. ... Therefore, when we hear the Sacramental word called to mind, let us understand the promise

Chapter XIX: The Word is Consecratory

which the minister has clearly preached leads the people by hand the more the sign aims and directs us." However, before we either prove or refute something, we must diligently explain the teaching of Calvin.

Firstly, therefore, we must remark that Calvin and the rest of our adversaries think and speak one way on Baptism and another on the Eucharist, which are the only two that they consider properly to be Sacraments. In Baptism, they require two kinds of words; in the Eucharist, only one. Accordingly, in Baptism they require in the first place a word of preaching, whereby the divine promise is proposed and explained by the minister. Then, they require that, while he sprinkles with water, at the same time the words, "I baptize you in the name of the Father, and of the Son, and of the Holy Spirit," should be said. That much is clear both from Calvin's little book *On the Formula for Administering the Sacraments*, and from Melanchthon in *Loci Communes* (chapter on baptism), as well as from their daily practice. Lastly, it is clear from the fact that Catholics do not rebaptize those whom the Lutherans and Calvinists baptize. Nevertheless, it would have to be done if they did not apply the true form of the Sacrament while they baptized.

Moreover, in the Sacrament of the Eucharist the Calvinists (as is clear from the formula of Calvin), do not require any other word than instruction. In the first place they bid the institution of the Sacrament to be recited from 1 Cor. 11, nearly in that way in which we recite the reading from the same epistle in the Mass for the instruction of the people. Then, a preacher applies the explanation, and at length, they distribute the bread and wine without any sign of the cross or another word or sacred rite. Another formula is extant, from the English who reside in Geneva, wherein after the reading of the Epistle to the Corinthians and a sermon, thanksgiving follows in words that have been devised, which the minister pronounces out loud, and at length, without any words of consecration, the bread and wine is distributed.

The Lutherans, however, do not all act in the same way. Rather, some recite the words of institution as a mere history, others recite with the intention to consecrate, others recite nothing. For more on these opinions, see Chemnitz (*Exam.*, 2 par., p. 346).

From this it follows that our adversaries have true Baptism, but not true Eucharist, except perhaps for a certain few, namely those who applied the words and were ordained priests in the Church.

Secondly, we must note that when Calvin says the Sacramental word is a sermon, he can be understood in two ways: *a)* in one way, to mean the sermon is an essential part of the Sacrament, so that without a sermon there is no Sacrament; *b)* in the second way, to mean the sermon is not part of the Sacrament, but is merely required that the Sacrament be received fruitfully.

It is very probable that the Lutherans, who apart from the sermon apply the words of consecration in all the Sacraments, do not require a sermon for the essence, but only to acquire the fruit. Hence, with them there will be no argument in this place, with the exception of those who do not advance the very Sacramental words to consecrate, but to instruct, and clearly call it preaching of the Gospel, as Brenz does (*Württemberg Confession*, c. *de Eucharistia*).

Calvin seems now and then to speak on the word as sermon, as a thing distinct from the Sacrament. In the *Institutes* (4, 14 § 3) he says the Sacrament is like an appendage to the word; nevertheless, he more often speaks on it as an essential part of the Sacrament. In the words cited above, he says the Sacrament is constituted from two things, the sign and the word, and through the word he says he understands the sermon. Likewise, (*ibid*), he explains the saying of St. Augustine, "without the word, what is water except [just] water?" on the word of preaching. There, without a doubt, he posits the word in regard to the essence of a Sacrament. In the same place Augustine, and Calvin from Augustine, says, "Without the word, what is water but water?" i.e., the water without the word is not a Sacrament, rather a profane element. In addition, if a word in the form of a sermon did not concern the essence of a Sacrament, in the Eucharist, there would be no word concerning the essence among the Calvinists, seeing that they have no other word in that Sacrament but a sermon. Then, in his commentary on Ephesians 5:26, when Calvin is explaining the verse, "Cleansing it by the laver of water in the word of life," he says, "It appears there is no legitimate observance of the signs in the Papacy, for they boast that they have a word per se, but the fact is there is an incantation in its place, because they murmur it in an unknown language, and in this way, rather more as if it were more fixed on a dead element than men; there is no explanation of the mystery to the people, which alone causes a dead element to begin to be a Sacrament." Note the last words.

Lastly, Theodore Beza removes all doubt when he wrote this way in a book titled *Summa Doctrinae de Re Sacramentaria*, "What is the formal cause of the Sacraments? The ordination of God has been embraced in his very word and explained by his very minister according to his command; not the very pronunciation of those words, however, nor any force hiding in them." From this we understand that those words of Baptism, "I Baptize you in the name of the Father, and of the Son, and of the Holy Spirit," are recited by Calvinists while water is sprinkled, but those words are not the form of the Sacrament among them, rather, the preceding preaching is the form. The latter, however, pertain to the rite, as Beza indicates a little later (*ibid.*), and they do not advance them to consecrate the water, rather, that the people should also be thereby instructed.

We must note *thirdly*, there are three things in which we disagree with the Calvinists that we will show in order. *a*) First, we teach that in every Sacrament it is necessary to pronounce certain words that were instituted

Chapter XIX: The Word is Consecratory

by God in the very action of the Sacrament; they teach it is only necessary in Baptism. *b)* Secondly, we teach that a word in the form of a sermon is not necessary to the essence of the Sacrament; but they assert that it is required. *c)* Thirdly, we teach that fixed, consecratory words that have been devised are required for the essence of the Sacraments, which are properly called sacramental words; they deny the whole thing, and call it a magical incantation. Even the words of Baptism, as I said, they do not recite while they sprinkle the water to consecrate it, but to instruct the people, that these words are a certain part of the sermon, in which, as I said, Brenz and others among the Lutherans agree with the Calvinists. This is the reasoning why they use the vernacular, and we use Latin in the Sacraments; for they mean to teach the people who do not understand Latin, we invoke God to sanctify the element, seeing that God understands all languages.

1) Therefore, the first proposition: *Not only in Baptism, but even in the rest of the Sacraments, words are required in the very celebration of the mystery.* It is proven: For in the Eucharist, the Lord, while he blessed bread, pronounced fixed words, namely, "This is my body, which is given for you," and then commanded that we do the same thing, "Do this in my commemoration" (Luke 22:19). Therefore, even we ought to use fixed words, if we will to do what he did and commanded us [to do].

Perhaps they will say that Christ commanded that we do what he did, but not that we use the words which he said. We respond that "do this" refers to the whole action of Christ, so that he embraces the words also. That which (that I might now pass over other arguments) we learn from the tradition and use of the Catholic Church, which tradition, if it is not received, then even the form of Baptism will be called into doubt. From where, I ask, is it gathered that while water is sprinkled, the words "I baptize you in the name of the Father and the Son and the Holy Spirit," must be said? Certainly not from any place other than the words of Mathew 28:19, "Teach all nations, baptizing them in the name of the Father, and of the Son, and of the Holy Spirit." From this passage, however, it is not certainly gathered, unless the tradition of the Church is received. The Lord does not say, "I baptize you in the name of the Father," etc., so it will be enough if we shall say sprinkling water, "In the name of the Father, and of the Son," etc.

Next, the Lord did not say, "say in the name of the Father," etc., but he only said, "Baptizing them in the name of the Father," etc. Such words do not compel us to say, "In the name of the Father" etc., but only that we baptize *by the authority of God*, namely as his ministers, which can happen even if we were to say nothing; that fact can be shown from other similar passages. In Mark 16:17, the Lord says, "In my name they shall cast out demons, ... let them impose hands upon the sick, and they will be well." Still, it was not necessary for the Apostles, when they wanted to cure someone, to say out loud, "In the name of the Lord," but it was enough if they would think it. In Acts 9:40, Peter raised Tabitha and in Acts 14:9 Paul healed a lame man without any mention of the name of Christ. So also in Matt. 18:20, the Lord says, "Where there will be two or three gathered in my name, there I am in their midst." Nevertheless, it is not necessary that those who are gathered in the name of Christ should verbally say, "We are gathered in the name of Christ"; rather, it is enough if they come together in the authority of Christ. Lastly, in John 5:43, the Lord says, "I come in the name of my Father, and you did not receive me: if another will come in his own name, you will receive him"; where some other thing is not signified by a name, except authority.

As a result, the fact that we should say in Baptism, "I baptize you in the name of the Father, and of the Son, and of the Holy Spirit," cannot be gathered for certain from Scripture alone, but from Scripture *joined with the explanation and praxis of the Church.* Now, if in Baptism the authority of the Church is received, why not also in the Eucharist and the rest of the Sacraments?

The same thing can be shown in regard to the other Sacraments, although it is not very necessary, seeing that they are not received by our adversaries. It is clear in Confirmation that words were applied in Acts 8:15 where the Apostles, imposing hands prayed at the same time. From there, Cyprian says (*Epist. Ad Jubajanum*): "The Holy Spirit is called and infused upon the baptized in the imposition of hands." St. Ambrose holds the same thing (*de Sacram.* 3,2), "After the font, it remains that a perfection would take place, when, by the invocation of the priest the Holy Spirit is infused." Jerome holds the same thing (*Contra Lucif.*) as well as Augustine (*de Bapt.* 3, 16).

In the Sacrament of Penance, words are also required, as is clear from that of John 20:23, "Whose sins you forgive are forgiven them." From there, St. John Chrysostom, in his commentary on that passage, says God uses both the hand and tongue of the priest to absolve," and St. Leo (*Epist.* 91 *ad Theod.*), says that after Baptism God ordained the remedy of Penance in such a way, that forgiveness cannot be obtained except by the supplications of the priests.

St. Ambrose (on 1 Tim. 4) teaches that in the Sacrament of Order words are required, "The 'impositions of hands' [1 Tim. 4:14] are the mystical words whereby the designated man is sanctioned to the work, receiving the authority, by the witness of his conscience, that in turn he would dare to offer the sacrifice of the Lord to God." Jerome speaks likewise on Isaiah 58, that ordination of clergy takes place by the invoking of the voice and the imposition of hands.

In the Sacrament of Anointing of the Sick, words are clearly required from James 6:14, "Let him bring in the priests of the Church, and let them pray over him, anointing him with oil in the name of the Lord."

Lastly, in Matrimony the matter is clear, since mutual consent cannot be constituted unless it is expressed in words or equivalent signs. Therefore,

Chapter XIX: The Word is Consecratory

even Calvin, in his book on the *Form of Administering the Sacraments*, although he does not hold Matrimony as a Sacrament, nevertheless, willed it to be celebrated in the Church, and prescribed a certain form of words.

2) The second proposition: *A word in the form of a sermon is not required for the essence of any Sacrament.* It is proven firstly, by a negative argument from the authority of Scripture, which our adversaries are accustomed to make great use of, and should, since it would not be fitting to do anything in divine matters without the word of God, and they recognize nothing as the word of God but what has been written. So, in the Scriptures, mention is made of Baptism, first in John 3:5, "Unless a man will be reborn, etc."; then in John 4:1-2, where we find that the Lord baptized through his disciples; likewise in Mark 16:16, "He that will believe and be baptized will be saved." Titus 3:5, "He saved us by the laver of regeneration." 1 Peter 3:21, "Baptism saves you." In these passages, no mention is made of a word, let alone a sermon.

There are only two passages that mention words. One is Eph. 5:26, "Cleansing it by the laver of water in the word of life." The other is Matt. 28:19, "Teach all nations, baptizing them in the name of the Father, and of the Son, and of the Holy Spirit."

The first passage should be explained through the latter, both because this is a general rule even celebrated by our adversaries, namely to explain one Scripture by another when it can be done; and because Chrysostom, Theodoret, Theophylactus, Anselm, and other interpreters teach in this way. They say that "in the word of life," means "in the name of the Father, and of the Son, and of the Holy Spirit." One exception is Jerome, who in his commentary on this passage understands "through the word of life" to mean doctrine. Nevertheless, we must observe that Jerome omitted the literal exposition, and only explained it mystically, i.e., as he says, tropologically. For, he does not understand Baptism by laver of regeneration, but any cleansing which takes place through doctrine. All interpreters who explain it literally, however, understand Baptism for the laver, and for the word they understand the invocation of the Trinity.

So there only remains the passage of Matt. 28:19, "Teach all nations, baptizing them," etc. We do not deny that in this passage it is commanded that instruction should precede Baptism; nay more, we teach and do this very thing. We do not baptize any adults unless they have already received much instruction for a long time. Rather, we deny that a sermon is prescribed as an *essential* part of the Sacrament in this passage; nay more, we assert that in this passage doctrine is clearly distinguished from the Sacrament. St. Jerome distinguishes in this way in his commentary of the passage, "The particular order enjoined upon the Apostles, that first they teach all nations, then plunge them into the Sacrament of faith, and after faith and Baptism, they instruct them in what must be observed."

Hence, what we said about Baptism can also be said about the Eucharist.

Neither the Lord (Matt. 26), nor Paul (1 Cor. 11) say a sermon should be done when celebrating the Lord's Supper, nor did the Lord himself give any sermon, nor explain the force of the Eucharist (Which still, Calvin thinks is necessary) in the very celebration of the Supper. Later, he gave the longest sermon, which John describes (14-16), but it had no pertinence to the Supper, it was both given after the Supper and also, the Lord did not explain anything on the Supper in it. Therefore, Calvin should have considered from which Gospel he learned that a sermon is the form of the Sacrament.

It is proven secondly, that a sermon does not regard the essence of a Sacrament. If it were so, the offices of preaching and Baptism would not be distinguished. Whoever would preach, would baptize by this fact, seeing that he administers the form of Baptism, and vice versa, whoever would baptize, preaches, since Baptism would formally be nothing other than a sermon. St. Paul contradicts this teaching when he says in 1 Cor. 1:17, "Christ did not send me to baptize, but to preach the Gospel." In such a passage, a commentary (which is attributed to Ambrose) clearly attests: he shows it is much less to baptize than to preach, from the fact that whoever baptizes, only pronounces certain solemn words and pours water, which is very easy. For this reason, Peter (Acts 10:48), after he had preached to Cornelius, did not baptize him, but commanded him to be baptized by inferior ministers. However, according to Calvin, Peter himself should be said to have baptized, since he applied the form of Baptism.

Thirdly, if the form of Baptism were a sermon, there would be as great a variety of Baptism as there are sermons, since not everyone preaches in the same way. But Baptism is one, just as there is one God and Lord, as the Apostle witnesses (Eph. 4:5), as well as the Nicene-Constantinoplan Creed.

Fourthly, if the form of Baptism were a sermon, they would hold the Baptism of a heretic to be false, and hence they would have to be rebaptized, for the preaching of heretics cannot be true. Yet the Church approves the Baptism of any heretic you like, provided the prescribed words are given, i.e., "In the name of the Father, and of the Son, and of the Holy Spirit," even if they add the most perverse sermon and explanation, as St. Augustine teaches (*de Baptismo* 3, 15), "If Marcion consecrated Baptism with the Evangelical words, in the name of the Father, and the Son, and the Holy Spirit, the Sacrament was complete, although his faith expressed by the same words was other than what Catholic truth teaches, and was not uninjured, rather stained with fabulous falsehoods. For, under the same words (i.e., in the name of the Father, and of the Son, and of the Holy Spirit), not only Marcion, or Valentinus, Arius, or Eunomius, but the very carnal children of the Church, if they were asked individually for an accurate explanation of their opinions, would probably show a diversity of opinions as numerous as those who held them. For, the animal man does not receive the things of the Spirit of God. Can it, however, be said on account of this,

Chapter XIX: The Word is Consecratory

that they do not receive the complete Sacrament?"

Fifthly, the Baptism of Catholics is given without any sermon. Even if catechetical instruction, sermons, and a lot of preaching precedes it, nevertheless, on the day in which the Baptism takes place, a sermon is not customarily given. Just the same, Calvin does not command Catholics to be rebaptized, he rather more upholds that their Baptism is true (*Instit.* 4, 15 §16), "Such in the present day are our 'Catabaptists,' who deny that we are duly baptized, because we were baptized in the Papacy by wicked men and idolaters; hence they furiously insist on anabaptism." How is this consistent, that a sermon is the form of Baptism and still without the sermon a true Baptism can be given? How do those words of the *Institutes* agree with those words of the same Calvin on Ephesians 5 (*loc. cit.*), where he says there is no legitimate observance of signs among the Papists because they lack an explanation to the people, which alone causes the dead element to begin to be a Sacrament?

Sixthly, if the form of Baptism is a sermon, then certainly children should not be baptized. A sermon should not be given where there is no one to hear and understand it, for Sirach 32:6 wisely advises, "Where there is no hearing, do not pour out a word." But children understand nothing, are not attentive, nor can they be; so a sermon should not be made for them, and for this reason, should not and cannot be baptized.

This argument is usually answered in two ways. Some, such as the Lutherans, would have it that children perceive a sermon. We refuted them above with the dilemma of St. Augustine in his epistle to Dardanus. They either have the use of reason, or they do not; if they do not have it, then they do not understand; if they do, then they are sacrilegious, who refuse the Sacrament, as is clear.

Others, such as Calvin (*Instit.* 4, 16 §20), say that children do not usefully perceive the Sacrament for that period of time, nevertheless, they perceive the true Sacrament which is going to profit them later. This solution is not sufficient, for if the preaching of the word is of the essence of Baptism, no less than water, certainly they should perceive it no less than the water, otherwise it will be useless, but it will also be no Sacrament at all. If water were sprinkled by a minister, and did not touch the infant, no man would say he is baptized; therefore, if the sermon takes place, and is not perceived by the infant, no Calvinist should say that he is baptized. Moreover, a sermon is not truly perceived except when it is understood; for he is not said to perceive a sermon, which properly is a type of instruction, who is not instructed, even if he heard a certain sound. Therefore, infants do not perceive the form of a Sacrament, and for this reason it is not a Sacrament. So, let the Calvinists become Anabaptists, or let them cease to require a sermon for the essence of a Sacrament.

3) The third proposition: *A certain form of words is required for the essence of a Sacrament, which do not so much instruct those standing about,*

as they consecrate and sanctify the element. This is not only against Calvin, but also against Brenz and certain other Lutherans, who would have it that the very words of consecration are pronounced to instruct the people, not to consecrate the matter, and therefore, they think it is unlawful if these words are pronounced in Latin in the presence of a people ignorant of the Latin language.

This proposition is proven in that *a)* the words prescribed by the Lord in Baptism do not have the form of instruction, but *of invocation and benediction.* It is proven from Christ's very manner of speech. He does not say, "Teach all nations in the name of the Father, and of the Son and of the Holy Spirit," but, "Baptizing them in the name of the Father," etc. where those words, *in the name of the Father,* etc. regard the act of *baptism,* not the act of teaching; hence they sound out the invocation of the Trinity over the sprinkling of water, not the declaration of the mystery to those listening. Next, if it is permitted to explain Scripture by another Scripture, it will be clear that *In the name of the Father,* etc., sounds out an invocation, not an instruction. This form of speaking is received in this way in other passages, such as Mark 17:17, "They will cast out demons in my name"; in Acts 3:6, "In the name of Jesus Christ, the Nazarene, rise and walk." Matt. 7:22, "Did we not cast out demons in your name?"; and other places (*passim*). Lastly, if these words were to pertain to instruction, certainly they would be very imperfect, for not only should they be instructed on the Trinity, who are Baptized, but also on the Incarnation, the Lord's Passion, and especially on the promise of grace on account of the merit of Christ, none of which are mentioned in these words.

b) Secondly, the words which are said in the mystery of the Eucharist by the Apostle are called words of blessing, which certainly do not sound like an instruction, but *a consecration,* as we see in 1 Cor. 10:16, "The chalice of benediction, which we bless, is it not the participation of the blood of Christ?" The same argument can be introduced from the other Sacraments, if our adversaries received them. Nevertheless, see what we said in confirmation of the first proposition.

c) Thirdly, it is proven from the words of the Apostle in 1 Cor. 1:13, "Was Paul crucified for you, or were you baptized in the name of Paul?" There, the Apostle means to show that the authors of the Sacraments are not the men who administer them, but *God;* from there he proves it, because they are not given in the name of the ministers, but in the name of *God,* i.e., of the Father, and of the Son, and of the Holy Spirit. Therefore, the name in the words of the Sacraments means invocation, whereby authority is gathered. Wherefore, Chrysostom (*Hom. 3 on 1 Cor.*) says, "Do not say to me, who baptized, but in whose name; who baptizes is not required, rather, whom we invoke in Baptism." See Optatus of Mileve (*Contra Parmenianum,* 5) for more on this passage and on this discussion in general.

d) Fourthly, the same is proven in the tradition of Councils. The Council

Chapter XIX: The Word is Consecratory

of Nicaea (can. 19) commands the Paulianists to be rebaptized, and the Council of Laodicea (can. 8) decreed the same thing for the Cataphrygians. On the other hand, the first Council of Arles (can. 8), which was celebrated around the same time, and Syricius (*Epist.* 1, c. 1) command that Arians not be rebaptized. No reason can be given for the difference apart from what Innocent I gives (epist. 22 c. 5) that the Paulianists and Cataphrygians not only disbelieved the Trinity, but did not baptize with the invocation of the Trinity; but the Arians, although they did not believe the Trinity was one in essence, nevertheless, baptized in the name of the Father and the Son and the Holy Spirit. Certainly, inasmuch to instruction and explanation, the Arians erred in regard to the Trinity as much as the Paulianists and Cataphrygians; therefore, it is not instruction, but *invocation* that accomplishes Baptism.

e) Fifthly, it is proven from the Fathers, who do not recall instruction, but invocation and consecration when they speak on the words of the Sacraments. Dionysius the Areopagate (*Eccl. Hierarch.*) calls the words of the Sacraments τὰς τελεστικὰς ἐπικλήσεος, i.e., consecratory invocations. Justin (*Apol. Ad Anton. Pium*) says, "There is pronounced over him who chooses to be born again, and has repented of his sins, the name of God the Father and Lord of the universe; he who leads to the laver the person that is to be washed calling him by this name alone. ... And in the name of Jesus Christ, who was crucified ..., and in the name of the Holy Spirit, ... he who is illuminated is washed." St. Basil (*de Spiritu Sancto*, 15), says, "In three immersions, and with three invocations, the great mystery of Baptism is performed." Cyril (*Cat. 3*) says, "Simple water, through the invocation of the Holy Spirit, Christ and the Father, obtains sanctity."

Athanasius (*Serm.* 3 *Contra Arianos*), in regard to the means, says, "Why is the name of the Son recalled together with the Father when we are initiated in Baptism? For, that the Father is insufficient is a forbidden thing to say, etc.," where he teaches that the three persons are named in Baptism, not because one does not suffice to sanctify men, but because they are inseparable on account of the unity of nature; for this reason, he would have it, those words of Baptism are not said to instruct the people, as the heretics dream up, but to *invoke God*, who sanctifies us through Baptism.

St. Gregory of Nyssa (*de Baptismo*) says, "Stop contending with me: resist, if you can, those words of the Lord which gave to men the rule of the baptismal invocation. What says the Lord's command? 'Baptizing them in the name of the Father and of the Son and of the Holy Spirit.'"

Cyprian, or whoever was the author of the *Sermon on Christ's Baptism*, near the beginning says, "The solemnity of words, the invocation of the sacred name, and the signs attributed to the ministerial Apostolic institutions of priests, celebrate the visible Sacrament; the Holy Spirit forms and effects the thing itself, and as the author invisibly applies the hand of the whole goodness to visible consecrations."

Ambrose (*de Sacramentis* 2, 5) says, "The priest comes, says the prayer at the font, and while invoking the name of the Father, the presence of the Son and the Holy Spirit, he uses heavenly words. They are heavenly words, which are Christ's, because we baptize in the name of the Father, and of the Son, and of the Holy Spirit. So if the presence of the Trinity is present at the word of a man for the invocation of a Saint, how much more will he be present in that place where the eternal word operates?" He says similar things on the words of the Eucharist (*de Sacramentis* 4, 4).

Augustine (*de Baptismo* 3, 10) says, "Nor is the water 'profane and adulterous' over which the name of God is invoked, even though it be invoked by profane and adulterous persons, because neither the creature itself of water, nor the name invoked, is adulterous. Yet, the Baptism of Christ, consecrated by the words of the Gospel, is necessarily holy, however polluted and unclean its ministers may be, because its inherent sanctity cannot be polluted, and the divine excellence abides in its Sacrament." Again (*ibid.* 5, 20) he says, "So if what is said in the gospel, that 'God does not hear sinners' [John 9:31], to the extent that the Sacraments cannot be celebrated by a sinner, how then does God hear a murderer praying, either over the water of baptism, or over the oil, or over the Eucharist, or over the heads of those on whom his hand is laid? All which things are nevertheless done, and are valid, even by murderers."

CHAPTER XX

Objections Are Answered

THE objections of Calvin remain to be answered. In the first place, he advances the testimony of St. Augustine (*Tract. in Joan.* 80), where St. Augustine says, "From where does the water have so great a virtue, as in touching the body to cleanse the soul, save by the operation of the word, and that not because it is believed?" Calvin adds, "Except by the operation of the word, not because it is said, but because it is believed. Even in the word itself a passing sound is one thing, an abiding virtue another; this is the word of faith, which we preach. This is why, in Acts of the Apostles, it says: 'Cleansing their hearts by faith,' and Peter the Apostle, 'So Baptism saves us, not the laying aside of filthy flesh, but an examination of good conscience.' This is the word of faith which we preach."

I respond: This passage customarily distorts a few things, although still, it could not be that obscure given that it is a certain part of a sermon given to the people, unless perhaps we believe that St. Augustine usually preached by riddles, so that one would have to be Oedipus to understand. Therefore, I will relate what others think and refute those which do not seem rightly said.

First, Calvin contends this whole passage must be understood in regard to a sermon, but he is clearly deceived. Firstly, because Augustine says, "Take away the word, what is water but water?" But when you have taken away the word of a sermon, the water of Baptism is not mere water, but *sacred and sacramental* water, for among us there is no sermon in Baptism, and still Calvin affirms our Baptism is a true Sacrament (*Instit.* 4, 15 §16).

Secondly, Augustine says, "The word is added to the element, and becomes a Sacrament." A sermon, however, is not added to the element, rather, *it precedes* it, as Calvin himself teaches (*ibid*, 4, 14 §3). Otherwise, he should have said that the element is added to the word and becomes a Sacrament.

Thirdly, Augustine says, "From where does the water have so great a virtue, as in touching the body to cleanse the soul, save by the operation of the word? ... The cleansing by no means is attributed to a frail and faulty element, except that it is added in the word." There, Augustine affirms that water itself has the force of cleansing, but does not have it of itself, rather, *from the word*. Yet, a sermon bestows nothing to the water, for the whole is related to instruct those that listen to it, not to sanctify water. Nay more, the objection which Calvin raises in his commentary on Ephesians 5 is very absurd, because in the Sacraments we bring words to consecrate the element itself, not to instruct the people.

Fourthly, Augustine says, "In this word Baptism is also consecrated so that it can cleanse." However, the same Augustine teaches the word, whereby Baptism is consecrated, is that invocation, "In the name of the Father, and of the Son, and of the Holy Spirit." He speaks this way in his work *On Baptism* (3, 15), "If Marcion consecrated Baptism with the Evangelical words, in the name of the Father, and the Son, and the Holy Spirit, the Sacrament was complete." He repeats the same thing in numerous places.

Fifthly, Augustine says, "This word of faith only avails in the Church of God, that through the very believing, offering, blessing, moistening, even the smallest, cleanses the infant, although it is not yet old enough to believe unto justice, and confess by mouth unto salvation." The word of a sermon, however, is of no benefit except to those who believe *in act*, as is known; as a result, Augustine does not speak about the word as it is in a sermon.

Consequently, since we have rejected the opinion of Calvin, some Catholics teach that Augustine does not speak about the word of a sermon, nor of a consecration, but the institution of the Sacrament; for in his mode he effects a Sacrament, consecrates waters, cleanses the infant, etc.

Still, this explanation cannot be admitted. Firstly, because it does not remove the difficulty, which our adversary objects to us, from those words, "not because it is said, but because it is believed," and from those, "This is the word of faith which we preach." Augustine repeats these words three times in this place.

None of these squares with the words of institution of a Sacrament, for the words of institution do not have force because they are believed, rather, *because the Lord said them*, and he alone could make Sacraments from elements. The words of institution are not properly the word of faith which we preach, for in the same place, St. Augustine explains what this word of faith is when he says, "Because if you will have confessed in your mouth that Jesus is Lord, and believe in your heart that God raised him from the dead, you will be saved."

Secondly, Augustine, does not recognize another word in the Sacrament apart from the word which he is speaking about; rather, "a mere element," as is clear from those words, "Take away the word, and what is water but water?"; and "the word approaches the element, and a Sacrament is made"; and "From where does the water have so great a virtue, as in touching the body to cleanse the soul, save by the operation of the word?" Therefore, it is not a word of institution, since it is certain, apart from the word of institution, that Sacraments are constituted from words and elements, not bare elements.

Likewise, there is another opinion of Catholics, that Augustine speaks only on the ceremonial or consecratory word. Such an opinion is better than the other two, but still has this one unsuitability, that it cannot account for

Chapter XX: Objections are Answered

the reason why Augustine lays out the words of Romans 10:8, "this is the word of faith which we preach. Because if you confess in your heart" etc.; and again, why a little later he suborns Acts 15:9, "cleansing their hearts by faith"; and 1 Peter 3:21, "Non the laying aside of the filth of the flesh, but the examination of a good conscience"; and lastly, that of John 15:3, "Now you are clean on account of the word which I spoke to you." You cannot get to the words of consecration from any of these except through supreme force, and as I said above, we would make a riddle from a sermon meant for the people.

So I say, in this place Augustine did not always speak on the same word, rather here on the Sacramental word, then on the word as in a sermon, which becomes plain from the arguments already made.

Someone will say: Thus, Augustine lives in perpetual equivocation, since he takes up the term "word" differently in the same sentences (e.g., when he said, "From where does the water have so great a virtue, as in touching the body to cleanse the soul, save by the operation of the word?" and then adds, "Not because it is said, but because it is believed," where he clearly speaks on the word in the form of a sermon). Hence, either previously he was speaking about the word in the form of a sermon, or committed a vicious equivocation.

Besides, to prove water has force from the word, he advances the testimony of St. Paul from Romans 10:8, "This is the word of faith which we preach. Because if you confess, etc." and that of Acts 15:9, "cleansing their hearts by faith," and 1 Peter 3:21, "Not the laying aside the filth of the flesh, but the examination of a good conscience." He adds, "This is the word of faith, which we preach." What, I ask, does Augustine prove if he speaks equivocally on the word?

Lastly, in the last sermon, when he said that by water, an infant is cleansed through the word, he immediately adds, "This whole thing happens through the word, on which the Lord says, 'You have already been cleansed on account of the word, because I spoke to you.'" Such words must necessarily be understood on the Lord's sermon. This is why they should even be understood to be superior from a word in the form of a sermon, and not on the sacramental word, as we said previously, or in these words there will be an intolerable equivocation.

I respond: There is no equivocation in the words of Augustine. Accordingly, he took up to explain the words of the Lord in John 15:3, "You have already been cleansed on account of the word which I spoke to you." While he explained these words, he posed a question to himself: why did not Christ rather say, you have already been cleansed on account of Baptism, in which you have been washed? For, even if the aforesaid Word cleanses, insofar as it begets faith—the very beginning of justification—nevertheless, even Baptism cleanses at the very moment that it washes the filth of all sins.

He answers himself: Christ said, "You have been cleansed on account of the word," and he did not say, you are cleansed on account of Baptism, because in all cleansing, whether it takes place in the Sacrament, or outside the Sacrament, the cleansing force always arises from the word. If the cleansing took place outside the Sacrament, necessarily it would happen through actual faith; but faith, from hearing, hearing from the word of Christ (Rom. 10:17). Since the cleansing takes place in the Sacrament, it is indeed the element which cleanses, but the word of consecration is joined to so it can cleanse. Thus, cleansing always arises from the word. This is why St. Augustine, on those words of the Lord, "You have been cleansed on account of the word which I spoke to you," does not restrict it to the word in the form of preaching, but receives it *generally*; and in the whole rest of the sermon he tries to prove that one thing, all cleansing takes place through the word. Consequently, he advances the arguments and testimonies indiscriminately, here on the sacramental word, there on the word in the form of a sermon, because for each he proves in the same way that it is the *word* which cleanses.

From this foundation those three passages will be easily explained, where there seems to be a vicious equivocation. The first passage, "From where does the water have so great a virtue, as in touching the body to cleanse the soul, save by the operation of the word; not because it is said, but because it is believed?" These words are understood by some to have been said because, unless faith is present, either the proper faith in adults, or supplied in children, the Sacrament effects nothing. But this is not said rightly. Although faith is required in adults as a certain disposition to receive the Sacrament fruitfully, nevertheless, it is not faith which gives the power of cleansing to the element; consequently, water does not have the force of cleansing because I believe, but because it is *a Sacrament instituted by God*.

Augustine asks, however, how water gets its power, not whom the water benefits. So, "Not because it is said, but because it is believed," means the Sacramental word does not give power to the water, as it is a certain natural thing, i.e., striking the air, so that the word would be no better than the element; but as it is a *spiritual* thing, and recognizable by faith alone, namely, as it contains the invocation of the Trinity (just as also the sign of the cross, and the name of Jesus is honorable, and has the force to work miracles and compel demons, not as it is a natural thing and perceptible in a corporeal sense, but as *it represents a divine thing*). So the sense is, "The word, not because it is said, but because it is believed," i.e., not insofar as it is perceived by ears, but insofar as it is perceived by faith.

Moreover, that this is the true sense of this citation is clear from the following words, "For, even in the word itself a passing sound is one thing, and the power remaining another." There, when he calls the word a passing sound, it is because it is said, but when he calls the word, the power

Chapter XX: Objections are Answered

remaining, it is because it is believed.

Besides, "because it is believed" either signifies that it is believed in act, or that it is the object of faith, and hence a thing perceptible by faith; moreover, it cannot mean that it is believed in act. No actual faith is rigorously necessary for Baptism. Actual faith is not required for the one receiving baptism, as is clear from infants, whom Augustine in this place says are most truly cleansed by the word in the Sacrament, even if they do not avail to believe in their heart and confess by their mouth. The faith of the minister is not required, nor that of the parents, nor of anyone offering and receiving it that you like, as the same Augustine proves in *Epist.* 23 *Ad Bonifacium*, where he says children are truly cleansed even if they are baptized, even if they are offered by infidels. Therefore, whose actual faith is required if not that of the recipient, or of the minister, or of the sponsor?

Some will say: the faith of the Church is required. What if no one in the Church were to exercise the act of faith while the infant is baptized by the infidel? To argue from the impossible, what if the whole Church perished, and still any Turk you like, who does not know our affairs, were to baptize an infant, with the intention of doing what Christ instituted and the Church did? Certainly, he would be baptized. Nevertheless, it is true what Augustine and others say that infants are baptized in the faith of their parents, or the Church, because *de facto*, if no one were faithful, certainly no one is moved to baptize infants; but therefore, actual faith is not so required, that Baptism would be fruitless without it.

Here, we must diligently remark that Augustine does not deny the word itself, as it is said, and as it is a sensible thing, has a virtue; for if water itself has the virtue of changing, how much more the word, even as a sensible thing? Yet, he denies that virtue is from the word, *as it is a sensible thing*. Therefore, the whole Sacrament has the virtue, but has it from the word, as the word is a spiritual thing, and is recognizable by faith alone.

The other passage was difficult, where Augustine suborns Romans 10:8, Acts 15:9, and 1 Peter 3:31. *I respond* that those passages are not suborned to prove that the power to change something is in the water from the word, but to prove *in general*, the word has the power to change; that is Augustine's scope, as we said. Because it has already been proved from it, that the sacramental word gives the power to change to the element, he proves the same thing from the testimonies of those Scriptures. Those passages show that the hearts of men are cleansed by faith, but faith is born from the word of preaching, from which it follows that the word has the power to change.

The third difficult passage was at the end of the sermon, where after he had said that infants are cleansed in the sacramental word, he added, "This whole thing takes place through the word, on which the Lord says, 'Now you are clean, on account of the word which I spoke to you.'" Here, the response is that Augustine did not restrict these words of the Lord to the sermon which the Lord spoke after the Last Supper, but are understood on the word *generally*, so the sense will be: You are clean on account of my word, or because you heard me preaching and believed, or whereby you have been sanctified in Baptism. And that is enough for that citation of Augustine, and especially on the argument of Calvin.

The next objection is of Calvin, Brenz, Chemnitz and others, that the species is a kind of magical incantation, to murmur certain words over water, bread, or another mute element of this sort.

This is not so much an objection as it is a horrible blasphemy. In the first place, there are two things which are condemned in magical incantations. One, that some think in certain figures, or words there is a natural power to effect something; this is indeed superstition, seeing that it is constituted for certain that neither figures nor words have any natural power to effect something. The second, that some suppose the figures or words have of themselves no power, still, it is applied from an arrangement made with the devil to effect certain things; this is properly a magical incantation, and the greatest sin.

Hence, we all affirm the Sacramental words have no natural power. Thus, we say *divine institution* is required, that they might bring to effect, by God's institution, what they cannot do of themselves. This is a mere calumny of Calvin (4, 14 §4), that we only use a din of words without sense, and faith to consecrate the element; and Chemnitz (*Exam*. Part. 2 p. 101) says we place the power in syllables and characters while neglecting the sense of the words. These are mere lies; we do not place the power in characters, nor in a sound or the number of syllables, rather *in the sense and signification*, and that is from the institution of Christ.

Accordingly, all Catholics affirm that truly the Sacrament is completed whichever language we use, provided that the sense is the same; even if the same words are said or written in different languages, have different characters, a different sound, or a different number of syllables. Therefore, it follows that we think, as we truly do think, by that arrangement and promise of Christ, they have force. If it is magic, what else would follow except that Christ were the devil? Since all magic depends upon an arrangement with the devil, whereas the force of the Sacramental words would depend upon an arrangement of Christ, it manifestly follows that either nothing in our Sacraments is magic, or Christ is the devil. So, our adversaries have landed at this horrible impiety, that they make a devil out of Christ.

They will say that they do not make Christ the devil because Christ did not institute the pronunciation of words over mute elements. Now, we have sufficiently proved that Christ instituted it. Moreover, I ask them, whether they believe Christ could institute signs of this sort, which have the power to work something from his arrangement? I do not think they will deny it, unless they would deny Christ is God.

Chapter XX: Objections are Answered

In Num. 5:18, God instituted certain words which were to be said over water, and he willed it to be the power of those words to grant the power to the waters to kill adulterous women on the spot if they drank from them. Likewise, in Num. 21:8, he instituted that those who gaze upon a bronze serpent, would be immediately cured from the bite of the fiery serpents. And Christ himself, did he not drive out illnesses with words, the imposition of hands, or even mud? Therefore, Christ could institute this, that sacramental words would have force by his arrangement.

Again, I ask whether, if Christ instituted it, which it is clear he could have done, would it be magic or not? If they would say it was going to be magic, clearly, they affirm Christ is the devil; if they deny it was going to be magic, they could not for any reason call us magicians; for we only do what we believe Christ instituted. Moreover, if it were the case that Christ did not institute it, we would simply be deceived, but we would not, for our part, be guilty of the crime of magic.

Lastly, words and magical signs do not have any power, for the devil cannot give power to things. Rather, the devil only works in their presence. On the other hand, words and sacramental signs have power from God to work what they signify. For this reason, they act more wonderfully and sublimely by far than any incantations ever could.

The *third* objection of Calvin is taken from the authority of Christ, the Apostles, the primitive Church, and God himself, "We needn't labor to prove, when it is hardly obscure, that what Christ did, what he commanded us to do, what the Apostles follow, what the purer Church observed, nay more what has been known even from the beginning of the world, as often as God offered some sign to the holy fathers, it was an inseparable bond of doctrine, without which our senses were rendered astonished by the bare sight. Therefore, since we hear mention made on the sacramental word, we understand the promise which with a clear voice, preached by the minister leads the people by hand, to that which the sign aims and directs us."

We also do not need to labor in response. For, it is hardly an obscure fact, that Christ did not preface a sermon when he consecrated the Eucharist, and later commanded us to do the same thing. See Matt. 26, Luke 22, and 1 Cor. 11. It is also known that the Apostles and the Fathers followed, from these testimonies, which we cited a little earlier. Calvin advances no testimony apart from one of Augustine, which we already explained. Lastly, we do not deny that even God, when he gave signs to the Fathers, explained their power and we must do the same when we instruct Catechumens; but Calvin does not rightly gather from there that the sacramental word is nothing other than a sermon. For, to preach is one thing, to celebrate the Sacraments another; both should be done, but times and duties must still be distinguished.

CHAPTER XXI

The Things and Words of the Sacraments Were Determined in Such a Way That One May Not Add, Subtract or Take Anything Away

THE *third* question follows on the intrinsic causes that both things and words are so certain and determined that nothing in them can be changed. Truly, among Catholics there is almost no disagreement, and the matter requires more explanation than debate.

Among the old heretics there was no lack of those who perverted both the things and words of the Sacraments, and especially among the Gnostics, (see Irenaeus 1, 9 & 18, and Epiphanius *haeres.* 26). At the same time, however, all who use the Sacraments hold that the things and words are determined, and as much as possible do not recede from the words prescribed in the Gospel. Augustine says in this way (*De Baptismo* 7, 25), "Heretics are more easily found, who altogether do not baptize, than those who do not baptize in those words."

But in our time Martin Luther, the boldest of all heretics, devised a new heresy, namely that certain words are not required in the Sacraments. He speaks in this way in *The Babylonian Captivity*, in the chapter on Baptism, "Baptism is handed down in any manner you like, and provided it is not in the name of man, but in the name of God, then truly it saves; nay more I do not doubt if anyone received it in the name of the Lord, even if an impious minister would not give it in the Lord's name, truly he would be baptized in the name of the Lord." Therefore, according to Luther, if anyone would say, "I baptize you in the name of Luther, and of Catharine his wife, or even in the name of the devil, it will be a true Baptism, provided the recipient would receive it in the name of the Lord.

Later, Luther retracted this error. In his first homily on Baptism, given in 1535, he speaks in this way, "Christ clearly expressed which ceremonies he willed and he prescribed the form; such as those signs and no others, those very words, no others are used here. ... If you plunge an infant in water, and do not add the words of baptism, but you were to pronounce the Lord's prayer, or certain other words from Scripture, it would not be a true Baptism. ... If anyone would pronounce over the bread and wine before him, not the words of the Sacrament, but either of the Decalogue, or the Apostle's Creed, or some sacred sentence or Psalm, it would not be the true body and blood of Christ." He holds similar things in his 3rd *Homily on*

Chapter XXI: Nothing May Be Added or Removed

Baptism, held in 1540.

Although Luther retracted his error, nevertheless Brenz seems to approve more of the prior opinion of Luther. Accordingly, in his *Catechism* (on Baptism) he does not take much care for the prescribed form of Baptism from Christ, nor does Zwingli (*de Vera et Falsa Relig.*, c. Baptismo), on which we will speak about in the next book (2, 3). And duly, the earlier opinion of Luther, as manifestly opposed to the truth, is so much more suited to the principles of Lutheran Theology than the later opinion. If the Sacraments were chiefly instituted to arouse and sustain faith, there is no difference between the words or things which we use, provided that faith can be aroused and sustained in them. Therefore, not only must this error be destroyed, but I must establish a few propositions to prove the matter.

a) The first proposition: *Certain things that were also determined by God himself should be in the Sacraments.* This proposition, inasmuch as it regards the Sacraments of the New Law, is not denied by heretics, and is most certain among Catholics. They assert it in one way, and we in another. They show from their general principle, that no worship pleases God except the one which he instituted; the rest pertain to, ἐθελοθρησκείαν, and traditions of men. Such an argument is weak, as we have often shown in other places. Catholics prove it from this principle. Because the Sacraments of the New Law are a cause of grace and justification, "you are washed, you are sanctified" (1 Cor. 6:11) "cleansing it with the laver of water and in the word of life" (Eph. 5:26). Now, no one can give grace except God; therefore, only God can determine the things which pertain to the essence of the Sacraments.

In regard to the Sacraments of the Mosaic Law and the law of nature, there seem to be some doubts. Still, if they were truly sacraments, as they really were, it must altogether be supposed that the matter of those Sacraments was determined by God. In the first place, it is certain, *de facto*, that nearly all of the Sacraments which came to our notice, were determined by God. Circumcision was a Sacrament of the law of nature, and it is certain that God determined what had to be done, how and at what time (Gen. 17:10 *seqq*.). We can prove the same from many other verses. So, the old Sacraments were figures and types of our Sacraments. Now, to determine certain things, which infallibly signify some future thing, cannot be accommodated to anyone except God, who knows these future things for certain. Then, even if the old Sacraments did not effect justifying grace, nevertheless, they effected *legal cleanliness and led into the people of God*; no man can determine something to effect legal cleanliness, or introduce one into a certain society, except for the one who is the author of that law and society.

We must also note with St. Thomas (III q. 60 a. 5 ad 3), that in every law there was a matter of the Sacrament determined by God, but not always in the same manner. For in the natural law, because the law was not written on tablets nor promulgated by men or angels, but prescribed interiorly, and also inspired in the hearts of men, so also even the Sacraments were inspired by particular Patriarchs, such as Adam, Noah, Abraham, who then taught others. Truly, because the Mosaic law was promulgated by Moses, and publicly written on tablets, so also the Sacraments of that time that were handed down by God through Moses, were also passed on through letters. Thus, because the author of the New Law is the Incarnate Word, therefore, he also determined our Sacraments.

2) The second proposition: *Not only things, but even words were determined by God in the Sacraments of the New Law, so that it is not lawful for anyone to change them.* This proposition must be explained to be rightly understood. Therefore, we must note:

a) Firstly, a variation of form can happen in six ways: namely, by the *addition* of some term; the *removal* of some term; the *change* of some term; by taking away or changing some syllable; *transposition,* i.e., the variation of the order of saying them, such as by pronouncing one part of the form, and then by resting for some space or reaching out for something while speaking; and at length, by completing the pronunciation of the form.

b) Secondly, we must note there is a twofold integrity of the Sacramental form, one *substantial,* the other *accidental.* The substantial consists in only the sense, or signification of the words, but not in the sound, or number of the syllables. This is why as often as the words are varied, by adding, removing, changing, transposing, corrupting, interrupting, the substantial integrity always remains, provided the same sense remains, and vice versa, the slightest variation destroys the substantial integrity, if the sense should perish, just as if anyone would say by changing merely one letter: "I baptize you in the name of the Mother, and the Son and the Holy Spirit," he does not have the substantial form. The accidental integrity consists in all the rest, i.e., in the whole sound, order and number of syllables.

c) Thirdly, judgment on these changes, whether they are substantial or accidental, should not be mathematical, but *moral,* so that then it must be judged that the sense of the words is preserved when the listeners understand and judge that what is customarily signified by the untouched words has in fact been signified, even if otherwise the words will be pronounced in a very corrupted fashion. An example can be found in what Pope Zachariah relates (*epist. Ad Bonifacium,* also cited by Gratian in can. *Retulerunt, de Consecrat. Distinction* 4). Certain men, due to a lack of training in the Latin language baptized in these words, "*Ego te baptizo in nomine Patria, et Filia, et Spiritua Sancta.*" Such words, if they are received properly, do not signify *Pater, et Filius, et Spiritus Sanctus,* and especially if they are pronounced apart; nevertheless, the Supreme Pontiff judged most prudently, that the substance of the form was not changed, because it could easily be understood what they meant to say, both from the very action of baptizing itself, and even from the union with the word in the name;

Chapter XXI: Nothing May Be Added or Removed

he did not say, "*In nomine Patriae, et Filiae*,"[5] which the rule of grammar would demand if he had meant in earnest to change the form, but, "*in nomine Patria et Filia*." Seeing that they mean nothing of themselves, it is a sign that he meant to say that which others say, when they say "*In nomine Patris, et Filii*, etc."

For equal reasoning, we must make a judgment on interruption: If anyone will say while consecrating the Eucharist: *Hoc est cor-*, and then recite one Psalm, or rest for a notable space, and then at length would add, *pus meum*, without a doubt, in the judgement of the prudent, it must not be thought that he had said, "*Hoc est corpus meum*." But if after anyone said, *Hoc est cor—*, and he would suffer some brief emptiness of mind, and still also rest for a space, before he would add, *pus meum*, it would not be considered that the sense of the form perished.

d) Fourthly, we must note that it is not licit, as we say in the conclusion, to change the form of the words in any way, whether through that change the integrity of the substantial form removed, or only the accidental. This is the difference, that when the form is substantially changed, the Sacrament is not brought to completion; therefore, that integrity is said to be *necessaria necessitate Sacramenti*.[6] On the other hand, when it is only changed accidentally, the Sacrament is performed, but he sins because he changes it in this way, and therefore, this integrity is said to be necessary only by the *necessity of precept*.

e) Note *fifthly*, on the side of the form of the words a Sacrament is never rendered invalid unless the substantial integrity is really lacking. Still, it can happen in another way, that when there is only an accidental corruption the Sacrament does not come about, namely, if he who changes the form accidentally wishes to introduce a new rite, as Zacharias teaches (*can. Retulerunt, de Consecratione*, dist. 4; St. Thomas III q. 60 art. 7 ad 3 and art. 8 in the body of the article). The words of these authorities are not rightly explained by all.

Therefore, we must advert whether he, who intends to introduce a new rite, intends to introduce a new essential rite in respect to the *whole* Church of Christ universally, i.e., which was not previously in the very true and universal Church, or intends to introduce a new rite in respect to *some* Church which he thinks is false.

If he intends to introduce a new [rite] *absolutely*, then the Sacrament does not take place; not because the form is lacking, but rather, the *intention*. He is convicted of not doing what the Church does, seeing that he meant to introduce a rite which was never in the true and universal Church. This is what St. Thomas teaches (*loc. cit.*), anyone that intends to introduce a

---

5 Translator's note: *In nomine Patriae et filiae* in the possessive would be grammatically required here, not the subject form *Patria et Filia*. Thus, it is evidence that the ministers simply erred rather than meant to change the form.

6 Necessary by the necessity of the Sacrament.

new rite always gives the reason why he does not complete the Sacrament because he does not have the intention of the Church.

Now, if he intended to introduce a new rite, not absolutely, but only in respect *of some* Church, which he thinks is false and meanwhile intends to do what the true Church does; then the Sacrament is carried out, even if he is deceived in distinguishing the true Church. For example, let us say a Greek, baptizes with these words, "The servant of Christ is baptized in the name of the Father, and of the Son and of the Holy Spirit"; now, let's say that by doing so he intends to introduce a substantial rite, against a necessary rite of the Roman Church, so that he means to persuade that a Sacrament is not carried out if anyone should say, "I baptize you in the name of the Father and of the Son and of the Holy Spirit." If, he still intends to do what the true Church, whatever it is, does, then he truly baptized, his error notwithstanding. In that Baptism the substantial form is found and the intention of the true Church in general, which everyone agrees suffices; for his error in regard to the Sacrament, or the Church, does not invalidate the Sacrament, as all Catholics teach, who teach that the Sacraments handed on by heretics are valid. The minister is not held to intend to do what the Roman Church does; otherwise no heretic would truly baptize. Rather, only that which the *true Church of Christ* does, in which nevertheless, the intention is virtually included, so that he would intend to do what the Roman Church intends, because it alone is the true Church.

Therefore, what Paludanus says (4 dist. 3 q. 1 art. 3), that a Sacrament is not always invalid when someone intends to introduce a new rite, is true, but not against St. Thomas, as he perhaps thought. Nay more, St. Thomas did not say "When anyone means to introduce a new rite the Sacrament is not completed," but that *it does not seem* the Sacrament is completed, because, namely, it can happen that a Sacrament is carried out, but is presumed not to be completed because it is presumed that due intention was not present.

Now, in regard to what Domingo del Soto says (qu. 1 art. 8), that the Greeks truly baptize with the words the servant of Christ is baptized, etc., because the Roman Church tolerates that rite; so, if the Roman Church were to solemnly condemn that rite as invalid, then it would be that they do not truly baptize. This is not absolutely true, since if the Roman Church were to condemn that rite as an accidental corruption of form, then they would certainly sin, but they would still truly baptize. If, on the other hand, the Roman Church were truly to condemn it as a substantial corruption, then they would not truly baptize, but the reason would not be, as del Soto says, that the intention would be lacking, rather because the *substantial form* would be lacking.

Now that these things have been explained in this way, we will prove our proposition against the rashness of Luther and Brenz. *Firstly*, the

Chapter XXI: Nothing May Be Added or Removed

Sacraments were instituted by God, as our adversaries concede. Therefore, the particular part of the Sacrament, namely the form of words, were instituted by God. Consequently, anyone who changes it sins against God and often does not complete the Sacrament, namely when he changes it substantially. If the Sacrament depends on the institution of God, certainly it will not be a Sacrament when we do not do what he instituted.

Secondly: To change the matter of the Sacraments is a grave sacrilege, and the Sacrament would not be completed, as our adversaries concede. Why therefore, would the same reasoning not hold on the form, which consists in words?

Thirdly: To add to the words of Scripture, or change them is not lawful by any consideration. As a result, the words of the Sacraments should not and cannot be changed in any way, especially when the words of Scripture were instituted merely to signify, while the words of the Sacraments were instituted both to signify and sanctify.

Fourthly: The same is proven from the testimonies of the Fathers. Irenaeus (1, 18) rebukes certain heretics who changed the form of words prescribed by Christ in the Sacrament of Baptism. Tertullian (*de Baptismo*) says, "The law of immersion was imposed, and the form prescribed: 'Go,' he says, 'to all nations, immersing them in the name of the Father, and of the Son and of the Holy Spirit'." Cyprian (*epist. ad Jubajanum*) holds the same thing. Likewise, Athanasius (*serm.* 3 *Contra Arianos*) and Basil (*Hom. On Holy Baptism*), as well as the others who wrote against the Arians, use this argument to prove the divinity of the three persons, that we are commanded to express the three persons in Baptism. Likewise, Basil says in his work *On the Holy Spirit* (c. 12), that whoever removes or adds to the prescribed words in the Sacrament of Baptism cuts himself off from grace. Didymus (*de Spiritu Sancto* 2) says, "Whoever omits one of the prescribed names, neither attains the completion of the Sacrament, nor frees a man from his sins." Augustine (*Contra Donatistas*, 6, 25) says, "The Evangelical words are certain, without which Baptism cannot be consecrated." Damascene (*de Fide* 4, 16) says, "The Lord explained what form of words must be applied in Baptism, saying: Baptizing them, etc." The first Council of Arles agrees (can. 8), which commands an examination to be made on what form of words the Arians use when they baptize.

CHAPTER XXII

On the End and Necessity of the Sacraments

WE will explain three things in regard to the final cause of the Sacraments. *First*, we will speak on the end itself; *secondly*, on the necessity, which is discerned from the end; *thirdly*, we will defend the teaching of the Church against the lies, and calumnies of the heretics. What pertains to the first can be asked in two ways, when it is a question of what is the end of the Sacraments: a) *First*, to ascertain for what end did God institute the Sacraments and b) *secondly*, why to attain that end did he institute such means, when he could through other means, and that end could be attained without any means.

The first question has already been explained in the disputation on the definition of a Sacrament; we already showed that the Sacraments were instituted to justify men, but, as they are signs and the instrumental causes of God's grace.

The second question is easy, and has no controversy over it. Certain authors gather many arguments, both on the side of God, and on the side of man, and on the side of the Sacraments themselves, why it was useful to institute the Sacraments, i.e., sensible signs, to justify men. But these are the particular reasons.

1) *First*, because it was congruent with human nature, which is constituted of body and spirit. Chrysostom speaks in this way in *Hom. 60 ad Populum*, and *83 on Matthew*, "If you were incorporeal, then bare incorporeal gifts would be given to you, but because the soul has been inserted in the body, it is offered to you in intelligible sensible things." Gregory Nazianzen and Gregory of Nyssa teach similar things in their sermons on Baptism.

2) *Second*, it would more clearly appear that grace, which is given through the Sacraments, is from God alone. If it were given through some spiritual actions, men could suspect that they are justified by the proper force of that action; moreover, now when through corporal and abject things so excellent a gift is given, there is no place left for such a suspicion. For which reason the Lord, in John 9:6, gave sight to the blind man with spit and mud, not some precious ointment, and that he meant to subject the world to himself through poor and obscure men.

3) *Third*, that they are at the same time instruments of justification and signs, whereby the faithful are discerned from infidels, and whereby the people of God are gathered, and whereby also, God is worshipped in sacred

Chapter XXII: The Necessity of the Sacraments

ceremonies. There cannot be signs to discern some from others, nor even ceremonies of religion, unless they are external and sensible. See the many arguments cited by Hugh (*de Sacramentis* 1, p. 9 c. 3) and Lombard, as well as the Doctors in 4, 1, as well as St. Thomas (*Contra Gentes* 4, 56), and from more recent authors such as William Alanus (*de Sacr. In Genere*, c. 24).

In regard to the *second*, on necessity, there is a twofold necessity. One is called the necessity of precept, the other the necessity of means, although sometimes these two necessities are joined; for in this very matter, that something is a means to necessary salvation, at the same time it is also a natural precept if it is placed in our power. Nevertheless, this is the difference, that although someone from invincible ignorance, or another just reason does not fulfill the precept, he suffers no detriment, but if someone does not take up the necessary means, he suffers great detriment, because he does not attain the end, although it happens from invincible ignorance. For example, the Sacrament of Confirmation is a precept, but it is not a necessary means for salvation *simpliciter*; consequently, one who neglected to receive a Sacrament of this sort sins, but if he did not receive it for a legitimate cause, he does not sin, nor is his salvation impeded. On the other hand, because Baptism in fact, or in desire is a precept and a medium; therefore, anyone who is not baptized, or certainly does not desire Baptism, is not saved, even if it happens from ignorance or impotency.

Again, the necessity of means is rather a necessity *simpliciter*, in the way that wings are necessary to fly, or, *ad bene esse*,[7] in the way that a horse is necessary to make a journey. Lastly, each necessity is either absolute and natural, as in the posited examples, or from the institution and will of another, in the way that in games to reach the goal is a necessary means to the prize. It is also partly from the institution, partly from the natural congruence, as when a general will concede to his soldiers to pillage some city if they had taken it by force. From these what the necessity of the Sacraments is can easily be understood.

1) Thus, the *first* proposition is: *No Sacrament has absolute necessity, rather, all of their necessity depends upon the precept and divine institution connected to natural congruence.* It is certain that God could justify men without any Sacraments, there is no controversy over this.

2) The *second* proposition: *All the Sacraments are necessary by the necessity of precept, although not in each individual.* There is no controversy about this proposition with the heretics.

3) The *third* proposition: *Baptism and Penance are necessary, posited by divine institution, by the necessity of means simpliciter. Baptism is necessary to all, Penance to those who offend mortally.* In this matter we do not agree. Our adversaries affirm that the Sacraments are necessary because they are precepts, and even necessary as a useful means; nevertheless, they do not acknowledge any Sacrament as necessary *simpliciter*, as a means. And

---

[7] Translator's note: In regard to well-being.

the reason is, since faith alone justifies, Sacraments are only applied to arouse and nourish faith. Otherwise, without the Sacraments, faith can be begotten by the word alone, nourished, increased, so no Sacrament is necessary *simpliciter*. This controversy will be treated on the disputation on Baptism and Penance. Now, two clear passages of Scripture will suffice, "Unless a man be born again of water and the Holy Spirit, he cannot enter the kingdom of God" (John 3:5) and "Unless you do penance, you will all perish likewise" (Luke 13:3).

The *fourth* proposition: *The Eucharist, Confirmation, and Extreme Unction are necessary by the necessity of means to be well, having been posited by divine institution.* In this we do not agree, insofar as we number Confirmation and Anointing among the Sacraments, but we will address this in another place. Insofar as the Eucharist, we agree that it is in precept, but that it is necessary *ad bene esse* as a *means*, we seem to agree, but really, we do not. They say the Sacraments are necessary as a means instituted by Christ, but so explain the matter that weakens this necessity to the point that it is almost abolished (Calvin, *Antidote*, and Chemnitz in *Exam.*). They would have it that the Sacraments are only useful to nourish faith, because they represent to the eyes what the word offers to the ears. This is why the *Apology for the Augsburg Confession* (art. 13) compares the Sacraments to a picture. Just as pictures cannot be called necessary for salvation, except perhaps for very unlearned men, so in this way neither are the Sacraments according to their opinion. Chemnitz (*loc. cit.*) tries to refute this similitude on the picture, and show I know not what greater necessity, but he cannot deny that similitude in the *Apologia*, which he professes to follow in all things. Besides, he says the same thing in other words, for he would have it that a Sacrament is nothing other than a rite in which a promise is visibly represented in the word. Therefore, they really do not acknowledge a necessity, although they lie about doing so, seeing they acknowledge only a sort of weak utility of the Sacraments.

5) The *fifth* proposition: *The order is necessary not for each man, rather for the universal Church herself by the necessity of means simpliciter, positing divine institution.*

6) The *sixth* proposition: *Matrimony is necessary* ad bene esse, *not for every man, but for the universal Church.* On this there is no controversy. See St. Thomas 3, q. 65, art. 4.

In regard to the *third*, the lies and calumnies of Calvin and Chemnitz against the Council of Trent, Sess. 7 can. 4, are refuted, where it is a question of the necessity of the Sacrament. These are the words of the Council, "If anyone will say that the Sacraments of the New Law are not necessary for salvation, but superfluous, and without them or desire of them, men obtain the grace of justification from God by faith alone, even if all [of them] are not necessary for each man, *anathema sit.*" By such a canon, the Council defines three things. *a) Firstly*, the Sacraments are not

Chapter XXII: The Necessity of the Sacraments 109

superfluous for salvation, but necessary; that which was defined against the Anabaptists and Zwinglians, who (as we saw above in the disputation on the *Definition of a Sacrament*), held that the Sacraments were useful to discern faithful from pagans, but not to obtain salvation. Calvin and Chemnitz also gladly admit this part of the definition. *b) Secondly*, certain Sacraments are so necessary that without them, or the desire for them, a man cannot obtain salvation. This is against the Lutherans and the Calvinists, who only attribute necessity of this sort to faith. *c) Thirdly*, not all of the Sacraments are necessary to each man; that is asserted on account of Order and Matrimony. In each part of that definition they only rebuke what we number among these Sacraments; but we are going to speak of this in another place. Now, let us come to the lies.

Calvin so calumniates this Canon in his *Antidote*, "Here, the good fathers, for all their foolishness, do not perceive that whatever grace is conferred upon us by the Sacraments, is nevertheless to be ascribed to faith. He that separates faith from the Sacraments, acts as if he were to take the soul away from the body. Therefore, as we do not exclude the doctrine of the gospel when we say that we obtain the grace of Christ by faith alone, so neither do we exclude the Sacraments, the nature of which is the same as they are seals of the Gospel."

By such words he rebukes that part of the Canon where the Council condemns those who say that men are justified by faith alone without the Sacraments. He finds fault with the fact that he thinks the Council condemned Lutheran's opinion without understanding it. Even if the Lutherans affirmed that faith alone justifies and hence the Sacraments do not justify, still, they also admit the Sacraments justify in some manner. Namely, they do not deny that God justifies, and the passion of Christ justifies, and even a sermon in some manner justifies. For, God is said to justify, remitting sins on his authority and receiving us in grace, Christ is said to meritoriously justify, because he merited grace for us and the remission of sins. The word and Sacrament justify instrumentally insofar as they arouse and nourish faith, which embraces justification. Moreover, faith justifies because immediately, like a kind of spiritual hand, it takes hold of justification; in such a manner faith has no assistant in the work of justification. Thus, in Calvin's view, the Council ineptly gathers that the Lutherans exclude the Sacraments from justification because they teach faith alone justifies.

Chemnitz has a similar calumny (p. 80), "What must particularly be observed is that they oppose the necessity of the Sacraments to justification by faith alone. On the contrary, the things which are necessary to salvation must be distinguished, as Christ meriting, the Father giving, the organs or instruments of the word and Sacraments through which the Holy Spirit offers, applies, seals, increases and confirms the benefits of the New Testament among believers, and at length faith, which apprehends and receives those benefits. These individual things, in their own way, and in their degree were ordained for our salvation. Just as it does not follow that the Sacraments are necessary for salvation, therefore Christ alone did not acquire it by his own merit, so also it does not follow that the Sacraments are necessary for salvation, therefore, we do not receive the grace of justification by faith alone."

This is a calumny, and a manifest lie. For the Council rightly understood their opinion, and properly condemned the very thing which they teach. Really, the Council did not condemn them because they excluded the Sacraments from justification in any way you like, but because they exclude *from immediate reception, and application of justification*, which they attribute to faith alone. Catholic faith does not admit that the grace of justification is obtained by men or applied to them by faith alone; rather, it would have it that the Sacraments are necessarily required for it, so much so that if faith exists in someone, no matter how great, still it does not justify unless the Sacrament is also present in fact or in desire. Nay more, the Sacrament is more required than faith. For without the Sacrament in fact or in desire, no man is justified, neither a child nor an adult; without faith some are justified, such as children who have no proper faith, by which they receive justification, and still they are justified through the Sacrament of faith.

For this reason, what Calvin says is also refuted, that whatever grace conferred to us through the Sacraments is imputed to faith. That is false. Grace, which is conferred through the Sacraments, is imputed to the virtue of the Sacraments themselves and the institution of Christ, not of faith; for faith does not give force to the Sacraments, but only disposes the subject, as we said above.

Now, Martin Chemnitz (2 part. *Exam.*, p. 79 *et seqq.*), says that snares lurk in each utterance of this canon; moreover, he uncovers five snares. *Firstly*, he says, "In the beginning the method of composition in this canon must be considered. Peculiar snares lurk in nearly each utterance. ... The remaining rites, such as Confirmation, Extreme Unction, auricular Confession, Satisfaction, etc., they would have it are Sacraments necessary for salvation, *simpliciter*."

This is clearly a lie, both from the fact that the Council does not add the word *simpliciter*, and also because the common teaching of theologians, from which a Council never recedes, teaches that only three Sacraments are necessary *simpliciter*: Baptism, for all, and Penance for all who sin after Baptism, and Order for the universal Church itself. Without the rest, men can be saved provided there is no negligence or scorn. See St. Thomas Aquinas (III q. 65, art. 4).

Secondly, in this way Chemnitz says the same thing, "No sane man ever understood justification by faith alone in this way, as if it excluded the grace of God, the merit of Christ, as well as the ministry of the word and

Chapter XXII: The Necessity of the Sacraments

the Sacraments."

This is another lie. For, even if Chemnitz and Calvin were to teach that faith alone should not be opposed to the Sacraments in the business of justification, just as it is not opposed to the grace of God and the merit of Christ, nevertheless Luther, whom Chemnitz would never deny to be a sane man, in many places created an opposition between faith alone and the Sacraments, and so clearly taught that men are justified by faith alone, that no part of justification pertained to the Sacraments. In *On the Babylonian Captivity*, on Baptism, he says, "Baptism justifies no man, nor does it benefit any, rather the faith in the word of the promise." In his *Assertion of the First Article*, he says, "We say that neither the Sacraments of the New or Old Testament, but faith alone justifies." And in his book against John Cochlaeus, he says, "No part of justification can be attributed to Baptism." He certainly did not say the Grace of God, or the merit of Christ does not justify, nor benefit any, and no part of justification can be attributed to the grace of God or the merit of Christ. Thus, Luther opposed justification by faith alone to the Sacraments, though he still did not oppose it to the grace of God or the merit of Christ. So also, Melanchthon, whom Chemnitz would never say was insane, in *Locis*, for the year 1522, says, "Signs do not justify, as the Apostle says, Circumcision is nothing, so Baptism is nothing, participation of the Lord's table is nothing." I ask whether Melanchthon said the grace of God does not justify, and the grace of God is nothing? Consequently, the older Lutherans only opposed faith alone to the Sacraments, which they did not oppose to grace and the merit of Christ. Hence, the Council condemned at the same time these profane expressions of the old Lutherans, and the opinion which Calvin and Chemnitz follow, although they refrain from the words.

Thirdly, Chemnitz speaks in this way (*ibid.*), "They do not only relate the necessity of the Sacraments to the extent that they are instrumental causes whereby the grace of justification is conveyed and shown to us by God, but they speak about obtaining or receiving the grace of justification. They do not wish this to be attributed to faith alone, but attach the necessity of the Sacraments, i.e., they understand our work which we do in the reception of the Sacraments, so that faith alone does not receive the grace of justification, but faith together with the dignity or merit of this our work."

But here, Chemnitz shamefully lies, seeing that not one of us Catholics attributes the justification which we receive in the Sacraments to the dignity or merits of our work, but *to the divine institution* and *work of Christ*. For Baptism, or any other Sacrament is not our work, nor does it depend upon our dignity or merit; otherwise, the Sacraments conferred on the impious would be useless; but both Catholics and even Lutherans defend the contrary against the Donatists.

Fourthly, Chemnitz adds, "This is why they call them Sacraments of the

New Law, to be a mutual relation of law and our works even in the very use of the Sacrament."

Here he also groundlessly accuses us. By "law," the Council does not understand a precept, whereby a work is commanded, but *the New Testament*, for the Sacrament of the New Law means the same as a Sacrament instituted by Christ, who is the author of the New Testament, or Law.

Fifthly, he adds, most ineptly, "Thus they term *votum*, this is, a promise of a certain work, to receive the grace of justification."

Who does not marvel at the ignorance or impudence of this censor? He either does not know that *votum*, in the words of the Council, does not mean a promise, but a *desire*; or he labors much just to quibble. Certainly, when the Council says that the Sacraments or the desire [*votum*] are necessary, by *votum* they meant *desire* [*voluntatem*]. For as St. Augustine teaches (*On Baptism*, 4, 23), the thief was saved without Baptism, not because he lacked the desire to receive it, rather the necessity to receive it was not yet present. Now, that is enough on Chemnitz' trifling, and on the final cause of the Sacraments.

CHAPTER XXIII

Christ Alone Is the Author of the Sacraments

ON the efficient cause of the Sacraments, there are four controversies, as many as there are canons on the matter in the seventh session of the Council of Trent. We must observe that to understand these better, the Theologians consider a threefold efficient cause in the Sacraments: *one* principal and altogether independent, in which they say there is the power of authority; the *second*, instrumental, but of a united instrument, in which they say there is a power of excellence. The *third* instrumental, but of a separate instrument; in which they say there is a ministerial power.

The *first* cause by the consent of all is God, for he alone can give grace from authority and hence institute the Sacraments, which effect grace, or also infallibly signify it. The *second* cause is Christ as man, for the humanity of Christ is a united instrument to divinity by the hypostatic union, and therefore to Christ, as man, a certain ministerial power is attributed because it has been derived from dignity. Nevertheless, it is called a power of excellence because it is suited to Christ alone. The *third* cause is any other minister of the Sacraments you like. On the first cause, there is no question, on the second, one controversy, on the third, three.

1) Therefore, the *first* question is: whether Christ alone is the author of the Sacraments of the New Law. Our adversaries teach two specific things. *Firstly*, the Sacraments, namely Baptism, and the Eucharist, which are the only ones they regard as true Sacraments were instituted by Christ, while the rest were not. Calvin teaches in this way (*Antid. Conc.* Sess. 7 can. 1) as well as Chemnitz (*Exam.* 2 part. P. 13). Moreover, Chemnitz cites Cyprian in his sermon *On the Washing of Feet*; likewise Hugh of St. Victor (*de Sacramentis*, 2, p. 15, c. 2) as well as Peter Lombard (4 dist. 23) who deny all the Sacraments were instituted by Christ. He could add Alexander of Hales who says (4 par. Q. 24, mem. 1) the Sacrament of Confirmation was established by the Church after the death of the Apostles in the Council of Meldensis. It seems that St. Bonaventure thought likewise (4 dist. 7 art. 1 q. 1). Besides, the same Alexander (q. 59 membr. 3) and Bonaventure (dist. 18, art. 1 q. 3) as well as Marsilius of Padua (4 q. 14) say the Sacrament of Penance was not instituted by Christ, but by the Apostles.

On the other hand, the Council of Trent placed this as an error (sess. 7 can. 1) which is of this kind, "If anyone says the Sacraments of the New Law were not all instituted by our Lord Jesus Christ, *anathema sit.*" That canon should not be understood in such a way as if the Council meant the Sacraments were instituted by Christ immediately or mediately, but only *immediately*, for otherwise the Council would have posited that canon in vain since no man ever doubted whether God instituted the Sacraments at least mediately. The same Council, sess. 14, can. 1, arguing on the Sacrament of Extreme Unction, explains itself when it says that Sacrament was instituted by Christ himself, promulgated by Blessed James the Apostle. *Lastly,* if the Sacraments were only mediately instituted by Christ, the same thing could be said about the Sacraments and all other Ecclesiastical ceremonies; for they were all instituted by Christ mediately, because, without a doubt, he gave to the Church the power to institute and inspire, that it would institute and assist, lest it would err in the institution. Nevertheless, the same Council does not speak in the same way about the Sacraments and other ceremonies. For in sess. 21, ch. 2, the Church has the power of changing and instituting in regard to the Sacraments, save for their substance.

Therefore, this very true teaching of the Council can be confirmed with these arguments: *a)* In the Scriptures the Apostles are not called anything but dispensers and ministers of the mysteries of God (1 Cor. 4:1), "Let man think of us this way, as ministers of Christ and dispensers of the mysteries of God." So, they themselves did not institute, but only promulgated and administered the Sacraments that Christ had instituted.

b) Secondly, the Sacraments of the Old Law were instituted immediately by God, but merely promulgated by Moses, as is clear from the books of Exodus and Leviticus, where always, when something new was instituted, we read, "Thus spoke the Lord to Moses." Thus, it was more proper that the more excellent Sacraments of the New Law were instituted by God himself.

c) The Fathers affirm it. Cyprian, or whoever was the author of the sermon *On the Washing of Feet*, says, "The supreme priest himself is the institutor and author of his own sacrament; in what remains, men had the Holy Spirit as a teacher." There you see, not the Sacraments (as Chemnitz falsely cites), but certain other rites were instituted by men, according to Cyprian. Ambrose (*de Sacramentis*, 4, 4), says, "Who is the author of the Sacraments but the Lord Jesus?" Augustine (*Doctrina Christiana*, 3, 9) says firstly, the Lord himself, then the Apostolic discipline handed on the Sacraments to the Churches. The same in Epistle 18, c. 1, he makes God the author of the Sacraments.

To the other testimonies which Chemnitz alleges, we respond: Cyprian held the contrary, as we showed above. Hugh and Lombard, however, for "institution" meant to understand *promulgation*, in the way that even the Old Law is called the law of Moses, when still, Moses did not properly institute it, but only promulgated it. The same answer can be given to the testimonies of those who say the Sacrament of Penance was instituted by the Apostles. The same authors say Christ instituted Absolution, and insinuated Confession; this is why he did not leave the institution to the

Chapter XXIII: The Author of the Sacraments

Apostles as much as a *declaration*, although they call it an institution. Hence, what Alexander of Hales and Bonaventure say on the Sacrament of Confirmation cannot be defended. It is certain from the testimony of Pope Fabian, Dionysius the Areopagite, Cyprian, Tertullian, and other ancients, that the Sacrament of Confirmation existed a long time before the times of the Council of Meldensis. (See Dionysius, *de Ecclesiastica Hierarchia*, ch. On Baptism; Tertullian, *De Resurrectione Carnis*; Fabian, in *Epist. Ad Orientales*; Cyprian, *Epistles* 2, 1; and in the sermon on Chrism). But the Council did not declare anything except that the one who approaches the Sacrament of Confirmation should fast, as is clear from Gratian (can. *Ut Episcopi, de Consecrate*. Dist. 5), and nothing else is extent from this Council. More will be argued on this whole question in the individual Sacraments.

CHAPTER XXIV

The Ordinary Minister of the Sacraments Is Not Any Baptized Man You Like

THE second question is on the ministerial cause in confecting the Sacraments and the ministers: Who properly is the minister of the Sacraments in the Church? Our adversaries disagree much among themselves as well as us on this question.

Martin Luther says two false things, and opposes himself. First, he says that all are altogether ministers, not only men, but even demons. He speaks this way in his works on *Private Mass* and the *Anointing of the Priesthood*, published in 1534, "I will not say what the Papists say; none of the Angels, nor Mary herself can consecrate. On the other hand, I say if the devil himself were to come, and I were to ascertain the devil is so insinuated in the office of the pastor of the Church, in the appearance of a man, called to preach and publicly taught, baptized, celebrated Mass and absolved from sins in the Church, and exercised such an office according to the institution of Christ, then I would be compelled to affirm that the Sacraments are not inefficacious, but we receive true Baptism, the true Gospel, true Absolution, the true Sacrament of the body and blood of Christ."

Moreover, he shows that our faith, as well as the dignity and efficacy of the Sacraments do not rest upon the quality of person, but the words and ordination of Christ. So, whether he is good or evil, anointed or not anointed, legitimately called or not so called, whether Satan or an Angel, he effects the same provided he preserves the ordination of Christ. He also shows that Judas, who was a member of the devil, preached and baptized no less than the other Apostles. Why, therefore, can the devil not perform what his members can?

The other thing which Luther says, is that all baptized men have the power to administer all the Sacraments, even if, so as to avoid confusion, it is not fitting that all use this power, but only those who are legitimately called. He makes an exception for three cases. *a)* When someone is in a private place, such as his home; *b)* When no other man is present, and necessity demands it; *c)* when someone else is present, but does not administer them rightly, so that I must do it, according to 1 Cor. 14:30, "If a thing will be revealed to one sitting, let the first be silent."

That this is his opinion is clear from the following. In his book *On the Babylonian Captivity*, in the chapter on Order, he says, "Let any man that reckons himself to be a Christian be certain, we are all equally priests, i.e.,

Chapter XXIV: The Ordinary Minister

the same in the word, and have the same power in whichever Sacrament, but it is not lawful for anyone to use this very power, except by the consent of the community or the calling of an elder." A little later, "What if they are compelled to admit that we are all equally priests, as many of us that have been baptized, just as we really are, etc." Likewise, in the articles condemned by Leo X, in article 13, where he says, "Where there is no priest, any Christian you like can equally [function], even if they be a woman or a boy." Then, in the assertion of a certain article he renders the argument, "For anyone that has been baptized has the Spirit of Christ; moreover, where there is the Spirit of Christ, there the power and freedom of all." Likewise, in the book which he published against the Bull of Leo, in the year 1520, he says, "I defend and embrace with the full trust of my spirit, those articles condemned in the said bull, and I affirm that the same ought to be held by all faithful Christians, under the penalty of eternal damnation. ... The last thing which I have I shall give, namely this life and blood of mine. It is better that I be killed a thousand times than retract one syllable of the articles which they have condemned."

Now we must note in passing, later Luther revised some things from the same articles, namely 36 on free will, which in the assertion, he called the primary foundation of his whole doctrine. In that article, he says free will is a thing from title alone, and in the assertion he explains that it must be so understood, as according to the doctrine of Wycliffe, everything comes about from absolute necessity. Indeed, he clearly revised that in his *Saxon Visitation*, where he teaches that a man is free of will in civil works, and not everything comes about from necessity.

In his replies, found in his book *On the Abrogation of Private Mass*, published in 1521, he purposely teaches and shows that all Christians have the same power in the word and administration of the Sacraments, when he says, "By the unconquered Scriptures we strengthen that legitimate and sole ministry of the word that is common to all Christians, as it were priesthood and sacrifice." Later he shows with some examples of Scripture, that even women are allowed to preach. Likewise, in his book *ad Pragenses*, on instituting ministers of the Church, which he published in 1523, he says, "There is no priest, especially in the New Testament, rather he is born, not ordained, he is rather created; born in baptism, all Christians are altogether priests." In the same place, he amply shows that all Christians have the ability to preach, baptize, consecrate as well as to bind and loose from Baptism. He holds these words on the keys, "Let the lies of men cease. The keys are of the whole Church and any of its members you like, both in law and in use, and in every manner." Later, he still warns that it is not lawful for each man to use this right, except in necessity, but he must await a calling and election of the multitude.

From all this he deduces two corollaries. *One*, that public ministers do not differ from the rest in respect to power or some dignity, but only in the use of power. *Two*, that it follows from the first, a minister can become a layman, just as ministers are made from laymen. Hence, his arguments will be set aside for later when they will be answered. Thus, this is the teaching of Luther.

John Calvin is on an altogether different spectrum. Not only does he refuse to concede that the devil, or women, or any Christians you like could preach and administer the Sacraments, but he so severely defends that only certain men, legitimately called have this power, that he would not even concede it to the laity to baptize in necessity, especially women. He writes this way in the *Antidote* on sess. 7 can. 10, "No sane man makes all Christians equal in the word and administration of the Sacraments; not only because it is fitting for everything in the Church to be managed decently and in order, but also, because ministers are ordained by the singular mandate of Christ for that purpose. ... Moreover, where do they find the office of baptizing enjoined on women, as they permit them to do?" He teaches the same thing profusely in the *Institutes* (4, 3, §10, and ch. 15). Therefore, we have no controversy with Calvin in this place. His denial of the ability to baptize for laity and women in a time of necessity will be refuted in the disputation on Baptism.

Martin Chemnitz, while laying out the whole matter, does not sufficiently make clear what he thinks, according to his custom. When discussing Session 7 can. 10 of the Council of Trent, which holds, "If anyone will say that all Christians have the same power in the word and administration of all the Sacraments, *anathema sit*," he says three things. *First*, he asks whether the canon was placed to condemn the teaching of Luther, or a mutilated and depraved form, "Luther never supposed that any Christian could or should indiscriminately arrogate to himself or usurp the ministry of the word and the administration of the Sacraments in the Church without a legitimate calling." (*loc. cit.* p. 138).

But Chemnitz should distinguish power from execution. If he speaks on the *execution*, it is true that Luther did not think anyone could or should arrogate to himself this ministry without a legitimate calling. Yet the Council did not condemn that in Luther, for all affirm it is true. If he speaks on the *power*, it is false that Luther did not teach this, as the passages we provided demonstrate. It is also the very thing which the Council condemned. Nor can it be said that the teaching of Luther was mutilated or corrupted by the Council. The Council ought not describe the whole book of Luther, or relate the things which he wrote well within it; rather it was enough to relate the things which they were going to condemn.

Then, Chemnitz adds, the Council speaks fraudulently, "Obliquely, and as if doing something, they reach for this axiom: No man, even if legitimately chosen and called by the Church according to the prescribed word of God, has any power in the word and administration of the Sacraments and the Sacraments that they administer are not true and efficacious unless he has

Chapter XXIV: The Ordinary Minister

been anointed and shaved by some bishop. Let the reader understand these snares are hiding in this canon."

But the canon is absolutely clear, and Chemnitz rather holds snares of his simple intellect, for the Council does not say one has no power in the administration of those Sacraments who has not been anointed and shaved by a bishop. The Council was well aware, in regard to the Sacraments of Baptism and Matrimony, that ordination is not necessarily required, but it does say one does not have the power over *all* the Sacraments, to condemn the teaching of Luther which attributes power to the laity, even for Eucharist and Penance. *Lastly*, the Council did not name "anointed and shaved," for anointing and shaving are accidental ceremonies, and the essence of Ordination can consist without them. Therefore, Chemnitz hides snares in his words.

Thirdly, he says the teaching of the Canon is true as the words sound, but still does not rightly explain the matter, "On the other hand, in regard to the teaching of this tenth canon, just as the words have been placed, it is pertinent that I respond clearly and plainly. If anyone were to suppose, that any Christian you like without a peculiar and legitimate calling is permitted to usurp the power and exercise the ministry of the Word, and the Sacraments in the Church, he would be rightly condemned by law."

But Chemnitz does not rightly explain the Council, for it does not condemn those who say it is lawful for anyone without a calling to usurp ministry. Nobody says that; hence, it was not necessary for the canon. Rather, they condemned those who say Christians have the power to administer the word and *all* the Sacraments, because Luther so said, and it seems Chemnitz believes it although he did not dare clearly declare it. So the doctrine of the Church must be proposed and proven, which can be embraced in two propositions.

a) The *first* proposition: *The Minister of the Sacraments should be a man, but not an angel, whether good or bad.* This is against Luther and common among Theologians.

Nevertheless, it must be observed that if perhaps a good angel were to administer some Sacrament, we would have to hold it as approved because it would be certain that it was done from an extraordinary divine dispensation. This is why Nicephorus (22, 20) relates that St. Amphilochius was ordained a bishop by angels, and that was held approved by the bishops of his province. If, however, the devil would do it the Sacrament would have to be repeated, because the devil does not have the power, nor could he receive a peculiar dispensation of God, but rather he would usurp it to deceive.

This proposition is proven, *firstly*, in regard to the essence of the Sacraments, as a true and natural element is required, so also a true and natural word. Now, only a man speaks truly and naturally; for to speak is an action of a living body through the instrument of the tongue and palate.

Therefore, neither a good angel nor a bad one can confect the Sacraments, as St. Thomas rightly teaches (I q. 41 art. 3 ad 4). Angels also cannot properly speak through an assumed body.

Secondly, even if angels could apply true words and true bodies, nevertheless, they would not for that reason effect a true Sacrament. A Sacrament is a sign and cause of infallible grace; moreover, they do not have elements and words naturally, but only as they are assumed by God, as instruments of justification. Therefore, they are not true Sacraments, when they are applied by anyone, rather, when they are applied by one to *whom God commits it*. This is why, if the words with which Christ and the Apostles did miracles were not advanced by anyone, they would have had the same force. For if anyone would say to a lame man, "Rise and walk," it would do nothing unless it was taken up by God, as an instrument to perform the miracle; so he cannot confect true Sacraments, unless he has authority from God. God gave this authority to men alone, not to angels, whether good or bad. In Matt. 28:19, he said to men, "Going, teach all nations, baptizing them in the name of the Father, etc." Likewise, in Luke 22:19, he said to men alone, "Do this in commemoration of me," and in John 20:23, he said to men alone, "Whose sins you remit, etc." For this reason, Ephesians 4:8 says, "Christ ascending on high, led captivity captive; he gave gifts to men"; where through gifts he understands different ministries that are in the Church, for he had said before in verse 7, "But to every one of us is given grace, according to the measure of the giving of Christ"; and then, in verse 11, "And he gave some Apostles, and some Prophets, and other some evangelists, and others pastors and doctors"; lastly, in Hebrews 5:1, "Every priest taken from men has been constituted for men, etc." This is why Chrysostom (*On the Priesthood*, 3) clearly witnesses that it was not conceded to angels but to men to administer the Sacraments, and he holds the same thing in *Homily 85 on John*, near the end.

Thirdly, it is confirmed from the doctrine of Luther. He himself would have it that the foundation of the power in the word and the Sacraments is Baptism (*loc. cit.*), but this foundation lacks the angels, both good and bad. Likewise, in his *Homily on Baptism*, and elsewhere, he teaches the words and elements do not suffice, rather the command of God is required, but God never commanded angels to confect the Sacraments, therefore, etc.

Neither do Luther's arguments on behalf of the devil conclude the matter. In regard to his *first* argument, we concede that the efficacy of the Sacraments does not depend upon *any* quality of the minister. It does not depend upon an accidental quality, such as goodness. Nevertheless, it does depend upon an *essential* quality, without which he would not be a true minister, such a quality in the first place is that he be a man.

To the *second*, we affirm that Judas was also a member of the devil and ministered true Sacraments; but we deny the same is suited to the devil. Judas, not as a member of the devil, but as *a minister of Christ* administered

Chapter XXIV: The Ordinary Minister

the Sacrament; moreover, Judas was a minister of Christ because he was a true man, and received the power to baptize from Christ. Neither of these suit the devil.

b) The *second* proposition: *A true minister of the Sacraments (with the exception of Baptism and Matrimony) is not any man you like, even baptized, but only he that has been ritually ordained by the Church.*

Note the exception of Baptism, because on account of the supreme necessity of this Sacrament, the Church always understood that any man can confer it; we will speak more of this on the matter of Baptism. Likewise, Matrimony is excepted, because, seeing that Matrimony consists in the mutual contract of the spouses, it cannot happen in any other way than that those contracting it are the ministers.

This proposition is proven against the Lutherans. *Firstly*, from the Scriptures, which teach in the Church there are different offices that are not suited to all, such as in Romans 12:6, 1 Cor. 12:5, Ephes. 4:11, "He has placed some as Apostles, some as Prophets, etc." and 1 Cor. 12:29, "are all Apostles, and all prophets? etc." Therefore, the same can be said on pastors and doctors, the same who are named. They cannot respond, this is a question of use, as the Lutherans say, not on power. For certainly the Apostles did not have Apostolic power before they received it from Christ; therefore, they did not receive the use only, but the *power* itself.

Secondly, from that of Hebrews 5:4, "No man takes honor to himself, except he that is called by God, just as Aaron." Therefore, not every member of the people of God is a priest by this fact. This passage also cannot be understood only on the exercise, for Aaron, before he was called to the priesthood by God, did not have either use or power. *Besides*, to assume honor is not to carry out power, but to *receive* it. That is also confirmed from the following verse 5, "So even Christ did not glorify himself that he might become a high priest." Therefore, to assume honor is to become a high priest, but not to exercise the priesthood.

Thirdly, the Apostles were baptized, and they baptized before the passion of Christ. That they baptized is found in John 4:2, because they had been baptized, as Augustine teaches (*Epist.* 108 *ad Seleucianum*), and it is not believable that they were commanded by Christ to baptize before they themselves were baptized. They received the power to consecrate the Eucharist later in Luke 22:19, when they heard, "Do this in my commemoration." Similarly, they received the power to absolve later in John 20:23, "whose sins you remit." Therefore, they did not receive it in Baptism.

Fourthly, if every Christian receives this power in Baptism, therefore, they receive it because then, as Luther says, they are anointed by the grace of the Holy Spirit, and hence, they become spiritual priests. But this is false; it does not follow that they who, while they are baptized, do not receive grace, and they who later perish, did not truly confer the Sacraments;

which, nevertheless, Luther rightly denies against the Anabaptists. The answer cannot also be made that the character suffices, for the Lutherans do not acknowledge any character.

Fifthly, if every Christian has this power, no one can be deprived of its use unless as a punishment for a great crime. Yet, among the Lutherans many are deprived from the use of this power without any fault. Their objection from confusion that would arise in the Church, if everyone used this power is also not opposed to us. They can exercise this ministry in turn; or certainly, they should not be able to be repulsed, who want to minister, when there are few ministers, even if they have not been called by a magistrate. But they repel those who have not been called; as a result, they either do them an injury, or they should affirm that they do not have the power.

Sixthly, in the Old Law, where the Sacraments were imperfect, still not all could administer them, but *only* priests. The answer does not avail, if someone were to say Christians are made spiritual priests in their baptism, for even they become spiritual priests in Circumcision, and all could offer spiritual sacrifices. Nay more, what St. Peter said about all Christians, "But you are a chosen nation, a royal priesthood" (1 Pet. 2:9), Moses had already said the same thing in regard to all the Israelites in Exodus 19:6, and nevertheless, King Ozias was punished with leprosy because he willed to exercise the sacerdotal office (2 Chron. 26:19).

CHAPTER XXV

The Arguments of Luther Are Answered

From these points it will be easy to respond to Luther's arguments. First, in his book *On the Abrogation of Private Mass*, he proposes six Scriptures, whereby he shows all Christians are equally priests. His first is of 1 Pet. 2:5, "Be as living stones built up as a spiritual house, a holy priesthood, to offer up spiritual sacrifices, acceptable to God by Jesus Christ." *Ibid.*, v. 9, "but you are a chosen nation, a royal priesthood." Third, *ibid.* v. 9, "to declare his virtues, who has called you out of darkness into his marvelous light." There, Christians are said to be called for this purpose, to announce, i.e., to preach the virtue of Christ; therefore, all Christians can and should preach, because that is the especial office of priesthood. The fourth is Apoc. 5:10, "and has made us a kingdom of priests for our God, and we shall reign on earth." The fifth is Apoc. 20:6, "They will be priests of God and Christ." The sixth, is 2 Cor. 3:6, "who made us suitable ministers of the New Testament."

Besides this he adds certain passages to prove that women can preach: Joel 2:28, "Your sons and daughters will prophecy." Acts 21:9, "There were four virgin daughters prophesying with Philip." In Exod. 15:20, Miriam prophesied. In Judges 4:6, Deborah taught Baruch. In 4 Kings 22:15, Holda gave counsel to king Josias. In Luke 1:46, the Virgin Mary prophesied. In 1 Cor. 11:5, it says, "Let a woman pray and prophesy with her head covered. From such a passage he thinks another of the same Apostle is explained in 1 Cor. 14:34, "Let women be silent in church." In the first passage, he speaks absolutely. In the second he forbids women to speak when men are present and willing and able to speak.

Again, in his book *On the Institution of Ministers to the People of Prague*, he shows this in two ways. *Firstly*, by this argument: Christ is a priest. In Psalm 109 [110]:4, it says, "You are a priest forever." All Christians are brethren of Christ, for in Psalm 21 [22]:23, it says, "I will announce your name to my brethren," and in Psalm 44[45]:8, "God has anointed you with the oil of gladness apart from your fellows." Therefore, all Christians are priests.

Secondly, he shows it from the offices of priests, which are to preach, baptize, consecrate, absolve, sacrifice, pray for others, and judge on doctrines. That all can preach, he shows from three Scriptures. *Firstly*, from 1 Pet. 2:9; "To declare his virtues." Secondly, from 1 Cor. 11:26, "As often as you will eat this bread, etc. you will announce the death of the Lord." To announce the death of the Lord is to preach. Thirdly, from 1 Cor. 14:26,

"As often as you come together, every one of you has a psalm, a doctrine, a revelation"; in verse 31, "You all can prophesy one by one." Luther is rather triumphant due to these passages, "This is why it is enough, powerfully and clearly strengthened by these passages, the chief ministry of the word is altogether one in the Church, and common to all Christians, not only by law, but even by precept. This is why the priesthood will not be any but one and common, that nothing shall avail against this divine lightning, not an infinite number of Fathers, countless Councils, eternal custom and the universal multitude of the world, upon which straw the shaved goblins rely to establish their priesthood."

That all can baptize he shows from the use of our Church. The church even concedes to women that they can baptize, and hence, administer the word, for Baptism is not constituted without the word.

That all can consecrate the Eucharist he shows *firstly* because in Luke 22:19 Christ said to all in the supper, "Do this in my commemoration." Likewise, *secondly*, because Paul, in 1 Cor. 11, addresses the whole Church, and he says in verse 23, "I have received from the Lord what he also handed on to you." Then *thirdly*, he shows it because it is greater to baptize and preach than to consecrate. From preaching and Baptism the remission of sins is given, from the consecration nothing follows, except the stupefaction of the priest over his power and dignity.

That all can absolve, he proves from that of Matt. 18:18, "Whatsoever you bind on earth, etc."

That all can sacrifice, he shows because there is no Sacrifice in the Church but that according to Paul in Romans 12:1, we are commanded "to show *our bodies a living host, holy, pleasing to God.*"

That all can pray for others, he shows because the Lord's prayer is common, and in it we pray for others.

That all can judge and discern dogmas, he proves in two ways: *firstly*, from the Scriptures, which command that we flee false prophets. In John 10:27, "My sheep hear my voice." Matt. 7:15, "Beware of false prophets"; *secondly*, from the words of Paul in 1 Cor. 14:30, "But if anything is revealed to another sitting by, let the first hold his peace." Here, Luther triumphs and would have it that it is lawful for anyone to judge the Roman Church, although she sits as mother and teacher of Churches. These are the arguments from his book *De Instituendis Ministris*. Lastly, he adds this argument, which he makes in the *assertion*, art. 13, "He that has been baptized has the Spirit of Christ; where the Spirit of Christ is, there all power and liberty."

To the *first, second, fourth and fifth* passages, I respond: those passages are understood on the *spiritual* priesthood, whereby we offer spiritual sacrifices, i.e., good works, and especially praises and prayers; that is a priesthood common to all pious men. Apart from this priesthood there is another *properly* speaking, whereby a sacrifice properly speaking is offered,

Chapter XXV: Argumens of Luther Are Answered

and to whose office it pertains to minister the word and the Sacraments to the people.

This is obviously the case. *Firstly*, from the passages themselves, for in 1 Pet. 2:5, we find, "offering spiritual sacrifices." He added *spiritual*, for the distinction of sacrifices which are not spiritually and mystically, but properly sacrificed. Likewise, in Apoc. 5:10, and 20:6, seeing that in the Apocalypse it is a question on the Priesthood *of the blessed* in heaven, which certainly exists for no other reason than to offer praise.

Secondly, the same is proven because the words of St. Paul are taken from Exod. 19:6, where the same thing is said about the Hebrews, which St. Peter attributes to Christians. In the Old Testament not all were priests properly so called, but only the *sons* and *posterity* of Aaron, and still they were all spiritual priests.

Thirdly, because both Peter in his epistle, and John in the Apocalypse join the kingdom with priesthood. So, therefore, all are Christian priests, just as they are all kings.

Fourthly, these passages are only understood on *holy* and *pious* Christians, not on sinners who are not a holy nation as Peter calls them, but a priesthood, or external ministry suited also to sinners, from the teaching both of Catholics and of Lutherans.

Now, to the *third* passage, "to declare virtues, etc.," I respond: St. Peter does not command that all Christians publicly preach the word of God, but *to give thanks to God*, and praise him on account of his benefits. As Bede rightly explains, Peter alludes to the "Canticle of the Hebrews" (Let us sing gloriously to the Lord..., Exod. 15:1, *seqq.*), which they sang because they were liberated from Egypt after the crossing of the Red Sea. He would have it in the same way that Christians freed from servitude to the devil by the waters of Baptism sing a canticle of thanksgiving and praise the power of the Redeemer in earnest. Oecumenius is not wrong when he adds that Peter also meant that all Christians, not only in words but good works will proclaim the power of God, so that their life will be like a type of sermon to the Gentiles, according to Matt. 5:16, "That they may see your good works and glorify the Father, etc." In this way, even many other passages are understood, such as Psalm 18:1, "Let the heavens announce the glory of God, and the firmament proclaim the works of his hands," and 1 Tim. 2:10, "Just as it is fitting for women professing," in Greek: ἐπαγγελλομένους, announcing "piety through good works"; and again in verse 12, "I do not permit a woman to teach." There you see women are commanded to announce piety, and lest perhaps some might think, being deceived by the Lutheran interpretation, it is also lawful for them to preach, he adds, "Through good works," and, "I do not permit a woman to teach."

To the sixth, "He made us suitable ministers, etc." *I respond:* He does not speak about all Christians, rather, *only about himself and the rest of his fellow Apostles.* He compares himself with Moses, who was a minister of the Old Testament, and says that he supplied letters written in stone while he and his colleagues supplied the spirit, etc. Now, it is certain in the Old Testament that not all were ministers, and promulgators of the Law, but only Moses. Besides, in the whole preceding chapter he speaks about himself, and similarly at the beginning of Chapter 3 when he says, "Do we begin again to commend ourselves? Or do we need letters of commendation to you or for you, as some do?"

To those passages on behalf of women, *I respond:* It is one thing to prophesize, i.e., to predict the future, and another to prophesize, i.e., to preach or interpret the Scriptures. *Firstly,* it is not properly the office of the priest, or an Ecclesiastical prelate, rather, it is *gratia gratis data,*[8] which can also be suited to lay men or women. Certainly David, Elijah, Elisha, Isaiah, and many others who were not priests, still prophesied, and nearly all the passages brought forward are understood on this kind of prophesying. The *second* kind is proper to priests and does not suit women, because it is for women to be subservient, not in charge. This is also the argument which St. Paul advances in 1 Cor. 14:34, "Let women be silent in the Churches; it is not permitted for them to speak, but to be subject." Nevertheless, God is not for that reason prohibited in a way that he could *extraordinarily* concede to women that they teach men, as it happened for Deborah in ancient times, and two hundred years ago St. Catherine of Siena. Nevertheless, this privilege does not make a law.

To the argument, that because Christ is a priest and all Christians his brethren, *I respond:* This argument concludes nothing. *Firstly,* because Christ is not an Aaronic priest, but *according to the order of Melchisedech.* In the Aaronic priesthood it had place that all the brothers were priests; but in the priesthood according to Melchisedech, only the firstborn was a priest.

Besides, even in the Aaronic priesthood, only the natural born sons were priests, but not the adoptive; moreover, Christians are *adoptive* brothers of Christ, not natural.

Lastly, if all the things which are suitable for Christ were also fitting for all of us, why do we all not do miracles and predict the future?

To the argument taken from the *first* office of the priest, *I respond:* these three passages prove nothing. 1 Peter 2:9, "to proclaim virtues," is understood on *private* praise, not on sermons, as we said. That of 1 Cor. 11:26, "You will proclaim the Lord's death," is understood on the commemoration of the Lord's Passion, which we do not by preaching, but *by receiving the Eucharist,* otherwise all those who receive the Eucharist should preach, which is impossible. That of 1 Cor. 14:31, "You all can prophesy, so that all will learn and exhort all," is not understood on all Christians, but on all *who have these gifts,* for he says in v. 26, "Every one of you has a psalm, has a tongue, etc." Certainly, they do not all have the gift of tongues, seeing that Paul says the same thing in 1 Cor. 12:4, "Now there are diversities of graces,

---

8   Translator's note: A grace given gratuitously.

Chapter XXV: Argumens of Luther Are Answered

etc." and in verse 29, "Do all speak in tongues?" Today, there are none who have a gift of this sort. Therefore, Paul meant to say, each of you, who boast on account of these gifts use them orderly *ad aedificationem*. Add, *secondly*, that he does not speak on a public sermon, which is proper for priests, but on pious collations, and exhortations, which they used when they came together, as I will speak about a little later. Therefore, without cause does Luther scorn the Fathers, countless Councils, eternal custom, and the whole multitude of the world on account of these three passages so poorly understood.

To the *second* from the second office, *I respond:* Among us, women baptize *in the case of necessity* and from *permission*, not from an office; in this way it is also permitted to Jews and Turks on account of the supreme necessity of the Sacrament. Therefore, it does not follow because a Turk can baptize, therefore he can supply all the Sacraments, or therefore he is a true priest. Likewise, it does not follow that a woman can baptize, therefore she can supply all of the Sacraments, or therefore she is a priest. Nor is it true that no man baptizes without preaching; for the word, which is advanced in Baptism, is not in the form of a sermon, as we proved above, rather it is *consecratory*.

To the argument from the *third* office, *I respond,* "Do this" was not said to all, otherwise women and children would be held to consecrate the Eucharist, for equal reasoning that, "I received from the Lord what I handed down to you," does not mean the power to consecrate was handed down to all. Rather, the *saying, explanation, and declaration* of what the Lord had instituted was handed down to all. Lastly, the power to consecrate is greater than to baptize, just as through Baptism the remission of sins is given, so even through the holy Eucharist, "He that eats this bread, will live forever" (John 6:59). Besides, through consecration the conversion of bread takes place, even if Luther would have it otherwise, which does not take place through Baptism.

To the argument from the *fourth* office, *I respond,* "Whatsoever you will bind on earth, etc." is understood to have been said to the Church, concerning which he also says (*ibid.*), "Tell it to the Church, and if he will not hear the Church, etc." That the Lord would show the judgment of the Church must not be scorned, he added that promise, "whatever you will bind." Hence, the Church binds and looses, but through her *prelates*, not through anyone altogether, just as the body speaks through the tongue, not through the hand, and a University determines propositions, but through Doctors, not through students. Moreover, it shows clearly the praxis of the Church in all ages.

To the argument from the *fifth* office, *I respond:* We deny that in the Church there is no other sacrifice than the mortification of vices. An altar is not required for this sacrifice, but there is an altar in the Church, as is clear from Hebrews 13:10, "We have an altar on which those who serve the tabernacle do not have the power to eat." More will be said on this in another place.

To the argument from the *sixth* office, *I respond:* It is not for the priest to pray in any way whatsoever, but to pray *publicly*, and as a *public person* to intercede for the whole people, as Chrysostom teaches (*de Sacerdotio*, 6).

To the argument from the *seventh* office, *I respond:* Those passages, "My sheep hear my voice; they do not hear the voice of a foreigner; beware of false prophets," teach that all men should judge on dogmas, not indeed by examining them according to the rule of Scripture, as the heretics would have it, for if all could do that, there would be no need of pastors in the Church, but by examining them according to a doctrine *already handed down*, and to the doctrine *of other pastors*. All can easily judge whether a doctrine is new, and then should hold it suspect. Besides, The Lord does not call foreigners and false prophets ordinary pastors, but extraordinary, *who come on their own*, as all the heretics come.

Now to that "If it has been revealed to one sitting by, let the first be silent," in which Luther triumphs, it is not understood except on certain collations on which Paul argues in that passage, not on the public preaching of a pastor and much less on the public judgment of a Council or the Supreme Pontiff. That fact is clear *firstly* from the use of the Church. It is unheard of that while a public sermon is being made, it was permitted to someone nearby to speak, and much less was it ever permitted for private men to oppose the judgment of the whole Church.

Secondly, we are not held to believe everyone saying something was revealed to them, particularly in a serious matter and especially if that revelation is contrary to the doctrine of ordinary pastors; otherwise, the way would be open to every heresy. For, there is no heresiarch who does not present his doctrines as the truest revelation of God.

Thirdly, it is clear from those words, "Let two or three prophets speak, and the rest judge." It is not fitting that two or three should preach, but it is well suited that in some spiritual collation two or three might speak. Additionally, Justin explaining the custom of the first Church in the *Second Apology*, distinguished preaching, which was only granted to one in authority, from a spiritual collation, which was usually in the same place after a sermon and took place between the Sacraments.

To the *last* argument: He that has been baptized has the Spirit of Christ; where the Spirit of Christ is, there all power and liberty.

I respond: Firstly, the major proposition is not universally true. Many are baptized who do not receive the Spirit of Christ because they were baptized without faith or penance; many receive, who later lose it and still do not lose Baptism. *Secondly*, the minor proposition is false. A great many have the Spirit of Christ, who still do not have power over all things, since they cannot speak in different tongues, nor foretell the future, nor cure the sick, nor raise the dead.

CHAPTER XXVI

Faith Is Not Required, or the Goodness of the Minister, for the Sacraments to Be Efficacious

The *third* question follows, on the qualities of the minister of the Sacraments, whether faith or charity is necessarily required, to the extent that heretics, infidels, schismatics, and bad Catholics could not confect the Sacraments. We do not, however, ask whether they sin by conferring the Sacraments, for that is properly a scholastic question, but only whether it is *invalid*, whatever infidels or wicked men do, even if, otherwise they were legitimately ordained as priests or bishops, and omit nothing from those which pertain to the substance of the Sacraments.

Now, there seems to be no, or almost no controversy on this in our time. Even though Luther says several times that the Spirit of Christ, which is received in Baptism, is the foundation of the power to confer the Sacraments, from which it follows that only the good, who have the Spirit of Christ, efficaciously confer the Sacrament, nevertheless, he taught the same thing later, but did not require faith or the goodness of the minister, seeing that he holds the devil could efficaciously supply the Sacraments, as we said above. The *Augsburg Confession* (art. 8) affirms the Sacraments are efficacious, although they are supplied by hypocrites and bad men. Calvin holds the same thing (*Inst*. 4, 15 §16). This is why in his *Antidote to the Council of Trent*, in regard to Sess. 7 can. 12, where it anathema is declared to those who deny the efficacy of the Sacraments if they are supplied by the wicked, he writes nothing else, except this word, "Amen." Lastly, Chemnitz (*Exam*. 2 part. p. 115) affirms that the sess. 7 can. 12 of Trent does not displease him.

1) It is usually attributed to the Hussites and the Anabaptists that opinion that the Sacraments are not efficacious unless they are supplied by good and faithful ministers. Really, it is a marvel if the Hussites think this way, seeing that they customarily seek ordinations of their priests from the Roman Pontiff, yet still they hold the Roman Pontiff and all Catholic bishops as heretics. Certainly, if the Hussites hold their ordinations are valid, whom they suppose to be heretic, how much easier would it be to hold the Baptism they confer as valid? This is clear from the book of Luther to the Senate of Prague, where he dissuades the Bohemian Hussites from seeking ordinations from the Romans, since they, according to the Romans, and the Romans, according to them, are heretics. So, the fact that John Hus, in the articles which were condemned in the Council of Constance (sess.

14), says a bad prelate or one already known to be ambiguously a shepherd, is no bishop while he is in mortal sin, means either it is only understood in regard to *jurisdiction*, or certainly in this regard the Hussites do not follow their teacher.

Chemnitz (*loc. cit.*) attributes this error to the Anabaptists, but because their doctrine is in many places hidden, and not publicly divulged, we do not know upon what foundations it rests. This is why in this place it will be enough to show what the errors were on this matter in ancient times, and then, by what Fathers and by what arguments those errors were refuted, and lastly, how their objections were answered.

In regard to the *first*, in the 3rd century the error began to arise in Asia and Africa that the Sacraments which are given by heretics and schismatics are not valid after their separation from Catholic unity. From the Asiatics, Eusebius (*Hist.* 7, 6) relates it from the *Epistle* of Dionysius of Alexandria. In regard to the Africans, it is certain both from the same Eusebius (7, 2) and from Augustine (*de Baptismo* 2, 7), where he also shows that the first author of this error was Agrippinus, the bishop of Carthage, the predecessor of St. Cyprian. Vincent of Lerins more clearly witnesses it in his *Commonitory*, where he says Agrippinus was the first of all mortals to consider rebaptizing.

St. Cyprian followed his predecessor with many African bishops, still, not in such a way that he separated from the unity of the Church on that account, as is clear from the epistles to Quintus, Pompeius, and Jubajanus; for this reason he was never held as a heretic. There are not lacking those who assert that later Cyprian revised his teaching, such as St. Augustine (*Epist.* 48 *ad Vincentium*); just the same, even the other Bishops, who defined that error with Cyprian revised their teaching, being moved by the authority of Stephan, the Roman Pontiff, as St. Jerome writes in his *Dialogue Against the Luciferians*.

A little later, the Donatist heretics followed, who pertinaciously held the same error, and enlarged upon it. In the first place, Agrippinus and Cyprian did not hold as heretics those who thought the contrary; this is why they did not rebaptize those who were baptized by Catholics, even if they held the contrary opinion to them. The Donatists, however, rebaptized even Catholics, whom they regarded as heretics. St. Augustine writes in this way in *de Unico Baptismo* (c. 13) comparing the Donatists with Agrippinus and Cyprian, "To rebaptize heretics, which they are said to have done, then was a human error; but to rebaptize Catholics, which these men still do, is always from diabolic presumption."

Secondly, the Donatists defended their error after a definition of the Church in a general Council, which is proper for heretics. Agrippinus, and Cyprian did not see any absolute definition of the Church, as Augustine witnesses (*de Baptismo*, 2, 7-9).

Thirdly, Cyprian only rejected the Sacraments handed down by heretics

Chapter XXVI: The Efficacy of the Sacraments

and schismatics, i.e., by those who were outside the Church, but he did not reject the Sacraments handed down by bad ministers within the Church herself, as Augustine demonstrates (*loc. cit.* 2,3; *Contra Parm.* 2). Now, some of the Donatists excluded all manifest sinners from the administration of the Sacraments, as Augustine witnesses (*Contra Parm.*, 1, 10); some excluded wicked men as a whole, even those who were secretly bad, as Augustine also relates (*Contra Cresconium*, 2, 28).

After the Donatists, the Luciferians taught the same error. St. Jerome witnesses in his *Dialogue Against the Luciferians*, that they admitted the Baptism conferred by heretics, but not ordination; although Hilary, a certain deacon, as Jerome says (*ibid.*), would not even admit Baptism.

Then in the time of St. Bernard, there were some men called Apostolics, who denied that wicked men can efficaciously supply the Sacraments, as he witnesses in *Sermon* 66 on the *Canticles*. Later, the Albigensians taught the same thing, as St. Antoninus relates (*Summa Theologica*, par. 4, tit. 11, ca. 7 §5).

Between both of those were the Waldensians, who conceded to good laity the ministry of the Sacraments and also withdrew the same from bad priests, as St. Antoninus relates (*loc. cit.*, par. 4, tit. 11, cap. 7 §2) St. Thomas also regarded this when he says there is a certain error that all the good and none of the bad are suitable ministers of the Sacraments (*Contra Gentes*, 4, 77), which is altogether the same error as the one which Luther said at the beginning, that all those, and only those, who have the Spirit of Christ are priests.

Lastly, after all of these came John Wycliffe, who enriched this heresy in no small way. For not only sinners, whether secret or manifest, but even those who are good in the present, but at some point in the future, would be bad, i.e., those foreknown, he denies can confect the Sacraments. On this error, see the Council of Constance (sess. 8) and Thomas Waldens (2, 14).

Now to the *second*: Many saints and ancient Roman Pontiffs refuted this error. The first of these was St. Stephen, Pope and Martyr, as Eusebius relates (*Hist.* 7, 2 *seqq.*), then, Pope Syricius (*Epist.* 1 *ad Himerium*), Innocent I (*Epist.* 22 *ad Macedoniae Episcopos*), Leo (*Epist.* 77 *ad Nicetam*), Anastasius II (*Epist. Ad Anastasium Imperatorem*), and others.

Secondly, Councils condemned this heresy, firstly in the Council of Nicaea as St. Augustine frequently witnesses in *de Baptismo* (2, 3-9) and other places, but because he never calls it the Council of Nicaea, many are uncertain about which Council he is speaking. Nevertheless, there is no reason for doubt; he calls the Council *plenary of the whole world*. Augustine did not know a Council of the whole world except for Nicaea, for there were only four general Councils that took place in Augustine's lifetime: Nicaea, Sardica, Constantinople I, and Ephesus. From these, Ephesus was called shortly before his death and celebrated after it, which we gather from the epistle of the Africans to the Emperor Theodosius the younger.

The Council of Constantinople did not treat on this question.

Add that Augustine (*de Baptismo* 2, 9) testified that there was a plenary Council celebrated before he was born, in which this truth was defined. It is certain that Nicaea was the only Council celebrated before Augustine was born. Nicaea took place in 327, while Augustine was born in 357. The Council of Constantinople took place in 383 (see the *Chronicle* of Eusebius, with the addition of Prosper of Aquitaine). The Council of Sardica did not treat on this question and it was not known to Augustine, as we showed in our disputation on the right of appeal, and the 6th Council of Carthage.[9]

Besides, in the Council of Nicaea, (can. 19), the Paulianists are commanded to be rebaptized, from which it is clearly deduced that the Baptism of other heretics was approved by the Council.

Lastly (because one thing would suffice), St. Jerome, in his *Dialogue Against the Luciferians*, speaks in this way, "The Council of Nicaea received all heretics, with the exception of the disciples of Paul of Samosata," where he clearly says the Baptism of all heretics was approved by the Council of Nicaea, with the exception of certain men, who namely did not use a legitimate form.

Not long after the First Council of Carthage condemned this same error (can. 1), while Gratus the Bishop presided, in the times of the Emperor Constantine, St. Augustine recalls this same Council (*De Baptismo*, 2, 2). Likewise, the First Council of Arles (can. 8), in the same time and much later, the Council of Constance (sess. 8) and the Council of Trent (sess. 7, can. 12).

Thirdly, a great many Doctors refuted it, and especially Augustine in all of his books against the Donatists. Optatus (*Contra Parmenianum*), Jerome (*Dialogue Against the Luciferians*), St. Gregory Nazianzen (*Oration on Baptism*), St. Thomas (*Contra Gentes*, 4, 77), and Thomas Waldens (tom. 2), where he also advances the testimonies of many.

2) Hence, the particular arguments which they use are three. *a)* Firstly, they advance the tradition, the ancient custom from the time of the Apostles. Pope St. Stephen especially makes use of this argument, as St. Cyprian witnesses (*Epist. ad Pompejum*). St. Augustine uses the same argument (*de Baptismo*, 2, 9), "By the strength of custom, the whole world is bound, and this alone was enough to oppose those who wish to introduce novelty." St. Vincent of Lerins, in his *Commonitory*, says that this argument alone availed in the Catholic Church, introduced by tradition and custom of the Church, that in this one thing the case of St. Cyprian was conquered, who fought with supreme eloquence, and the most frequent Council of holy Bishops and many testimonies of the divine Scripture, against the truth.

From that we understand Luther with his own, has a contrary spirit to which the ancient and true Church of Christ held. Luther, on account of one poorly understood testimony of Scripture scorned eternal custom,

---

9   Translator's note: See *On the Roman Pontiff*, book 2, ch. 26.

Chapter XXVI: The Efficacy of the Sacraments

as he himself says in his book *On the Abrogation of Mass* and in his book *On Instituting Ministers* to the people of Prague. Now, the ancient Church explained all of the testimonies which Cyprian advanced with his own by the custom of two or three hundred years, and rightly, because it was certain that the perpetual custom of the universal Church cannot be opposed with the word of God, and custom is clearer than the word itself. In this way they rightly judged that the word of God must be interpreted by custom, not that custom must be abolished due to an ambiguous and obscure passage of Scripture, as the Lutherans of today demand that we must do.

b) Secondly, they advance the argument founded on the word of God, which can be concluded by this syllogism. The minister of the Sacraments works by virtue and divine authority, but God does not take the power he gave from a minister on account of sin or infidelity, therefore etc.

The major is proven. The Scriptures everywhere teach this. John 1:33, "This is he who baptized in the Holy Spirit." Therefore, *Christ* is the principal author in Baptism, not the minister, as Augustine profusely deduces from this verse (*Tract. in Joan.*, 5). 1 Cor. 3:7 says, "Therefore, neither he that plants is anything, nor he that waters, but it is God who gives the increase." Besides, if ministers baptized by their own power, there would be different Baptisms; some would be better than others, for the diversity of merits and the excellence of those who baptize; but Baptism is one (Eph. 4:5). Likewise, the Apostles never call Baptism *their own*, which they conferred upon others, although they still called the Gospel which they preached their own (Rom. 16:25; 2 Tim. 2:8) "according to my Gospel." Therefore, in Baptism, they recognized nothing of their own, except being a mere minister. Lastly, it was just that the Sacraments would not depend upon human virtue, lest men would be accustomed to trust in men, when it is written, "Cursed is the man who trusts in man" (Jeremiah 17:5).

Now the minor proposition is proven. For, the authority to confer the Sacraments is not *gratia gratum faciens*, but *gratia gratis data*; therefore, it is not so opposed with the wickedness of life that it cannot exist together with it. It is certain that a grace of this sort can exist in sinners, as is clear from Caiaphas, who prophesied when he was still very wicked (John 11:51), likewise, on those in Matt. 7:22 who say, "Did we not cast out demons in your name? etc."

Secondly, the authority to confer the Sacraments is not given for the utility of the one having it, but *for others*; therefore, it was not suitable that it be taken away on account of the sin of the one having it, so that one will be punished for the fault of another.

Thirdly, God does not take the power of jurisdiction away on account of sin, as is clear in 1 Pet. 2:18 where the Apostle commands that Christians be obedient to their masters, not only the good but even the *severe*, and again (*ibid.* v. 13), he commands them to be obedient to kings and other

Gentile magistrates who were infidels. Therefore, how much less is the power of order taken away? If the power is taken away to punish someone that has it, the power of jurisdiction is more to be taken away than order, because it is loved more, and hence he is punished more for whom it is taken away. Besides, the power of jurisdiction depends more upon the goodness of one's life than the power of order, for the passions are more under dominion in command, than in supplying the Sacraments, as is obvious from experience.

Fourthly, God does not take natural potencies for natural works away from men on account of sin, as is known; therefore, he should not take away supernatural power for supernatural goods, in which the merit of the worker does not consist. For, God provides for the good of the whole Church no less than the good of this world.

Fifthly, Judas was a sinner and reprobate, and nevertheless he baptized, as Augustine gathers (*Trac. in Jo.*, 5) from John 4:2, "He was not baptizing, but his disciples." Augustine also teaches that Judas efficaciously baptized, because we do not read that those whom he baptized were later rebaptized.

c) The *third* argument is taken from similar things. For, in the first place, among the Jews circumcised by Samaritans, whom the Jews considered heretics, they were not circumcised again, but were rather admitted, as having been properly circumcised (Augustine, *Contra Cresco.*, 1,31). Then, the word of God is efficaciously preached by the wicked, as Augustine gathers (*de Baptismo* 4, 11) from Matt. 23:3, "Whatsoever he will say to you, observe and do; but do not do according to their works," and Philip. 1:17-18, "Certain men, from contention, preach Christ not sincerely; supposing that they raise affliction to my bonds. But what then? So that by all means, whether by occasion, or by truth, Christ be preached; in this also I rejoice, yea, and will rejoice." Besides, he relates nothing to the efficacy of the sower and planting, as the same Augustine supposes (*Contra Cresc.* 3,8), whether one has washed his hands or they are dirty, provided the seed is good and the ground fertile, and there is no want of the heat of the sun and the rains from heaven. Likewise, as St. Gregory Nazianzen teaches in his orations *On Baptism*, an iron seal no less properly imprints the image of the king than a gold seal. Likewise, as the same Augustine teaches (*de Baptismo*, 3, 10), the light of the sun or even a lamp is not polluted even if it passes through mud and filthy places. Lastly, Augustine also (*Tract. in Jo.* 5) relates whether water to irrigate courtyards should pass through a stone canal or a silver one.

3) In regard to the *third*: St. Augustine diligently refuted the arguments of the heretics in seven books against the Donatists. This is the breakdown of those arguments:

a) First, no man gives what he does not have; heretics and the impious do not have the remission of sins, therefore they do not give it. This is why they do not efficaciously supply the Sacraments.

Chapter XXVI: The Efficacy of the Sacraments

I respond to the minor. Heretics do not have remission of sins formally, nevertheless, they have it *ministerially*, in the same way that a servant who often does not have one coin, nevertheless bestows many gold coins from his master to another. Both in natural things as well as in man-made, the effect should not be similar to the instrument, but to the principal cause. Heat does not have the formal substance of fire, nor does a pick-ax the form of a chair; and nevertheless, they effect them instrumentally.

Add to this that the Sacrament must be distinguished from its effect, and among the effects must be distinguished the character from grace, for all of these things can be separated from each other. It can happen that a heretic would baptize, and he confers the character and grace as if he baptized an infant. Likewise, when a man who is baptized places the obstacle of infidelity because he believes the heretic and the Baptism does not confer grace, it is not empty on that account, since it effects the character. Besides, to confer neither the character nor grace, as if one were to give Extreme Unction to a sick heretic, nevertheless, he still administers a true and efficacious Sacrament, although it works nothing in the recipient on account of his indisposition. Here we must note with Augustine (*de Baptismo* 6, 1) this was the particular reason for the error of Cyprian and others, who did not distinguish between the Sacraments, as well as their use and effect.

b) The *second* argument is against the preceding answer: He that does not have the Holy Spirit cannot remit sins, for it was said in John 20:22, "Receive the Holy Spirit; whose sins you forgive, they will be forgiven them." Heretics, on the other hand, as well as the impious, do not have the Holy Spirit, *ergo, etc.*

I respond by denying the minor. Accordingly, by "Holy Spirit" in that passage we understand the power to remit sins, as Chrysostom and Cyril understand on this passage. Moreover, this power can exist without *gratia gratum faciens*. By Holy Spirit, any gifts you like can be understood, although they do not make a man holy, as is clear from 1 Cor. 12:7, "The manifestation of the Spirit is given for the profit of every man. To one the word of wisdom is given by the Spirit, and to another, etc.," and in 1 Cor. 14:32, "the Spirits of the Prophets has been subjected to the prophets," where, the Spirit calls the good of prophesying a gift from the Holy Spirit.

It can also be said that the Lord willed to signify in those words, "Receive the Holy Spirit, …" that the effect of the Sacraments particularly depends upon the virtue of the Holy Spirit; hence, it is necessary that the Spirit at least assists, and so is received at least as assisting and working in the Sacraments, although he does not work in the minister himself. Moreover, the Holy Spirit always assists in his Sacraments (as Augustine rightly teaches, *de Baptismo* 3, 10), even if the minister were an adulterer or a murderer, because the Sacrament is never adulterous.

Lastly, because there are not lacking those who understand through the Holy Spirit in this passage that grace and the character are bestowed, and they are diffused in our hearts, namely Ambrose (*Serm.* 10 *on Psalm* 118) and Augustine (in his commentary on John 20), therefore, we can add that the grace of the Holy Spirit is given through sacred Ordination with the power to forgive sins, but from there it is not rightly gathered that those who do not have grace cannot forgive sins. That grace is not the same with the power to forgive sins, nor is it so joined with it that it could not be separated, for it is not given, as some hold, that one can forgive sins but that he would not offend God in so holy a ministry if he remained an enemy of God but presumed to reconcile others.

c) The *third* argument: The Sacraments belong to the Catholic Church alone, which Christ founded, but the heretics are outside the Church in the synagogue of Satan.

I respond: The Sacraments always belong to the Church, even if they are sometimes found outside the Church. This is why when those baptized by heretics come to the Church, what belongs to the Church must be acknowledged, Baptism, and it is retained, but the error will be corrected. Otherwise, even the Gospel, and many other good and true things would have to be repudiated, which are sometimes found among the heretics.

Lastly, certain citations of the Fathers can be advanced, such as St. Athanasius (*Serm.* 3 *Contra Arianos*) where he says that all heretics have useless water. Likewise, St. Ambrose (*de Mysteriis*, 4) where he says, "The Baptism of unbelievers does not heal," and Leo (*Epist.* 77 *ad Nicetam*), where he says no heretic gives sanctification through the Sacraments.

I respond: Athanasius says two things. First, he speaks in this way, "The Arians come into danger, lest they might lose the integrity of the mystery; but I speak about Baptism." Secondly, he absolutely denies the Baptism of the Arians, or of other heretics cleanses, "The man who simply says, 'O Lord,' he is not the one who gives legitimate Baptism, rather those who express the name and have right faith." In the first citation, he argues on the very *substance* of the Sacrament and therefore he does not say that absolutely the Baptism of the Arians is not whole, rather, he says it is *dangerous*, lest at some point it would not be whole, because, namely, it was easy for them to corrupt the form and for the name of the Father and the Son, they would say the creator and the one made, as he says in the same place. In the second citation, he does not argue on the substance, but the *utility* of the Sacrament, and therefore, those who are absolutely heretics and lack right faith cannot sanctify those whom they baptize, because it is understood in regard to those who consent to their heresy. Ambrose and Leo as well as others speak in the same way. This is why these Fathers never say that the Baptism of heretics must be repeated, because they certainly would have if they were speaking on the substance.

CHAPTER XXVII

The Intention to Do What the Church Does is Required

THE *last* question remains on the ministerial cause: Whether the intention of the minister is necessary for the completion of the Sacrament. There will be four parts of this question. *Firstly*, we will explain the teaching of the heretics. *Secondly*, the teaching of Catholics will be explained as one and vindicated from the lies of our adversaries. *Thirdly*, we will confirm the truth. *Fourthly*, we will answer objections.

1) Regarding the *first*, a new heresy arose in our time, that the intention is not required in the minister of the Sacrament, rather, the Sacrament is altogether completed if the thing and words are present even if the minister carries out the action with a joke, or laughing, or feigning, and lyingly. The first author of this opinion was Luther. He writes this way in his work *On the Babylonian Captivity*, "I do not doubt, if anyone would receive it in the name of the Lord, even if an impious minister would not give it in the name of the Lord, truly he has been baptized in the Lord's name. For, the power of Baptism is not placed so much in conferring, as in the faith of the one receiving, just as an example is read on a certain mime baptized as a joke." In article 12, of those which Pope Leo X condemned he says, "If a priest does not absolve in earnest, but as a joke, nevertheless, if [the penitent] believes he has been absolved, he has truly been absolved." In the assertion he confirms the very same thing. Still, in his book on *Private Mass*, published in 1534, he shows the same with three arguments, which we will refute shortly.

John Calvin followed Luther in his *Antidote to the Council of Trent* (sess. 7, can. 11), "When they write this nonsense on the intention to consecrate, it has been advanced from sophistry and no probable reason. ... I declare, only for the most holy institution of Christ, that if some epicurean, inwardly grinning at the whole action, were to administer the Supper to me according to the command of Christ and the legitimate rule given by him and in due form, I would not doubt that the bread and the cup extended by his hand are pledges to me of the body and blood of Christ." Tilman Hesch teaches the same thing in his book on the *Six Hundred errors of the Popes*, (locus 15).

Martin Chemnitz also holds the same thing (*Exam. Conc. Trid.*, 2 part., p. 141 *seq.*), where he treats on the matter profusely. Although on page 146 he teaches the sacramental action should not be a mocking gesture or a ridiculous game, in which he seems to agree with us, nevertheless, he understands this only on the outward action, not the internal intention. Later, on page 154, he teaches the Sacrament is true, although a minister would administer a Sacrament with a joking mind, and he contends this throughout the whole disputation, that the efficacy of the Sacrament does not depend upon the intention of the minister in any way. He also argues on p. 1045, where it is a question on absolution that, "There should be no anxiety in conscience on the intention of the minister, but if the Evangelical word is announced, faith apprehending it, it constitutes him absolved before God, whatever the mind of the priest."

It seems Ambrose Catharinus is close to this teaching of the heretics, since in his little work on the intention of the minister of the Sacraments, he distinguishes a two-fold intention, one of doing *simpliciter* the outward action, which the Church does, the other, of doing the external action not *simpliciter*, but as a Sacramental, or, with a mind of celebrating the mystery which Christ instituted, and the Church celebrates. He says the first intention is required, but denies the second. Therefore, if anyone, while he baptizes a child, intends to pour water over him and say, "I baptize you" according to Catharinus it will be a true Sacrament, even if he intends to pour water and only say those words to wash dirt off of the body of the child, or to make a joke in that way. I do not see how that opinion differs from the teaching of Chemnitz and the other heretics, except that Catharinus subjected himself to the Apostolic See and the Council at the end of that work; the heretics mock both.

2) In regard to the *second*, the teaching of Catholics is that the intention of doing what the Church does is required. It is expressly held in this way in the Council of Trent, sess. 7, can. 11, as well as the Council of Florence, in the *Instruction to the Armenians*.

In this place, we must note certain things. *Firstly*, it is not so required that the minister have a general intention of doing what the Church does, that he could not have a particular intention; nay more, it is better to have a particular intention, i.e., to confer the Sacrament of Baptism, Absolution, Confirmation, consecrate the Eucharist, etc. For one who does not know our mysteries, it is sufficient if he intends in general to do what the Church does; and this is what the Councils teach.

Secondly, it is not necessary to intend to do what the Roman Church does, but what the *true* Church does, whichever it is, or what Christ instituted, or what Christians do, for they all come down to the same thing.

Someone might ask: What if someone were to intend to do what some particular false Church does, although he thinks it is a true Church, such as Geneva, and he explicitly does not intend to do what the Roman Church does? *I respond:* That also suffices. Anyone who intends to do what the Church of Geneva does, intends to do what the universal Church does. He intends to do the same thing which such a Church does, because he thinks it is a member of the true universal Church, although he is deceived in

Chapter XXVII: To Do What the Church Does

the recognition of the true Church. Moreover, an error of the minister in regard to the Church does not abolish the efficacy of the Sacrament, rather that would be a *defect of intention*. This is the reason why, in the Catholic Church, those who were baptized by the Genevans are not rebaptized, although, nevertheless, when they baptize they intend to do what the Church of Geneva does, and not what the Roman Church does. Add the fact that, although the Roman Church is the true Church, and the Church of Geneva false, they do not differ in regard to the substance of Baptism, rather, only on *accidental ceremonies*. Although, if any Catholic would intend to baptize in the way the Geneva ministers administer, and not the way Catholic priests do, he would intend a true Baptism in regard to the *substance*, but without the accidental ceremonies. Hence, he would confer a true Sacrament, although he would sin, and being suspect of heresy, could be justly punished.

Thirdly, actual intention is not necessarily required, nor does a habitual intention suffice, but a *virtual* intention is required and suffices, although one must pay attention to apply an *actual* intention. It is called *actual* when the minister has such an intention in act; such an intention is not required as some scrupulous man does, that we would say verbally, or mentally those formal words: I intend to do this, or I will to do this. Rather, it is only required that a man is present in mind and would do what he does attentively. For that intention is said in an act that has been exercised, as Cajetan says, and as we said, it is not necessary to supply it; because it is not in our power for our thought not to be distracted at some point, even when we carry out the holiest of things. *Habitual* is said to be a certain inclination, or promptitude from an infused or acquired habit, such as can be present even in sleep, and this, without a doubt, does not suffice. The act proceeding from this is not human and deliberate, otherwise it could be said that a man was baptized by someone who was sleeping or drunk, he would be truly baptized. *Virtual* is said to be when an actual intention is not there at the present moment on account of some wandering of the mind, nevertheless, it was present a little earlier and the operation is done in virtue of that. This is required by the consent of all, if an actual intention is not present, and it suffices. This is also not opposed to the doctrine of St. Thomas, although he says a habitual intention suffices (III q. 64, art. 8). As he himself explains, *virtual* is understood through habitual, for he only calls to mind actual and habitual intention. On the other hand, Scotus and Gabriel, as well as other later authors, for the sake of greater clarity, made the threefold distinction, and called virtual what St. Thomas calls habitual, and added another habitual, which St. Thomas omitted.

Lastly, we must note that on this doctrine, Catholic doctors wonderfully agree, with the one exception of Catharinus, but that will become clear from the refutation of the lies of Tilman and Chemnitz.

a) Firstly, each author says (*loc. cit.*) that the Council of Trent defined that a Sacrament is not valid unless the minister intends not only the act, but also the *finis Sacramenti*, i.e., he intends that, for which the Sacrament was instituted, which clearly differs from our teaching.

Now this is a pure lie. The Council, in the whole of canon 11, does not name the *finis Sacramenti*, nor does the Council say as our adversaries seem to have gathered, that the minister must intend to do what the Church intends, but what the Church *does*. Hence, what the Church does is not signifying the *finis* (end), but the action. Next, it is certain from praxis. The ancient Church did not rebaptize those children who had been baptized by the Pelagians, nor do we rebaptize those who were baptized by the Zwinglians and Calvinists, and still, we know all of them to baptize without the intention of the true end, which is to remove original sin. Nevertheless, we do not mean that it was defined by the Council what Catharinus and Chemnitz would have preferred, namely, that the minister only intends to do an external act, which the Church does; there was no reason to define that, since no man ever denied it, nor could deny it. Lastly, anyone who intends to do an external act, but not in earnest, he does not intend to do what the Church does rather, he means to *feign* what the Church does, Just as those soldiers who genuflected while saying to Christ, "Hail king of the Jews!" Truly they meant to genuflect and to say those words, still, because they did not do it in earnest, but as a joke, no man would say they intended to do what men do when they adore their Kings rather, they intended to *feign adoration*.

b) Secondly, Chemnitz says that the scholastics disagreed among themselves, because Peter Lombard, and Innocent IV would have it that the intention of doing what Christ instituted suffices. Alexander of Hales and Gabriel Biel would have it that the intention of the *finis Sacramenti* is also required.

Really, the Scholastics do not truly disagree if they are correctly understood, for all in 4 Sent. (dist. 6) teach the very thing which Peter Lombard teaches, nor are Alexander of Hales and Gabriel exceptions to this. Hales (*Summa* 4 part. 13, memb. 1 art. 2) says that the intention of the *finis Sacramenti* is required in the minister, but he understands through "intention of the *finis* the *whole and completed action*," and in this way he says the same thing which the others say, just using different words. That this is so is obvious from the same citation, where he distinguishes a twofold end, one intrinsic to the work, which is nothing other than the *terminus* and complement of the action; the other extrinsic, which is the fruit and utility of the work, e.g. in the Sacrament the intrinsic end is the ceremony completed, ritually joined with things and words; the extrinsic end is the remission of sins. Moreover, Alexander affirms the intention of the first end is necessarily required, but not the second.

Hence, Gabriel (4 dist. 6 q. 1, concl. 3), says the intention of the minister is required, not only in respect of the act of baptizing, as of an object, but

Chapter XXVII: To Do What the Church Does

also in respect of the effect, as of the end. Gabriel, however, takes up all of these from Scotus (4 dist. 6 qu. 5). Both, as they themselves explain, understand by "act" an object, the very *external* act, of the sort that one could also intend, who baptizes as a joke; such an intention we also say does not suffice. Rather, through the effect as an end, they understand a certain *general and remote* end, not a particular and proximate one. For, they mean it is required that the minister intends the effect of grace, or salvation, but only as he intends to do in the baptized, which Christians do in them whom they baptize, for Scotus explains it in this way. Moreover, this is nothing else than to say the intention is required in respect to the work, not as it is a type of natural work and could be done as a joke, but as it is a *sacred* work, or as it is *a ceremony which Christ instituted, or which Christians use*. Yet, this opinion falls into place with that which all Catholics teach.

3) Now, in regard to the *third*, the teaching of the Church is proven. *a)* The *first* argument: Just as a certain form of words is necessarily required to determine the indifference of the matter, so something else is required, whereby the indifference of the form is determined. For those words, "I baptize you," and similar things, can have different signification. To baptize is to imbue with water, moreover a man imbues himself in water to wash away the filth of the body, or to refresh himself when he does so for his health. Nothing can be produced in which this indifference of form would be determined, except for the intention of the minister who advances those words, as well as his whole action, *ergo, etc.* Now, they will perhaps say that it is determined by the intention of the recipient; but this is false. For here we are arguing on the action of the *minister*, not about the action of the recipient. The action of one, however, cannot be determined by the intention of the other. Besides, what would happen when those who cannot intend anything are baptized, such as infants? Will they say it is determined by the institution of Christ? On the contrary, if the institution of Christ would see to it that those words would signify it, provided they were advanced outwardly without any order to the intention of the one speaking them, why would a true Sacrament be confected if a parrot advanced the words?

b) The *second* argument is taken from the kind of ministry, for ministers of the Sacraments are instruments of God, but *animated* instruments *using reason*. There we must note that one man can be an instrument of some agent in many ways.

Firstly, according to the corporal members alone, if anyone uses the hand of another to take something, or if he compels him to bear a burden, which can be done without any will of his.

Secondly, through the corporal members and the sensory powers, so if anyone would command a servant to read or show something to him, or to be attentive and look at something, and to relate what he sees, the will of the servant is not required, unless whereby he would will to do the outward act. Even if he did not significantly intend to read, nevertheless, if he wills to advance these words, he satisfies his office, because his master does not use anything for an instrument except his tongue and eyes, etc.

Thirdly, by the corporal members, the sensory powers, and even reason. Just as if a king were to constitute governors and judges in cities to declare the law in his name and govern the people. In that type of situation, not only the body and the senses, but even prudence and the will are instruments. For, a king determines particular actions, but leaves them in the will of the instrument. This is why, in such matters not is power necessarily required, but also *the will* and hence, the intention to exercise actions. One is not truly freed, whom the judge absolves without intention, although it seems he is outwardly freed. Ministers of the Sacraments, however, are of this third kind, as is clear from the Scriptures. In Matt. 24:45, it is said, "Who do you suppose is a faithful and prudent servant, whom his master has constituted over his household?" There, fidelity and prudence indicate the servant is such a man, that it is in his will to do and not to do; for this, fidelity and prudence are required. Besides, those who have been put in charge are called to do so "with carefulness" (Romans 12:8), and again, "Obey your prelates" (Hebrews 13:7). Lastly, Christ did not determine particular actions, but said, "Whose sins you forgive, they are forgiven them" (John 20:23), where he manifestly leaves it to their will to bind or loose. This reasoning plainly convicts the matter, for instruments of this sort are chiefly instruments through *the will* and *intention*; if these are taken away, they cease to be instruments.

c) The *third* argument is taken from the distinction between speculative and practical words. Everyone says that speculative words have the same force, because they hold their whole efficacy in signifying. This is because the words show the same thing whether they are said by a sober man or a drunk one, or even by a parrot, or by Balaam's ass, provided it is not an ambiguous signification, because then, as we said, it should be determined by the intention of the one saying it. Practical words, however, which, apart from the signification have efficiency, are not efficacious unless a man who has *the power and the will to do what the words signify* would say them. That is clear from induction. The commands of kings, and judges are efficacious, not the commands of private men. Similarly, those who have a gift of miracles efficaciously command the dead and demons, but not others, even if they use the same words. The reason is, seeing that when the words, per se and naturally, are not operative, it is necessary that then they are only efficacious when said by one who has power. This is why the Apostle says in regard to the power to prophesy (1 Cor. 14:32), "the spirits of prophets, subjected to the prophets." The same thing is clear from experience: if a king, without intention, as in a dream, were to command somebody to be killed, the command is not usually given to execution because it is not certain whether he meant it, although the king could command it. It is certain, however, that the words of the Sacraments are

Chapter XXVII: To Do What the Church Does 143

practical words, since they are not instruments of justification; therefore, they require power and the will, and hence, *intention.*

What if someone would object that the words of the Sacraments have, in themselves, the operative power from the institution of Christ, hence their efficacy does not depend on the intention or power of the minister?

The response should be that there are two opinions of theologians. Some would have it that in the very minister there is also an operative power efficiently and instrumentally, as there is in the Sacrament (Cajetan, 3 part. Q. 64 art. 1; del Soto, 4 dist. 1 q. 5, art. 1; Ledesma, ibid). Following this opinion the answer is easy. In the sacramental words there is an operative power, but *dependent upon the minister.* Then only the words have efficacy, provided they are joined with the power which is in the minister.

Yet, others suppose the minister does not have in himself any efficient force in respect to justification, rather that it is only in the Sacrament. The minister alone, however, suits it, by applying the Sacraments, in the same way that one who plants and waters (with whom the Apostle compares ministers of the Church in 1 Cor. 3:6), does not produce efficiently and physically the fruit of the trees, but *applies* the agency. It seems some men feel St. Thomas argues in this way (III q. 64, art. 1, *ad* 1). It should not be inferred, therefore, that the ministers, according to this opinion, do not truly and properly consecrate, absolve, wash, reconcile, etc. This is the difference between voluntary agency and other things, that the other things are not properly said to do, when they alone apply the agency, for it is not said properly the cat burned down the house if he caused the fire, but it is said the house burnt in that *case.* Voluntary agency, on the other hand, when they apply the agency in earnest is most properly said to act. For, even a doctor properly cures the sick man when he applies salutary medicine, and properly kills him when he means to give him poison in place of medicine. According to this opinion, the answer is given to the objection which was posed, that the Sacramental words do not have power, and hence are not Sacramental except when moved by God, as *instruments,* but they are not moved by God as instruments except when they are pronounced by the man to whom he has consigned them. This is why the Sacramental words always, in some way, depend upon the power and will of the minister. Although the first opinion seems more probable; nevertheless, the second rightly answers each argument.

d) The *fourth* argument is from the absurdity, which would otherwise follow (as Hugh of St. Victor notes, *de Sacramentis,* 2, 6, c. 13). *Firstly,* if some father were to bring his son to the bath, and while he submerged the boy made the sign of the cross over him in a Christian fashion and said, "I wash you in the name of the Father, and of the Son, and of the Holy Spirit," namely invoking God, that the boy would behave and not struggle against his bath, and thinking nothing about Baptism, then that boy should be considered to have been baptized, if the intention of the one baptizing is not required; for the matter and form advanced in some degree or other would suffice. Still, this is plainly ridiculous.

Secondly, if a priest read the gospel at table as they customarily do at the table of prelates and religious, and among what was to be read he was to pronounce these words, "This is my body," and "this is my blood," now the all the bread and wine on that table would be consecrated, if the intention were not required.

Thirdly, if when bringing in a maidservant, someone would say, "I accept you as my own," understanding, but not expressing a maidservant, and she would say to him, "I receive you as my own," (understanding a master, not expressing it), now they would be married.

CHAPTER XXVIII

The Arguments Are Answered

It remains to answer the arguments. *Firstly*, of Luther; *secondly* of Calvin; thirdly *of Chemnitz*; fourthly of *Catharinus*.

1) The *first* argument of Luther is from the *Assertion of the Articles* (art. 12) where it is said from every intention, the Word of God arouses faith in the one hearing. Yet, faith is what justifies, therefore, the sacramental word, advance from whatever intention, is efficacious. He strengthens his argument from Philip. 1:18. The Apostle rejoices that the word was preached from any intention, even if some preached to rouse hatred against Paul, because namely even in that way the word could be fruitful; therefore, in the same way the word in the Sacraments, even if it is advanced as a joke, will still be useful.

Secondly, Luther confirms it in his book *On Private Mass*, from the fact that Alexander, the bishop of Alexandria, is read to have held the Baptism valid which Athanasius as a boy conferred upon other boys as a joke. Likewise, from the fact that it is read in other histories in regard to certain Gentile guests, who baptized one of them to mock Christians, and still he was immediately converted when the water touched him, from which we understand that it was a true Baptism.

I respond: the *first* argument rightly proves among those who agree with Luther, that the Sacraments were only instituted to arouse faith and only faith justifies, but among us it concludes nothing of the sort. For, even if we were to concede that the word, advanced from any intention, can arouse faith, nevertheless, we do not concede the word advanced by any intention can have *sacramental effect*. The notion of the distinction is that to arouse faith, no efficiency is required, rather, a signification suffices, as is known.

To the confirmation, I say: It is one thing to intend not to preach, and another to intend to preach, but *for a bad end*. Paul, speaks about the latter, and in this way we concede that Baptism is true and efficacious when a minister intends to truly baptize, although on account of a bad end. Someone will say, "Even the one who intends not to preach in earnest, nevertheless, if he advances the words of preaching, he will bear fruit." Therefore, etc.

I respond: The notion of the word in the form of a sermon, and a sacramental word is not the same thing. Words of preaching are, if I may say so, *speculative* words, which do not depend upon intention; sacramental words are *practical*, which, as we proved, depend upon intention.

Moreover, although these arguments conclude the matter in Luther's way, that it is not the right way is clear from these same arguments. They yield the conclusion that words alone without water or another element suffice; likewise, they conclude that the Sacraments can be conferred by a drunk man, or even by a magpie.

I respond to the *second* confirmation: The Sacraments can be conferred as a joke in two ways (as Hugh explains, *loc. cit.*). *a)* In one way, that those who play at it, truly intend to confer the Sacraments, but on account of recreation, in the way in which some men can truly be said to offer the Sacraments, but for the purpose of making money. This game does not impede the truth of the Sacrament, because this joke is extrinsic to the sacramental action itself. In the other mode, those who make a game of it do not intend to truly confer the Sacraments, but to ridicule and deceive, just as those who clothed Christ in purple and said, "Hail king of the Jews," and did not intend to make him king, but to mock him. This game impedes the truth of the Sacrament, because this joke is intrinsic to the action.

Therefore, I say, the game of Athanasius was of the first sort; for he truly willed to baptize, but received the action as the matter for a game and delight. That it is so is gathered from history itself (Ruffinus (*Hist.* 10, 14; Sozomen 2, 16; and Nicephorus 8, 40). These authors write that Athanasius only baptized Catechumens, and that he applied all the ceremonies of the Church, and also the fact that boys customarily played these games in earnest e.g., when one pretends he is a king, others servants, or they play at besieging some place, truly their king intends to command, and they intend to obey and in earnest they attack some place, and others defend it in earnest, but these are called sports, because they are puerile and taken up for the sake of pleasure. Nicephorus writes a similar history on his own time (3).

To that about the farcical baptism, *I respond:* nothing in that history is against us. The first who wrote it was (as far as I know) Ado of Trier in his *Martyrology* (8 Kalend. Sept.[10]). Later writers received the story from him, such as Vincentius in his *Speculo Historiali* (12, 102), and St. Antoninus (*Summa Historialis*, 1 part. Tit. 8 cap. 1 §9). Moreover, Ado writes that a mime, Genesius by name, in the presence of the Emperor Diocletian, for the sake of mocking Christian mysteries, feigned that he was sick, and demanded Baptism. Then, by the command of the Emperor, a priest and exorcist were fetched, who baptized him. When he was asked by the priest what he sought, he immediately converted, not play-acting, but *in earnest*, to answer that he sought the grace of Christ. So he was truly baptized, and in earnest, when even the priest intended to baptize him and he intended to receive baptism, although the emperor still believed him to be play acting, see Surius (tom. 4, in *vita S. Genesius*).

---

10   Translator's note: 25 August.

Chapter XXVIII: The Arguments Are Answered

2) The second argument is of Calvin (*Antidotum*) and Chemnitz (*Exam.* 2 part., *loc. cit.*) who thence take up the argument: If the efficacy of the Sacrament depends on the intention of the minister, then the certitude which a man ought to have on the effect of the Sacrament would perish, as well as spiritual consolation, because no man can be certain about another's intention.

I respond: A man should not seek infallible certitude on his salvation or justification in this world; that kind of certitude belongs to divine faith. This is not suited to this state, on which the Apostle speaks in 1 Cor. 10:12, "He that stands, let him see to it lest he falls," and in Philipp. 2:12, "Work out your salvation with fear and trembling." See Augustine on this matter (*On the Good of Perseverance*, 2, 13; as well as *On Rebuke and Grace*, 13). Now, *human and moral* certitude, which would suffice that a man be at rest, we have from the Sacraments, even if they depend on another's intention. For, it is very easy to have an intention, there is no reason to doubt whether the minister had an intention, unless it were to come about from an outward sign, and this suffices that a man should not seek to be baptized again, but to relax regarding the Baptism he received.

Note that the Lutherans are compelled to confess this, even if they don't want to. For they are baptized while they are still infants, in the custom of Catholics; moreover, when they come to adolescence, they cannot remember, nor do they know whether they had Baptism, unless they wish to believe their parents. Therefore, they believe their parents, who still can be deceived, and is at ease with it. How much more at ease will a man be with his own baptism, when he sees that he is baptized, and understands the words, and does not have any notion that the minister has a contrary intention, if a man is at ease who only believes his parents or friends that he was baptized?

3) The *third* argument of Chemnitz is on the authority of St. Augustine (*de Baptismo* 7, 53), where he does not dare to define whether Baptism conferred as a joke should be held [valid], but says one must wait for the revelation of God. Some men add another passage of Augustine (*Tract. in Jo.*, 5), where he seems to say that Baptism conferred by a drunk man is valid, and still it is certain that drunkards do not have intention.

Chemnitz also adds Pope Innocent IV, who by the testimony of Angelus (*Summa*), felt that it is not required for the truth of the Sacrament that the minister should purpose to do in his mind what the Church does. Indeed, if he should conceive the contrary in his mind, i.e., to not do what the Church does, still it would appear what he meant to do, so it is sufficient.

I respond: The passage of Augustine is against our adversaries. In the first place, Augustine says he is uncertain on the matter because it has been defined by no Council, "It is safe for us not to advance in setting forth a view which has neither been conceived in any Catholic regional Council nor established in a plenary one with any rashness of judgment. Rather, there should be care to assert with a confident voice that in the governance of our Lord God and Savior Jesus Christ, the consensus of the universal Church has been strengthened." Now, however, the matter has been defined in two general Councils: Florence and Trent. Not only is it not related that they have been received by the Lutherans, but neither was Nicaea received by the Donatists in the case of Anabaptism, and still, Augustine everywhere affirms the matter as certain and defined on the authority of that Council. Then, in the same place, when Augustine says we must not seek the revelation of God as to whether anabaptism was handed down as a joke, without true intention to confirm it is valid, clearly he witnesses that it is not certain from the Scriptures, as our adversaries boast. Besides, without a doubt, we do better by far according to the teaching of Augustine by baptizing those who are baptized without intention, than the Lutherans by not doing so. In a doubtful matter it is better to repeat Baptism, at least *sub conditione*, than to expose oneself to the danger of losing Baptism. To the other passage of Augustine, the response is easy; he does not say the Baptism of a drunkard is valid, but of an alcoholic.

To the authority of Innocent, *I respond*: Chemnitz, as is his custom, does not faithfully recite his opinion. For Innocent (cap. *Si Quis Puerum*, extrav. *de Baptismo*, etc.), after he had said the Sacrament is valid even if the minister did not keep in mind to do what the Church does, added, "Provided he intended to baptize," which Chemnitz omitted. Innocent repeats not only once, but three times, that the Baptism is not valid if the minister does not intend to baptize, but merely to wash the body.

Wherefore, those words of Innocent IV, "even if he does not have in mind to do what the Church does," can be understood in two ways: in one way, on that which the Church does, *in regard to the substance of the action*, in the other, *in regard to the effect of that action*. Innocent understood it in the latter mode, and this is the sense: Even if a minister did not have it in mind to do what the Church does (i.e., to justify man from sins), because without a doubt, he thinks that ceremony does not have such a power; nevertheless, if he truly intends to do the ceremony which the Church does, that is enough. Chemnitz takes it in the first mode, but wrongly, because Innocent holds the contradictory teaching three times in the same place. This is why Chemnitz also falsely imposes upon Innocent, that he said the Sacrament is valid if it only appears the minister meant to baptize, even if he really did not intend to do so. For Innocent does not say it, nor can it be gathered from his words.

4) The *fourth* argument is of Catharinus, on the authority of St. Thomas, Chrysostom, and Pope Nicholas. Now, St. Thomas (III q. 64 art. 8 ad 2) says that for the completion of the Sacrament the intention of the Church is sufficient, which is expressed in the very form of words; nothing else is required on the side of the minister. Now, he holds more clearly in 4 dist. 6 q. 1 art. 2, where he says the mental intention of the minister is not

Chapter XXVIII: The Arguments Are Answered 149

required, rather the expression of words suffices, in which the intention of the Church is contained. Chrysostom (*Homily 85 in Joan.*) says, "The priest offers hand and tongue, and it would be unjust if we, approaching our salvation, should stumble on account of the malice of another." Pope Nicholas, when he was asked regarding the consultations of the Bulgarians whether someone had to be rebaptized if he were baptized by a Jew, he responded not if he were in the name of the Father, and of the Son, and of the Holy Spirit; in that place there is no mention of intention.

Lastly, Catharinus adds the argument that it seems excessively hard that God placed the salvation of men into the will of an impious minister, and that our justification would be rendered uncertain. Now, that argument has been answered, nevertheless, another of his can be supplied (*loc. cit.*), that among men, when a master contracts with another through a servant, or sends a gift to another, it is not required that the servant do it by some intention.

I respond: In regard to St. Thomas, he teaches that an internal intention of the minister is required. In III, q. 64, art. 8, in the body of the article, he says the things which are done in the Sacraments need to be determined through the intention of the minister because they can be applied to many uses. Likewise, in response *ad primum*, he says the minister, because he is an animate instrument, should apply himself to the work through intention, whereby he intends to do what Christ does, as well as the Church. Likewise, in his response *ad tertium*, an actual intention is not necessary, but a habitual one suffices, and he explains then it is habitual when from the beginning of the work, he intends to do in act what the Church does. Likewise, in art. 9, *ad primum*, he says the Sacrament is true even if the minister believes the Sacrament avails to nothing, provided he intends to do what the Church does. Lastly, in article 10, he says very clearly, that the intention of conferring the Sacrament is required in the minister, but not to play or joke, and without that intention the Sacrament is not completed. Now, what St. Thomas added is not opposed to us, when he says, "Especially when the intention is manifested outwardly" (*ibid.*). He means to say: When the minister has the intention to not confer a Sacrament, but to joke, even when he does not manifest it, then the Sacrament is null; but it is more than null, if he manifests an intention [not to perform a Sacrament], because in the first mode it is nothing in the sight of God, in the second manner, it is null in the sight of God and men.

I respond to the objection which Catharinus (with Cajetan and Domingo del Soto) makes from *ad 2* in the 8th article of St. Thomas. When St. Thomas says a mental intention is not required for the completion of the Sacrament, but an external conveyance of words, he is not speaking about the completion of the Sacrament *simpliciter*, but on the completion *in the sight of men*, which suffices for human certitude and to pacify the mind, so that nothing else is required. This is proven in two ways. *a)*

Firstly, because in the second argument, St. Thomas makes this objection: If a mental intention were required, there could be no certainty that he received a Sacrament. Therefore, the response should be understood on the completion of the Sacrament in regard to *certitude*, but not absolutely. b) *Secondly*, because in this answer St. Thomas added that an external conveyance of the form suffices, *unless a contrary intention of the minister or the recipient is expressed*; such an addition stands best, if it is a question on certitude, as is clear. It is false, however, if it is a question on the completion of the Sacrament absolutely, as Catharinus would have it. For if the internal intention of the minister were not required, except to pronounce those words, then certainly it would be a true Sacrament if the minister were to express the contrary intention in this way: I do not intend to baptize, but invalidate the Sacrament, and therefore I want to say these words, I baptize you in the name of Father, and of the Son and of the Holy Spirit. Nay more, even if he expressed derision by an outward gesture and said these words ironically, it would still be a Sacrament. St. Thomas, however, teaches the contrary, as we made clear.

I respond to the citation from Chrysostom: Chrysostom speaks on the uprightness of the ministers and meant to say the efficacy of the Sacraments does not depend upon the goodness of the ministers, but on the goodness of God alone. This is why, when he says, "The priest offers hand and tongue," he excludes *virtues*, not the intention of the minister. For he means to say that the minister is the instrument of God, not the principal agent. From this, however, because the minister is an instrument, it follows that he does not act in his own virtue, to the extent that faith, hope, charity or any virtue of his is not required. Nevertheless, it does not follow that intention is not required, nay more, the contrary rather follows, that it is required since a man is an animate and rational instrument, and hence, he should be moved by God according to his nature (i.e., by the medium of his own election and intention).

Someone will say, following Chrysostom's reasoning, namely, that it would be unjust that the malice of one man shoudl harm another, he also concludes the Sacraments should not depend upon the intention of the minister, because then the malice of the minister could harm the recipients of the Sacraments, namely if he secretly removed his intention.

I respond: That reasoning concludes the matter in respect to *uprightness*, but not on intention, for two reasons. *Firstly*, if the Sacraments would depend upon the goodness, it would happen often enough that the malice of one would harm the other, because a great many are evil and the Sacraments could not be valid which are given by infidels or heretics, or public sinners during some urgent necessity. If, however, they depend upon the intention, the malice of the minister will very rarely harm the recipients. Everyone can have intention, and there is no reason why they would not. *Secondly*, because it is just that the Sacraments do not depend upon a quality of the

Chapter XXVIII: The Arguments Are Answered

minister, which is not altogether necessary for the minister himself, such as uprightness is. Conversely, it would not be equally just that they do not depend upon that quality, without which the minister would not be a minister, such as intention. Add that if this reasoning would prove the matter, the Sacraments do not depend upon the intention of handing down the Sacraments in earnest; it is also proven that this does not depend upon the intention of doing that external act, which Catharinus and the heretics alone admit. For, even in this mode, it can happen that the malice of the minister would harm the recipient, such as if someone refused to say the words or to dump out the water at a time when no other could be found willing and able to do it.

Through this the argument of Catharinus is also answered, because it would be very hard for the salvation of men to be in the arbitrary will of an impious minister, for he is compelled also in some case to affirm it. It should also not seem hard that God permits something so as not to destroy human nature, otherwise, it would also seem hard that God left in the will of a tyrant the lives of many innocents.

To the authority of Pope Nicholas, I say he was not anxious about intention, both because it is ordinarily present and because the Church does not judge on internal matters.

To the *last* argument, from human custom, the answer is clear from our third answer.

ON THE SACRAMENTS IN GENERAL

BOOK II

ON THE EFFECT, NUMBER AND CEREMONIES OF THE SACRAMENTS

THE FOURTH CONTROVERSY

On the Effect of the Sacraments

The Partition of This Controversy

There are three parts to this controversy. First, whether the Sacraments of the New Law are true causes of justification, *ex opere operato*; second, whether to be a true cause of justification *ex opere operato* is proper to the Sacraments of the New Law, or in common with the Sacraments of the Old Law; third, whether the Sacraments of the New Law impress a character on the soul. The first question is divided into four headings: *a) First*, we will explain the state of the question; *b)* we will advance the teachings of the heretics; *c)* we will confirm the truth; *d)* we will answer objections.

CHAPTER I

What Is the State of the Question on the Efficacy of the Sacraments?

WHAT pertains to the *first*, we must explain what it is that we are asking when we make a disputation on the efficacy of the Sacraments *ex opere operato*. Our adversaries relate it as a hateful teaching of Catholics, but they explain it incorrectly.

Therefore, we must note four things. 1) *Firstly*, the state of the question is not that which Calvin posits in the *Institutes* (4, 14 §17) when he says, "Here, it is only a question of whether the Lord operates by a proper and intrinsic virtue (as they say), or resigns his office to external signs." Now, no man ever disputed this question, because he would have to have asked whether the Sacraments are the *primary* causes, which never came into the mind of anyone but a madman. So, we only ask whether they are *instruments of God*, that is whether God justifies us *through the Sacraments*, but not whether the Sacraments justify us without God. In the same way, no man ever asked whether a carpenter at work resigns his office to the saw, since it is certain that the saw does nothing without the carpenter.

From that it follows that it is a lie and a most vain calumny of the heretics, who say we take men away from Christ, and from his passion, and hinder them with symbols, because we teach the Sacraments are causes of justification. On the contrary, we bring men more to Christ and his passion in this very matter, because we say the Sacraments are instruments of Christ, in which he applies to us the merit of his passion; unless perhaps, it were to be said one draws men from the fire, when he says heat is an instrument whereby the fire heats. Nevertheless, Calvin speaks in this way in the same place, "Because it leads souls headlong to destruction, in deriving a cause of righteousness from the Sacraments, it entangles miserable minds, already of their own accord too much inclined to the world, in a superstitious notion, which makes them acquiesce in the spectacle of a corporeal object rather than in God himself." Luther, as well as others, holds similar things.

2) *Secondly*, it must be known that there is no controversy on the manner in which the Sacraments are causes, i.e., whether by achieving the effect physically, or only morally, and if physically, whether through some inherent quality, or through the motion of God alone. These things do not pertain to a question of faith; rather, only generally, *whether the Sacraments are true and proper instrumental causes of justification*, that truly because of this very thing which someone is baptized, it would follow that he was justified. All Catholics agree on this, as Luther himself affirms in his work *On the Babylonian Captivity*, in the chapter on Baptism, "What a great number think there is some secret spiritual power in the word and water, which is worked in the soul of the man receiving the grace of God. From these, others opposing it, state that nothing is of power in the Sacraments, but grace given by God alone, because he assists from an arrangement that he instituted in the Sacraments; nevertheless, they all concede this, the Sacraments are efficacious signs of grace."

This suffices for faith and for the legitimate use of the Sacraments, in the way that in the miracles of Christ it was not required that the men who were about to be cured knew in what kind of cause the fringes of Christ's garment would heal; it was enough that they would know and believe a touch of this kind of fringe brought healing. It was also not necessary that the Apostles themselves, who cured by imposing their hands, knew how it happened. Likewise, it is not necessary that either the ministers or the recipients of the Sacraments know how the Sacraments are causes of justification.

Add that this is common with many mysteries of faith. Namely, we only hold that something exists from the Scriptures, and nevertheless, we are unaware of the manner, such as that God is three and one, Christ is God and man, the same bodies rise according to the number of persons, the whole Christ is in the Eucharist, etc., so also, in this it is enough to prove from the Scriptures that the Sacraments are able to be causes of grace;

Chapter I: State of the Question

how it happens is very difficult to understand, much less explain. Little wonder, since if in regard to natural things, which God made, although they fall under sense, a man cannot find the reason, as Solomon says (Eccl. 8:17), how much more can an exact reasoning not be rendered in regard to supernatural things? Nevertheless, the Scholastics do not dispute on these matters in vain, to show in various ways what the faith teaches can be defended, and they say many things with probability; moreover, the rest of these do not pertain to faith.

This is why our adversaries, and chiefly Chemnitz (*Exam. Conc. Trid.* 2 part. c. On the Efficacy of the Sacrament & *de opere operato*), as well as Hesch (*600 Errors of the Popes*, t. 15, on the Sacraments), do not act rightly when they rebuke and oppose the opinions of the Scholastics on the manner of efficiency of the Sacraments, as if we believe these pertain to the faith of the Catholic Church.

3) *Thirdly*, we must remark on what it means to confer grace *ex opere operato*. Our adversaries find fault with this term, as a novelty, and they explain the teaching itself poorly. Calvin (*Antidote*, sess. 7, can. 8) calls it a monster of words, to confer grace *ex opere operato*. Chemnitz (*loc. cit.*, p. 115) says that in advancing these words, the Council did not preserve the form of sound words which Paul commands in 2 Tim. 1:13.

There is no reason why there should be a great contention regarding the term. This is no novelty, except that it is against the rule of grammar, since *operatum* is in the passive voice. But this is not new. Even in Hebrews 13:16, "Talibus enim hostiis promeretur Deus,"[11] *promeretur* is technically in the passive voice. Moreover, St. Augustine (Psalm 138) prefers to say *ossum ossi* instead of *os ossis*[12], so that he would be better understood. As he says, "Better for the grammarians to throw a fit than the people not understand us."

What pertains to the matter at hand, they say we understand two things from the phrase *ex opere operato*, which are, nevertheless, both false and opposed to themselves. *a) Firstly*, they assert that *ex opere operato* signifies a meritorious work or dignity of the work on the side of the minister or the recipient. Luther first explained the matter very badly in *The Babylonian Captivity* (c. on Baptism), where he says that papists made the precept on the Sacrament a work of faith. In other words, papists think the Sacraments give grace because the one who receives the Sacrament does a good work commanded by God. Next, Calvin (*Instit.* 4, 14 §26) says, "All the trifling taLk. of the sophists concerning *opus operatum*, is not only false, but opposed to the very nature of the Sacraments which God instituted so that believers, who are empty and devoid of all good, might bring nothing apart from their neediness. Hence it follows, that in receiving them they

---

11 "God deserves well of such sacrifices."

12 Translator's note: *Os*, in classical Latin, is the proper subject form of "bone," whereas *ossum* was normative in Augustine's time.

do nothing which merits praise, and that in this action (which in their regard is only passive), no work can be ascribed to them." He holds the same thing in the *Antidote* (sess. 7, can. 8), where he does not otherwise refute that the Sacraments confer grace *ex opere operato*, except that it is absurd for the efficacy of the Sacrament to depend upon the merits of men. Finally, Chemnitz (*loc. cit.*, p. 95) says, "There are those who constituted the power of the Sacraments in the work itself, whereby the Sacraments are either celebrated or received, so that the Sacraments would be said to confer grace from the dignity and merit of the worker, because either he that celebrates or he that receives exercises it."

This is a false exposition, and a witness to their ignorance, or malice, as is clear from the fact that all Catholics oppose a work *ex opere operato* to a work *ex opere operantis*. They understand by *ex opere operantis* a good or meritorious work of the worker himself. Next, since both Catholics and Lutherans teach against the Donatists that the efficacy of the Sacraments does not depend upon the goodness of the minister, how could it come into someone's mind that Catholics believe the Sacraments confer grace from the dignity and merit of the minister? There can be no doubt that a good work and merit depend upon the goodness of the worker, since in Matt. 7:18 we read that "a bad tree cannot bear good fruit." For equal reasoning, seeing that all Catholics teach the Sacraments confer grace (and often the first grace, so that they would make a man pass from being impious to just), how could it happen that they would believe the Sacraments confer grace from the dignity and merit of the recipient? If he that receives the Sacrament could do good and meritorious works before the reception of the Sacrament, he would not be impious, but just.

b) The *second* exposition is false, that to confer grace *ex opere operato* is to confer grace to the sinner without faith, and a good motion of the heart of the same sinner, so that the force of the work that has been worked would be devised to exclude faith and internal penance in the business of justification. Luther (*Babyl. Cap.*, on Baptism) says, "Hence, they are impelled to only attribute to the Sacraments of the New Law, that they decree these are beneficial even to those who are in mortal sin, nor is faith or grace required." Calvin, in the *Antiodote* (sess. 7, can. 5), says, "They fabricate a magical force present within the Sacraments, which are efficacious without faith," and in Canon 8, "If it is conceded to them, as they demand, that grace is acquired in the Sacraments *ex opere operato*, then part of the merit is separated from faith, so that the use of the Sacrament would avail of itself for salvation." Chemnitz (*loc. cit.*, p. 125) says, "The papists defend the opinion of *opus operatum*, namely that through the Sacraments grace is conferred upon the recipients in such a way that a good interior motion is not required in the recipient." Melanchthon holds similar things in the *Augsburg Confession* (art. 13), as well as the *Apologia* for the same, and Hesch in his book on the *600 errors of the Popes* (tit. 15).

Chapter I: State of the Question

But this exposition is opposed to the first. If *ex opere operato* is the meritorious work of the recipient, how can it happen that the work which has been worked would exclude faith, since without faith no good merit can be understood? "Without faith it is impossible to please God" (Heb. 11:6). Besides, the exposition is also false, as well as a mere calumny and lie. The Council of Trent itself, in its 6th session, chapter 6, clearly teaches that the beginning of justification takes place by faith and penance, and all theologians teach the same thing, as above in chapter 2 we showed in refutation of the lies.

Therefore, to understand what *ex opere operato* means, we must note that many things cooperate in the justification which someone receives when he partakes of the Sacraments; namely, on the side of God, the will of the one using a sensible thing; on the side of Christ, his passion; on the side of the minister, the power, will, and goodness; on the side of the recipient, will, faith, and penance; lastly, on the side of the Sacrament, the outward action itself, which arises from the due application of the form and matter. It remains from all these things, that which actively, and proximately, as well as instrumentally effects the grace of justification is alone that external action which is called a Sacrament, and this is called the *opus operatum*, by receiving in the passive voice (*operatum*) so that it is the same thing for the Sacrament to confer grace *ex opere operato*, as to confer grace *from the force of the very Sacramental action instituted by God for this purpose*, not from the merit of the agent or the recipient. St. Augustine (*de Baptismo* 4, 24) expresses it in these words, "For him [the infant] the Sacrament avails much of itself." The will of God, which uses the Sacrament, actively cooperates, but it is the *principal* cause. The passion of Christ cooperates, but it is the *meritorious* cause, not the effective cause, since it is not in the act but in the past, although it objectively remains in the mind of God. The power and will of the minister necessarily cooperates, but they are *remote* causes; they are required to effect the Sacramental action itself, which is worked immediately after. The uprightness of the minister is required, that the minister himself would not sin while administering the Sacraments, nevertheless, it is not itself the cause of grace in the recipient, nor does it help the recipient by way of *impetration* and *example*. Will, faith, and penance in an adult recipient are necessarily required as *dispositions* on the side of the subject, not as active causes, since faith and penance do not effect Sacramental grace, nor do they give the efficacy of the Sacrament. Rather, they only remove the obstacles which impede the Sacrament from exercising its efficacy. This is why in children, where the disposition is not required, justification does not come about without these things.

We can provide an example in a natural thing. If to burn wood, it is first necessary for the wood to be dried, then a fire struck from a flint, then the fire applied to the wood, and so at length the burning would happen, nobody would say the immediate cause of the fire is the drying, or striking of fire from the flint, or application of the fire to the wood, rather, the fire alone as the primary cause, and the heat or warming as the instrumental cause.

4) *Fourthly,* we must note the deceit and ignorance of Chemnitz. In his *Examination of the Council of Trent* (2 part., *de opere operato*), he upholds that certain Catholics, such as Gropper and Alonso de Castro rightly explain what *ex opere operato* means; but, he adds, no other Catholics think in this way, nor the Council of Trent itself, and therefore the whole controversy remains. But poor Chemnitz could not understand them, or certainly refused to, "Certain doctors, Gropper and Alonso de Castro, planned to do injury to the Scholastic doctors, as if they taught on the opinion of *ex opere operato*, the Sacraments confer grace without faith in the recipient; but they say they meant nothing other in their disputation on *opere operato* than the truth of the Sacraments is not from the dignity of the worker, or estimated by merit, but is from the institution, power, and work of God the author....If the Popes meant this when they dispute on *opere operato*, because the opinion is true, there would be no controversy. Now, all the Scholastics of old did not suppose this, and now not even the Popes mean this when they contend for the opinion on *opere operato*, but by far, nourish another monster under those exotic words, and force it upon the Church."

There are three falsehoods in these words:

a) First, when he says Gropper and Alonso planned to do injury to the Scholastics, etc., rather they spoke truly as we have often shown, and will prove again shortly.

b) Second, when he says there would be no controversy if all Catholics would say the same thing, as Gropper and Alonso. But really, we all say the same thing and still the controversy remains. For those two authors not only say the Sacraments do not take their efficacy from the dignity of the minister, and do not exclude faith, which pleases Chemnitz and us, but they also say the Sacraments have true efficacy, or efficiency to produce grace from the divine institution, which cannot please Chemnitz, since he (as we will show) attributes no efficiency to the Sacraments, except to nourish faith by way of the object representing the divine promise.

c) Third, when he says that neither the Scholastics of old nor the Popes understand *ex opere operato* in the way that Gropper and Alonso explain it, namely that they do not exclude faith. That this is a lie will become plain from the refutation of his argument.

First, he proves it because all the Scholastics say the Sacraments of the New Law give grace *ex opere operato*, whereas the Sacraments of the Old Law gave it *ex opere operantis*. But if *ex opere operato* would exclude the dignity of the minister, even Circumcision would have given grace *ex opere operato*, since the malice of the minister brought no harm to the one being circumcised. So, it is not from the teaching of the Scholastics that *ex opere operato* only excludes the dignity of the minister, but even faith and the

Chapter I: State of the Question

internal motion of the recipient, which pertains to *ex opere operantis*, and they were necessary in the Old Law.

I respond to the first: Some Scholastics, such as Gabriel (whom Chemnitz cites later), when they say, the Sacraments of the Old Law did not confer grace *ex opere operato*, they make an exception for Circumcision; hence, Chemnitz's argument does not avail against us.

I say secondly: *ex opere operato* not only excludes the dignity of the minister, but even faith and an internal motion from the efficiency of Sacramental grace. As we said, even if these were required in adults, nevertheless, they are not such things that they effect the grace, rather the *Sacrament* itself, as an instrument of God. In the Sacraments of the Old Law, however, the Sacrament itself did not properly work grace, but either the faith and devotion of the recipient, or of the whole Synagogue, or something else, as we will say shortly. Therefore, Chemnitz's argument proves that *ex opere operato* from the teaching of the Scholastics excludes faith and an internal motion from the efficiency of Sacramental grace; still, he does not prove what he meant to prove, namely that they exclude faith and an internal motion *simpliciter,* so that the Sacraments (according to their calumny) confer grace to the recipients without that faith and without that internal conversion of heart.

Secondly, he shows from Gabriel Biel, who, in 4 dist. 1 q. 3, says it then is an *opus operatum*, when an internal motion is not required.

I respond: He perversely cites Gabriel; that author adds by what motion *de congruo* or *de condigno* grace is merited. Therefore, Gabriel did not exclude an internal motion disposing toward grace, but *meritorious of grace.* Even if that disposition could be meritorious of grace *de congruo*, or even of an increase of grace *de condigno* if it were an act proceeding from charity; nevertheless, one is a grace which is given on account of a disposition; the other, which is given by the force of the Sacrament, as the author himself explains (4 dist. 4 q. 2 concl. 4, *ad primum*).

Thirdly, he proves it from Paludanus (4 dist. 1 q. 1 concl. 2 prob 4), who says it is not required in the Sacraments that a man dispose himself. Rather, the disposition is effected by the Sacrament itself, and this is to cause grace *ex opere operato.*

I respond: Chemnitz did not understand Paludanus. That author does not speak on the disposition, which is the internal movement of the recipient, such as faith and penance, since he expressly says such movements are required in the Sacraments (*loc. cit.*, q. 5), rather, he speaks about a certain *final disposition*, to which he thinks grace immediately follows, and he says that disposition is the character in three Sacraments; in others, a certain adornment of the soul. Since Paludanus could not understand how the Sacrament effects grace, he devised that opinion that it would effect a certain disposition to which grace immediately follows. On this matter, it is appropriate for the Scholastics to dispute.

Fourthly, he proves it from Marsilius of Padua (4 sent. Q. 2 art. 2), and Mensingerus (*In Joan.* 6), who distinguish *opus operatum* against the internal devotion of the operator.

I respond: They distinguish, not to altogether exclude it, rather, to exclude it from *efficiency*, as we said.

Fifthly, he proves it from St. Thomas, Paludanus, and Gabriel, who say Mass benefits even those who do not have penance in heart, *ex opere operato*.

I respond: They speak on *the sacrifice*, not on the Sacrament. Moreover, the Sacrifice benefits the impenitent by way of *impetration*, because it obtains conversion and penance for them. Our prayers operate in the same way, although they do not do it as efficaciously.

Sixthly, it is proven from the fact that many Catholics show the Sacraments effect grace *ex opere operato*, because Baptism benefits children who do not have faith or any internal motion. Therefore, in that way, they exclude faith and an interior movement in adults, since they hold even in adults, the Sacraments have force *ex opere operato*.

I respond: Catholics most efficaciously prove by the example of children, the efficacy of the Sacraments does not depend upon any quality of the recipient. Nevertheless, it does not follow that they exclude faith and penance in adults, for this is asked of adults, as dispositions. Children do not need such dispositions, as we will show in the proper place.

Next, Chemnitz tries to show that the Council of Trent meant to exclude faith and an internal movement by the term *ex opere operato*. *Firstly*, because when the Scholastics explained *opus operatum* in different ways, and some meant to exclude an internal motion; others did not. The Council, in can 8, admitting *opus operatum* simply, and not rather more restricting it to the latter than to the former explanation, is thought to have approved all.

I respond: It is false that any Scholastic taught that an internal motion is excluded by *opere operato*. Next, if it were so, the Council would have approved nothing, but only defined *in general*, that the Sacraments confer grace *ex opere operato*.

Secondly, Chemnitz argues that when the Council, in can. 12, defines that the Sacraments do not depend on the dignity of the minister, as a result, in this can. 8, by *opus operatum*, it does not understand the Sacrament does not depend upon the dignity of the minister, just as Gropper explains *opus operatum*, but something else, namely that faith of the recipient is not required.

I respond: That the Sacraments also confer grace *ex opere operato* does not properly mean a negation, i.e., not to depend upon the dignity of the minister. Rather, it means an *affirmation*, i.e., the Sacraments by their own force effect grace, from which the negation follows, that it does not depend upon the dignity of the minister or the recipient. Therefore, the Council in

Chapter I: State of the Question

can. 8, defined that affirmation against the Lutherans; next, can. 12, defined the negation against the Donatists and the Anabaptists.

Thirdly, Chemnitz argues: Because the Council in its 8th Canon, does not oppose *opus operatum* to faith, it therefore understands faith to be excluded through a work *opus operatum*.

I respond: If the antecedent were true, the consequent can be denied; if the Council would oppose *opus operatum* to faith, it would understand faith to be excluded from the efficiency of Sacramental grace, but not excluded *simpliciter*. Nevertheless, the antecedent is false, because the Council does not oppose *opus operatum* to faith, but to faith *alone*. Even Chemnitz remarked on that later in his book.

Apart from these arguments, Chemnitz adds two express lies, whereby he closes his disputation on the term *ex opere operato*. For, not only did he impose this absurd explanation of *ex opere operato* on the theologians, but he even pretends that he has already refuted those theologians, so they no longer dare to defend that opinion, "The popish writers have already run from the challenge, nor do they manifestly dare to make a defense of this axiom, that the use of the Sacraments without faith will save the recipients." Now, as we have shown, this was never an axiom of the Popes, but a lie of the Lutherans. Next, as a clever man, he investigates the reasons why the Scholastics fell into so absurd an error, and he posits two causes. One, that when they read in Augustine (*de Baptismo* 3, 14) that there is no difference toward the integrity of the Sacrament, whereby faith is imbued, and the recipient of the Sacrament, and they failed to notice that Augustine speaks on the substance of the Sacrament, not its utility and fruit; thence, they supposed that faith is not required for the Sacraments to be beneficial. The other, is that when they read in Augustine (*Epist.* 23), that children without faith profitably received the Sacrament, because they do not place an obstacle of contrary thought, they thought the notion is the same for children and adults.

But these are frivolous, nay, even false causes. For, all theologians in 4 dist. 4 distinguish a Sacrament from the *res Sacramenti*, and they teach the Sacraments can be received, even without faith and penance, but not the *res Sacramenti*, i.e., grace. Besides, the Council of Trent (sess. 7, can. 13) teaches on Baptism that Baptism benefits infants without their having actual faith. Still, in sess. 6, c. 6 & 8, and sess. 14, cap. 4, and elsewhere, it teaches that in adults faith and penance are necessarily required for them to be able to be justified, and the Catholic Church has always taught that way.

CHAPTER II

The Teaching of the Heretics on the Efficacy of the Sacraments

In regard to the second, whether justification is proper to the Sacraments of the New Law, there was an ancient heresy of the Messalians, in the 4th century, who taught that men are not justified by the Sacraments of Baptism, Eucharist, and the others, but by prayer alone. This is related by St. John Damascene in his book *On Heresies*, where he describes their teaching, "Baptism does not perfect men, nor do the divine Sacraments which they have received atone for the filth of the soul, but only the prayers which they rightly pour forth." The Armenians also and the new Cathars, if we believe Guido, denied that the Sacraments confer grace.

Now, passing over all these, the Lutherans sometimes write on this matter in such a way that it seems that they do not dissent from Catholics, but sometimes they clearly write the contrary. Nevertheless, they remain in the same teaching, which is that the Sacraments do not immediately have any efficacy in respect to grace, but are a bare sign, but effect something mediately, insofar as they rouse or nourish faith, which justifies man. Yet this very thing, namely to rouse faith, the Sacraments do not do except by representation. They would have it that the Sacraments cooperate with justification in the same way as the preaching of the word, except that preaching is applied to the ears, and arouses faith through hearing, while the Sacraments are applied to the eyes, and they arouse faith by sight.

Luther and Melanchthon openly proposed this opinion in the beginning, but they clearly said what they thought, namely that the Sacraments effect nothing. Moreover, we must note the passages against Chemnitz, who impudently says that Luther always and in earnest condemned that profane opinion against the Sacramentarians, "that the Sacraments are not organs and instrumental causes of grace, but only call to mind the nature of a picture, and arouse faith."

Now, let us listen to Luther in 1520, in his book *On the Babylonian Captivity*, where he says, "Baptism justifies no man, nor is it of any use; but faith in the word of the promise, to which Baptism is added, this justifies…. The same God, who saves us through Baptism and bread, saved Abel through sacrifice, Noah through the Ark, Abraham through Circumcision, and all others by their signs." A little later he numbers the Sacraments of the Old Law, which he did not believe were inferior to the Sacraments of the New Law in regard to their efficacy, namely the sign given to Gideon in the dew and fleece, the sign given to Manoah in sacrifice (Judges 13:16),

Chapter II: Teaching of the Heretics on Efficacy   165

and the sign offered to Ahaz in Isa. 7:11. Then he concludes, "Our signs, or Sacraments, and those of the Fathers hold a connecting word of promise, which demands faith, and it can be completed by no work of another; therefore, they are signs or Sacraments of justification, because they are Sacraments of justifying faith, and not of a work, from where their whole efficacy is faith itself, and not an operation. For, who believes them, he fulfills them, even if he does nothing....It cannot be true that the efficacious force of justification is in the Sacraments, or these are efficacious signs of grace; for all of these are said in the loss of faith." Likewise, in 1521, in his assertion of the first article, he writes in this way, "We say neither the Sacraments of the Old Law nor the New justify, rather, faith alone." Likewise, in 1523, in his book against Cochlaeus, "No part of justification can be attributed to Baptism; otherwise, if any part would justify, it would not be lawful to deny that Baptism without faith justifies. Since, however, it is denied, faith alone is rightly left."

Melanchthon, in *Loci Theologici* (published in 1522, in the chapter on Signs), says that he shudders at the error of the Scholastics, that the Sacraments justify, and adds, "They do not justify, as the Apostle says, 'Circumcision is nothing'; consequently, Baptism is nothing, and the participation of the Lord's table is nothing. Rather, they are witnesses καὶ σφραγίδες [and the sign] of the divine will toward you." He says the same thing in the *Apologia* (published in 1530, art. 13), that the Sacrament is the sign of the promise, and like a picture of a word. In his book against the Anabaptists, "Just as the will of God is shown in the word, or promise, so also it is showed in the sign, just like a picture....It is beneficial to keep in mind that the Sacraments do not justify." There you see that similitude to a picture, which Chemnitz execrates with great force, and still he professes to be a follower of the *Apologia* in the beginning of the second part of the *Examination*.

The Sacramentarians followed Luther and Melanchthon, and from them Calvin, who uses the similitude of the picture in the *Institutes* 4, 14 §17, "It remains fixed, there are no other parts of the Sacraments apart from the word of God; such are, to offer and propose Christ to us, and in him the treasury of heavenly grace....We must beware lest the Sacraments lead us into that error, namely that we would think some hidden virtue has been connected to and fixed to the Sacraments, whereby they confer, of themselves, the grace of the Holy Spirit to us. It is an error, although the Sacraments are described a little more magnificently by the Fathers to amplify their dignity, this is the only duty divinely enjoined upon them, to testify to us and ratify the benevolence of God in us. ... The Sacraments are to us from God, because messengers of joyous things from men, or pledges to ratify covenants, inasmuch as what is not bestowed of itself, something of grace but declares and shows, and also (as they are deposits and tokens), they make us ratified, which has been given to us by divine largess." Then in §18, Calvin uses the example of a rainbow, the fleece of Gideon, and others which Luther uses.

Hence, the same Luther in his later books was convicted (as it has the appearance of truth) by the arguments of Catholics, who wrote otherwise by far. In his homily *On Baptism*, which he published in 1535, near the beginning of the second part, he so holds that "baptism was instituted for this purpose, to serve us, benefit us, give to us, not something carnal or corporeal, but eternal grace, eternal cleanliness, sanctity, and eternal life." In homil. 2 *On Baptism*, which he gave in 1540, he says, "It cannot happen that Baptism does not do what it was instituted for, namely regeneration and renewal of the Holy Spirit....Baptism only has power and energy that a man, who was conceived and born in sin, shall be regenerated in the sight of God, and a man who before that was condemned to death is now a son of God. Who can attain and partake of this glory and power of most holy Baptism in his senses, thought, and intellect? ... John willed to signify by these words that Baptism is very efficacious, and of such power that it can wash away sins, drown and suffocate death, cleanse and heal all vices and filth."

More recent Lutherans imitate this manner of speech, and first among them is Chemnitz. In his *Examination* (2 part. p. 98), where he cited some Scriptures for the efficacy of the Sacraments against the Anabaptists and the Sacramentarians, he so adds that "these very manifest testimonies, which attribute efficacy to the Sacraments, and these are the kind that explain they are not perverted by some moralizing interpretation from their simple and genuine meaning, which the proper meaning of the terms shows. The Fathers understood these testimonies simply, just as they sound." On page 101 he adds, "The Sacraments are instrumental causes, so that through those means, or organs, the Father wills to show, give, and apply his grace; the Son communicates his merit to believers, the Holy Spirit exercises his efficacy for the salvation of every believer." He certainly speaks very much like a Catholic. Calvin also does not rarely speak in the way that Catholics do. In the *Antidote* (sess. 7, can. 5) he says, "We must always repeat in our memory, the Sacraments are nothing other than instrumental causes to confer grace to us," and in can. 6, "If there is anyone who denies the grace which they prefigure is contained in the Sacraments, we condemn them."

Just the same, neither Luther, nor Calvin, nor even Chemnitz, receded from that first opinion, which really attributes no efficiency to the Sacraments. For, when they say the Sacraments are instrumental causes that both confer grace and are efficacious, they always understand, *by the medium of faith*, so that they do nothing else than arouse or nourish faith, which alone justifies.

Calvin (*ibid*, can. 5) explains how the Sacraments are instrumental causes of grace and says then, at length, the Sacraments have their effect if they serve faith. On can. 8, he says that grace effects the Sacraments in us

Chapter II: Teaching of the Heretics on Efficacy

in the same manner which it causes the word of God to be preached. Now it is certain that the word does not effect, except by arousing, or nurturing faith. Lastly, Theodore Beza (as we noted above), in his book *De Summa Rei Sacramentariae*, q. 2, explains the opinion of Calvin, his teacher, in this way, "Where does the efficacy of the Sacraments come from? From the operation of the Holy Spirit *in solidum*, but not by signs, except insofar as the interior senses are moved by those external objects."

Chemnitz also (p. 101 *et seqq.*), explaining accurately in what manner the Sacraments are efficacious, at length concluded they are efficacious in the way in which that very promise, or the word of the promise is efficacious. On p. 102, he says, "The word, and the Sacraments show us where faith should seek, and where it can find Christ the mediator, the Father, and the Holy Spirit." On p. 105, explaining how faith in the Sacraments justifies, he says, "It has not been thought that faith receives grace without a medium, or organ of the word and the Sacraments; for the object of faith is the word and the Sacraments, nay more, in the word and the Sacraments the true object of faith is the merit of Christ, the grace of God, and the efficacy of the Spirit. Consequently, faith justifies because it apprehends and receives these things in the word and the Sacraments in this sense: Just as the faith of the word, so also the faith of the Sacrament is said to justify."

Lastly, whatever Catholic words the Lutherans use, they cannot, in any way, understand what we do, namely, that the Sacraments are true and immediate causes of justification. They could, if they were to withdraw from their very first principle, *faith alone justifies*, which to this point they have not done.

CHAPTER III

That the Sacraments Confer Grace Ex Opere Operato Is Proven from the Scriptures

It remains now that we prove the Sacraments are true instrumental causes of grace. So as not to labor in vain, we must prove at the same time, that the Sacraments are a cause other than preaching. For they usually respond to all of our testimonies that the Sacraments are true causes of grace, but by exciting faith, just as in Romans 1:16, the word of the Gospel called, "The power of God in the salvation of all believers."

We shall advance six classes of arguments. The first will be from the Scriptures of the New Testament, where it is expressly found. The second from the prophecies of the Prophets, and from the figures of the Old Testament. Thirdly, from Councils. Fourthly, from the Greek Fathers. Fifthly, from the Latin Fathers. Sixthly, from reason.

The First Class of testimonies: From the New Testament

1) The *first* testimony is of Matthew 3:11 and the parallels in Mark 1:8, Luke 3:16, and John 1:26. There, John the Baptist says, "I baptize you with water, he will baptize you with the Holy Spirit." With such words there is no doubt, that the only distinction posited between the efficacy of John's Baptism and Christ's is constituted between water and the Spirit. Now, the Baptism of John was efficacious to nourish faith, no less than the Baptism of Christ. In John's Baptism, there was an external washing and the word of the promise, seeing that he preached a Baptism of penance for the remission of sins (Luke 3:3), and he was preaching together with the faith in the Mediator, saying that they would believe in him that was going to come (Act. 19:4).

Calvin responds to this argument (*Commentary on Matthew* 3) that the efficacy of John's and Christ's Baptism was the same, but the distinction which John places in water and the Spirit he says consists in the fact that John was a minister of an outward rite, but Christ was the author of internal sanctification. But if it is thus, then John should not have said, "I baptize ... he will baptize," but, "I baptize ... he baptizes." Besides, if the force of each Baptism was the same, why, in Acts 19:5, did Paul command those whom he heard were baptized with the Baptism of John to be baptized in the Baptism of Christ?

Calvin responds in his *Commentary on Acts* 19, that they were not baptized again, but only visibly received the gift of the Holy Spirit, and

Chapter III: *Opere Operato* Proven from Scripture

this is signified in the words, "When they heard these things, they were baptized in the name of the Lord Jesus." Now, apart from the fact that this would be a vicious equivocation, since in the whole narration the name of Baptism is received for Baptism of water, if this were so, then everyone would be allowed to pervert the Scriptures if he could twist words so clear into another thing. In the same passage, verse 6, Luke added soon after, "And when Paul imposed hands upon them, the Holy Spirit came upon them, and they spoke in tongues and prophesied." Therefore, that "they were baptized" did not signify they visibly received the gift of the Holy Spirit.

Calvin answers: The later words are an explanation of the first. But Luke did not say, "They were baptized, and when he imposed hands, etc." Rather, "they were baptized: for when he imposed hands, etc.," or certainly, they were Baptized, and he imposed hands on them, etc. The explanations are customarily made in this way. However, the phrase, "when they heard these things, they were baptized in the name of the Lord Jesus, and when Paul imposed hands upon them, the Holy Spirit came" evidently shows these were two actions done at different times: Baptism and the imposition of hands. Lastly, let us compare this passage with another of the same author, namely Acts 8:12, where we similarly find Baptism in the name of the Lord Jesus and the imposition of hands, then it becomes crystal clear that for "Baptism," true Baptism is understood in both passages.

2) The *second* testimony is of Mark 16:16, "Whoever believes and will be baptized, will be saved." Here, the force of saving is attributed to Baptism. But it does not save except by justifying and washing the filth of sin.

Nor can one answer that it saves by arousing faith. In the first place, in this passage faith precedes. It is inept to say, firstly the effect is placed, and then its cause. Just as it would be absurd to say, "whoever will be cured, and receive medicine"; so it would be absurd to say, "whoever believes and will be baptized," if Baptism is a cause of faith. This is why, to hear the word of God is truly a cause of faith, and in Scripture it always precedes, as in John 5:24, "He that hears the word and believes, has eternal life," and in John 6:45, "Everyman who has heard, and learned, comes to me." Therefore, faith is not an effect of Baptism, since it precedes, but rather more is the *disposition* for it.

Thereafter *ad hominem*: in this place Christ did not join the Sacrament with preaching, as our adversaries do; for he does not say, "He that will hear the word, and will be baptized"; rather, he joined it with *faith*, which is the effect of the word. So, just as among our adversaries, faith immediately justifies by applying the merits of Christ, but not by arousing some other cause; why do they not affirm in the same way that Baptism immediately justifies by applying the merits of Christ, since Christ speaks in the same way on faith and Baptism?

3) The *third* testimony is of John 3:5, "Unless a man be born again

from water and the Holy Spirit, he cannot enter the kingdom of God." This passage clearly makes Baptism of water the cause of new birth, for the preposition *from* [*ex*] means this, as is clear in all similar utterances.

It cannot be said that to be reborn from water is to be reborn from faith, which excites the water. *Firstly*, Christ would have had to say, "Unless a man be born from the word and the Holy Spirit," since the more principal cause of arousing faith is the word, rather than water. *Secondly*, then the discourse of Christ would be altogether unintelligible. Since he said nothing previously about faith, who could divine that he was handing down a method of arousing faith? *Thirdly*, the proposition would be false, "Except a man be reborn, etc." If faith alone justifies, it would not pertain to salvation from where faith is aroused, whether from water, or from wine, or from another thing. It is also certain that faith can be aroused in many ways without Baptism of water; for a sermon suffices more than enough to arouse faith.

Calvin could not respond to this passage in any other way than by denying it is a question of baptism; but even before him, Zwingli and Bucer denied it. Therefore, Calvin, in his *Commentary* as well as the *Institutes* (4, 16, §25), denies it should be understood in regard to Baptism, but only an internal renewal. Thus, through water he would have it that the Holy Spirit is understood, and this is the sense: unless a man will be born again from water, i.e., from the Holy Spirit, who cleanses in the form of water, etc.

But *a)* All authors have hitherto understood this passage on Baptism: Justin Martyr (*2nd Apologia*); Tertullian (*de Baptismo*), Cyprian (*ad Quirinium* 3, 25); Ambrose (*de Spiritu Sancto* 3, 11); Jerome (*on Ezechiel* 16), likewise Basil, Gregory Nazianzen, Gregory of Nyssa (*Serm. On Baptism*); lastly, all the interpreters of this passage, Origen, Chrysostom, Augustine, Cyril, Bede, Theophylactus, Euthymius, and others.

b) Secondly, if we are allowed to play with the Scriptures, we could deny Baptism of water. For everywhere we would understand by the word "water" the Holy Spirit, and in that manner, we will be allowed to overturn every other mystery.

c) Thirdly, we cannot deny that such an utterance is forced, and absurd, and unusual in the Scriptures. The example which Calvin advances from Matt. 3:11, "He will baptize you in the Holy Spirit, and with fire," does not avail. There, he means through fire, the same Holy Spirit is understood that has the similitude with fire. Through fire, outward fire can most rightly be understood, which descended visibly upon the Apostles on the day of Pentecost, or the fire of tribulation, or the fire of Purgatory; Bede touches upon these in his *Commentary on Luke* 3. Besides, in this passage, fire is placed after the Holy Spirit, and it is not so absurd, that after one term another is placed whereby it is declared. Conversely, in John 3:5, the Lord placed water before the Holy Spirit; it would be very absurd for the declaration to be placed first, then that which is going to be declared. It

Chapter III: *Opere Operato* Proven from Scripture

cannot be denied that water, if it is received for the Holy Spirit, would be placed to declare the effect of the Holy Spirit, which is to cleanse.

d) Fourthly, if in this passage water would not be placed except to explain the effect of the Holy Spirit, it would badly be joined with the word "to be born again," for water, if only its meaning were to be expected, does not give birth, but washes and refreshes. Therefore, either the Lord should have said, "Unless a man be cleansed with water, and the Holy Spirit," or, "Unless a man will be born again from seed, and the Holy Spirit." Therefore, water does not only declare the effect of the Holy Spirit in this passage, but properly signifies water, as it cooperates Sacramentally to spiritual regeneration.

4) The *fourth* testimony is Acts 2:38, "Do penance, and be baptized every one of you in the name of Jesus Christ." Acts 22:16 is similar to it, "Rise up, and be baptized, and wash away your sins, invoking his name." In these passages, the remission of sins is attributed to Baptism, and it cannot be said that it is done because Baptism arouses faith, for those whom Peter is addressing in Acts 2 already believed, as Luke indicates in the same passage. After they heard Peter's sermon, they repented in their heart, and said (v. 37) "What shall we do, men and brethren?" Peter, however, did not say, "You must believe," or "believe more." Rather, he said, "Do penance, and be baptized, etc." For equal reasoning, Paul, to whom Ananias said, in Acts 22:16, "Be baptized, and wash away your sins," already believed, and needed to do penance for three days, fasting.

Calvin answers both in his *Commentary* on Acts and in the *Institutes* (4, 15, §18). He argues that to be baptized in remission of sins, or to wash away sins in Baptism, is nothing else than to receive testimony, or the seal of justification that has been received, and to fortify or confirm faith.

Yet (to omit what we have already proven, that the Sacraments cannot be seals, or certainly are false seals, since the minister does not know whether the man to whom he applies the divine seal is truly justified), who does not marvel at this new trope, whereby to wash away sins signifies to receive the seal of justification that has already been received? It is unheard of that an action signified is placed to signify a sign, and that future action is posited to signify a past sign. The examples would be, if anyone were to say, "drink wine," it would be absurd to say he meant to signify, "look at the ivy which hangs upon the inn." For equal reasoning, if it were said to an emperor returning with victory, "Conquer the enemies," and it were said to signify, "receive the triumph as a sign of a past victory," the utterance would be absolutely absurd. You cannot rightly say, "conquer the enemy," to a man that already fought and conquered.

5) The *fifth* testimony is of Acts 8:18. "And when Simon saw that the Holy Spirit was given by the imposition of hands of the Apostles, ..." 2 Tim. 1:6 is similar to this passage, "I admonish you to stir up the grace of God which is in you, by the imposition of my hands." Even if these passages are

understood in regard to the Sacraments of Confirmation and Ordination, which many of our adversaries do not accept as proper Sacraments, nevertheless, if the Sacraments, as they would have it, are improperly said to be true causes of grace, how much more are Sacraments properly so called? Hence, in these passages the imposition of hands is very clearly asserted as the cause of grace, as is clear from the particle *by*. Nor can it be said that the imposition of hands is the cause of grace by arousing faith. All of these men, who, by the imposition of hands received the grace of the Holy Spirit, already believed and were baptized.

6) The *sixth* testimony is of 1 Cor. 10:17, "We who are many, are one body, all who partake in the one bread." There, to participate in the one bread is placed for the cause of being one body. In the Greek it is even more clear, "ὅτι γὰρ πάντες ἐν τοῦ ἑνὸς ἄρτου μετέχομεν." We all participate in one body. However, how are we one body because we partake of the one bread, except because that bread nourishes and increases the life of this body? In bodily matters, because the same food nourishes the members of the same body, therefore, we most rightly prove that some members are members of the same body if they are nourished by the same bread. This is why if you take away true causality from the Sacrament of the altar, it cannot be proved that we are one body because we partake of the same Eucharist. It is similar to this passage of 1 Cor. 12:13, "We are all in one Spirit, in one body of the baptized." There, Paul proves we are one body because by Baptism we receive one Spirit. But the argument effects nothing if Baptism does not confer the Spirit.

7) The *seventh* testimony is of Ephesians 5:25, "Christ loved the Church, and gave himself for her...cleansing her with the laver of water in the word of life." This passage is similar to Titus 3:5, "He saved us by the laver of regeneration." There, we are most clearly told that we are cleansed and saved by the laver of water and through the laver. Both signify an instrumental cause.

Calvin responds, in his *Commentary* for this passage, that Baptism is properly said to be the laver of the soul and is an efficacious symbol. This is because God, while he shows this sign, at the same time also operates what he signifies through it.

On the other hand, *per accidens*, justification is joined in this way, which God alone does with Baptism; hence, we are no more properly said to be cleansed and saved through Baptism than through any other action you like, which is then done at the same time. Nor can Baptism truly be called the laver of regeneration, if through it, God does not wash us, although at the same time he washes us.

Now, if one were to say that God cleanses us through Baptism, because showing that symbol, he calls forth faith which cleanses, one could also say men become drunk by ivy, because it hangs in the inns, or because the ivy calls out to buy wine, since afterward the wine inebriates.

Chapter III: *Opere Operato* Proven from Scripture

8) The *eighth* testimony is of 1 Peter 3:21, "Baptism, being of a like form, saves you also, not the putting away of the filth of the flesh, rather, the examination of a good conscience towards God." Here, we have *firstly*, Baptism saves us. Next, it saves us in a similar way, whereby formerly in the time of Noah a few were saved by water. Otherwise, that water truly and efficiently saved those who were in the ark, namely, taking the ark on high. Lastly, we have the distinction between the Baptisms of the Jews, and ours. The former remove the filth of the flesh; ours purify the conscience. As a result, just as the Baptisms of the Jews truly removed the filth of the flesh, not only by signifying, but also *in effect*, so also our Baptism truly washes the conscience, not only by signifying, but also *in effect*.

CHAPTER IV

The Second Class of Testimonies: The Prophecies of the Prophets

FIRSTLY, in Isaiah 1:11: where he said, "Why do you offer me the multitude of your victims, says the Lord? I am full, I desire not the holocausts of rams, and fat of fatlings, and the blood of calves, lambs, and goats." To which he adds in verse 16, "Be washed, and be clean." St. Jerome and St. Cyril, in their commentary, as well as St. Cyril of Jerusalem (*Catheces.* 1), Theodoret (Ps. 50), and Basil (in *Orat.* 13, which is on Baptism) explain it literally on Baptism, which succeeded the old expiations. The fact that Baptism has the force of cleansing is clear from the words of verse 16, "Be washed, and be clean." In other words, Be baptized, and in that way you will be cleansed. This is why St. Jerome relates this passage in the following manner, "In place of the ancient victims, and holocausts, ... I favor the religion of the Gospel, that you be baptized in my blood through the laver of regeneration, which alone can forgive sins." There, by *alone*, he did not exclude God, the merit of Christ, faith, and any other kind, but *the Jewish sacrifices and ceremonies.*

Secondly, Ezekiel 36:25 says, "I will pour out clean water over you, and you will be cleansed of all your iniquities, ... and I will give you a new heart, etc." Jerome and Theodoret, in their commentary on this passage, understand Baptism, as well as Cyprian (1, last epistle; and 4, 7), where St. Jerome remarks that through the sprinkling of the water of Baptism, not only are sins cleansed, but even a new heart and new spirit are given.

Thirdly, St. Jerome (*Epist.* 83 *ad Oceanum*) says that Micah 7:19 prophesies the *grace of Baptism*, "He will cast all of our sins into the depth of the sea." Rupert also understands this passage in this way, as well as Augustine (on *Ps. 113*). Now, to be sunk in the sea not only signifies it is extinguished, but really it is extinguished by the force of the waters.

Fourthly, Zachariah 13:1, "On that day there will be a fountain open to the house of David, and the inhabitants of Jerusalem; for the washing of the sinner, and of the menstruating woman." Jerome and Rupert, in their commentary, explain this passage on Baptism, which has the force to cleanse sins.

Fifthly, David in Psalm 50:8, "Sprinkle me with hyssop, etc." However, we will speak on this a little later, in the explanation of the sixth figure.

Chapter IV: *Opere Operato* Proven by the Prophets

Figures of the Sacraments

1) The first is of Genesis 1:2, "The Spirit of God is borne upon the waters." The Hebrew expresses the purpose for which it is borne upon the waters, namely, to render them fertile. From there, fish and birds were going to procreate, as it is said later. The word מְרַחֶפֶת *merachepheth*, means *it brooded over*, in the fashion of hens maintaining their nest, and the eggs with heat, as Jerome says in *Questions in Genesis*. This was, however, a figure of Baptism, which is constituted from water and the Holy Spirit, as Tertullian teaches (*de Baptismo*), and Jerome (*Epist.* 83 *ad Oceanum*). So, as water receives a certain vital force from the beginning of the world from the Holy Spirit that living things would procreate, so also Baptism receives the force to procreate new men from the Holy Spirit. As Tertullian says, "So, in Baptism, there is no wonder if the waters are able to bring life" (*De Baptismo* 3, 21). He also calls Christians little fish, because they are born from the waters. This is why the capital letters of the Sibylline verses make ἰχθὺς, i.e., fish, and they mean *Jesus Christ, Son of God, Savior*.[13] Augustine remarks on this in *City of God* (18, 23) as well as Prosper (*de Praedictionibus* 2, 29), and before both of them, Optatus of Mileve (*Cont. Parm.* 3), "Hence, it is the fish, who in Baptism, is inserted into the fountain-like waves through the invocation, that what was water, shall be called a fishpond from the fish, whose fish contain the name according to the Greek pneumonic in one name for each letter the throng of the names of the saints, ἰχθὺς, which means Jesus Christ, Son of God, Savior." And St. Jerome, alluding to this in *Epist.* 43 *ad Bonosum*, says, "Just as an ἰχθὺς the Son seeks a watery place."

2) The *second* figure is of Genesis 7:7, on the flood saving Noah and the others who were on the ark, which St. Peter explains in 1:3, which we spoke of earlier.

3) The *third* figure is of Genesis 17:11 & *seqq.*, on circumcision, on which Paul says in Coloss. 2:11, "You were circumcised with a circumcision not done by hands, in the despoiling of the body of the flesh, rather, in the circumcision of Christ: you were buried with him in Baptism." Although circumcision truly and efficiently cut the flesh, still, it was not a mere testimony of cutting, etc.

4) The *fourth* figure is from Exodus 14:27, *et seqq.*, the drowning of the Egyptians in the Red Sea, and the crossing of the sons of Israel; St. Paul speaks of this in 1 Cor. 10:2, "They were all baptized in Moses, in the cloud, and in the sea." Then in verse 11, he says, "All of these things happened to them in a figure." Therefore, the Red Sea was a figure of Baptism, but the cloud overshadowing them, a figure of the Holy Spirit. Just as the Red Sea truly drowned the Egyptians and liberated the Israelites, so also Baptism truly destroys sins and saves souls. See Cyprian (*Epist.* 4, 7), Augustine

---

13 Ιησους Χριστος, Θεου Υιος, Σοτερ.

(*Tract. In Jo.* 11 & 13) and Jerome (*Epist.* 82 *ad Oceanum*).

5) The *fifth* figure is Exodus 16:17, on the manna falling from heaven and the water bubbling out of the rock, which were figures of the Eucharist, the body and blood of the Lord, and St. Paul explains them in the same way. The manna, however, and that water truly refreshed and revived the bodies of the Israelites, and were not testimonies or seals. Consequently, the Eucharist truly refreshes souls; otherwise, the figure would be better than the thing prefigured.

6) The *sixth* is of Numbers 19:9, on the lustral waters which had the ash of a red cow. This was a figure of Baptism, as St. Augustine writes in *Questions on Numbers* 33. There, we must remark from the same Augustine, that there were three things necessary in this expiation: the ash of a red cow, water, and hyssop, in which water was sprinkled. The ash of the cow signified the death and merits of Christ; the water, Baptism, which applies the merits of Christ; the Hyssop, the lowly grace, having roots in the rock, signifies faith, without which Baptism is not given to adults, and if perhaps it were given, it would not profit him. Thus, just as in that expiation, hyssop does not cleanse, rather, water having force from the ash of the cow and the sprinkled hyssop, so in Baptism it is not faith, which properly cleanses sins in Baptism, but water having force from the passion of Christ and received with faith. To these expiations, both prefiguring and prefigured, David looks when he says in Psalm 50:8, "Sprinkle me with hyssop and I shall be clean; wash me, and I will be whiter than snow." He looks to that purgation, which he knew was prefigured, through the expiation of water, which was being sprinkled with hyssop, as Theodoret explains in his commentary on this passage.

7) The *seventh* figure is of Joshua 4:10, on the crossing of the sons of Israel through the Jordan to the promised land, under Joshua's leadership. Ambrose teaches that this was a figure of Baptism (*In Luke 1*), "He preceded in spirit, and in the power of Elijah," and Augustine on Psalm 113 [114]:3, "And you, O Jordan flowed back." Nobody said through the waters of the Jordan the sons of Israel did not cross to the promise land but it was merely a promise of crossing.

8) The *eighth* is in 4 Kings [2 Kings] 5:14, on Naam the Syrian cured from leprosy by the laver of the Jordan (see St. Ambrose's commentary on Luke 4, and *De Sacramentis* 2, 4). Rightly, the water of the Jordan truly cured that Syrian; it was not the seal of a promise.

9) The *ninth* is John 5:2, on the Probatic Pool, which is a very manifest figure, celebrated by many Fathers such as Tertullian (*de Baptismo*), Ambrose (*de Spiritu Sancto* 1, 7), Chrysostom, Cyril, and Theophylactus in their commentaries on this passage. Chrysostom explains this figure most beautifully, and added that God willed to show the efficacy of Baptism by these different figures, lest it would seem unbelievable, "Baptism was going to be full of the greatest power and grace, cleanse sins, and make one

Chapter IV: *Opere Operato* Proven by the Prophets

living from the dead, etc." Rightly unless it were so, as Chrysostom says, the figure would be more excellent than the very thing prefigured.

10) The *tenth* is John 9:7, on the man born blind, whom the Lord illuminated by the water of Siloe, on which see Ambrose (*Epist. 75 ad Bellicium*), and Augustine (*Tract. in Jo.* 44).

We must note two things in regard to these passages of Scripture. *a) First*, that since Scripture so often speaks in prophecies, figures, and clear words regarding the Sacraments, nevertheless it does not even once say the force of the Sacraments consists in rousing or nourishing faith. Rather, it always explains that they consist in cleansing sins and purifying the soul. Really, by this fact, if we carefully assess the matter in earnest, it is evidently gathered that the teaching of the heretics is absolutely false. How is it believable that the immediate and clear end of the Sacraments is never found in Scripture, when it so often impresses the mediate end?

b) Secondly, what if it were lawful to deny the Sacraments truly and immediately sanctify, when Scripture so clearly teaches this? For the same reasoning, it could be denied that faith justifies, which our adversaries affirm (*passim*). For, the Scriptures attribute nothing to faith which they do not also attribute to the Sacraments. For example, it is said in Luke 7:50, "Your faith has saved you," and in 1 Pet. 3:21, it is said, "Baptism saved you." Likewise, on faith, in John 5:24, "Who believes him that sent me, has eternal life." On the Sacraments, in John 6:59, "Who eats this bread will live forever." On faith, Acts 15:9, "Purifying their hearts by faith." On the Sacraments, Ephes. 5:26, "Cleansing it in the laver of water in the word of life." On faith, Romans 3:28, "We regard a man justified by faith." On the Sacraments, Tit. 3:5, "He saved us by the laver of regeneration." On faith, Romans 5:1, "Therefore, justified by faith." On the Sacraments, John 3:5, "Unless a man be born again of water and the Holy Spirit, etc."

CHAPTER V

The Third Class of Arguments: From Councils

THE Council of Nicaea, which was recently translated from Greek and published by Alphonsus Pisanus in a heading which is titled δικτύπωσις, the doctrine on Baptism, before the eighth canon, "Our Baptism must not be considered by the eyes of the body, but the mind; you see water, consider the power of God hidden in the waters....A man descended [into it], being guilty of sin and detained by the corruption of servitude and there he was baptized; he ascended, however, from that servitude, free from sins, a son of God, as both heir, and coheir of Christ."

The First Council of Constantinople, in the Creed, "We believe in one Baptism for the remission of sins."

The Council of Mileve, c. 2, "Since children cannot commit sins in themselves, therefore, they are truly baptized in the remission of sins, so that what they derive from generation will be cleansed in regeneration." But certainly, in children Baptism cannot be the cause of the remission of sins by arousing faith.

The Second Council of Orange (can. 5), "We also believe this according to Catholic faith, that since they have received grace through Baptism, all who have been baptized may and must obtain those things which pertain to salvation by the assistance and cooperation of Christ, if they wish to labor faithfully." Note, this cannot be explained in regard to arousing faith. A little later the same Council says that faith was inspired by God first so that we would faithfully pine for the Sacraments. Besides, even if faith, according to our adversaries, justifies from sins, nevertheless, it does not give grace to perform our duties well. But Baptism, according to this Council, gives grace to perform our duties well.

Add to these the more recent Councils of Florence and Trent.

CHAPTER VI

The Fourth Class of Testimonies: From the Greek Fathers

Now from the Greek Fathers. Justin Martyr, in his *Apology to the Emperor Antoninus*, says, "We obtain remission for sins already committed in water, etc." And previously, he had said that no man is lead to Baptism unless he already believed. He holds similar things in the *Dialogue with Trypho*.

Clement of Alexandria (*Paedagog.* 1, 6) says, "This work is described in many ways, grace, illumination, completion, and laver; laver, through which we wash away sins; grace, whereby the penalties due for sins are remitted; illumination, through which we gaze upon that holy, and salutary light; completion, however, we say because it lacks nothing. What is lacking to a man who knows God? etc."

Origen (*hom.* 14 *in Luke* 14, 2) says, "Children are baptized in remission for sins. ... And because through the Sacrament of Baptism the filth of birth is laid aside, for that reason, children are baptized."

Cyril (*Catech.* 3), says, "Dead in sins you went down, up you rose living in justice." See the whole *Catechesis*. And in the preface for it, he says, "This purpose of Baptism is truly great; the liberation of captivity, the remission of sins, the regeneration of the soul, the vehicle to heaven, etc."

Basil (*de Spiritu Sancto*, 15) poses the objection of the heretics: So, if the Holy Spirit is equal to the Father and the Son, because we are baptized in him, water will also be equal to the Father and the Son, because we are baptized in it. Then he answers, "If grace is in the water, it is not from the nature of water, but the excellence of the Spirit, etc." According to our adversaries, he ought to have said the water does nothing, and in this way would immediately answer the objection. On the contrary, Basil affirms that in water there is a power, but says it is not in the water by its nature, rather the force of the *Holy Spirit*. See also *Homil.* 13, which is an exhortation to Baptism; there he holds the same thing very clearly. See also Gregory Nazianzen, (*Orat. in Sancta Lumina*, and *Orat. in Sanctum Lavacrum*).

Gregory of Nyssa (*de Baptismo*) says, "Baptism is the expiation of sins, the remission of crimes, the cause of renewal and regeneration." A little further on, explaining how it happens, he brings forward many examples of the things whereby God performed miracles, such as the staff of Aaron and other things, and adds, "All of these things, though they were matter without soul or sense, were made the means for the performance of the great marvels wrought by them, when they received the power of God. Now, by a similar train of reasoning, water also though it is nothing else but water, renews the man to spiritual regeneration, when the grace from above sanctifies it. If anyone again is uncertain, asking how the water and the sacramental act that is performed therein regenerates, I most justly reply to him, 'Show me the manner of that generation which is after the flesh, and I will explain to you the power of regeneration in the soul.' You will say, perhaps, by way of giving an account of the matter, 'It is the cause of the seed which makes the man.' Learn from us in return, that sanctified water cleanses and illuminates the man."

There, we must note that the teaching of Gregory cannot be reduced to what that heretics say, namely that the Sacraments operate by objectively moving one to faith. *Firstly*, he compares the water of Baptism with the rod of Aaron, which efficiently causes miracles. *Secondly*, he compares it to a woman, which is the efficient cause of man, as he says. *Thirdly*, he denies water effects anything unless it receives a certain supernatural force, but to objectively move through the manner of a sign, no supernatural power is required. Lastly, the question which he proposes, "How can water regenerate," would make no sense if it only operated objectively.

Chrysostom (*Hom. 39 in Gen.*) says, "What Circumcision does [in the Old Law] is in the laying aside of flesh; [in the New] Baptism acts in laying aside of sins." Likewise, in *Hom. 24 in Joan.*, he teaches extensively that we must believe the words of Christ, asserting that water has the force to regenerate, although the manner would be above reason. In *Hom. 25* he says, "What the womb is for the embryo, water is for the faithful. Accordingly, he is made and formed in the water. First it was said, 'Let the waters produce creeping creatures;' from the time in which Christ steps out into the channel of the Jordan, no more does water produce creeping creatures, but rational and spiritual souls." See the same thing in *Hom. 35 in Joan., Hom. 1 in Acts, Hom. To the Neophytes*, where he enumerates ten effects of Baptism, which also work in children, and among so many effects it never came into his mind to place arousing faith; which is the only thing our adversaries acknowledge.

Cyril of Alexandria (*in John*, 2, 42) says, "In the same manner, when water has been heated more intensely by the power of fire, it does not burn differently than the fire itself; so also by the operation of the Holy Spirit, water, whereby the body of the baptized is washed, is reformed to divine virtue and power." There you see that water is in this way an instrument of God, just as the heat in warm water is the instrument of fire to warm it.

Theodoret (on *Hebrews* 10), on the verse *Our hearts have been sprinkled from an evil conscience, our bodies washed with clean water*, says, "In the law they used to use sprinklings, and they frequently washed the body; the men, however, who established life from the New Testament, cleanse the soul by most holy Baptism and render the conscience free from previous faults." See the same author in *Epitome Divinorum Decret.*, on Baptism, Damascene (*de Fide* 4, 10), Theophylactus (*on John* 3 & 5), and Oecumenius (on *Hebrews* 10).

CHAPTER VII

The Same Is Proven from the Latin Fathers

From the Latin Fathers, Tertullian (*de Baptismo*) says, "Water was the first to produce that which had life, that it might be no wonder in Baptism if waters know how to give life." Likewise, in his book *On the Resurrection of the Flesh*, he proves the body is going to rise again because the Sacraments are applied to the body, that it would transfer their effects to the soul, "The flesh is washed that the soul be cleansed; the flesh is anointed that the soul be consecrated; the flesh is signed that the soul is fortified; the flesh is overshadowed by the imposition of hands that the soul would be illuminated with the Spirit; the flesh is fed with the body and blood of Christ that the soul would be fed lavishly by God." There, he enumerates different effects of the Sacraments; hence, he did not think the Sacraments only arouse faith.

Cyprian (*Epist.* 2, 2) writes to Donatus, that before he was baptized, he could hardly be persuaded to believe what Christians preached in regard to the power of Baptism, namely that it immediately changes man, washes away sins, and infuses virtues; nevertheless, he later learned by his own experience:

"I once thought it a difficult matter, particularly difficult in respect to my way of life at the time, that a man should be capable of being born again, a truth which the divine mercy had announced for my salvation, and that a man animated for a new life in the laver of saving water should be able to lay aside what he had previously been; and although retaining all his bodily structure, should be himself changed in heart and soul. I asked, how is such a conversion possible? ... After that, by the help of a fruitful stream, the stain of former years had been washed away, and a light from above, serene and pure, had been infused into my reconciled heart; after that, by the agency of the Spirit breathed from heaven, a second birth had restored me to a new man, then, in a wondrous manner, etc." In such words we must note two things. *Firstly*, if the Sacraments only objectively move the mind to belief, as our adversaries say, it was not the reason why Cyprian believed the effect of Baptism with difficulty; this effect is not more difficult than the idea that the word of God preached avails to arouse faith. *Secondly*, note that Cyprian says Baptism works *immediately* and *swiftly*, and renews man. He would not have said this if he believed Baptism only moved the mind objectively, then it would not ordinarily have its effect right away. Otherwise, from the same sign, as even from the same words, some would be moved more quickly, others more slowly, and others not at all.

He teaches likewise (*Epist.* 3, 8 *ad Figum*), that infants must be baptized even before the eighth day (namely, if threatened by danger of death), to receive the remission of sin. Pope Syricius commands the same thing (*Epist.* 1, cap. 2). Now, if Baptism only arouses faith, and only benefits infants by the notion that when they become adults they will remember, etc., why does Cyprian want infants who are about to die to be baptized? Likewise, he speaks (*Epist.* 4, 7, *ad Magnum*) of how the poison of a scorpion and a serpent is extinguished in water; so the devil struggles and resists exorcists before Baptism; but in Baptism he loses all power. All of this would certainly be ridiculous if the Sacraments only operated objectively. See also his sermons *On the Baptism of Christ, on the Lord's Supper*, and *On the Anointing of Chrism*. Gaudentius holds similar things (*Tract. de Exod.*).

Lactantius (*De Divino Praemio* 7, 5) says, "When a man purified by the heavenly laver lays aside infancy with every sin of his prior life, after he has received an increase of divine vigor, he becomes a perfect and full man."

Pope Sylvester (as Nicephorus relates in 7, 33), when he baptized Constantine, he spoke in this way, "This water conceived by divine power through the invocation of the Trinity, just as it outwardly washes the body of man, so inwardly the soul from filth, and cleansing wickedness, causes it to shine with the rays of the sun."

Ambrose (*De Poenit.* 2, 2) says, "It seemed impossible that water could wash away sins. And Naam the Syrian did not believe his leprosy could be cleansed by water; but what was impossible, God made possible, since he is the only one that bestows grace upon us." (See also *de Sacramentis*, 1, 4-5; 3,1 and *de Mysteriis* 3& 9, as well as his commentary on Luke 9, c. 3, and *On the Holy Spirit* 3,11).

Jerome (*Epistle* 83 *ad Oceanum*) says, "A little later I will teach on how much force Baptism has, as well as what grace water sanctified in Christ has." Later, where he asserts a great many testimonies and figures, he says, "Let my days come to an end if I would want to lay aside everything which pertains to the power of Baptism." See the same in his *Dialogue against the Luciferians*, as well as *Against the Pelagians*, book 3.

Optatus (*Contra Parmenianum* 5) says, "Baptism of Christians confected [in the name of] the Trinity confers grace; if it is repeated, it causes a loss of life." There, you see *firstly*, he clearly asserts the Sacrament confers grace. Next, what this author says, that repeating Baptism causes harm, clearly shows it does not only work by objectively arousing faith, since in that way it would be advantageous to repeat it. See (*ibid*) many things on the power of the Sacraments.

Augustine (*de Baptismo* 4, 22) says, "I find not only the passion for the name of Christ is such a thing that, when one is lacking Baptism, can supply, but also faith and conversion of heart, if perhaps he cannot run to celebrate the mystery of Baptism due to the difficulties of time." Therefore,

Chapter VII: *Opere Operato* Proven by the Latins

if on the one hand martyrdom, and on the other faith with conversion of heart supplies in place of Baptism, it manifestly follows that it does not justify by arousing faith, but by immediately applying the merits of Christ, and *immediately justifying*. He also proves the Sacrament of Baptism is of much benefit to infants, even if they do not have faith from Circumcision, which is given on the eighth day, "So why did he command, that after every male infant be circumcised on the eighth day, who could not yet believe in heart, that justice was imputed to him except because the very Sacrament availed him much per se?" (*ibid.*, 24) There, Augustine teaches that the Sacrament did not work by arousing faith, but *by effecting* of its own force. The same Augustine (*Contra Faustum* 19, 11) says, "The power of the Sacraments infallibly avails a great deal, and only scoffers will treat them lightly. Without them piety cannot be completed, so only the impious neglect them." But if they only objectively arouse faith, they would not infallibly avail a great deal, and would hardly avail at all. No man would say in regard to a sermon that it infallibly avails a great deal, when very often some men are scarcely moved by many sermons, and still, Luther affirms in his book against John Cochlaeus, that a sermon is more efficacious than Baptism. That would be very true if it were a question on the efficacy of imparting faith. The same Augustine (*Tract. in Jo.* 80) says, "How is it that water has such a power to influence the body and wash the heart? ... By no means would cleansing from a stream be attributed to a fallible element, unless it were added in the word."

Pope Leo (*Serm.* 4 *de Natali Domini*) says, "The water of Baptism has the nature of a virginal womb, while the same Spirit fills the font who also filled the Virgin, so that sin, which the sacred conception emptied of all its power in the womb, the mystical washing removes it in the font." In *Serm.* 5, he says, "He placed the source, which he took up in the womb of the Virgin, in the springs of Baptism; he gave to water, what he gave to his Mother. For the power of the most high, and the overshadowing of the Holy Spirit, which he caused so that Mary would give birth to the savior, he does the same thing that the flowing water would regenerate the believer."

The author of the homily on the Sacrament of the Lord's body, which is contained in the homilies of Eusebius of Emesa, and in St. Jerome (*Tom.* 9) says, "Just as at the nod of the Lord's command, immediately the high heaven, the depth of the waves, and the vastness of the world came into being from nothing; so equal power in the spiritual Sacraments supply power to the words, and the effect serves the thing...." In the same place, from the force of the Sacrament of Baptism, whereby it immediately changes and renews a man in regard to the soul, he proves that it shouldn't seem incredible if the Sacramental words change the substance of bread into the flesh of Christ. There, without a doubt, an objective operation to provoke faith has no place. In the consecration of the Eucharist the words do not change the bread by arousing faith in it. This author places similar force in the consecration in respect to bread as in Baptism in respect to the soul.

Gregory the Great (*Epist.* 9, 39 *ad Theodistam Patritiam*) teaches in Baptism all sins are truly forgiven, just as the Egyptians really died in the Red Sea, "Therefore, he that says sins are not completely forgiven in Baptism, let him say the Egyptians in the Red Sea are not truly dead."

Then, St. Bernard (that I might pass over more recent authors), in his *Sermon on the Lord's Supper*, says, "The Sacrament of the Lord's body does two things in us, namely it both diminishes sense in lesser things, and altogether abolishes consent to graver sins. If any one of you do not notice the movements of anger, hatred, or lust, or other things of this sort so often or so keenly, let him give thanks to the body and blood of the Lord, because the power of the Sacrament works in him." His words cannot be taken to mean nourishing the effect of faith, for St. Bernard does not only say that through the Sacraments sins are forgiven, which the Lutherans would have it takes place through faith apprehending the justice of Christ and the benevolence of God, rather, he also says the force of the Sacrament works in us so that we will not consent to sins, which cannot happen by faith alone, nor do our adversaries say it can happen.

The heretics respond in different ways to this argument from the Fathers. Melanchthon, in the *Apologia*, art. 13, boldly speaks in this way, "No letter from the ancient writers can be proffered in support of the Scholastics in this matter."

Luther (*Contra Cochlaeum*) acknowledges the passages of Augustine which Cochlaeus cites, and in his fashion scorns them, "But if there are some from the Fathers who felt the Sacraments justify by their own power, even be it Augustine, as Cochlaeus contends, I am not moved in the slightest; they are sayings of men, and often opposed to themselves, and are mostly in a human sense outside the teaching of the Scriptures." It is certainly more believable that so many holy Fathers understood the Scripture better than one Luther, which he also would have conceded if the spirit of pride had not clearly blinded him.

Calvin answers (*Instit.* 4, 14 §26) that the Fathers speak hyperbolically, "Perhaps, those immoderate praises of the Sacraments which are read in the ancients about our signs deceived the sophists; Such as what we read in Augustine, that the Sacraments of the Old Law only promised a savior, while ours give salvation. These, and similar figures of speech, since they did not advert to their hyperbolic nature, promulgated their hyperbolic dogmas." This is a very ruinous escape, for as many Fathers as have been cited relate these marvelous effects to the omnipotence of God. Now, no omnipotence is necessary where the words are not true and proper, but hyperbolic. Besides, the Fathers themselves at some time warn that they do not speak hyperbolically, such as Chrysostom (*Hom.* 4 *ad Baptizandos*), where, when he said souls are perfectly washed and cleansed in Baptism,

Chapter VII: *Opere Operato* Proven by the Latins

he warns that he does not say these things for the sake of ambition, i.e., amplification and the desire to show eloquence. Augustine (*Epist.* 23) says in regard to the end, that anyone who does not believe it can happen that little children without actual faith are saved through the Sacrament, is an infidel. From which we understand, he did not hand down hyperbolic utterances, but dogmas of faith. Lastly, if Calvin were to say one or another of the Fathers used hyperbole in a laudatory oration, it could be tolerated. Now, that all the Greek and Latin Fathers, not only in their sermons, but even in their dogmatic books, epistles, or commentaries on the Scriptures speak hyperbolically, is not at all believable.

Chemnitz (*Examination*, 2 part. p. 98) says Scripture clearly attributes the force of justifying to the Sacraments, nor can these places be twisted through a trope into another sense, and so it must be understood from the Fathers. Nevertheless, he later explains all these on the efficiency through the arousal of faith, which we have already refuted.

CHAPTER VIII

The Sixth Class of Arguments: From Reason

We must observe that to more easily understand the efficacy of the arguments, there are double words and the remaining signs. There are certain ones not instituted to any other end than to *signify*, which can *theoretically* be called signs. Others were instituted to *sign* and *effect* something, which on account of that can be called *practical*. Moreover, they differ because the former immediately work nothing by their own force but only represent an object, and if perhaps some effect follows, it does not follow from the force of that sign, but from another place. The latter operate immediately and by their own certain virtue. For example, when someone warns another that the enemy is here, he immediately flees, otherwise, that admonition is not the immediate cause of that flight. Hence, the admonition was of the first kind of sign. For equal reasoning, a man that runs to the inn after he has seen the sign for it is not immediately moved by the sign, but by the apprehension of things which he needs, and which that sign represents. Hence, it is not properly a practical sign, as we receive it here, for, sometimes, we customarily call practical signs all those which refer to the work, whether mediately or immediately, in the way it was received in the disputation on the intention of the minister. For then, we called all imperative words practical; but here, we call these very things theoretical; we say practical, however, which apart from signification they have efficiency, in the way a seal is truly a practical sign, because it not only represents an image, but also imprints it in wax.

These different signs, however, are recognized from another distinction, for theoretical words and signs are not employed except to those who understand them. Since they do not operate except by representing something to the mind, it is foolish to apply these signs where there is no use of the mind. Now, words and practical signs can be applied even to inanimate things, and not only to those who do not understand them, but to those who do not even understand them, in the way in Scripture that Joshua commanded the sun and moon (Jos. 10:12), "O sun, move not toward Gabaon, nor you, O moon, toward the valley of Ajalon." In Matthew 8:26, the Lord commanded the sea and wind. In Matt. 9:25, Luke 7:14 and John 11:43, he commanded the dead, and Peter in Acts 9:40, "Tabitha, rise." In Matt. 17:19, "If you have the faith of a mustard seed, you will say to this mountain, move hence, etc." So also, what pertains to other signs, Moses struck the rock to give water (Exod. 17:6), and the Lord put his fingers into

Chapter VIII: *Opere Operato* Proven by Reason

the ear of the deaf and mute man, and also touched his tongue to cure him.

Thus, the controversy between us and the heretics is that they make Sacraments signs of the first kind, while they affirm these do not justify except by arousing faith; we make them of the second kind. This is why if we are able to show the Sacraments are signs of the second kind, we will have won our case.

1) Therefore, the *first* argument: The Sacraments are rightly applied to those who do not understand them; therefore, they are signs of the second kind and truly justify not by arousing faith in the manner of a sermon, but by immediately effecting holiness. The manifest consequence is from the aforesaid. The antecedent is proven because infants, the deaf, insane, and those sleeping are duly baptized. The characteristic example is found in Augustine (*Confess.* 4, 4) on a certain man that was baptized while he was placed outside himself by the force of illness, and altogether did not know what was done in his regard; nevertheless, the Sacrament was very advantageous to him. Add that the 4th Council of Carthage (can. 76), as well as the 1st Council of Orange (can. 12), Augustine (*de Adulterinis Conjugiis* 1, 26 & 28), and Leo (*Epist.* 91 *ad Theodorum*) teach the Sacraments of Baptism and Absolution can be conferred even to those who are in danger of death, although they are oppressed by the strength of a plague and do not have the use of reason or the senses, provided it is certain that before they would have desired Sacraments of this sort. Now surely, it would be rather inept to preach to them or apply signs to arouse faith.

2) The *second* argument: Sacramental words and signs depend upon divine institution, and cannot be instituted by men on their own authority; therefore, they are not mere signs, as the words of preaching, rather, *practical* signs, and have the force to effect something supernatural. The antecedent is conceded by our adversaries, as we proved above. The consequent is proved; if Sacramental words and signs are bare signs instituted to arouse the mind, they could easily be instituted by men and would have the same force. For, it does not matter for a bare signification who instituted it, provided it represents the same object. Why is it important who placed the signs in the inn? Do the Hebrew words written by God on the tablets not mean in the same way the Greek and Latin words written by men? Do the trumpets, which God commanded to be made in Numbers 10:2, incite men to war in the same way as the profane trumpets of the heathen? Therefore, in the same way, if Peter, or Paul, or any other man you like instituted Baptism and the Eucharist, those signs would have the same force which they have now. Yet, certainly that cannot be said according to the teaching of Catholics, who hold these Sacraments not only signify, but also *effect* that which they could not of themselves.

3) The *third* argument: The Sacraments do not only depend on the institution of God, but also on their very use, for he is the one who baptizes through his ministers, consecrates, absolves, etc. Therefore, they are not

bare signs instituted to arouse faith, such as sermons; rather, they effect something besides. Our adversaries concede the antecedent, and it was proven above in the question on the efficiency of the Sacraments, from that verse of John 1:33, "This is he who baptizes," from Chrysostom in *Hom. 83 in Matt.*, as well as Augustine in *Tr. in Joan.* 5, and from others. The consequent is proved. For words and the other signs to signify as well as arouse faith in the soul by representation, it is of no importance from whom they proceed. Whether it is the Lord or a slave that speaks, the words always signify the same thing; trumpets no more arouse men to war if they are blown by the emperor than by a mere trumpeter. So, if Sacramental signs necessarily depend upon God, as principal causes, which are worked through ministers, we are compelled to affirm these do not only signify, but also effect something.

4) The *fourth* argument: The Sacraments do not only depend upon God as the institutor and principal agent, but also upon the passion and death of Christ, as we proved above in the beginning of the question on the efficiency of the Sacraments, on account of which the Fathers teach in a common consensus, that the Sacraments flowed from the pierced side of Christ. This is why even many of the Fathers teach that Christ willed to be baptized, that by the touch of his most clean flesh he would give to water the force of cleansing, as Ambrose teaches (on *Luke* 2, 12), Nazianzen (*Orat. in Sancta Lumina*), Chrysostom (*Hom. 25 in Joannem*), Bede (on *Luke* 3), and others; and even Luther himself affirms the same thing in his *Hom. On Baptism*. Therefore, the Sacraments do not only work by representing an object, in the fashion of a sermon, but by truly *effecting*. Otherwise, they would neither need the merits of Christ, nor for Christ to give them any power. Just as a sermon would not rightly be said to emanate from the side of Christ, nor is Christ said to give any power to a sermon to signify because the words stand on their own, so also we would not rightly say the Sacraments issue from the side of Christ, or Christ gave any force to them.

5) The *fifth* argument: The Sacraments were instituted to render us certain about the remission of sins and the grace of God, so they do not only work objectively by representing in the fashion of a sermon, but *by effecting* what they really signify. The antecedent is admitted by all, but especially by our adversaries. Catholics teach from the Sacraments a certain moral certitude of the remission of sins is begotten in us, still, not an infallible one. Although the Sacraments are of themselves infallibly efficacious, nevertheless, it can happen that they are not efficacious for us on account of our not being disposed. But our adversaries hold that absolute certitude is begotten from the Sacraments, and they rebuke us as if we were asking men to be uncertain about the efficacy of the Sacraments. This is clear from Luther in his book on the *Babylonian Captivity* (ch. On Baptism), from Chemnitz (*Examin.* 2 part. ch. *On the Intention of the Minister*), and others. The consequent is proven: If the Sacraments only

Chapter VIII: *Opere Operato* Proven by Reason 189

operate by signifying and arousing faith, they advance no certitude. Then the Sacrament would depend upon our faith, not upon the institution of Christ, which is to abolish true certitude of the efficacy of the Sacrament, as Luther affirms in his book *Against the Anabaptists*, published in 1528, where he profusely insists that the Sacraments should not depend upon the faith of the ministers or the recipients, but on the institution of God alone, lest their efficacy would be rendered uncertain.

The answer cannot be made that the Sacraments advance infallible certitude because they infallibly arouse faith, which infallibly justifies; accordingly, we learn the contrary from experience. How many men are there who are baptized and still do not believe? If a sermon, which is more efficacious than the Sacraments, according to Luther (*Contra Cochlaeum*), does not infallibly arouse faith, as we experience, how much less will the Sacraments infallibly arouse faith? So, if the Sacraments advance any certitude, it is that they effect what they signify *ex opere operato*.

6) The *sixth* argument: The Sacraments stand in a contrary manner to faith and the word therefore, they do not work in the same way. The antecedent is proven. The word of God precedes faith, but follows the Sacraments, accordingly, "Faith through hearing" (Romans 10:17). This is why the word is preached to infidels and any sort of heretic, so that they will begin to believe. Yet, the Sacraments at least require faith in adults, nor can they rightly be conferred except upon those who already believe. This is why, in Acts 8:36, when the Eunuch said, "Behold water, what prevents me from being baptized?" Philip answers, "If you believe with all your heart, it can be done." It was always the custom in the Church that men who want to be Christians must first become Catechumens and be sufficiently instructed for a while, and they will not be baptized unless they are instructed, as well as being firm and stable in faith. Justin, in his Apology to Antoninus Pius, while explaining the customs of the Church says, "Whoever has been persuaded and believes the things we hand down and say are true, and undertake to be able to live accordingly, they are instructed to pray and beg God with fasting for the remission of their past sins, and we pray and fast with them. Then, we bring them where there is water, and they are regenerated in the same manner in which we ourselves were regenerated." From this it follows that the teaching of the heretics is not only false, but also very inept.

7) The *seventh* argument: The Sacraments are no less efficacious if they are given in the Greek or Latin language, which the recipient of the Sacrament does not understand, than if they were given in the vernacular, which everyone understands. So, they do not operate in the fashion of a sermon, but have their effect apart from the arousal of faith. The consequence is clear, because if they are worked in the fashion of a sermon, they would effect nothing unless they were given in the vernacular. The antecedent is proven because the Lutherans and Calvinists admit our Baptism, which is

always given in Latin; for they do not rebaptize those whom we baptized.

8) The *eighth* argument: If the Sacraments work by arousing faith, there would not be any reason why they would be applied to learned men who can read the Scriptures, or even the ignorant who listen to sermons; Scripture and a sermon arouse faith much better than Baptism or the Eucharist. Therefore, it would be better to read one chapter of the Bible in place of Baptism. Moreover, even the image of Baptism depicted on a tablet could cause the same thing which Baptism causes, for it makes a visible promise and arouses faith, and this would be better than Baptism because it always remains, while Baptism is done once, and passes.

9) The *ninth* argument: The Sacraments do not benefit any but the recipients, even if many others are present and hear and see what is done; otherwise, it would not be necessary for individuals to be baptized, and communicate with the body of the Lord. Rather, it would be enough that one be baptized, or communicate in the presence of a whole multitude. As a result, they do not work in the manner of a sermon, by arousing faith. The consequent is clear. If they did work in the manner of a sermon, they would benefit all who hear them; for everyone that is present can be roused to faith, while the promise of God is pronounced and placed in a visible sign before the eyes. Nor does it make a difference that the Sacrament seems to be only directed to one, seeing that even a sermon can be directed to one man, and still, it arouses everyone who hears it to faith.

Besides, while the minister baptizes and says, "I baptize you"; he does not mean to say, "I wash you from sins" (according to the Lutherans), rather, "I witness to you the remission of sins," as Melanchthon (*Loci*, c. On Baptism), Calvin (*Inst.* 4, 15, §15), and the rest of our adversaries are compelled to explain it. Hence, this witness is not beneficial to the one who is baptized except that at the same time he thinks and believes that God is well disposed toward him through Christ, as they themselves affirm. Everyone, however, that is present can think and believe the same thing; accordingly, the promise is common, and what is said to one is suitable to all. Therefore, God is not well disposed to the man that is baptized because he is baptized (according to the teaching of the Lutherans), but the witness of Baptism is true, that God is well disposed to him provided he apprehends this benevolence of God by faith.

10) The *tenth* argument: If the Sacraments only operate by signifying, there is no difference between our Sacraments and the Sacraments of the Old Law. They also signified the grace of Christ and the remission of sins, and could arouse faith. But we will demonstrate that this is false in the following question.

CHAPTER IX

Objections Taken from the Scriptures Are Answered

Now we are going to answer the arguments of Luther, Melanchthon, Calvin, Chemnitz, and others, which are partly taken from the Scriptures, partly from the Fathers, and partly from reason.

So, let us begin from the first class of arguments. 1) The *first* argument is taken from Habak. 2:4, and Rom. 1:17, as well as Hebrews 10:38, "The just man lives by faith," the Scripture says, but it does not say the just man lives by the Sacraments. Therefore, the Sacraments do not justify except by arousing faith. It is confirmed from similar passages, such as Rom. 4:3, "Abraham believed God, and justice was reputed to him," and Rom. 10:10, "He believed in heart unto justice." Paul did not add, "And the Sacrament is received in body unto justice." Luther teaches likewise in the *Bab. Capt.*, on Baptism, as well as in the *Assert.* of art. 1.

I respond: a) Scripture does not say the just man lives by faith *alone*, hence it's place is left for the Sacraments. Otherwise, not only the Sacraments, but even God, the merit of Christ, and other things would be excluded, which, the Lutherans themselves do not mean to be excluded; Scripture does not say the just man lives by God or by the merit of Christ.

b) Even if Scripture does not say in these words that the just man lives by the Sacraments, nevertheless, it says the same thing in other words. When it says a man is regenerated through Baptism (John 3:5, Tit. 3:5), what else does it say except Baptism gives life?

c) Those words of the Prophet, "The just man lives by faith," do not literally signify a man becomes just or is reputed so by faith, as the Lutherans would have it. Rather, they signify the just man, from the faith which he has, constantly awaits what God promised, and he does not become despondent, or give up, even if the promises seem to be delayed. Anyone who spends time on that passage of Habakkuk, as well as that of Paul to the Hebrews, will not doubt this is the true sense, and both passages treat on patience and longanimity. "If he delays," the Prophet says, and the Apostle from him, "wait for him, because coming he will come, and not tarry. Behold, the unbelieving man, his soul will not be right in himself, but the just shall live by faith." To the confirmation, I respond in the same manner: Paul attributed justification to faith, but not to faith *alone*. Besides, Scripture attributes the same thing in other passages to the Sacrament, as in Acts 2:38, "Be baptized, every one of you in the name of Jesus Christ in remission for sins," and in Acts 22:16, "Be baptized and wash your sins by the invocation of his name."

2) The *second* argument is from Mark 16:16, "He that will believe and be baptized will be saved, but he that will not believe will be condemned." Luther (*loc. cit.*), in his first argument, draws the conclusion from this testimony in two ways. *Firstly*: He that believes and is baptized has been saved, but who does not believe is damned, even if he were baptized; therefore, not Baptism, but faith saves. Secondly, the Lord speaks in this way, "he that will not believe will be condemned." He does not say the man who was not baptized will be condemned; therefore, faith alone saves, not Baptism.

I respond: a) The consequent is bad. The only thing that can be gathered from that antecedent is that Baptism alone does not save, but not, "therefore Baptism does not save." Otherwise, from the fact that Paul says in 1 Cor. 13:1 (*et seqq.*) that faith is of no benefit without charity, we could gather, therefore faith is of no benefit. *b)* I say to the *second*, the Lord did not say that he that will not be baptized will be condemned; not because this is not very true, seeing that the same Lord said, "Unless a man be reborn of water and the Holy Spirit, he cannot enter into the kingdom of God" (John 3:5), but because it was not necessary to say this since it would be understood per se from the fact that he said, "He that will not believe will be condemned." Who does not believe, consequently, does not wish to be baptized, and even if he would, it would be of no benefit to him. Now in the affirmation, it behooves us to add Baptism to faith, because not everyone who believes is baptized. There are similar arguments from the general to the specific. Negatively: it is not an animal, therefore not a man, is a valid statement. Affirmatively: It is an animal, therefore it is a man, is an invalid statement.

3) The *third* argument is taken from Paul in Rom. 4:10. Melanchthon (*Apol.* Art. 13) says from this that "Paul protests" (namely against the scholastics, teaching the Sacraments justify *ex opere operato*), and denies Abraham was justified by Circumcision, but says circumcision is a sign put forward to arouse our faith. Therefore, in the same manner, the Christian Sacraments do not justify, except by arousing faith.

I respond: a) Paul does not say Circumcision was a sign put forward to arouse faith; rather, it was given to Abraham, *as a sign of the justice of faith*, i.e., this privilege was conceded to Abraham, that he would be the first to have the Sacrament of Circumcision, because his obedience and faith merited it. This was, however, a testimony of the justice of his faith, as we adverted in chapter 17 of the last book. Therefore, this passage does not bear on the matter, for Circumcision was a sign of the justice of faith for Abraham alone, and for him it was not a sign arousing faith, but a testimony of the faith *that he already had*.

b) Secondly, the notion of Circumcision and Baptism are not the same. In regard to Circumcision, Paul says, "Circumcision is nothing" (1 Cor.

Chapter IX: Objections from Reason Answered 193

7:19). On Baptism, however, he says, "The laver of regeneration has saved you" (Tit. 3:5). We will say more on this later.

4) The *fourth* argument is of Zwingli (*On True and False Religion*), who advances Luke 5:21: *Who can forgive sins except God alone?* Then he says, "The Pharisees understood only God, but not the Sacraments, can justify, according to that of Isaiah 43:25, 'I am he who blots out iniquities.'"

I respond: The blindness of the heretics is truly wondrous; they would rather prefer to believe the Pharisees than Christ! If the Pharisees said, "Who can forgive sins except God alone?" in the same place Christ cured the paralytic to show he, *as a man*, can forgive sins. "That you would know, that the Son of man has the power on earth to forgive sins. Then he said to the paralytic, take up your matt, etc." Besides, didn't Christ say to men in John 20:23, "Whose sins you forgive are forgiven them"? Nevertheless, the words of Isaiah are not false for that reason. He speaks on one who forgives sins by *his own authority*, which, without a doubt, is God alone.

5) The *fifth* argument is of Chemnitz, from Ephesians 5:26, where the Apostle says, "Cleansing it with the laver of water in the word of life." There, Paul attributes the whole force of Baptism to the word. But the word works by exciting faith, for "faith from hearing, but hearing from the word of Christ" (Rom. 10:17). Chemnitz also adds the verse of 1 Pet. 3:21, "Baptism has saved you, not the laying aside of the flesh, but the examination of a good conscience in God through the resurrection of Jesus Christ." There, Baptism is said to save through the resurrection, i.e., through faith in the resurrection.

I respond: In Ephes. 5:26, by "word of life," a sermon is not understood, whose effect is faith, rather *the form of the Sacrament*, i.e., the consecratory and practical word, not one in the form of a sermon; all the interpreters explain it in this way, as we showed above on the question on the form of the Sacrament. Hence, St. Peter does not say Baptism saves by faith in the resurrection, but *through the resurrection*, i.e., as Bede explains on this passage, because when we are baptized, we represent the resurrection of Christ by emerging from water, and because Baptism causes us to waLk. in the newness of life by justifying us, in the way Christ, through the resurrection, began to live a new life, just as Paul says in Rom. 6:9. A similar phrase is in Romans 4:25, where Paul says, "Christ was betrayed on account of our sins, and he rose again for the sake of our justification." That is the same thing as if one were to say that by the passion of Christ we die to sin, by the resurrection of Christ we begin to live in the life of justice; where, without a doubt, the preposition *by* does not signify a meritorious cause, but an *exemplary* cause, for Christ did not merit by rising again, since he was outside of the means and state to merit.

CHAPTER X

Objections Taken from the Fathers Are Answered

FIRSTLY, they object from Augustine, who says not the Sacrament, but the faith of the Sacrament justifies. Martin Luther cites this teaching without the name of Augustine, as a common proverb (*Babyl. Capt.*, on Baptism), and in his assertion of the articles, art. 1. Yet, in his book against Cochlaeus, he cites Augustine by name. Melanchthon also does that in the *Apologia*, art. 13, where after he had said that no letter could be produced from the Fathers on behalf of the teaching of the Scholastics, he added, "Nay more, Augustine says the contrary, that faith of the Sacrament, not the Sacrament justifies."

I respond: Augustine says nothing of the sort in clear words, but rather the contrary. In *Epist.* 23 *ad Bonifacium*, Augustine says children are faithful and are saved if they die after Baptism because, even though they do not have faith nevertheless, they have the Sacrament of faith. This is the same thing as if one were to say faith does not save children, rather, the Sacrament of faith. Perhaps Luther gathers that opinion from *Tract. in Joan.* 80, where Augustine says the heart is cleansed by the water of Baptism, by the agency of the word, not because it is said, but because it is believed. Now, we have already shown in the question on the form of the Sacrament that "because it is believed" does not mean the act of faith, but *the object*. Nevertheless, if that opinion were found clearly expressed in some place, without a doubt it would need to be explained for that time alone in which someone cannot have the Sacrament; in a necessity of this sort the faith of the Sacrament suffices with the desire of it, as Augustine says (*de Baptismo* 4, 22), just as on the other hand, in infants who cannot have actual faith, the Sacrament of faith suffices, just as we have already shown from *Epistle* 23.

Secondly, they advance the words of Augustine from *Question on the Old and New Testament*, qu. 59, "A man that supposes Baptism consists in carnal reason, this is not spiritual; nor will he be able to obtain a heavenly gift who believes he is transformed by water, not by faith."

I respond: firstly, the book cited is not of Augustine, but of some heretic who teaches many things against faith, as well as against Augustine, such as in qu. 21 that a woman was not created in God's image, and in quest. 109, that Melchisedech was the Holy Spirit, and in q. 123, that Adam did not have the Holy Spirit.

Secondly I say, the testimony that has been brought forward is not

Chapter X: Objections from the Fathers Answered

against us, but on our side. This author speaks about the *formal* cause of justification, not on the efficient cause, and he says a man is changed and renewed not by the outward washing, as if our Baptism were nothing other than cleansing the flesh, as the Baptism of the Jews was, but through faith, which, when it is completed and living, formally cleanses and justifies, according to that of Peter in Acts 15:9, "Purifying their hearts by faith." This faith (i.e., formal justification) however, this author says is given in Baptism, "water is discerned, but the one that is not seen, the Spirit, works that faith be in it." There, he cannot speak on imperfect and inchoate faith, which, according to us, disposes to justification and which, according to the Lutherans, apprehends justification, for that should precede Baptism. Therefore, he speaks on perfect faith, which is infused in Baptism and which formally justifies. The Council of Trent defines the same thing in sess. 6, ch. 7.

Thirdly, Calvin (*Instit.* 4, 14) advances another passage of St. Augustine from *Quest. in Levit.* 3, q. 84, where Augustine says two things: *a)* The minister, as a man only offers the visible Sacrament while God offers invisible grace; and *b)* these two are so separated, that in certain things the Sacrament is sensible without invisible grace, as in Simon Magus when he was baptized by Philip, and in certain things invisible grace without the Sacrament, such as in the good thief.

I respond: To the first, a man administers the Sacraments in two ways. In *one* way, by doing what he can from his own natural power. In the *second* way, by applying the Sacraments as instruments moved by God and elevated to perform a supernatural action. In the first way, we truly say that a man does not justify, but only washes the body, or something of this sort; Augustine speaks in this manner. In the second way, we truly say a man justifies, but not by any other action than that which God himself uses to justify. Moreover, in regard to this manner of explanation, St. Jerome, commenting on Isaiah 4 says, "A man offers water, but God the Holy Spirit." I say to the *second*, it can be separated, not because the sensible Sacrament is not the cause of invisible grace, but its effect can be impeded by an obstacle or the indisposition of the subject, and because God can give his grace even without the Sacrament.

Fourthly, they usually advance another citation from Augustine (*de Trin.* 15, 26) where he says that only God can give the Holy Spirit, and therefore the Apostles did not give the Holy Spirit to men upon whom they imposed their hands, rather they prayed and he descended.

I respond: The gifts of the Holy Spirit are one thing, and the Holy Spirit himself is another. The gifts of the Holy Spirit give the Sacraments; no one can properly give the Holy Spirit himself except the one from whom he proceeds. It could also be said that the Holy Spirit cannot be given *by one's own authority*, but by God, from whom he proceeds. Nevertheless, he is given to men *instrumentally*. In Acts 8:17, we read that the Holy Spirit was given by the hands of the Apostles, which Augustine affirms (*ibid.*).

Fifthly, they advance these words from Augustine (*Contra Faustum* 19, 16), "What are the corporeal Sacraments, except certain visible words?" Hence, he supposes it is gathered that the Sacraments do not justify except in the fashion of a sermon, or a picture, which only acts by representing.

I respond: In that passage, Augustine assigns one effect, or signification, of the Sacrament, but not on that account does he deny the rest, which he often posited elsewhere. This is why in that place it is only a question on the signification. The reason was that he was disputing on the Sacraments in general, i.e., on the Sacraments of both Testaments; hence, he was obliged to posit the effect common to all the Sacraments. The reason why, however, he called the Sacraments visible words, is that he was disputing against the Manicheans, who found fault with the change of the old Sacraments into the new, and said necessarily the words were changed after the arrival of Christ; for when the ancients said "Christ will come, die and rise," we should say "He came, he died, and he rose." Thence, Augustine gathers, even the Sacraments needed to be changed, lest they would signify something false. Moreover, to demonstrate the most suitable similitude, he said, "What are the Sacraments (namely in regard to the signification) except visible words?"

Sixthly, Chemnitz advances another citation of Augustine (*City of God* 21, 25), where Augustine rebukes those who think that because they receive the Sacraments of Baptism and the Lord's Supper, they cannot be damned, even if they do not preserve faith or a good life. They seem to have altogether felt the Sacraments justify *ex opere operato*, so that they were justified by its force, not faith.

I respond: Augustine rightly rebukes them, not only because they believed the Sacraments justify *ex opere operato*, but they believed they could not lose grace and salvation once it was acquired in the Sacrament by any sins they committed later. Such an opinion is not ours, but rather Martin Luther's, who said, "You see how rich a Christian and baptized man is, who even willing, cannot lose his salvation no matter how many sins he commits, unless he refuses to believe?" (*On the Babylonian Capt.*, on Baptism).

Seventhly, it is customarily objected that Bernard says, "Just as a canonist is bestowed with a book, an Abbot with a staff, a Bishop with a ring, so divisions of grace are handed down in different Sacraments." (*Serm. de Coena Domini*).

I respond: Bernard does not compare the Sacraments with a book, staff, and ring by the notion of efficiency, but only by the notion *of the diversity of the Sacraments*. Otherwise, he teaches in the same sermon that the Sacraments confer grace, as we cited above.

Lastly, they advance Tertullian (*de Poenitentia*), who calls Baptism the seal of faith; Basil speaks the same way *In Eunom.*, and *On the Holy Spirit*,

Chapter X: Objections from the Fathers Answered

c. 12.

But we responded to these in book 1, ch. 17, where we showed that Baptism is called the seal of faith, not because it arouses faith, but because through Baptism it is witnessed that the man who is baptized believes, and also that the Church in baptizing gives him a public witness of his faith. Nevertheless, the Fathers truly attribute this to baptism, but they do not deny it also has more excellent effects, nay more, they also assert them, as I showed above.

CHAPTER XI

The Objections Taken from Reason Are Answered

1) THE *first* argument is of Luther (*Babyl. Capt.*, on Baptism) and Melanchthon (*Apol.* Art. 13), as well as others. In every Sacrament the word of the promise is required; where the promise is, there faith which receives the promise is necessarily demanded. Therefore, it is faith which immediately operates and justifies. Luther confirms it, because many are saved by faith without the Sacrament, such as those who do not have a means whereby they may be baptized, and vice versa, those who have the Sacrament without faith are damned. Therefore, it is the faith in the Sacrament which justifies, not the Sacrament.

I respond: This argument, which is still very common amongst our adversaries, errs in three ways. *a) First*, the word of the promise is indeed required in the institution of the Sacrament, but it is not required in the very *use* of the sacrament; that much is clear. Men who baptize do not say, "He that believes and is baptized will be saved," which is the promise. Rather, they say, "I baptize you in the name of the Father, etc." Those who consecrate the Eucharist do not say, "He who eats this bread will live forever." Rather, "This is my body." And they that absolve do not say, "Whose sins you forgive," but, "I absolve you." Hence, here we are arguing about the *use* of the Sacrament, not the institution. We do argue on the effect of the Sacrament, but the Sacrament operates while we use it. This is why the argument is not to the point, and what it assumes is false. *b) Secondly*, even if the promise, and consequently faith, were always required in the use, it could not be concluded for this reason that it is faith which immediately justifies. Let us say that faith is required as a *condition* to apply the Sacrament to a man. It would be like a physician that offers a remedy and promises health; the sick man is required to have that faith which receives that promise in earnest and assents to the physician. Nevertheless, it is not that faith which heals the sick man, but the remedy, although without faith he would not receive it; so also, etc. *c) Thirdly*, even if the promise and faith were also required in the Sacrament to justify, still, one could not conclude from this what they conclude, that faith alone acts, but the Sacrament effects nothing. Rather, one would have to conclude that each is necessary, and one without the other does not suffice.

I respond to the confirmation: faith and the Sacrament [of Baptism] can seem equal in this matter. Just as in a case of necessity someone can be saved without the Sacrament *in re*, provided he would have a desire

Chapter XI: Objections from Reason are Answered 199

for it as well as faith and penance. Vice versa, children are saved without actual faith through the Sacrament alone, just as in adults, while a man that has the Sacrament and does not want to believe is condemned, so also, a man who has faith, and does not want to receive the Sacrament is damned. Whereby, we understand that each is required when it can be had, and each justifies, but in a different way. The Sacrament actively justifies as an instrument of God; faith and penance justify, as dispositions and, according to some, as meritorious causes *de congruo*. Now, the grace is not the same (as we said above) which is given by the force of the Sacrament, and that which is given without the Sacrament on account of a disposition, or merit of faith and penance *de congruo*.

2) The *second* argument is of Zwingli (*De Vera et Falsa religione*, c. de Sacramentis). God alone knows the hearts of men; therefore, he alone can cleanse them. As a result, the Sacraments do not justify. It is confirmed, because if the Sacraments would justify *ex opere operato*, God would be obligated by the Sacraments, and naturally, he could not cause a man not to be justified if he received the Sacrament.

I respond: The argument proves the Sacraments are not principal causes; it does not, however, prove they are not instrumental causes. It is not necessary for the Sacrament to know the heart and conscience; rather, it is enough if *God* knows, who works through the Sacraments.

I say in regard to the confirmation, God is not bound to the Sacraments, but vice versa, the Sacraments are bound to God. God can justify without the Sacraments, but the Sacraments cannot justify without God. The fact, however, that God cannot take justification away from one who faithfully receives the Sacraments is not, therefore, because God is bound to the Sacraments, but because he is bound (if one may speak this way) *to his truth*; so he cannot be unfaithful to his own promise. Furthermore, all these arguments, if they would conclude the matter, would also conclude that men cannot be justified by Christ's blood or by faith in Christ; the blood of Christ does not scrutinize hearts nor penetrate the soul more than the Sacraments. Just as it seems absurd to our adversaries that God is bound in some way to the Sacraments, so it should seem absurd for the blood of Christ to be bound to our faith. Nevertheless, our adversaries teach nothing more often than we are justified by the blood of Christ, and faith in it.

3) The *third* argument is of Calvin (*Instit.* 4, 14, §14). Those who say the Sacraments justify, drag men away from God and see to it that in a spectacle they embrace a corporeal thing, not God himself.

I respond: a) If the argument had any validity, it would prove that in the Old Testament, God should not have put forward the bronze serpent, since when men looked upon it, they were healed. Nay more, God should not have become incarnate, lest men would embrace a corporeal thing in a spectacle.

b) Secondly, I answer that the contrary follows from our doctrine. When we say the Sacraments do not have power of themselves, but it is God who works through them, in this very thing we draw men to God. It is in the same way in which the men who were cured by Christ, either by the touch of the fringe of his garment or even by spit and mud, did not embrace the fringe, spit, and mud, but acknowledged and praised the power of Christ.

4) The *fourth* argument is of Chemnitz (*Exam.* 2 part., ch. On the Efficacy of the Sacrament). The word of God and the Sacraments justify in the same way, but the word only justifies by arousing faith; therefore, the Sacraments only justify by arousing faith. He proves the major proposition firstly, because just as Scripture says the Sacraments justify, so also it says the word justifies, as in Romans 1:16, "The Gospel is the power of God in the salvation of every believer." Secondly, he proves it because in justification through the Sacraments two things come together like hands. One is of God offering grace, the other is of man receiving it. The hand of God is the word and the Sacraments; the hand of man is faith. Thus, neither the word nor the Sacrament benefit anything, unless they are received in faith, and if anything is beneficial, it is so because it is received in faith. "The word of hearing did not profit them, not being mixed with faith of what they heard."

I respond: It is false that the word and the Sacrament justify in the same way; nay more, as we said above, they justify in such a different way, that one, i.e., the word, precedes faith and the other, i.e., the Sacrament, follows faith.

Now I answer the first proof. *a)* By the Gospel, in that place a sermon is not understood, rather *the mysteries* of the Gospel themselves, such as the incarnation, the passion, the Sacraments, etc. *b) Secondly*, if the Gospel were received for a sermon, I say in the same place it is explained how the Gospel saves, for the Apostle adds that "the Justice of God is revealed in it from faith in faith." Now, no Scripture explains the manner of salvation of the Sacraments. *c) Thirdly*, I say, Scripture attributes to both the word and the Sacrament the force of testifying, but never says they justify *in the same way;* nor are we allowed immediately to gather from the fact that we read the word and the Sacrament justify, that they justify *in the same way;* otherwise, we would also be allowed to conclude that the word justifies in the same way in which God, or faith, or the passion of Christ justify. All of these are said to justify in the Scriptures, and still, Chemnitz would not admit that these justify in the same way.

I respond to the *second proof:* The word and the Sacraments can be called the hand of God, through which grace and justice come to us, but not in the same manner. A hand can have many duties, both to extend something and also to work. Hence, the word can be called a hand because *it offers salvation*, but not because it really does or applies it. On the other hand, the Sacrament may be called a hand because it really applies the merit of Christ and works grace. The difference of which is an evident sign that the

Chapter XI: Objections from Reason are Answered   201

word is not preached except to those understanding it, nor is it profitable unless it is understood and believed. On the contrary, the Sacrament is produced, and is beneficial even for those who do not understand it, such as infants and the mentally disabled. For equal reasoning, faith can be called our hand, not as Chemnitz would have it, that it apprehends the promise, and that very thing alone justifies in this way; rather, because *it removes obstacles and disposes the soul*, where such a disposition necessarily resides. Otherwise, not only would Baptism not be profitable to infants or the mentally disabled, but not even adults and the sane, if in the very moment of Baptism they were distracted in their attention, for then faith does not apprehend the promises.

5) The *last* argument is of Zwingli: It cannot happen that the Sacraments, which are lowly and material things, would penetrate to the soul; therefore, they do not cleanse the filth of sin, which resides in the soul.

Zwingli confirms this argument *firstly*: If the Sacraments could work in any manner in the soul, it should happen by the action which they have in the body, as Augustine says about water, which touches the body and washes it; but often the Sacraments do not even touch the body itself. When a man is absolved, it is not necessary for the Sacrament of Penance that the sound of words or the hand of the priest reach him. For equal reasoning, Matrimony can be done by nods alone, or even between those who are absent from each other. Next, it is not necessary that the words of consecration really reach the bread to consecrate it, for these words can be said so silently, and in such a distance, that the moving air does not arrive on the bread. Then in Baptism itself, the same thing can be proven, for the power should be in the words.

Secondly: Justification is a more noble and difficult work than the creation of the world, as Augustine teaches (*Tract. in Joan.*, 82), and it is clear because in justification the creation of grace is found, which is a certain divine and supernatural thing; but no creature can be an instrument of creation, as St. Thomas teaches (I, q. 45, art. 45).

Thirdly: Zwingli says that justification takes place in an instant; the Sacraments cannot work in an instant, therefore they cannot justify. The minor is proven. For some cause cannot work except when it exists; but the Sacramental action, since it is successive, cannot exist in an infant. To explain it further, successive things do not exist except while they come into being, for they consist in a certain flux. This is why there is no instant one can assign in which a successive thing would exist, or even any part of it; rather, there is only an instant one can assign in which a certain indivisible copulation of a successive thing. Such a copulation is not a successive thing, nor part of it for the successive things essentially require a certain extension. Therefore, it cannot be understood that a successive thing acts, except successively, and hence in time, when there is no instant where that very thing exists, and cannot do it because it does not exist, or certainly when it does not exist.

Fourthly: There is either some divinely superadded power in the Sacraments, or there is not. If there is not, therefore, they cannot achieve a supernatural effect, for it is unintelligible that something would altogether remain just as it was before and receives nothing, and still cannot do what it could not before. If it is, then it is either a corporeal power or a spiritual one. If corporeal, it will not be able to effect a spiritual thing, nor act in a spiritual thing, hence it is of no benefit. This is because the superadded power is required, because the Sacrament cannot act in the soul, which is a spirit, nor can it produce grace, which is spiritual. If, however, it is a spiritual power, then it cannot be in a corporeal Sacrament, for it is not a spiritual accident and indivisible in a corporeal subject, and by extension, cannot be received; for everything which is received, is received by the mode of the recipient.

Besides, *fifthly:* That sort of power would either be whole in any part of the Sacrament you like, or part of it in one part of the Sacrament and part in another. Not the first, because then it would follow that it does not depend upon a subject in existence, nor would it properly adhere. This is why it would be a substance, not an accident. Likewise, when any word you like has been brought forth, the effect would immediately be produced, which no man concedes. Also, not the second, because then it would be corporeal, and besides, when the first word is brought forth part of the power would immediately perish, and when the second, the other part would perish. Thus, that power, whether whole or in a greater part would perish, before the effect would begin to be produced. This is why that power in the parts of the Sacrament preceding the effect was redundant.

Sixthly: Either that power is only in the words, or only in the element, or in both. If only in the words, how does the Eucharist justify when it is consumed? If only in the elements, how do the words of consecration of the Eucharist operate? If in both, either the power will be the same, and this cannot be, since one accident cannot be in two subjects, or there will be two powers, and then there will be two powers in the Sacrament, which seems absurd. If you say that they will be two partial powers, then conversely, because then they would have to cooperate at the same time with the work. Yet, sometimes it happens that one part of the Sacrament is applied a long time after another, as when a man confesses today, and will be absolved tomorrow.

Lastly, it is beyond comprehension (as Chemnitz says), why this power would exist when it arrives, when it would cease to exist, etc.

***

We can answer these arguments in three ways. *Firstly*, it could be, if someone meant to confess ignorance in regard to knots of this sort and still satisfy the heretics, nay more, even block up their mouths. We are indeed held to render an account of that, hope which is in us (1 Pet. 3:15), but we

Chapter XI: Objections from Reason are Answered

are held to do so from the beginnings *of faith*, not from Metaphysics. St. Augustine (*On the Merits and Remission of Sins* 3, 4), when speaking on arguments against the manner of treating original sin, says, "I, even if I may not avail to answer arguments of this kind, I still see that we must adhere to the Scripture, etc." In *Epistle* 29 *to Jerome*, he says that he, if asked how the sin of Adam is propagated to his posterity, customarily answers, "I confess that I do not know this, as many other things." Nevertheless, not for that reason did there lack a defense of faith, rather he very keenly defended it, showing that it must be believed that original sin is propagated to Adam's posterity, although we do not know how it happens, because Scripture and tradition teach it, as well as the custom of the Church.

Secondly, someone could answer that the Sacraments are true causes of justification, but *moral*, not physical, in the way that the true cause of a homicide is that someone commanded it to be done, although he did not touch the man that was killed. Now, this response can be defended, save for faith, which they uphold from more recent authors such as Ledesma (4 dist. 1 q. 3 art. 1) and Melchior Cano (*Relectione de Sacramentis*). Many of the old Scholastics seem to have felt the same way, such as Bonaventure, Scotus, Durandus, Richard, Ockham, Marsilius, Gabriel in their commentaries on 4 dist. 1 or 2, who teach the Sacraments truly justify, and nevertheless hold only God produces grace in regard to the presence of the Sacraments, so that they are not physical causes except those things without which the effect could not come about. Just the same, I think it by far the more probable and safer opinion, which gives true efficacy to the Sacraments. This is because the Fathers teach (*passim*) that the Sacraments do not act unless they first receive power, or blessing, or sanctification from God, and they relate the effect of the Sacrament to the omnipotence of God, as well as compare it with the true efficient causes, as we saw above. *b*) Next, because there would be no difference between the mode of action of the Sacraments and magical signs. *c*) Then, because then man would not be a minister of God in the very Sacramental action, rather a man would offer a sign by his action, and God by another action, who would infuse grace after that sign was seen, as when one shows a bill to a merchant, and he gives money. Now, the Scriptures teach that God is the one who baptizes through man, as we showed above.

Thirdly, we can answer with St. Thomas (III q. 62, art. 4) that the Sacraments are the efficient causes, not only physical, but also *instrumental*; the divinely endowed power, however, is not some new spiritual or corporeal quality adhering in them, rather, it is only the *motion*, or *use* of God. By this fact, God uses this Sacramental action to produce grace, elevates it, and causes it to touch a supernatural effect, which it could not attain if it were moved by anyone else.

To understand this matter, we must note four things.

1) There is a great difference between the instruments which God uses,

and those which men use. In fact, there are five differences. *a)* The *first* is that man needs a twofold application: one in which he applies himself to the instrument, such as taking up an axe in his hand; the second, whereby he applies the instrument to the work. The former motion is in the man himself, the second is in the instrument. God, however, does not need the first application; he is immutable and absolutely present to all things, hence he has already been applied. This is why that motion, whereby God moves the Sacraments, is the mere application of the Sacrament to a work, and it is in the Sacrament itself, not in God.

b) The *second* difference is that man needs an instrument naturally suited to that work. A man could not cut wood with iron, unless that iron were also sharpened. God does not need that sort of suitability for an instrument; he is not helped by an instrument, since he could do everything by himself, rather, he uses an instrument because he is pleased to do so, or to honor a creature, or certainly, to show his power in it, just as if someone meant on purpose to write with a pen that was hardly suitable. From which it follows that it is not necessary to place some inherent quality in the Sacraments which formally completes it, rather, it is enough if God means to use a Sacrament; he does not need a suitable instrument.

c) The *third* difference is that when a man uses an instrument, it is necessary that, apart from the motion of man himself whereby the instrument is moved, the instrument itself also fits the task which is proper to it by its own natural power. For example, when a carpenter uses an axe to make a chair, it is not enough for him to move the axe skillfully, rather, it is also necessary that the axe would cut; and when nature uses heat for nutrition, it is required that the heat warms what is proper to it, by the medium of that action, nature uses heat to convert food into flesh. Now, when God uses some instrument, it is not necessary that the instrument do something by its own power in the subject; if perhaps it acts, that operation is not the cause of divine effect, as a type of operation, but only *as the thing* which God means to apply to do this. Hence, we see in the use of many Sacraments that no proper and natural action is found for them, as is clear from Absolution, Matrimony, and the consecration of the Eucharist. In others, a proper action is found, such as washing or anointing, but as I said, that insofar as it is a natural action, it is not a cause, rather, it is *like a certain thing*. From which it follows, as a motion, or use of God in the Sacraments, it is not only a power of agency impressed in the instrument, but it is the whole power, and notion whereby they act. So that which is the sharpness and force of the agent impressed in the axe, that whole is only the motion of God in the Sacraments.

d) The *fourth* difference follows from these two, that a man cannot use anything for an instrument of his work; but God can and really does use very different things to produce the same thing.

e) The *fifth* difference follows from the preceding differences, that a

Chapter XI: Objections from Reason are Answered

man cannot use an instrument unless it touches the thing in which the effect is going to be produced, since the instrument should work in regard to its proper subject and corporeal action; but the corporeal action is not without contact. On the other hand, God can always, through something which is in one place, act on another thing that is very remote from the place, seeing that he does not need the proper operation of that thing.

2) *Secondly*, we must remark, everyone concedes that God can use any instrument, no matter how inept, provided first he would make those instruments suitable. Yet certainly, it is not necessary that he do so rather, God can effect whatever he wants by an inept instrument while it remains inept in the way the best scribe can so skillfully use an unsuitable pen, that through it he will form the letters beautifully. We have an example in John 5:4, where after the Angel went down and moved the water, by that water being so moved all sickness was cured. Moreover, this was a figure of Baptism, as we taught above. This is why the Fathers, imitating this manner of speech, often say the Sacraments do not act unless the Holy Spirit first would come down into them. (See Tertullian, *de Baptismo*; Ambrose *de Spiritu Sancto* 1, 7; Chrysostom on *John* 5; and on the same passage, Theophylactus, and Theophilus of Alexandria *Paschali*, 1). For equal reasoning, when God willed to convert the world through the preaching of the Gospel, he could choose eloquent men, or certainly render unlearned men the most eloquent for this task. Yet, he did not wish to use this means, but chose unlearned men, and those who spoke simply, impolitely, and lacking all style, and through them, converted the world.

3) *Thirdly*, we must remark that the sacramental power is sometimes in the element, sometimes in the word, and sometimes in both, for, the sacramental action is properly the action of the minister giving the Sacrament, not the action of the recipient. The reception is our work, but the Sacrament is not our work, rather God's. As a result, the action of the minister is that which God uses as an instrument to justify. So, when the minister uses things and words, as in Baptism, Confirmation, and Extreme Unction, then God also uses things and words, and hence, the power of God is in both. These two must come together, otherwise nothing would happen. Still, when the minister does not use anything but words, the matter of the Sacrament is not present on the side of the recipient, or certainly, would not be applied by the minister to act; then the power is not present except in words. So, it is in the Sacrament of Absolution and Matrimony, and in the consecration of the Eucharist; for the minister does not apply the sins of the penitent to absolve him, nor bread to consecrate something, but words to consecrate the bread. Hence, it is not repugnant to the Sacrament of Penance that on one day the penitent would confess his sins, and on the next day he would be absolved; the operative power is not in the sins, but in the absolution alone. Nevertheless, in the consecration of the Eucharist the presence of bread is required, not because the operative

power is in the bread, but because, unless the bread were present, it would not be the matter in which the Sacrament acts. In absolution, even if there is no confession in the present, because it has already been made, nevertheless the man is, upon whom Absolution falls. Lastly, sometimes the minister uses the element alone, as when he extends the Eucharist, and then the power is in the element alone.

4) *Fourthly*, we must remark that justifying grace is not properly created, nor is it produced from the natural power of the soul, rather, it is produced from the obediential potency,[14] or natural capacity. Hence, St. Thomas does not oppose himself when he says that no creature can instrumentally be suited for creation, and nevertheless, the Sacraments are suited for the production of grace in the soul. I explain: A thing is properly said to be created which is made independently from the subject; conversely, something is said to be produced which depends upon its subject, is made in it, exists in it, and operates in it. Therefore, the rational soul is truly created, although it is made in the body, because it does not necessarily depend upon the body. This is clearly because when separated it can operate, and first subsists in itself by nature before it is infused in the body. Yet, grace is a certain spiritual quality, which depends in every way on the subject, as is clear: this is why it is produced. Now, it is not produced from a natural potency, because there is no such potency in man. Otherwise grace would be a natural thing; where there is a natural potency, there is a natural act. Nor is it opposed, that grace cannot be made except by God, for even the soul cannot be created except by God, and nevertheless, it is a natural thing, because matter is in the natural potency to the soul. Therefore, grace does not give man a natural being, but a supernatural being. Nevertheless, there is a natural capacity in man for grace; naturally, it is fitting for a man to be able to receive grace, as Augustine teaches (*de Praedesinatione Sanctorum*, 5), and that capacity can be called an obediential potency (as then it would be a natural potency) nevertheless, it is such a thing, that it can become whatever God wills, and this is called an obediential potency.

Nor is the production of grace from the obediential potency opposed to the fact that the theologians, as well as the Council of Trent (sess. 6, cap. 7) say grace is infused, for the infusion is opposed to *acquisition*, not production. So, infused knowledge is distinguished from acquired, not because they are both produced from the potency of the intellect, but because one is acquired by one's own labor, the other is given by God alone without labor. If knowledge of natural things is rightly said to be infused, such as what God gave to Adam and Solomon without their having labored for it, although it was produced from the natural potency, how much more rightly will grace be said to be infused, which is not given by God alone, and does not correspond to that natural potency?

---

14 Translator's note: The *potentia obedientialis* means that which is actualized solely through obedience to the creator.

Chapter XI: Objections from Reason are Answered

From these, I respond to Zwingli's argument by denying the consequent. A corporeal and lowly thing can act in the soul, not by its own nature, rather *by the power of God.* Augustine (*Tract. in Joan.* 80) did not fear to say, "Water touches the body, and washes the heart." A true and corporeal fire both restrains and tortures the demons; nay more, we also experience affection in our soul from the emotions of the body in a wonderful manner, even though our souls are spirits. How do these bodies of ours retain souls, as in a prison? The soul cannot depart from the body when it wills, and still, the body is a body, and the soul a spirit.

I have already answered the *first confirmation*, it does not need contact, which does not act through its own proper and natural action.

To the *second confirmation*, I say *a)* that citation of Augustine does not bear on the matter. When Augustine says it is better to justify the impious than to create heaven and earth, he did not mean it is more difficult to infuse the habit of grace in the soul than to create heaven; rather, he meant to say (as he explains himself in the same place) that it is a work *of greater mercy* to justify the impious than to create heaven, and it is also more *noble*, because heaven and earth will pass away, but the salvation of the elect will not. Moreover, in the same place, he says the faithful cooperate with God in their justification, hence, the faithful have claim to a greater work than it was to create heaven and earth. *b)* It is not impossible for a creature to be suited, as a mere instrument of God, to a true creation. St. Thomas, however (*loc. cit.*), denies it in regard to a creature, which would be suited by disposing the subject through a proper action. *c) Thirdly*, I have already shown that grace is not properly created.

To the *third confirmation*, it can be said that the last intrinsic is not given successively in any way, and therefore, justification takes place in the last *sensible* part, not in the last *simpliciter*, which is nothing. Or, it must be said that justification takes place in that instant, in which the Sacramental action is finished. Although the action would cease negatively, in regard to its parts, i.e., it does not exist by its first part, nevertheless, it ceases affirmatively, i.e., it exists by the last part of it, *inasmuch as to its terminus*. For, as in the line the last part cannot be assigned, nevertheless, the last point can be assigned, whereby the line is terminated, so, in time and motion. Now (they say), then it is not a Sacramental action. I respond, then it is the greatest, in the way in which a successive thing can exist. For the thing successively is never existing through its parts *in re*, but always has a certain indivisible thing, which is either a beginning, or an end, or continuative of a successive thing, and through it, it is said to exist; and then it is perfectly said to exist when that indivisible thing terminates the action. It is clear in time: it is not said to have been an hour except when it ends. The same thing is clear in prayer, which perfectly signifies when its *terminus* is advanced.

To the *fourth confirmation*, I have already said that power is corporeal, because it is the motion of a corporeal thing, although it can be called spiritual by reason of the cause and effect.

To the *fifth confirmation*, I say that power is partly in one part of the Sacrament, partly in another; hence little by little it perishes insofar as the parts of the Sacrament perish. Still, they were not redundant. That particle works in the power of all that preceded. Just as prayer also perfectly gives its signification when the last word is advanced, nevertheless, that still effects nothing unless other things would have preceded; the *terminus* of motion is acquired by the last that has been changed, which still could not anything, except that they preceded the rest.

To the *sixth confirmation*, I have already responded; at one point, the power is in the words, at another, in the element, or in both, etc.

To the *last confirmation*, I say, it seems a difficult matter to them, because they imagine a spiritual quality should be constituted in a corporeal thing, but they who suppose it is not a necessary quality of the same thing, do not suffer any difficulty in the matter.

CHAPTER XII

The Controversy on the Difference between the Sacraments of the Old Law and the New is Explained

THE next question follows on the effect of the Sacrament; whether to justify *ex opere operato* is proper to the Sacraments of the New Law, or is common with the Sacraments of the Old Law. There will be four parts of this question. We will explain *firstly*, the teaching of the heretics; *secondly*, the teaching of Catholics; *thirdly*, we will prove the truth; *fourthly*, we will answer objections.

In regard to *the first question*, all Catholics and heretics agree that there are at least six differences between the Sacraments of the New and Old Law. 1) *First*, that now there are other external rites than there were then, as is known. 2) That now there are fewer Sacraments than there were then. 3) That ours are easier, as is clear from Circumcision and Baptism, as well as others. 4) That ours are more noble, at least by the notion of the author, because ours were established and promulgated immediately by Christ, while the Mosaic, if they were not established by Moses, they were at least promulgated by him. 5) That the Old were figures of the New. 6) The former were given for a time, i.e., until the arrival of the Messiah; ours will endure as long as the world will endure. All of these are gathered from Augustine (*Epist.* 118 *ad Januarium*; *de Doct. Christ.* 3, 9; *Contra Faustum* 19, 13; on Ps. 73).

The question, however, is whether apart from these difficulties, there is a distinction in the principal effect, which is to justify from sin. The heretics of this time place almost no distinction, although they do not have sufficient agreement among themselves.

In the first place, the Anabaptists, as well as the followers of Carlstadt and Zwingli (as we showed above) attribute nothing to our Sacraments except to discern the faithful from the infidels, or that they are like a profession of fidelity, or to admonish us to good works. They are compelled to attribute more to the Sacraments of the Old Testament than the New. Circumcision, which always remains and can be discerned, better distinguishes a Jew from a non-Jew than Baptism, which is seen once and passes. By the same reasoning, Circumcision better admonishes fidelity and good works than Baptism, since it is permanent, more concentrated, and more sensible, etc.

Luther, however, who would have it that our Sacraments arouse faith, attributed the same thing to the Old Sacraments. This is why he speaks this way in his book *On the Babylonian Captivity*, c. On Baptism, "It is an error that the Sacraments of the New Law differ from the Sacraments of the Old Law, belonging to the efficacy of the signification, i.e., that ours efficaciously signify by doing what they prefigure, the old do not." He repeats the same thing in *Assert.* artic. 1.

It must be noted, however, that Luther distinguishes two kinds of the old signs, in *de Babylon. Capt.*, (c. On Baptism): He says they were certain things which had the word of the promise connected, and hence, demand faith, as the sign of the rainbow was given to Noah, the sign of the dew in the fleece of Gideon, the sign in the turning back of the sun given by Isaiah to king Hezekiah, and other things. Otherwise, he says these were true Sacraments and equal to ours in regard to efficacy. Now, he says there were others, which did not have the connected promise, such as all those legal ceremonies, whereby men made expiation, garments, temples, etc., and also, he says these were not properly Sacraments, and they were by far more inferior to our Sacraments. This is why, in *Hom. 1 on Bapt.*, he seriously inveighs against the Anabaptists, who attributed no more to our Baptism than the washings of the Jews; as if he attributed much to Baptism, who did not regard the rainbow as equal to it. Hence, from this distinction, another error of Luther is gathered, or rather more a contradiction, that he did not want the Sacraments to be those things which were called Sacraments by all the ancients, such as Jewish washings, the Paschal Lamb, Sacrifices, and similar things, and vice versa, held as Sacraments things which nobody held or dreamed to be so, such as the rainbow, the fleece of Gideon, the shade of the hour-glass of Ahaz, and similar things.

Now Calvin agreed with Luther, that the Sacraments of the Old Law justify in the same way that ours do, namely by nourishing faith, "This dogma of the Scholastics, whereby so great a difference is made between the Sacraments of the Old and the New Law, that the former did nothing but foreshadow the grace of God, while the latter actually confer that it, must be altogether exploded" (*Instit.* 4, 14, §23). He holds similar things in the *Antidote*, (sess. 7 can. 2). Nevertheless, Calvin dissents from Luther in two things. *Firstly*, because he supposes the Sacraments of the New Law give grace more abundantly than the Old, because namely, they more clearly arouse faith, and hence greater faith justifies more. In the *Antidote* (*loc. cit.*) he says, "Still, we also do not deny that more abundant grace is secured under the reign of Christ." Luther, however, altogether equates the Sacraments of the Old and New. *Secondly*, Luther (as we showed) did not hold that all the Jewish ceremonies were Sacraments and equal to ours, but only those which have the connected promises. Calvin holds all those ceremonies as Sacraments, which give grace, although not as copiously as ours. In the *Instit.* (*ibid.*§21), he numbers the purifications of the Jews among the Sacraments, and again (*ibid.*, §26), he teaches the same thing more extensively. Although both err, what Calvin teaches is less absurd than Luther.

Chemnitz (*Exam. Conc. Trid.*) partly follows Luther and partly Calvin.

Chapter XII: Difference between Old and New Law

On pp. 60 and 70, he admits the distinction of Luther on the double kind of ancient signs; on p. 74, he admits, with Calvin, grace is more abundantly given in the Sacraments of the New than in the Old; while he agrees with both in condemning the doctrine of the Church. That is enough on the teaching of the heretics.

CHAPTER XIII

The Teachings of Catholics Are Explained

Now in regard to the *second* question, all Catholics agree that the Sacraments of the Old Law, which are properly called Mosaic, do not confer grace *ex opere operato*. All theologians teach this in their commentaries on 4 dist. 1, and the Council of Florence defined the same thing (*Instruct. Armen.*). The Council of Trent (sess. 7 can. 2) also taught this, albeit more briefly and obscurely, since it was not necessary owing to the fact that the matter was already defined.

Here we must note that these Councils did not define (as Chemnitz calumniates and lies in 2part. *Exam.*, pp. 58, and 59) that the ancient Fathers did not hold the grace of God from the merit of Christ, or held it without any organ, or medium, by applying the merits of Christ. The Councils say nothing of these, but merely assert this is the distinction between the Sacraments of the Old Law and the New, because ours *confer* grace, while the old only *signify* it.

The consequent, however, is not that the ancient Fathers did not have grace, or had it without an organ applying the merits of Christ. Even if they did not have it through the Sacraments, nevertheless, they had through faith, as even now adults through faith and true contrition are justified, before they really come to the Sacrament.

Even if Catholics agree among themselves on this principle, and disagree with the heretics of this time, still, there are also two questions among them. These are opinions on which I will speak briefly, since it is necessary, partly to explain the proposed controversy, partly to refute the calumnies of the heretics.

Therefore, one question is on the Sacraments of the Old Law, except for Circumcision, whether they would at least justify *ex opere operantis*. There are two opinions. The *first* is of Lombard (4 dist. 1) who denies it; he says the Old Sacraments did not justify, even if they were received in faith and charity, because they were given to be burdens, not to justify. The *second* is common to the theologians, that all the old Sacraments justify *ex opere operantis*, that is, by the faith and devotion of the recipient, and this is the truest opinion. The teaching of the Apostle in Romans 2:13 is generally true, "Doers of the law will be justified." Although this justification is not properly sacramental, rather, it is common to all good works, which are done in charity, nor is the justification first, but second. Chemnitz makes a lot of noise about this (*Exam.* 2 part. p. 58), arguing this opinion directly, and under the opposite brow, as it were, is repugnant to Paul,

Chapter XIII: The Teaching of Catholics Explained

who expressly teaches Abraham was not justified by works (Rom. 4:2), but what he says arises from mere ignorance. Paul speaks about works, which are done *only by the power of free will*, and we affirm that nobody was ever justified by such works. Theologians, however, when they say the Sacraments of the Old Law justified *ex opere operantis*, they speak about a work which arises *from the grace of God*. They call an *opus operantis* faith, charity, obedience, which are all the gifts of God, seeing that they would not have them without special help of God. Paul is speaking about such works when he says in Rom. 2:13, "Doers of the law will be justified," and James in his epistle (2:21) says, "Was Abraham justified by works?"

The other question is about Circumcision, which is not properly a Mosaic Sacrament, but of the law of nature; wherefore, John 7:22, "Circumcision is not from Moses, but from the Fathers." Hence, there are two opinions on Circumcision. The *first* opinion is of Alexander of Hales (4 q. 7 memb. 7 art. 4), Bonaventure, Scotus, and Gabriel (4 dist. 1) who admit Circumcision confers justification *ex opere operato*. Now, many arguments are opposed to this teaching. *Firstly*, the Scriptures, which say the Sacraments of the Old Law were in want of elements, they do not exclude Circumcision, nay more, they especially speak about that, as we will show. *Secondly*, the Councils of Florence, and Trent attribute the force of justification to our Sacraments alone. Some make the argument that these Councils, when they deny that the Sacraments of the Old Law justify, only speak about the Mosaic Sacraments, i.e., those promulgated by Moses, but not about Circumcision, which was a Sacrament of the law of nature given to Abraham, not to Moses. I say that this does not avail, for the Councils intended to explain the *excellence* of the Sacraments of the New Law; such an excellence is no less obscured if the Sacraments of the law of nature were equal with ours than if it were attributed to the Sacraments of the written law. Besides, seeing that God proceeded in steps in the law and gave a more imperfect law in the state of nature than in the state of the written law, and in the latter state more imperfect than in the state of the Gospel; then he certainly did the same thing in the Sacraments. Hence, if the Mosaic Sacraments did not justify, how much less do the Sacraments of the law of nature.

Nevertheless, here we must remark that this first opinion does not find favor with the heretics of this time, although they equate some ancient Sacrament with ours. The heretics, when they make the Sacraments of the Old Law equal with those of the New, they do not extol the Old, but, disparage and reject the New; this opinion, on the other hand, does not cast out the New, but extols the Old.

The *second* opinion is of St. Thomas (III. Q. 70, art. 4) and his disciples, Capreolus, del Soto, Ledesma, and others on 4 dist. 1 & 2, who teach that Circumcision did not justify by its own force, but still justified, insofar as *it was a protestation of faith, and applied faith*. Therefore, these authors would have it, that the Sacraments of the Old Law justified from the merit of the passion of Christ, as we are justified, but this merit is applied to us through the Sacraments, whereas to the Jews it was only by faith; nevertheless, such faith required the Sacrament of Circumcision as a condition *sine qua non*. This opinion without a doubt is more probable, but because it is not our intention to defend it, except for faith, against the heretics, let us pass these over to the third heading.

CHAPTER XIV

It Is Proven That No Sacrament of the Law of Nature or of the Written Law Justified Ex Opere Operato

Now we must prove the truth. We will prove, however, that no Sacrament of the Law of nature or the Written Law justified *ex opere operato*, or in the manner whereby the Sacraments of the New Law justify, against all the heretics of this time, and in some way, even against those who attribute justification *ex opere operato* to Circumcision.

The *first* passage is from the Prophets, Psalm 39:7, "You refused Sacrifice and oblation, but you perfected my ears. You have not demanded a burnt offering, even for sin." There, Scripture does not deny that God willed sacrifices since he commanded it to be done, but denies he meant it *to expiate sin*. The second passage is Psalm 50:17, "If you wanted a sacrifice [namely to expiate sin], indeed I would have given it; you will not delight in holocausts. A sacrifice to God is a contrite spirit, etc." There, Scripture opposes Sacrifice to contrition, and what it denies on the one hand, it affirms on the other; it would not do that if both were suited to justification, nor would it rightly be said now that God does not wish Baptism, but contrition. The third passage is of Isaiah 1:11 & 12, "Why do you offer me the multitude of your victims, says the Lord? ... Who required this from your hands?" The fourth passage is of Jeremiah 11:15, "Shall the holy flesh take away from you your crimes, in which you have boasted?" There, he speaks on the Sacrifice for sin. Certainly, he would not say about Baptism, "Does Baptism take away your crimes?" The *fifth* passage is of Amos 5:22, "If you offer me holocausts and gifts, I will not receive them; neither will I regard the vows of your fat beasts." Hence, if the Sacrifices did not justify, how much less did the other ceremonies justify? No ceremonies have clearer promises in regard to the remission of sins than the Sacrifices.

Now, the same can be proven from the words of the Apostles. The *first* passage is from Romans 3:1-2, "What advantage then, has the Jew, or what is the profit of circumcision? Much every way. First indeed, because the words of God were committed to them." There, the word, *first* (even as Calvin and Peter Martyr witness in their commentaries) is not an ordinal number; it is as if Paul meant to advance many advantages of Circumcision, but signifies the *chief*, or *particular* benefit, for he does not advance any others. So, by Paul's own words, the circumcised Jews only excel the uncircumcised Gentiles because they have the law of God, and the prophets; therefore, Circumcision did not justify. Otherwise, the Jews would have been more excellent than the Gentiles even by justice, which

Paul explicitly intended to refute. This is why, a little after verse 9 he added, "What then? Do we excel them? No, not so. For we have charged (i.e., we brought the cause and show) both Jews and Greeks that they are all under sin." There, even if Paul had said the Jews excel the Gentiles on account of Circumcision, because they believed the utterance of God, nevertheless, now he denies the Jews excel the Gentiles, because they do not excel inasmuch as it pertains to justification, which is the very question; for all, both circumcised and uncircumcised, are sinners. With such words, he very clearly teaches that Circumcision did not justify. He did not intend to say that no one was just before the arrival of Christ, seeing that it is certain the Patriarchs, Prophets, and many Gentiles were just, such as Melchisedech, Job, and others. Rather, he meant to say that they were not just from the very fact that they were circumcised, or uncircumcised, but from the fact that *they believed in the Christ who was going to come*. In verse 20, the Apostle says, "Because by the works of the law no flesh shall be justified before his sight." Who would deny that Circumcision was a work of the law? In verse 29 he continues, "Is he the God of the Jews only? Is he not also of the Gentiles? Yes, of the Gentiles also. For it is one God, that justifies circumcision by faith, and uncircumcision through faith." In other words, God is the God of all, so how believable is it that he gave a remedy against sin to the Jews alone? Hence, we can make the argument another way: Is God merely the God of men and not women? Who would believe that God gave a remedy which is only beneficial to men?

The *second* passage is Romans 4:10, where the Apostle explicitly proves that Abraham was not justified in Circumcision, but in uncircumcision. Thus, from there he warns that Circumcision was not given to justify. If the man to whom it was first given was not justified by it, how much less will others be justified by it?

The *third* passage is 1 Cor. 7:19, "Circumcision is nothing, and uncircumcision is nothing." There, Paul shows disdain for circumcision as he does for uncircumcision, since it is a question of justification.

The *fourth* passage is Gal. 4:9, "How do you turn again to the weak and needy elements, which you desire to serve again?" By "elements" he understands *Circumcision*, on which he particularly speaks in this epistle, and at the same time, other legal ceremonies also, and he would not have spoken rightly when he calls them weak and needy if they justified. In the same place (verse 3) he says the Jews, like children, were serving the elements of this world, yet we are men fully grown, but such a difference would not at all be true if the Sacraments of the New did not have another power than those of the Jews.

The *fifth* passage is of Gal. 6:15, "Neither Circumcision nor uncircumcision avails for anything, rather a new creation." There, we see the new creation opposed to Circumcision and uncircumcision? That would be inept if Circumcision effected a new creation.

The *sixth* passage is Philipp. 3:6, where Paul says he thinks the justice which is in the law is a detriment, and he repeats this many times; but certainly, he would not have said it if a man were justified by any legal ceremonies. This is why in verse 2, he contemptuously calls Circumcision mutilation, "Beware the mutilation." As Chrysostom explains, one is mutilated because clearly, he is robbed by cutting too short; he is mutilated because he is rashly, and apart from any skill, cut in vain. In the same place, the Apostle says that he has no trust in the flesh, and through trust in the flesh, he explains trust in Circumcision, and other things of this kind.

The *seventh* passage is from Col. 2:16, where all of the Old Sacraments are called shadows of future things: the body of Christ. But if ours had the same force, they would still be shadows. He says (*ibid.* v. 11), "You were circumcised with a Circumcision not made by hand, in the despoiling of the body of the flesh, but in the Circumcision of Christ, and buried with him in Baptism." There, Paul calls Circumcision not made by hand, and hence Baptism was not made by hand, because God is the principal agent baptizing. Likewise, he attributes nothing to Circumcision except the despoiling of the flesh, and he opposes it to Baptism. Moreover, we must remark that in the Greek text, we find, "In despoiling of the flesh of the sins of the flesh," and hence, this part (*in despoilment*) must be joined with "you were circumcised," but not with "Circumcision made by hand," so the sense is: You have been circumcised in the despoiling of the body of sins, not in the Circumcision made by hands, but the spiritual Circumcision of Christ, buried with him in Baptism. From that text the same argument is taken up, but in another way: For, as the Greek Fathers explain it (Chrysostom, Theodoret, Theophylactus), Paul teaches the Jewish Circumcision was a laying bare of one foreskin, but our Circumcision is the despoilment of the whole body of sins.

The *eighth* is Hebrews 7:18, "The former commandment is made reprobate, because of its weakness and uselessness." He speaks however, on the mandated ceremonials, the most particular of which was in regard to Circumcision.

The *ninth* passage is Hebrews 9:10, where he says that the old ceremonies were justices of the flesh, and sanctified the wicked, but only to the cleansing of the flesh.

The *tenth* passage is Hebrews 10:1, where he says the law was a shadow, not the very image of things, nor could it make those approaching it perfect; nor could it take away sins and cleanse the conscience; and God refused hosts and oblations, nor did they please him, which should be understood in the order to justification *ex opere operato*, for otherwise it cannot be denied, that they pleased him on account of the obedience and devotion of those offering them. They are called the sweetest odor before the Lord (Levit. 1:13).

Now, let us see what our adversaries have in response to these passages.

Luther and Lutherans answer, the Scriptures, when they deny the Old Sacraments justify, should be understood on those which do not have a connection to the promise.

Yet the passages they present to us speak expressly about Circumcision, which everyone concedes had a connected promise. Then, no Jewish ceremonies had a promise more express than Sacrifices and ablutions. In Leviticus 4:5-6, the remission of sins is promised to the one offering the sacrifice. Again in Levit. 20:21-22, sanctification is promised to those who wash with water, as the law commands; and still in Hebrews 10:4, the Apostle clearly says it is impossible for sins to be remitted by the Jewish sacrifices and ablutions.

Chemnitz (*Exam.* 2 part., p. 63), after the answer of Luther, proposes another which is also of Calvin (4 *Inst.* 14 §23 &25), as well as of Peter Martyr (on 1 Cor. 7), namely that when Scripture rebukes the Old Sacraments as useless, it does not speak on them *secundum se*, but as wrongly being understood by the Jews, i.e., in regard to bare ceremonies, without the promise and faith in Christ. It is very true that the Old Sacraments were useless for their recipients if they did not have faith.

On the contrary, 1) there is no question between us and the heretics, as to whether the Old Sacraments are beneficial from faith. Everyone upholds that, and this is what the Scholastics say and the heretics wrongly rebuke: the Old Sacraments were useful *ex opere operantis*. Still, the question is, whether from the divine institution they were useful besides *as Sacraments*. That utility *ex opere operantis* is not properly of the Sacraments, rather it is common to every good work.

2) The fact that Sacraments without the promise and faith, are of no benefit, not only suits the Sacraments of the Old Law, but also the New, as our adversaries themselves teach, and still Paul so distinguishes the new from the old, that he says ours save, regenerate, cleanse, and justify (Eph. 5:25, Tit. 3:5, 1 Cor. 1:2), while the old are poor elements, avail nothing, and are nothing (1 Cor. 7:19, Gal. 5:2, Hebr. 10:1, and other places).

3) The Apostle says in these passages that those ceremonies were powerless to justify, where he says they were shadows and figures of our things (Col. 2:17; 1 Cor. 10:11; Heb. 10:1). Therefore, the Apostle meant the Sacraments were useless to justify, not only as they were falsely explained by the Jews, but also *secundum se*, and as they were Sacraments instituted by God. They could be called figures not as they were wrongly explained by the Jews, but as they were Sacraments instituted by God. They were not figures for the men who thought nothing about Christ, but only those who were assenting to that rite.

Lastly, if Paul only meant to say the Old Sacraments without faith were not beneficial, he would not have made the comparison with the foreskin, nor would he have said, "Circumcision is nothing, and the foreskin is nothing (1 Cor. 7:19), or, "Neither is circumcision of any use, nor the

Chapter XIV: O.T. Doesn't Justify ex Opere Operato   219

foreskin" (Gal. 6:25). For the foreskin not only without faith is nothing, and avails nothing, but it is *absolutely* nothing, and is of no use.

Apart from this answer, Calvin makes use of three others. *One* is from the *Institutes* (4, 14 §22), that Paul speaks on the Old Sacraments, not absolutely, but comparatively, and especially Col. 2:17, where the Old Sacraments are called *shadows*. Calvin says that Paul did not mean to weaken the efficacy of those Sacraments, but to magnify the efficacy of ours, which give a more abundant grace than the Old.

On the contrary, if our Sacraments only differ from the Old because ours give greater grace, but the older less, then Paul would not have rightly said they are nothing and of no use, nor would he have compared Circumcision with the foreskin, nor even would he distinguish the Old as a shadow from the body. For, a shadow is not a lesser body, rather *nothing*, nor does it have anything except the similitude of a body. Nay more, in Hebrews 10:1, he so weakens the Old Sacraments, that he says they were not images, but *shadows*. For the image has a positive and real similitude to the body; but the shadow has a *privative* similitude, which is also nothing.

The *second* answer of Calvin (*ibid.*, §24) is that Paul speaks on the Sacraments of the Old Law for that time, which was already abrogated through Christ.

On the contrary, in Romans 2:25, Paul says, "Circumcision indeed benefits if you observe the law." There, he shows that he speaks about that which was suitable for Circumcision when it was still in force. After the abrogation it was not useful, but harmful, as the same Paul says in Gal. 3:11. Thus, Paul means to say Circumcision, when it was in force, was useful, not that it would itself justify, but because the circumcised preserved the law of God, and could more easily know the will of God than others. Paul also explains in 3:1, "Of what use is Circumcision? Much, every way, etc." Likewise, in 1 Cor. 7:19, where he says Circumcision is nothing, he speaks for the time in which it was in force; for a little earlier, before verse 18, he had said, "Is any man circumcised? Let him not procure uncircumcision. Is any man uncircumcised? Let him not be circumcised." The sense is that it will be the same whether someone would come to the faith of Christ from Judaism or from paganism. Therefore, he speaks on those who were circumcised while the law was in force, and later came to the faith of Christ, and warns them not to put themselves above the others on account of the Circumcision they once received, because it is nothing. Besides, in Gal. 4:3, he says the ancient fathers were serving under the elements of this world. Likewise, in Philip. 3:3, he says he did not trust in the flesh, i.e., did not glory (as he explains in the same place), because he was circumcised on the eighth day. Hence, he scorns Circumcision, which he had received when it was in force. Likewise, in Col. 2: 17 and Heb. 10:1, he calls them shadows and figures. Moreover, they were not shadows and figures except before their abrogation. Again, in Heb. 7:18, he says they were abrogated on account of their weakness and uselessness. Lastly, in Heb. 10:4, he avowedly teaches that it was impossible that sins be expiated by the sacrifices and washings, and on that account, Christ came to complete what they could not do.

The *third* answer of Calvin (*ibid.* §25) says the ceremonies of the law are called shades, not because they have no solidity, but because their complement was suspended in a certain measure, even to Christ. He also adds that because they are called shadows, they should not be received in regard to efficacy, but in regard to the mode of signification, because namely, they signified future things, ours signify past things.

On the contrary: *Firstly*, this answer plainly destroys the text. Paul does not only make these ceremonies shadows, but he calls it the *shadow* itself. *Secondly*, if they were only shades, because the complement was suspended even to Christ, i.e., because they were representing something which had not yet come, ours could also be called shades, since they represent the resurrection and future glory. *Thirdly*, it is impudently asserted; Paul does not argue in regard to efficacy, but only on the manner of signification. The words, "It is nothing, avails nothing, needy elements, weak, useless, cannot expiate sins," and similar things, cannot be explained except on efficacy. Lastly, the question of the Apostle with the Jews was on *efficacy* and on justification, not on the manner of signification. The Jews were not so stupid that they did not understand that the Old Sacraments signified future things, if they believed the Messiah was going to come. That is sufficient for the first argument.

CHAPTER XV

The Same Is Proven from the Fathers

WE must also prove this distinction from the Fathers, both as a thing that must be more confirmed and because Chemnitz (*Exam.* 2 part. p. 56-60) holds that we only place one thing, and that from Augustine, which still he tries to snatch away from us. We will advance twenty ancient authors from Hebrews, Greeks, Latins, apart from Augustine.

1) Philo (*de Circumcisione*), explaining all the reasons for Circumcision, which he affirms he received from the ancients, neither says nor even subtly insinuates that it was instituted as a remedy for sin.

2) Josephus (*Antiq.* 1, 12) does not give any other reason for Circumcision than to distinguish the posterity of Abraham from the other nations. Nevertheless, if anyone could know why Circumcision was instituted, it would especially be those who were Jews and very learned, and who also lived in the time when the Law was in force.

3) Justin Martyr (*Dialogue with Trypho*) says, "Moreover, from the fact that women cannot be circumcised, we understand that Circumcision was given for the sake of a sign, not a work of justice." Furthermore, in nearly the whole *Dialogue* he shows this; Circumcision did not justify, but was only given to distinguish the Jews from others.

4) Dionysius the Areopagate (*Hier. Eccl.* Part 1, 5) teaches that the church is a medium between the synagogue and the heavenly country. The synagogue had carnal Sacraments, both as shadows and figures; the heavenly Jerusalem has the bare truth without any corporeal signs. Our Church shares features of both, because it has corporeal signs, and at the same time, spiritual gifts.

5) Irenaeus (4, 30) says, "God did not give Circumcision as the crown of justice, rather, in a sign to keep the race of Abraham recognizable. ... And because a man is not justified by this, rather, he showed in a sign given to the people that Abraham himself believed God without Circumcision, and it was reputed to him unto justice." See also *ibid.*, 28-29, 32 & 34.

6) Origen (*Contra Celsum* 2) says Christians duly laid aside Circumcision, the Sabbath, and similar things, because they were carnal and corporeal things, and passed to the spiritual law of God. Likewise, in *Homily* 3 *on Genesis*, where he explains the precept of Circumcision, he makes an opposition between that carnal Circumcision of the Jews and the spiritual Circumcision of Christians; hence, he merely means there is a difference between the Old Sacraments and ours, inasmuch as there is a difference between flesh and spirit.

7) Eusebius of Caesarea (*Demonst. Evang.* 1, 10; *hist.* 1,1) beautifully teaches why the carnal Sacraments, and sacrifices were given to those first parents, as certain elements and foreshadowings of spiritual things.

8) Eusebius of Emesa (*Hom. in Sabatto Post Primam Dominicam Quadragesimae*), commenting on the verse *Let us make three tents here* says, "The first tent is the synagogue; the second, the Church; the third, heaven. The first was a shadow and a figure; the second in a figure and truth, the third, in truth alone. In the first the way is shown; in the second, discovered; in the third, possessed. The Sacraments of the Church do not merely teach and show the remedy, as the Sacraments of the synagogue, but they rather more *are* the medicine, and remission of sins.

9) Athanasius, in his oration on the verse *All things have been given to me by my father*, profusely teaches that Circumcision was nothing other than a shadow and figure of Baptism, which is the true and spiritual Circumcision.

10) Epiphanius (*Panarion*, haeres. 8, which is of the Epicureans) says, "Formerly, Circumcision was carnal, which served the time even to the great Circumcision, i.e., Baptism, which circumcises us from sins."

11) Basil (*de Spiritu Sancto*, 14) says, "The same prejudicial comparison is made also in the case of Baptism by all who judge the reality by the shadow, and comparing the typified with the type, attempt by means of Moses and the sea to disparage at once the whole dispensation of the Gospel....Why then, do you compare Baptisms, which have only the name in common, while the distinction between the things themselves is as great as might be that of dream and reality, that of the shadow and figures with substantial existence?"

12) John Chrysostom (*Hom.* 27 *in Gen.*) says, "Pay attention to the fact that God willed to establish Circumcision as the law, not because it can effect something for the salvation of the soul, but for Jewish children to bear this token of gratitude as a sign and seal, and that it was not lawful for them to mix in marital commerce with the gentiles. Hence, Blessed Paul calls this a sign, saying, "And he gave the sign of Circumcision as a seal, for Circumcision itself does not lead to justice." See the same thing in *Hom.* 39 as well as 40 on *Genesis*, and his homily *On the betrayal of Judas*, *Hom.* 7 on *Romans*, and *Hom.* 14 on *Hebrews*.

13) Cyril teaches the same thing (in *Julianum* 10), and 14) Theodoret (*Quaest.* 67 *in Gen.* as well as *ad Graecos* 7), 15) Damascene (*de Fide* 4, 10, 14, & 26), 16) Theophylactus on *Romans* 2, and 17) Oecumenius on *Rom.* 4.

From the Latins:

18) Tertullian (*Contra Judaeos* 1) says, "If Circumcision cleanses a man, seeing that God made Adam uncircumcised, why did he not circumcise him after the fall, if Circumcision cleanses? ... God provided this Circumcision as a sign that he did not give it for salvation." He proves the same thing from the prophets, that the Sacrifices and the Sacraments of the Jews did

Chapter XV: Proven from the Fathers

not justify; where he also calls their Sacraments carnal, and ours spiritual.

19) St. Cyprian (*Contra Judaeos* 1, 9) opposes the carnal Circumcision of the Jews to the spiritual Circumcision of Christians, and he adds that Adam, Enoch, Noah, and Melchisedech were just without Circumcision, "because the sign of the seed was of no benefit." Therefore, (*Epist.* 3, 8 *ad Fidum*) he says the carnal Circumcision, when the spiritual came about, evaporated like a shadow at the onset of the light.

20) St. Ambrose (in *Epist.* 72 *ad Irenaeum*) says, "The sign is a corporeal Circumcision, the truth is a spiritual Circumcision; the former cuts off a member, the latter, sin." Then in his commentary on Romans 4 (if he is the author) says, "Therefore, Circumcision does not have any dignity, rather, it is only a sign, because the sons of Abraham usually received a sign that they would be known as his sons, who, believing God received this sign, to imitate their father in faith." You can find the same thing in his book *On Abraham* (1, 4), where he argues about Circumcision, and in *De Sacramentis* (1, 4 &6) and *de Mysteriis*, c. 8&9.

21) St. Jerome (on *Galatians 3*) gives the reason why Circumcision was instituted, and not even the slightest word suggests that it was a remedy for sin, "Because Christ would arise from the seed of Abraham, and from Abraham, even to Christ many ages were going to pass, by God's providence, lest the progeny of his beloved Abraham would be mixed with the other nations, and little by little his family became uncertain, he marked the Israelite flock with the mark of Circumcision. Next, for forty years in the desert not a man was circumcised; nay more, they were only living without the mixing of another nation. Immediately, as that people crossed the banks of the Jordan, Circumcision was necessarily going to provide against the error of mixing with the Gentiles. When, however, following Jesus' lead, the circumcised people is described, it signifies that in the desert Circumcision ceased, which was reasonably carried out in Egypt, and by our Lord Jesus Christ the spiritual Circumcision cleansed believers." He says the same thing in his commentary on *Isaiah* 1, that God rejected the Jewish ceremonies, and was pleased by the laver of Baptism, "This alone can cleanse sins."

Lastly, St. Augustine (in *Ps.* 73 [74]) says, "The Sacraments are not the same; because there are some Sacraments giving salvation, and some promising a Savior. The Sacraments of the New Testament give salvation; while the Sacraments of the Old Testament promised a Savior."

Chemnitz and Calvin both respond to this citation. Chemnitz (*Exam.* P. 59 & 60) answers that Augustine spoke on the Old Sacraments, which did not have a promise connected to them, but were mere signs, according to Luther's distinction.

This answer does not avail, because Augustine speaks in general on the Old Sacraments, and especially on the Sacrifices, and says they were all changed because they did not give salvation. Besides, when Augustine says the former Sacraments promised a Savior, he seems to speak particularly on those which had a promise connected to them. How would they not have a connected promise, if they promised a Savior?

Secondly, he answers with Calvin (*Inst.* 4, 14 §26) that Augustine does not speak on the efficacy of the Sacraments, but on their signification; he only meant this difference between the Old Sacraments and ours, that the Old signified Christ was coming, ours signify he has already been produced and given.

On the contrary, Augustine does not say our Sacraments signify a Savior, but *give salvation*. Besides, in the same place he says, "The Sacraments were changed, they became easier, fewer, more salutary, and happier." This pertains to the *efficacy*, not the signification. Next, Augustine clearly places the distinction in regard to efficacy in other places. In *Epist.* 19 to Jerome, he says, "Why will I not say the precepts of those Old Sacraments were not good because men were not justified by them? They are shadows announcing grace, whereby we are justified." What could be clearer? Doesn't Augustine altogether say the very thing which the Council of Florence later defined? Then, in *Contra Faustum* (19, 13), he says, "The Sacraments of the New Law were instituted in a greater power and a better utility." So, our Sacraments excel the ancient ones in *utility and power*, not merely in signification. Then, in his *Tractates on John* (43), he says, "In the Sacrifices there was no expiation of sins, but a shadow of future things." In his *Questions on Numbers*, he says, "If we attend to the Old Sacraments per say, by no arrangement could they heal; but if one were to inquire after what the new Sacraments really are, the cleansing of sins will be found in them." That is enough from the testimonies of the Fathers.

CHAPTER XVI

The Same Is Proven from Arguments That Have Their Foundation in the Scriptures

THE *first* argument: A Sacrament, for it to be able to justify, should have an absolute promise of grace connected to it: No such thing existed in the Old Law; thus, none of them justified. The major proposition is most certain among our adversaries, for Luther asserts it in his *Assertion of the Articles*, art. 1. Melanchthon (*Loc. Com.*, published in 1558, tit. *De Sacramentis*), Calvin (*Instit.* 4, 14, §3), and finally Chemnitz (*Exam.* 2 part. p. 42), all posit in the very definition of a Sacrament, that it should have the promise of grace, and not any grace, but *the remission of sins*. Lastly, they are compelled to admit this, since they would have it that the Sacraments justify by arousing faith; for faith among them does not justify, except by apprehending the promise of forgiveness.

The minor proposition is proven. *Firstly*, from the Apostle in Hebrews 8:6, "But now he has obtained a better ministry, by how much also he is a mediator of a better testament, which is ratified on better promises." Later, in verse 12, explaining how these promises of the New Testament are better, he advances the verse of Jeremiah 31:34, "I will forgive their iniquity, and I will remember their sin no more."

Secondly, from St. Augustine (in Ps. 72), where he says the promises of the Old Testament as well of the New are different, as even the Sacraments themselves are different; the former promised earthly things, now they promise heavenly things.

Thirdly, it is proved from Luther himself. In *Babylonian Captivity*, in the chapter on the Eucharist, he speaks in this way, "The Old Testament was a promise given through Moses, not of the remission of sins, or of eternal things, but temporal, namely the land of Canaan, whereby no man was renewed in the spirit; wherefore, it was even fitting to slay mindless beasts as a figure of Christ, in whose blood the same Testament was confirmed, seeing that the Testament is determined by the blood, and the promise by the holocaust." There he offers for us a clearly insoluble argument against himself, for he expressly calls to mind the promise. One cannot make the response that he speaks about the Sacraments which do not have a promise connected to them, since he expressly mentions the promise. Besides, a little before that citation he posits the examples of the rainbow, or the fleece of Gideon, the hour-glass of Ahaz, and similar things, and says that these things were only signs of earthly promises, and still in the following chapter, which is on Baptism, he would have it that these very things are properly Sacraments and equal to ours. Next, Calvin denies this minor proposition. In the *Institutes* (4, 16 §4) he says that the promise of the Sacraments of the Old and New Testament is one and the same. Thus, the minor is proven.

Fourthly, from individual things that are said about the Sacraments among them. Luther enumerates among the Sacraments, the Sacrifice of Abel, the rainbow, the fleece of Gideon, and the hourglass of Ahaz, but none of these have the promise of the remission of sins. On the Sacrifice of Abel we read nothing except that it pleased God after it was done. The rainbow only had the promise of temporal salvation; for this reason in Genesis 9:12, it is said that it was given as a covenant, not only to man, but all the beasts of the earth and every reptile. Similarly, in the fleece of Gideon, and the hourglass of Ahaz, these signs were made to confirm the promise of victory against temporal enemies. In regard to the other Sacraments, such as Circumcision, the Sacrifices for sin, the Manna, the Red Sea, and other things I will show the same thing in the answer to the argumentation.

2) The *second* argument: The whole Old Law itself is distinguished from the New in this: the Old does not justify, while the New does. As a result, it cannot happen that the Old Sacraments, which were a certain part of that law, would justify. The antecedent is proven: *a)* firstly from what is said in John 1:17, "The law was given through Moses, grace and truth came through Jesus Christ." How is this true, if the Mosaic Sacraments conferred grace? *b)* Secondly, in 2 Cor. 3:6, it is called the letter that slays, while the New, the spirit giving life. But why was the Old not a spirit giving life, if its Sacraments justified? *c)* Thirdly, in Gal. 4:24, it is said what was begotten in servitude brought our freedom. But how, if that grace also conferred what frees from the servitude of sin? *d)* Lastly, it is called the *Old* Testament, because it pertains to the old man; it did not understand the idea of renewal. On the other hand, our Testament is called *New*, because it renews, as Augustine teaches (*Against the Two Epistles of Pelag.*, 3, 4). This is why the Apostle also calls Baptism the laver of renewal (Tit. 3:5). Nevertheless, it does not follow from this that there was no justification from sin in the holy men of the Old Testament; for there was, but not by the agency of the Old Testament, or through its Sacraments; rather, through the agency of the *New* Testament, to which the former pertained, and it was pertaining to the participation in it by faith and desire.

3) The *third* argument: The promise in the Sacraments, which was instituted to justify, cannot be fulfilled unless it is received in faith, as our adversaries say. Now, the promises connected to the Old Sacraments were fulfilled, even if men did not believe; thus, these Sacraments were not instituted to justify. The minor is proven, for the promise of God was connected to the heavenly rainbow, which is a true Sacrament for Luther, but it was only in regard to never again destroying the world with a flood

Chapter XVI: Proven from Scriptural Arguments

of water. That promise will be fulfilled, even if men do not believe. So also, the promise that was connected to Circumcision, was to make Abraham the father of many nations, and to give the land of the promise to his posterity, as is clear from Gen. 17:4, Rom. 4:18, which without a doubt was going to be fulfilled, whether men believed or not. This is why, the Apostle in Rom. 3:3 says, "Shall their unbelief cause the trust of God to be without effect? God forbid. God is true, and every man a liar."

4) The *fourth* argument: Holy Scripture says that our Sacraments save, regenerate, and justify, as we proved above. No such thing is ever read in regard to the Old Sacraments, as will be clear in the answer to the arguments; therefore, they rashly assert that they are equal in regard to efficacy.

CHAPTER XVII

We Answer the Objections

Our adversaries have five arguments.

1) The *first* is from Genesis 17:14, where God speaks about Circumcision, "The male, whose foreskin will not have been circumcised, that soul shall be erased from his people; because he has broken my covenant." Both some Catholics (who think Circumcision justified *ex opere operato*) and heretics (who do not acknowledge a distinction between the Sacraments of the New and Old Testament) take their argument from this passage.

Firstly, these Catholics, having followed Augustine in *City of God* (16, 17), argue in this way. God threatened every masculine Hebrew child, even infants, to perish forever unless he was circumcised, therefore, through Circumcision male children were freed from eternal death.

Calvin, however (*Instit.* 4, 16 §3&4) argues in this way: The promise which is in Baptism is the same in Circumcision, namely the remission of sins and eternal life; therefore, they do not differ except in their outward rite, or sign. He probes the antecedent from Gen. 17:7, where Circumcision is instituted, God said to Abraham, "I will be your God, and of your seed after you." Commenting on this, Calvin says, "In such words the promise of eternal life is contained; in the way that Christ is interpreted, who thence proves the resurrection in Matt. 22:32 from the fact that God is called the God of Abraham, Isaac and Jacob, for he is not a God of the dead, but the living. Therefore, it is the same thing to say I will be your God, and I will give you eternal life. But the first entry to God is through the remission of sins, therefore, God also promised a remission of sins when he says, 'I will be your God, and the God of your seed.'" He offers a confirmation of his argument from the very fact that the Apostle, in Eph. 2:12, says: The Gentiles, who were uncircumcised, were without God, without Christ, without hope, and foreign to his promises. Therefore, men obtained all of these things by Circumcision.

I respond to the argument of certain Catholics: The whole force of that argument depends upon two terms which are found in the Greek text, ἡμέρα ὀγδόῃ, which St. Augustine uses. The Greek reads this way, "And an uncircumcised male, whose foreskin will not be circumcised on the eighth day [τῇ ἡμέρᾳ τῇ ὀγδόῃ], that soul will perish from his people. There, the words *On the eighth day* are added by the Septuagint; they are not found in the Hebrew codices, nor in the Chaldean paraphrase, nor in the Latin Vulgate. Hence, on account of those two words, *On the eighth day*, St. Augustine was compelled to explain this passage in regard to infants,

Chapter XVII: Objections Answered 229

and say God threatened this penalty to uncircumcised children; and so he was further compelled to explain the following words, "Because they have broken my covenant," in regard to original sin, and on the covenant made with Adam on not eating from the tree of the knowledge of good and evil, which only children could violate; and hence, lastly, he was compelled to explain the words, "That soul will perish," in regard to eternal death, which is due to original sin. (See Augustine in *City of God*, 16, 27; *On Original Sin*, 2, 30-31; *On Matrimony* 2, *On Concupiscence*, 11). If we were to remove those words, *on the eighth day* from the text, as they truly should be removed, the whole argument falls apart. We would not be compelled to explain this passage in regard to children; nay more, we would be compelled to explain this passage only in regard to adults, so that the sense would be, a male Hebrew, who refuses to be circumcised, or to circumcise his son, will perish from his people, because he was disobedient to the precept I gave regarding Circumcision. From such an opinion it would no more follow that Circumcision justifies than whatever precept of the law, for God threatens death a thousand times more for not keeping his precepts.

The sense of this passage is shown in three ways. *a)* Firstly, from the words, "because he broke my covenant." Even if St. Augustine explained this passage on the covenant made with Adam, nevertheless, it is as clear as day that this should be explained on the covenant with Abraham in regard to circumcising male children. For, in that chapter the covenant of God is named eight times, and it is always received for the covenant of Circumcision. What could be clearer than the exposition of God himself in the same chapter, "This is my covenant, which you will observe, every male child among you will be circumcised"? Hence, the reason for the threat in this passage is not original sin, but *actual* sin, i.e., a transgression of the precept on Circumcision, a sin that adults alone are capable of transgressing.

b) Secondly, it is proven from the punishment, "that soul will perish from his people." These words do not signify eternal death, or hell, but some *temporal* penalty. "From his people" signifies it; he does not say he will absolutely perish, but he will perish *from the people*, i.e., he will be separated from his people, either by corporeal death, or by a certain thing like excommunication. The Hebrew term רַת (*karath*) properly means to cut off from the people. And this penalty is placed everywhere in Scripture against all who would omit some ceremony, as is clear from Exodus 12:15, 31:14; Leviticus 7:20, 17:9, 18:29, 19:8, 20:3, and 23:29; Numbers 15:30 and 19:20. In the last passage it is said the soul of that man is going to perish from the people, who touches a dead body and does not wash himself with water. Such an omission certainly does not seem to be a crime meriting eternal death.

c) Thirdly, it is proven from Exodus 4:24, after the Lord wanted to kill Moses, because he had not circumcised his son. There, we clearly see the punishment is corporeal death, and it was imposed against an adult who was capable of actual sin, not infants. Although St. Augustine (*Quaest. In Exod.* 11, *de Baptismo* 4, 24) tries to show that the son of Moses, not Moses himself was in danger on account of being uncircumcised, nevertheless, the matter is absolutely clear. For, if God threatened death on a child, if he was not circumcised on the eighth day, what benefit would it be to the son of Moses if that Circumcision took place after he eighth day? Lastly, the text is very clear, "And while Moses was on his journey in the inn, the Lord met him, and threatened to kill him." Which him? None but Moses, about whom he was speaking in the nearest verse. Besides, it follows in verse 25, "Right away Sephora took a very sharp stone, and circumcised the foreskin of her son." If the verse, "He meant to kill him," were understood on the son of Moses, Scripture would have said, "She circumcised his foreskin, but not of her son. Besides, it adds that Sephora also said to Moses, "You are a bloody husband to me," i.e., I was going to lose my husband, unless I redeemed you by the blood of my son. This is why St. Jerome, in his commentary on Gal. 5, has no doubt that Moses was in danger in this passage, not his son.

Now *I respond* to Calvin's argument. I deny that a promise of the remission of sin and eternal life was connected to Circumcision. Firstly, it is opposed to the Apostle and Augustine, who, as we saw above, teach that the promises of the New Testament are better than the Old. Secondly, it is opposed to the first institution of Circumcision. When Abraham himself was first commanded, and the promise firstly made to him, he was already most just before Circumcision, as is clear from Gen. 12 (*et seqq.*) and from Paul in Rom. 4:3. So, the promise was not on the remission of sins. *Thirdly*, it is opposed to the very fact of Gen. 17:2, where we only read that when God enjoined Circumcision upon Abraham, he promised him and his posterity the land of Palestine. "I will place my covenant between me and you, and I will exceedingly multiply you," and in verse 4, "I AM, and my covenant is with you, and you will be a father of many nations. ... (v. 8) I will give to you and your seed the land of your pilgrimage, all the land of Canaan." The Apostle also teaches the same thing in Rom. 4:18. Now, it is true that this earthly promise was a figure of a spiritual and heavenly promise, which was going to be given to those who are not circumcised in the flesh, but in heart; the Patriarchs and Prophets understood this, as well as other perfect men of that time, as the Apostle says in Hebr. 11:4, *et seqq.*, as well as the elder Tobias in Tob. 2:18. Nevertheless, the earthly promise was connected to carnal Circumcision, and this alone pertained to the Old Testament. To assert the contrary, as Calvin does, is nothing other than to make the Gospel according to the law, and confuse everything.

To Calvin's proof, "I will be your God," *I respond:* The promise of eternal life or the remission of sins is not meant by these words, but only, as Chrysostom explains in his commentary on this passage, *the promise of a certain peculiar protection*, of the sort that should be given to a peculiar people, like the Israelites were, as we find in Deuteronomy (*passim*). In

Chapter XVII: Objections Answered

this way, God was not only the God of the good, but also of the wicked, provided they were from the people of Israel. Hence, those words do not mean the promise of the remission of sins; otherwise, God would only be the God of the just. Add that these very words do not sound as much like a promise of God, as they do an obligation of the people. It is the same thing to say, "I will be your God, and of your seed," as if he would have said, "You will not have another God but me," according to that of Jeremiah 24:7, "I will be their God, and they shall be my people," and that of Gen. 28:20, "If will be with me and guard me on the road on which I walk, and give me bread to eat ... the Lord shall be my God." But Calvin says, "God is not the God of the dead, but the living, as Christ says 'I will be your God' means the promise of eternal life." *I respond:* The words of Christ mean nothing other than God is not the God of those who do not exist, but of those who do, whether they are good or bad, blessed or damned. For, he means to prove against the error of the Sadducees, the souls of the dead are immortal, and therefore, not extinguished with the body, but really remain and live; but he proved it best from the words of God to Moses in Exod. 3:6, "I am the God of Abraham, Isaac and Jacob." Since they were already dead, as far as the body, they had to be alive insofar as the soul, or he would not have said, "God is their God," for God is not the God of those who do not exist.

Now, to the argument from Ephesians, *I respond:* The Gentiles were without God, without Christ, without hope, and without promises, not because they did not have Circumcision, but because they did not have *true faith, and knowledge of the true God*, and worshiped idols in place of God. Otherwise, even among the Gentiles, who acknowledge the true God as Job once did, and later Cornelius the Centurion and several others who were not without God, without Christ, and without hope, even if they were not circumcised.

2) The second argument is taken from Leviticus chapters 4, 5, & 6, particularly 6:2-7 where we read, "The soul which will sin, and despising the Lord, shall deny to his neighbor a thing delivered to his keeping, which was committed to his trust; or shall by force extort anything, or commit oppression; or shall find a thing lost and denying it, shall also swear falsely, or shall do any other of the many things, wherein men are wont to sin, being convicted of the offence, he shall restore all that he would have gotten by fraud, in the principal, and the fifth part besides to the owner, whom he wronged. Moreover, for his sin he shall offer a ram without blemish out of the flock, and shall give it to the priest, according to the estimation and measure of the offence; and he shall pray for him before the Lord, and he shall have forgiveness for everything in doing of which he hath sinned." Here, we clearly see the remission of any sin you like promised, even perjury, which is numbered among the most serious, by offering Sacrifice. The argument is confirmed: If these ceremonies established by God, with such a characteristic promise of the remission of sins do not justify, then

Catholics ineptly gather from James 5:14, that Extreme Unction justifies. There, James speaks in the same way, "Is any man sick among you? Let him bring in the priests of the Church, and let them pray over him, anointing him with oil in the name of the Lord. And the prayer of faith shall save the sick man; and the Lord shall raise him up; and if he be in sins, they shall be forgiven him."

I respond: The old Sacrifices availed for the expiation of sin, *insofar as the temporal penalty and insofar as they expiated the legal uncleanliness*, not insofar as the sin and the penalty of hell, except inasmuch as they were certain signs professing faith in Christ, as the Theologians commonly teach (on 4 dist. 1), as well as St. Thomas (I IIae q. 103, a. 2), and Alphonsus Tostatus (*In Levit.* 1, 19).

This can also be proven in many ways. *a)* Firstly, because Scripture did not establish Sacrifices for every sin, but only for sins *of ignorance*, especially against the ceremonies of the law, as is clear from Levit. 4:2 and 5:17, and even for sins in regard to the loss of a neighbor in external things, and for perjury from the desire to keep another's possessions which were consigned to his trust, as is clear from Levit. 6:2-3. For other more serious sins, such as blasphemy, homicide, adultery, idolatry, no Sacrifice is found. Nor is it opposed that Levit. 6:3 says that by the sacrifice of a ram every kind of sin which men customarily commit is forgiven. There it is talking about every sin in regard to *taking away of another's possessions*, not about every sin *simpliciter*, otherwise the various Sacrifices for different sins would be placed in vain in previous chapters. Thus, if Sacrifices do not expiate every sin, but only certain ones, without a doubt they do not expiate in regard to sin, but only in regard to temporal punishment or legal uncleanliness. God never remits one sin in regard to fault and eternal punishment so as to remit all, and hence, the differences between those promises of the Old Testament, and the promises of the Sacrament of Extreme Unction are clear. James speaks absolutely about everyone, "If he is in sins, they shall be forgiven him" (Jas 5:15).

Secondly, it is proven because the old Sacrifices, as St. Thomas notes (*loc. cit.*), did not please God of themselves, but from *the devotion and obedience of those offering them*, as is clear. In Proverbs 15:8, the sacrificial victims of the impious are said to be abominable before God. In Sirach 34:23, "The most High does not approve the gifts of the wicked." In Isaiah 1, where the Lord said he refused the sacrifices of the Israelites, he adds in verse 15, "Your hands are full of blood." In Malachi 2:2, God says to the wicked priests, "I will curse your blessings." In 1 Kings [1 Samuel] 15:22 he says, "Does the Lord desire holocausts and victims, and not rather that the voice of the Lord should be obeyed?" Lastly, in Gen. 4:4, "The Lord regarded Abel and his offerings, but he did not regard Cain and his offerings." For this reason, St. Gregory (*Moral.* 22, 12) says, "Oblation did not know to appease the wrath of the Judge, except that it would be pleasing on the side

Chapter XVII: Objections Answered

of the cleanliness of the one offering. ... This is why Abel did not please with offerings, but the offerings of Abel were pleasing." From there we gather that the Sacrifices did not avail to the expiation of sin. Either those who gave the direction for an offering to be made were just or unjust. If just, they did not need the remission of sins; if unjust, his sacrifice was of no value, as we have already showed. Someone will say the merit of the priest making the offering could avail for the unjust man. But the merits of one cannot, for certain and infallibly, confer the first grace on another. Here, however, the absolute promise in regard to the remission of sins is placed; therefore, it is proper to understand this about remission, inasmuch as it is only for *a temporal penalty*.

Thirdly, Ezekiel 18, when it is a discussion on the remission of sins, never mentions Sacrifices. Nay more, the other prophets, as well as Paul, clearly teach that the sins of souls cannot be expiated by Sacrifices. Otherwise, we would be compelled to affirm that the Scriptures contradict themselves, if in Leviticus it was not a question of anything but *legal uncleanliness*, or the remission of *a temporal penalty*.

3) The third argument is taken from 1 Cor. 10:3, where the Apostle, speaking about the manna of the Hebrews, and the water flowing from the rock, says, "They ate the same spiritual food, and drank the same spiritual drink." Calvin makes much of this argument (*Instit.* 4, 14 §23), "The Apostle speaks in no more glittering terms of the one than of the other when he says that the fathers ate the same spiritual food as we do, and explains that such food was Christ. Who will presume to regard as an empty sign that which gave a manifestation to the Jews of true communion with Christ? ... First, he makes them equal to us in the Sacraments, and leaves us not one jot of privilege." Peter Martyr insists on the same argument in his commentary on 1 Cor. 10, as well as Chemnitz in the *Examination* (2 part., p. 67).

Now, this argument has four difficulties for us. *a)* They emphasize a particle (*eandem*). If the ancient Jews ate the same food in the manna, which we eat in the Eucharist, certainly the manna and the Eucharist will be of the same power. *b)* Secondly, they focus on the particle *spiritualem*. If that food and drink were spiritual, certainly they would have the same effect, hence they will not be empty corporeal signs. *c)* Thirdly, they focus on the state of the question. The Apostle (as they say) meant to alert Christians, lest they would trust too much in the reception of the Sacraments, and so they would not believe that they were all saved because they received Baptism and Eucharist, unless they would also persevere in good works; but the Apostle argues from examples of the ancients, who equally benefitted from similar Sacraments, although they did not keep themselves from sin. Thus, it would be fitting that their Sacraments and ours be of the same dignity and efficacy, if Paul's argument were to have some validity. *d)* Fourthly, they confirm from Augustine, who disputed on this passage of Paul (*Tract. in Joan.* 26), and says the Sacraments of the Jews were different from ours in signs, but really, what is signified is equal; different in the visible species, equal in the spiritual power.

I respond: Calvin, and Chemnitz oppose themselves. In the first place, Calvin and Chemnitz (*loc. cit.*) would have it the manna, as well as the water gushing from the rock, nay more the crossing of the Red Sea, were Sacraments among the Jews, as well as justifying Sacraments, such as Baptism and Eucharist are with us. Now, they themselves previously rejected that these were Sacraments. Calvin in the *Institutes* (4, 14 §19) says the Sacraments, on which we argue, were ordinary ceremonies, not something which was done once or again. Chemnitz (*loc. cit.*, p. 41) also placed in his definition of a Sacrament, that it be a ceremony which endures as long as religion endures. It is certain, however, the manna, water from the rock, and the crossing of the Red Sea were no such things. They were not ceremonies, and endured for a brief space of time. Next, Calvin says that the Old Sacraments are equal to ours in such a way, that no unique prerogative is left to ours; and nevertheless, earlier in the same chapter (14, §22), he said our Sacraments are more excellent, for the very reason that they confer a more abundant grace. Then Chemnitz opposes himself in a more serious manner. In this place he admits with Calvin that the Eucharist is in nothing more excellent than the manna of the Jews was, and he does not notice the fact that Calvin advances the argument to prove that the Lord's body was not in the Eucharist, except as a figure, just as it was in the manna, which is contrary to what the Lutherans and Chemnitz himself teaches (in 2 part. exam. p. 332).

Now with these things out of the way, *I respond* to the first part of the argument. When Scripture says, "They ate the same food," it does not mean to say ours and theirs was the same food, but their food was all the same; this is the sense. All the Jews ate the same manna, and still not all pleased God. This is shown: *a)* Firstly, the former were not Sacraments, but ours are Sacraments, as we have shown. *b)* Secondly, these were common also to the beasts, for even beasts drank from the water that gushed from the rock, and crossed the Red Sea. Dogs, chickens, and similar household animals ate the manna as their food, and this did not happen in some case, or by someone's malice, the way it can also happen that the signs of the Eucharist are devoured by animals; rather, God willed and instituted the manna for this purpose. God brought water forth from the rock that men and beasts of burden would drink, and opened the sea, and caused the manna to rain down, so that men and beasts would cross, and live. *c)* Thirdly, because we read that no promise was made to those eating the manna or drinking that water, or by crossing the Red Sea; our Sacraments, however, have the fullest promises. Here, our adversaries clearly run into difficulties.

Peter Martyr, in his *Commentary* on 1 Cor. 10, tries to extricate himself. He poses the question, where are the promises connected to the Red Sea, and the manna, and answers in this way, "I reckon these are what we read

Chapter XVII: Objections Answered

in Exodus and in Numbers. In Exodus they were clearly admonished to see to it that they saw the mighty works of God. And you will find this same thing written about the manna, if you diligently search through everything." Now, such testimonies of our adversaries are poor and destitute, for, if they had something, they would mark down the very place of the Scripture, not declare that we must search it out. Moreover, I have looked in earnest for these promises, and I have not found any but these. In Exodus 14:13, Moses says to the sons of Israel as they are preparing to cross the Red Sea, "Stand and see the great wonders of God; for the Egyptians, whom you now see, you will not see again. The Lord will fight for you, and you will be silent." Yet, this is a temporal promise, and was immediately fulfilled by the slaying of the Egyptians in the Red Sea, as we read there (*ibid.*). Again, in Exodus 16, the manna is shown to the people, as well as the quails, but no promise is added, except for what we find in verse 12, "In the evening you will eat meat, and in the morning, you will be filled with bread." Then, in Exodus 17:6, as well as Num. 20:8, the water is brought forth from the rock. But there is no promise except this, "When you will bring forth water from the rock, the whole multitude shall drink, as well as their animals."

Peter Martyr sees these are earthly promises, and for that reason, so as not to appear to have surrendered, he tries to elicit the promise of the remission of sins from these promises. He uses this reasoning: The limit of evils, and the root of all others is sin; therefore, when we seek to be freed from some evil, whatever that is, then tacitly we seek to be freed from sin. So, in the same way, whatever goods God promises or shows, depend upon reconciliation with him, as well as his grace and favor.

Really, it would be easier to draw water from a rock than to draw out the promise of reconciliation from these passages of Scripture. Even if the sin of Adam was the occasion of all evils, nevertheless, the afflictions of this life are not so connected with sins that they cannot be separated. Men often sin, and still they are not punished in this life; often men that do not sin are also afflicted, as is clear from St. Job, and Tobit, and others, who were not afflicted on account of sins, but to exercise virtues. On the other hand, in respect to good things, God often gives an abundance of temporal things to those whom he is not going to give his grace, as well as eternal life, or to reward their good moral works, or other reasons, and not give temporal goods to those whom he is going to give eternal life, as is clear from Luke 16 in the example of the rich man, and the beggar, as well as nearly everywhere in the Scriptures. It is clear from Nebuchadnezzar, Cyrus, and others, to whom God subjected the world, although still they were never his friends (See Augustine *City of God*, 5, 12 & 15). Therefore, Peter Martyr very clearly errs when he says any good you like, which God gives, depends upon reconciliation with God and his grace. Nor does it follow that since God promised the people of the Jews a victory over their enemies, or an abundance of food and drink, therefore he promised remission of sins and eternal life. St. Basil (*de Spiritu Sancto*, 14) proves there was no spiritual promise in the passing of the Red Sea, the manna, the water from the rock, etc., and he says that anyone who would equate those signs with ours weakens the universal Evangelical dispensation [from the law]. He says, "What remission of sins, what renewal of life took place in the sea? What spiritual gift is given through Moses? What death to sin took place there?"

To the second part of the argument, *I say:* The manna and the water gushing from the rock are called spiritual food and drink, not because of the effect, but on account of the *cause and signification*. On account of the cause, because it was produced through a miracle by the work of angels, as Chrysostom and Theophylactus show on this passage. This is why in Ps. 77[78]:25, the manna is called the bread of angels, "Man ate the bread of angels." Certainly, it is not called the bread of angels because the angels ate it, but because the angels *made* it. On the water, the Apostle explains the same thing, why the drink is said to be spiritual, "they drank of the spiritual rock that followed them, and the rock was Christ." (1 Cor. 10:4). There, it was not the water itself, which they drank, that he calls spiritual, but *the rock*, which was the cause of that water, and he taught them that the true cause of that water was not the corporeal and visible rock, which laid fixed to the ground, but another, invisible rock, i.e., the providence of Christ, God, which never deserted them. This is why, when the Apostle says, "They drank from the spiritual rock," the sense is not—as Calvin supposes—that they drank from the spiritual rock, i.e., Christ, rather because they drank water from the spiritual rock, i.e., Christ, *flowing from the efficient cause*, as it were. Moreover, the Apostle does not compare the water with Christ, but the rock, which was the cause of the water. This whole explanation is confirmed from John 6:49, "Your fathers ate manna in the desert, and they died, ... he that eats this bread, will live forever." There, the Lord is absolutely clear when he teaches that the manna of the Jews was not a spiritual food, in regard to its effect, in the way the Eucharist is, since those who ate the manna died.

Calvin answers this (*Instit.* 4, 14 §25), as well as Peter Martyr (*loc. cit.*), that Christ accommodated himself to the rude opinion of the Jews, who thought the manna was nothing other than food for the stomach. Thus, Christ did not assert that he was about to give them a better food than the manna really was, rather what the manna was according to the rude opinion of the Jews.

On the contrary, either the Jews rightly supposed manna was merely corporeal food, or they did not. If rightly, then our Eucharist is by far better, since it is spiritual food; if not rightly, then the Lord approved their error, and did not speak clearly, nay more, not even truly. Accordingly, even he asserted that food was merely corporeal when he says, "Your fathers ate the manna, and they died." Before that even more clearly, when they gloried in the fact that their fathers ate manna in the desert, and boasted that this

Chapter XVII: Objections Answered   237

bread was like heavenly bread, Christ said, "Moses did not give you bread from heaven, but my Father gives you true bread from heaven," i.e., as Cyril rightly explains in his commentary on John (3, 34), as well as Chrysostom (*hom. in Joan.* 44), the manna was not really heavenly bread, but earthly, although it is from heaven, that is it came down from the air; but the truly heavenly bread is this very thing, which now the Father gives you.

Additionally, Chrysostom (*Hom. 45 in Joan.*) agrees with us, "Notice how he makes a distinction between this bread and the manna from the purpose of each one; to show that the manna offers nothing great, he adds: Our Fathers ate manna, etc." Likewise, Cyril (*loc. cit.* 4, 11) in regard to the manna of the Jews, introduces Christ speaking in this way, "I am the bread of life; that [the manna] was merely a figure, an image, and shadow."

To the third part of the argument, *I respond:* The scope of the Apostle was not to show that one must not place too much trust in the Sacraments, but rather more, not to *abuse* the Sacraments. If he meant to show that one should not place too much trust in the Sacraments, he would have taken up an example of the Jews in the true Jewish Sacraments, such as Circumcision and the Paschal Lamb, and similar things. He takes up, however, other things which were indeed a figure of our Sacraments but were still not Sacraments themselves, as we showed above. Besides, it is clear from the context itself. In chapter 8, he exhorted Christians not to eat food offered to idols, lest they would give offense to the weak in that way; then in chapter 9 he shows by his own example that it is fitting not to offend weak brethren; then in chapter 10 he treats the question on food offered to idols, and proves these must not be eaten, because it is a very shameful thing to pass from the table of the Lord to the table of demons; i.e., it is a sign of great ingratitude against Christ, and of great irreverence toward the Sacraments themselves. As a result, he advances examples of the Jews to show this very thing. Hence, it is not required (as Calvin would have it), that we attribute equal force to the Red Sea and Baptism, to the manna and the Eucharist. Inasmuch as they are inferior things, so much the more the argument of Paul is stronger. If the Jews were punished because they scorned the figures of our Sacraments and were ungrateful to God, from whom they received those benefits, how much more justly are Christians to be punished who scorn the Sacraments themselves and are ungrateful to God, from whom they receive by far greater benefits?

To the fourth part of the argument, *I respond:* St. Augustine never says our Sacraments and the Old are equal in regard to their efficacy, but only in regard to their *signification,* or the *rem significatam,* because they all exceedingly signify the same Christ. See Augustine not only in *Tract. in Joan.* 26 & 45, which our adversaries cite, but also in *Psalm* 72 & 77, as well as *Tract. in Joan.* 11, and *Hom.* 27 from his *Book of 50 Homilies.* Everywhere he repeats the same thing: the signs were different, but one thing was signified, i.e., Christ. Moreover, those words which Calvin cites from *Tract.*

in Joan. 26, "They are different in visible species, equal in spiritual power," have not been adduced in their entirety and in good faith. For Augustine speaks in this way, "The old were one thing, ours another, but in the visible species, nevertheless they signify this same spiritual power," i.e., they were different signs, nevertheless, in regard to the spiritual force power to signify, they were the same because they signified the same thing. He said this a little more clearly earlier in that tract, "They were different in signs, but in the thing which is signified, they are equal." Nor could Augustine say in any manner what Calvin attributes to him, that the Old Sacraments were equal to ours in regard to efficacy, since On *Psalm 72*, he had said ours are more wholesome and happier, and in *Contra Faustum* (19, 13) he said ours are greater in virtue, better in utility.

We must observe one thing here. The exposition of Augustine, who understands *by same spiritual food*, Paul in 1 Cor. 10:3 to mean the old and new Sacraments are the same in regard to the power to signify, and thence, that food is called spiritual, is not against us, as we have already shown. Nevertheless, it must not necessarily be followed, for if through spiritual food we were to understand food spiritually understood, as Augustine would have it, then only the just would have eaten it. This is what Augustine upholds, and he notes that Paul said, "Our fathers ate the same spiritual food," not, however, *your fathers*, because he is only speaking about the just, who are similar to us. But Christ, in John 6:59, said, "Your fathers ate the manna," not *our fathers*, because the Lord spoke on the wicked Jews who did not eat that food spiritually. But this is opposed to the words of the Apostle, who says, "Our fathers all ate the same spiritual food." Through *all*, he understands not merely all the just, but all absolutely, both the good and the bad who were in the desert. For he added, "But a great many of them did not please God," and a little before he had said, "Our Fathers were all under a cloud, and they all crossed the Red Sea." Certainly, not only the good, but also the wicked were under a cloud, and they crossed the sea. Therefore, the exposition of Chrysostom and Cyril (as well as of other interpreters), whom we followed above, is truer. It should be no wonder if we favor Chrysostom's exposition of this passage in favor of Augustine, since he wrote his commentary explicitly on this Epistle of St. Paul, while Augustine, however, explained this passage in passing in his commentary on John.

4) The *fourth* argument Chemnitz takes from Paul in Coloss. 2:11, "In whom also you are circumcised with the circumcision not made by hand, in despoiling of the body of the flesh." Chemnitz says (*loc. cit.* p. 66), "Paul, by interchanging the terms Circumcision and Baptism, signifies we who in the New Testament have the despoiling of the body of the sins of the flesh, received and now possess the same thing that the circumcised in the Old Testament received through Circumcision."

I respond: This argument concludes nothing. Even if Paul calls Baptism

Chapter XVII: Objections Answered

Circumcision, because Circumcision was a figure of Baptism, still it does not follow from there that the effect of each was the same. Rather, it follows that they are not the same, since the force of the figure and the thing prefigured could not be the same. This is why the same Apostle calls the Jewish Circumcision made by hand, but he denies that ours is made by hand, because the one who principally baptizes is God, not a man. Moreover, Paul does not attribute the effect of Circumcision to Baptism, for to despoil from the body of sins, i.e., from the body the guilt of sins, and render a man purely spiritual, Paul attributes only to Christian Circumcision, i.e., Baptism. The Jewish Circumcision did not circumcise the whole body, but only one part.

5) The *fifth* argument is of Chemnitz (*loc. cit.* p. 67), from Paul in Hebrews 13:8, "Christ is the same, yesterday, today, and forever."

I respond: If this argument concluded anything, it only concludes the Sacraments of the Old Law signified the same thing which ours do, namely Christ, who was hidden in the Old Testament in figures and prophecies. Not even this concludes the matter. The Apostle speaks about *faith and doctrine*, not about Sacraments; he means Christ to be believed to be eternal, not temporal, as the heretics dreamed up.[15]

---

15 *Recognitium n. II*: In book 2, after ch. 17, I felt the reader must be advised that in the whole preceding disputation I never intended to deny that in Circumcision original sin was usually remitted, but only that circumcision itself did not remit sin *by its own power, and ex opere operato*, as Baptism does. Later, in ch. 26, I clearly made the exception of Circumcision, when I said, "The old Sacraments were not instituted to remit sins," although some of the Fathers, whom I adduced to prove that none of the old Sacraments conferred grace *ex opere operato*, they seem at some time to signify that Circumcision in no way availed to the remission of sins nevertheless, I am not unaware that St. Augustine, as well as the Fathers and Doctors who lived after his times, handed down in a great consensus that original sin was remitted in Circumcision, namely St. Gregory (*Moral.* 4, 2). The author of the sermons on the *Cardinal Works of Christ*, in the *Serm. On Circumcision*, which is falsely attributed to St. Cyprian; Bede (*Quaest. Var.*, 15; *ad Luc.* 2), Bernard (*Epist.* 77), and lastly Lombard in the *Sentences*, 4, dist. 1, which all Scholastic Theologians follow, and Pope Innocent III (*c. Majores, de Baptismo et Ejus Effectu*); I will not have dared, nor will any pious Doctor with me, to scorn such a consensus of Doctors, especially with the added teaching of a Supreme Pontiff.

CHAPTER XVIII

On the Character

Now we come to the *third* question on the effect of the Sacraments, which is on the character. Namely, do the Sacraments impress some indelible character on the soul? We will say three things: 1) *Firstly*, what our adversaries suppose in regard to the character; 2) *secondly*, what is the opinion and teaching of Catholics on the character; 3) *thirdly*, we will prove this truth from Scripture, the Fathers and argumentation. From all this the arguments of our adversaries will evaporate.

In regard to the *first*, John Wycliffe (*Trialogi* 4, 15), as Thomas Waldens witnesses (*de Sacramentis* 2, 109), upholds the Sacramental Character can be proven from neither Scripture nor reason. All the heretics of this time teach the same thing, especially John Calvin (*Antidote to the Council of Trent*, sess. 7, c. 9) and Chemnitz (*Examination of the Council of Trent*, 2 part., p. 127 et *seqq.*), as well as Tilman Hesch (*On the Errors of the Papists* tit. 5).

Chemnitz uses three arguments. *First*, that in the Scriptures and the Fathers, there is a marvelous silence about the character. This argument is also of Calvin, and what we will say on that will make the whole house of cards tumble.

The *second* is, that among themselves, even the Scholastics are uncertain; he shows it from Gabriel Biel. This argument will also evaporate in short order.

The *third*, that the first author, or the inventor of the character was Pope Innocent III, who partly decreed many things, and also partly made them, and among other things he took care to have Otho created Emperor, and later excommunicated and deposed him. In such an argument there are two lies. One, that Innocent III was the first to devise the character, which is a lie. The same Innocent (cap. *Majores, extra de Baptismo*) relates the opinion of certain men, saying that anyone who is baptized against his will, receives only the character, like those who are feigned to be baptized. Therefore, he was not the first to devise the character. The other, that the same Pope was evil; for he was one of the most praiseworthy of Popes. That I might pass over his works, his books *On the Contempt of the World*, his sermons and epistles, which breath piety, are praised by all historians as the best and most learned, and to skip Italians, we can name Blondus, Platina, and others if we would only hear the testimony of two Germans.

Albert Kranz, a German, and one who wrote Lutheran contentions, and thus was led by neither hatred nor love, says (*Metropolis* 8, 1), "[Innocent

Chapter XVIII: On the Character

III] wrote and constituted many praiseworthy things." Again (*ibid.* 12, 2) he says, "Pope Innocent III excelled much in doctrine and magnificent things, and that age had no equal." The same author, in *Saxoniae* (7, 37), writes that the Emperor Otho was a rebel against the Church and therefore, nothing prospered for him, and at length he died in great sorrow and contrition on account of that sin, to the extent that he even bid the lowliest servants of his house to tread upon his neck as a sign of penance. All this certainly teaches that the Emperor, not the Pope, had erred.

The Abbot of Ursperg, likewise a German, and who lived in the time of Innocent, was not well disposed toward him because he was attached to the Emperor Philip, who was the Pope's enemy, and at length, is the only one Chemnitz cites against Innocent. This author, I say, understood the man rightly, for, where he writes about the Emperor Philip, he says it must not be believed that the Pope preferred his will to God's, although he was opposed to Philip; in other words, the Pope did not have evil intentions, but did not favor Philip due to some false information. Later, speaking about the excommunication of Otho, the Abbot says that Otho invaded the Papal states as an enemy against an oath sworn to the Lord, so as to usurp the Papal states. Likewise, he adds that Pope Innocent wanted to bear all the injuries for the good of peace, and still, he could not even bend Otho's obstinacy. He also says the Pope, as a strong man trusting in the Lord, carried through the difficult business, namely the deposition of Otho, an expedition for aid to the Holy Land and a very great General Council that was advantageous to the Church.

CHAPTER XIX

The Teaching of Catholics in Regard to the Character

IN regard to the *second*, we will include a few propositions, whereby I shall draw together the answers of all the questions which Chemnitz touches upon, and from which he says nothing is certain.

1) The first: *Some spiritual sign is impressed upon the soul in certain Sacraments, which is called a character.* This is expressly held by all Catholics who comment on the *Sentences* 4, dist. 6, and it is expressly held in the general Councils of Florence (*Instruct. Armen.*), and Trent (sess. 7 can. 9). Moreover, we must note that some theologians, such as Durandus (4, dist. 4 q. 1) and Scotus (dist. 6 q. 9) as well as Gabriel Biel (*ibid.*, q. 2) admit the character, but teach certain things which seem to favor Chemnitz. Firstly, Durandus says, a character is not something real that is distinct from the soul, but only *respectum rationis*; nevertheless, in the same place he says that the character exists should not be denied, and all theologians say this. Therefore, the hesitation of Durandus is not on the character, whether it exists, but *what* it might be. Moreover, all the others agree the character is something real that is distinct from the soul. Scotus was uncertain about the notion of proving the character and says it cannot be proven from some manifest testimony of Scripture, or even the Fathers; nevertheless, on account of the authority of the Church, he did not doubt it is most certain that a character is imparted. Gabriel was also uncertain whether the Church had defined it. Nevertheless, he says it would be presumptuous to deny the character for he uses these words in the end of the first *dubium*. All the rest teach the character can be proved not only by the authority of the Church, but even the Scriptures and the Fathers. Therefore, there was no question among the Scholastics except on the *way* to prove the character.

The term "character," however, the Scholastics took up from Augustine, who uses this word all the time, other Fathers before Augustine call it *a sign*, or a *signaculum*, not a character; still it is the same thing. Character is the Greek term, and signifies the form, or figure, and this word is found in the Greek codex of the Scriptures in Hebrews 1:3 and in the Vulgate in Apocalypse 13:16, although in those places it is not a question of the Sacraments, but other matters.

2) The second proposition: *The character is not a relation, but an absolute quality.* This is common, with the exception of Scotus and Durandus. Durandus (*loc. cit.*) teaches the character is an *ens rationis*, i.e., a relation arriving from deputation to a certain office, the quality of relation that

Chapter XIX: Catholic Teaching on the Character 243

is in teachers, judges, etc. Such an opinion is scarcely distinguished from the heresy of this time and seems to have been expressly condemned in Councils, which, if Durandus could have seen, without a doubt he would have taught differently. The heretics do not deny, nor could they, whether there is some *relatio rationis* in ministers, which is not in others who are not deputed to ministry. Hence, the Council of Trent, when it declares anathema to those denying the character, and intended to condemn some error, without a doubt it condemned those who deny the character is real.

Scotus would have it that it is a real relation, but certainly, that can hardly be defended. The character, by the consensus of all, is produced through the sacramental action; relations are not produced. Rather, they arise from the production of a proximate foundation. Besides, what would be the foundation of this relation? The soul? But then there would be a character in every man. Is it faith or grace? Yet, without these, there cannot be a character. I know Scotus constituted a certain genus of relation, to which an action is able to exist. But we have not proposed to broadly dispute these matters, nor are there lacking some who accurately refuted that opinion of Scotus. Certainly, the very word "character," does it not signify something which is a relation? Lastly, the manner of speech of the Fathers, who say the character is impressed and fixed, and for that reason we are consecrated and signed, describes an absolute thing. Therefore, the character is an *absolute* quality, from which arises the relation of similitude to Christ, to whom we are configured by the character.

3) The third proposition: *The character has three offices, to make one suitable for divine worship, to configure to Christ, and to distinguish from others.* I explain: *a)* The first office is *to make one suitable*. The character is a certain spiritual and supernatural power, partly active, partly passive. For only three Sacraments impress a character, Baptism, Confirmation, and Order. The character of Baptism is a passive power; it makes a man suitable to receive all the other Sacraments, and without it no reception of the other Sacraments is valid. The character of Order is an active power to administer the Sacraments to others. The character of Confirmation has both: for it also makes one suited to receive the other Sacraments, and it also makes one suited to profess the faith. Nevertheless, this character of Confirmation seems principally to be more active than passive. Furthermore, here we must note that this power does not seem to be physical, but moral. For, the character does not touch upon the effect, but is only said to operate because wherever such a character exists, God is present *ex pacto*, and he comes in to produce the supernatural effect, which he does not do where there is not such a character.

b) The second office arises from the first, since this power is derived from Christ and is a certain participation, as it were, in the power of Christ who, as the supreme priest, has all power in the Sacraments. Consequently, the character configures us to Christ, and makes us more similar to him than others are who do not have the character.

c) The third office arises from the second, since, by the character we are configured to Christ by a certain special notion, thence it happens that one group of men are distinguished from others, such as priests from laity, confirmed laity from the unconfirmed, and baptized laity from the unbaptized. Thus, it is understood from there why the theologians say the character is a Sacrament, and the *res Sacramenti*, since the outward sign is such a Sacrament, grace however, is the *res tantum*. The character is an effect of the sensible Sacrament, and so it is called a *res* [thing], and at the same time it is a sign, because a man is consecrated to God, and a soldier of Christ, etc., nay more, even of grace, which is either present, or was present, unless an obstacle were placed in the way.

4) The fourth proposition: *The Sacramental character is only in the soul, as in a subject.* Note, all agree that the character is adhesively in the soul. Accidents do not adhere to an accident, but to a substance; nevertheless, one accident can be in another in two ways. *Firstly*, because by that medium it is in the substance, in the way that corporeal accidents are in a quantity. *Secondly*, because it perfects the operation of some other accident, the way faith is said to be in the intellect, while hope and charity are in the will. In this way, some place the character in the intellect, as necessary to exercise acts of the intellect. Others place it in the will because they think it disposes to charity, which is in the will. Others place it simply in the substance of the soul, and this seems truer, because it is not a habit, or an operative power. This is why the Councils of Florence and Trent say it is impressed in the soul.

5) The fifth proposition: *The character is indelible.* This is held in the aforementioned Councils, and conceded by all. The reason is *a posteriori*, because it is certain the Sacraments, which impress the character, cannot be repeated. *A priori* many reasons are adduced, but the most principal is because the character does not have a contrary and exists in an incorruptible subject. It is not like the habit of faith and the other virtues, which are removed by contrary acts; rather it is like a power according to certain men, or like a form, even a figure according to others. It happens that the character is a certain consecration of the soul; the consecration however, lasts as long as the consecrated thing endures.

6) The sixth proposition: *Only three Sacraments impress the character: Baptism, Confirmation, and Order.* This is also held in the aforesaid Councils, and conceded by all. The reason is the same *a posteriori*, which is the conclusion above. *A priori*, it is difficult and hardly necessary to give an account. It is principally adduced because in these three a man receives a new power, and is deputed to a new ministry through a new consecration, and in a certain measure changes his state; hence, he receives a new sign. In Baptism, a man passes from the devil to Christ, and is enrolled in his household, and receives the power to participate in the Sacraments and

other goods of the Church of Christ. In Confirmation, he is enrolled in the army of Christ, to bear his standard on his forehead, and receives strength and power, so from that office he will fight against demons. In the Sacrament of Order, he is enrolled in the number of generals, and put in charge of this army, and receives the power to distribute the goods of his master to others. In the other Sacraments, no change of state takes place, nor is a man deputed to a new ministry, nor does he receive a new power. Rather, he is either nourished spiritually, as in the Eucharist, or he receives the medicine against the illness and wounds of sins, as in the Sacrament of Penance, or receives the remedy against the remnants of sin, as in Extreme Unction, or lastly, he receives the remedy against concupiscence, as in Matrimony.

7) The seventh proposition: *Neither Circumcision nor any Sacrament of the Old Law impressed a character on the soul.* Thus St. Thomas (III q. 63 art. 1). Scotus thought the contrary on Circumcision in 4 dist. 6, q. 9 ad 1, but the truer opinion is of St. Thomas, for Circumcision impressed a character in the body, and in that way it was a figure of Baptism, which was going to impress a character on the soul. Besides, the character is impressed on us to receive, or administer supernatural works, whereas no works of the Sacraments of the Old Law were supernatural. Lastly, since Scotus had taught Circumcision confers grace *ex opere operato*, it is not without reason that he attributed the impression of a character to Circumcision. But we, who teach Circumcision had no force of itself apart from cutting back the flesh, we should consequently deny the power to impress a spiritual character.

8) The eighth proposition: *No character in Christ was created.* This is also the teaching of St. Thomas in III, q. 63, art. 5. The reason is that the character is a certain participation in the priesthood of Christ; therefore, it is only in those who have this priesthood through participation. Likewise, to be signed with a character is for sheep, slaves, soldiers, and lastly subjects, who are received by a superior for some ministry; but Christ is the pastor, general, Lord, etc. Besides, Christ did not receive any Sacraments of the New Law apart from the Eucharist; therefore, he did not receive their characters. Lastly, we need the character that God would run with us as if by arrangement to the Sacramental actions; but Christ did not need any to run with him by arrangement, since he is the principal cause as God and the united instrumental cause as man. No one makes an arrangement with himself, or with his arm from a concurrence.

CHAPTER XX

The Character Is Proven from the Scriptures

In regard to the third, we must prove from the divine letters that the character exists. In the meantime, we must observe that it is not to be marveled at that there are not as many testimonies found as express on the character as are found on grace. Grace is the principal effect, the character is *secondary*. Likewise, grace is the effect of all the Sacraments, while the character is only of *some* of them. Moreover, the true notion of a Sacrament can exist without a character. Lastly, the knowledge of grace is more necessary than of the character. Just the same, there are not lacking passages of Scripture from which the character can be gathered, especially joined with the explanation of the Fathers and of the Church, without which no Ecclesiastical dogma can altogether be established for certain.

1) The first testimony is of 2 Cor. 1:21-22, "He that anointed us is God, who also has sealed us, and given the pledge of the Spirit in our hearts." Here, three effects are posited for the Sacrament of Confirmation, in which we are properly anointed, and signed, both outwardly and inwardly. *Firstly*, the anointing, which without a doubt takes place by *gratiam gratum facientem*, for the oil heals the sick, renders the members robust, illuminates, consoles, etc., in the way justifying grace does. *Secondly*, it is a sign, or certain seal, whereby we are consecrated to God and deputed to his worship; through this we understand the character which the Fathers everywhere call a sign and seal. *Thirdly*, a pledge of the spirit, i.e., the testimony of a good conscience, which follows justification, and is like a pledge of future glory, for, nothing in this world is more joyful than the testimony of a good conscience; this is peace, which surpasses every sense. Nobody can answer that through this sign only the external Sacrament is understood, whereby promises are sealed, as our adversaries would have it. This is because Paul speaks about a sealing *of the heart*, not the body, as also from an *internal* anointing, and internal testimony, and because Paul says we are sealed, he does not speak of promises, otherwise, he would have to say the promises are sealed; Paul speaks in the same way on the sign and anointing. See Ambrose (*On the Holy Spirit* 1, 6), as well as Haymo and Theodoret on this passage.

2) The second passage is Ephes. 1:13, "In whom also believing, you were signed with the Holy Spirit of promise, who is the pledge of our inheritance." Here note that *believing*, in Greek is in the past tense, πισεύσαντες, i.e., after you believed. This is why he speaks about Baptism, which is given after faith; he says in Baptism the seal is given by the virtue of the Holy

Spirit. And in this way both Greeks and Latins explain it in regard to the seal, which is received in Baptism (Chrysostom, Theophylactus, Jerome, Haymo, Bede, Anselm, and others). Nor can we say here it is a question of the seal of promises to excite faith, seeing that this seal is given after faith.

3) The third passage is Ephes. 4:30, "Do not grieve the holy Spirit of God; whereby you are sealed unto the day of redemption." There, by *day of redemption* he understands the day of regeneration through Baptism, as Haymo and Oecumenius remark. Nor is the phrase *unto the day* against us, because the Apostle customarily takes up the preposition εἰς, which is joined with the accusative, in place of the preposition ἐν, which is joined with a dative in Greek, and an ablative in Latin, as in 2 Tim. 4:18, "He will save me unto his heavenly kingdom," i.e., in his heavenly kingdom.

Calvin explains all of these passages in his *Commentary* in regard to the seal of promises which God makes in hearts, so that faith will be all the more strengthened. It is contrary, however, to the manner of speech of the Apostle, who always says "we are sealed." It would be very improper and uncustomary speech to say men are sealed, in place of sealing the promises made to man.

Next the figure and prophecy of the Old Testament. Circumcision was a figure of Baptism, by the agreement of all. But Circumcision was not merely a cutting away of the flesh whereby justification from sin was signified, but it also left in the flesh a certain thing like a brand, through which Jews were discerned from non-Jews; if such a brand signified anything, certainly, it was signifying the character which Christians bear in the soul, whereby they will forever be discerned from non-Christians. The prophecy is held in Isaiah 66:18-19, where the Lord, speaking about the calling of the nations, says, "All nations and tongues will come, and they will see my glory, and I will set a sign among them." Although by this sign the sign of the cross can be understood, or something else, nevertheless, nothing is opposed if we were to say the character is understood, especially when we see Paul speak about a certain internal spiritual sign, and it is fitting to explain Scripture by Scripture when it can be done.

Some add another figure from Exod. 12:7, where the posts and lintels are signed in the blood of the lamb. Some add the prophecy of Ezechiel 9:4, "Mark a Thau upon the foreheads of the men that sigh and mourn." But these passages are not to the matter. They are explained by the Fathers in regard to the sign of the cross, which is inscribed on the foreheads, and rightly, for Ezechiel names the forehead and the lintels signify the same thing, since what is in the entryway of a house, that is the forehead on a man. This is why, even in Apocalypse 7:3, where a similar seal is found, the forehead is also named, "until we will sign the servants of our God on their foreheads." Besides, in each place all those who are signed are said to be saved, and there is not any among them who are not saved. But certainly, this does not suit the character; for many are damned with the character and many will be saved without it. But everyone who is signed with the cross of Christ, and in his blood will be saved, that is, to whom the merit of the crucifixion is applied, whose figure is the sign of the cross; nobody will be saved, to whom this merit is not applied. (See Cyprian, *Contra Demetrianum*; Jerome in *Ezechiel* 9, Gaudentius, tract. 5 in *Exod.*).

CHAPTER XXI

The Character Is Proven from the Fathers

DIONYSIUS the Areopagate, in his *Ecclesiastical Hierarchy* (2, §1), says Baptism forms a man to receive the other Sacraments. We call that formation the character. He says the same thing (§3) on those who are baptized, "The divine Majesty admits this man inwardly as part of his consort, and bestows his light, then also some sign."

Cyril of Jerusalem (in the Prologue of his *Catechetical Lectures*), describing Baptism through its effects, calls regeneration "the remission of sins, the holy and indelible seal." Likewise, he says, "The Holy Spirit, in the time of Baptism, seals your soul" (*Cateches*. 4). And again, "He, to this day, seals souls in Baptism" (*ibid.*, 16, 24). See also *Catech*. 17.

Basil, in his thirteenth *Oration*, which is an exhortation to Baptism says, "God gives tokens to those fighting under him. ... How will the angel claim you for his own, how will he snatch you up from your enemies, if he does not recognize the seal? ... The treasure that has been sealed is not easily robbed by thieves. Sheep that have been marked may approach a trap with little danger." Later, defining Baptism through its effects, he speaks of the *inviolable seal*.

Gregory Nazianzen, in his *Oration on the Holy Laver*, uses a similar phrase, that Baptism is a seal whereby the faithful are preserved, and by such a sign we are recognized as a possession of God.

Chrysostom (*Hom. 2 in Epist. Ad Ephes.*) says, "Moreover, the same marked us in the character of the Holy Spirit. ... The Israelites were also marked, but by the mark of Circumcision, just as cattle; but as sons we are marked in the Holy Spirit." In *Hom.* 14, he says we are signed as the Lord's flock.

Epiphanius in the *Panarion* (*Haeres*. 8, which is of the Epicureans), after he said Circumcision was a carnal wound and a carnal seal, he adds in regard to Baptism, "He circumcises us from sins, and marks us in the name of God," and in *Haeres*. 30, he calls Baptism the *seal of Christ*.

Ambrose (*On the Holy Spirit*, 1, 6) says, "We are signed in the spirit, as his brilliance and image, and we are enabled to possess grace, which his indeed a spiritual seal. Likewise (*de Mysteriis* 7), he says, "Recall that you have received the spiritual seal."

Augustine (*On Baptism* 6, 1) says that this was approved in a general Council, "It is clear enough to the pastors of the Catholic Church dispersed throughout the whole world, by whom the original custom was later confirmed by the authority of a plenary Council, so that even the sheep who strayed outside, and had received the character of the Lord from false plunderers without, when it comes to the salvation of Christian unity, are corrected from error, freed from captivity, and healed of their wound, nevertheless, the Lord's character is recognized rather than rejected in it." See the same thing in other places (*Epistles* 23; 50; and 204; *Tract. in John* 5 & 6; *Contra Parmen.* 2, 13; *Contra Lit. Petil.* 2, 109; *Contra Cresconium* 1, 30). You can also see similar things in Theodoret in his commentary on 2 Cor. 1, as well as Haymo, Primasius, Anselm, Theophylactus, Oecumenius (*On Eph.* 1 & 4), and Damascene *de fide*, 4, 10.

Now, one could only make the response to these passages from the Fathers that they are not talking about a character, or a seal, which is what we say, but an outward symbol. Augustine (*Serm. De gestis cum Emerito*) says three things, which seem to favor this answer. *Firstly*, he says the outward character is recognized, and being recognized, it is approved. *Secondly*, he says that if Donatus were baptized in the name of Donatus, he would be affixed with the character of Donatus on the soul. *Thirdly*, he says the character is the very invocation of the Trinity, which takes place in Baptism, "I particularly attend to faith in the name of the Father, and of the Son, and of the Holy Spirit. That is the character of my general; in regard to that mark he commanded his soldiers, or rather more companions, to impress it upon the men whom they gather into his quarters, saying, 'Go, baptize the nations in the name of the Father, and of the Son, and of the Holy Spirit.'"

I respond: The character with Augustine and the other Fathers cannot be an outward symbol or a Sacrament. *Firstly*, the Fathers say this seal is in the *soul*, not in the body, such as Cyril; or it is *spiritual*, as Ambrose; or they oppose it to the brand of Circumcision, which was on the body, such as Epiphanius and Chrysostom. Lastly it is even a type of *consecration*, as Augustine says (*Contra Epist. Parmen.* 2, 13). Certainly, the soul is properly consecrated, not the body, according to that of Tertullian (*de Resurrectione Carnis*), "The flesh is anointed to consecrate the soul." *Secondly*, they say it adheres and remains, which is not suitable to an outward symbol that does not remain except while it is being done. Augustine (*Contr. Parm.*, 2, 13) says, "The Christian Sacraments adhere no less than a corporeal mark; we see that apostates do not lose them, which, on that account, are not restored to them after they have come back to their senses, because they could not be lost." The other Fathers, who hold the same thing, say it is an *indelible seal*, such as Cyril, Nazianzen, and others. Moreover, the statements brought forward from Augustine (*loc. cit.*) observe it, where he says the character is affixed, impressed, borne, and other things, which cannot be accommodated to a passing action. *Thirdly*, if the Fathers were to call the character an outward symbol or seal, all the Sacraments would impress a character, since they are all outward symbols sealing a promise, as they say. So why did no Father ever say the Eucharist impresses a

Chapter XXI: The Fathers on the Character

character?

Now, against the passages brought forward from Augustine *I respond:* A character can be seen outwardly and recognized, not in itself, but *in its cause*. When we recognize someone has been duly baptized, at the same time we recognize the character fastened to him, because this is the effect, which always and necessarily follows its cause. That this is sufficient is clear, since we do not even see an external act after it has taken place. This is why Augustine could not rightly speak about an outward symbol that is seen and acknowledged when men who were baptized by heretics come to the Church.

To that bit on the character of Donatus, I say Augustine speaks *hypothetically*, not absolutely; he means to say, if Donatus could confer a Sacrament in his own name, it would impress his character. Otherwise, Augustine was not unaware that Baptism conferred in the name of Donatus would both not impress a character on the soul, and also not be an outward Sacrament.

To the last, I say the invocation of the Trinity, and the whole outward symbol can be called a character, not impressed, but *impressing*. Just as the same image is in the seal and in the wax, whereas the image of the seal is the character impressing, and the character in the wax has been impressed, so the outward Sacrament, and especially the form of the Sacrament, is the character impressing, since the character soon follows its conferral in the soul, and it follows from the force and impression of the Sacrament.

CHAPTER XXII

The Character Is Shown from Argumentation

THE *first* argument is taken from divine liberality and custom. God differs from men in this, that men, when they enjoin some duty upon men, do not attribute something internal, whereby they become suited to that office. When they love something, they do not make it good and beautiful, rather, they love because it is so; when they want to be loved by others, or to be believed, or have men hope in them, they do not attribute to them some internal power, by which they love, hope, or believe. God, however, when he loves, he makes it good by loving, and beautiful by infusing grace, and when he wishes to be believed, hoped in, and loved, he infuses the habits of faith, hope, and charity. Thus, in the same way it is believable that when God assigns someone, and consecrates him to either give or receive the Sacraments, or other ministries, he does not do it through a simple assignment, as men normally do, but by infusing certain qualities, whereby they become fitting and suited for these kinds of offices, or ministries, and we call these qualities *characters*.

The *second* argument: Baptism, by the common opinion (with the exception of Anabaptists), confers something Sacramental, even if it were to be given and perceived without faith. Eucharist and Absolution confer nothing without faith; therefore, Baptism has some Sacramental effect apart from grace. The same argument can also be made in regard to Confirmation and Order. The antecedent is proven: A man that is baptized by infidels, and communicates with them in unbelief is also truly said to be properly baptized provided the due rite was observed, as well as the form of words with intention. The Lutherans and Calvinists do not deny it, but one who is absolved without faith is not truly absolved, and he that receives the Eucharist without faith does not truly communicate with the Lord's body, according to Calvin. According to Catholics, he indeed takes the true body of the Lord with his mouth, but receives nothing in his soul apart from sin. Therefore, some Sacramental effect remains from Baptism, which is not grace, since grace is not given without faith, and it is not the outward action itself, because that is also found in the Eucharist and Absolution. As a result, it is some other permanent thing in the soul, and we call this *the character*. Otherwise, let our adversaries explain why without faith a man is truly baptized, and not truly absolved, or does not truly communicate with the Lord's body. And this was the ancient question of the Donatists, who did not think Baptism had any effect other than to give grace, and therefore, they thought Baptism received without faith was empty.

Chapter XXII: Arguments Proving the Character   253

The *third* argument: Baptism cannot be repeated if it was once validly conferred, which is also the case for Confirmation and Order, the rest can, as we know in regard to Eucharist and Absolution. The true cause of this distinction cannot be assigned except by the character, so it is necessary to uphold that a certain character is impressed through these Sacraments. The major proposition has been received by all, even the heretics of this time, with the exception of the Anabaptists. The minor is proven: In the first place, if a character is posited, it will be the particular reason for the distinction. So, certain Sacraments cannot be repeated because once they have been given they always remain in effect; the grace, which is the sole effect of the Sacraments, can easily be lost and often is. Besides, even if at times it is not lost, still it can be increased, and thus the Sacrament can be repeated so that grace will increase. The character cannot be increased by repetition of the same Sacrament. Add, that grace is not a Sacrament, but merely the effect of the Sacrament. Consequently, this argument rightly shows why some Sacraments are not repeated, while others are, as the Councils of Florence and Trent teach. If, however, this argument were not admitted, no other sufficient account could be given, which I will show from the refutation of what Calvin and Chemnitz advance.

Calvin (*Inst.* 4, 18, §19) says that Baptism cannot be repeated because it is the entrance into the Church, as well as a certain initiation in faith. For this reason, just as God is one, in whom we believe, and there is one Church, in which we enter, so also Baptism is one.

This is not a strong argument. *Firstly*, because those who are baptized by heretics, and believe them, do not enter into the Church, nor are they initiated to faith, as is clear from the fact that among heretics there is neither Church, nor faith; therefore, they would be able to be baptized again. *Secondly*, those who are baptized in the Catholic Church, and later through heresy and apostasy depart from it, should again, if they wish to be saved, enter into the Church and be initiated to faith; so, why can't they be baptized again? This is why Calvin's argument would prove something, if a baptized man could not go out from the Church, or lose the faith, which still is certainly false. *Thirdly*, we no less enter into the Church and are initiated to faith through the word than through Baptism, but the word can be repeated so that we might be strengthened all the more in faith, and we might adhere more strongly to the Church; so why could Baptism also not be repeated? *Fourthly*, ordination is not an initiation to faith, nor an entry into the Church, and still it cannot be repeated, as Augustine teaches (*de Baptismo* 1, 1).

Chemnitz (*Exam.* 2 part. p. 133) already posited one reason not in his name, but in the name of the Scholastic, Gabriel Biel. The divine institution is the reason why some Sacraments can be repeated, and others cannot. Yet this argument hardly avails, for not without great reason would God forbid something so useful to be repeated. Men who cannot assign any reason why God would forbid a thing rashly say God forbade it. How do they know God forbade it? The Scriptures do not clearly say it. On the other hand, if you were to flee to the tradition of the Fathers and the Councils, both teach together that God willed that certain Sacraments impress a character while others do not.

Chemnitz himself (*ibid.*, p. 136) sends us to another place, where he promises that he will give very solid reasons from Scripture, and furnishes it later (pp. 238-240) while examining Trent's Canon 11 on Baptism. But there he posits four reasons, which he admits are not too strong, then another four which are very strong.

The first from the weaker arguments is that Baptism signifies the death of Christ; but Christ only died once. This does not avail, for the Eucharist also signifies the death of Christ (1 Cor. 11:26), and yet it can be repeated. All the Sacrifices of the Jews also signified the death of Christ, and still, they were frequently repeated. They will say these are not similar, because by Baptism we ourselves are put to death with Christ; we die to sin, just as he died in body. On the other hand, either the force of Chemnitz's argument is taken from the fact that the death of Christ, which is one, is represented through Baptism, or because we die to sin. If they will say the first, the argument concludes nothing, because what was done once can be represented more often, as is clear from plays, where deeds that were once done are represented; inasmuch as for this purpose, *per accidens*, is it that we also die in Baptism. If they would say the second, then the argument also concludes nothing, because the same man can die with Christ often, if, namely, he would sin often and repent of his sins as often. Besides, Ordination is not a representation of the death of Christ, and still it cannot be repeated. Thus, that it is a representation of the death of Christ is not the true reason forbidding its repetition.

His *second* argument from the weaker ones, is that in John 13:10 it is said, "He that is washed, does not need but to wash his feet, but is clean wholly." This is not a strong argument because he speaks about a man who is really clean. This is why a man that became unclean again after Baptism would not be forbidden from being baptized again by this testimony.

The *third* argument from the weaker ones is because in Hebrews 6:4 it is said, "It is impossible for those who were once illuminated, ... to be renewed again to penance," where, through illumination Baptism is understood. This does not avail, because Paul speaks about those who were once illuminated and renewed, i.e., *justified*, as is clear from the words "renewed again." This is why they could at least be justified in a second baptism, who were not in the first.

The *fourth* argument from the weaker ones is because in Ephesians 4:5, it is said "One Baptism." This is not a strong argument. It is called one Baptism because only the Baptism of Christ is salutary, and it is celebrated in one certain rite. Otherwise, there is also said to be one faith in the same

Chapter XXII: Arguments Proving the Character

place, and in 1 Cor. 10:17, the Eucharist is called one bread; nevertheless, we repeat the confession of faith as well as the reception of the Eucharist. If anyone loses the faith, he may and must acquire it again, and still he cannot receive Baptism again.

Now, the *first* argument from the stronger group is that the arrangement of God with us that was begun in Baptism is perpetual. God does not follow the common rule, "The one breaking trust, his trust is broken." Rather, he always keeps his agreement, even if we should be unfaithful. "Shall their infidelity make the faith of God without effect? God forbid" (Rom. 3:3). This is why, when we sin after Baptism, there is no need for a new arrangement, but it is enough to run back to that which was once begun in Baptism.

This argument is weaker than the others. Firstly, in Hebrews 6:4, Paul rejects that a man who has sinned after Baptism can return to the arrangement of Baptism. Therefore, he does not say it is impossible to be baptized again, but "It is impossible to be renewed again," i.e., a man cannot more fully return to the friendship of God and the remission of all sin and penalty with the ease that he once did in Baptism. Rather, he needs a laborious penance, fasting, tears, etc.; hence, he needs another arrangement of God more severe than what the first was.

Secondly, when someone is baptized without faith, God does not make any arrangement with him, for the arrangement is among two consenting parties. This is why even Chemnitz says not only is grace offered by Baptism, but also shown, applied, and given. Yet certainly, it is neither applied nor given to a man who does not believe, therefore, at least they could be rebaptized according to that argument, who received Baptism without faith, which is false as our adversaries also concede.

Thirdly, just as Baptism is an arrangement, so also the word of God, especially according to our adversaries, who say the word and the Sacrament stand in altogether the same way in justification. Yet, the word is repeated daily.

Fourthly, the Eucharist contains an arrangement with God no less than Baptism, and still it can be repeated.

Lastly, it is false that the arrangement of God is perpetual for the one who breaks trust with God, so that the promise must be preserved, and however he conducts himself toward the one to whom the promise was made. Now, the promises of God are conditional. He promises that he will be a father and spouse in Baptism, if we will persevere as sons and spouses; otherwise, the same God says, "I will speak suddenly against a nation, and against a kingdom, to root out and to pulldown, and to destroy it. If that nation against which I have spoken, shall repent of their evil, I will also repent of the evil that I have devised to do to them" (Jer. 18:7). What Chemnitz adduces from Romans 3:3, "Shall their infidelity make the faith of God without effect? God forbid," is understood from *absolute* promises, of the sort that sending the Messiah was, but Baptism was not this sort of promise. At least, it depends upon the faith of the recipient, as our adversaries themselves teach; hence, it is not absolute.

The *second* of Chemnitz's very strong arguments is that nothing was ever written about repeating Baptism; while on the others it has been written, such as on the Eucharist in 1 Cor. 11:26, "As often as you will do this," and on Penance in Matt. 18:22, "I do not say to you even seven times, but seven times seven." Now, this argument does not avail much. That I might pass over the fact that this passage of Matthew is not understood in regard to the Sacrament of Penance, but on *bearing with injustice*, we can answer Chemnitz what Luther answered Carlstadt (*Contra Coelestes Prophetas*, on the term Sacrament), that while it is not written that Baptism should be repeated, it is also not written that it must not be repeated. Augustine (*On the Trinity.* 7, 4) speaks in this way on the name of three persons, "We say in God there are three persons, not because Scripture says it, but because it does not contradict it," and so we could also rebaptize not because Scripture says it, but because it does not contradict it, and such a Baptism is a good and very useful thing, if it were not a danger of sacrilege on account of the character that had already been impressed.

The *third* of Chemnitz's very strong arguments is that we do not have an example in the Scriptures of a second Baptism; besides, Circumcision, which is a figure of Baptism, was only received once. Now, this is similar to the previous argument, for in Scripture we also do not have an example of someone who was forbidden to be baptized; nay more, according to our adversaries we have an example of second Baptism. In Acts 19:5, Paul commanded those to be baptized who were baptized by John the Baptist, and according to all Lutherans, and Chemnitz himself, this had the same force and efficacy as the Baptism of Christ and John. So, if we only seek examples of Scripture, it would be altogether fitting to rebaptize. So our adversaries ought to open their eyes and understand; after the Baptism of John one could be rebaptized, because it did not have an indelible effect in the soul, as the Baptism of Christ has. If we were to regard the examples of the Fathers, the Lutherans should altogether rebaptize. Cyprian, and other Africans, and some in Asia rebaptized, moreover they resisted the Roman Church, which refused to rebaptize, as is clear from Eusebius (*Hist.* 7). Why do our adversaries not prefer to follow the African and Asian Fathers in this matter than the Roman Church, as they usually do in all other matters?

What Chemnitz advances from Circumcision, however, favors us. Circumcision was not repeated, because it impressed an indelible character in the flesh.

The *fourth* of his stronger arguments is that through Baptism we are born spiritually. However, there is only one spiritual birth, as there is one bodily birth. This is why Nicodemus asks (Jo. 3:4), "How can a man be born when he is old?" He was rightly judging about bodily birth.

Chemnitz has stolen this argument from Catholics, for St. Thomas

Chapter XXII: Arguments Proving the Character

holds this in III q. 66, a. 9. There is this difference between Catholics and Chemnitz, that Catholics use it as a certain congruity, and at the same time, they know the true cause is the impression of the character. The Councils of Florence and Trent, that we have already cited, posit the only argument as the true one. But Chemnitz, after rejecting the true cause, embraces that congruity as a very strong argument.

So, I will show that even this argument is not strong. In the first place, a man not only through Baptism, but also through faith and the word of God, is born spiritually, as our adversaries concede, and is clear from Paul in 1 Cor. 4:15, "I begot you through the Gospel," and nevertheless, acts of faith and sermons are often repeated. Besides, *secondly*, even if bodily generation is one naturally nevertheless, it can be repeated supernaturally, and indeed it will really be repeated in the resurrection, which the Lord calls regeneration in Matt. 19:38. So, since Baptism is a supernatural generation, what forbids it from being repeated? *Thirdly*, even if bodily generation in no way can be repeated, still, the reason for spiritual generation is not the same. Just as bodily death is only one, so is bodily birth. But spiritual death is manifold, as is clear. So why could spiritual generation also not be manifold? *Fourthly*, Ordination is not a generation, and still it cannot be repeated. Lastly, those who are baptized without faith are really not regenerated, and still they cannot be rebaptized; on the other hand, those who were regenerated before Baptism through faith, contrition, and the desire for Baptism, are baptized later just the same, as is clear from Cornelius (Acts 10:48). Therefore, that is not the reason.

THE FIFTH CONTROVERSY

On the Number and Order of the Sacraments

The fifth Controversy, which is on the number of the Sacraments, has four parts. Firstly, we will explain the teachings of the heretics. Secondly, we will prove the truth of the Catholic faith. Thirdly, we will refute the arguments of our adversaries. Fourthly, we will add something about the order of the Sacraments by way of an appendix.

CHAPTER XXIII

What the Heretics Suppose about the Number of the Sacraments

Now for what pertains to the first point, our adversaries have great disagreement amongst themselves on the number of the Sacraments. Luther paved the way for all of them in his work *On the Babylonian Captivity*. In that little book, published in 1520, he taught many things. In the beginning of the book, he says there was only one Sacrament, if one is going to speak according to the use of Scripture. Still, in the same book, the seven Sacraments are denied, and three were posited for the time being: Baptism, the bread, and Penance. In the end of the book he says, if we prefer to speak more rigidly, Baptism and the bread are the only two Sacraments. In the middle of the book (in the chapter on Confirmation), he does not condemn seven Sacraments, but only denies they can be proven from Scripture. But this does not line up with the beginning of the book, where he says that he must deny there are seven, and posits three; for it is not one thing to condemn and another to deny that there are seven Sacraments. From this inconstancy of Luther, the different sects of Lutherans arose, as well as the teachings of other heretics which I will enumerate briefly.

1) The *first* is of Luther, that there is only one Sacrament, although there are a great many sacramental signs (*loc. cit.*). But he did not have followers in this opinion; all others posit more, and suppose that they posit these according to the use of Scripture.

2) The *second* opinion is of those who only number two Sacraments properly so called, Baptism and Eucharist. This, as I said, Luther showed in his work *On the Babylonian Captivity*. Melanchthon thought the same (*Loci Theo.* Published in 1521 and 1522, in the chapter on signs) where he only acknowledges these two. Likewise, Illyricus in the *Antwerp Confession* (c. 11 on the Sacraments and 18 on Absolution). Nicholas Selenccerus (*Paedagog.* 2 part. on the Sacraments) and Chemnitz (*Exam.* 2 part. on the number of the Sacraments, p. 12 et *seqq*).

3) The *third* opinion is of those who number three Sacraments Baptism, Eucharist, and Penance. This is more common and more received among Lutherans. In the first place, Luther, even if he preferred the rigid interpretation of only two, still he also said there were three, and later always repeated it, as in the year 1523 (*Ad Pragenses de Instituendis Ministris*), and in 1534 (*de Missa Privata*), and lastly in 1545, which was the last year of his life, in his assertions against the Doctors of Louvain. He holds this in his 35th Assertion, "Penance, with the power of the absolving keys, we gladly confess to be a Sacrament, for it has the promise, and faith in the remission of sins on account of Christ." Nearly every Catechism of the Lutherans, as the Catechisms of Melanchthon, Brenz, and others. Likewise, their ritual books, or *Agenda*, and lastly, the *Apologia for the Augsburg Confession*, art. 13.

Here we must note that Illyricus and Chemnitz cannot be defended from perjury and defection from the Augsburg Confession. As Tilman Hesch relates (*de Praesentia Corporis Christi in Coena*), when the Lutherans are promoted to a degree or pastorship, they swear on the words of the Confession and its Apology. But Illyricus, in his *Apology for the Antwerp Confession* (c. 18), and Chemnitz (*Exam.* 2 part., p. 44 & 903) respond that the *Apology for the Augsburg Confession* called Penance a Sacrament broadly, when it is not truly and properly a Sacrament. Now, the answer does not avail because the *Apologia* has these words, "If we call the Sacraments rites which have the command of God, and to which the promise of grace is added, it is easy to judge what the Sacraments properly are. ... So truly, Baptism, the Lord's Supper, and Absolution (the Sacrament of Penance) are Sacraments, since these rites have the command of God, and the promise of grace." Besides, the only reason that Chemnitz does not hold Absolution properly to be a Sacrament is because it does not have a rite commanded by God. On the other hand, the Apologia professes that Absolution has a rite commanded by God. So, by the teaching of the *Apologia*, Absolution is most truly a Sacrament.

4) The *fourth* opinion is of Zwingli (*de Vera et Falsa Religione*). In the chapter on the Sacraments, he teaches that there are only two: Baptism, and the Supper. Nevertheless, in his chapter on Matrimony, he also adds Matrimony as a Sacrament. It is true that Zwingli did not gladly call Matrimony a Sacrament, but the reason is not that he thought the

Chapter XXIII: The Number According to Heretics

definition of a Sacrament was unsuitable for Matrimony, rather, because he feared that by the word Sacrament the dignity of Matrimony would be obscured and stained; for he says the word Matrimony, or wedlock, is far more illustrious than Sacrament.

5) The *fifth* opinion is of Calvin, who numbers three Sacraments, but not the same as Luther and Zwingli. He would have it that Baptism, the Lord's Supper, and Ordination are Sacraments. Even if in the *Institutes* (4, 18, §19-20) he says that Baptism and the Supper are the only two Sacraments, nevertheless, a little later (19 §31, and earlier in 14 §20) he also numbers Ordination among the true Sacraments and teaches that although he had taught that there are only two Sacraments, he spoke on the ordinary Sacraments common to the whole Church. Hence, even in the *Antidote to the Council of Trent* (sess. 7, can. 1), he only rejects four from the number of the Sacraments: Confirmation, Penance, Extreme Unction, and Matrimony. Hence, he admits three.

6) The *sixth* opinion is composed of Lutheranism, Calvinism, and of others, who receive four Sacraments: Baptism, the Supper, Penance, and Ordination. This is the opinion of Melanchthon, who, although he had posited with Luther that there are only two Sacraments, and later three, still in the edition of *Loci Theologii* published in 1536, 1552, and 1558 (which was the last edition), he says this in the chapter on the number of the Sacraments, "I am especially pleased to also add Ordination, as they call it, i.e., the calling to the ministry of the Gospel, because this is also commanded by the Gospel mandate, and has a promise added to it, etc." In the whole chapter he profusely proves that Ordination is a Sacrament, and hence there are four Sacraments. Luke Lossius, in his *Catechism* published in 1557, teaches the same opinion, although in the 1554 edition he held there were only three.

7) The *seventh* opinion, composed from Lutheranism, Calvinism, and Zwinglianism, is not clearly, but obscurely of Melanchthon. In the last edition of *Loci*, published in 1558, although he makes only four Sacraments, still, he put forward that a fifth be added, i.e., Matrimony, with Zwingli. He affirms Matrimony is a sign of a sacred thing, and has a divine mandate, and has a connected promise. He says only one thing is lacking, that it existed before Christ. But this should not have impeded him Matrimony would be no less a Sacrament, because according to his own teaching, the Baptism of John was the truest Sacrament, and the same with our Baptism, and still it was before Christ. So, just as he would have it that Baptism was a Sacrament because it was received and confirmed before Christ, why not Matrimony for the same reason?

8) The *eighth* opinion is that there are six Sacraments. Lindanus attributes this in his *Tabulis Analyticis* to William Postellus, in his *Panthenosia*; later he died as a Catholic.

9) The *ninth* opinion is that there are seven Sacraments. Although

we hold there are seven by Catholic faith, still, this teaching for them an *opinion*, cannot be faith; for a man who is a heretic in one article simply lacks faith. Therefore, this opinion is of other Lutherans, who prefer to follow what Luther had said in the beginning, that he did not condemn seven Sacraments, although he said in the same book that he rejects seven sacraments. John Sleidanus (*Hist*.20) two years after the death of Luther in 1548, in a certain little Council in Leipzig, determined that Confirmation and Extreme Unction were rites conferring grace, and so seven Sacraments must be received. In that little Council, many theologians were present from Wittenberg and Leipzig, and with them Melanchthon, and then Surius writes in his history that they began to be called soft Lutherans, in his *History* for the year 1548. This is why Matthias Illyricus, in his book titled *The Exhortation of Illyricus to the Constancy in the Recognition of the Religion of Jesus Christ*, and the *Augsburg Confession*, asks why what he calls the *Interim* of Leipzig restored the seven Sacraments of the Papists. Then in the preface of the seventh Century of the *Centuries of Magdeburg*, the heresiarch does not hesitate to call the leaders the heads of the soft, or political Lutherans.

From all this one may gather *firstly* that the inconstancy of Luther and Melanchthon, as particular fathers of the Lutherans, is marvelous in such a serious matter. *Secondly*, the true Church cannot exist among our adversaries. A particular mark of a true Church is a consensus in the doctrine of the Sacraments among them. Luther holds this in his book *On the Marks of the Church*, as well as the *Augsburg Confession* and its *Apologia* (art. 7). They agree to such an extent that they still cannot enumerate the Sacraments in a common consensus. But if any of them should drag the Church to themselves, I wonder if they would not be ashamed on account of their fewness. Hence, it is also gathered *thirdly*, that a heresy of this sort cannot endure for a long time, for every kingdom divided against itself will be laid desolate. This is why Luther himself annotated this on Psalm 5, "No heretics were ever conquered by force, or by a trick, but by mutual dissension; nor does Christ fight with them otherwise, than by sending among them the spirit of dizziness, just as among the Sichimitas (Jud. 9), and among the workers of the tower of Babel (Gen. 11), and in the New Law, among the Arians, Donatists, and Pelagians." Hilary wrote the same thing much earlier, in *de Trinitate* 7.

CHAPTER XXIV

Catholic Truth on the Number of the Seven Sacraments Is Proven from Scripture and the Fathers

REGARDING the *second* point, the teaching of Catholics is one. There were always seven Sacraments, which is proven in three ways: 1) *Firstly*, from the testimonies of Scripture and the Fathers, which, although they do not number the Sacraments, nevertheless, they really witness that all of these seven Sacraments are true and proper; 2) *secondly*, from the other testimonies of Councils and Doctors, which precisely posit that number as seven; 3) *thirdly*, from arguments and certain congruities.

1) In regard to the first class of testimonies, we must note three things: *a)* Firstly, our adversaries should not ask us to show the explicit declaration that the number of the Sacraments is seven in the Scriptures or the Fathers. They cannot show a declaration that there are two, or three, or four, because Scripture and the Fathers did not write a Catechism in the way that we do on account of the multitude of heresies; rather, they only hand down these things in different passages. This is also not proper to the Sacraments, but common to all other things. Scripture relates the miracles of Christ, and never counts how many there were; it hands down articles of faith, and does not say how many there are. Later, the Apostles published a creed of twelve articles for certain reasons. So also, it cannot be known from Scripture how many books are canonical, but Councils later published the Canon, and a certain number, which they learned from tradition.

b) Secondly, we must note that our adversaries should not ask us to show in the Scriptures that Confession, or Ordination, and similar things are explicitly called Sacraments. We do not dispute on the name, but on the *thing*. They will not show this word is attributed to Baptism or the Eucharist, but only to Matrimony, which still nearly all the heretics deny is a true Sacrament. On the other hand, we will find the word Sacrament in Scripture attributed to many things which by the consent of all are not Sacraments, which we are arguing about now; such as in Ephesians 1:9, the proposal to call the Gentiles to faith is called the Sacrament of the will of God. In 1 Tim. 3:16, the incarnation of the Word is called the Sacrament of piety. In Apoc. 17:7, a certain sign imprinted on the forehead of a woman is called the Sacrament of the woman, who represents Babylon.

c) Thirdly, we must note that it altogether suffices if we show from Scripture and the Fathers that the definition of a Sacrament is suited to rites that are no fewer and no more than seven. Although we may not agree in the explanation of the definition of the Sacrament (as we profusely showed above in Book 1, nevertheless, we agree on a certain general definition, namely that the Sacraments are rites, or outward and sensible signs, which have a connected promise of justifying grace by the divine institution. Now that we have noted these things let us proceed to the proof.

That Baptism Is a Sacrament

Firstly, there is no question on Baptism, for the rite is expressed in "the laver of water in the word of life" (Ephes. 5:26); and in the institution and command in John 3:5, "Unless a man be born again." Matt. 28, "Baptizing them." And the promise of grace from Mark 16:16, "He who believes and will be baptized, will be saved." And Tit. 3:5, "He saved us through the laver." All the Fathers whom we cited above in the question of the effects of the Sacraments teach the same thing.

That Eucharist Is a Sacrament

On the Eucharist there is no question, for it has a rite (Matt. 26:26 and 1 Cor. 11:23), "He took bread, and giving things, broke, etc.," and an institution and mandate in the same place (v. 24), "Do this." And in John 6:54, "Unless you will eat, etc.," and the promise of grace in John 6:59, "He that eats this bread will live forever." The Fathers also teach the same thing. Augustine (*epist.* 118, 1) where, when he said Christ instituted the Sacraments in a very small number, by a most excellent signification, excellent observation, he posits Baptism and Eucharist as an example.

That Confirmation Is a Sacrament

In regard to Confirmation, we have an outward rite and imposition of hands (Act. 8:17; 19:6). We have the effect of grace in the same place, for the Holy Spirit is given by the hands of the Apostles by the same phrase which was said in Tit. 3:5 on Baptism, "By the laver of regeneration he saved you." The institution and command are not expressly found in the Scripture; nevertheless, it is clearly gathered (*loc. cit.*). The Apostles would never have confidently and ordinarily imposed hands to share the grace of the Holy Spirit unless the Lord commanded it. They were not unaware that no man could institute a ceremony in which the grace of the Holy Spirit would follow. Even Chemnitz (*Exam.* 2 part. p. 13), the *Apologia for the Augsburg Confession*, art. 13, and Calvin (*Instit.* 4, 19 §2) affirm that no man can cause an external symbol to contain a certain promise of grace. Hence, it is must be the case that either the Apostles were rash, which no man would say, or that they had a command of Christ. It was, however, an ordinary and necessary ceremony, and it was not enough to pray to God for the coming

Chapter XXIV: Number According to Catholics

of the Holy Spirit. From that it is gathered that the primary Apostles, Peter and John alone, took up the labor and journey, that they would go from Jerusalem to Samaria to impose hands on those whom Philip the deacon had baptized, since they could pray for them while remaining in Jerusalem.

Moreover, we must note that the imposition of hands was joined with anointing and the sign of the cross; these are done at the same time, while chrism is smeared in the sign of the cross on the forehead of those being confirmed, and that by the ministry of a Bishop's hand. This is why Dionysius (*de Ecclesiast. Hierarch.*, 2, 3 & 4, 3) clearly calls to mind Chrism in the Sacrament, and Tertullian (*de Resurrectione Carnis*), posits Confirmation in the same order with Baptism and the Eucharist, "The flesh is washed, so that the soul will be free from stain; it is anointed that the soul be consecrated, etc." In his work *de Praescriptionibus*, teaching the devil imitated Christian Sacraments, he places an example in these two, "He baptizes some, his own believers, ... and sets his marks on the foreheads of his soldiers." In his book *On Baptism* he states, "From here, hands are imposed through blessing, calling and inviting the Holy Spirit." There you see, Tertullian is a very ancient author, and he posits all three things, anointing, the sign of the cross on the forehead, and the imposition of hands.

Likewise, Cyprian (*Epist.* 1, 12;; 2, 1) merely calls anointing the imposition of hands and besides, clearly calls it a *Sacrament*. In *Epist.* 2, 1, speaking on Baptism and Confirmation, he says, "Then they are fully sanctified, and can be sons of God, if the they are born in each Sacrament." Augustine (*Contra lit. Petiliani*, 2, 104) says, "The Sacrament of Chrism is sacrosanct, in the kind of visible seals, just as Baptism itself."

On Penance

John 20:23 says, "Whose sins you forgive are forgiven them, and whose sins you retain, they are retained." Here, we have firstly the rite, namely outward, and a judicial absolution, which is a sign of the inward, which is done by God through the outward word, as an instrument. Secondly, we have the promise of grace, "They are forgiven them." Thirdly, we have a command (*ibid.* v. 21), "Just as my Father sent me, so also I send you." This is why the Apostle, in 2 Cor. 5:18, says, "God gave us the ministry of reconciliation," and in verse 20, "We exercise the legation for Christ."

Ambrose (*de Poenitentia* 1, 7), says, "What is the difference whether priests vindicate this right given to them through Penance or the laver? One thing is in each ministry. Now someone will say that the grace of the mysteries works in the laver. What about in Penance? Is the name of God not worked?"

Cyril (on *John* 12, 56) compares the reconciliation of penitents with Baptism.

Augustine (*de Baptismo*, 5, 20) also numbers Reconciliation with Baptism, Eucharist, and Confirmation by the imposition of hands; and in Psalm 146, on the verse *Who binds up their griefs*, he calls the Sacrament the reconciliation of penitents with clear words, "What are these bandages? Temporal Sacraments. The medicinal bandages are for our grief, meanwhile temporal Sacraments whereby we have consolation." Later, he says these Sacraments are the Eucharist and the imposition of hands of a priest in Penance, which will not be in Heaven.

On Extreme Unction

In James 5:14, we have the rite, "Let them pray over him, anointing him with oil in the name of the Lord." Likewise, the promise in verse 15, "And the Lord will lift him up, and if he is in sins, they will be forgiven him." Lastly, the command is evidently gathered from the fact that the Apostle would not dare absolutely to promise such an effect, unless he received it from the Lord, as we showed above, even by the testimony of the *Apology*, Calvin, and Chemnitz.

From the Fathers, Innocent I (*Epist.* 1, 8 *ad Decentium*) speaking on the holy oil of the sick, "[This anointing] may not be given to penitents, inasmuch as it is a kind of Sacrament. To persons whom the other Sacraments are denied, how can it be thought that one kind of Sacrament can be conceded?"

Bernard, in the life of St. Malachi, writes that he was called to anoint a dying woman, but while delayed with the anointing, she died. Malachi, however, was so vehemently sorrowful that she died without the grace of the Sacrament; therefore, he prayed for a long time and wept, until he recalled her from the dead, and then, at length, anointed her and she was altogether healed. Bernard writes, "He anointed her, knowing sins were remitted in this Sacrament.

On the Sacrament of Order

We have an outward rite, the laying on of hands (1 Tim. 4:14). Likewise, the promise of grace in the same place, "Do not the neglect grace which is in you, which was given to you through prophecy, with the imposition of hands of the priest." In 2 Tim. 1:6, he says, "I admonish you to stir up the grace of God which is in you through the imposition of my hands." Lastly, the institution and command of Ephes. 4:11, "He gave certain men as Apostles, certain as prophets, others Evangelists, others, pastors and teachers., etc." Besides, the Apostle knows how grace was given to Timothy through the imposition of hands; if he did not learn it from God, by what sign is grace conferred?

Augustine in *Contra Parmeniani* (2, 13), speaking about Baptism and

Chapter XXIV: Number According to Catholics

Ordination, says, "Both are Sacraments, and by a certain consecration both are given to a man, the former when he is baptized, the latter when he is ordained. Therefore, in the Catholic Church, it is unlawful to repeat either." He has similar things in *De Baptismo*, 1, 1.

On Matrimony

We have the very word Sacrament used in conjunction with this in Eph. 5:23, "This is a great Sacrament." Likewise, the external rite, i.e., the visible contract between man and woman; the Apostle says in regard to this, that it is a great Sacrament, as Chrysostom and Jerome explain on this passage, who also cites Nazianzen, and all others. We also have the divine institution in Matt. 19:6, "What God has joined, let no man separate." Lastly, we gather that grace is connected to it from this very passage of Paul. The union of men and women signifies the union of Christ with the Church. But that union is twofold: *a)* one, by conformity to nature, which happened in the incarnation, and this joined Christ not only with the Church, but even with the whole human race; *b)* the other is by grace and charity, and this is with the Church alone; and by reason of this Christ is said to be the bridegroom, and the Church the spouse, according to that of 2 Cor. 11:2, "I have espoused you to one husband that I may present you as a chaste virgin to Christ." Therefore, for the matrimony of a man and woman to be able signify each union of Christ with the Church, it is not only necessary for there to be a certain natural and carnal union among spouses, such as is found even among the Gentiles; but also a *spiritual* union arising from grace and charity. Hence, this Sacrament confers that grace so that the signification would be completed. This is why Paul (Ephes. 5:25) often warns men to love their wives as Christ loved the Church; and women to be subject to their husbands, as the Church is subject to Christ; and he gave the reason, because this, their union, is the Sacrament of Christ and the Church.

Now from the Fathers, Augustine (*passim*) teaches this very thing, "In our marriages, the sanctity of the Sacrament avails more than the fertility of the womb." (*de Bono Conjugali* 18). In chapter 24, he also says, "The good of marriage throughout all nations and men is for the sake of procreation, and the faith of chastity; moreover, inasmuch as what pertains to the people of God, also in the sanctity of the Sacrament, by reason of which it is also unlawful, after a divorce, to marry another." These suffice for this place, since we will advance more in the disputation on individual Sacraments.

Washing of Feet Is Not a Sacrament

Now it remains for us to prove that there are no more Sacraments than the aforesaid seven. Now truly, the Fathers called many things a Sacrament apart from these seven. Pope Alexander I (*Epist.* 1) calls holy water a Sacrament. Augustine calls the sign of the cross a Sacrament (*Contra Faustum* 19, 14, & *On Ps.* 141), and he also calls the ceremonies which proceed Baptism, such as exorcisms and similar things, Sacraments (in *Ps.* 65; *de symbol* 4, 1). Lastly, he calls a certain blessed bread which was given to Catechumens a Sacrament (*On the Merit and Remission of Sins* 2, 26). Next, St. Ambrose (*de Sacramentis*, 3, 1) and Cyprian (*Serm. On the Washing of Feet*), as well as Bernard (*Serm. de Coena Domini*), contend that the washing of the feet, which the Lord instituted in John 13:14 is a Sacrament. None of these present any difficulty apart from the last.

In the first place, neither holy water, nor the sign of the cross, nor blessed bread, nor the exorcism and other ceremonies preceding Baptism are found in Scripture; hence, our adversaries cannot hold them to be Sacraments. Next, all of those ceremonies are given before Baptism, as is certain from the same citations of Augustine. But Baptism, by the consensus of all, is the first of all Sacraments, a door as it were. Then, none of them have the promise of *gratia gratum faciens*. Furthermore, it is not certain whether they were instituted by Christ or by the Apostles, whereas only Christ could establish true Sacraments.

The greater difficulty appears in the washing of feet. In John 13:12 we have an outward rite, the very washing of feet, and likewise the promise of grace in verse 8, "If I do not wash you, you will have no share with me." Likewise, a mandate of God in verse 15, "I gave you an example," and in verse 14, "And you should wash one another's feet." Likewise, these words reveal there is a mystery in verse 7, "You do not know what I do now, but you will hereafter." Lastly, those testimonies of the Fathers, Ambrose, Cyprian, Bernard, whose testimony Chemnitz adduces (*loc. cit.* p. 32) to prove there are more than seven Sacraments, if they were established on the testimonies of the Fathers.

I respond: That washing of feet has nothing in common with Sacraments properly so called and can only be said called a Sacrament *broadly speaking*; to the extent that everything called a Sacrament has a mystical sense and figures, as well as types of other things. That washing was really a sign of the humility and charity of Christ. Likewise, it was a sign of the purity with which men ought to approach the Eucharist; therefore, Christ did this immediately before the institution of the Eucharist. Lastly, it was a sign and a certain figure of purgation, which we were going to have through the passion of Christ, as Cyril explains in this passage.

That it was not, however, a Sacrament properly so-called, is clear firstly because we do not have a promise of justifying grace, for that of verse 8, "Unless I wash you, you will have no share with me," does not literally promise grace, but *threatens punishment* on account of disobedience, as

Chrysostom, Cyril and Basil (*on Baptism* 1, 2) explain on this passage. If Peter obstinately refused that washing, he would have been damned; not because he lacked the washing of his feet, but because he would have sinned against Christ and that *obedience* would be lacking. Still, it can mystically signify, as Augustine explained on this passage, that even the just need Christ to wash them daily from venial sins, which are like the filth which adheres to their feet on account of living in human society. Now, this does not suffice to effect a Sacrament, because here it is a question on the washing of venial sins which do not need *gratia gratum faciens*. This is why the Lord says in verse 10, "He that has been washed does not need to wash his feet, but is wholly clean." In other words, he is clean simply, and absolutely, since he would be just; nevertheless, he still needs washing from venial sins. Besides, we do not have from this passage that washing of feet really takes away venial sins; otherwise, we would have to wash our feet daily. Rather, only that *one* washing, whereby the Lord washed the feet of his disciples, was a figure of the internal washing which we receive from Christ. Therefore, the washing of feet itself is not a Sacrament properly so-called.

Secondly, we do not have a command, or institution of using this rite frequently, which is required in every Sacrament; otherwise, all men who do not use those ceremonies would sin daily. Although these ceremonies were once customary in certain Churches immediately after Baptism, nevertheless, it was never received in all of them, nor in the Roman Church itself, as Ambrose witnesses (*loc. cit.*). Nor is the command in the following verses opposed to us, v. 15, "I have given you an example" v. 14, "And you should wash one another's feet," and v. 7, "What I do, you do not know now, but you will know hereafter." This command instructs *humility* and *charity*, as Chrysostom and Cyril explain, but not the material washing of feet itself, as is clear from the praxis of the Church, for Christians never supposed they had a special command on the washing of feet.

It is easy to respond to the earlier passages of the Fathers. Ambrose calls it a Sacrament and mystery, because it was preserved in his Church as *a sacred ceremony*, and as some Sacramental; nevertheless, he did not think this washing is a Sacrament properly so called, from the fact that he affirms mortal sins are not forgiven by that washing, but *certain remnants of original sin*. Furthermore, he says he does not find fault with the Roman Church where these ceremonies were not in use, but he could not say that if he thought it was a true Sacrament. Hence, Cyprian and Bernard, if we read them carefully, do not say the material washing of feet itself is a Sacrament whereby men are sanctified; they only say that *unique* washing of the feet of the Apostles which Christ did was a Sacrament, because he signified by that something sacred, which we should do daily, i.e., the expiation of venial sins, which Christ does in us daily through prayer, fasting, humility, and the exercise of piety toward our neighbors, from which we are freed. Rightly, if they would have thought washing of feet was a Sacrament, it would behoove us to daily wash each other's feet, according to that opinion, for they say this Sacrament is a daily expiation of sins.

CHAPTER XXV

That There Are Seven Sacraments Is Proven from Later Councils and Doctors

THE second proof is taken from the testimonies which precisely place the number of seven, and these testimonies are three. 1) The *first* is of all Theologians, and hence of the whole Church for at least 1500 years. Peter Lombard (4, dist. 2) and all Theologians thereafter hand down that there are seven Sacraments. Lombard did not write anything new, but found what was in the use of the Church, which is an argument of the greatest weight. If it were false, what we say, then the whole Church perniciously erred for 1500 years. Truly, if the Sacraments were fewer, it would be a great impiety and superstition, as well as a great deception to souls, to have held these as Sacraments for so long, when they really weren't. But if there were more, it would be a great impiety to have scorned the true Sacraments of God for so long, as well as a great detriment to souls. *Secondly*, it is a more pernicious error in regard to the Sacraments than in regard to other dogmas, for the rest are almost speculative, and ignorance of them excuses many simple men. However, the recognition of the Sacraments pertains to praxis, and to the praxis of individual men. *Thirdly*, a genuine use of the Sacraments pertains to the marks of the Church, by the common opinion of all the heretics of this time. This is why if, for these 1500 years, there was an error in the Sacraments as grave as this, consequently, it should be said the Church perished throughout the world, for in this time, they will not easily find men who felt otherwise about the Sacraments. Even the Hussites and Waldenses, who were nearly the only heretics before Luther appeared on the scene, received seven Sacraments. On the Hussites it is clear from the Council of Constance (sess. 15, art. 8) and in regard to the Waldensians, Luther affirms this in the book he wrote to them.

2) The *second* testimony is of the Council of Florence, in its institution of the Armenians, where the seven Sacraments are asserted and explained. Here, we must note two lies of Chemnitz. In his *Examination* (2 part. p. 35) he says that while the number of the Sacraments being seven was attempted among the Greeks, it was forced on the Armenians. He added that the Armenians were converted to the faith by St. Bartholomew, and after a thousand and more years at length received the number of the Sacraments to be seven from the Roman Pontiff. Here he lies. In the first place, when he says the Council tried this number among the Greeks, in other words he means the Council Fathers attempted to persuade the

Greeks, but could not. Now in the whole Council, there was altogether no discussion on the number of the Sacraments with the Greeks, and it is clear from the Council documents which are extant in both Greek and Latin. Nay more, this instruction for the Armenians was given with the approval of the whole Council a little before its dissolution, as we read in the decree of Eugene IV, where the institution is found. From which we understand, the Greeks altogether felt the same as the Latins in regard to the number of the Sacraments; otherwise, the Greeks would not have so easily approved the instruction without any question. That can also be confirmed by the testimony of Jeremiah, the Patriarch of Constantinople, who, in the very censure which he published against the errors of the Lutherans, witnesses that the Greeks number and receive seven Sacraments. He speaks this way in chapter 7, "Likewise, in the Catholic Church there are seven divine Sacraments, Baptism, Anointing of Sacred Oil, Holy Communion, Order, Matrimony, Penance, Extreme Unction."

In the second place, Chemnitz lies when he says this number of the Sacraments was forced upon the Armenians, since they were ignorant of them for a thousand years and more. Now (as we read in the decree of Eugene) before the union of the Armenians with the Latins, conferences were held between them on the faith of the Trinity, and of the Incarnation, of the Sacraments, and the books of each nation were accepted, and then at length the formula of the instruction was prescribed. The fact is it was not intruded; rather, after mature discussion, they received it, and really, they would not have so easily accepted it except they saw the conformity with the ancient rites and books of their Church. *Add*, that in the same instruction, the doctrine on the three divine persons and the two natures of Christ was handed down to the Armenians. So, if, as Chemnitz says, the number of seven Sacraments was intruded on them, why does he not also say the number of divine persons and nature of Christ were intruded on them?

3) The *third* testimony is the Council of Trent (sess. 7, can. 1) where an Anathema is added against those denying that there are seven true and proper Sacraments. Such a testimony ought to suffice even if we had nothing else, if we were to abolish the authority of the present Church, and the present Council, the decrees of all other Councils could be called into doubt, nay more the whole Christian faith. This was always the custom among Christians, that when controversies arose the Bishops who then lived would give a definition. Besides, the strength of all of the ancient Councils, as well as all dogmas depends upon the authority of the present Church. We do not have an infallible testimony that these were Councils, and were legitimate, and defined this or that, except because the Church which is now, and cannot err, so senses and teaches. That certain historians call these Councils to mind cannot produce any faith except human, the basis for which can be false.

CHAPTER XXVI

The Same Is Proven from Congruous Argumentation

CATHOLIC doctors usually confirm that the number of the Sacraments is seven from various congruous arguments. The *first* is from the similitude of the spiritual and bodily life. Accordingly, in bodily life, certain things are required on the side of individual men and certain things on the side of the whole commonwealth. On the side of individual men three things are required per se: generation, increase, and nutrition; and two things *per accidens*: the remedy against disease, if it should happen that a man becomes ill, and a remedy against the remnants of disease, so that he may perfectly regain his health. On the side of the commonwealth two things are required. Firstly, parents who propagate the corporeal life of man. Secondly, princes and magistrates, who order and rule them. The spiritual life works in the same way. *Firstly*, regeneration is required, which is through Baptism. Secondly, increase, through confirmation. Thirdly, nourishment, through the Eucharist. Fourthly, remedy against disease, if it should happen that a regenerated man sins, and that is through Penance. Fifthly, the remedy against the remnants of sins, through extreme unction. Sixthly, on the side of the common wealth, matrimony, whereby men are propagated, and deputed for the worship of God. Seventhly, Holy Orders, whereby they are ruled and governed.

2) The *second* argument is from the number of sins and wounds. Baptism is especially against original sin, Penance against actual and mortal. Extreme Unction against the remnants of sins, Confirmation against weakness, Eucharist against malice, Matrimony against concupiscence, Order against ignorance.

3) The *third* argument is taken from the number of virtues. Baptism corresponds to faith, Confirmation to hope, the Eucharist to charity, Penance to justice, Extreme Unction to fortitude, Order to prudence, and Matrimony to temperance.

4) The *fourth* argument is taken from the frequency of the number seven in expiations. See Exodus 29:30; Leviticus 4:6, 8:11, 13:4, 14:8, 15:13, 16:14, 23:18; Numbers 19:4; Deut. 16:3; 2 Chron. 29:21; Job 42:8. In all those passages you will always see seven animals offered in expiation, or seven days, or blood sprinkled seven times, etc. This is also why in 4 [2] Kings 5:10, Naaman was commanded to be washed seven times to cleanse leprosy. See St. Thomas (4 dist. 2, q. 1; III q. 65, art. 1, and *Contra Gentes* 4, 58).

Now Chemnitz, in his *Exam.* (2 part. p. 16-18), says three things about these arguments. *a)* Firstly, he asserts that they are the principal foundations and demonstrations of our teaching. He says, "These are the demonstrations, these foundations, in which the number of seven Sacraments has been brought into the Church, and it was received by the Scholastic writers." *b)* Secondly, he says these demonstrations do not avail because otherwise we would be able to prove there were seven Sacraments in the Old Law, since even then there were virtues, as well as sins, the spiritual and bodily life. *c)* Thirdly, he says if the number of the Sacraments ought to be taken from the frequency of numbers in Scripture, there could be three Sacraments, or even twelve, or more, because there are many numbers that are frequent and sacred in the Scriptures.

But these are trifles. In the first place, no Theologian ever said these were the foundations and proofs, but only *suitable arguments supposing faith*. The Scholastics are wont to make it that what we hold from faith should show it is not opposed to reason, but rather more in conformity with it. Still, Chemnitz's argument concludes nothing, namely that it would behoove us also to find seven Sacraments in the Old Law. For the Old Sacraments (as we showed above) were not instituted to perfect men in the spiritual life, nor to be a remedy for sin, save for Circumcision, but only to signify the Christian mysteries, and certain other purposes. Ours, on the other hand, were instituted as a remedy for sin, to justify and perfect men in the spiritual life, as is very clearly deduced from the Scriptures. Therefore, these arguments from suitability rightly stand, if they are applied to our Sacraments, but not if they are applied to the Old. Lastly, that argument of Chemnitz on the variety of numbers frequently found in the Scriptures concludes nothing, for the argument of Catholics is taken from the numbers which signify the *expiation of sins*, but not from any numbers you like. Hence, in the Scripture, the number seven is so frequent in expiations that the whole Scripture seems to shout that at some point a time would come in which seven notable and very efficacious remedies would be given by God in expiation of sins.

CHAPTER XXVII
Objections Are Answered

It remains that we refute the objections of our adversaries, which are partly from Scripture, partly from the Fathers, and partly from reason.

1) Firstly, they advance three arguments from Scripture. The first is a negative argument, because the Scriptures never hand down that there are seven Sacraments. The second is affirmative, because Scripture only teaches there are two Sacraments. John 19:34, blood and water flowed from the side of Christ, i.e., Eucharist and Baptism (as Chrysostom, Cyril, and Theophylactus explain in this passage, as well as Damascene in *de Fide* 4, 10, and Augustine in *de Symbolo* 2, 6, & *Tract. in Joan.* 9, and other places). Third, because the Scriptures do not only not posit seven and only two, but they also deny there are seven. In Apoc. 17:7, the Angel calls the Sacrament a beast which has seven heads, from which it seems to signify, the number of seven Sacraments pertains to Antichrist, who is described by that beast. These are the arguments of Chemnitz from Scripture, which he has in *Examination*, 2 part. pp. 18 & 50. But these are mere trifles.

To the *first*, we answered above that Scripture does not ever expressly name seven, nor two nor three.

To the *second*, that passage of John cannot be badly explained to mean the Eucharist and Baptism through blood and water, as nearly all the Greeks explain it, but the other Sacraments are not excluded for that reason. Only two things are posited, because these are more *common* and more *principal*, and from these the same judgment can be made on the rest. Just as in Heb. 6:2, Paul only posits two Sacraments, Baptism and the imposition of hands, i.e., Confirmation, "Not again laying the foundation of penance from dead works, and of faith towards God, of the doctrine of Baptisms, and the imposition of hands." There, by the imposition of hands, Chrysostom, Theodoret, Theophylactus, Oecumenius, and others understand Confirmation, which was given after Baptism; he does not call to mind the Eucharist, which was given at the same time with Baptism and Confirmation (as even now it is given when adults are baptized).

Nevertheless, I say *secondly*, it is not necessary to follow that exposition of the Greeks on the blood and the water, for other equally great expositors explain it otherwise. Cyril (*Cat.* 3), and Jerome (*Epist.* 83 *ad Oceanum*) understand through blood and water, two Baptisms are signified, one in blood, i.e., Martyrdom, and the other in water. Ambrose (*in Lucam* 10, 105) as well as Leo (*epist.* 4), and Augustine, as well as Bede (*in Joan.* 19) understand through the blood, the price of redemption, through water, Baptism. This also seems especially to be the literal exposition, that we would understand from the side of Christ Baptism flowed, which has all of its force from the blood of Christ. So, it did not say water and blood went out, so that the order would demand it be a question on Baptism and the Eucharist, since Baptism precedes Eucharist. Rather, it said; "Blood flowed, and also water," i.e., *the price and application of that price*. This is also confirmed from 1 John 5:6, "This is the one who came through water and blood, Jesus Christ, not in water only, but in water and blood," where it seems John himself explains the mystery which he placed in John 19:34, and at the same time shows the difference between the Baptism of Christ and of John, because John came in water only, i.e., he conferred a Baptism that was not efficacious; but Christ conferred the most efficacious Baptism, since he gave water mixed in his blood.

To the *third* I respond, Chemnitz is positively blasphemous when he calls the Sacraments of Christ the head of the beast. He is compelled, whether he wills or no, also to number the Sacraments among the heads of the beast which he holds for true Sacraments, namely Baptism and the Eucharist, for these are from the number of those seven. Add that John does not say these seven heads are the seven Sacraments, but one sacrament; hence, (if one may be permitted to taLk. nonsense) it squares more in Luther, who said there is one Sacrament, and many Sacramental signs. Lastly, John himself interprets those seven heads as *seven kings*, from which the whole blasphemous edifice of Chemnitz falls to ruin.

2) Now from the Fathers. *Firstly*, Calvin (*Inst.* 4 19 § 3) says that when the Fathers speak properly about the Sacraments they are content with two, Baptism, and the Eucharist. He shows it from Augustine (*Doct. Christ.* 3, 9; *Epist.* 118). Calvin also adds a proof. Augustine usually seeks mysteries as much as possible in numbers. Then Calvin says, "Moreover, he is usually more curious in the numbers that must be observed, than would be necessary; and still he never wrote that the number of the Sacraments was seven."

Chemnitz (*Exam.*, 2 part., p. 25 *et seqq.*) asserts three things from the fathers. *a)* Firstly, if we were to speak properly about the Sacraments, the ancient Fathers did not acknowledge any but two, Baptism and Eucharist. He shows it from Justin (*Apologia* 2), from Irenaeus, and from Tertullian (*Against Marcion*, 2, 4; *de Corona*), and likewise from Cyril (*Cathec.*), and from Ambrose (*de Sacramentis, de Mysteriis*). The last two authors expressly treat on the Sacraments, and still they do not posit any but two.

b) Secondly, he affirms the more recent Fathers posit more Sacraments than two, but fewer than seven, while speaking properly on the Sacraments. He shows it from Dionysius, whom he says we feign to be the Areopagate who, in his *Ecclesiastical Hierarchy*, explains only four Sacraments, Baptism, Eucharist, Confirmation, and Order. Likewise, from Gregory (*can. Multi*

Chapter XXVII: Objections are Answered

Saecularium, 1, q. 1, cited by Gratian), who posits three, Baptism, Chrism [Confirmation], and the Eucharist. Then from Rabanus and Paschasius (*de Coena Domini*). Lastly, from an uncertain author, who wrote under the name of Cyprian, on the cardinal works of Christ, for this author in his sermon on the Lord's Supper, on the washing of feet, and on Chrism, posits fewer than seven.

c) Thirdly, he affirms that when the Fathers speak broadly about the Sacraments, they number more than seven. He shows it from various citations from Augustine. From all of this he gathers that among the ancients there are not seven Sacraments properly or improperly speaking, but fewer or more.

I respond first to all these arguments: None of the Fathers ever wrote that the Sacraments were not seven, or that they were only two or three; rather, they only mentioned some of the Sacraments for their own purpose and said nothing of the others. They do not, however, oppose the Theologians who asserted seven Sacraments, when they neither deny there are seven nor say there are only two or three. Add the fact that the same Fathers mention only one Sacrament in many places and none in others. This is why according to Chemnitz's dialectic, it would behoove him to gather there is only one Sacrament, or even none. So, it should be enough that the Fathers in different places, or certainly different Fathers of the same age, call to mind all of the seven Sacraments in some place, as we have shown above. Now that we have prefaced this answer, I will also answer the individual Fathers.

First, we will answer the testimonies that Calvin cited from Augustine. Augustine, in those two citations, does not say there are only two, rather, he places two for the sake of example. That is clear from the same citations. In *Doctrina Christiana* (3, 9) he so holds, "The Lord Himself, and Apostolic discipline, have handed down to us a few rites in place of many, and these are easy to do, most majestic in their meaning and most sacred in the observance, just as the Sacrament of Baptism and the celebration of the Lord's body and blood." There, you see the particle "just as" clearly shows these are examples. So also in *Epistle* 118, where Augustine said we have very few Sacraments in number, most excellent in meaning, easy in observance, and adds, "just as Baptism and the communication of the Lord's body, and something else is commended by the Scripture." There, you also see examples, and it is also shown there are more than two. He repeats the fact more clearly commenting on Psalm 103, on the words, *You covered the higher rooms of it with water.* "Look," he says, "at the gifts of the Church itself, the gift of the Sacraments of Baptism, in the Eucharist, in the rest of the Holy Sacraments." In *Epist.* 119 to the same Januarius (c. 7), he says, "For the celebration of the Sacraments we use sensible things, water, wheat, wine and oil." There you see, the matter of all the Sacraments is counted, save for Penance and Matrimony, since those two do not have any consecrated matter.

Additionally, even if in certain places Augustine does not call to mind any but two, still in other places he expressly posits more, and especially in regard to Confirmation and Orders, he affirms these are Sacraments, just like Baptism (*Contra lit. Petiliani*, 2, 104; *Contra Parmen.* 2, 13). Consequently, Calvin impudently lies when he says that Augustine was content with only two Sacraments.

In regard to Confirmation, I throw the argument back at the author. If St. Augustine only believed there were two Sacraments and was more curious than was fitting in the mysteries of numbers, why did he not indicate what mysteries were hidden in the number of two Sacraments? Besides, it is not true that St. Augustine was as curious as Calvin says in the mysteries of numbers. He was not unaware that there are twelve articles of faith, three Theological virtues, Ten Commandments, and many other things of this sort. Nevertheless, Augustine wrote nothing in regard to the mysteries of such numbers. So consequently, he did not write on the mysteries of the number of seven Sacraments, lest Calvin would accuse him of curiosity in these matters.

Now I come to the passages cited by Chemnitz. To the passage of Justin, *I respond:* In his *Apologia*, Justin calls to mind two Sacraments because *the argument at hand required it*; he answered those things which the pagans objected, which were two things. Firstly, that Christians were atheists, because they did not worship the gods. Secondly, that in their gatherings they did many foul and wicked things, especially devouring human flesh, and therefore, they did not admit any to their gatherings apart from their own. In regard to such calumnies, see Tertullian in the *Apologeticus*, and Minutius Felix in *Octavius*. So, Justin responds to these two things, and so especially treats in that part of the *Apology* on faith, and teaches that Christians are not atheists, since they worship the three divine persons and besides, venerate the Angels, etc. Then, in the second part he treats on the meeting, and in passing mentions Baptism to teach that it is only lawful for the baptized to be present at the gathering, and briefly explains what Christians do on each Sunday in their gathering, where necessarily he should treat on the Eucharist because this particular mystery was in the gathering, and chiefly in this regard things had wrongly gone out about Christians, they were thought to eat the flesh of some young man. In regard to the other Sacraments, it was not necessary to speak, partly because these were unknown to the pagans and partly because they were exercised without calumny.

I respond to Irenaeus, that Irenaeus never instituted a disputation on the Sacraments, rather for the opportunity of places only recalled one or another. In 1, 9 he treats on the Eucharist, refuting the nonsense of a certain Mark in regard to the Eucharist, and in chapter 18 treats on Baptism, refuting the nonsense of other heretics of that time in regard to Baptism.

Chapter XXVII: Objections are Answered

Again in 4, 32-34, he treats on the Sacrifices of the Old Law, as well as the New, and therefore, at the same time also makes an argument on the Eucharist. Likewise, in 1, 2 he treats on Penance, and in 3, 4 he calls to mind Confession. Nor is it opposed that he does not call Penance a Sacrament, for he does not call Baptism or the Eucharist Sacrament.

The same thing can be said in regard to Tertullian: He never established a disputation on the Sacraments; rather, he particularly distinguished four in his book on the resurrection of the flesh: Baptism, Chrism [Confirmation], Eucharist, and Ordination. Nor does Chemnitz's commentary avail, that Tertullian did not make Chrism and the imposition of hands new Sacraments, but held these were ceremonies connected to Baptism. Really, Tertullian distinguishes these four, and attributes the proper effects to each. Besides, if it were a question of the ceremonies of Baptism, he would not have placed the imposition of hands after the Eucharist.

But let us see the citations which Chemnitz brings forward. Firstly, he advances the first book against Marcion. But that place favors us, for in that book he never says that there are two Sacraments; rather, he says in the Sacraments the true God willed to use water, bread, and oil, which are materials that are consecrated in five Sacraments. Nor did Tertullian call to mind the other two, because he only meant to show that our God is the true Creator of elements and of the other sensible things, against the error of Marcion, who denied it. He does this admirably well, because if another God had created these things, our God would not have used them in his Sacraments.

Secondly, Chemnitz adduces book four *Against Marcion*, where in the margin at number 51, there is an annotation of Blessed Rhenanus, "Baptism and Eucharist, two Sacraments of the primitive Church." Such an annotation deceived Chemnitz. In that place Tertullian does not say these two are the only Sacraments, rather he rebukes Marcion because he would not admit anyone to these Sacraments unless they condemned Matrimony.

Thirdly, he brings forward the book *de Corona Militis*, where none are named but Baptism and the Eucharist. Chemnitz, however, does not notice that in this book there is no question on the Sacraments, but on the *ceremonies* of the Church, which are not found in Scripture, but from Tradition. This is why there he enumerates different traditions in regard to these Sacraments, and lest we would think that Sacraments are not one thing, and ceremonies another, he adds, "For these and other disciplines of this sort, if you ask for the law of the Scriptures, you will find none; tradition is shown to you to be the author, custom their confirmation, and faith their observation."

To Cyril and Ambrose I say two things. Firstly, it is false that they only acknowledged two Sacraments, since both, in the books which Chemnitz cited, call to mind Confirmation as a Sacrament distinct from Baptism and the Eucharist. This is clear from Cyril in *Catech*. 3 and from Ambrose in *de*

Sacrament. 3, 2, and on those initiated in the mysteries, c. 7.

Secondly, I say, it is no wonder if these authors in these books only treat on three of the Sacraments, for they write expressly to Catechumens, and they instituted them from these things which are done at the time of Baptism. Hence, when adults are baptized, three Sacraments are administered to them on the same day: Baptism, Confirmation, and the Eucharist. This is certain both from the praxis which is in the Church today and from the books of Ambrose that have been cited, where the whole order of Baptism and what follows is described. This is why Amphilochius, in his life of St. Basil, writes this way on his Baptism, "Bishop Maximinus baptized Basil and Eubulus, and anointing them with the sacred Chrism, gave to them life-giving communion."

To the argument from Dionysius the Areopagate, I say that in his book on the *Ecclesiastical Hierarchy* he only discussed the matter to point out very name and *solemn* actions of the Hierarch, i.e., the Bishop. Therefore, he treats on Baptism and Eucharist, which the Bishop customarily administered with a solemn rite. Likewise, in regard to the consecration of oil and on the Ordination of clerics, which can only be done by Bishops; the other three he omits, for, in Extreme Unction, it is conferred by a priest in private; Matrimony does not need any ministry of the priests in regard to its essence, even if the presence of the pastor is altogether required by a decree of the council of Trent; and the blessing, which the Church usually gives in weddings, is celebrated by the priest in private. Lastly, Bishops indeed once solemnly imposed Penance, and then in holy week absolved the penitents; but it seems that began after the death of the Apostles, when sins began to be multiplied. This is why it is rather more an argument for the antiquity of these books. Nevertheless, Dionysius was not unaware of the Sacrament of Penance, since he calls it to mind in his epistle to Demophilus.

To Gregory, I say the words of that Canon do not seem to be of Gregory, since they are not found in his works, but they are extant in Isidore (*Etymolog.* 6, 19); but whichever they are, that author does not posit anything but certain examples.

Rabanus, in his books on the institution of clergy, treats on all the Sacraments which are suited to clerics (*de Ordine* 1, 6), and in the same book (c. 24) on Baptism, Confirmation, and the Eucharist, in 2, 29, on Penance, in ch. 11 (*ibid.*) on Extreme Unction. He only omits Marriage, because it does not pertain to clergy.

Paschasius, in his book *de Coena Domini*, why is it surprising that he did not treat on anything but the Eucharist, when this alone is what the subject of his book requires? Lastly, Cyprian, or whoever is the author of the sermons on *The Cardinal Works of Christ*, does not call to mind all the Sacraments, because he only explains the Sacraments *which the Lord instituted in the Supper*, which are Eucharist, Chrism, and Ordination. See

Chapter XXVII: Objections are Answered

the sermons on the Lord's Supper, on the washing of feet, and on Chrism. To the other passages of Chemnitz, it is not necessary to respond, because we affirm the Sacraments taken *broadly* are more than seven.[16]

In the last place, Chemnitz argues from reason and proves there are only two Sacraments, because only two suit the definition of a Sacrament. But for this to be able to affect anything, he confects a new definition, and that is very long; he places as many particles as it takes to make it appear the other five Sacraments are excluded. But we diligently refuted this definition above in the disputation on the definition of a Sacrament.

---

16 *Recognitium* no. 3: I said Cyprian, or the author of *The Cardinal Works of Christ, on the Washing of Feet, and on Chrism*, explained three Sacraments, which the Lord instituted in the Supper, which are the Eucharist, Chrism, and Ordination; but I did not rightly say the author explained the Sacraments, which Christ instituted in the Supper, when I should have rather said, that author explained the mysteries which the Church celebrates on the day of the Lord's supper, which are the institution of the Eucharist, the washing of feet, the reconciliation of penitents, and the confection of chrism.

CHAPTER XXVIII

On the Order and Comparison of the Sacraments of the New Law among Themselves

THIS one thing remains for the end of this question on the number of the Sacraments, that we should also show their order. This is one of the errors of the Lutherans, that there is no Sacrament which is more excellent than another. Luther speaks this way in his work *On Establishing Ministers to the People of Prague*, "One Sacrament cannot be more worthy than another, since they all consist in the word of God." Now, the Calvinists are compelled to say the same thing for even greater reason, since they do not place the body of Christ in the Eucharist, except as a figure of speech, there is no other reason why they should value it above Baptism. Nor do the Lutherans have a reason why they would value the Eucharist above Baptism. Even if they affirm that the true body of Christ is in the bread, still they are compelled to place the same body of Christ in the same manner in the water of Baptism, since they place it everywhere. Furthermore, there is also no reason when they attribute the same effect to each Sacrament, namely to seal the promises and to nourish faith.

On the other hand, the Council of Trent placed this error (sess. 7 can. 3) in which anathema is said to those who make the seven Sacraments of the New Law equal. In regard to this Canon, and the whole issue, we must make a few remarks. 1) The *first* is that Calvin (*Antidote*) and Chemnitz (*Exam.* 2 part. p. 75 *et seqq.*), altogether ignore the state of the present question and turn the whole issue into jokes and calumnies. They both say that they must especially keep this canon, since they do not make the seven Sacraments equal, nay more, only place a distinction between Baptism and the Eucharist on the one hand, and the remaining five on the other, so they might say that the first two are the institution of Christ, but the rest are inventions of men. But this (as I said) is to ignore the state of the question. The Council, when it says anathema to those who make the seven Sacraments equal, does not place the force of the argument on the number being seven, but *in the notion of a Sacrament*. This is the sense of the canon: if anyone makes the Sacraments of the New Law equal (which in can. 1 we said are seven), so that one is no more worthy than another, *anathema sit*. That this is the sense, however, is clear for two reasons: *a*) Because the Council in its canons, condemns the errors of the Lutherans, which was not that they made Confirmation equal to Baptism, or some other argument of the same thing in regard to those they do not hold

Chapter XXVIII: Sacraments of Old and New Law

as Sacraments; rather, because they do not posit a distinction *of dignity* between Baptism and the Eucharist. *b)* Secondly, because it is also clear from the Council itself. Within sess. 3 can. 3, it asserts the Eucharist excels all the other Sacraments; the Council does not make such a comparison in the others.

2) Note *secondly*, that Chemnitz, after ignoring the true reason for this canon, posits certain other ones, namely, that the Council wanted to renew an ancient contumely, that Chrism excels Baptism. Likewise, that the Sacrament of Order excels the others, because it brings with it the riches to be offered to it. Lastly, that the Sacrament of Order is so much more excellent than Marriage, that it cannot remain together with it. But all of these are mere calumnies and trifles that are very worthy of their authors. The Council, as I said, especially intended to condemn the error of the Lutherans on the equality of Baptism and the Eucharist, and so these censors should respond to it. We do not say the Sacrament of Order is opposed to the Sacrament of Matrimony, but the *act* of Matrimony contains something indecent to the priestly state. For if lay men should restrain themselves from their wives for a time for the sake of prayer (1 Cor. 7:4), certainly, the conjugal act impedes prayer, and much more the Sacrifice. Otherwise, we do ordain true married men, although they are *continent*, as priests.

3) Note *thirdly*, the seven Sacraments, although they are of the same genus and hence all truly and properly Sacraments, nevertheless, differ in species and according to the different notions, there are none which do not excel another for someone. Baptism excels all the others in regard to *the effect of remitting sins*; for it remits original sin which no other Sacrament remits; likewise, it remits all actual sins and every penalty due to them, which the other Sacraments do not.

Confirmation excels the others, and even Baptism itself (even if the Lutherans would not have it so), in regard to the *effect of grace to act well*. In that Sacrament the fullness of the Holy Spirit is conferred, and Confirmation is a certain perfection as well as consummation of Baptism; it presupposes the whole effect of Baptism, and a more copious superadded grace. This is why it is said to the Apostles in Luke 24:49, "Sit in the city, until you are clothed with the power from on high." Before the effect of Confirmation, which they received on the day of Pentecost, although they were baptized, they were terrified, so that they all fled in the passion; but later, once they had received the Holy Spirit, they became very courageous. This is why Cyprian (*Epist.* 2, 1) and Cornelius (*Epist. Ad Fabium*, cited by Eusebius in 6, 33) did not fear to say that those Christians who lack the Sacrament of Chrism are not fully sanctified, nor perfected Christians, even if Calvin and Chemnitz call this an ancient contumely.

The Eucharist excels all others in regard to *the very substance of the Sacrament*. The rest are certain from the sensible thing, and the certain power of acting shared to them by God through motion, but the Eucharist is not only a certain operative power, rather it truly contains Christ, the very author of that power.

Penance excels the rest by *necessity*, save for Baptism alone, with which it possesses a common excellence.

Extreme Unction excels Penance in some mode, in regard to the *effect of grace*, just as Confirmation excels Baptism. For it presupposes the whole effect of penance, and a more copious superadded grace, which can not only blot out all sins that are present, but even removes the remnants of sins.

Order excels all the others except for Confirmation by reason of the minister, for it can only be conferred by a Bishop. Nay more, it even seems to excel Confirmation in this matter, for sometimes by a dispensation, Confirmation can be conferred by a simple priest, whereas Holy Orders, and especially the priesthood, is never conferred by any except Bishops. Besides, Order excels the rest in regard to something proper to itself, that it constituted men in a higher degree than other Christians are, not (as the nonsense Chemnitz talks) because it conveys riches offered to it.

Lastly, Matrimony excels by *signification*; it signifies the union of Christ with the Church, which is why the Apostle calls it *a great Sacrament* (Eph. 5:32).

4) Note *fourthly*, the Eucharist excels all *simpliciter*. Its excellence is in the very substance of the Sacrament, and besides, this Sacrament is the consummation of all other Sacraments. This is why it is also customarily conferred after each one, when they are given to adults. However, we are going to speak of this matter in another place.

5) Note *fifthly*, the order which the Council preserves in enumerating the Sacraments is not the order of dignity. Rather, it *firstly* places five, which pertain to all, *then* two, which do not, and in the first five the order of time in which they ought to be received by their nature is preserved. *a)* Firstly, Baptism is given; secondly, Confirmation; thirdly, the Eucharist. This order is preserved when adults are baptized, and it is the natural order. Fourthly, penance is given, if it happens that one sins after Baptism; fifthly, Extreme Unction at the end of life. After these five, which are common to everyone, the other two are placed, which are not suited to everyone: Order and Matrimony, and Order is indeed placed earlier than Matrimony because Order is more excellent. Here, the notion of time should not be considered, since these two Sacraments are not joined in one man except *per accidens*.

THE SIXTH CONTROVERSY

On the Ceremonies of the Sacraments in General

ON the rites of the individual Sacraments we will argue in their proper places. Here, we are only going to dispute on rites in general. We instituted the last controversy to dispute on them, not only because they are very dignified matters, which is known, but all the more so that there would be no canon of the Council of Trent on the Sacraments in general which we will not have defended. Hitherto, we have defended all apart from the last, which says anathema to those who scorn the ceremonies of the Church, or suppose they can be omitted without sin (Sess. 7, can. 13).

There will be four parts of this question. The first, on the term, definition, and partition of ceremonies. Second, on the state of the case, as well as the errors and lies of the heretics. Third, on the explanation and proof of the truth. The fourth will be on the objections of our adversaries.

CHAPTER XXIX

On the Name, Definition, and Partition of Ceremonies

WHAT pertains to the first, we must preface certain things to understand the state of the case. The first, is what ceremonies are. There are ceremonies that are outward acts of religion which do not have praise for any other reason than they are done for the honor of God. Religion, which is the most noble of the moral virtues, has three acts, as any other virtue you like. First, the internal act, the elicited act, which is to will the honor due to God and to give worship. Secondly, an external act corresponding to the internal, which is any outward action; it is not good and praiseworthy for any reason except that it is to worship God, such as a Sacrifice, genuflection, and similar things. Thirdly, the *actum imperatum*, i.e., the act of any virtue you like, which is appointed by religion to the honor of God. In this way, fasting, almsgiving, and other things that can be called that kind of act of religion, when they are done to worship God, although otherwise they are also acts of other virtues. St. James said in regard to this third act (1:27), that religion is to visit orphans, and to guard oneself without blemish from this world. St. Augustine (*Enchirid.* 3) said God is worshiped by faith, hope, and charity. From these three acts, the first is in no way a ceremony; the third is also not a ceremony, except insofar as it is commanded by religion; the second is properly and simply a ceremony, and on that we are disputing in this place.

Now what pertains to the term. In Hebrew, ceremonies are called חֻקִּים (*chukim*), a term which signifies not so much an outward action itself as a law, or statute, whereby that action is commanded. This is why in the New Testament, the Jewish ceremonies are usually called the "law," such as in Matt. 11:13, "The Law and the Prophets even to John," and Gal. 5:3, "I testify again to every man circumcising himself, that he is a debtor to do the whole law." The Greek everywhere has the word δικαιώματα, i.e., justifications, because they were rites instituted to justify and cleanse man. The Latin translators nearly always render the term "*caeremoniam*" in the Old Testament for the Hebrew word חֻקִּים *chukim*. This Latin word, comes from the name of the town of Caere, as Livy would have it (book 5) and Valerius Maximus (1, 1), because in that town the sacred Roman rites were preserved during the time when the Galls pillaged Rome. Or, perhaps more rightly it gets its name from going without something (*carendo*), that they would be ceremonies, *caremonia* as it were, as St. Augustine supposes (*Retract.* 2, 38 as well as Gellius 4, 9 and Macrobius *Saturnal.* 2, 3) for the reason that certain ceremonies were instituted which involved abstinence, and therefore, going without (*carendo*) things, just like the sort which are found among the Jews go without the use of pork, and nearly all the votaries of the Nazarites, who forwent the use of wine, and many other things of their own will.

Now we come to the partition. There are five partitions of ceremonies. 1) The *first* partition is taken from the end, or effect. Certain ones were instituted to justify, such as the Sacraments, and on these we have not yet treated; certain ones have spiritual effects, such as to coerce demons, as in exorcism, holy water, etc.; certain ones were only for adornment and signification, such as a white garment for neophytes, the light of candles, etc., and we are arguing on these.

2) The *second* partition is taken from the efficient cause, i.e., from the institutor. Some were instituted in a certain measure by nature itself, which can be called natural things, such as: to look up to heaven when we pray to God; to raise your hands; to genuflect; and to strike the chest. Nature itself teaches us these things, which is why they are common with the pagans and certain sects. Some were instituted by God, such as many in the Old Testament and some Sacraments in the New; these are called *divine* ceremonies. Lastly, some were instituted by the Apostles or their successors, which are called *Ecclesiastical*. There is a similar partition of words, for there are certain ceremonies of visible words. We see certain

Chapter XXIX: Definition of Ceremonies

words are natural, such as those in which we express different emotions, for in that way, everyone cries, sighs, laughs, etc. Others were instituted by God, as in Gen. 1:1, the words heaven and earth, the sea, and in other places the names of some great men; lastly, others were instituted by men, as in Gen. 2:20, where Adam imposed names upon all living things.

3) The *third* partition is taken from the formal cause. Some ceremonies are the immediate worship of God, such as sacrifice, prayer, adoration, etc. Some dispose one to worship God, such as fasting, celibacy, bitterness of life, etc. Some are instruments of divine cult, such as Churches, altars, chalices, etc.

4) The *fourth* partition is from the material cause or from the material object. Some ceremonies exist in regard to persons, such as exorcisms, breathings, sprinkling with ashes, etc. Some in regard to place, such as the consecration of a Church, some in regard to time, such as feast days, vigils, Lent, and so also the times that have been determined for the celebration of the Sacraments. Some in regard to the manner, such as that the Sacraments are administered in Latin. Lastly, some in regard to things themselves, such as blessings of water, oil, vestments, palms, etc.

5) The *fifth* partition is taken from accidents, such as the fact that some are universal and some are particular. For example, fasting on the Sabbath in the times of St. Augustine was preserved at Rome, but not in Milan; and on the other hand, washing of feet after Baptism was preserved in Milan, but not at Rome. See Augustine (*Epist.* 118) and Ambrose (*de Sacramentis* 3, 1). The same is the case for other temporal matters, such as abstinence from blood and suffocated animals (Act. 15:29). Others are perpetual, such as the rites of the Sacraments. Lastly, some are of precept, while others are free. On such matters see Augustine (*loc. cit.*).

CHAPTER XXX

On the State of the Case

Now, to understand the state of the case, we must observe three things. 1) *Firstly*, our adversaries agree with us in several things. *a)* They affirm that some ceremonies are necessary for the administration of the Sacraments, apart from those ceremonies in which the essence of the Sacraments are contained. *b)* These ceremonies must be applied, which have a mandate or example in Scripture, such as prayers, thanksgiving, exhortations, and psalmody. These were in use among the Apostles, as is clear in 1 Cor. 14:18, and 1 Tim. 2:1. *c)* They affirm the Church can establish in regard to these ceremonies which are found in the Scriptures, a certain order and manner in which they should be preserved, lest there be confusion (Luther in his book *On Pious Ceremonies* and in his book *On the Formula of the Mass*, Calvin in the *Institutes* 4, 10 §14, and Chemnitz *Exam.* 2 part. p. 171). Lastly, so many Agendas, which nearly each Church publishes of its events, prove the same thing.

2) *Secondly*, we must observe that our adversaries rebuke many things in doctrine regarding the ceremonies of Catholics, but these are all their lies, not our dogmas. This is why we must note and separate all of them, so that the true state of the case would appear.

Thus, Chemnitz (*Exam.* 2 part. p. 157 *et seqq.*) attributes all these to us. Firstly, that the Council of Trent approved any rite you like devised by men, no matter how absurd. Calvin holds the same in the *Antidote* for sess. 7 can. 13. This is, however, false, for the Council did not approve anything except the rites received by the universal Church, which Augustine approves to such an extent that he says to dispute against these is the most insolent insanity.

Secondly, that we assert rites must be retained which are repugnant to the word of God. Thirdly, that the Pope can change what was instituted by Christ. Fourthly, that it is a mortal sin and worthy of anathema, to change even the least thing in these ceremonies. Calvin holds the same thing (*loc. cit.*). Fifthly, that we value human ceremonies above divine precepts. Calvin holds the same (*Instit.* 4, 10; *Confession in Apolog.* Art. 15 et ult.). Sixthly, that we suppose without these human rites the Sacraments do not have truth and efficacy. That is most clearly a very impudent lie; Tilman Hesch holds the same lie in his book *On the 600 Errors of the Popes* (tit. 15, error 13). Seventhly, that we attribute some spiritual force in each ceremony. Eighthly, that we attribute to some ceremonies the efficacy of the Sacraments,

Chapter XXX: State of the Question

such as the Paschal Candle. Luther holds something similar in his final homily on Baptism, where he says that Catholics suppose holy water and similar consecrated things are Sacraments, although the same Luther says the contrary in his book *On the Babylonian Captivity* in the chapter on Order. Ninthly, that we prefer our ceremonies to the very Sacraments of Christ. Calvin holds the same thing in the *Antidote*, where he impudently lies that we value salt, oil, and spit above the water of Baptism. Tenthly, that Tertullian and Cyprian taught from the error of the Montanists that exorcisms and anointing have spiritual effects. Now, we have never read that the Montanists taught any such thing, rather, we read it everywhere in all the Fathers. Eleventhly, that Cyprian and Cornelius attributed to Anointing the effect of Baptism, and that later, by the witness of Peter Lombard, these opinions were corrected, and now the Council of Trent has again renewed them. These are all lies. Cornelius and Cyprian do not speak on Ecclesiastical ceremonies, but on the Sacrament of *Confirmation*; they do not attribute to it the effect of Baptism, but another that is its own. Nor is there extant in Peter Lombard any word on the correction of this opinion; only the correction of the error of Cyprian on Anabaptism in the sentences (4, dist. 6).

Others add to these, that we think the particular cult of God consists in these ceremonies (Calvin *Instit.* 4, 10 §9 &12), likewise the *Augsburg Confession*, art. 26, which is on the distinction of food). Likewise, through these ceremonies men are justified, and in a certain measure succeed in place of Christ. Calvin holds the same thing (*loc. cit.* §15, and the *Apologia Confess.*, art. 15). Now, all of these are lies and do not pertain to the state of the question. All we Catholics affirm that Ecclesiastical ceremonies are not a particular worship nor does the essence and efficacy of the Sacraments depend upon them nor do they have the power to justify, as the Sacraments have, hence they are inferior to the Sacraments nor are the approved rights opposed with the word of God nor are they excessively multiplied, so that in their multitude religion, which they ought to serve, goes to ruin in a certain measure. For farmers desire in their vines apart from grapes also foliage, whereby they are adorned and the grapes are assisted; but if too much foliage grows and would impede, rather than help them, they are cut back. So, it is done in rites of this sort, as Augustine teaches (*Epist.* 119, 19). Thus, in this we agree with our adversaries.

3) Note *thirdly*, the whole controversy consists in six headings. *a)* The first is whether some ceremonies were established by Christ or the Apostles, which are not found in Scripture rather, discerned from tradition alone. *b)* The second is whether the ceremonies which are not Sacraments have any spiritual force, such as to coerce demons. *c)* The third is whether the Church could institute new ceremonies. *d)* The fourth, whether it could institute these, that the faithful would be held in conscience to preserve them, even short of scandal. *e)* The fifth, whether ceremonies of this sort

are good and meritorious and some part of the divine cult. *f)* Sixth, whether the Sacraments must be celebrated and administered in the Latin language.

To all of these Catholics respond in the affirmative. To the same headings, save for the third, nearly all the Lutherans and Calvinists respond in the negative; on the third, they do not agree among themselves. Luther (*de Formula Missae; de Piis Caeremoniis, Confess. Aug.* art. 15 & 26), as well as Melanchthon (in *Loci,* tit. On ceremonies) and Illyricus (*Apologia pro Confess. Antwerp.* C. 10), and the Lutherans in common, affirm the Church can institute some ceremonies for instruction, as well as the splendor and order of the Church, provided there is no obligation and opinion of worship. But Calvin (*Instit.* 4, 10 §11) contends that it is not licit in any way, and Brenz seems to think the same thing (*Würtemberg Confession,* chapter on Ceremonies). He says the Church can institute a disposition for sermons, readings, feasts, and other things, which are celebrated following the mandates or examples of Scripture; but it is not lawful to fabricate new rites to overshadow the truth, now made clear in the Gospel, by such things as lighting candles in the daytime, to use banners or crosses to signify the victory of Christ, etc. Chemnitz then, teaches the same thing (p. 166). After he said it is a hard question, whether men are permitted to add to some rites which the Son of God instituted by any counsel you like, he added that nothing must be added to the divine institution, or taken away, and those who make the additions, it seems to them as if the ceremonies instituted by Christ were not suitable and sufficient enough.

CHAPTER XXXI

The Truth Is Explained and Defended

Now to explain and prove the truth, we advance certain propositions. 1) First: *Christ or the Apostles instituted certain ceremonies, which we do not have from any Scripture, but from Tradition alone.*

This is going to be proved profusely when the discussion is on individual Sacraments. Now, we will briefly prove from the fact that the Sacrament of Chrism is most holy, just as the Sacrament of Baptism (as Augustine affirms, *Contra lit. Pet.* 2, 104), but God alone can institute Sacraments; thus, Christ instituted the Sacrament of Chrism, and still, we have no mention of Chrism in Scripture. Likewise, 1 Cor. 11:34, the Apostle says, "I will arrange the rest when I come." Just the same, he later wrote nothing on the rite of the Sacrament of the Eucharist, which it was a question of in that letter; nor is it believable that he did not make good on what he promised, or his laws later fell away. This is why St. Augustine affirms (*Epist.* 118), among other things, that the laws of the Apostles were that we should receive the Eucharist while fasting; and the Apostle promised it, with the other rites which the Church preserves, when he said, "I will dispose the rest when I come." Basil (*de Spiritu Sancto*, 27) enumerates many things, and firstly, the sign of the Cross, which the Apostles instituted, came from Tradition alone and was not written. For equal reasoning, Christ himself established the mixing of water with wine in the Eucharist, as Cyprian asserts (2, 3), and from him, Augustine (*Doctr. Christ.* 3, 21), and still, it is not expressly found in Scripture. More on these elsewhere.

2) The second proposition: *Some ceremonies have spiritual force.* We must also speak on this elsewhere. In the meantime, we will prove it from the sign of the cross. All the Fathers constantly affirm that the forehead must be armed and fortified against all the snares of the demons, and that it has a marvelous power. See Tertullian (*Scorpiacus*), Origen (*Homil.* 6 in Exod. 15), Cyprian (*Epist.* 4, 6), Lactantius (4, 26 & 27), Nazianzen (*Orat.* 1 in *Julianum*), Nyssa (*Life of Gregory Thaumaturgus*), Epiphanius (*Panarion*, haer. 30), Chrysostom (*Homil.* That Christ is God), Ephrem (*de Armature Spirituali*), Palladius (*Hist. Lausiaca* 2, 54), Jerome (*Life of Hilarion*), Sulpitius (*Life of St. Martin*), Augustine (*de Civit. Dei* 22, 8), Prudentius (*Hymn. Ante Somnum*), Paulinus (*Natal.* 8).

But in the name of all, let us hear St. Athanasius in his work *On the Incarnation and Salutary Arrival of the Lord*, "By the sign of the Cross, all magic is stopped, and all witchcraft evaporates to nothing. ... Let him approach who would test by experience what we have just said, and in the very presence of the deceit of demons, and the imposture of oracles, not to mention the marvels of magic, let him use the sign of that Cross which is laughed at among men, and he shall see how by that means the demons are put to flight, oracles cease, and all magic and witchcraft is brought to ruin."

Moreover, we must observe that the sign of the cross terrifies demons in three ways: *a)* Firstly, from the apprehension of the demons themselves; *b)* secondly, from the devotion of man; *c)* thirdly, it is principally from the institution of God, and so works *ex opere operato*. There can be no doubt as to the first, since the demon, when he sees the sign of the cross being made, remembers that he was defeated by the cross of Christ, and hence shudders at that sign of his downfall and flees just as dogs flee when they see sticks or stones. Next, this sign has force from the devotion of the man making the sign, in the way in which vocal prayer has force. This is because the sign of the cross is a certain invocation of the merits of Christ crucified expressed in a sign; we speak in heart, mouth, and nods. Therefore, to use the sign of the cross to oppose the devil and any evil you like, is to use the passion of Christ, i.e., to call upon God through the merits of Christ. This is why then, the effect proceeds more from the internal faith and devotion, than from the figure of the cross itself, just as when we pray using our voice, and obtain what we ask, that impetration is not attributed to the sound of our voice, but faith and devotion. Apart from these two ways, there is also a third from the institution of God and *ex opere operato*. Often the Jews, or pagans, without true faith or devotion are helped by the sign of the cross, as is clear in regard to Julian the Apostate (cited by St. Gregory Nazianzen, *in Julianum Orat.* 1), and from Josephus, a Jew, cited by Epiphanius (*Pan. Haer.* 30); and from another Jew cited by Gregory (*Dialog.* 3,3). This is why St. Augustine (83 *Questions*, 79) says, "Little wonder that these signs avail when they are put to use by good Christians. Even when they are usurped by strangers who altogether have not given their name to the militia, just the same, they avail because of the honor of the mist distinguished general....When, however, powers of this sort do not yield to these signs, God himself restrains them by secret ways when he judges it just and also useful, for in no way would any spirits dare to scorn these signs; they tremble at them, whenever they see them."

3) The third proposition: *The Church can institute new ceremonies, not to justify the impious, but for other spiritual effects.* Note, for the explanation, ceremonies instituted by the Church are useful in three ways. *a)* Firstly, to adorn and represent some mystery of religion, and in that way to assist the unlearned; and on this there is no debate among Catholics. *b)* Secondly, to cure illness and expel demons, and cleanse venial sins, as well as other kinds of things, and that is through the manner of impetration, as when the Church blesses candles, palms, fields, etc. These avail to those effects, to which they were instituted by the force of the prayers of the Church,

Chapter XXXI: The Truth is Defended

which are heard without a doubt, and on this there is no question among Catholics. *c)* In the third way, it is probable that the Church is able to institute ceremonies of this sort to the same effects, through the application of the merits of Christ; so that *ex opere operato* they produce those effects, in the way the Sacraments justify *ex opere operato*. Without a doubt, Christ merited for his Church, not only grace and glory but also all other benefits, which can be useful to it. To obtain grace and justification of the impious, he instituted the Sacraments, in which these merits are applied; nor is it lawful now to institute other signs to that principal effect. To the other lesser benefits he left the power to the Church to institute signs whereby his merits are applied. Some dispute in this way, but this is not even that certain, especially since we see these signs do not have an infallible effect. Although it could be said they have an infallible effect *if it is useful for men*, but not absolutely, because often it is not expedient for us to obtain these benefits, in the way that we normally speak about Extreme Unction, in regard to the effect of healing the body.

Whatever this case is with this, our proposition only asserts against the heretics that it is lawful for the Church to institute new ceremonies, not to justify from mortal sins, but *for other ends*. It is proved *firstly* from the examples of the Synagogue, or of private men in the Old Testament. There is not any reason why the Church of God could not do, without the express command of God (although not without God's inspiration), what some private men or the Synagogue could do in the Old Testament. In Gen. 28:18, Jacob, when he was not yet a Patriarch but a private man, devised a new ceremony by God's action, although without an explicit mandate. There, he erected a stone as a placard, pouring oil over it, and he called the name of that place Bethel, in memory of the vision which he had in that place. Likewise, the Synagogue of the Jews, added a new feast which Mordechai had created, for all to celebrate, which God did not institute in the Law, as we have it in Esther 9:17. It was done in the time of Judith in addition of another feast, as we read in Judith 16:31, "The day of the festivity of this victory is received by the Hebrews in the number of holy days, and is religiously observed by the Jews from that time until this day." Now, the fact that this book is not received by the heretics presents no obstacle to this argument. It is sufficient for us if they have the faith in it which they have in Livy or Sallust, for here it is not a question on some hidden dogma, but on the history deeds. We have a similar thing in 1 Maccab. 4:59, where a new feast of dedication of the altar was instituted, for which a feast was celebrated, and even the Lord himself ascended into Jerusalem for it (John 10:23).

Secondly, it is proven from the example of the Apostles. In Act. 15:29, the Apostles gathered in a Council and instituted a new ceremony, namely that the Gentiles should abstain from blood and suffocated animals, which God certainly never commanded except to the Jews, and besides, the Jewish law was emptied and abrogated by the death of Christ. This is why these ceremonies of the Apostles were truly new, instituted for another end, which was formerly Jewish; thus, it is called the doctrine of the Apostles (Act. 16:4). Besides, we already proved above that the Apostles instituted many other things, although they are not found in the Scripture. There is no reason why the Church cannot do now what it did then, for the Apostles did not do it from some new revelation conceded to them, but from *the ordinary power* to govern the Church, as is clear from the fact that they compelled a Council, and after gathering opinions, decreed what they judged to be useful.

Thirdly, if the Church could not do it, or it were incompatible on the side of the Church, or on the side of the ceremonies, or on the side of novelty (i.e., the Church could not do it either because it did not have the authority to establish something, or because the ceremonies, as Brenz says, are proper to the Old Testament, hence they are not suitable for the New Testament, or because it is not lawful for someone to add ceremonies to what was instituted by Christ). None of these, however, can be said. That the Church can establish something is manifestly clear even from the fact that from the beginning of the faith in each age, Councils were celebrated, which always published canons; to condemn all Councils would be manifest insanity (to pass over the great many arguments with which we have proven this in other places). That ceremonies are not repugnant to the New Law is clear from the Sacraments instituted by Christ, which are the truest ceremonies, as even our adversaries concede. Then, that novelty itself is not repugnant is clear, because the Lord never forbade that we would add ceremonies to more suitably and usefully administer his Sacraments. Nay more, since the Lord instituted very few ceremonies, he did not hand down the *manner* in which they should be administered rather, he left it without any doubt to the providence of the Pastors of his Church, as St. Augustine rightly teaches (*Epist.* 118 c. 6).

4) The fourth proposition: *The ceremonies instituted by the Church cannot be omitted without sin, even short of scandal.* This depends on another question, whether laws oblige in conscience, which we disputed in *On the Roman Pontiff*, book 4 ch. 15 *et seqq.* The particular reason is from Paul in Romans 13:1-2, "There is no power but from God, such were ordained by God; therefore, he that resists that power, resists the ordination of God. Those who resist acquire damnation for themselves." Then in v. 5, "Therefore, be subject by necessity, not only on account of wrath, but even on account of conscience." Such an opinion, even if it is applied by the Apostle in particular temporal Princes, when he added in verse 4, "If you do evil, fear; for not without cause does he bear a sword," nevertheless, it is the *general* opinion on all those having power, as Calvin concedes (*Instit.* 4, 10 §5), and it is clear from the words in v. 1, "There is no power but from God." This proposition is equivalent to this: All power is from God. There is,

Chapter XXXI: The Truth is Defended

however, in the Church a certain power of those put in charge of others, it cannot be denied, since Scripture everywhere teaches it, as in Romans 12:8, "He that rules with anxious care," 2 Cor. 13:10, "I write these things, since I am absent, that when I am there I may not deal more severely, according to the power which the Lord has given me," and in Hebrews 13:17, "Obey those placed over you." Therefore, it is effected, that those who do not preserve the laws of the Church would sin in conscience. All of these show it, "They resist the ordination of God," "They acquire damnation for themselves," "Be subject from necessity," "Not only on account of wrath, but also on account of conscience." (See more in *On the Rom. Pontiff*, loc. cit.).

But in particular, the fact that ceremonies are not all of free observance is proven from the fact that on account of ceremonies grievous dissensions arose in the Church and laws were imposed with the most severe penalties in regard to ceremonies, and at length they were held as heretics who did not obey. All of these are manifest arguments that the matter is not free. Dissensions do not arise from free affairs.

a) The first dissension was on account of legal ceremonies which the Apostles quieted down in Acts 15:28, where they say, "It has seemed to the Holy Spirit and to us, to lay no further burden upon you than these necessary things: that you abstain from things sacrificed to idols, and from blood, etc." They would not call a legal ceremony a *burden*, nor a *necessary thing* unless it obliged in conscience.

b) The second dissension was on the day of Easter, namely, regarding another ceremony. The Church made this ceremony so important that Pope Victor I was willing to separate the whole of Asia from the unity of the faith because the Asiatics refused to obey in this matter. Eusebius is a witness (*Hist.* 5, 25). Then, the Council of Nicaea came together chiefly on account of this very question, as Epiphanius writes (*Pan.* Haer. 70), as well as Constantine in his epistle cited by Eusebius (*Life of Constantine*, 3) and Athanasius (*Epist. de synodis Arimini et Selueciae*), where he also adds the Council of Nicaea commanded in clear words that everyone should obey. The Council of Antioch, also celebrated a little later, in canon 1, excommunicated those who did not keep the law of the Council of Nicaea on Easter. *Lastly*, the Fathers held them as heretics who willed to preserve that ceremony in a different way, as is clear from Epiphanius (*Pan.* Haer. 50), Augustine (*Haeres.* 29), and Theodoret (*de Fabulis Haereticorum*, 3).

c) The third dissension was on the rite of Baptism, whether the heretics were truly baptized. That dissension also aroused much of the Church, and from there many Councils were held, and at length the Donatists were held as heretics, because they would not submit to the definition of a general Council. See Eusebius (*Hist.* 6, 3) and Augustine in most of the seventh volume.

Later there were some dissensions on the choice of foods, on the times of fasting, on days of feasts, pilgrimages, vigils, candles and other ceremonies, on account of which the Encratitae are counted as heretics by Epiphanius (*Pan.* Haers. 46) and Augustine (*Haer.* 23). Then, the Manichees, who rejected a great many ceremonies of the Church (Augustine, *Contra Faustum* 20, 3 & 4). Then, the Eustaniani, cited by Socrates (2, 33) and the followers of Aërius, cited by Epiphanius (*Pan.* Haer. 75) and Augustine (haeres. 53). Then Vigilantius, cited by Jerome (*Contra Vigilantium*). Thence, Claudius of Zurich, cited by Jona in his three books on Sacred Images. Then, the Petrobrusians, cited by Bernard (*Epist.* 240). Thence, the Waldenses, cited by Guido in his *Summa de Haereticis*; and the Thaborites, cited by Aeneas Sylvius (*de Origine Bohemorum*, c. 35). Lastly, John Wycliffee, cited by Thomas Waldens (tom. 3 *de Sacramentalibus*).

Lastly, this proposition is proved, because if the observation of ceremonies were free, it would be impossible for it to be able to come about that some order and uniformity would be preserved in the Church. If now uniformity is hardly preserved in certain particular things, when it is so severely commanded, what would happen if it was a free affair? Still, the Apostle commands (1 Cor. 14:40) that everything be done genuinely and following order. Such reasoning moved Calvin to will his ceremonies be ratified by law. In the *Institutes* (4, 20 §27), he says that the Church would be disemboweled, deformed, and dissipated if ever it were lawful to change the ceremonies. In §31, he says ceremonies should be kept with a free conscience, nevertheless, in such a way that they are not held in contempt, nor passed over with supine negligence, and later he says it is not a crime if through imprudence or forgetfulness something is omitted; there he shows it is a crime if through contempt, or crass negligence they were omitted. But the Church teaches nothing else on its ceremonies.

5) The fifth proposition: *The ceremonies are not indifferent things, but are useful, meritorious, and a certain part of divine worship*. We are going to prove all of these in parts. In the first place, that the ceremonies are useful, is proven by these reasons: *a)* Ceremonies, as they arise from internal pious affection and devotion, so they also preserve it, nourish it, increase it, as St. Augustine teaches (*de Cura pro Mortuis* 5, and *Epist.* 119, 11, as well as *Confess.* 9, 6&7). We ourselves experience this when we enter basilicas ceremonially adorned with crosses and sacred images, fitted out with altars and burning lamps, we easily conceive devotion; on the other hand, when we enter the churches of the heretics, where there is nothing except a seat for preaching, and a wooden table to make a supper, we seem to have entered a profane hall, not the house of God.

b) The second utility is that ceremonies not only help the affections, but even the understanding, as Augustine teaches (*Epist.* 119, 7), and for the unlearned, ceremonies serve in place of Scripture or pictures. Furthermore, in certain times some dogmas were better persuaded by ancient ceremonies than many testimonies. Certainly, Augustine clearly thought he proved that original sin is in infants before Baptism because according to the use

Chapter XXXI: The Truth is Defended

of the Church they are exorcized, and breathed upon, and bidden through the mouths of those carrying them to renounce the devil and his works (*On the Merit and Remission of Sins* 1, 34, in *Julianum* 6, 2).

c) The third utility is that they assist the memory. Unless we were to yearly represent the Lord's birth, apparition, passion, and other mysteries of redemption with ceremonies, so many characteristic benefits would be easily forgotten.

d) The fourth is to arouse faith. We easily exercise faith when we are armed against the devil with the sign of the cross, or holy water, or similar things. By that ceremony we publicly give witness that we believe for certain that the power of the Crucifix is so great, that merely its image puts demons to flight.

e) Fifth is the preservation of religion. Ceremonies supply it lest religion would become cheap and scorned, and little by little perish. The excellence of our religion is because it is spiritual, we do not easily perceive it because we are corporeal. Therefore, bare mysteries are not proposed to us, rather they are clothed and adorned that a certain outward majesty should throw itself before the senses, and they are perceived with a greater reverence by the mind itself. Therefore, ceremonies are to religion what salt is to meat, and the skin to the marrow. This is why Augustine rightly affirms (*Contra Faustum* 19, 11) that no religion, whether true or false, can exist without ceremonies. So among the ancients, to be a theologian was nothing other than to know the gods by what ceremonies they were worshipped, as can be understood from Plato in his *Dialogue on Rule*. Among the Jews the highest thing was to know the ceremonies, as is clear from Exodus 18:20, where Jethro advises Moses to consign civil judgments to others while he taught the people the ceremonies and the rite of worship. Among Christians also, knowledge of ceremonies was of the highest value, which even the one question on Easter abundantly demonstrates. The same fact is gathered from Basil (*Epist.* 63), Leo (*Epist.* 4), and Innocent (*Epist.* 1 *ad Decentium*) who rebuked bishops that ignored ceremonies.

f) The sixth is the distinction of Catholics from heretics. Although the Sacraments are types of symbols whereby we are discerned from unbelievers, nevertheless, we can hardly be distinguished from heretics by the Sacraments; rather, we are best distinguished by ceremonies. In this time, the sign of the Cross, abstinence from meat on Friday, and similar things are the best signs distinguishing Catholics from heretics. For this reason, in the very beginning of the Church the Apostles changed the Sabbath to Sunday, lest we would seem to Judaize. Epiphanius, at the end of the *Panarion*, written against all heresies, reviewed the ceremonies of the Church to point out certain ones like marks, whereby the Church was discerned from all sects. Hence, holy men always preferred to die than be compelled to omit some ceremony, when they understood that only deserters cast away the sign of the militia. St. Eleazar is a witness to this (2

Macc. 6:28), since he preferred to be slain than to pretend to eat pork, lest in that way it would seem that he had defected from his religion. Later, the seven Maccabee brothers followed him (2 Macc. 7:2). There is also a witness in the man Tertullian presents in his book *de Corona Militis*, chapter 1, who preferred to die than be crowned with laurels like the rest of the soldiers, because among Christians it was not lawful to take part.

Moreover, the fact that they are *meritorious*, and please God, is proven: all works of virtues please God, and among God they merit the reward, if they are done, as they should be, with Faith and Charity. Ceremonies are, however, works of virtues. At the very least they are acts of religion, often they are also acts of religion and some other virtue at the same time, and lastly, when they are commanded, they are also acts of obedience. *Secondly*, the outward profession of faith pleases God, as is clear in Matt. 10:32, "He that will confess me, etc." and Romans 10:10, "Oral confession is unto salvation." Now, in ceremonies we profess faith, as is clear, because the Turk no less recognizes that I am a Christian if he sees me venerate the Cross, than if I say I am a Christian. This is why even our adversaries affirm that we publicly witness the faith through the Sacraments. Thirdly, faith, hope, charity, devotion, and every good inward act pleases God, therefore, outward acts will also please God which are partly effects of inward things, and partly increase and preserve the things themselves (as we said). This is why in Exodus 17:11, when Moses prays with elevated hands, the people of God conquered, when he lowered his hands, they were conquered.

The fact that it can be called part of divine worship, however, is proved: natural reason itself teaches man, who is constituted from soul and body, should honor and worship God both in the soul through interior acts, and in the body through outward acts. This is why Cyprian (*Serm. On the Lord's Prayer*) says, "We think we stand under the sight of God; the habit of body and the manner of voice is pleasing to the divine eyes." Secondly, all other virtues, although they are principally constituted in the soul, nevertheless, are not consummated through outward acts, as is clear in regard to Temperance and Fortitude, and other things. Why, therefore, do we not say the same about religion? It is also confirmed, because if vocal prayer, by the consensus of all, is the worship of God, why not also bodily adoration? Just as vocal prayer is worship, because it is a sign of internal adoration. Thirdly, nature teaches that God must be worshiped in the best way, since he is the greatest being. But a man worships more in body and soul than he does in the soul alone; therefore, God can be worshiped by corporeal ceremonies. Fourthly, God is truly offended, and affixed with ignominy not only by an internal act, but also an external one; so he must be honored not only by the internal act, but also but the external.

Now, our adversaries answer all of these things. They do not deny that God may and must be worshiped with some ceremonies; rather, they deny it in regard to ceremonies devised by men. No cult pleases God which he

Chapter XXXI: The Truth is Defended

himself did not institute, or certainly, for which he did not give testimony in his word.

On the other hand: Either it is required that in particular, and expressly, God approved worship, or it suffices if in general and in virtue he approved it. The first cannot be said, namely that worship which God did not expressly approve does not please him. Without a doubt, the worship of Abel pleased him, who offered the fat of his flock (Gen. 4:4, Heb. 11:4), and still, God did not command this worship. Likewise, the worship of Jacob pleased him, when he erected the stone as a monument in Gen. 28:18, and the worship of the Blessed Virgin, who vowed perpetual virginity, which God never commanded; therefore, it is enough if God commended something *in general*. Calvin also admits this in the *Institutes* (4, 10, §30), where, when he wants to prove kneeling in prayer is good, nay more divine, he advances that testimony of the Apostle (1 Cor. 14:40), "Everything should be done genuinely, and according to order," and says kneeling is good and divine, because in general it is indicated by Paul in that decorum, which he prescribes in prayer. Now in this way, all of our ceremonies are good and divine, because they are shown *in general* to be approved by God in many ways. *Firstly*, in this very testimony of Paul kneeling is no more included than lit candles, and sacred vessels, as well as other kinds of things. *Secondly*, when God commands overseers to be obeyed, in general he commands all Ecclesiastical laws to be kept, several of which regard ceremonies. Lastly, God is the author of all virtues. In Wisdom 8:7, it is said of divine wisdom, "it teaches sobriety and prudence, as well as justice, and virtue, in which there is nothing more useful to man in this life." There, the four Cardinal virtues are enumerated, to which all the others are reduced. So, God teaches and commends religion, which is a part of justice, and hence, the outward cult, which is a certain part of religion.

6) The *sixth* proposition: *It was very wisely instituted, that in the Latin Church, the Sacraments be administered in Latin.* Note *firstly*, when it is a question on the language in which the Sacraments should be administered, an exception should be made for Matrimony. Matrimony consists in mutual consent, and necessarily requires words, or a nod, so that both parties understand. Similarly, the confession of sins should be done in a language known to both, although the confession is not so much a Sacrament as the *matter of the sacrament*.

Note *secondly*, there is no divine law about which language the Sacraments should be administered in, nor does it pertain to the essence of the Sacraments. So, Baptism will be valid if it is administered in Latin, or Italian, or another language; nevertheless, on account of many serious reasons, it has seemed to the Church and to the Holy Spirit himself, who rules it, that the Sacraments should not be administered in the vernacular except in the case of necessity.

Note *thirdly*, we speak about the Latin Church; in the Greek Church they do rightly when they use Greek, and in the Churches of Syria when they use Aramaic. For the administration of the Sacraments, a vernacular language is not required, but one which is not altogether unknown, at least for the learned; otherwise, pastors and the necessary ministers would not be found. Moreover, the Greek, Aramaic and Latin languages are of this sort: they are not vernacular, and still each is common and known to experts in their regions. The same could almost be said about Arabic which now is common to many orientals, and in that language the Divine Office is celebrated; but the vernacular Arabic is different from the Arabic which they use in sacred rites.

This proposition is proven *firstly* from the ancient custom of the Church. The Latin Church always administered the Sacraments in Latin, even when the Latin language had ceased to be the common language. That is clear from Isidore, Alcuin, Amalarius, Rabanus, Strabo, Micrologus, Rupert, and Thomas Waldens, who wrote on the divine offices in Spain, France, Germany, Italy, and England, in times where Latin was not the common language, and they clearly teach the Sacraments were customarily administered in the Latin language. They describe the whole rite in Latin, and the formal words which one must use. Besides, in the administration of the Sacraments, some parts of the Divine Scripture are read, especially among our adversaries, but in those times the Scriptures were only available in Hebrew, Greek, and Latin, as is clear from Bede (*Hist.* 1, 1) where he says that in England in his time there were four vernacular languages, but Latin was common to all because of the Scriptures. Rabanus also (*de Instit. Cleric.* 3, 8) says in his age the Scriptures were not extant in any but these three languages. Lastly, our adversaries do not advance a German, or French, or even Spanish or Italian version of the Scriptures, except from a few years ago. They could object that there was a Gothic edition, which Ulphilas, the bishop of the Goths is said to have made (*Tripartita Historia* 8, 13, and which is also cited by Socrates 4, 27). That bishop, however, did not embark on that task until he was an Arian, along with his whole people. Add lastly, two examples which clearly show at one time there was no use of the vernacular in the celebration of the Sacraments. One is of the Moravians, who, as Aeneas Sylvius cites in his *Origi. Bohemorum*, ch. 13, obtained from the Roman Pontiff the right to celebrate the divine offices in the Slavonic language. The other is of the Bohemians, to whom Gregory VII refused, when they asked (*loc. cit.* book 7). But if the use of the vernacular was common then, they would not have sought permission.

Secondly, it is proven from reason. There is no necessity which compels the Sacraments to be administered in the vernacular, and on the other hand, there are many unsuitable things that would follow if it were done. That there is no necessity is proven. If there were any necessity, it would be particularly for those who partake of the Sacraments to understand what is said. But this is not a true necessity, For the words of the Sacraments are

Chapter XXXI: The Truth is Defended

either directed to the elements, such as the consecration of the Eucharist the blessing of water and oil, the elements, however, understand no language, or they are directed to God, as the deprecatory form of words, such as in Extreme Unction; God, however, understands all languages. Or, they are directed to persons, but to be consecrated or absolved, not, however, to be instructed and taught, as in Baptism and Absolution, and hence, it is *per accidens* if the person understands what sign it is, because they are very truly and efficaciously baptized and reconciled even if they do not have the use of reason, as is clear in the Baptism of infants, and in the Reconciliation of the sick who have lost their senses; such can be reconciled, as they are also baptized, if they lack Baptism, as Augustine teaches (*de Adulterinis Conjugiis* 1, 26 & 28) as well as the fourth Council of Carthage (can. 76), and Leo I (*Epist.* 91 *ad Theodorum*). Add, that there are almost no adults in the Latin Church so unlearned, who do not understand the words of the Sacraments, even if they are in Latin, or certainly would not understand in general that through these words, such and such a Sacrament is ministered to them.

It is unsuitable, however, if we use the vernacular. This is clear firstly because it would impede the common use of Churches. They could not come together in the churches of the Germans, English, Italians, Polish, French, Spanish, nor vice versa. It would do much harm to the unity and communication which should exist between the members of the one body. Besides, Christians would be compelled to go without the divine offices outside of their regions.

Secondly, the Sacraments require a certain majesty and reverence, which is certainly better preserved if we use a language that is not the common vernacular. In the same way it is proper that in the administration of the Sacraments we use a house, garments, instruments, all other than what we use in ordinary and daily life, so it seems proper that we use another language. It is not that we dream up, as Chemnitz supposes, that the Latin language is more sacred than others, but in this matter we say that which is not common has more veneration.

Thirdly, it is expedient that the words of the Sacraments be professed in the same way by all, so that the danger of change or deviation would be avoided. It will easily be preserved if everyone were to use the same language; very difficult if they used different ones.

Fourthly, if the Sacraments were administered in the vernacular, the gates of ignorance would be opened wide, for the ministers will be content if they knew how to read. Therefore, little by little, the Latin language would be forgotten, and as a result they will not read the Fathers, and hence they would not understand the Scriptures.

CHAPTER XXXII

The Objections Against Ceremonies Are Answered

JOHN CALVIN (*Instit.* 4, 10) makes many objections against ceremonies, which we will refute in order.

1) Calvin takes the first argument (*loc. cit.* §2) from the Apostle in 1 Cor. 7:35, "Paul employed great caution in this matter, he did not dare to even impose a fetter on anyone thing, and for good reason; he certainly foresaw how great a wound would be inflicted on the conscience if these things should be made necessary which the Lord has left free."

I respond: The Apostle argues in that place on virginal continence, which the Lord did not command, but *counseled*, and it was certainly right for the Apostle not to command that which the Lord wished to be a counsel. Yet, the notion of other things is not the same, on which the Lord commanded nothing in particular. These things can be either commanded by the Church or counseled, insofar the things themselves require it. This is why the same Apostle, who refused to command continence, commanded many other things, and besides, in 2 Thess. 3:14, he speaks in this way, "And if any do not obey our word by this epistle, note him and do not keep company with him, that he may be confounded." And the Apostles in Acts 15:29 imposed upon the Gentiles the burden to abstain from blood, strangled animals and said it was necessary, nevertheless the Lord left it free.

2) The second argument is in §8, "The Apostle, in the epistle to the Colossians, maintains that the doctrine of the true worship of God must not be sought from men, because the Lord has faithfully and fully taught us in the way which he is to be worshipped. To prove this, he says in the first chapter, that all wisdom is contained in the Gospel, that the man of God may be made perfect in Christ. In the beginning of the second chapter, he says that all the treasures of wisdom and knowledge are hidden in Christ, and from this he concludes that believers should beware of being led away from the flock of Christ by vain philosophy, according to the constitutions of men. In the end of the chapter, he still more decisively condemns all ἐθελοθρησκείας, that is, fictitious modes of worship which men devise by themselves or receive from others, and all precepts whatsoever which they dare to deliver at their own hand concerning the worship of God."

I respond: First, that epistle to the Colossians contains nothing against ecclesiastical laws in regard to ceremonies. As is certain from Chrysostom, Ambrose, Theodoret, Theophylactus, and Oecumenius, it was written against Simon Magus, and other heretics and imposters of that time who persuaded men that they must approach the supreme God by certain angels

Chapter XXXII: The Objections Are Answered

and Christ did not suffice. Besides, they forced upon Christians ceremonies that were partly Jewish and partly pagan. Thus, in the first chapter, he treats profusely on the excellence of Christ, and says he is the head of all, and over all things, and the angels depend upon him as their author. Then in chapter 2, he warns them not to be deceived by philosophy, namely that of Plato and similar authors, which the followers of Simon and the Gnostics used, and at the same time convicted them because they kept the Sabbath and new moons, which are Jewish, and were purged by Christ; and because they should abstain from certain foods as unclean; and that they waLk. in the religion of the angels, thinking they can ascend to God only through them. All these things are false and superstitious.

Lastly, I respond to the individual propositions of Calvin. *a)* The first is: *Christ has fully instructed us on the true worship of God*. I respond that, it is true on the *general* instruction, but not on the particular, as Calvin himself affirms later in §30, where he argues on kneeling.

b) The second is: *The Apostle teaches the doctrine of the true worship of God must not be sought from men.*

I respond: He teaches we must not seek from men who teach *contrary* to Christ, as the Philosophers and followers of Simon did; but it would be right to seek from men who build upon Christ, and follow his rule, and the doctrine they teach in particular, which he only pointed out in general. In Luke 10:16, he also says, "He that hears you, hears me."

c) The third is: *The Apostle condemns all human and voluntary worship.*

I respond: When Paul says human and voluntary worship, he means it is *merely* human, and devised by our own talent, i.e., *one who is not in conformity with the faith and principles of the doctrine of Christ;* however, the things which are taught by the Church are not merely human, since they were instituted under God's inspiration. This is why in 1 Cor. 14, after Paul instituted different rites in the Church in regard to the order of prophesying, and speaking, and that women should be silent, in regard to which the Lord expressly commanded nothing, the Apostle adds in verse 37, "If anyone seems to be a prophet, or spiritual, let him be acquainted with the things that I write to you, that they are the commands of the Lord." Here, he calls them commands of the Lord because they were given under his inspiration, therefore he wills them to be learned by spiritual men. If they were express precepts of the Lord, then it would not be necessary to learn these things in the spirit.

3) The *third* argument is in §9, "The Apostle (Gal. 5:1) in no way suffers the consciences of the faithful to be reduced into servitude Consequently, it is not lawful to institute ceremonies which oblige in conscience."

I respond: Paul speaks on *Jewish* servitude, whereby they served under an ancient law, not, however, in regard to obedience of any law you like. The same Apostle teaches otherwise in Romans 13:5, to obey power, "not only on account of wrath, but also conscience." There we must note, the ancient law is called the yoke of servitude, not because it obliged in conscience (which is common to every true law), but because it was *very difficult and laborious*, and did not have grace connected with it, whereby one could be filled with the love of justice. This is why a man either was or was not filled with fear of punishment (it cannot be denied that some were filled with that love of justice, such as the Patriarchs, and Prophets, and many others were, but they did not have that from the law, rather the grace of the New Testament), and in that way it pressed and weighed down in the fashion of the heaviest yoke. Moreover, the Apostle deterred the Galatians from this yoke. Since they willed to be circumcised, they were cut away from the grace of Christ, and at the same time, obliged themselves to keep the whole law, which was altogether to return to the state of the Old Testament. Therefore, Calvin treats the Scriptures with the worst faith, while he twists them from the true sense to sanction his heresy.

4) The *fourth* argument, is from §10 & 15, "In Matthew 15:3, the Lord rebukes traditions of men; and he does the same in Isaiah 29:13; 'In vain do they worship me with the commands of men.'"

I respond: In §10 there are many lies so impudent, that all the soap of Geneva could never wash them away! Namely, that Catholics forbid marriage and allow prostitution and that they judge it a more serious matter if anyone would imbue the slightest taste of meat on Friday than if they daily polluted their whole body with a prostitute, etc. Now I say to those Scriptures, which are everywhere asserted by Melanchthon, Brenz, Chemnitz, and others, that the Lord rebukes three things that were customarily done in the Jewish ceremonies. *a)* Firstly, certain things opposed with the commands of God, such as they were in Matt. 15:5, and Mark 7:11, that sons would give what was necessary for their parents to the priests. *b)* Secondly, that many of the Jewish traditions of the Pharisees were inane and altogether useless, such as to wash one's hands as often as possible. Moreover, the Lord calls these two kinds of ceremonies commands of men, because they stood on only human authority. *c)* Thirdly, the fact that they kept certain other good and useful things, but sinned in that they constituted the highest point of religion in them, and did these more than divine commands; the Lord speaks on this in Matt. 23:23, but he does not call these human traditions, rather he says, "These things you ought to have done, and not to have passed over." Christian ceremonies approved by the Church, however, are not of the first or second kind, and our adversaries do not any longer advance arguments, but only lies to prove the contrary. Yet, if there really were some among more unlearned Catholics, who made more of ceremonies than divine commands, we think they must be corrected. We do not approve of whatever men do, otherwise we would approve many sins, rather, *that which they ought to do according to the sound doctrine of the Church.*

5) The *fifth* argument is in §12, "The Romans have taken their system

Chapter XXXII: The Objections Are Answered 305

partly from the frenzies of the gentiles, partly, like apes, they have rashly imitated the ancient rites of the Jews, with which we have nothing more to do than with the sacrifices of animals and other things."

I respond: First, the Manichees once made the same argument, as cited by Augustine (*Contra Faustum* 20, 4) and Vigilantius, as cited by Jerome (*Contra Vigilantium*), namely that the Church retained rites in imitation of the Gentiles. Therefore, Calvin should acknowledge who his forefathers were. Secondly, I say, if that argument were valid, one should also abolish Baptism and the Lord's Supper, for even the Gentiles used Baptism when they were initiated in the sacred rites of Mithras; and they also celebrated a Sacrament of bread, as Tertullian relates (*De Praescript.*). The Jews also frequently used expiations through water, and they did not lack the shewbread. I say thirdly, it should not seem a marvel, if our ceremonies have some similitude with the Jewish, since the latter were figures of ours, as we read in 1 Cor. 10:11. By the same notion, little wonder if sometimes our rites have a similarity with the rites of the Gentiles. For the devil, who always wants to be the ape of God, imitated Jewish rites instituted by God, as Tertullian notes (*loc. cit.*), which he said were figures of ours. I say fourthly, although there may be some similitude among our rites and the rites of the Gentiles as well as the Jews in the outward symbol, nevertheless, there is absolutely the greatest difference. From the end and intention the external actions take their species. The rites of the Gentiles were done to worship demons, ours are done to worship the true God; consequently, there is as much difference between theirs and ours as there is between a sacred thing and a sacrilege, between piety and impiety, and between God and the devil. Moreover, even the sacrifices of the Gentiles and the Jews were the same, and nevertheless, the former were idolatrous, the latter pious and religious. Jerome responds to Vigilantius in this way, and Augustine to the Manichees (*loc. cit.*). The Jewish rites were good, but they heralded Christ would come; ours, likewise, are good, but different from theirs, because they are partly a memorial of the past, and partly to signify future glory.

6) The *sixth* argument, in §13, is taken from Augustine (*Epist.* 119, 19), who laments that some men have so burdened he Church with a multitude of ceremonies, that the condition of the Jews would be more tolerable. *I respond*: Augustine speaks on ceremonies which *private* men, and especially foolish women imposed on themselves. The same Augustine, speaking in the same place on redundant ceremonies, says this, "In my view, everything of this sort, which is neither contained in the authorities of the Holy Scriptures, nor found in the statutes of Councils of Bishops, nor fortified by the custom of the universal Church, but are innumerably varied in different customs, must be removed."

7) Calvin's *seventh* argument is in §14, "God willed there to be this distinction between us and the Jews: He taught them, like children, through sensible signs, but we as men more simply, without such signs. That is clear

from John 4:23, where the Lord says, 'The hour comes in which true adorers will worship the Father in spirit and truth.' Moreover, in Gal. 4:3, the Apostle compares the Jews to children abiding under a tutor." Chemnitz makes the same argument (*Exam.* p. 166), where he says shadows and figures were proper to the Old Testament, but we are admonished in the New Law by the light of the Word of God, not shadows. Brenz holds something similar in the last chapter of the *Württemberg Confession*, which is on ceremonies.

I respond: The distinction between the Jews and Christians, which pertains to ceremonies, can be understood in two ways. *a)* One, that they had only outward ceremonies, but we have only the light of the word, both spiritual and simple truth. This seems to sound like the words of our adversaries, especially Chemnitz, but it is manifestly false. The Jews also had the light of the word apart from ceremonies, from where Psalm 118 [119]:105 says, "Your word is a lamp to my feet." God required of them not only external worship, but also internal. In Isa. 29:13, God rebukes the Jews when he said, "This people glorifies me with their mouth and lips, but their heart is far from me." On the other hand, Christians, apart from the light of the word, also have the sensible Sacraments, which are shadows and figures of past and future things. Just as outward and sensible Sacraments are not opposed to the new Testament, as is known, so other ceremonies are not opposed. The Christian Church, although it dwells in a great light with respect to the synagogue, nevertheless, it also dwells in a shadow with respect to the heavenly Jerusalem. We waLk. by faith, which is obscure, and not through sight.

In another way, that distinction can be understood in that Jewish worship, insofar as it is Jewish, i.e., of the Old Testament, was principally external and corporeal; Christian worship, i.e., of the New Testament, is principally internal and spiritual. This is very true, since the internal and spiritual worship proceeds from the Spirit of faith and charity, which spirit is the very grace of the new Testament, and could in no way be found in the Old Law. This is why Paul, in 2 Cor. 3:6, calls the Old Testament the letter, and the New, the spirit. In John 1:17, the former is called the law, the latter, grace. Lastly, in John 4:24 that "in spirit and truth" signifies Christian worship is in the spirit, as opposed to Jewish which was in the body, and it is in truth, as opposed to the same Jewish worship, which consisted in shadows and figures, as Chrysostom, Cyril and Euthymius explain. Although Theophylactus and St. Thomas do not understand it badly in their commentary of this same passage, namely that "In spirit" is opposed to Jewish worship which was bodily and "in truth" opposed to the worship of the Samaritans, which was mixed with falsity and error. Wherefore, a little earlier, the Lord had said, "Not on this mountain," namely Gerizim, where the Samaritans worshipped, "Nor in Jerusalem will you adore the father." In other words: Hereafter you will not worship God falsely, nor with Jewish worship, especially corporeally, but with Christian worship, which will be

Chapter XXXII: The Objections Are Answered

in spirit and truth, i.e., spiritual and purified from every error.

Nevertheless, we must observe, that although Jewish worship in the Old Testament was corporeal, nevertheless, it did not please God without the spiritual, and therefore, God also asked spiritual worship of them, as we showed from Is. 29:13. Yet, those who furnished it did not have it from the Old Testament, but from the grace of the *New*. For equal reason, although Christian worship is principally spiritual, nevertheless, it cannot exist in this pilgrimage without bodily worship, and thus, it admits Sacraments and other ceremonies which serve spiritual worship.

8) The *eighth* argument is from §15, "Whatever commendation works have, they have it in respect of obedience, which are the only thing God regards, as he testifies by the prophet, 'I did not command in regard to sacrifices and victims, but only that by hearing you would hear my voice' (Jer. 7:22; 1 Kings [1 Samuel] 15:22). Does God want Sacrifice, and that the voice of God be obeyed no longer? Consequently, ceremonies, which God did not institute, do not please him, nor can they be meritorious." He strengthens his argument in the same place. Since our ceremonies are both not meritorious, but useless, since they are hardly understood by anyone.

I respond: The antecedent is false and against the very clear Scriptures, for the sacrifice of Abel pleased God (Heb. 11:4), although God did not command it. In 1 Cor. 7:38, "He that does not marry, does better." In the same place in regard to a widow, "She will be more blessed if she remains so," and still in the same place he asserts he does not have it from precept not to marry, even for a second time. In 1 Cor. 9;15, he also contends it was licit for him to live on the goods of others to whom he preached, and still he preferred to live on his own labor, so as to have a greater reward. These words show this very thing, "It is better for me to die, than that any man should take away my glory." Hence, these Scriptures value obedience over sacrifices. But it is not permitted to conclude, that sacrifices which were not commanded merit nothing; rather, they do, even if they are offered with faith and devotion, since the contrary is certain from the Scriptures, as we have already shown. To his confirmation, I respond: The ceremonies of the Church are easily understood, at least *in general*, as is clear if anyone runs through the ceremonies taken from person, time and things. Now, if some ceremonies are not understood by all, such as the multitude of vestments and signs in Mass, nevertheless, they do not lack utility even among the most unlearned, since without a doubt they unite veneration with sacred things. Certainly, the Jews understood a little, but they did not receive them in vain.

9) The *ninth* argument is from §17, "Does not the law which was once given to the Church endure forever? 'What things soever I command you, observe to do it; you shall not add unto it, nor take away from it' (Deut. 12:32). And in another place, 'Add you not unto his words, lest he reprove you, and you are found a liar' (Prov. 30:6)."

I respond: In these passages, the Lord does not forbid any addition. By the word, either the sacred books are understood, or the moral precepts, or the judicial, or the ceremonial, we will always find that an addition was made. After Deuteronomy, where that prohibition of addition to the words of the Lord is found, all the other sacred books were written, not only the histories, but even the prophetical books as well as the whole New Testament. Likewise, there are many moral precepts in the Prophets and in the books of Solomon, which seem to have been added to the Pentateuch. David added a judicial precept, that in war they should divide the spoils equally among those who fight and those who guard the baggage (1 Kings 30:24). Later, the Jews added ceremonial laws in regard to new feast days (Esther 9:28; Judith 16:31; and 1 Macc. 4:59). Thus, the Lord forbade a *corrupting* addition, and it is the same thing, "Do not add or take away." In other words, keep what I command wholly and perfectly. It is clear from the reason which is given in Proverbs 30:6, "Lest he reprove you, and you are found a liar." He cannot be called a liar and a forgerer, who institutes a new ceremony, provided nothing impedes the ceremonies of God; rather, he is called a liar and a forger who corrupts the words of God, or his precepts. This corruption, however, may take place in two ways. *a)* In one way, if anyone adds something to the very words or precepts of God, or takes away something whereby they are corrupted. For example, if during the Sacrifices of Christ a man would offer bread without wine, or bread, wine and honey. *b)* In the second way, if anyone would put up a non-canonical book in place of the word of God, or some ceremony he invented in place of a Sacrament; or on the other hand, to remove a truly canonical book or a true Sacrament from the number of sacred books or Sacraments. The heretics commit this very sin when they deny many sacred books are canonical and remove five Sacraments from the number of the Sacraments. We see the same thing in the corruption of money; they are called forgerers who either corrupt the money itself, by adding tin to silver, or by diminishing the silver itself; or who intrude money they minted themselves in place of the money of the prince. They will find none of these in the ceremonies of the Church.

10) The *tenth* argument is from §23, where Calvin takes up three examples from Scripture. In 4 Kings 17:25, those who were worshiping in Samaria are related to have been torn apart by wild animals, because they worshiped God with new ceremonies that God did not establish. In 4 Kings 16:14, Ahaz is rebuked because he placed a new altar in the temple, which was able to be seen as an adornment of the temple. "And still we see," Calvin says, "how the Spirit detests the audacious attempt, and for no other reason except that inventions of men are impure corruptions in the worship of God." Referring to 4 Kings 21:5, Calvin says, "The guilt of Manasses is aggravated by the circumstance of having erected a new altar at Jerusalem."

Chapter XXXII: The Objections Are Answered

I respond: Calvin uses bad faith in all of these examples, as is his custom. In 4 Kings 17:25, the Samaritans are not reproved because they worshiped God with new ceremonies, but because from the beginning, "they did not fear the Lord, nor worship," nay more, they were Gentiles, nor did they know the law of God; then, however, they were thoroughly taught the law of God, and at the same time began to worship God, as well as their idols. In 4 Kings 16:14, Ahaz is rebuked, not because he constructed a new altar in the temple, but because he commanded *a new altar to the similitude of the altar of idols* which was in Damascus to be made in the temple of the Lord, and he removed the Lord's altar from its place, that he might set up that idolatrous altar. Lastly, in 4 Kings 21:5, Manassas not only placed a new altar in the temple, but sanctified it to *idols*. Scripture speaks thus, "He built altars for all the host of heaven in the two courts of the temple of the Lord," and in verse 7, "He also set an idol of the grove, which he had made, in the temple of the Lord." Otherwise, to erect a new altar in the temple of the Lord would not be a crime, for in 3 Kings 8:64, we read that Solomon commanded the middle part of the hall to be sanctified to offer holocausts, because the bronze altar, on which they should be offered, was not capable of such a multitude of victims; then Solomon offered twenty-two thousand oxen, and a hundred and twenty thousand sheep. Yet, that is enough from Calvin. Melanchthon treats the Scriptures in similar bad faith, for in his *Apologia for the Augsburg Confession* (art. 15), he advances this argument apart from the others. Firstly, Ezechiel 20:18, "'Do not waLk. in the statutes of your fathers.' Therefore, it is not lawful to institute new cults without a command from God." Ezechiel, however, speaks about *idolatrous* fathers; Scripture speaks otherwise in Proverbs 22:28, "Do not transgress the ancient boundaries, which your fathers placed for you." Likewise, Melanchthon argues secondly "If it is lawful for men to establish worship, now the worship of all the Gentiles is going to be approved, and even those things which Jeroboam instituted." Remarkable! As if it would be licit to fashion an unjust law, if one were permitted to fashion a new law. Thirdly, he adds, "Daniel 11:30, signifies new human cults are the very form of Antichrist. So he says: 'He will worship the God Maozim in his place, and the God whom their Fathers knew.'" This is also an excellent argument, as if to worship the true God in a new cult, is also to worship a new god, i.e., a false and fictitious god.

THE END OF THE BOOKS ON THE SACRAMENTS IN GENERAL

AD HONOREM DEI

THE SECOND GENERAL CONTROVERSY

ON BAPTISM AND CONFIRMATION
Explained in Two Books

The Argument and Partition of the Disputation on Baptism

The subjects which are customarily discussed on Baptism can be recalled to nine headings. First, on the name and definition. Second, on the matter. Third, on the form. Fourth, on the necessity. Fifth, on the minister. Sixth, on the recipients. Seventh, on the effects. Eighth, on the comparison of Baptism of Christ and that of John; that comparison turns upon the particular effects. Ninth, on the rite and ceremonies. In explaining all such controversies, we will focus particularly on two ends: One, that we might defend the canons on the Council of Trent on Baptism, which are contained in its seventh session, against the *Antidote* of Calvin and the *Examination* of Chemnitz. The second, the opinions of specific heretics of this time, and we shall well understand the arguments, and with God's help, efficaciously refute them.

BOOK I

ON BAPTISM

CHAPTER I

On the Name, Definition, and Partition of Baptism.

There is no disagreement over the term "Baptism," since everyone uses this term because it is found everywhere in the Scriptures. Βάπτισμα properly means *immersion*. Ordinarily, Baptism is done through immersion to represent the burial of Christ, according to that of Col. 2:12, "buried with him in Baptism." The Fathers, however, have many other names, in regard to which see Clement (*Paedagogi* 1, 6), Nazianzen (*Oration on Baptism*), and Chrysostom (*Hom. ad Baptizatos*), who call Baptism *illumination, grace, a gift, seal, mystery, cleansing*, and certain other terms; but the characteristic and most common term is φωτισμὸς, i.e, *illumination*. Apart from the three cited Fathers, all the later Greeks use it, and before them, Dionysius the Areopagate (*de Eccles. Hierarch.* c. 2). In fact, even Paul himself uses it in Heb. 6:4, when he says, "It is impossible for those who were once illuminated, etc." and in 10:32, "Call to mind the former days, wherein being illuminated, you endured a great fight of afflictions." From there, Cyril of Jerusalem, in his *Catecheses* on Baptism, calls them *Catecheses of the Illuminated.* Baptism, however, is called an illumination, because the habit of faith is infused in it.

Now with what pertains to the definition, St. Thomas (III, q. 66, art. 1) advances some definitions, but the Roman Catechism gave the most suitable definition from the Scriptures, "Baptism is the Sacrament of regeneration through water in the word of life." Such a definition is partly taken from John 3:5, partly from Paul in Eph. 5:26. In the first place, it is posited as a *Sacrament*, which is the genus. Then it is added, *of regeneration*, which is a difference narrowing the genus, and distinguishing it from the Sacraments of the Old Law. Thirdly, it is added *through water*, which is another difference still drawing it more and distinguishing it from the other Sacraments of the New Law. Even if the others are not properly said to regenerate, nevertheless, they justify the impious, and especially Penance. The justification of the impious, however, especially of a heretic or apostate, is scarcely different or not at all from regeneration. This is why in Gal. 4:19, Paul says, "my little children, of whom I am in labor again." But when it is added, *through water*, the difference is already clear, for the reconciliation of penitents is not a regeneration through water, but *a certain reformation, and a recalling from hell as it were*.

Here we must observe, the Sacrament of Baptism is not the water itself, which is a permanent thing, but the washing, which is a passing thing. Therefore, Baptism is the Sacrament of regeneration through water, i.e., an outward sign sanctifying through the sprinkling of water. Lastly, it is added, *in the word of life*, that the form of the Sacrament is also expressed, which is *the particular* part of the essence.

Melanchthon (*Loci Com.*, published in 1558, tit. On Sacrifice) defined Baptism in this way, "Baptism is a sign, in which God causes grace within us and receives us." But this definition would be suited to every Sacrament, in fact, even to the word itself, which still is not a Sacrament.

Calvin (*Instit.* 4, 15 1) defines it in this way, "Baptism is the sign of initiation, in which we desire the society of the Church, that we would be reckoned to be grafted among the sons of God in Christ." Such a definition has many vices. It is neither essential, since it does not touch upon any part of the essence of Baptism, nor does it explain the effect, or the principal end of this Sacrament. The principal end, according to Catholics, and really, according to the Scriptures, is to justify and regenerate; according to Calvin (as he adds, *ibid.*), it is to nourish faith after the fashion of a sealed charter; such an end is not explained in the definition, but only a certain secondary end, which is to witness the fidelity which we owe to God and the Church, and so to be acknowledged and numbered among the sons of God.

Moreover, this very definition is also suited to Circumcision. Circumcision was a sign of initiation, in which the Jews desired the society of the Church and to be grafted in Christ. Even if the body of the Jews is called the Synagogue, when it is distinguished contrary to the Church, nevertheless, it *absolutely was the Church*, and the Church of the true God before it denied Christ. Christ himself, although he was not a man in the time of the Synagogue except in its last days, nevertheless as God, was always the head of the whole Church. Nay more, even as a man that was going to come and suffer, he was then already the head, to whom the Jews were joined through faith and grafted in. This is why in 1 Cor. 10:9, the Jews in the desert are said to have tempted Christ, and in Apoc. 13:8, it is said, "The lamb was slain from the beginning of the world." The same definition seems to suit the preaching of the word of God, for we are also initiated in the word of God, and we desire to be grafted into the Church, and in Christ.

CHAPTER II

On the Matter of Baptism

On the matter there is almost no dissension, even if some errors existed on this matter at some point, or even exist now. The first was the error of the Manicheans (as Augustine witnesses in *de Haer.* 46), who held Baptism should not be applied in water, because they thought not God, but the devil created water, or even other corporeal things. The Marcionists were more modest, who even if they believed water was the work of the evil principle, i.e., the devil, not of the good God, still they applied water in Baptism on account of Christ's command. Theodoret relates (*Fabl. Haeret.* 1), that he had seen a certain old Marcionite, who upheld that water must be applied in the mystery, and still so hated it, that he preferred to wash his face in *his own spit* rather than water, lest it would seem that he needed its creator.

The second error was of the Seleuci and Hermiae, who excluded water from Baptism, basing their actions on the authority of Scripture, which everywhere compares the Baptism of John with the Baptism of Christ, and always affirms that John baptized in water, while Christ baptized in the Holy Spirit and fire (Matt. 3:11, Luke 3:16, John 1:26, Act. 1:5). Philastrius relates this error (*de Haeres.*), as well as Augustine (*de Haeres.* C. 59).

The third error on the same foundation was of the Jacobites, who in place of baptismal water impressed the sign of the cross on their foreheads with a burning iron. Bernard Lutzenburg is a witness of this in his *Catalogue of Heretics*.

The fourth error is of the Paulicianians, who (as Euthymius witnesses in *Panopliae* 2 part., tit. 21), substituted the words "I am living water," in place of the element of water in Baptism.

The fifth error is of Luther, who in *Symposiacis Coloquiis* (c. 17) was asked whether it was lawful to baptize in miLk. or beer if there was no water available. He first answered, "It must be consigned to divine judgment." Then, he added that whatever can be called a bath is suitable to baptize. But certainly, no man ever doubted whether a bath could be carried out with wine, and milk, let alone beer.

The Council of Trent decreed against all this nonsense, in sess. 7 can. 2, that *true* and *natural* water is required for Baptism. From that we understand two things. *Firstly*, no liquid is a matter for Baptism which is not true and natural water. *Secondly*, all true and natural water, however much it is accidentally altered and changed, is suitable matter for Baptism. That is crystal clear from the Scriptures, for in John 3:5, it is said, "from water and the Holy Spirit."

Likewise, in the same place the rivalry of the disciples of John arose, because they saw Christ baptize his disciples in water, as even John had done it. Act. 8:36, "Behold the water, what prevents me from being Baptized?" Ephes. 5:26, "In the laver of water in the word of life." In 1 Cor. 10:1, Paul compares Baptism to the Red Sea. In 1 Pet. 3:21, Peter compares the same Baptism to the flood. Lastly, the Prophets also expressly predicted Baptism of water, as in Ez. 36:25, "I will pour upon you clean water." But why God chose water over another element, the authors render an account, advancing the different properties of water, which you can see in St. Thomas (III. 66, a. 3), and William of Paris (*de Sacramentis, de Baptismo*).

No, the testimonies which the Seleucians advance do not conclude anything. They do not teach a distinction between John's Baptism and Christ's, that one is only in water and the other only in the Spirit, or fire; rather, that one was in water only, the other not only in water, but in *water and the Spirit*, as it is said in John 3:5. This is why in 1 John 5:6, "This is he, who came through water and blood, not in water only, but in water and blood." Moreover, what is added about fire in Matt. 3:11 and Lk. 3:16 does not mean fire as some elemental thing, as the Jacobites foolishly supposed, but a certain *heavenly* and *divine* fire, which is why it is joined with Holy Spirit. That fire, however, can either signify the fiery tongues which descended on the Apostles on the day of Pentecost, or the fire of purgatory, as Jerome (on *Matt.* 3) and Bede (on *Luke* 3) teach. Or, even the fire of divine judgment, as Hilary explains (on *Matt.* 2); or lastly, the fire of tribulation in this life, which is lacking in none of the baptized, as the author of the imperfect work on Matthew 3 explains.

Chemnitz notes nothing against this canon, except that it is not necessary for water to be exorcized and blessed, if true and natural water suffices. But he gathers it badly, for even if *holy water is not required for the substance of the Sacrament, still, it is rightly instituted*, as we will address below.

CHAPTER III

On the Form of Baptism

ALTHOUGH in our time nearly everyone admits the form of Baptism *in regard to what pertains to praxis*, which is the singular providence of God lest innumerable infants would perish, nevertheless, there were and are serious errors in this matter. The *first* was of certain men, who in the very time of the Apostles baptized in the name of three without a beginning, i.e., of three Fathers, or in the name of three Sons, or three Paracletes. Such an error is related and condemned in can. 48 (49) of the Apostles.

The *second* was of the Gnostics, who, as Irenaeus witnesses (1, 18), baptized in the name of the Unknown Father, in the truth of the Mother of all, and in the name of Jesus descending.

The *third* was of the Cataphrygans and the Paulianists, who did not baptize in the name of the Father, and of the Son, and of the Holy Spirit, as Innocent I witnesses (*Epist.* 22, 5). As a result, the Council of Nicaea (can. 19) and Laodicea (can. 8) commanded such to be baptized again.

The *fourth* was of certain Arians, who baptized in the name of the Father, through the Son, in the Holy Spirit. As Nicephorus relates (13, 35), an Arian Bishop by the name of Deuterius wanted to baptize in this way, but, by a divine miracle, the water immediately vanished. Likewise, other Arians did not preserve the true form of Baptism, as is clear from the first Council of Arles (can. 8), where Arians who return to the Church are commanded to be asked under what form of words they were baptized; for not all were baptized in the same way. Also, many of those Catholics were rebaptized, as Augustine witnesses (*de Haeres.* c 49).

The *fifth* error was of certain Eunomians, who did not baptize in the name of three persons, but in the death of the Lord, as Socrates relates (5, 23).

The *sixth* was of the Greeks, who at a certain time applied their form, wherein they say, N. the servant of Christ is baptized in the name of the Father, and of the Son, and of the Holy Spirit, so that they would dare to rebaptize Latins who were baptized in the words, "I baptize you, etc." The fourth Lateran Council condemns this error, in c. 4. There, they did not condemn the form which the Greeks used to Baptize, because it does not differ from ours in substance, as it was declared in the last session of the Council of Florence. Rather, the *error* of the Greeks which the Council condemned was that they made bold to condemn our form without any reason or cause.

The *seventh* error is of Luther, Zwingli, and Brenz, who, although they teach the customary form must be used, nevertheless, do not think it is necessary to the substance of Baptism. Luther (*On the Babylonian Captivity*, c. On Baptism), asserts, "Baptism is valid in whatever words it is conferred, provided it is not given in the name of a man but in the name of the Lord." Nay more, he adds that even if an impious minister would not give it in the name of the Lord, nevertheless it is valid if it is received in the name of the Lord. Zwingli (*On True and False Religion*, on Baptism) clearly teaches it is not necessary for there to be any certain form of words in Baptism, although he says that he does not forbid one from using the sacred words already received. This is why a certain Zwinglian, as John of Eck relates (*Hom.* 10, on Baptism), baptized "in the *names* of the Father, and of the Son, and of the Holy Spirit," which is manifest Arianism. Name signifies power and authority in Scripture, "In my name demons shall be cast out," (Mk. 16:17) and John 5:43, "I came in the name of my Father." As there is one God in three persons, so one name, one power, one authority. This is why Ambrose (*de Sacramentis*, 2, 7) and Jerome (*on Eph.* 4) note that in Baptism a threefold sprinkling is done, and still it is not said in the names, but in the name of the Father, and of the Son, and of the Holy Spirit. Brenz, in his Catechism, in the chapter on Baptism, writes that the Baptism is true if, after the Catechumen has recited the Creed, the minister were to speak in this way, "I heard from you the confession of your faith, that you believe in God the Father, the Son, and Holy Spirit. In this confession I plunge you in water, so that by this sign you will certainly be grafted in Christ. Go in peace." Still, he advises that the customary form of the Church must be preserved. It is well that he does so advise, otherwise the Baptism would not be valid.

Apart from these errors, there is a certain disagreeable opinion of many Catholics, who suppose that the invocation of only one divine person, and especially of Christ, suffices for Baptism. It appears that Ambrose thought this way (*de Spiritu Sancto*, 1, 3) as well as Bede (in *Acts* 10), who cites the words of Ambrose. Bernard (*Epist.* 340 *to Henry*) teaches that it seems to him Baptism would be valid if someone conferred it from ignorance, "in the name of God, and of the holy and true cross." Likewise, Hugh of St. Victor (*de Sacramentis* 2, part. 6, c. 2), and Peter Lombard (4 dist. 3), and lastly, Pope Nicholas (*Epist. to the Bulgarians*, as it is contained in *can. A quodam Judaeo*, de consec. dist. 4), who defined nothing, but advanced the authority of Ambrose, and seems to have approved it.

The foundation for this is of two authors. First, the authority of the Apostles, who baptized in the name of Christ, as we see in Acts 8:12, 10:48, and 19:5. Second, because in each divine person all three are implicitly contained. Whoever says the Father, at the same time says the Son and the Spirit of his mouth. Who says Christ, says the unbegotten, i.e., the Father; the anointed, i.e., the Son; and the anointing, i.e., the Holy Spirit. Who says the Holy Spirit says the Father and the Son, from whom he is spirated. Now, the particular foundation of all authors after Ambrose, is the authority of

Chapter III: The Form of Baptism

Ambrose himself; this is why if perhaps Ambrose did not mean to say what his words seem to say, the foundation of that opinion falls to ruin.

Whatever the case is in this matter, it is certain that Baptism given in the name of Christ or another divine person without expression of the others, should either absolutely, or at least conditionally, be repeated, as all the more serious Theologians rightly teach in 4, dist. 3.

Thus, this is the true form of Baptism: *Ego te baptizo in nomine Patris, et Filii, et Spiritus Sancti.* There, the pronoun *Ego* does not pertain to the essence. Although it should not be omitted since it is prescribed by the Church, nevertheless, if it were omitted, the Baptism would be whole, because the person of the minister is sufficiently expressed in the word *Baptizo*.[17]

Hence that this is the true and necessary form of Baptism is gathered from the Gospel; but it is not evidently so from the Gospel alone; rather, we are compelled to have recourse to *tradition* and *the declaration of the Church*. We must note this against Calvin and other heretics, who prescribe this form in the rite of Baptism and use the same, when they refuse traditions but only admit Scripture. In the Gospel, we only have one testimony, in Matt. 28:19, "Going, teach all nations, baptizing them in the name of the Father, and of the Son, and of the Holy Spirit." From such words, if they were considered alone, we are not compelled to say "I baptize you," just as when we preach, we are not compelled to say "I teach you,"; rather, we seem to satisfy it if we baptize and teach, even if we do not express what we do in words. For equal reasoning, it is not evidently gathered from this passage alone that it is fitting to say "In the name of the Father, and of the Son, and of the Holy Spirit," for this passage could be explained, either on *faith* in the Trinity, that we would baptize in the faith of the Trinity, or even concerning *authority*, that is, that we baptize by the authority received from God. Just the same, when we read in Mark 16:17, "In my name demons will be cast out, etc.," nevertheless, if we were to join the authority of the Church to this passage of the Gospel, it will be constituted for certain, that all those words pertain to the form of Baptism.

In the first place, we must say, "I baptize," or something of this sort, in which the action of the minister is expressed, as the Council of Florence teaches in its *Instruction to the Armenians*; Pope Alexander III also teaches it (*Extravagantes, de Baptismo et Ejus Effectu,* cap. *Si Quis Puerum*); every Catechism and ritual book teaches it, even the most ancient. Lastly, even reason teaches it. Only the words "In the name of the Father, and of the Son, and of the Holy Spirit," even with that external washing, do not determinately signify something which should be signified in this

---

17 Translator's note: This holds for Latin and other languages which do not require a personal pronoun to indicate the 1st person of the verb. In Latin, *Ego* is not necessary because *Baptizo* means "I baptize," but the subject pronoun is added for emphasis or distinction.

Sacrament. Now, that washing could be done to refresh, or to cure from some disease, and the help of the Holy Trinity would rightly be invoked for this purpose. Therefore, the word *Baptizo* must be added, which from Ecclesiastical use signifies washing from filth, not just of the flesh, but also of *the spirit*.

Next, a different person from the minister must be expressed, which we do through the pronoun *Te* [you], and hence, nobody may baptize themselves; apart from the testimonies already advanced, Innocent III teaches it in clear words (*Extra.*, de *Baptismo et Ejus Effectu*, c. *Debitum*).

Then, that the three divine persons must be expressed, apart from the testimonies already advanced, two Supreme Pontiffs teach this, Pelagius (can. *Se Revera*, and can. *Multi Sunt*), as well as Pope Zachariah (can. *In Synodo de consecrate.* distinc. 4), because they affirm Baptism is not valid if it were given in the name of the Lord or in the name of Christ, unless the three persons are clearly expressed. The tradition of all the Fathers confirms the same thing, who affirm Baptism should be given in the name of the Father, and of the Son, and of the Holy Spirit. See also St. Gregory of Nyssa (*de Baptismo*), Chrysostom (*ad Ephes.* on the verse, *Cleansing it in the Laver*), Nazianzen in his *Orat.* on the Holy Laver; Damascene (4, 10) and Theophylactus (on *Matt.* 28). Then from the Latins, Tertullian (*Contra Praxeam & de Corona*), Cyprian (*Epist. Ad Jubajanum*), Hilary (*de Synodis*); Ambrose (*de Sacramentis* 2,5&7; *de Mysteriis* 4), Jerome (*ad Ephes.* 4), Syricius (*Epist.* 1), Innocent (*Epist.* 22), Augustine (*de Baptismo* 6, 25), Leo (*Epist.* 4), Fulgentius (*de Incarnatione et gratia Christi*, c. 11), and Gregory (*Epist.* 9, 61).

On the other hand, the arguments which we have posited on behalf of the opinion of those who believe Baptism is valid if it were given in the name of Christ alone conclude nothing at all. To the first example from the Apostles, some Scholastics answer the Apostles did it from a certain peculiar dispensation of God. But since that dispensation is not read in Scripture, nor in any Council, nor in the Fathers, those who deny the Apostles baptized in any other way than in the name of the Father, and of the Son, and of the Holy Spirit are on more solid ground. It is also confirmed from Acts 19:3, when a certain man said to Paul, "We have not so much as heard whether there is a Holy Spirit." Such words indicate, that even in *his time*, in the very form of Baptism the Holy Spirit was customarily named. Since it is certain that Baptism was never given in the name of the Holy Spirit alone, it follows that it was given in the name of the three persons. Furthermore, since in the Canons of the Apostles those who baptize in any other way than in the name of the Father, and of the Son, and of the Holy Spirit are condemned, and the most ancient Fathers who either saw the Apostles or their disciples, such as Dionysius and Justin, prescribe the same form of Baptism, it is not at all believable that the Apostles baptized any differently.

Chapter III: The Form of Baptism

What Luke says in Acts 8:12, 1g0:48, and 19:5, however, that the Apostles baptized in the name of the Lord Jesus, can be understood in many ways, namely that they were said to baptize in the *faith* of the Lord Jesus, or in the *authority* of the Lord Jesus, or in the Baptism *instituted* by Christ, or lastly, in the name of the Lord Jesus, but *not alone*, but joined with the Father and the Holy Spirit. Perhaps, the name of Christ is commended more, so they were saying, "I baptize you in the name of the Father, and his Son Jesus Christ, and the Holy Spirit."

Hilary, Basil, and Fulgentius seem to have understood these passages in this way. Hilary (*de Synodis*) enumerates various passages of Scripture, which seem to oppose themselves unless they are correctly understood. Among other apparent contradictions, he posits these passages from Matt. 28, where the Apostles were commanded to baptize in the name of the Father, and of the Son, and of the Holy Spirit, and then in Acts where they are related to have baptized in the name of Christ. Although Hilary does not explain how these must be understood, nevertheless, from his manner of speech and from other similar passages that have the appearance of contradiction, it is gathered that he thought the Apostles baptized in the name of the Father, and of the Son, and of the Holy Spirit; otherwise, as he says, they would be guilty, as trespassers of a divine rule given to them. Luke showed this very thing as briefly as possible in Acts by expressing the name of Christ and not denying the names of the other persons. Fulgentius, *On the Incarnation and Grace of Christ*, 11, very clearly says the Apostles baptized in the name of the Father, and of the Son, and of the Holy Spirit, and this very thing is to baptize in the name of the Lord Jesus, as it is said in Acts 2:38, or in the death of Christ, as it is said in Romans 6:3. Basil (*de Spiritu Sancto*, 12), writes in the name of the Son, all the persons are understood, since Scripture says the Apostles baptized in the name of Christ; hence, the Apostles really baptized in the name of the Father, and of the Son, and of the Holy Spirit, not in the name of Christ alone. There, St. Basil means in one person, all are understood, which pertains to the words of St. Luke in Acts, but not to the form of Baptism itself. Some also suppose that Ambrose spoke in this way, and Bede from him, since he adduces the same testimonies, and speaks on the same matter, and very frequently was wont to make the sentences of Basil his own; certainly, the Roman Catechism (on *Baptism*) joins Ambrose with Basil in this matter.

To the *second* argument I respond: The implicit mention of the three persons does not suffice in Baptism, both because the Lord, in the Gospel, as well as all the Fathers hand down that it must be explicit; and also, because the Sacraments are outward and sensible signs, hence it is necessary to sound out the invocation of the three persons outwardly and sensibly; nor does it suffice if the invocation of one person were said aloud, but the others were conceived only in the mind, which is, when they would be invoked implicitly.

CHAPTER IV

On the Necessity and Institution of Baptism

WE have spoken on the material and formal cause; now we must speak on the necessity, which seems to pertain to the final cause. First, there is no question whether by the divine mandate of Christ, Baptism is necessary for salvation, for Calvin also affirms this in his *Antidote to the Council of Trent*, sess. 7 can. 5. The controversy is whether it is necessary as the means to salvation, so that if anyone were not baptized, he would perish even if perhaps he is excused from violation of the precept due to ignorance. This controversy is of particular importance in children, who are not capable of the precept. There are three questions, however. 1) *First*, whether Baptism is necessary. 2) *Second*, when it began to be necessary. 3) *Third*, whether it can be supplied by martyrdom or penance, which are called Baptisms, the former of blood, the latter of flame [desire].

1) On the *first* question, there was once the heresy of the Pelagians, that Baptism was not necessary for the remission of original sin, but only *to obtain the kingdom of heaven*; as Augustine witnesses (*de haeres*. c. 69).

But our heretics are far bolder than the Pelagians, since they not only deny that Baptism is necessary for the remission of sin, but also deny it is necessary for the kingdom of heaven. In the first place, John Wycliffee denied it (Thomas Waldens, t. 2, c. 96). Next, Zwingli (*On True and False Religion*) denies clearly enough that Baptism is necessary for salvation, saying it is nothing but an outward symbol. Martin Bucer (on *Matt*. 3) teaches the same thing, but from another foundation, namely because children of the predestined are saved even without Baptism; those who are not predestined, however, are damned even with Baptism. John Calvin (*Antidote*, sess. 6 c. 5; *Instit*. 4, 16 §24, & 25) teaches the children of the faithful are saints and members of the Church, even without Baptism, and if they die they are saved. His foundation is that he supposes original sin is not imputed to the sons of the faithful, and that it is from the force of the covenant of God with Abraham (Gen. 17:7), "I will be your God, and the God of your seed," that we succeed through Christ into the posterity of Abraham. Peter Martyr holds the same in his *Commentary on 1 ad Cor.*, c. 7, from the words, "Otherwise your children should be unclean, but now they are holy." There, he clearly says the sons of the faithful are saved without Baptism, and advances the same arguments as Calvin. Henry Bullinger, the successor to Zwingli in the Zurich synagogue, holds the same thing, citing the same passage. Nevertheless, there seems to be this difference between Bullinger, and Calvin: that Calvin only makes them saints before Baptism,

Chapter IV: The Necessity of Baptism

who are born from faithful parents; Bullinger, however, in his book *De Testamento*, or the sole and eternal covenant of God, teaches it is enough if parents were faithful at *some point*, although later they are not, when children are born to them. Nay more, he even seems to say it is enough if their ancestors were faithful, even if their immediate parents are not. From which it follows, according to the opinion of this man, without a doubt all children are saved, for they are rare who do not have someone among their ancestors who was faithful.

The Council of Trent posited against these errors in sess. 7, can. 2, "If anyone shall say that Baptism is not necessary for salvation, *anathema sit*." This truth is proven firstly from the express word of God (John 3:5), "Unless a man will be born again of water and the Holy Spirit, he cannot enter into the kingdom of God." Such words do not sound like a precept, but a *medium*, as Augustine shows (*On the Merits and Remission of Sins*, c. 30), where he accurately examines this passage. And it is also clear from the reason which is given in verse 6 and 7:"What is born of the flesh is flesh, ... you must be born again." The Lord indicates that men are born carnal, and sinners, and thus slaves to sin. Hence it is necessary for there to be a remedy against these evils, and Baptism will hereafter be that remedy. The same thing is convicted from the figure of the bronze serpent, which the Lord posits in the same place. In this way he wills rebirth through faith and his Baptism to be the remedy against eternal death, just as the bronze serpent was once the sole remedy against the bite of the serpent. Therefore, the verse, "Unless a man be born again, etc.," is the same as if one were to say, "Unless you eat, you will not live"; or "Unless you take medicine, you will not recover your health." This does not signify a precept, but a *necessary medium*. Our adversaries do not dispute on this matter; rather, they attempt to twist the passage by various expositions, so that it could not be gathered that water is necessary.

Calvin (*Antidote, loc. cit.*) says two things: *a)* Firstly, according to some Fathers water is received for mortification; Chemnitz holds the same thing in his *Examination* for can. 2, sess. 7, but names Basil as the one who understood mortification for water. But this is vain, for Basil, in his book *On the Holy Spirit* (cap. 15), does not explain what the word water literally signifies in John 3:5, but presupposing it means true and natural water, asks why water is joined to the spirit in Baptism. He gives the reason, that water signifies the mortification of sinners, but the Spirit the resurrection of virtues.

b) Secondly, Calvin says that in this passage water is *an adjective of the spirit* and its sense: One must be born from the Spirit, who cleanses just as water. Now, we refuted this exposition above (book 2 cap. 3), where we advanced fifteen testimonies of the Fathers, who understand this passage on the water of Baptism; and besides, we confirmed the same thing with a few arguments.

Peter Martyr, in his commentary on 1 Cor. 7, apart from this explanation of Calvin which he does not find fault with, advances another, that there is no force of action in the conjunction "By water and the spirit." It is enough if men are reborn from the Spirit, in the way that it is said in Rom. 10:10, "It is believed from the heart unto justice, and the confession by mouth is unto salvation." There, you have the same copulative particle, and nevertheless, faith and confession of mouth are not of the same necessity. But this is a poor escape. In the first place, confession of mouth and faith of the heart are not related to the same end or effect; faith of the heart is necessary to acquire justice, confession of the mouth to not lose salvation. Now in Baptism, spirit and water pertain to the *same* regeneration; this is why those passages are not similar. Besides, if the force of action is not in the copulative, certainly it will be equivalent to a disjunctive; thence, however, it would follow that water without the spirit would be enough to be reborn, which is absolutely absurd. What Peter Martyr says, that Christ willed that we be reborn of the Spirit, he says gratuitously; if the conjunction *and* is received copulatively, both are necessary, if disjunctively, one or the other suffices, whichever it is.

Zwingli (on Mark 1), explains Baptism by a sermon. Brenz (on Matt. 3) explains the whole passage of the Gospel, *Unless a man be born again*, in regard to repentance, so that the sense would be: Unless a man would do penance, he will not enter into the kingdom of heaven. Wycliffe, as Waldens witnesses (tom. 2 c. 101), understands by water in John 3:5 that water which flowed from the side of Christ, so that the sense would be: Unless a man be reborn from the water, which flows from my side, i.e., from my passion, etc.

But these and similar things they have dreamed up are easily refuted. *Firstly*, from the common consensus of the Fathers cited above. Although this passage is explained in such different ways by men of this and the previous age, prudent men can do no better, even if they were not Christians, than to appeal to the judgment of the ancients, who explained this passage before these modern disputes.

Secondly, they are refuted by the common axiom of Theologians, whereby we are taught to understand Scripture according to the propriety of words, where we are not compelled by an apparent absurdity. Otherwise, we could twist every passage—even the clearest— if it were permissible to invent new senses. Hence, our adversaries show no absurd thing would follow if by "water" in this passage, they understand water, except that thence their heresy is refuted.

Thirdly, because if in this passage we do not understand water from the word "water," it will be difficult to establish that the Sacrament of Baptism consists in water, which still everyone in this time affirms, both Catholics and heretics. The rest of the passages of Scripture where water is mentioned in Baptism, such as Acts 8:12 and Ephes. 5:26, while they certainly prove

Chapter IV: The Necessity of Baptism

men can be baptized in water, still do not show they cannot be baptized in other liquids. Besides, these passages can be twisted to metaphors no less than John 3:5. As a result, the Council of Trent, in its 7th session, can. 2, rightly says anathema to all who twist this passage to metaphors, and do not understand it in regard to *true and natural* water, as the words sound.

2) In the second place, the same truth is proven from the tradition of the Church and the Fathers. The Church always believed infants perished if they passed form this life without Baptism. *First*, we have the testimonies of the Councils of Carthage and Milevitanus (cited by Augustine, *Epist*. 90 & 92), in which the opinion of those who supposed infants are saved without Baptism is expressly condemned. The Council of Trent agrees with this in sess. 6, can. 3 and sess. 7, can. 5.

Secondly, we have the testimonies of Pope Syricius (*Epist. ad Himericum*, 2) and Pope Innocent I (*Epist. 26 to the Council of Milevitanus*), who teach that children altogether perish if they die without Baptism. Likewise, Leo I (*Epist. 80/78 to the Bishops of Campania*), where he says in danger of life men must be baptized at any point so that they would not lack the necessary liberation.

Thirdly, we have testimonies of nearly all the Fathers who expressly teach the same thing (Irenaeus 3, 19; Origen *ad Rom*. 6; Nazianzen *orat. In sanctum lavarcum*; Basil *orat. 13 on the exhortation of Baptism*; Cyprian *Epist*. 3, 8 *to Fidus*; Ambrose *de Abraham* 2, last chapter; Jerome *Contra Pelagianos* 3; Augustine *On the Merit and Remission of Sins* 1, 16, 23-24 & 27, *Epist*. 28, *On the Origin of the Soul* 2, 12 and 3, 9; Proser of Aquitaine *On the Calling of the Gentiles* 2, 8; Fulgentius *de fide ad Petrum* 30; Bernard *Serm. 66 in cant*.; Peter of Cluny *Epist. Contra Petrobrusianos*). Let us, however, hear one or another testimony of Augustine in the name of others. In *On the Origin of the Soul* 3, 9, he says, "Do not believe, do not say, do not teach, that infants prevented from being Baptized by death can obtain the forgiveness of original sin if you wish to be a Catholic." Again, in *Epist*. 20 to Jerome, "Whoever will say that in Christ even children who depart from this life without the participation of the Sacrament will enter eternal life, this man certainly goes against the Apostolic preaching and condemns the whole Church; this is why whenever you see a man hasten and run with children to be baptized, it is because he believes without a doubt they altogether otherwise cannot be brought to life in Christ."

Lastly, it is proven from an argument taken from the foundations of our adversaries. Their foundation is that the sons of Christians are born free from the reality of original sin, not because they do not have the sin but because it is not imputed to them, since they are sons of the saints. This foundation can easily be overturned. *Firstly*, because Jacob and Esau were the sons of the best father, Isaac, and yet God chose Jacob, but hated Esau before they could do something good or bad (Rom. 9:13). Therefore, the sons of the saints are not born saints.

Peter Martyr answers this in his *Commentary on 1 Cor. 7* and says the sons of the saints are born saints when they are predestined; nevertheless, we do not know who are the ones that are predestined, therefore, we may have good hope in regard to all the sons of the saints until they betray their reprobation through bad works. This response is inept; if it so stood, it really will not matter if one is born from the faithful or infidels, and good hope will be maintained for all infants, for it most often happens that the sons of the faithful are reprobate, and the sons of infidels are predestined. Besides, if the sons of the faithful are not predestined, they are not born saints, and Peter Martyr Vermigli badly brings forward Calvin, following that promise of Gen. 17:7, "I will be your God, and the God of your seed."

Vermigli answers that promise was not universal but only had place among the predestined. But this is said gratuitously, for the words of Scripture are *absolute*, nor is there any mention of predestination in that chapter. Lastly, that promise is rendered inane if the condition of predestination is going to be attached; for thence neither parents nor sons can take consolation, since they do not know whether they are predestined. It is similar, if a king would say to someone, "I am giving you this city for yourself and your posterity, nevertheless, I will only concede it to your posterity at my pleasure."

Secondly, David was the son of a faithful man, and still, in Psalm 50:6, he says, "I was conceived in iniquity, and in sins my mother conceived me." The Apostle was also the son of saints, as he himself affirms in 2 Cor. 12:14, and still in Ephes. 2:3 he says, "Even we were by nature sons of wrath."

They answer: These are said about the corruption of nature and the sin which is really present, not from the reality, which is not in the sons of the faithful, since sin is not imputed to them. But certainly, that he is a son of wrath clearly pronounces a reality, for a son of wrath is not any but he who is liable to punishment and vengeance. He is not, however, liable to punishment to whom sin is not imputed. This is why Paul does not say "We are sons of wrath," but "*We were*," and still according to our adversaries, sin always remains, even after Baptism.

Thirdly, the passages of the Apostle Paul are general in regard to original sin: in Rom. 5:11, "In whom we have all sinned," and 2 Cor. 5:14, "Christ died for all therefore, all have died." These passages cannot be explained on the vice of nature, nor on the reality; otherwise, no man would have the reality. Nor can it be said that the sons of the faithful contract original sin, but soon it is forgiven to them before they are born. If the sons of the faithful are thus sanctified, namely because they are sons of the faithful, then they will begin to be saints at the very moment in which they begin to be sons of the faithful. Yet they begin to be sons of the faithful, in the very moment in which they begin *to exist simply*; therefore, they never have original sin, which is against Paul and against those or our adversaries who admit original sin, and they do not advert that they contradict themselves.

Chapter IV: The Necessity of Baptism

Fourthly, the foundation of our adversaries is opposed to the axiom of all the Fathers, nay more, of all Christians, which is that Christians *are not born, but made*, as Jerome (*Epist. 7 ad Laetam*), Tertullian (*Apologeticus* 17), and others say (*passim*). Now, according to Calvin and Martyr, Christians are born, not made.

3) Now, let us see their arguments. *a) Firstly*, they object to that of Gen. 17:7, "I will be your God, and the God of your seed." This was certainly said to Abraham and his posterity, but we succeed into the posterity of Abraham through Christ. Christ breaks down the barrier which separated us from the people of God.

I respond: That promise, as we showed above in the question in regard to the difference of the Sacraments of the New and Old Law, was not literally a promise of remission of sin, but *of peculiar protection and governance, as well as earthly happiness*. Nevertheless, in a certain mystical sense, it was also spiritual promises and of remission of sins and eternal life, and pertains to us; but it descends to us, not by carnal generation of parents, but *by the spiritual regeneration of Christ*. The Apostle in Rom. 4:12, 9:8; Gal. 3:7 and 4:28, clearly teaches they are true sons of Abraham, not who are sons of the flesh, but who are sons of faith, i.e., those who imitate the faith of Abraham. So then, we begin according to the Apostle to be sons of Abraham, since we begin to be faithful, but they do not become sons except when they are baptized, for to be baptized is to believe, as Augustine says (*Merit and Remiss. of Sins* 1, 27). Besides, reason teaches the same thing. Through carnal generation we cannot become sons of Abraham, since our parents did not descend from Abraham, but because Christ was truly the son of Abraham, then even we begin to be sons of Abraham when we begin to be sons, or brothers, of Christ. It is certain however, this does not happen except through Baptism. For this reason John 1:13 says, "They were not born from blood, nor from the will of the flesh, nor from the will of man, but from God," and John 3:7, "You must be born again." See Augustine (*Epist.* 200 *ad Aselicum*).

b) Secondly, they object to the verse of the Apostle in 1 Cor. 7:14, "Your children would be unclean, but now they are holy."

I respond with Augustine (*Merit and Remiss. of Sins* 3,12) that whatever is meant through this sanctity of children, it cannot be understood in the way which our adversaries would have it, that the children become holy without Baptism. In the same place, Paul says the unfaithful spouse is sanctified by the faithful one, and still, it would be quite stupid to believe the unfaithful spouse obtains remission of sins without conversion to God and the Baptism of Christ simply because they adhere to a faithful spouse.

Hence, there are three explanations of the Fathers on this passage. One, children are called holy *by a certain civil sanctity*, which is clearly legitimate, not spurious. This is of the commentary which is attributed to Ambrose, as well as St. Thomas and Anselm on this passage.

Peter Martyr Vermigli refutes this explanation, because they are legitimate sons, even if each spouse were an infidel, and still the Apostle says children are born holy from one faithful spouse, the other an infidel, because the infidel is sanctified through the faithful; therefore, some other sanctity must be acknowledged in this passage.

Yet, he poorly rebukes this explanation, for the notion of a marriage between two infidels is one thing, and one between a faithful and infidel another. When both spouses are infidels, the marriage without a doubt is legitimate, as a type of civil contract, nor can there be any doubt about the fact, as there also cannot be a doubt when each is among the faithful. But when one is faithful, the other is an infidel, it can be doubted whether the marriage is legitimate on account of a disparity of religion, for it seems the faithful is polluted on account of the cohabitation with an infidel. Therefore, the Apostle warns Christians that even if the Matrimony is legitimate, the faithful spouse is not polluted on account of cohabitation with the infidel spouse, but on the contrary, the infidel spouse is sanctified by the faithful spouse; the greater force is of faith than infidelity. He proves that there is also a legitimate wedlock in such a disparity of religion from the fact that their sons are not reckoned unclean, i.e., in disrepute and spurious, but holy, i.e., *legitimate, and free from civil ignominy.*

The second exposition is the sons of these spouses are called holy because they are consecrated to God by the faithful spouse, and become Christians through Baptism, and are reared in the fear of God. The Apostle exhorts Christian spouses that they should not depart from their spouse if they are an infidel, and he gives the reason that the infidel is sanctified by the faithful, i.e., either converted to the faith, or certainly are well disposed to the faith since they do not shudder at the manner of life of the faithful spouse; from there it also follows that the sons are holy, i.e., *they become Christians.* Certainly however, it would not happen if the infidel spouse were to refuse to dwell with the faithful, or the infidel spouse were not sanctified by the faithful; for then, the sons would follow the infidel parent, and hence, be unclean, and they would be infidels. Tertullian explained it in this way (*ad Uxorum* 2), and from him St. Jerome (*in Jovin.* 1, *Epist.* 153 to *Paulinus*), and Augustine (*Merit and Remiss.* 2, 26; 3, 12, *On the Sermon on the Mount* 1, 27).

Peter Martyr Vermigli also seizes upon this exposition, that he would firm up his heresy from this passage of the Apostle. For, it often happens that those who beget sons from whoring about should see to it that they become Christians and nurtured in fear of God, as Augustine did with his son Adeodatus, and nevertheless, no man from there would prove the union with a prostitute is holy. Paul, however, proves that wedlock is holy even of an infidel with a member of the faithful, because from thence holy children are born.

But Peter Martyr unduly rebukes this exposition. Carnal commerce

Chapter IV: The Necessity of Baptism

with a prostitute is a thing that is bad *per se*, and therefore cannot become holy because it took place with a member of the faithful. Nor can it become praiseworthy and be retained, even if children are born from it who become Christians, for evil things cannot be done so that good will come of it (Rom. 3:8). Now, the marriage of infidels is a good thing, and therefore, it can be become better, if one of them would be converted to the faith; and they can be commended and persuaded in perseverance in such a marriage, on account of the good which follows from it, that their sons become Christians.

The *third* exposition is of others, as Augustine and Anselm relate (*loc. cit.*), who say the infidel spouse is sanctified by the faithful, because they learn to keep the laws of wedlock and not abuse Matrimony. The infidels who do not know God, even if they are legitimately married, still often abuse Matrimony, and do not abstain from conjugal relations during the time of menstruation, nor do they always preserve the natural mode of action. From there, however, wedlock is polluted, and sons are born unclean. Their children and their parents are freed from pollution, however, through this, that the infidel consent to dwell with the faithful, and hence preserve the laws of chaste wedlock.

c) The *third* argument of Calvin: Baptism is profaned when it is given to those who do not pertain to Christ, in the way that the seal of the king is profaned when it is sealed on a false document.

I respond: Baptism is not profaned when it is given to the unclean, but on the contrary, rather sanctifies and cleanses the unclean. It is not a seal of the grace that has been received, as Calvin dreams up, rather, it is an instrument *conferring grace*, and a sign of the grace which is then given.

d) The *fourth* argument: The infants of the Jews, who died before the eighth day, could not be circumcised, and still it does not have the appearance of truth that they perished; therefore, they were saved without Circumcision. The same notion, however, prevails for Baptism among Christians, and Circumcision among the Jews.

I respond: The whole argument is constituted from uncertain things. In the first place, many of the Fathers (as we said above) deny Circumcision was given as a remedy for sin. Next, we do not know whether before the eighth day they held the infants of the Jews had some remedy, and what it was. Then, the notion of Christians and Jews is not the same. Now, a certain remedy has been determined by Christ, and indeed as common and easy as possible, apart from which it is not lawful to create something else; in the Old Testament, however, what was done cannot be known for certain, since Scripture says nothing. We know one thing for certain from Scripture: that every man born of sinners was not saved, except through the passion of Christ applied through certain means, as Augustine profusely teaches in his three books on *Merits and Remission of Sins*, and in his four books *On the Origin of the Soul*.

e) The *fifth* argument: If Baptism is necessary, untold numbers of infants will perish without any fault of their own, which seems foreign to the mercy of God. This is the argument of Peter Martyr, and was also of certain Catholics such as Cajetan, Gabriel Biel, and others, although they did not teach the sons of Christians are born holy, but still tried to discover another remedy for children apart from Baptism.

But we respond with Augustine (*On the Good of Perseverance* 2, 12) and Prosper (*de Vocatione Gentium* 2, 8): the judgments of God and why he would permit so many children to perish are secret; still, he is most just. Even if children are not baptized through no fault of their own, still, they do not perish without fault, since they have original sin. Those who set up another remedy apart from Baptism very clearly oppose themselves to the Gospel, Councils, Fathers, and also the consensus of the universal Church, for, as Augustine says, "There is no other reason a man hastens into the Church and runs with infants in danger to Baptism, except because it is certain there is no other remedy" (*Epist.* 28). It seems, however, the men who confect these things do not think the care of infants pertains more to God than to them, and when Christ asserted that Baptism is necessary (John 3:5), he knew well that many would be deprived of that remedy through no fault of their own, and it would be very easy for God, if he willed, to provide Baptism for all infants, just as he really provides for all the elect. What Bucer and Vermigli say, that infants that have been predestined are also saved without Baptism is said very ineptly, as Augustine shows in his work *On the Origin of the Soul* (3, 10). God has most efficaciously provided the remedy for the salvation of those whom he predestined. Hence, all who die in infancy, if they were predestined, without a doubt are baptized, and conversely, if they are reprobate, they are not baptized.

CHAPTER V

On the Time in Which Baptism Began to be Necessary

THERE is a question among Theologians in regard to the time in which Baptism began to be necessary. Now, because there is no controversy with the heretics, I will only explain in a few propositions what seems to me to be the more probable opinion.

1) The first proposition: *Baptism was instituted before the Lord's Passion.* Mark, it cannot be denied that Christ had some Baptism in use before the Passion. In John 3:22 & 4:2, Christ is said to have Baptized through his disciples. Now, there can be a doubt whether that Baptism was the Sacrament which we now have, and on which mention is made in Matt. 28:19, or whether it was a certain preparation for the Sacrament of Baptism that was going to be instituted later, just as the Baptism of John was. Chrysostom (*Homil.* 28 in Joan.) and Theophylactus (on *John* 3) clearly teach that Baptism, with which the disciples of Christ baptized in John 3:22 did not remit sins and was only in water without the Spirit; nor was there any difference between the Baptism of the disciples of Christ and John, rather both were a preparation and therefore, Christ did not baptize per se, but through the disciples, because it was not fitting for him to baptize without the Spirit. It seems that St. Leo the Great taught the same thing (*Epist.* 4,3 *ad Episcopos Siciliae*) when he says, "The very nature of the act teaches us that it is the recognized day [i.e., the day of resurrection] for the general reception of the grace, on which the power of the gift and the character of the action originated. And this is strongly corroborated by the consideration that the Lord Jesus Christ Himself, after he rose from the dead, handed on both the form and power of baptizing to his disciples, in whose person all the chiefs of the churches received their instructions with these words, 'Go ye and teach all nations, baptizing them in the name of the Father and of the Son and of the Holy Spirit.' On which of course he might have instructed them even before his passion, had he not especially wished it to be understood that the grace of regeneration began with His resurrection." Still, what we said is more probable. Cyril teaches in earnest (*in John* 2, 57 *seqq.*), and Augustine (*Tract. in Joan.* 13 & 15; *Epist.* 108 *ad Seleucianum*), as well as Hugh of St. Victor (*de Sacramentis* 2, part. 6, cap. 4).

This is the more common assertion of Theologians, with Peter Lombard in 4 dist. 3. This is the argument. *Firstly*, because in John 4:1, it is said that Christ baptized, although he did not baptize himself, rather his disciples, as the Evangelist adds in verse 2. So, that Baptism was properly the Baptism *of Christ*, as distinguished from the Baptism of John; otherwise, not he, but

John would be said to have baptized them, whom the disciples of Christ baptized. If, however, it was properly the Baptism of Christ, necessarily it was in water and spirit, not in water only, for Scripture always posits this distinction between Christ and John, that the latter only baptized in water, while the former in water and also in the Spirit. It would not be fitting for Christ to institute an empty ceremony, or usurp the office of John to himself, namely to baptize in water alone. Additionally in John 1:33, it is said concerning Christ in the present, "He is the one who baptizes in the Holy Spirit."

Secondly, this same thing is proven, because in Acts 19:5 we read that those whom John had baptized were *rebaptized*. Now, we never read that those whom the disciples of Christ baptized before his passion were rebaptized. It is certainly very probable (as Augustine teaches in *Epist.* 108) the Apostles were not baptized unless it was before Christ's passion.

Thirdly, the Fathers teach in a common consensus that Christ, when he was baptized in the Jordan, gave the waters the power to sanctify, as is clear from Tertullian (*Contra Judaeos*), Hilary (*in Matt.* 2), Ambrose (on *Luc.* 2, 12), Jerome (*Dialog. Contra Luciferianos*), Nazianzen (in his *Oration on the Holy Light*), Bede (on *Luc.* 3), and others. Now certainly, the waters would not have the force of sanctifying except from that time in which they began to be the matter of Baptism.

Lastly, the foundation of the contrary assertion is not solid. Chrysostom and Theophylactus alone advance for that verse of John 7:39, "The spirit was not yet given because Jesus was not yet glorified." This passage is understood *on the plenitude of the Holy Spirit*, which began to be given visibly in Pentecost; otherwise, all the saints had the Holy Spirit even before the passion of Christ.

2) The second proposition: *The Baptism of Christ was instituted when the Lord himself was baptized by John in the Jordan.* Note: On this matter, i.e., at which point of time Christ instituted Baptism, there are a great many opinions among the Scholastics, but the more common and probable is the one which we follow. This was also embraced by the *Catechism of the Council of Trent*, as well as Peter Lombard with St. Thomas and others commenting on 4, dist. 3.

Note besides, we do not mean to say that Christ, on the day of his Baptism, taught the matter or form of Baptism in words, for it is false. Rather, he first established and decreed what he later declared to Nicodemus in John 3:3, and in another time to his disciples, that water is the matter of Baptism and as it's form, the invocation of the three divine persons. He determined the waters for the matter of Baptism, since these by the touch of his most clean flesh, he deigned to consecrate and illumine, as the Fathers teach (*loc. cit.*). At the same time he determined the form, when in his Baptism the whole Trinity sensibly appeared, as is clear from Matt. 3:16. After Christ was baptized, the heavens were opened, and the voice of the Father thundered, and the Holy Spirit appeared in the appearance of a dove, and the Son of God himself taken up in the flesh was present; there also at the same time (as Hilary witnesses, *loc. cit.*), the effect of Baptism was declared to have been instituted by Christ, namely, heaven is opened for the baptized, and sons are adopted by the Father, and filled with the Holy Spirit, etc.

3) The third proposition: *The Baptism of Christ was not necessary by the necessity of means or the necessity of precept before the death of Christ.* It is proved, because even to the death of Christ the ancient law retained its force, as is clear, because Christ preserved it even to death. On the day before he was to suffer, he preserved the ceremony of the Paschal Lamb, and in Matt. 23:3, he warned men to keep and do what the Scribes and Pharisees taught from the seat of Moses. Consequently, even Circumcision, if it was given as a remedy for sin, was in force even to the death of Christ. Therefore, during that whole time the Baptism of Christ was not necessary as a means to salvation, seeing that without it men could, even if they were children, be justified. This is why that of John 3:5, "Unless a man be born again, etc." does not signify from that day in which the Lord spoke with Nicodemus Baptism was necessary, but signifies it was going to be necessary in the New Law, *after the legal ceremonies ceased*, as Bernard explains (*Epist. 77 to Hugh*). What Fulgentius says (*de Fide ad Petrum*, 3) must be explained in the same way: From the time in which it was said, "Unless a man be reborn," no man could be saved without Baptism, he means by the word time, not the very day on which it was said, but the time *of the New Law*. Lastly, that also of Luke 16:16, "The Law and the Prophets even to John," does not mean then the law ceased in regard to the force or obligation, but *in regard to the preaching*; John was the last of the prophets. Wherefore, it is added, "From that time the kingdom of God is preached." Besides, in the death of Christ, the efficacy of the ceremonies and the whole Old Law ceased; therefore, the power of Circumcision also ceased. Therefore, even to that time the Old Law had force. Hence, that in the death of Christ the force of the law ceased, is clear from the Gospel of Matt. 27:51, "The veil was torn," and John 19:30, "It has been consummated." Likewise, from the Apostle in Rom. 7:4, "You have become dead to the law through the body of Christ." Likewise, nearly all the ceremonies of the law were figures of Christ (Col. 2:17 & Heb. 10:1). Christ, however, fulfilled the work of redemption in death.

4) The fourth proposition: *The Baptism of Christ began to be necessary by the necessity of means as well as the necessity of precept from the day of Pentecost.* Note, the Old Law ceased in the death of Christ *simply*, because then the reason for the law ceased universally. Nevertheless, on account of ignorance of this fact, the Old Law still obliged the Jews until the public promulgation of the Gospel. On the other hand, the Evangelical law, as well as the Christian Sacraments were founded and also very beneficial

before the death of Christ; just the same, they did not have the force of precept until after the solemn promulgation, as the Council of Trent says about Baptism (sess. 6, cap. 4). The reason is because the promulgation is in regard to the essence of the law, as St. Thomas teaches (I IIae q. 90 a. 4). The solemn promulgation of the New Law, however, took place on the day of Pentecost. This is proved: *a)* Firstly, because, as we said, the Old Law was in force even to the death of Christ, but from that time even to Pentecost neither Christ nor the Apostles publicly spoke to the people. *b)* Secondly, the New Law should not be promulgated solemnly until after all the mysteries of redemption were completed. *c)* Thirdly, the Old Law was solemnly promulgated on Mount Sinai in the fiftieth day after the first Pasch of the Jews; therefore, the New Law ought to have been promulgated on the fiftieth day after the first Pasch of Christians. That promulgation of the law was a figure of the promulgation of the Gospel, as Augustine (*Epist.* 119), and Leo (*Serm.* 1 *On Pentecost*), and others teach. *d)* Fourthly, all the conditions necessary for promulgation agree with the first sermon which Peter gave on the day of Pentecost (Acts 2). It was held in the royal city of Jerusalem, when all men of all nations were present, as Luke witnesses, by a supreme herald of the Gospel, which the Apostle Peter was, and in that sermon particular headings of the whole Evangelical doctrine were understood. Lastly, the use of the Sacraments began immediately after.

CHAPTER VI

On Baptism of Blood and Desire

The question pertains to the last part of the disputation on the necessity of Baptism, whether Baptism of water can be supplied by martyrdom, both in children and in adults, and through true conversion of heart in adults.

Martin Chemnitz (2 part. *Examination*, pp. 90-92) admits these three Baptisms, and says that from ancient times these three Baptisms, blood, flame, and water, were eloquently distinguished. He disagrees, however, with Catholics in the manner of explanation; he would not have it that martyrdom or penance remit sins as Baptism of water, rather he argues that only faith, which embraces Christ in the time of martyrdom and penance, is what justifies it. Illyricus also (*Cent.* 5, 4, col. 517) says that Prosper acted against the word of God, and with great injury when he equated Martyrdom to Baptism. But Illyricus does not advance arguments. Chemnitz, on the other hand, shows that martyrdom and penance are our works, but it would be absurd and impious for our works to be equal to the blood of Christ and the power of Baptism. He gives a confirmation from Augustine, who in *On Baptism against the Donatists* (4, 22) says the good thief who hung on the Cross next to Christ did not obtain the remission of sins by his own passion, but from faith embracing Christ; Cyprian had taught the contrary of that, but then Augustine refuted it (*loc. cit.*).

This assertion of Chemnitz is not only false, but also opposes itself, and is not without its own lies. Seeing that the same Chemnitz everywhere teaches with his master Luther that only faith justifies even in the very Baptism of water, does he not clearly oppose himself when he says martyrdom and Penance do not remit sin in the way in which Baptism does, because in them only faith justifies? There are also two lies in this assertion of Chemnitz. The first, when he says that Augustine asserts the good thief was justified by faith alone embracing Christ. Augustine does not say this, rather that the good thief was justified *by faith and a conversion of the heart*. Secondly, when he says that Cyprian, who believed martyrdom justifies in the way in which Baptism does, was refuted by Augustine. This is an impudent lie, since Augustine not only did not refute Cyprian, but praises his teaching. He speaks in this way, "That the place of Baptism is sometimes supplied by martyrdom is supported by an argument by no means trivial, which the blessed Cyprian adduces from the thief, to whom, though he was not baptized, it was yet said, 'Today shall you be with me in Paradise.'" A little later, Augustine teaches the thief cannot be called a martyr, or saved by Baptism of blood, rather, Baptism of flame; but in this he speaks to confirm the teaching of Cyprian, for if Baptism of flame justifies, how much more Baptism of blood, as Cyprian had said. To explain the whole matter, I will posit some propositions.

1) The first proposition: *It is rightly called martyrdom, and is a certain type of Baptism.* This proposition is proven from a twofold reasoning. *Firstly*, because the divine Scripture and the Holy Fathers customarily name Baptism martyrdom, as in Mk. 10:38, "Can you drink the chalice which I will drink? Or be baptized in the Baptism with which I am baptized? The Fathers teach the same thing. Tertullian (*de Baptismo*), speaking about martyrdom, says, "This is the Baptism which renders the laver of regeneration when it has not been received, or restores it when lost." Prosper, in epigrams:

And whatever the mystical form of the sacred laver imparts,
The glory of martyrdom wholly satisfies.

Cyprian, in the preface to his book *On the Exhortation of Martyrdom*, says that martyrdom is a Baptism, and indeed more excellent than the Baptism of water. Ambrose on Ps. 118 (serm. 3) distinguishes three Baptisms, one of water, the other of blood, and the third of purgatory in another life. Jerome (*On Eph.* 4:4), commenting on the verse "*One Baptism*," distinguishes the Baptism of water from the Baptism of martyrdom. Augustine in *de Civit. Dei* 13,7; *Epist.* 108 *ad Seleucianum*; *On the Origin of the Soul* 9; *On Baptism* 4, 21-22. Cyril, in *Catech.* 3, also posits these two Baptisms, as also Nazianzen (*Orat. in Sancta Lumina*), Damascene (4, 10), Bernard (*Epist.* 77), and Hugh of St. Victor (*de Sacram.* 2, part. 6, c. 7).

The *second* reason is that martyrdom agrees with the Baptism of water in three effects: firstly, that without a doubt it configures a man to the passion and death of Christ; secondly, it remits original sin and all the other crimes, if there are any; thirdly, among the Sacraments it is proper to Baptism alone.

Nevertheless, here we must observe that these are not all equally certain. Now, the first is certain, that martyrdom is a configuration to the death of Christ, as is known, and a more noble configuration than Baptism of water; because the former is real, the latter is Sacramental. Likewise, it is certain among all, that it remits all penalty, so that martyrs immediately obtain the crown. That much is clear from the fact that the Church never prays for the souls of martyrs, but rather commends itself to them. As St. Augustine says, "Whoever prays for a martyr does him an injury" (*Serm.* 17 *de Verbis Apostoli*; Innocent, cap. *cum Marthae* extra, *de Celebration Missarum*). This is why Cyprian (*Epist.* 4,2 *ad Antonianum*), comparing martyrs with other dying Christians, says, "It is one thing to be forgiven, and another to obtain glory; it is one thing to be sent into prison and not go out from there until the last farthing is paid, and another immediately to receive the reward of faith and virtue; it is one thing to be corrected, tortured by long suffering and cleansed for a long time in the fire and at length to be freed from sins, and another to have cleansed all sins in martyrdom; and lastly, it is one thing to wait upon the sentence of the Lord on the day of Judgment, and another to be crowned by the Lord straightaway."

On the second effect there is a greater difficulty. There are not lacking theologians who teach that martyrdom does not confer grace *ex opere operato*, but merely *ex opere operantis*, nor does it give any degree of grace apart from that which corresponds to the merit of charity of the martyr himself (Domingo del Soto, and Ledesma in 4 dist. 3, q. 1, art. 11). Martyrdom received without charity is of no benefit, as Paul says in 1 Cor. 13:3. However, a man that is in charity is without a doubt in grace. This is also why we believe all true martyrs have true, nay more, even supreme charity before they undergo martyrdom, according to that of John 15:13, "Greater love than this no man has, that he gives up his life for his friends."

The more probable assertion is that martyrdom confers the first grace *ex opere operato*, so that if someone approaches martyrdom while still in sin, nevertheless, without attachment to some sin and with faith, and inchoate love, and at least imperfect penance of the sort that is also required before Baptism of water, he will be justified *ex opere operato*, and saved by virtue of martyrdom. St. Thomas teaches expressly in this way (4 dist. Q. 3 art. 3 ad 1, & q. 4), as well as John Major, Gabriel Biel, and others on the same 4, dist. 4. It is proved, *firstly*, from the martyrdom of infants. It is certain that infants killed for Christ are not only saved, but also held by the Church in the number of the martyrs, as is clear from the feast of the Holy Innocents, which Bernard calls to mind in his *Sermon on the Innocents*, and before him Augustine (*de lib. Arbit.* 3, 23; *Epist.* 28 *to Jerome*), and before Augustine, Origen (*Hom.* 3 *in diversos locos Evangelii*), and Cyprian (*Epist.* 4, 6 *ad Thibaritanos*). But children cannot do anything, and they are sinners before they are baptized with Baptism of water, or blood.

Some answer that the Innocents were circumcised, hence they were justified before martyrdom. Still, this is nothing. It is uncertain whether they were all circumcised; in fact, it is very probable and nearly certain that they were not all circumcised. Herod slew all boys who were in Bethlehem and its confines, and he did not only command the sons of Jews to be slain, but altogether every child; perhaps there were not a few Gentiles among them. Besides, he commanded all infants two years and younger to be slain; hence they also, who had not yet attained to the eighth day, on which alone they could be circumcised. *Lastly*, it is not de fide that Circumcision justifies, and still the Church absolutely believes for certain that all those infants are saved. Besides, the Church not only honors the Innocents as saved, but also as *martyrs*; therefore, the passion they received for Christ conferred something to them *ex opere operato*. What del Soto answers, that this is a privilege of children does not avail, since it is asserted without any foundation. If martyrdom benefits infants *ex opere operato*, why not adults?

Certainly, it is no less a martyrdom, no less potent and efficacious for adults than infants, but on the contrary, rather more noble and efficacious.

Secondly, it is proved from the argumentation of St. Thomas. The grace which is given in martyrdom, the remission of all punishment, cannot be *ex opere operantis*. It would either be from the endurance of punishment, or from the fervor of charity. Not from the endurance of punishment, because many martyrs were previously wicked men who had merited death a thousand times over, and, without a doubt, a certain light death by beheading was not sufficient satisfaction, and still if they are truly martyrs, all punishments are forgiven them. There are also many confessors who often suffered more than martyrs, and still the whole of their punishment is not always forgiven. Also, it cannot be attributed to the merit of charity; for many holy confessors had greater charity than many martyrs, and yet they did not have forgiveness of all punishment; martyrs, however, even if they did not have any but one degree of charity, nevertheless, by the very fact that they are martyrs, have the forgiveness of all punishment. Consequently, we must affirm that martyrdom is *ex opere operato*, i.e., it confers grace by the arrangement and institution of Christ. Now, if martyrdom confers grace *ex opere operato*, certainly it can also confer the first grace, for the only thing that would seem to stand in the way is that it would not to have force *ex opere operato*.

Thirdly, the Church never examines whether a man had grace beforehand to venerate them as a holy martyr; rather, it honors them all indifferently when it is certain they were slain for Christ in the confession of faith and the unity of the Church. Heretics and schismatics cannot be martyrs, since they place an obstacle to the grace of God through the sin of infidelity and schism, in which act they persevere.

Fourthly, if martyrdom does not confer the first grace *ex opere operato* but only works by the fervor of charity, then Baptism of blood would not truly be distinguished from Baptism of flame, rather both would be Baptism of flame, since both would consist in internal conversion and a motion of the soul toward God. But really, Baptism of blood is distinguished from Baptism of flame because the very shedding of blood in martyrdom supplies Baptism, but in Baptism of flame, however, it is only an internal conversion and inspiration of the Holy Spirit.

Fifthly, let us say there was someone seized in persecution who would rather die than deny Christ, and really dies, and still did not have true contrition but only a certain attrition for his sins before martyrdom, and then did not have a greater disposition than that which is necessary for Baptism of water. He will either be justified and saved, or not; if so, then martyrdom gives the first grace *ex opere operato*. He would not be able to merit something before martyrdom since he would not have been just. If he was not saved, then Baptism of blood does not supply for Baptism of water; for he is truly baptized in his own blood, and truly a martyr, since

Chapter VI: Baptism of Blood and Desire 341

he died for the true faith. As a result, it must be affirmed that he is justified *ex opere operato*.

Sixthly, and lastly, this seems altogether to have been the teaching of the Fathers. Cyprian, in his *Epistle* to Jubajanus, says, "Can the force of Baptism be greater or stronger than confession and martyrdom?" Likewise, Augustine (*City of God* 13,7), "Whoever has not received the laver of regeneration and dies for the confession of Christ, it is of the same value to forgive sins as if they were washed in the sacred font of Baptism." These will be false if Baptism confers the first grace and also forgives sins even in regard to guilt, while martyrdom can do neither. In this way, the power of Baptism of water will be greater by far than the power of Baptism of blood, yet the Fathers teach the contrary.

There is an argument which is customarily made from two passages of Scripture. 1 Cor. 13:3, "If I should deliver my body to be burned, and have not charity, it profits me nothing." John 15:13, "Greater love than this no man has, that he would lay aside his life for his friends." *I respond:* these passages do not give the conclusion that a martyr, before his martyrdom, must have true charity and hence be justified. The first place does not require that charity precedes, but that it *accompanies* other goods, for without charity nothing suffices for salvation. This is also very true, seeing that martyrdom profits nothing if the martyr departs this life without charity. But he cannot depart without charity when grace is infused by the force of that martyrdom and the arrangement and privilege of God, and hence, charity. Moreover, the fact that on account of this passage of Paul it is not necessary for charity to precede the martyrdom itself, at least in time, is clear because the same Paul says that without charity, faith and knowledge profit nothing; nevertheless, ordinarily faith, and often even knowledge, are earlier in man than charity, yet if faith and knowledge always remain without charity, they do not save a man, as the Apostle rightly said. Add the fact that what the Apostle says about martyrdom can also be said about Baptism; a man that has Baptism, if he would not have charity, he is not saved, and still, nobody denies that Baptism gives the first grace.

The second passage teaches that supreme charity *on the side of the work* is to lay down his life for a friend, because man has something greater which he would give for his friend than his life. Nevertheless, this passage does not teach that everyone who gives his life for a friend has supreme charity in regard to the habit, or internal act, as is known, since many who did not give their life had greater charity than those who gave it, as is clear from the Blessed Virgin, St. John the Evangelist, and others. Besides, even if a man lays aside his life for the love of Christ, he has, without a doubt, true charity, as this passage of the Gospel teaches, and a great many martyrs appeared to be such men; nevertheless, it can also happen that someone is not yet fully justified, taken up for martyrdom, decrees to lay aside life, not on account of charity for God, which he does not yet have, as much as out of fear of hell or hope of heavenly reward. Certainly, it cannot be said of such a man that he had true charity; still, he did well by laying aside his life in confession of Christ and is a martyr, i.e., a witness of the truth. We also say in regard to men of this sort, their sins are remitted them and grace is infused upon them from the martyrdom *ex opere operato*.

2) The second proposition: *Perfect conversion and penance are rightly called Baptism of desire* [lit. of wind], *and it supplies for Baptism of water, at least in necessity.* Note: Baptism of desire is not said to be any conversion you like, but *perfect*, which includes true contrition and charity and at the same time, also a desire for Baptism.

Note *secondly*, this proposition was not as certain among the Fathers as the previous one. In regard to martyrdom, none of the Fathers that I know of denied that it supplied for Baptism of water, but in regard to conversion and penance, there are not lacking some who denied it. A book titled *On the Ecclesiastical Dogmas*, which is falsely attributed to St. Augustine, clearly says in chapter 74 that a Catechumen cannot be saved even if he lived in good works unless he will have been cleansed by Baptism of water or blood. There were also some men in the time of St. Bernard who supposed the same thing, as is clear from his 77th *Epistle*.

Yet, there cannot be any doubt that it must be believed that true conversion supplies for Baptism of water, since it is not from contempt, but from necessity that some men die without Baptism of water. It is expressly held in Ezechiel 18:21, "If the wicked man will have done penance for his sins, ... I will no longer remember his iniquities." Ambrose teaches the same thing in his *Oration* on the death of Valerian the younger, "The man whom I was to baptize, I have lost, but he has not lost the grace in which he hoped." Augustine says the same thing (*de Baptismo* 4,22), as well as Bernard (*loc. cit.*), and after them Innocent III (cap. *Apostolicam de Presbytero non Baptizato*), from where even the Council of Trent (sess. 6 can. 4) says Baptism is necessary *in fact or in desire*. Lastly, true conversion agrees with martyrdom and with the Baptism of water in the use of the term Baptism and in its two effects; consequently, it is believable that it also agrees in another effect, which is to forgive sin and justify man, and in that manner, it supplies for Baptism of water. The antecedent is proven. Firstly, in regard to the term Baptism, we read in Mk. 1:4 as well as Lk. 3:3, "Preaching the Baptism of penance in remission of sins," and in 1 Cor. 15:29, "What will they do who are baptized for the dead? If the dead do not rise, then why are they baptized for them?" A no more suitable exposition can be given for this passage than if we were to understand by Baptism the work of penance and affliction, which the living take up on behalf of the souls of the dead. Besides, if penance configures a man to the passion of Christ, as martyrdom does, although not as perfectly as martyrdom, perfect contrition also forgives the whole punishment, just as it was in the conversion of Mary Magdalene, the good thief, and others. Baptism

Chapter VI: Baptism of Blood and Desire

of flame is also not absolutely and simply called an internal conversion, except when it is so perfect and fervent that it removes every blight of sin. Otherwise, it if did not remove all punishment, as much as there was, it is not a Baptism, except imperfectly.

3) The third proposition: *Both martyrdom and penance remit sins, but not "faith alone, whereby martyrs or penitents embrace Christ."* This is against Chemnitz, and it is proven from the Scriptures, the Fathers, and reason. *a)* Firstly, the Scriptures attribute remission of sins to passion itself and to penance. Matt. 10:39 & 16:24, "He that loses his life for my sake will find it." Mk. 8:34 and Lk. 9:24, "He that will lose his life for my sake, shall save it." Ezechiel 18:27, "When the wicked turns himself away from his wickedness, which he has done, and does judgment and justice, he shall save his soul alive." And in Lk. 7:47, it is said of the Magdalene, "Many sins have been forgiven her, because she has loved much." *b)* Secondly, the fathers cited above never attribute justification to faith alone, but to the very passion, or penance, and desire for Baptism. *c)* Thirdly, if faith alone operated in martyrdom and penance, there would not be three Baptisms but two, or rather only one. Hence, Chemnitz would not have spoken correctly when he says that the Fathers eloquently distinguish three Baptisms. What if he were to say there are three Baptisms which are three instruments to arouse faith? I would say, there would be many more, because there would be as many as there were instruments to arouse faith, as is clear.

Furthermore, the argument of Chemnitz does not conclude anything. We do not equate our works with the power of Baptism or the blood of Christ when we say through martyrdom and Penance sins are forgiven and supply Baptism; rather, we equate *the grace of God to the grace of God*, and the arrangement and institution of Christ to the arrangement and institution of Christ. Just as in Baptism of water, what chiefly operates is the divine institution as well as grace, so also in martyrdom and penance. The passion of the martyrs does not have the power to justify of itself, rather, *from the arrangement and promise of Christ*. Similarly in penance and conversion, it is only a certain disposition to which justification follows from the arrangement and promise of God. Additionally, the disposition itself is not especially our work, but God's, which firstly inspires penance and the love of martyrdom, and then helps to perfect it.

4) The fourth proposition: *Martyrdom and conversion to God, even if they are certain types of Baptism, nevertheless are not Sacraments.* It is proven *a)* firstly, because they do not have the essence of a Sacrament. In martyrdom, there is no form of words as to its essence; in conversion, there is neither a form of words nor an outward sensible sign, which is necessarily required. *b)* Secondly, the Sacraments are remedies against ordinary sin and suitable in every time. On the other hand, martyrdom is not an ordinary remedy, and it cannot be had in any time. *c)* Thirdly, the Sacraments are a cause of grace, just as actions of God through his ministers; but the slaying of the

martyrs is not an action of God through his minister, but the action of the devil through his accomplice. As it is a passion, however, it coincides only dispositively to justification, just as conversion or Baptism of flame. On the other hand, the Sacraments and martyrdom justify *ex opere operato* in a very different way. In the former, the *opus operatum* is an active cause of instrumental grace; in the latter, it is the disposition.

CHAPTER VII

On the Minister of Baptism

THE fifth controversy follows on the ministerial efficiency. In such a matter there is only one question: Whether the laity can baptize. Calvin devised a new heresy in the *Institutes* (4, 15 §20-22), where he teaches that it is not lawful for anyone to baptize, not even in extreme necessity, who is not an ordinary minister of the Church called and ordained to this purpose. He also repeats this in his *Antidote to the Council of Trent*, sess. 7, can. 10, on the Sacraments in general. He does not explain clearly enough whether he supposes that Baptism is not valid if it is given by a layman, or whether it is only not permitted without sin for the laity to baptize.

Hence, Catholic doctors uphold six pronouncements in a common consensus. *Firstly, ex officio,* the right to baptize *ordinarily* pertains to priests alone, i.e., to bishops and priests, nevertheless, it is suitable to priests in this way with subordination and dependency upon their bishops. In the same way that the power to absolve sins is given to priests in their ordination, and nevertheless, because to absolve from sins is an act of jurisdiction which is proper to bishops, as a result priests cannot use that power except in as much as the bishops concede it to them, so also it should be supposed in regard to the power to baptize. Hence, certain testimonies of the authors can be reconciled that would otherwise seem to be contrary. Certain men affirm simply that the duty to baptize pertains to priests, such as Isidore (*de Officiis Divinis*, 2 24). Others say priests cannot baptize without the faculty of the bishop, such as Tertullian (*de Baptismo*), and Jerome (*Dialogo contra Luciferianos*).

Secondly, they teach that *ex officio* it is also suitable for deacons to baptize, but *in the absence* of priests, or *by their command.* The same authors teach in this way, namely Tertullian and Jerome. Nor do Ignatius (*Epist. ad Heron.*) and Epiphanius (*Haeres.* 79) oppose them when they deny that the office of baptizing is unsuited to deacons, but proper for priests. This is because Epiphanius and Ignatius are speaking on the *ordinary* office, while Tertullian and Jerome are speaking about the *extraordinary office*, and they each rightly say that *ordinarily*, seeing that it pertains to the priests alone to baptize, *extraordinarily* it also pertains to deacons. Gelasius also holds this (*Epist.* 1 c. 9), and it is expressed in the very ordination of deacons.

Thirdly, Catholics teach that it is never lawful for the laity to baptize *solemnly*, nor even privately *while the priest is present*, or a deacon, or even when they are absent, *outside of a case of necessity.* Augustine teaches this (*Contra Parmen.* 2, 13), and his reasoning is that it is lawful for no one to usurp the office of another.

Fourthly, they teach that it is lawful for the laity to baptize in a case of necessity. I have never found any uncertainty about this in the Church, which is why the heresy of Calvin is new and unheard of.

Fifthly, they also teach that the unbaptized are permitted to give Baptism in a case of necessity, if they know the rite. Still, the Fathers seem to be uncertain about this. Tertullian (*de Baptismo*) makes the argument why it is lawful for the laity to baptize. He says, "Because what can equally be received by all can be equally given by all." Jerome (*loc. cit.*), imitating Tertullian, says, "We also know it is lawful for the laity, as someone receives, so also he can give." In the Council of Elibertinum (can. 38) it says the laity can baptize provided they themselves are baptized and have not been married twice. Augustine was likewise uncertain. In *Contra Parmen.* (2, 13), he proposes a question, whether the unbaptized could baptize, and says he does not dare to determine the matter since it has never been defined by any general Council. Likewise, Gregory II (*Epist. ad Bonifacium*, which is also cited by Gratian in can. *Quos a Paganis, de consecr.* Dist. 4) bids those baptized by pagans to be rebaptized.

Moreover, the matter has now been defined in a general Council, as Augustine desired. In the Council of Florence, it is held that in a case of necessity it is lawful for the laity, whether a man or a woman, Christian or pagan, to baptize provided the matter, form, and due intention are present. Pope Nicholas had decreed the same thing much earlier in the canon *A Quodam Judaeo* (*de consecr.* dist. 4, and the same thing is found *ibid.*, can. *Romanus*). The same reasoning is persuasive. Since faith is not required in the minister of Baptism, or goodness, or ordination, as is known, there is no reason why it would not be a true Baptism which is conferred by a pagan or a Jew, if those things which are necessary for the essence of Baptism are present.

Moreover, no testimony of those advancing the contrary convicts the matter, that it is not lawful to receive Baptism from one that has not been baptized. Gregory II is not believed to have commanded those baptized by a pagan to be rebaptized on account of a defect in the minister as much as *on account of the defect in the sacramental form*, which these pagans, perhaps due to inexperience, did not preserve. Augustine, however, even if he was uncertain, nevertheless was prepared to acquiesce to a general Council. And besides, in *de Baptismo* (7, 53), he clearly says if his opinion were asked, he would answer that Baptism is valid no matter who confers it and where, provided it is consecrated by sacramental words. The Council of Elibertinus asserted what was certain, baptized laymen licitly baptize; it did not expressly deny the contrary, but left it in doubt. Lastly, Tertullian and Jerome perhaps only meant that Baptism can be given to all, as it is received by all, i.e., because it is a Sacrament necessary to all; therefore, it can be received by all, and similarly it can be given by all, not that it is necessary

Chapter VII: The Minister of Baptism

that a man receive it before he can give it. I find this persuasive, both because the words seem to have this sense, and because if they had another sense, they would contain an absurd argument. It is not a good argument that this man has Baptism, therefore he can give baptism; otherwise, a priest could also ordain priests, and a deacon, deacons, because the former has the priesthood, and the latter the diaconate. Nor is it a good argument, if it were argued negatively, that this man does not have Baptism, therefore he cannot give it; otherwise, an impious minister could not justify others through words and the other Sacraments, because without a doubt he lacks justice and piety. Consequently, it is not required that he would formally have Baptism in himself, who is going to be the minister; rather, it is enough if he were to have it *virtually and ministerially*, in the way that everyone has it who has the use of reason, tongue, and hands, that they would be able intentionally to mention the words and sprinkle water.

Sixthly, they teach not only men, but even women can baptize in extreme necessity. This is held expressly by the Council of Florence, likewise, the fourth Council of Carthage (can. 100, as we will cite later), and Urban II (*Epist. ad Vitalem*), and it is also held in the can. *Super His* (30, 3). Lastly, the custom of the Church holds the same thing, as well as the clear argument which we just made on behalf of the unbaptized.

Now that all of these have been so constituted, it only remains that we prove, against Calvin, that it is lawful *in a case of necessity* for those who are not Ecclesiastical ministers to baptize. 1) It is proved *firstly* from the Old Testament. In Exodus 4:25, Sephora, the wife of Moses, circumcised her son, and in that way freed her husband from the danger of death. Circumcision was a figure of Baptism, and according to Calvin it altogether effected the same thing which Baptism does now, therefore, it will also be lawful in a case of necessity for women to baptize.

Now Calvin (*Inst.* 4, 15 §22) challenges this example with the most violent bile; he says Sephora was a stupid and rash woman, "What a foolish woman did is ignorantly drawn into example. ... I would have my readers focus on the fact that in no way did Sephora mean to perform a service to God. Seeing her son in danger, she frets and murmurs, and not without indignation throws down the foreskin on the ground, thus upbraiding her husband and taking offence at God. In short, it is plain that the whole business proceeded from a weakness of mind; she complains both against her husband and against God, because she is forced to spill the blood of her son. We may add, that however she might have conducted herself in all other respects, yet her temerity is inexcusable in this, in circumcising her son while her husband is present, and that husband not a mere private individual, but Moses, the chief prophet of God, and no greater than he ever arose in Israel. This was no more allowable in her than it would be today for women under the eye of a bishop."

Calvin, however, who convicts Sephora of temerity and a weakness of mind, does not notice that he does so from a mere weakness of mind and a fancy to disparage, with incredible temerity. I will begin from the last: Sephora did not sin because she circumcised her son while her husband was present, she did it after she had been *compelled* by Moses, or rather more, God. Although Moses was present, nevertheless, he could not do it himself since he was in the greatest difficulties, and altogether exhausted. The fact that Scripture says "the Lord met him, and wanted to slay him" either signifies that Rabbi Abenezra did not badly explain the passage, that a serious plague of divine origin was sent against Moses, or as our exegetes explain it, an Angel appeared to him with a naked sword, who troubled him right away and would not permit him to rest until Sephora circumcised her son, for then at length the Angel dismissed Moses. As a result, there can be no doubt that Moses, if he could have, would have circumcised his son himself, but because he could not, he gave a sign for his wife to do it. This is what Calvin himself, not knowing what he says and opposing himself, indicates when he says, "She complains both against her husband and against God, because she is forced to spill the blood of her son." If she was compelled by God and her husband, then she did not begin to circumcise her son rashly while Moses was present. Where is the temerity of Sephora, which Calvin says is inexcusable?

What Calvin says, however, that Sephora circumcised her son without the intention of serving God, and threw the foreskin on the ground and murmured against God and her husband, are mere lies without any foundation, and proceed from a mere desire to disparage. Scripture says no such thing. One is a particle that is added to the exposition of Lyranus, which perhaps deceived Calvin. When Scripture says "And dismissed him," after she had said "a bloody spouse you are to me," Lyranus explains it in such a way as if Sephora dismissed Moses and she departed from him with indignation on account of the circumcision of her son.

But Lyranus is deceived, as well as anyone else who explains it this way. The words "and dismissed him" cannot be referred to Sephora, but to the Angel who dismissed Moses, i.e., he ceased to disturb him when Sephora said she had carried out the Circumcision, "You are a bloody spouse to me," for the Hebrew voice is of the masculine gender וַיִּרֶף *vaijreph*, hence it cannot agree with Sephora, nor does רָפָה *rafah* mean to dismiss properly, in the way when one departs from another, but means to be mild or relaxed, i.e., to no longer pursue and disturb, which properly suits the angel, who was pleased on account of the Circumcision and ceased to disturb Moses. This is why the Septuagint adds the word "angel," καὶ ἀπῆλθεν ἀπὸ αὐτοῦ ὁ ἄγγελος. From there it is also gathered that Sephora pleased God, hence she was right and good, seeing that immediately he was pleased.

But Calvin responds to our consequent, "It is wrongly inferred from the fact that the angel of God was appeased after she took a stone and circumcised her son that God approved of her act. Otherwise, we would have

Chapter VII: The Minister of Baptism

to say that God was pleased with a worship which Gentiles brought from Assyria and set up in Samaria." But what is between that similitude? Those Gentiles who crossed from Assyria were torn apart by lions because they instituted false worship (4 Kings 17:25). Sephora, however, by circumcising her son, freed Moses from the danger of death. Now, if perchance Calvin would answer that he did not speak about the time in which the Gentiles worshiped their idols and were torn apart by lions, but on a later time in which they worshiped God together with their idols and were immune from the lions, I would object to the contrary: those Gentiles were freed from the lions because they worshiped the true God in a true rite, without a doubt they were informed by the Israelite priest, as it is related in the same place, not because they worshiped their idols at the same time or because they used some rite which they had devised. Although those Gentiles did not please God, nor could merit something from God when they worshiped God together with their idols, nevertheless, God willed to show what a difference there is between worship that he instituted and the impious superstitions of the Gentiles. Consequently, he sent the lions against those Gentiles when they worshiped their idols alone, and restrained the lions when they began to honor the true God with true worship.

2) *Secondly,* the same truth is proven from that passage which Calvin takes up as his chief argument, namely Matt. 28:19: *Going, teach all nations, baptizing them...,* he argues, "These were said to the Apostles alone, who were instituted as ministers of the Word and the Sacraments: therefore it is not lawful to usurp that office." Yet, we make our argument from this very passage. Although the ministry of the word is proper to the Apostles and the Bishops who succeed them, nevertheless, it is lawful for all; nay more, all are held in the point of necessity to teach and instruct the ignorant, especially when their eternal salvation is in danger. We have an example of this in Acts 18:26, regarding Aquila and his wife Priscilla, who, seeing a certain Apollo preach, since he did not keep the faith of the Lord well, they diligently instructed him.

Consequently, in that way, although the office of baptizing is proper to priests, still in necessity it is also lawful for the laity and women to baptize. It is lawful for an even greater reason, since it is more proper to Apostles and Bishops to preach than to Baptize. "Christ did not send me," Paul says in 1 Cor. 1:17, "to baptize, but to preach the gospel."

3) *Thirdly,* it is proven from examples of Scripture. In Acts 8:38, Philip the Deacon baptized. Although he was not a layman, certainly he was not an Apostle, nor a bishop, nor a priest; still, according to Calvin, only the Apostles received the power to baptize from Christ. He speaks in this way (*ibid.* §20), "Christ did not give a command to any men or women whatever to baptize, but to those whom he had appointed Apostles." Besides, in Acts 9:18, Ananias baptized Paul, who was neither an Apostle nor even a deacon, but clearly a layman. This took place in the first year

after the Lord's Passion, in such a time as there were not yet any ordinary bishops or priests apart from the Apostles, nor were there any deacons apart from seven. Likewise, in Acts 10:48, Peter commanded Cornelius and his household to be baptized by the brethren, who came with him. These brethren were most probably not Apostles nor deacons, but simple disciples. Lastly, in Acts 2:41, before any bishops, priests, or deacons were ordained, on the very first day of Pentecost three thousand men were baptized; but the Apostles could certainly not have properly done all of the Baptisms, so it was fitting that others would baptize, who were laymen. Even the seventy-two disciples in that time were laymen, for the Lord did not ordain priests except in the Last Supper, and there the Apostles alone.[18]

4) *Fourthly,* it is proven from the testimonies and examples of the

18   *Recognitio* n. IV. I said Ananias, when he baptized the Apostle Paul at Damascus, was neither a priest or a deacon, but a mere layman. It seems to me this is sufficiently proven from the fact that Paul's conversion and Baptism took place in the first year after the Lord's Passion. Later I noticed that there are some who place the conversion of St. Paul in the second year after the Lord's Passion, and would have it that this Ananias was a deacon; but we, in assigning the time of the conversion of St. Paul, followed Eusebius, who, in his *Chronicle*, places both the death of St. Stephen and the conversion of St. Paul in the year 34 A.D. and in the 19th year of the Emperor Tiberius. This time is sufficiently consistent with those things which the Apostle relates in Gal. 1:18 and 2:1, namely, "Three years after his conversion he came to Jerusalem to see Peter," and again, "after fourteen years he again returned to Jerusalem, and compared the Gospel with the rest of the Apostles." It is commonly believed that this took place in the eighteenth year from the Lord's Passion, when the first Council was celebrated at Jerusalem (Act. 15:6 *et seqq.*), for if you add one year to three and fourteen, which followed from the Lord's Passion, although not wholly, it will become 18 years. Nor does it stand in the way, what some say, that the martyrdom of St. Stephen could not have happened in the same year, since after Stephen's death many events are related in the Acts of the Apostles before the conversion of St. Paul which could not have happened in so short a time. I say this is not opposed, for what is related on the deeds of Philip the Deacon, it is not necessary that everything would happen before the conversion of St. Paul. In the same year, Philip could preach in Samaria, and Paul set out for Damascus; but St. Luke could not relate everything together. Whether

Chapter VII: The Minister of Baptism 351

Fathers. Tertullian, in his work *On Baptism*, where he said the right to baptize is properly suited to Bishops and priests, and still even deacons if the Bishop would permit it, adds, "Otherwise, even the laity have the right to baptize. "What can equally be received by all can be equally given by all." Alexander, the bishop of Alexandria, with his whole Church held as valid the Baptism which Athanasius while a boy and a layman conferred upon other boys, as Ruffinus witnesses (*Hist.* 10, 14). The Council of Nicaea, as Jerome testifies (*Contra Luciferianos*), decreed that the Baptism of heretics is valid, provided it is given according to the form of the Church. St. Stephen, the Pope and Martyr, had already defined the same thing, as Cyprian relates in his *Epistle to Pompejus*. Neither Stephen nor the Fathers of the Council of Nicaea were unaware that among some heresies there is not a true priesthood, hence they are laymen who baptized, although perhaps they might be called priests. The Council of Elibertinus, celebrated around this same time (can. 38), teaches that the lay faithful can baptize when one is far away from a Church and some Catechumen is near death. Ambrose, or the author of the *Commentary on the Epistles of Paul* attributed to him, in Eph. 4, says in the primitive Church it was lawful for everyone to preach and baptize on account of the fewness of ministers; but now that Ecclesiastical matters have been constituted in their order, it is not lawful for [minor] clergy and laity to preach or baptize. Certainly, what was lawful in the primitive Church due to the lack of ministers should, by the same reasoning, be lawful in any time of extreme necessity. Jerome, in his *Dialogue against the Luciferians*, says, "If necessity compels one to baptize, we know that it is also lawful for laymen." Augustine (*Contra Parm.* 2, 13) holds the same thing, as well as the fourth Council of Carthage, at which Augustine was present (can. 100). "A woman," it says, "should not presume to baptize except when necessity compels her." Although that exception, "except when necessity compels her," is not found in the volumes of Councils, nevertheless, Peter Lombard cites this Canon (*Sent.* 4 dist. 6) as well as Gratian (can. *Mulier, de consecrate.* dist. 4). Lastly, these authors teach the same thing on baptizing the laity: Gelasius (*epistol.* 1); Isidore (*de Officiis Divinis* 2, 24); and Lombard with every school, in 4 dist. 6; and lastly, the Council of Florence.

Still, Calvin responds to this argument as he is wont, "The practice which has been in use for many ages, and even almost from the very commencement of the Church, for laity to baptize in danger of death when

---

or not Ananias was a deacon in that time I think is uncertain; I wrote what I did from conjecture, not certain knowledge. Oecumenius affirms that Ananias was then a deacon, which he shows from the Canon of Clement, but Clement seems to signify the contrary in the *Apostolic Constitutions* (lib. 8); when he speaks about Philip and Ananias, he calls Philip a deacon and Ananias a faithful brother.

a minister could not be present in time, cannot, it seems to me, be defended by any firm reasoning" (4, 15 §20). This very thing is the most serious reason: in matters of this sort, what can we have that is greater than the *consensus of the whole Church*, a most ancient consensus, and also one that has come down to us even from the very beginning of the Church? Now, let us see what he advances to the contrary.

Firstly, Calvin objects with the command of Christ in Matt. 28:19, "Going, teach, etc.," because this pertains to the Apostles alone. *I respond*: It is not certain whether these were said to the Apostles alone. Although Matthew only mentions the eleven Apostles, still it is probable that then there were many more men present. These words seem to have been said on the day of the Ascension, on which day five hundred brethren were present with the Apostles, as Paul witnesses in 1 Cor. 16:6. Next, we can answer *secondly*, that Apostolic deeds explained that command. Since the Apostles ratified that Stephen, who was not an Apostle, would preach; and Philip, who was not an Apostle, would preach and baptize; and many others did the same thing who were neither Apostles nor deacons, such as Ananias and others, they clearly declared by the fact that in urgent necessity it is lawful for everyone to do what pertains to the special office of certain men. Just as at that time necessity to propagate the Church demanded it when there were too few ministers ordained for this purpose, so now when necessity demands it, when someone's life is in danger while the priests are away.

Secondly, Calvin objects that even the Fathers themselves were uncertain as to whether it could rightly happen that the laity would baptize in necessity, although they held and permitted this custom. He shows it from Augustine, who speaks this way in *Against the Epistle of Parmenian* (2, 13), "And if a layman was to be compelled by necessity to give Baptism, I do not know whether anyone would piously say the Baptism must be repeated. If it were to happen that no necessity would compel him, it is the usurpation of another's office, but if necessity would demand, there is no sin or venial sin."

I respond: This is no uncertainty of Augustine. The early words contain a rhetorical device, but it is plainly assertive. It is the same to say: I do not know whether someone has piously said it cannot not be affirmed except impiously. The later words mean it is a venial sin when the laity do not apply all diligence to find a priest to baptize. but there is no sin when diligence has been applied and a priest cannot be found, so they baptize.

Thirdly, Calvin makes an objection from the fourth Council of Carthage (can. 100), where it is forbidden for women to baptize.

I respond: The Council itself makes the exception in the *case of necessity*, as we showed above from Peter Lombard and Gratian. Besides, although the Council does not expressly make an exception, it is fitting to understand that case was excepted; just the same, when the Apostle forbids women to

Chapter VII: The Minister of Baptism

speak in 1 Cor. 14:34 and 1 Tim. 2:12, the exception is understood in the case of necessity. What Calvin answers here, that Baptism is not necessary, we already refuted in the controversy above.

Fourthly, Calvin objects from Tertullian and Epiphanius. The former, in his book *de Virginibus Velandis*, says, "It is not permitted for women to speak in Church, nor to teach, baptize, or offer." In his *On Baptism*, Tertullian says, "A petulant woman, who has usurped the power to teach, will of course not likewise give birth to the right for her to baptize." Epiphanius in the *Panarion* (haeres. 42, which is of Marcion), says, "[Marcion] permits even women to give Baptism, etc." In heresy 79, he says that it was not even granted to the most holy Mother of Christ to baptize, otherwise she would have baptized Christ rather than John.

I respond: These Fathers speak about the *public* ministry, not on the private ministry in the case of necessity. Tertullian says that it is not lawful for a woman to speak, teach, baptize, etc. in Church, and besides, he joins the office of giving Baptism with the office of sacrifice; sacrifice, however, is always public. So, just as it is not lawful for a woman to sacrifice, because it is a public office, so also it is not lawful for her to publicly baptize. Epiphanius is also clearly speaking about the *ordinary and public* ministry, because in heresy 79, where he says it is not lawful for a woman to give Baptism, he says in the same place that it is also not lawful for deacons; and still it is certain from the Scripture that it is lawful for deacons, at least extraordinarily.

Calvin's response is not valid, that Epiphanius pronounced it a laughing stock to give women the permission to baptize and did not make any exceptions. For in the very place where Epiphanius calls it a laughing stock, he speaks about the public ministry. It truly would be a laughing stock if a woman were to baptize in a Church while men were present. Little wonder if he did not add the exception for necessity; for he does not add it when he denied that deacons can baptize, because it was certain that it could be understood *per se*.

CHAPTER VIII

On the Baptism of Infants, against the Anabaptists

THE sixth controversy follows on those receiving Baptism. The whole question is on the Baptism of infants. Although we have already proved against Calvin that the Baptism of infants is necessary if they ought to be saved, still, it remains that we address two questions. One, with the Anabaptists, whether infants have the capacity for Baptism, or whether it is lawful to baptize infants. The second, with the Lutherans and Calvinists: What kind of faith is necessary in the Baptism of infants?

In regard to the first question, there was a heresy in the time of St. Bernard that taught it was not permitted to baptize infants. St. Bernard relates and refutes it in his *Sermons on the Canticles* (66) and in *Epist.* 240. The same heresy exists in this time, that of the Anabaptists, that it is not lawful to give Baptism except to adults who ask for Baptism themselves. All the Anabaptists agree in this error, although they permit disagreement in many matters among themselves, as Calvin witnesses in his *Instruction Against the Anabaptists*. Calvin also witnesses the same thing in the *Institutes* (4, 16 §29), that Michael Servetus and certain other Anabaptist teachers contended that Baptism should not be received until 30 years of age, the same age in which Christ received Baptism. This heresy arose in the year 1527, as Cochlaeus relates in the *Acts of Luther*. It seems that the originator of this heresy was Balthasar Pacimontanus, who was later burned in Vienna. This is what Cochlaeus calls him in the *Acts of Luther* for the year 1528, where he says that Luther wrote against him in the same year, although Balthasar confesses that he gathered this error from the writings of Luther, which is also very true, and we will demonstrate this in the following question.

The ministers of Transylvania, who published two books against the Trinity and the Lord's Incarnation in 1567, added 36 arguments against infant Baptism in those books. There, we see the greatest frenzy of Satan against the human race, since he was not content that innumerable souls of adults were lost through the Lutherans and the Sacramentarians, he also willed the souls of infants to be lost through the Anabaptists.

Apart from these heretics, two authors *obliquely* seem to have taught the same thing: Erasmus, in his preface to the *Paraphrase in Matthew*, where he taught that men who were baptized in infancy, when they became adults, should be questioned as to whether they thought it was valid, because it was promised in their name, and if they did not think it was valid, they must be dismissed free [of the obligations of the Sacrament]. Luis Vives,

Chapter VIII: The Baptism of Infants

in his annotation to *City of God* 1, 27, says that formerly, no man used to be baptized unless they were adults, and those who sought Baptism of themselves, and understood what it means to be baptized.

Now, the Catholic Church always taught that infants must be Baptized, which the Council of Trent again defined in a declaration with anathemas (sess. 7 can. 12-14 on Baptism). This truth is proved from three kinds of arguments.

1) *First*, it is taken from the Scriptures, and we have three arguments from the Scriptures. *a)* First, it is taken from a figure of the Old Testament. Circumcision was a figure of Baptism so manifest that Paul called Baptism Circumcision (Col. 2:11). But Circumcision was given to infants (Gen. 17:23), so why not also Baptism? The Anabaptists can easily elude this argument when the Lutherans and Calvinists propose it. This is because the Lutherans and Calvinists hold that the form of Baptism is a sermon, as we showed in the previous book, which cannot be said about Circumcision. It follows from this that infants could be circumcised but not baptized. Yet, when we propose it, since we do not require words in the form of a sermon for the essence of Baptism, but *consecratory words*, then the argument cannot be eluded.

b) The second argument is gathered from two passages of the Gospel, joined together in John 3:5, "Unless a man be reborn of water, etc." This passage proves that infants without Baptism perish forever; for it is the general threat of the Lord. But we do not yet have that infants can be baptized, for the Anabaptists will say that children perish because they do not have the capacity for that unique remedy. The fact that children do not perish, the Lord teaches in Matt. 19:14, Mk. 10:14, and Lk. 18:16, "Permit the children to come to me, ... to such is the kingdom of heaven." There, even Mark says the Lord embraced the children and blessed them. Still, how do children possess the kingdom of heaven, how does the Lord embrace and bless them, if they cannot be saved?

Two responses can be given to this passage. One, of the Anabaptists, that the Lord blessed in the persons of the children those in innocence and humility, not age; for he did not say the kingdom of heaven is for these, but *"such as these,"* from where Augustine (*Confess.* 1, 19) also says, "You, our King, commended the sign of humility in the stature of a child when you said, for such as these is the kingdom of heaven." The other, that the Gospel does not speak about infants, but children, who already have the use of reason. As Tertullian notes (*de Baptismo*), the Lord says, "Permit the children to come to me"; they do not come unless they are of greater stature, for infants can be carried, they cannot come.

However, neither response is solid. Even if the Lord meant to commend the humility and innocence of the children, as Augustine rightly teaches, nevertheless, at the same time he also indicated that the age of infancy is not foreign from the kingdom and salvation. When the Lord says,

"Permit the children to come to me," he speaks literally and historically about *true* children whom many offered for the Lord to bless them, as the three Evangelists witness, and the Apostles tried to prevent them from approaching. This is why that argument, "To such is the kingdom of heaven," ought to agree with *true* children. And besides, that this embrace and blessing was given to true children clearly shows they can pertain to the society and reign of Christ. Therefore, just as Isaac and Ishmael are allegorically two Covenants in Paul (Gal. 4:24), and still historically they were two true men, so also the infantile age is a type of humility, and still it is really suited to the kingdom of heaven.

The second answer is also solid. The words of the Evangelists signify children and infants. Matthew and Mark have παιδία, i.e., children. Luke has βρέφη i.e., infants. In the same place, Luke says they were *carried*, they did not come by their feet: προσέφερον δὲ αὐτῷ καὶ τὰ βρέφη, which is "They brought infants to him." Therefore, the term *venire* is received broadly for "to approach." Moreover, this argument which is really solid of itself, is still weak when it is produced by the Calvinists, for the Calvinists would not have it that John 3:5, "Unless a man be born again," be understood in regard to Baptism. Once this passage has been taken away, the later passage, which Calvin alone uses, does not convict the matter, since the Anabaptists could answer, according to Calvin's principles, that children pertain to Christ because they are born holy, or because they are predestined. So, Calvin saw how solidly he could resist the Anabaptists.

c) The third argument is gathered from those passages where whole households are said to be baptized, as in Acts 16:15, where Lydia is said to have been baptized with her whole house. In verse 33, on the prison guard, "He was baptized, and immediately his whole house." In 1 Cor. 1:16, Paul says, "I baptized the house of Stephen." But certainly, it would be rare in whole households for there not to be some infants. Calvin also uses this argument; but it is only a probable argument, not, however, clearly convincing. That is enough from Scripture.

2) The *second* class of arguments contains the testimonies of the Church, which always both taught and preserved it as the tradition of the Apostles. Melanchthon also uses this argument (*Loci* tit. *De Baptismo Parvulorum*), and he placed it as the strongest argument in his first attack, but the Anabaptists duly mock him for it. If tradition and the testimony of the ancient Church would avail in this matter, why would it not also avail in other points, such as in the assertion of Purgatory, the invocation of Saints, etc.? Consequently, this is our argument, not that of our adversaries.

First, we have the testimony of Dionysius the Areopagate (*Eccles. Hierarch.* last chapter), who affirms that the Apostles handed down that infants should be baptized. Justin Martyr, or whoever was the author of the *Questions* (q. 56), teaches the same thing where he says that baptized children are saved, while others are not. Irenaeus (2, 39) says all are saved

Chapter VIII: The Baptism of Infants

who are born again in Christ: infants, children, the young, and the old. Origen (*Romans* 5, 6) says, "The Church receives tradition from the Apostles, even to give Baptism to infants." Cyprian (*Epist.* 3, 8) writes that it seemed not only to himself, but to the whole Council, that children can be baptized, even before the eighth day. Jerome (*Contra Pelagianos*, lib. 3), says infants are baptized, and then lack all sin. Gregory Nazianzen (*Orat. in Sanctum lavacrum*), Basil (*Orat. Exhortat. ad Baptismum*), Chrysostom (*Hom. 1 ad Neophytos*) all teach the same thing. Augustine (*On Genes.* 10, 23) says, "The custom of mother Church in baptizing children must by no means be cast aside, nor considered superstitious in any way. It would altogether not be believed except that it is Apostolic tradition." He also repeats the same thing in *On Baptism* (1, 24), that infant Baptism is Apostolic tradition. He also says in *On the Merit and Remission of Sins* (1, 16), that the Pelagians did not dare to deny infant Baptism, because they saw how openly they would oppose the whole Church if they were to deny it. See also Prosper of Aquitaine (*On the Calling of the Gentiles* 2,8), who chiefly proves this in an argument against the Pelagians, that original sin is a given because infants are baptized, although they have no actual sin.

The Council of Miletevanus, among other canons decreed the following in these words, "Whoever denies that children must be baptized soon after birth, *anathema sit.*" The Council of Gerundense (Girona), celebrated in the 6th century, decreed in its fifth canon, that even on the very day in which they are born, infants can be baptized if it seems that they are in danger of death. The second Council of Braga (can. 7) also proves infant Baptism. So also, the general Council of Vienne, as we find it in *Clementina I, de Summa Trinit. Et Fide Catholica.*

Here express decrees of holy Popes on the matter may also be added. Clement I (*Const. Apost.* 6, 15), Syricius (*Epist.* 1, 2 *ad Himerium*), Innocent I (*Epist.* 26 *to the Council of Mileve*), Leo I (*Epist.* 84/86 *to the Bishop of Aquileia*), Innocent III (*Epist. to the Bishop of Arles*, which is also held in cap. *Majores*, on Baptism and its effect). From these it is gathered how false what Luis Vives says, that formerly nobody was put forward for holy Baptism until he became an adult.

3) The *third* class of arguments is constituted from reasoning. *a)* The first argument: Children can be saved, but outside the Church there is no salvation; therefore, it is necessary for them to enter the Church. The first proposition is proven both from the Scripture that has been cited (Matt. 19:14, *To such as these is the kingdom of heaven*) and also from the example of the Holy Innocents, whom the Church has always taught were saved, as we proved above in chapter 6. Furthermore, if children can also be partakers of the sin of Adam, why not also the grace of Christ? Otherwise, there would be greater sin than grace, the contrary of which the Apostle teaches in Rom. 6:14. The second proposition is absolutely certain. In Matt. 12:30, it is said, "Whoever is not with me is against me," and in the Creed, we

join the remission of sins with the Church, "I believe in the Holy Catholic Church, the communion of saints, the remission of sins." Thus, the Church is also compared with the Ark of Noah, because just as everything that was not in the ark perished during the flood, so also now, those who are not in the Church shall perish, as Jerome says (*Epist.* to Damasus on the word hypostasis). St. Cyprian famously said the same thing on the unity of the Church, "No man can have God as a father, who does not have the Church as a mother." See also Augustine (*On Baptism* 4, 1). Lastly, the fourth Lateran Council, under Innocent III, says in its first chapter, "The universal Church of the faithful is one, outside of which no man is saved."

Consequently, we hold that infants must enter the Church, but they can only do so through Baptism; therefore, it is necessary for them to be baptized. The assumption can be proven. *First*, from that of Paul in Rom. 8:30, "He called those whom he predestined; and he justified these whom he has called, and glorified those whom he has justified." Hence, we hold all the predestined are called, justified, glorified, and on the other hand, no one has been glorified unless first he was justified, no one is justified unless first he was called, no one is called according to the proposition, unless he had already been predestined. In infants, no calling can be devised except through Baptism. Then they are rightly called, since they are enrolled in the number of those called. Besides, in Acts 2:41, it is said, "Those who received his word were baptized, and they were added on that day about three thousand souls." There, we said that to be baptized is nothing other than to enter the Church. This is why the Fathers, in a common consensus, distinguish Catechumens from the faithful, and teach the former are not yet within the Church because they lack Baptism, nor can they be called faithful. See Nazianzen (*Orat. in Sanctum Lavacrum*), Chrysostom (*Hom.* 24 *in Joan.*), Cyril (*On John* 12, 50), Augustine (*Tr. in Joan.* 4), the Council of Florence in its *Instruction to the Armenians*. Lastly, a man cannot be joined to Christ and the Church except by faith, or the Sacrament, or both. The Anabaptists agree that children cannot be joined to Christ and the Church by faith; therefore, they should be joined by the Sacrament.

b) The *second* argument: If infants could not be baptized, there would be an impediment, either on the side of some divine prohibition, or the Sacrament, or on the side of the minister, or on the side of the recipient himself, or, lastly, on the side of the Church, which acquires a right over men in Baptism because it does not seem to be able to happen without their own will. However, none of these can be said. No divine prohibition exists. The Sacrament does not depend on anything but divine institution, otherwise it would not be certain nor would it impart lasting consolation; consequently, of itself it is always efficacious and works the same thing whether it is given to an adult or an infant. The minister, however, can equally pour water over an infant and advance the sacred words over him just as with an adult. On the side of the recipient a certain disposition

Chapter VIII: The Baptism of Infants

through actual faith and conversion to God is required in adults, but this is not required in infants. In adults that disposition is required through a twofold cause. *Firstly*, on account of the actual sins which they add to original sin. That sin which is committed through an actual turning away of one's own will from God, requires an actual conversion of one's own will toward God so as to be forgiven. *Secondly*, because God acts with things according to their natures, and so a man who has the use of free will is not justified by God unless he also agrees to it through assent of his free will. Neither cause is found in infants. They neither have the use of free will nor have they sinned through an actual turning away of their will from God, for they only have that *habitual* turning away, which can be removed by the infused habit of charity, and they sinned by the will of another. This is why it is just that the will of another would benefit them.

Lastly, the obligation which is born of Baptism does not stand in the way. In the first place, a man is not obligated except to those things which he has otherwise been obligated, or was going to be obligated. Everyone is held, even without Baptism, to keep divine law as well as to renounce the devil and all his allurements. Again, all are held to receive Baptism, and that by a divine command, and hence all are held to subject themselves to the Church and its precepts. The only difference between infants and adults is this: that the former, who are self-governing, should subject themselves to the Church of their own will, and unless they would do that, they will sin. The latter, because they are not self-governing, can be subjected to the Church by the will of their parents. Therefore, they have the will of another in place of right reason, which they would have if they were adults; hence, no injury is done to them, but rather a great benefit, since they are baptized, although the obligation to obey the Church follows from it. Yet, infants who lack parents and tutors and are baptized by someone not of his household cannot later protest, for those who baptize them act for their sake. Just as if someone would come upon a man that was lethally wounded who did not have the use of speech and reason, and since he bid him to be carried into a house and cured by doctors, certainly he could not later complain about that man, because he was obliged to pay the doctor's bill. If he were to complain, and refuse to pay, he would be condemned by every just judge.

CHAPTER IX

The Objections of the Anabaptists Are Answered

Now, it will be worthwhile to answer the thirty-six arguments which the ministers of Transylvania produce on their behalf.

1) The *first* argument: *Infant Baptism is never found in sacred rites, and we have no command or example concerning it, so it must be rejected.*

I respond: This is a strong argument against the Lutherans and anyone else who uses their principle. Yet, it does not avail against Catholics. Although we do not find an express command to baptize infants, still it is gathered clearly enough from the Scriptures, as we showed above. Besides, Apostolic tradition is no less an authority among us than Scripture; the Apostles speak in the same spirit with which they write. This is an Apostolic tradition, and thence we know, from where we know the Apostolic Scripture is Apostolic Scripture, namely from the testimonies of the ancient Church.

2) The *second* argument: *We have been commanded to teach first, then Baptize; therefore, infants must be taught before they are baptized: 'Go, teach all nations, baptizing them, etc.* (Matt. 28:19).

I respond: The Lord places the order in this place which the Apostles ought to preserve in the conversion of the Gentiles, to first instruct them, and then to baptize, and lastly to warn them that faith and Baptism do not suffice unless they would also add obedience of the law and good works. Therefore, he adds, "Teaching them to preserve everything whatever I have commanded you." Such an order must be preserved *when it can be done*, as the Church also diligently preservers when adults come to the faith. But if either on account of the incapacity of men or a defect of water not everything can be preserved, or not in that same order, certainly it is better to preserve something than nothing. If anyone were in the desert with a Gentile that was dying, where there was no water, he could teach and instruct him that he would believe. Then he would not sin against the precept of God, "Teach, baptizing," because it is understood, *when it can be done*. So, because infants do not have the capacity for doctrine, and are capable of Baptism, the order is changed for them, so that they are first baptized, lest perhaps they would perish without this singular assistance, and then when they mature, they are taught. Just the same, if an adult would come to the faith, and Baptism must be delayed for a just cause, nevertheless he will be taught and advised to observe the law of God. He would indeed be a very foolish man who would say that Catechumens should not preserve the law of God and live well because the Lord postponed Baptism so they might be advised on the obedience which must be furnished to the law.

Chapter IX: The Anabaptists Are Answered

3) The *third* argument: *Paul gloried and gave thanks to God because he baptized no man apart from Cajus, Crispus, and the house of Stephan* (1 Cor. 1:14-15). *How necessary infant Baptism is can be gathered from there. Besides, the fact is that Christ did not even baptize an adult, nor John the Baptist an infant.*

I respond: Our adversaries declare the fact that Christ, John, and Paul did not baptize infants but do not prove it; nay more, the contrary is more probable, at least in regard to Paul and John. In the house of Stephan, which Paul baptized, it is probable that there was some infant. Moreover, all Jerusalem went out to John, nay more, even all of Judaea, so that he would baptize them (Matt. 3:5 and Mark 1:5). Who would assert among all these that there was not any who brought his child? Christ, however, did not *ordinarily* baptize himself, but through his disciples (John 4:1). Still, without a doubt he baptized someone, or some, so that he would have men that were baptized, through whom he would baptize others, as Augustine writes (*Epist.* 108 *ad Seleucianus*). Evodius, the successor of the Apostle Peter in the episcopate of Antioch, writes that the Blessed Virgin and St. Peter were baptized by Christ himself (*cf.* Nicephorus *Hist.* 2, 3; Euthymius on *John* 3). Be that as it may, as they say, Christ, John, and Paul baptized no infant. So were infants not baptized? Or, were they not baptized in ancient times? Perhaps John baptized no infant because his Baptism was not necessary for infants; Christ and Paul were focused on greater things, and so consigned the office of baptizing to others, as is clear in regard to Christ in John 4:2, and in regard to Paul, in Acts 19:5.

4) The *fourth* argument: *The reprobate must not be baptized. Many infants are reprobate; thus, it should be withheld so they will not profane the Sacrament through our ignorance.*

I respond: Firstly, they would prove by the same argument that adults must not be baptized. *Secondly*, this argument rightly proves against Calvin, Bucer, and the like, who would have it that Baptism is a seal of the eternal benevolence of God. With us, however, it proves nothing. Even if a child perhaps will later be reprobate, still when it is baptized it is truly justified, and hence the Sacrament is not profaned since it is equally in him, and also in each of the elect, a true and efficacious sign of grace.

5) The *fifth* argument: *He that does not believe must be kept away from Baptism* (Act. 8:37); *If you believe, it is permitted. Infants do not believe* (Deut. 1:39) *nor do they know evil, or good.*

I respond: This argument is a proof against the Lutherans, who suppose the Sacraments are nothing other than instruments to nourish faith, but what it is that they think on this matter, we will explain in the following chapter, where we will also answer their argument. In the meantime, I say, someone else's faith suffices for an infant, just as another's sin harmed them.

6) The *sixth* argument: *For men to be compelled to Baptism is to grant*

more to the Sacrament than is right, as well as to strengthen the opinion of the Pope, who teaches no man can be saved without Baptism.

I respond: The argument most truly concludes the matter against Calvin, but not against Catholics.

7) The *seventh* argument: *Water has been joined with the Spirit* (John 3:5), *just as faith with Baptism* (Mark 16:16), *"he that will have believed and be baptized." But infants are insensible and cannot believe.*

I respond: What pertains to Scripture, the passage of John does not teach that the baptized should feel a motion of the Holy Spirit, as the Anabaptists believe, but only *the force of the water in Baptism is from the Holy Spirit*; and just as the water washes on the outside, so the Spirit washes inwardly, which can happen also while one is sleeping and insensible. That washing and inward renewal takes place through the infusion of habits, which can be infused without any action on our part. Now, in regard to what pertains to faith, Mark 16:16 is understood without any doubt concerning adults. It is preceded by "Preach the Gospel to every creature; whoever believes," but it would be stupid to preach to infants. *Furthermore,* that the Anabaptists are compelled to affirm this very thing, if they will to constitute it for themselves. They teach infants are saved without faith, and without Baptism, as Melanchthon witnesses (*Loci,* tit. *On Infant Baptism*). Add lastly, they do not lack the faith which is necessary to them, as we said above and will speak more of below.

8) The *eighth* argument: *The Church is obliged only to believe articles of faith; therefore, she should not be compelled to infant Baptism, since it is not an article of faith.*

I respond: It pertains to faith that infants can be baptized. Even if it is not expressly found in the Scriptures, still it is found in *Apostolic tradition.* Besides, it is clearly deduced from the Scriptures, as we already said. Still, the argument rightly settles the matter against Zwingli and Calvin, who do not admit tradition and think Baptism is not necessary, and also because they twist the passage of John 3:5, "Unless a man be born again, etc.," into metaphors.

9) The *ninth* argument: *If infants must be baptized, consequently they should also communicate, as antiquity showed, which was compelled to force empty washings of this sort as well as suppers upon children.*

I respond: The notion of Baptism and communion are not equal. Baptism is necessary for children, because otherwise they perish forever if they should die without Baptism, but Communion, just as the other Sacraments, is not necessary except for adults after Baptism. That fact is clear from their nature and effects. The Eucharist (that I might speak on that alone) was instituted to preserve and nourish the spiritual life acquired in Baptism, but corporeal food acts in corporeal matters, which preserve animal life. So, just as a body can live without food for a time, namely, as long as the natural heat will not have begun to consume a vital humor, so also without

Chapter IX: The Anabaptists Are Answered 363

the Eucharist the spiritual life can be preserved, as long as the heat of concupiscence will not begin to destroy the humor of grace and the virtues. Yet, that certainly does not happen in infants, rather, only in adults. This is why even the Lord himself, to show the Eucharist was not instituted for infants, refused to constitute it in milk, which is the sole nourishment for infants, but *bread and wine*, which properly pertain to adults alone. Moreover, some Fathers, for certain reasons, poured into the mouths of infants, whereby they could take the Eucharist, but these causes do not have place, and the Church does not do it for more important reasons. However, we are going to say more on this matter in another place.

10) The *tenth* argument: *Baptism is not given without penance* (Act. 2:38, Mk. 1:4), y*et infants do not know to do penance.*

I respond: Penance is necessary in the Baptism of *adults*, and what is discussed in those passages is because of the actual sins which adults committed; original sin is not a matter of penance. No man can rightly do penance for this sin, which he did not commit and which was not in his power; we ourselves do not commit original sin, rather we inherit it from Adam by natural propagation. This is why in Rom. 9:11 it is said in regard to infants, "Although they did nothing good or evil."

11) The *eleventh* argument: *Nazianzen, in his sermon on Baptism, desires Baptism to be delayed until children are able to make a response with their own faith. Augustine (*On Baptism*) writes that the Baptism of children was not established by Councils, but began in the time of Origen.* They add the testimony of Trismegistus, the Sybils, and Musculus.

I respond: Nazianzen wanted Baptism to be delayed until the third year for children to be able to respond in some way; nevertheless, he made an exception for *danger of death.* He would have it, that if a danger were seen, they could be baptized *at any time*, and he proves it from Circumcision and other arguments. Therefore, Nazianzen has two arguments against the Anabaptists: *One*, infants can be baptized at any time; *two*, Baptism was never to be delayed beyond the third year of infancy. Certainly, three-year-old children do not yet have the use of reason, nor can believe, nor do penance, nor furnish the other things which the Anabaptists want. Additionally, Nazianzen's counsel was not approved by other Fathers, for that advantage is scanty, and infants of this sort can incur great danger on account of unforeseen cases. The same should be said about Tertullian (*de Baptismo*), who gave the same counsel which Nazianzen later gave. On the other hand, the Anabaptists poorly and falsely cite Augustine. He does not refuse to say that infant Baptism was established by Councils because he means to weaken it, rather, to show that *it is more ancient than all Councils.* He speaks this way in *de Baptismo Infantium*, 4, "What the universal Church holds was always retained not as something instituted by Councils, rather, is rightly believed to have been handed down only by Apostolic authority." From such words the lie about infant Baptism being invented in the time of Origen is refuted, for Augustine neither says that infant Baptism was invented in the time of Origen, nor could he say it since he affirms it descends from Apostolic Tradition. Hence, we have no more regard for the testimony of the Lutheran Musculus than that of the Anabatists themselves. Trismegistus and the Sybils do not speak about the Baptism of Christ, but on some *pagan washing*, which means nothing to us.

12) The *twelfth* argument: *It is believed in heart to justice, confession is made by mouth unto salvation* (Rom. 10:10). *Children cannot do that.*

I respond with Augustine (*loc. cit., de Baptismo* 4, 24): This is what the Apostles handed down, that infants are saved by Baptism even if they do not believe in heart nor confess by mouth. Even if they do not have actual faith, still they have the *Sacrament of faith*; in the same way, vice versa the good thief did not have the Sacrament of faith and was saved by his faith and conversion to God. Thus, in necessity, *faith, and desire for the Sacrament* supplies for the defect, and conversely, the Sacrament of actual and proper faith supplies for the defect.

13) The *thirteenth* argument: *Since the Sacraments are perfect, they require perfect men. Infants are still imperfect, therefore, etc.*

I respond: Perfect things, if they are compared to the acting cause, do not suit any but the perfect; they cannot do perfect works unless the craftsmen are perfect. If they are compared to the *patient* cause, i.e., to the matter or subject, then they suit the imperfect, not the perfect, for their job is to perfect imperfect things. Baptism is this kind of thing in respect to men; it is a perfect Sacrament, which perfects imperfect men. It is similar to bodily medicine: perfect medicine is not given to those in perfect health, but those who are in very imperfect health, i.e., those who are very sick. This is why the Apostle, in Heb. 6:1, says it is for the imperfect to be baptized, "Leaving the discourse of our beginning in Christ, let us go on to things more perfect, not laying again the foundation of penance ..., and ... baptism, etc."

14) The *fourteenth* argument: *The Lord's Supper requires an outward confession of faith, and for that reason, children are kept away from it. Baptism also requires an external confession, since it is nothing else but a protestation of faith.*

I respond: Both the Lord's Supper and Baptism are outward professions of faith, and so by their reception we profess the faith, even if we would altogether say nothing in words. This is why, while children are baptized, they profess the faith, and would do the same if they were to communicate; that is not the reason why they are kept away from communion.

15) The *fifteenth* argument: *The symbols of Christ were ordained for his commemoration and preaching. Children can do none of these.*

I respond: Those who take up the symbols of Christ, by the very fact that they take these up, they commemorate and preach Christ; this is why even children do it. While they are submerged in water, they commemorate the death and burial of Christ; while when they are lifted from the water, they

Chapter IX: The Anabaptists Are Answered 365

commemorate the resurrection of Christ. The Apostle requires nothing else in Rom. 6:3.

16) The *sixteenth* argument: *Faith from hearing, hearing through the Word of God. If anyone will say infants have faith, you will show a new revelation of a new faith in them, because you cannot prove it from the word of God.*

I respond: This argument concludes the matter against the Lutherans, who posit actual faith in infants.

17) The *seventeenth* argument: *Christ was baptized at thirty years of age.*

St. Gregory Nazianzen responds to this, in his *Oration on the Holy Laver*, that we cannot do everything which Christ did *in the same way*, nor should we. He fasted *from all food*, and that just after his Baptism. We do it *in another way* and in another time. He gave the Eucharist in a little supper, after supper, and before his passion; we in Churches before supper, after the resurrection. Besides, add that Christ postponed Baptism to his thirtieth year, *both* because he did not need Baptism, *and* because there was no danger to him that he would be prevented by death, *and* because he had determined to begin his preaching with the auspices of a perfect age; in Baptism, however, he began to be acknowledged on account of miracles, which then happened. We, however, begin to need Baptism as soon as we are born, nor are we certain in regard to the time of our life, and then we are not baptized to begin in the world, but lest we would perish forever. Additionally, Christ was circumcised in infancy; what circumcision was for the Jews, Baptism is for us.

18) The *eighteenth* argument: *Whoever is baptized puts on Christ. Judge for yourselves whether infants put on Christ.*

I respond: Infants put on Christ, seeing that through the habit of grace infused in them, the old man departs and they put on the new. Moreover, it can be done without an act of one's own mind, as Paul teaches in Rom. 5:19, "As by disobedience of one man, many became sinners, so also by the obedience of one, many shall become just." Therefore, just as in this very thing, that someone is born from Adam he shares in the sin of Adam, even if he does not have the use of mind, so in this, that someone is reborn from Christ through Baptism he shares in the justice of Christ, and so he puts on Christ, although by age he does not have the use of reason.

19) The *nineteenth* argument: *The Sacraments of the New Testament are spiritual; infants are wholly carnal.*

I respond: Therefore, they receive spiritual Sacraments so that they will also become spiritual; such things truly take place by *habit*, not by act.

20) The *twentieth* argument: *The Apostles were fishers of men, not infants.*

I respond: As if infants are not men. Nevertheless, to fish is proper not to baptize, *but to preach*, and we affirm one must not preach to infants.

21) The *twenty-first* argument: *Those who approach the Sacraments should prove themselves* (1 Cor. 11:28). *Infants cannot do this, therefore, etc.*

I respond: The Apostle only said this in regard to the *Eucharist*, which requires that a man approach without being conscious of sin, otherwise he approaches unworthily to discern the body of the Lord. Furthermore, the Church rightly does not allow infants to communicate, since they cannot discern the Lord's body. In Baptism, such a proving is not required, for one can approach while conscious of sins, provided he is sorry that he sinned and has a purpose to live rightly, for Baptism was instituted to cleanse sins. Although, however, another type of proof is required for Baptism among adults, that they do not approach with a feigned mind nor with attachment to sin; nevertheless, in infants there is no proof necessary, since they cannot place an obstacle.

22) The *twenty-second* argument: *One who wishes to become a Christian should put on the new man after he has taken off the old. Infants cannot do this.*

I respond: We already said what is assumed is false. Although the major proposition is not absolutely true, since one that is wicked would also be a Christian, provided he receives Baptism and professes the faith of Christ.

23) The *twenty-third* argument: *The faithful steward gives food in due season, and looks to gray harvests, not fresh green and tender ones.*

I respond: The Church preserves this the best, which gives Baptism to children and not Communion, because it is always the time for Baptism, not, however, communion. Hence, regions gray for the harvest are said to be men disposed and suited to receive salvation, and infants are always of this sort; adults are not always of this sort, who are impeded by different desires and sins.

24) The *twenty-fourth* argument: *Those who can drink from the same cup are said to be brethren. Infants cannot, therefore, etc.*

I respond: Those who drink from the same cup are called brethren, but those who are reborn in Baptism are called brethren by a greater notion. Baptism makes us sons of God and brothers of Christ, and similarly of everyone else who has been reborn. However, to drink from the same cup is merely a *sign of fraternity*. This is why the Apostle spoke in regard to each: on Baptism (1 Cor. 12:13), "We were all baptized into one body in one Spirit"; on the Eucharist (1 Cor. 10:17), "One bread, and one body we are many." Conversely, to drink from different cups, so that some drink the chalice of Christ, and others drink the chalice of demons, is a sign of diversity and schism. If one did not drink from any chalice, such as children, it does not impede the fraternity which can be held from a different source, namely from *Baptism*, which truly makes us brothers in one Father, nay more, also members of the one body, "We were all baptized into one body in one Spirit" (1 Cor. 12:13). We also see this in other carnal matters; infants are sometimes brothers of adult men because they were begotten by the same father, although they do not eat the same bread, nor drink from the same cup.

Chapter IX: The Anabaptists Are Answered

25) The *twenty-fifth* argument: *Those who only take an outward share of the Sacraments take up nothing. Infants are only sprinkled with water, since they lack reason, therefore, etc.*

I respond: The assumption is false. Although infants lack the use of reason, nevertheless they do not lack a rational soul and its potencies, in which God can and does dwell through grace when they are baptized, as Augustine writes in *Epist. 57 ad Dardanum.* In that epistle he says it is a marvel and still true, that God would not dwell in many who know him, such as in philosophers, about whom Romans 1:21 speaks when it says, "When they knew God, they have not glorified him as God." On the other hand, he dwells in many who do not know him, such as in baptized children. In his book, *On the Merit and Remission of Sins* (1, 9), he says, "He gives the most hidden grace of his Spirit, which he secretly infused even in children."

26) The *twenty-sixth* argument: *He ought not be called to Christ who cannot be prepared by John the Baptist.*

I respond: It is true, *if preparation is needed*; children, however, do not need it. This is why the Lord says in Matt. 19:14, "Permit the children to come to me," nor did he command them to wait until they were prepared by John.

27) The *twenty-seventh* argument: *Baptism is the imbuing with doctrine and imposition of hands* (Heb. 6:2).

I respond: The Apostle does not say this, but speaks in this way, "Leaving the discourse of our beginning in Christ, let us go on to things more perfect, not laying again the foundation of penance from dead works and of faith towards God, of the doctrine of baptisms and imposition of hands, and of the resurrection of the dead and of eternal judgment." There, the verse "Baptisms of doctrine," must be joined with "not again laying the foundation." And the sense is: we should not return again to the foundation of doctrine handed down in regard to Baptism and the imposition of hands, i.e., on Confirmation; these are given to Catechumens in the beginning of faith, but now they should aim for higher things. This is why Baptism is not defined as the imbuing with doctrine; rather, it is asserted the doctrine on Baptism pertains to *beginners*, not to the perfect, which is against the Anabaptists, who would have it that Baptism is for the perfect.

28) The *twenty-eighth* argument: *Baptism is a mortification and washing in the name of Jesus* (Act. 22:16).

I respond: Even in children Baptism mortifies sin. Hence, that invocation is not on the substance of Baptism, rather it is suitable to be applied when it can be done.

29) The *twenty-ninth* argument: *Baptism is to be washed in body with water in certitude of faith, after a bad conscience has been cast aside* (Heb. 10:22).

I respond: The Apostle does not define Baptism in that passage, but warns the man who wishes to approach God that he should have full faith, a good conscience, and besides, Baptism. He speaks in this way, "Let us approach with a true heart in fullness of faith, having our hearts sprinkled from an evil conscience and our bodies washed with clean water."

30) The *thirtieth* argument: *Baptism is a laying aside of filth and sin, and to be buried with Christ* (Col. 2:12).

I respond: This also agrees with infants, who have original sin. Even if the Anabaptists reject it, nevertheless Paul affirms it in Rom. 5:12, "In whom all have sinned," and Eph. 2:3, "Even we were sons of wrath by nature."

31) The *thirty-first* argument: *Baptism is a promise of a good conscience toward God* (1 Pet. 3:21).

I respond: That is an *effect* of Baptism, not the very essence of Baptism. Hence, Baptism *fundamentally* causes this effect in infants, so that in this way we will say it will also act *formally* when they come to adulthood, for it washed sin, and from that washing later arises the testimony of a good conscience.

32) The *thirty-second* argument: *Baptism is the laver of regeneration and renewal of the Holy Spirit* (Tit. 3:5, & John 3:5), and 33) the *thirty-third* argument: *Baptism, which was prefigured by the prophets* (Ezech. 36:25; Zach. 13:1), *in no way pertains to infants.*

I respond: What they assume is false, from the very fact that they think infants do not have original sin; hence, they deny infants are regenerated or should be cleansed.

34) The *thirty-fourth* argument: *The Sacraments are solid food, but infants need milk.*

I respond: The Sacrament of the Eucharist is solid food, and as it was instituted under the species of bread, it is not given to children. Baptism, however, is not food, rather, *a regeneration*, which especially suits infants because they are customarily born. This is why the Apostle in Heb. 6:1 says Baptism is for the imperfect.

35) The *thirty-fifth* argument: *We must be animals first, and then spiritual* (1 Cor. 5). *The Sacraments are spiritual instruments; therefore, infants cannot be reborn in the spirit.*

I respond: The import of this argument seems to be: The Sacraments are spiritual things, therefore they are only suited to spiritual things. Infants are not spiritual things, as is gathered from the Apostle, who teaches we are first animals and then spiritual, thus the Sacraments are not suited to infants. Yet, in this argument the first consequent is bad. The Sacraments are spiritual in this way: *that they cause men to become spiritual beings from animal ones*, since they have the force to regenerate and renew (John 3:5 & Tit. 3:5).

36) The *thirty-sixth* argument: *No man will ever dare to baptize blind, deaf, and mute adults, how much less infants who can neither walk, nor hear, nor speak.*

Chapter IX: The Anabaptists Are Answered

I respond: Adults of this sort, if they can indicate their will in some manner whereby they wish to be baptized, or certainly would have shown it before they fell into that condition, altogether may and must be Baptized, as the third Council of Carthage clearly hands down (*Carthaginense* cap. 34), as well as the first Council of Arausicanum (can. 12) and Augustine (*de Adulterinis Conjugiis* 1, 26), in regard to the sick who suddenly become mute. If their will cannot be known, they are not baptized because in those who have the use of reason, their consent is required, as we said above, but in infants it is not required, since with them the consent *of others* suffices. Likewise, we do not know in regard to adults who are blind, mute, and deaf, whether they would place some obstacle, but we certainly know in regard to infants.

CHAPTER X

What Our Adversaries Suppose in Regard to the Faith Which Is Required in the Baptism of Children

THE second question remains, in regard to the faith with which children are baptized. There are two extreme opinions of the heretics on this matter, while the teaching of the Catholic Church falls in the mean.

1) The *first* opinion is of the Lutherans, who attribute actual faith, or something similar to actual faith, in children. First, Luther in 1520, in his book *On the Babylonian Captivity* (c. on Baptism), when he said, "All the Sacraments were established to nourish faith," ... "The Sacraments do not justify, nor benefit anyone, rather, faith alone," and again, "The Sacraments are not completed when they are done, but when they are believed." He seems to oppose the Baptism of children by these assertions. Then he objects to himself, "The Baptism of children, perhaps, is opposed to what has been said, since children do not understand the promise of God nor have the faith of Baptism." Then he answers himself and says two things. *a)* Firstly, infants believe. *b)* Secondly, they acquire faith not by the force of the Sacrament, but *through the prayer of the Church and the faith of their sponsors*, and he explains it this way: it is customarily said that children are aided by someone else's faith. Moreover, the fact that he speaks on actual faith of children, not on some habit, is clear from his words, "Just as the word of God is powerful when it is pronounced, it transforms the heart of the impious, which is no less unresponsive and incapable than any child, so through the prayer of the Church offering and believing, to which all things are possible, and when faith has been infused, the child is transformed, cleansed, and renewed." But certainly, an impious man, when he is transformed by the voice of the word of God so that he would wish to convert, is *actually* transformed, not habitually.

Likewise, Luther, in his book *Against Cochlaeus*, written in 1523, says, "We say infants at the font believe the force of the word, in which they are exorcized, and through the faith of the Church which offers them, and by its prayers obtains faith for them. Otherwise, they would be pure and intolerable lies when the minister asks of the child whether he believes? He is not going to baptize unless someone would answer 'I believe' for him in his place. Why would he ask whether he believes, if it is certain he does not believe, as Cochlaeus contends? Be it that Augustine sometimes speaks this way, yet it is enough for Cochlaeus for this to be so said by a man; we would have this saying proved by divine testimonies. We would assert that children are altogether not to be baptized if it is true that in

Chapter X: The Faith Required in Infant Baptism 371

Baptism they do not believe, lest the Sacrament and word of majesty were to be mocked. We ought, however, to deny to the sophists this error of faith in children." There, he clearly speaks about *actual* faith, not habitual faith. Neither Cochlaeus, Augustine, nor the Scholastics, whom he calls sophists, deny habitual faith in children. Besides, Luther would have it that faith is in children *before* Baptism, while they are exorcized and questioned; but that cannot be anything but *actual* faith, since habitual faith is not infused before Baptism, rather, in Baptism itself. Luther wrote the same thing to the Waldenses, where he says that it is better to altogether omit Baptism in children than to baptize them without faith, for if you receive a Sacrament without faith, you receive it with your great evil. He proves it from Mk. 16:16, "He that will believe and be baptized." Such a passage is understood on actual faith.

This assertion seemed very hard to all the others, and it begot three different sects. Some denied that infants must be baptized, since they altogether believed that without faith Baptism was useless, as Luther had said, and at the same time, held from certain experience that children do not believe since they clearly struggle and cry when they are baptized. These are the Anabaptists, whom we spoke of in the last chapter.

Others do not deny children must be baptized, but deny faith is required in children; these are the Sacramentarians, whom we will address shortly when we relate the second assertion.

Lastly, others deny neither faith nor Baptism of children, but try to soften and explain Luther's teaching. So, in 1536, the Lutherans came together in an assembly at Wittenberg, whose acts are extant in Cochlaeus (*Miscellaneorum* 3, tr. 8, c. 2). In that pseudo-synod, these pronouncements are found. First, the error of those who imagined that infants are saved without some action of their own is rejected. Second, even if we do not understand what kind of action of children it is, nevertheless, it is certain that new and holy motions take place in them, just as in John the Baptist, when he leapt in the womb. Third, although it must not be imagined that infants understand, nevertheless their movements and inclinations to believe and love God are similar to the movements of faith and love, and this must be understood when infants are said to believe.

The Lutherans seem commonly to follow this mitigation of Luther's teaching. Melanchthon in *Loci*, for the year 1558 (tit. *On the Baptism of Infants*), says, "In regard to infants this is sufficient enough to hold: The Holy Spirit is given to them in Baptism, who effects new movements, new inclinations in them toward God according to their measure." Brenz holds the same thing (*Apolog. Pro Confess. Württemberg*, on Baptism) and David Chytraeus in his *Catechism* (loc. 7, de Baptismo). Likewise, Illyricus, with the Centuriators (*Cent.* 2, c. 4, col. 63; *Cent.* 5, cap. 4, col. 517) rebukes Justin and Augustine, because they would have it that in Baptism infants do not believe with their own faith, but the faith of another. Lastly (to pass over the rest), Martin Chemnitz (*Examination of the Council of Trent* 2 part. sess. 7, can. 13, p. 528 *et seq.*) says there is a difficulty in understanding and explaining just how infants believe, "nevertheless, how this can be very simply understood is explained in the formula of Concord among the Theologians of Saxony and upper Germany, constituted in the year 1536, etc." He also briefly gives a summary of those items which we cited above from the Assembly at Wittenberg.

Here we must observe, however, that Chemnitz, by a marvelous fraud and deceit—nay more a clear lie—asserts that this opinion of the assembly at Wittenberg harmonizes with the assertions of Luther that we cited above; and again, that Luther agrees with Augustine; and conversely, that the Council of Trent dissents in this matter from the General Council of Vienne, because Vienne taught that in Baptism the habits of faith, hope, and charity are infused in Baptism, but the Council of Trent held that decree as so vile that it did not even mention it. We will refute such lies in short order. In the meantime, that is all for this first opinion.

2) The second opinion is on another extreme: in Baptism, no faith is necessary to infants. It seems that Luther first taught this. Although he wrote the things we cited above before the Anabaptists arose, nevertheless, after they appeared, he wrote a book against them in 1528, and when he came to this argument on the faith of infants, he said there is no difference whether they believe or not. This is because, as he says, Baptism is not founded on the minister, or the recipient, which is most uncertain, but upon the command and institution of God. He holds similar things in his *Homilies on Baptism* given in the year 1537 and 1540; still, this principle of Luther is not solid. Even if from the fact that the Sacrament does not depend upon our faith but on the divine institution, it would follow that it is always efficacious in itself, and still it does not follow that it is useful and fruitful *for us*, unless it is received with faith. Otherwise, even a man who approaches pretending to want Baptism, or who refused to stop sinning, would be cleansed by Baptism. Consequently, the Sacramentarians follow Luther in that which he wrote, that faith is not required; but they gather it from another foundation, namely from the promise made to Abraham and his seed, or certainly from divine predestination.

Calvin wanted to defend the first opinion of Luther, which we explained above, but he did not dare. Thus, he speaks this way in the *Institutes* (4, 16, §18), "It would not be safe to deprive the Lord from his ability to furnish them with knowledge of himself in any way he pleases." In (§19), "I would not rashly affirm that they are endowed with the same faith which we experience in ourselves, or have any knowledge at all resembling faith." In (§21), "If those upon whom the Lord has bestowed his election, after receiving the sign of regeneration, depart this life before they become adults, he, by the incomprehensible energy of his Spirit, renews them in the way which he alone sees to be expedient. Should they reach an age

Chapter X: The Faith Required in Infant Baptism

when they can be instructed in the meaning of Baptism, they will thereby be animated to greater zeal for renovation, the badge of which they will learn that they received in earliest infancy, in order that they might aspire to it during their whole lives." Theodore Beza holds the same thing in his *Confess.* (4, art. 48) and Peter Martyr Vermigli (on 1 Cor. 1 &7), where he clearly says that infants do not understand, nor believe, and still are rightly baptized, because they have already been sanctified and are made members of the Church through the gift of divine election and the promise made to their parents. Nay more, Wolfgang Musculus, who was present in the assembly at Wittenberg, later became a Sacramentarian and says (*Loci Communes*, tit. *De Paedobaptismo*) the Lutherans wrote ill-advisedly, if it is certain that infants who do not believe must not be baptized; and this was the occasion for Anabaptism.

3) The third opinion is of Catholics, that infants do not have actual faith and still do not lack all faith. Rather, they have *habitual* faith, and besides, believe with *someone else's* faith, even in the very *reception* of Baptism. To prove all these in order, we will posit propositions in the following chapter.

CHAPTER XI

It is Declared What Faith Is Required in the Baptism of Infants, and the Errors of Our Adversaries Are Refuted

1) THE first proposition: *Infants do not have actual faith.* This is against the first opinion of Luther. It is proved, *firstly*, because Scripture, in Deut. 1:39 and Jonah 4:11, affirms that infants cannot discern a difference between good and bad, nor does the time of Baptism ever make an exception for it. This is why Luther upholds it without the testimony of Scripture.

Secondly, the Fathers reject this opinion. Nazianzen (*Orat. on Holy Lights*) says that infants are sanctified without the sense of sanctification. Augustine, in *Epist.* 57 *ad Dardanum*, mocks this opinion of Luther because it injures human senses; and again in *Epist.* 23, *Tract. Jo.* (80), *On Baptism* (4, 24), and *On the Merit and Remission of Sins* (1, 20) he says children do not have faith which is in cognition; likewise, they do not have what Paul says, "It is believed in heart to justice." From such things, we understand Chemnitz (p. 258) altogether rashly and mendaciously wrote that the teaching of Luther in this matter is the same as that of Augustine. We showed above that Luther attributes *actual* faith itself to children, the contrary of which Augustine says in as many citations. Why does Luther, in his book *Against Cochlaeus*, affirm that he holds himself against Augustine in this question? Nevertheless, the impudent Chemnitz wanted to bring Luther and Augustine into agreement against their will with his own lie.

Thirdly, there is reason. Faith cannot arise in the mind, except from divine revelation, which is either immediately from God alone, or through the organ of the word of God, whether it is preached or read. Luther does not say faith is given to infants in the first way, but in the second when he says they believe through the force of the word whereby they are baptized, assisted by the prayers of the Church. Besides, that first manner is not ordinary, but *extraordinary*, and very rare, perhaps conceded to the prophets and Apostles alone. "Faith from hearing," Paul says in Rom. 10:17, speaking on the *ordinary way* in which faith is begotten. Now, if faith is immediately revealed to all infants, then it would be the ordinary manner, and all infants could be called prophets when they are Baptized. The fact that in the second way faith does not arise in infants is clear from manifest experience. If the word of exorcism begot faith, certainly it would be heard and understood by the infants, hence they would listen attentively; we observe the contrary. Next, exorcism is not related to teach faith, but to *coerce demons*. Then, this is to place a new miracle in the ears and mind of infants. Nor does the argument which Luther advances on prayers and the faith of the sponsors avail, for sometimes it happens that the sponsors, and the parents, and even those baptizing are infidels, and still Baptism would truly and usefully be given to infants, as Augustine teaches (*Epist.* 23). The force of the prayers and faith of the sponsors is not sufficient to obtain miracles infallibly. Lastly, if God causes a miracle in the *mind* of an infant, that it would believe in heart unto justice, why not also cause one in the *tongue*, so that it might confess by mouth unto salvation? That would be very easy, as the ass of Balaam shows, which spoke wisely by God's will in Num. 22:28.

Fourthly, it is proven from the argument of Augustine in *Epist.* 57, since it is certain that infants both cry and struggle in Baptism, if they truly understood (which is necessary if they ought to believe), what would actually happen is that a great sacrilege would be committed and they would not be washed, but rather, would be even more stained.

2) The *second* proposition: *While infants are baptized, they do not have any new movements and inclinations similar to acts of faith and love.* This is against the invention of the Wittenberg assembly, as well as Melanchthon, Chemnitz, and other Lutherans. It is proved *firstly*, because it is opposed to the word of God. These authors would have it that infants without understanding possess these very motions and that they are called faith, although improperly, and in that way, infants cannot be justified without some faith. Now, in the whole Scripture the word faith is never found to be defined this way, that it would indicate some motion without sense and without cognition, but rather more the contrary, as is clear from Rom. 10:17, "faith from hearing," and Heb. 11:3, "We understand by faith that the world was framed by the word of God," and so in regard to other places.

Secondly, it is opposed to reason. Either these motions and inclinations are in the body or in the soul. If in the body, they cannot be similar to acts of faith and love, which are in the soul, for corporeal things are not said to be similar to spiritual things, except metaphorically and through a type of analogy. Besides, it cannot happen that a motion and inclination to believe and love God would be corporeal, since God is a spiritual object as well as the highest, which can hardly be mentally obtained in some way. If, however, they are in the soul, then it all becomes a contradiction, because they are without cognition. What is a movement of the intellect, except to understand something? Otherwise, the intellect cannot be moved except by understanding, just as the eye cannot be moved except by seeing, nor the sense of hearing except by hearing. And how can the will be inclined except by a preceding cognition, since the object of the will is nothing other than *understanding the good?*

Thirdly, it is opposed to Luther himself, for he (*loci cit.*) previously posited that faith in infants, about which he had often said, is what alone justifies. It is certain, however, justifying is not a movement without cognition; otherwise, even the animals could be justified. Luther would have it that faith is begotten in infants from the hearing of the words of exorcism; hence, he does not posit faith without cognition. Besides, Luther would have it that faith is in children prior to Baptism, so that the answer could truly be given to the minister about to baptize that they believe, but the authors of this assertion say through Baptism those movements are given to children. Melanchthon speaks this way (*loc. cit.*), "The Holy Spirit is given to them in Baptism, who effects new movements and inclinations in them, etc." Similarly, Chemnitz (p. 259) says the Spirit of regeneration is poured upon infants when they are baptized, and works holy motions in them, etc. This is why Chemnitz falsely affirmed on a previous page that Luther supposed what he does.

Fourthly, it is opposed to the doctrine and principles common to all Lutherans. There is nothing more certain and common among them than that men are justified by faith alone, and the Sacrament is nothing other than an instrument *to arouse or nourish faith*. Certainly, if these movements of infants, without true faith suffice to justification and to receive Baptism usefully, it is false that men are justified by faith alone. Nor can they say these very motions are faith. When they speak about faith in the matter of justification, they always understand through faith *an apprehension of divine mercy*, which can be without cognition. Besides, since these movements are aroused immediately by God, as they would have it, and not through the Sacraments, which call forth faith in the manner of a sermon by outward senses, then certainly that principle which holds the Sacraments do not justify except by arousing faith in the manner of a sermon falls completely to ruin. So, if anyone would judge rightly, once the principles on justifying faith alone have been posited, the opinion of Luther, which attributes faith to infants, is less absurd than the Wittenberg assembly, which conceded the motion without cognition to the same. For Luther falsely devised a new miracle, but once that was assumed, everything that follows was constituted for certain. The latter, however, confect a miracle and by placing it destroy their own principles, and oppose themselves to clear reason.

3) The *third* proposition: *Infants are not justified without any faith*. This is against the Sacramentarians, and it is proved *a) firstly*, because Scripture affirms that faith is a necessary means to salvation, "The man who does not believe has already been judged" (John 3:18), from which passage, Augustine proves that baptized infants have some faith, (*On the Merit and Remission of Sins* 1, 33). In that passage the Lord does not speak in regard to the precept of belief, which, without a doubt, children are not held to, but in regard to the *means of salvation*. He had already said in verse 14, "Just as Moses lifted up the serpent in the desert, so the Son of man must be lifted up before man, that everyone who believes in him shall not perish, but have eternal life." He added in verse 18, "He that believes in him is not judged, but he that does not believe has already been judged." So, just as to look upon the bronze serpent was not a precept as much as a unique

remedy for salvation, so also in this passage of the Gospel, faith is asserted to be necessary as *a remedy*, not a precept.

b) Secondly, it is proven from Heb. 11:6, "Without faith it is impossible to please God." Likewise, Rom. 3:28, "We hold a man to be justified by faith," a point which Paul drives home as often as he can. Therefore, how can infants be justified and please God without any faith? But Calvin and Peter Martyr Vermigli say if God predestined infants, and promised that he would be their God, then without a doubt he will give them the Holy Spirit, and will justify them in some way known to himself, although not through faith. *I respond:* Predestination is not fulfilled except by that means *which has been revealed to us in the Scriptures.* Hence, the Apostle (Rom. 8:30) explains the means clearly enough when he says, "Whom he predestined, these he also called; those whom he called, these he justified; those whom he justified, he has also glorified." The same Apostle contends nothing else in the same epistle (Rom. 3-10) than justification does not come to pass without faith. Why would he attribute justification to infants without faith, and before the calling, i.e., before Baptism, by which means alone infants are able to be called? What else is it but to construct a new justification against the word of God?

4) The *fourth* proposition: *The habit of faith, hope, and charity is infused in infants during Baptism.* In the first place, this is certain among Catholics by the authority of Councils and Doctors. Although at some point there was a dispute as to whether infants received the habit of these virtues with justifying grace, nevertheless, it was always the more common opinion that these habits are infused upon infants by Baptism (St. Thomas III q. 69, art. 6; Scotus; Durandus; Gabriel Biel; and nearly all the rest commenting on the *Sentences* in 3, dist. 23). Moreover, the general Council of Vienne (as we find it in *Clement. I de Summa Trinitate et Fide Catholica*) defined this teaching is more probable, and more in conformity with the testimonies both of the Fathers and recent Theologians.

Furthermore, it is not the case that this teaching was not good enough for the Council of Trent, as Chemnitz boldly lies in his *Examination* (2 part., p. 261), for although the Council of Trent did not mention the Council of Vienne, nevertheless it received its teaching and defined it as certain. In sess. 5, in the decree on Original Sin, it defined that infants are justified in Baptism, so that if they were to die in that state, there is nothing which would delay them from entrance into heaven. Then, in sess. 6, c. 7, the Council defined that in Baptism all of the gifts of faith, hope, and charity are infused in Baptism, and adhere to the intellect.

Secondly, this same assertion can be gathered from the Scriptures, whereby we already proved that without faith infants cannot be saved. It is certain that faith does not properly mean anything except an act or habit, and at the same time it is certain that in infants there can be no act of faith; certainly, it follows that the habit is in them. Likewise, from the Scriptures we proved above that infants are rightly baptized, and by Baptism, justified and saved. Likewise, it is certain from the Scriptures that there is no justification without faith; therefore, it should also be certain that infants at least have *habitual* faith.

Thirdly, it is proven from the Fathers, who, although they do not expressly call to mind the habits, say the same thing in other words. All the Greek and many Latin Fathers say that Baptism is an *illumination,* and those who are baptized are illuminated. This is why Augustine also says (*Tract. in Joan.* 44) when the man born blind was anointed by Christ, he became a Catechumen in a certain measure, since he was illumined, he was also baptized in a certain measure. The Fathers, without a doubt, say it on account of faith, which is received in Baptism, which is the light of the heart, as St. Thomas explains (III q. 69 art. 5). The same thing is gathered from that of Act. 15:9, "By the faith purifying their hearts." Then lastly, because faith alone among the Theological virtues pertains to the intellect, in which justification consists, and that is acquired in Baptism. But an act of faith is not received in Baptism, for in adults the act precedes like a disposition; in infants there is no act of faith, therefore Baptism illuminates by reason of the habit which is infused in them. Additionally, Augustine, in *On the Merit and Remission of Sin* (1, 26), affirms that infants are not only cleansed through Baptism, but also illumined, because, as has been said, it cannot be done except through faith.

Fourthly, it is proven from reason. Baptized infants are called, and truly are, faithful, as Augustine teaches (*On the Merit and Remission of Sin* 1, 33), as well as the Council of Trent (sess. 7, can. 13). But we are not called the faithful by an act of faith, rather by a *habit* of faith, otherwise when we sleep or even when we are awake, were we not to think about the faith, we would not be among the faithful. This is why Augustine (*loc. cit.*), when he said children are among the faithful, adds, "This is acquired for them through the power of the Sacrament, as well as the answer of their sponsors." There he clearly means children are called faithful, both by the habit which is infused by the power of the Sacrament and also by the act of someone else's faith.

5) The *fifth* proposition: *Infants believe by act, partly while they are really baptized, partly by someone else's faith.* The first part is of Augustine (*On the Merit and Remission of Sins* 1, 27) where he says for infants to be baptized is itself to believe, because without a doubt the action itself is a profession of faith. He holds similar things in *Epist.* 23. The Church speaks in that way about the Holy Innocents, when it says they confessed not by speaking, but *by dying.* Nor can there be any controversy on this matter. The second part is against the temerity of Illyricus, Chemnitz, and others, who would have it that it is a papist error that infants are baptized in the faith of the Church. A consensus of the Fathers suffices to prove this assertion. In this way Justin Martyr teaches in *Quaest.* 56; Dionysius in

Chapter XI: The Heretics' Errors on Infant Baptism

On the Ecclesiastical Hierarchy; Ambrose, or whoever is the author of the *Commentary on Hebrews*, in ch. 11; Augustine in *On Free Will* (3, 23), where he says it is the teaching of the whole Church. Likewise, *Epistles* 23, 57, and 105; *On Baptism* 4, 24-25; and *Sermon* 10 and 14, on the words of the Apostle; Prosper in *On the Calling of the Gentiles* (2, 8); Bernard (*Sermons on the Canticles*); and at length the Council of Trent in sess. 7 can. 13.

In this place we must observe, however, that a twofold faith is required in Baptism. One is *actual*, which precedes Baptism, as a certain disposition, and it is this which is demanded of those about to be baptized when they are commanded to recite the Creed and are asked whether they believe. Which, for the most part, in the judgment of serious doctors, is not from a habit of faith, but *from the special assistance of God*. This is why the Fathers do not number Catechumens with such a faith among the faithful. The second is that which follows Baptism; it is also an *essential part of justification*, and is not an act, but a *habit*, and those about to be baptized understand this when they are asked what they seek, and they respond, "Faith, giving eternal life," as we have it in the Council of Trent (sess. 6, cap. 7) and in books which treat on the rite of Baptism. Now, when the Fathers say that infants are baptized in the faith of their parents, or the Church, they do not speak on the habit of faith, but on the *act of faith*. When we say children are baptized in the faith of their parents, the sense is not that infants are justified *formally* or are faithful by the faith of another, as Chemnitz and Illyricus incorrectly suppose (*loc. cit.*), where they even incorrectly cite Habakkuk 2:4; "the just man lives by his faith." No Catholic ever taught that children live by someone else's faith, rather, by *their habitual faith*. Nor is the sense, as Luther explains it, that faith is obtained for them, whereby they are justified by the faith and prayers of their sponsors and the Church. Children have justifying faith infused by the Sacrament *ex opere operato*, not from the ministers or the Church *ex opere operantis*. The sense, however, is that children do not have their own actual faith, which is required as a *disposition* to the Sacrament, rather *of someone else*.

Someone will say: What benefit is someone else's faith for an infant?

I respond: It is altogether of great benefit. *First*, it leads them to Baptism. As adults, unless they believe, they cannot come to Baptism. So also, unless parents, or some others who have care of infants, would believe, they do not bring them for Baptism. Consequently, just as each man's own faith is beneficial to him, because it is the cause of his own Baptism, so the faith of another is beneficial to an infant, because it is the reason that the infant is baptized. Conversely, the infidelity of a father is very harmful to an infant, because it is the reason why he would not be baptized. (See Prosper, *loc. cit.*). The second advantage is that in this way they honor and worship God while they profess the faith and renounce Satan, and fulfil what pertains to the rite of Baptism, at least through another's mouth, for God holds this service as valid when furnished through others, since they could not do it themselves. This is what Augustine often insists upon (*loc. cit.*).

From all of this it is gathered that the faith of another is not so necessary that the Baptism would not be true or fruitful if it were lacking, seeing that it does not regard the essence of justification or Baptism; nevertheless, it is necessary for the *solemnity of the rite* and ceremony, and often, as we said, for Baptism itself to be handed down to infants. If no man had faith, no one would see to it that infants be baptized. Now, it remains to answer their arguments, which are few and trifling.

The *first* argument is of Luther against the first proposition, "If infants do not believe, the Sacraments will be mocked by a lying sacrilege, while it is answered for the infant, 'I believe'."

I respond: There is no lie, for the one who answers "I believe" signifies the infant believes with his own act, but *through another*. As Augustine says (*Serm.* 10), "Mother Church applies the feet of others to infants so that they would come, the heart of others so that they would believe, the tongue of others so that they would confess." It is no injury, since they are burdened with the sin of another, i.e., contracted by another, although it truly and properly adheres in them.

The *second* argument, "In Matt. 18:6 it says, 'He that will scandalize one of these little ones, who believe in me.' Therefore, the little ones believe."

I respond: The little ones, on whom the Gospel speaks, were not infants, but full-grown children. The Lord called them to himself, and said they can be scandalized, but to come with their own feet and have the capacity for scandal does not agree with infants.

The *third* argument is against the second proposition, "John the Baptist leapt in the womb (Lk. 1:44), therefore it is no wonder if infants have new movements."

I respond: Firstly, one example does not make a general rule, as Augustine says on this matter in *Epist.* 57. Yet, since Chemnitz says by this example that he does not mean to prove it is so in all infants, but merely that it can be, I respond secondly: John the Baptist did not have a movement without cognition, as they suppose, for as Ambrose and Bede witness in their commentaries on this passage, John knew the Lord was present, and so leapt. The Gospel itself also, while it says that he leapt in joy, teaches clearly enough that he did not lack understanding.

The *fourth* argument is against the same proposition, "Infants can be saved because of what the Lord says in Mark 10:15: 'Unless a man receive the kingdom of heaven like a little child, he will not enter into it.' As a result, it is necessary for infants to receive the Holy Spirit, and hence some operation of it. But they cannot receive faith with cognition, therefore they cannot receive a new movement without cognition."

I respond: The last consequent does not avail, for infants can receive and really do receive the habit of faith, which is neither faith with cognition, nor a movement without cognition.

CHAPTER XII

What Are the True, or False Effects of Baptism

THE *seventh* controversy follows, on the effect of Baptism. There are two questions on this matter. One, on the true effects which Catholics acknowledge. The second on the false effects, which our adversaries attribute to Baptism.

Among Catholics, the true effects are three. *Firstly*, Baptism removes and truly destroys every sin and penalty. *Secondly*, it confers grace and divine gifts *ex opere operato*, whereby a man is truly and formally justified. *Thirdly*, it impresses an indelible character, on account of which it cannot be repeated. These are recalled to what the Fathers enumerate, especially Nazianzen in his *Oration on the Holy Laver* and Chrysostom in his *First Homily to the Neophytes,* that because it makes the soul beautiful, loved by God, resplendent, and that he seals it with a royal seal which makes him an heir of God and which opens the kingdom of heaven, and similar things. Our adversaries deny the first effect, for they say sins are not truly taken away by Baptism; rather, they are not *imputed*. They also reject the second, for they deny men are justified *ex opere operato* through the Sacraments, but only through faith. They absolutely deny the third, and consequently, they cannot give a sufficient reason as to why Baptism is not repeated. We already said enough on the second and third effects in the disputation on the *Sacraments in General*; here we will only argue on the first effect. This will be the first question: Does Baptism truly remove sins?

Moreover, our adversaries enumerate five other effects of Baptism. The *first* is that a baptized cannot be damned, even if he wants, unless he refuses to believe. The *second*, that Baptism frees one from obedience to the divine law. The *third*, that it would free him from the observance of human laws. *Fourth*, that it frees a man from all vows. *Fifth*, that the memory of Baptism alone justifies a man from the sins which he commits after Baptism. There certainly are not as many effects of Baptism as there are errors of the Lutherans, and they are duly condemned by the Council of Trent in sess. 7, in as many canons, 6-10. There will be another question in regard to these effects.

CHAPTER XIII

That Baptism Truly Takes Away Sin

Now, what pertains to the *first* question, there was an ancient heresy of the Origenists that not all sins were removed by Baptism, but only covered; moreover, sins were at length removed by death. A certain Epiphanius records that Proclus the Origenist held this position in his *Panarion* (haeres. 65) where he also posited the refutation of this heresy from the book of St. Methodius the Martyr *On the Resurrection*. The Messaliani seem to have later aroused the same heresy, as Theodoret witnesses (*On the Fables of the Heretics*, 4). Likewise, again, some in the time of St. Gregory, as he relates in his *Epistles* (9, 39 *ad Theoctistam Paritiam*).

In our day, all Lutherans teach the same thing, for Luther himself in the articles condemned by Leo X in 1520, art. 1, says, "To deny that sin remains in a child after Baptism is at the same time to disregard Paul and Christ." Then in his *Assertion* of the same article, "It is one thing for all sins to be remitted, and another to be removed; Baptism remits all things, but altogether removes nothing, rather, it begins to remove them." John Calvin holds similar things in his *Antidote to the Council of Trent*, sess. 6, where he refuted the decree on Original Sin, "Sin truly remains in us, nor is it immediately extinguished on one day by Baptism, rather because the guilt is destroyed, there is nothing in imputation." He holds the same thing in the *Institutes* (4, 15 §10 and 11), as does Melanchthon in his *Apologia for the Augsburg Confession*. Here we must note an outstanding lie, for Melanchthon says, "Augustine says sin is remitted in Baptism, not because it doesn't exist, but because it is not imputed." Moreover, Luther says the same thing in the *Assertion of the Articles* (2 art) and John Fisher convicted him of a lie, showing Augustine did not say this. The book of John Fisher was published in 1523, and still Melanchthon in 1530 again advanced the same lie. Besides, Cochlaeus witnesses in his discussion of the Augsburg Confession (art. 2) that Melanchthon himself was convicted by Eck, and confessed that he had badly cited that place in Augustine. Still the same lie, no matter how many times it was discovered and confuted, they again wrote in the *Book of Concord* on p. 59 of the Latin edition published in 1580, and they always repeat it when they publish that *Apologia*. Lastly, Martin Chemnitz, in his *Examination of the Council of Trent* (p. 430 et *seqq.*), defends the same thing, although more cautiously. He affirms *firstly*, that all sins are remitted in Baptism, to the extent that they are also taken away and destroyed, and only certain remnants of original sin remain. Nevertheless, he then adds that these remnants are a certain thing, which is evil, and the

Chapter XIII: Baptism Removes Sin

evil of sin, and according to the Scriptures are called sin, and that could damn a man if God wished to impute it [to him]. In other words, sin is remitted in Baptism, not because it is removed, but *because it is imputed.*

On the other hand, the Council of Trent, in Session 5, published a decree against this very serious and pernicious error in which it affirms that through Baptism, everything which has the notion of sin in a man is really taken away.

We must make this observation: the foundation of our adversaries is nothing else than that they suppose concupiscence itself, which for a certain fact remains even in the baptized until death, is truly and properly a sin. Although we do not agree with this, rather we oppose it, such a question is not for this place; rather, we will treat on it in the disputation on Original Sin, as is customary. Because this question is so joined with it that when one has been explained, the other is concluded, perhaps it could have been passed over in this place. Nevertheless, because there are other arguments whereby it is proven that Baptism removes all sins, and others whereby it is proved that concupiscence is not a sin, except improperly, therefore I have seen fit to treat the proposed question here, although, as I said, from the definition of one the definition of the other is also obtained.

Firstly, it is proved from the Scriptures that *in Baptism all sins are really taken away, so that they are not only not imputed, but there is nothing which can be imputed to sin.* Because there are many testimonies of Scripture, we will reduce these to a few headings.

1) The *first* is of those which have the words *cleansing, washing, taking away, destroying,* or *removing,* and similar words which are especially opposed with the manner of speech of our adversaries, particularly Luther; besides, they are unable, except very ineptly, to be explained through not being imputed, for it is rightly said someone takes away the ignorance or malice from another because it forgives a man, because he ignorantly or maliciously did something. Such passages are Psalm 50 [51]:4, "Destroy my iniquity, wash me more from my sins"; Micah 7:18, "You take away iniquity"; John 1:29, "Behold the lamb of God, behold he that takes away the sin of the world"; Ephes. 5:26, "Cleansing it in the laver." Chemnitz answers this (*Exam.* p. 501), that Paul did not say "He cleansed," but *cleansing* because daily he washes it until he would show it on the glorious day of judgment. But Chemnitz did not consider the verse which follows, "In the laver of water in the word of life." The cleansing through the laver of water, i.e., through Baptism, is not done daily, except in different men who come to Baptism. For each man is only baptized once, and then is cleansed and caused to be without stain and blemish, although daily Christ acts in different men, so that on the day of judgment he will show forth his whole body, i.e., all the elect, without stain and blemish.

2) The *second* heading is of those passages which say stains, or filth, or iniquities are taken away. According to our adversaries, sin is not taken

away by Baptism, except in regard to *guilt*, i.e, *in regard to being liable to punishment*. They would have it that the very filth of sin remains, which was the cause of that guilt. However, the terms *stain, filth, iniquity*, and similar things do not mean guilt, i.e., being liable to punishment, which can be taken away through non-imputation, but mean the very filth which they hold remains in a man. *Cant.* 4:7 says, "You are all beautiful, my love, and there is no stain in you." There is a similar passage of the Gospel (Jo. 13:10), "He that has washed, does not need to wash his feet, but is clean wholly." Gregory the Great considered this passage (*Epist*. 9, 39), for it truly cannot be said wholly clean, in which something remains, because he would have the very notion of a stain. Ez. 36:25, "I will pour clean water upon you, and you will be cleansed from all of your filth. Ephes. 1:4, "He chose us, ... that we would be holy and immaculate." Col. 1:22, "He reconciled in the body of his flesh through death, to show you holy and immaculate irreproachable." There you see, not only without stain, but nothing else which could be blameworthy. That is understood *insofar as it pertains to the very justification received from God*, for later men can very well fall, and do things worthy of blame. In this way, the evasion of Chemnitz is taken away. He responds on p. 496 *et seqq.* by objecting other passages where we are bid to be cleansed from all filth of the flesh and the spirit (2 Cor. 7) and cast off the old man and put on the new (Ephes. 4 and Col. 3). Now these, and similar things are understood either in regard to sins which are committed later, or on the mortification of the senses and inclinations which provoke one to evil action, although formally they are not sins.

3) The *third heading* is from the figures of Baptism. The figures that precede it are manifold. One, in Circumcision (Col. 2:11); the other in the Red Sea (1 Cor. 10:1); the third, cleansing the leper in the Jordan (4 Kings 5:14); the fourth, in the drowning of the swine (Matt. 8:32), which Nazianzen brings forward in his *Oration on the Holy Laver*. Fifth, in the Probatic Pool (John 5:2); sixth, in the washing and curing of the man born blind (John 9:7), which Augustine explains in *Tract. in Jo.* 44. But in Circumcision flesh was truly cut, not only through imputation. In the Red Sea the Egyptians, whom the Israelites previously served, were *truly and properly* drowned. This is why St. Gregory, treating on this passage (*Epist*. 9, 39) says, "Should a man say that in Baptism sins are not altogether forgiven, let him say that in the Red Sea the Egyptians did not truly die." The same thing can be said for other things.

4) The *fourth* heading contains those passages which compare the cleansing of justification in things that are truly and properly unclean. Psalm 50:8, "You will wash me, and I will be whiter than snow." Isa. 1:18, "If your sins have been as scarlet, they will be whitened like snow; and if they were red as crimson, they will be as white as wool." Isa. 44:22, "I blotted out, like a cloud, your iniquities, and your sins as a mist." Certainly, since solar rays dissolve the mist with their heat, so it causes these to disappear so that

Chapter XIII: Baptism Removes Sin 385

no darkness remains and a truly clear and peaceful sky appears.

5) The *fifth* heading contains a similitude of original sin. Rom. 5:19, "Just as through the disobedience of one man many became sinners, so through the obedience of one many were constituted just." But they were *truly* constituted sinners and *truly* lost justice, not only by imputation. In Jo. 3:6, "What was born of flesh is flesh, what is born from the spirit is spirit." The former are truly carnal, the latter, therefore, are truly spiritual. It is confirmed from that verse in 1 Cor. 15:22, "Just as all die in Adam, so all are brought to life in Christ." This passage is only understood about *true* death, and *true* resurrection, therefore the passages cited above are on *true* sin, and *true* justification.

6) The *sixth* contains the similitude of the death of Christ. Rom. 6:4, "We are buried with Christ through Baptism in death." In verse 2, "If we are dead, how will we live in him?" The same is repeated in Col. 2:12, and Augustine says on that passage, "In just the same way true death came to pass in him, so in you true remission of sins, and in just the same way the true resurrection in him, so in us true justification" (*Enchiridion*, 52). But the death and resurrection of Christ were true in every way, not, however true in regard to one thing and false in regard to another; therefore, even the remission of sin is true death of sin, not in regard to guilt alone, but *in regard to everything which has the notion of sin*.

7) The *seventh* heading contains those passages which teach that we are reborn by Baptism. Jo. 3:5, "Unless a man be reborn from water and the Holy Spirit." Tit. 3:5, "He saved us through the laver of regeneration." Col. 2:13, "When you were dead in sins, and the uncircumcision of your flesh, he gave life with him [Christ]." 1 Pet. 2:2, "As newborn babes." Certainly, that new generation and life require a true death of sins, and a true interior change, not, however, imputation alone. For how truly are we given life and reborn, if death still remains in us?

8) The *eighth* contains those verses which teach that light and darkness cannot dwell in us at the same time. 1 Cor. 10:21, "You cannot be a partaker of the Lord's table, and the table of demons." 2 Cor. 6:14-16, "What affinity is there between light and darkness? What participation is there of justice with iniquity? What peace is there between Christ and Belial? ... What harmony does the temple of God have with the temples of idols? For you are a temple of the living God." Our adversaries would have it that the devil dwells in us through sin, which they say is truly in us, and at the same time Christ through justification. Chemnitz answers (*loc. cit.* p. 501) that Paul teaches there cannot be mortal sin at the same time as the justice of faith. Papists, however, as he says, understand these passages badly, seeing that they deduce from there that the old and new, flesh and spirit, cannot consist at the same time, but in both he is deceived. When he upholds that there cannot be any mortal sin with justice of faith, what he understands it in regard to mortal sin is not according to its nature, but *from the mercy*

of God not imputing it. He would have it, with Luther, his teacher, that the sin worthy of eternal damnation always remains in us, but it becomes venial in believers, *because God does not impute it.* But this is against Paul, because a sin that is by its own nature mortal is truly in us after Baptism, consequently, there is iniquity in us, and therefore, darkness, therefore Belial; as a result, there is an affinity between light and darkness, justice and injustice, Christ and Belial, for iniquity does not cease to be iniquity because it is not punished, which is obvious. Hence, Catholics do not deny that there is in man the oldness of the flesh and the newness of the spirit when they affirm concupiscence is in us, which is the law of the members opposing the law of the mind (Rom. 7:23), but they deny it is a sin, except when we consent to its desires with our free will.

9) The *ninth* heading contains those passages which teach God hates sin. Psalm 5:6, "You hate all who work iniquity." Psalm 44 [45]:9, "You have loved justice and hated iniquity." Wisdom 14:9, "God hates the impious and his impiety." It comes about from these passages that either God altogether removes sins in justification, so that there is nothing which he can hate, or certainly he remits altogether nothing, not even being liable to punishment. If sin would remain, God would hate it; if he hates, he would mean to punish; if he meant to punish, he would not forgive. Therefore, to say God does not impute sins which truly remain and also refuses to punish them is a manifest contradiction according to the Holy Scriptures, which describe a most severe God as the enemy and avenger of sins.

The arguments of our adversaries prove nothing else but concupiscence is truly a sin, although we do not agree with them. We will answer all of these in the disputation on original sin.

CHAPTER XIV

That Baptism Does Not Make Men Impeccable

Now we come to the effects of Baptism which our adversaries invent. Since nearly all of the things which we are going to say here properly consider other discussion, and here it is only treated on account of the canons of the Council of Trent on Baptism, we will only briefly touch upon the matter, constituting as many propositions as there are canons of the Council.

1) The first proposition, therefore: *Baptism does not bring about a state of affairs where the baptized are unable to lose the grace of God unless they would refuse to believe.* This is expressly held in canon 6 of the Council of Trent. We must make a few brief remarks. A) Formerly, there were two errors among the ancients: One was of Jovinian, who, as Jerome (*Contra Jovinianum* 2) and Augustine (*de Haeres.* c. 82) relate, taught that a truly baptized man cannot sin any further, and if perhaps he sinned, he wasn't really baptized, but only received water. His specific argument comes from these words of 1 Jo. 3:9, "Whosoever is born of God does not commit sin, for his seed abides in him, and he cannot sin because he is born of God." Also, 1 Jo. 5:18, "A man born of God does not sin, rather, the generation of God preserves him." St. Jerome meticulously refuted this error (*loc. cit.*), and certainly the Divine Scriptures agree, as that verse of Rom. 11:20, "you stand in faith, do not think too high of yourself, but fear, etc.," and Hebr. 6:4, "It is impossible for those who were once illumined, etc.," 2 Petr. 2:21, "it was better for them not to know the way of justice, etc." Lastly, in Act. 8:13, clearly, we read that Simon believed, and received Baptism; and still in the same place we read of his ruin. Hence, the testimonies from the epistle of John were received in a *feigned sense* just as that of Matt. 7:18, "A good tree cannot bear bad fruit," namely, while the tree remained good. John only meant to show that true justice and charity cannot come together with mortal sin, and hence, he is not just who does evil. Augustine explains it in this way (*Tract. in Jo.* 5) as well as Jerome (*In Jovinianum* 2).

The other error was of certain men who, as Augustine relates (*City of God* 21, 25), were teaching that the baptized cannot be damned, even if they lived in the most depraved manner, provided he did not depart from the Catholic Church. Augustine refutes this error (*ibid.*) from the clearest testimonies of Scripture, and besides he wrote a whole book against this error, which is titled *On Faith and Works*. The particular Scriptures are Romans 8:13, "If you will live according to the flesh, you will die"; and 1 Cor. 6:9, "Do not wander, neither fornicators, thieves, nor adulterers, ... will possess the kingdom of God." Similar things are held in Gal. 5:21, Eph. 5:5,

1 Thess. 4:4, 1 Tim. 6:9, and other places, which are all said in regard to the baptized, as is clear from the same passages.

b) Note *secondly*, something from part of each error has been restored in our day. John Calvin restored the first error, who taught men are truly justified once and cannot ever depart from grace and salvation. In his *Antidote to the Council of Trent*, sess. 7 can. 7, he says in regard to Baptism that in Baptism as a charter of God we are rendered more certain on the perpetual grace of adoption. In the *Institutes* (3, 2 §11 and 12) he teaches that true faith once held cannot be lost and is a proper gift of the elect. The refutation of this error is not suited to the present treatise, since he does not attribute it to the power of Baptism, but predestination. The opinion of Calvin is clearly opposed to the Scriptures, since in Act. 8:13, Simon Magus believed and was baptized, and a little later he lost the faith and charity. Besides, if what Calvin supposes were true, there never would have been any apostates, nor from Catholics would any have become heretics, which is not only opposed to the consensus of the whole world, but even with the Scriptures. Acts 20:30, "From you men shall arise speaking perverse things, to draw away disciples after them." 1 Tim. 1:19, "Some have made a shipwreck concerning the faith." 1 Tim. 4:1, "In the last times some shall depart from the faith." 1 Tim. 6:10, "The root of all evil is the lust for money, which some, being greedy for it, have wandered from the faith." And 1 Jo. 2:19, "They went out from us."

Luther restored the second error in his book *On the Babylonian Captivity*, where he holds the very words which the Council condemned in its sixth canon. His disciples do not differ from him in that opinion, even if they do not approve of the manner of speech. Now, the proposition, *A man cannot be damned unless he refuses to believe*, can be understood in three ways. In the *first* way, the sense would be that there is no sin that is truly and in itself mortal, except unbelief. Our adversaries do not teach this; in fact, on the contrary they contend every work, even those *done in the best possible way* are mortal sins if God would judge them according to the rigor of justice. This is why Chemnitz, in his censure of Trent's sess. 7 can. 6, shows from the Scriptures that many sins can damn a man apart from incredulity.

In the *second* way, the sense would be that all sins are so joined with infidelity, and conversely, faith is so joined with justification, that faith cannot be present with any mortal sin; hence, he that has faith has no sin nor can he perish, and conversely, whoever sins thereby loses the faith. That is similar to what Catholics say about the virtue of charity, for charity really cannot be present with mortal sin, and therefore, no man with charity perishes, and no man is saved without it. Chemnitz would have it that this is the sense of the Lutheran proposition in his *Examination* (2 part. pp. 213 *et seqq.*), where he says Luther never felt present grace is lost by any mortal sin, but felt that a man can, through true faith, immediately return to grace.

Chapter XIV: Baptism Does Not Impart Impeccability

As sins destroy faith, so revivified faith destroys all sins.

In the *third* way, that proposition can be understood so that the sense would be that a man is able to retain faith while he sins at the same time, and through this, not lose the present grace of God, because although sins by their nature cause a man to be a sinner and an enemy of God, nevertheless, faith remaining in his heart makes it so they are not imputed to him and do not damn him. Chemnitz affirms this sense is Epicurean, and the Council rightly condemned the proposition understood in this sense, and even Calvin affirms this in his *Antidote* for this canon 6. Hence, license is given to baptized men to carry out any sins, provided at the same time they believe, and these are not imputed to them. Yet, in no way does Chemnitz concede this was the mind of Luther.

3) Note *thirdly*, that teaching of Luther was rightly condemned by the Council, for Luther said it in the third sense, although Chemnitz would not have it so, and besides, it is also heretical in the second sense which Chemnitz and Calvin admit. Yet, that the first was the mind of Luther is clear from his writings. In *On the Babylonian Captivity*, after he had said a baptized man cannot be condemned unless he refuses to believe, he adds, "No sins can damn him but unbelief alone; moreover, if faith would return or remain in the divine promise made to the baptized man, in that moment all the remaining sins shall be absorbed through the same faith." There you see him say *if faith would return or remain*. Thus, Luther *thought* faith can remain while someone sins, and through that faith sins are not imputed to him, *even while they are committed*. Although Chemnitz relates this sentence, it was not in good faith, since he omitted *or faith remains*. Likewise, in his book *On Christian Liberty*, Luther says, "Nothing makes a person good except faith; nor evil except unbelief." Likewise, in the question whether works make unto salvation, this is the first assertion: *There is no justification except in faith, so there is no sin except in unbelief.* The second assertion: *Justification properly is of faith in the fourth way; and sin of unbelief.* Likewise, in his book *On Monastic Vows*, "There are no evil works of a believer in Christ which could accuse and condemn him." Lastly, in *Sermon 1 on the Gospel* for the second day of Pentecost, on the verse *God so loved the world*, he says, "Where there is faith, there sin does no harm." He adds, "In this way God makes the sins of believers nothing in themselves, in the way a father makes nothing of the trifles of infants playing." There he is clearly speaking about sins *which are committed in act*, and would have it they do no harm because they are covered or excused by faith.

The fact that even in the second sense that proposition is false is clear because it is opposed to Paul in 1 Cor. 13:2, "If I have all faith, so that I would move mountains, but not have charity, I am nothing." There, Paul teaches that faith can exist without charity, and hence, a man with true faith is condemned. The response is made to this that Paul speaks on the faith of miracles, not on justifying faith. *But on the contrary*, the faith of miracles is nothing other than Catholic faith excelling and justifying in its mode. This is why Paul, speaking on the same faith later on, numbers it with the other Theological virtues, "Now faith, hope, and charity remain." In this passage he says, "If I have all faith." Besides, according to the Lutherans, there is no reason why justifying faith itself cannot remain with sin, for it is nothing other than *trust in divine mercy*, as they everywhere define it. What, however, forbids someone from being able to trust while he stole, or committed adultery, that God would not impute the action to sin? Lastly, if a sin that has been committed is able to remain with faith, which still is truly a sin and *adheres* in the justified, as our adversaries say, why not also a sin which *is being committed?* Certainly, if sin could not exist with faith, it would not exist by the notion of past or present time, but by the notion of the malice and vileness of the sin itself. Now, a sin already committed with its whole malice and vileness remains with present faith. Therefore, it can also be done with present faith. This is why they are compelled, if they do not wish to destroy their own principles, to admit that third sense with Luther, which they still affirm is Epicurean, and duly condemned by the Council of Trent.

CHAPTER XV

Men Are Not Freed from Keeping the Law of God by Baptism

THE second proposition follows from the second effect of Baptism: *Baptism does not bring about a state of affairs where a man is under obligation to faith alone, but not to fulfill the universal law of Christ*. This is held in the Council of Trent, sess. 7, can. 7. Moreover, we must make some observations.

1) *Firstly*, the proposition that a baptized man is freed from keeping the divine law may be understood in two ways. *a)* In one way, to act against that law would not be unjust or a sin, as if the law were abrogated. Our adversaries do not teach this, nay more, they would have it that all the works of the just are sins because they never fulfill the law as it should be fulfilled. In this sense, Chemnitz affirms the canon of the Council was rightly placed and the contrary opinion is a blasphemy against Baptism itself (*Exam.* 2 part. p. 216). So, there is no controversy on this sense.

b) In the second way, it can be understood that to act against the law would be a sin, and still *it will not be imputed to those who have faith*, nor does justification or salvation depend upon fulfilling the law, but *only upon mercy*, which is apprehended through faith. All Lutherans teach in this sense (although some speak more cautiously, others more freely), that Christians are not obliged to the divine law, but only to *faith*. Nay more, in this they constitute the summit of evangelical liberty, as is clear from Luther's book *On Monastic Vows* where he says the liberty of the Gospel consists in this, that a pious conscience is free from all works, though not from doing them since he would have it these are done as a fruit of faith, rather, free from *accusing and defending*, because no works are so bad which avail to accuse a believer and condemn him, no work is so good that they can defend and justify him. Likewise, in his *Commentary on Gal.* ch. 2, he set up this dialogue, "What if conscience would declare you sinned? Answer, I have sinned. So, will God punish and damn you? No. At least the law of God says this. But the law has nothing to do with me. Why? Because I have liberty." John Calvin teaches the same thing clearly enough in the *Institutes* (3, 29 §2, 4 and 7).

2) *Secondly*, note what our adversaries suppose in regard to the canon of the Council. Calvin, in his *Antidote*, acknowledges canon 7 of the Council was placed against him and his followers, and he clearly professes the contrary.

Now Chemnitz, in his *Examination* of the same canon, acts fraudulently, as he is wont, and passes over that sense, in which they customarily deny one is obliged to fulfil the law, and he badly explains the teaching of that Council, so as to refute it, and of Luther, so as to defend it. Thus, he says two things. *Firstly*, Luther did not teach that Christians are free from obedience to the law of God, but only this: the grace of Baptism and justification do not depend upon the condition of observance of the law, as if no man would be justified unless previously he had merited it through the full observance of the law, but in fact, it is freely given through faith. *Secondly*, he says the Council meant to define that justification, which is in Baptism, depends upon the condition of fulfilling the law, and because the Council did not clearly say this, he gathers it in this way, that the Council borrowed the phrase of Galat. 5, "He that is circumcised is obligated to do the whole law." Paul did not say those words, however, according to his own mind, but explained the mind and abuse of the Pseudo-apostles, who supposed the whole law must be fulfilled for this purpose, that the circumcised would obtain the grace of God. Consequently (Chemnitz says), the Council Fathers felt the same about the grace of Baptism, namely that it depends upon the condition of fulfilling the law of Christ. Then, he also makes up two sophisms attributed to the Council for this dogma, which he also answers. The *first* is that we renounce Satan in Baptism and profess ourselves to serve God. Thence, the Council gathers the grace of Baptism does not depend upon faith alone, but also on condition of the law. *Second*, because we are not baptized in Moses, but in Christ, i.e., not in the law, but in the Gospel. The Council Fathers placed *the law* in place of the Gospel, to indicate that the grace of Baptism depends upon the law.

Each utterance of Chemnitz is filled with a lie. First, Luther's teaching is so clearly expressed by Luther himself, that Chemnitz can in no way be excused. Luther speaks this way in his book *On Christian Liberty*, "A Christian man is in need of no work, no law, since through faith he is free from every law." Likewise, in the prologue to his *Commentary on Galatians*, he says, "The supreme Christian art and wisdom is to not know the law, to be unaware of works, and all active justice. ... The law does not pertain to the new man." He teaches similar things everywhere in the same *Commentary*, as well as in his work *On Monastic Vows*, and in other places. Since he supposes the law is impossible, and all works, even of the most holy men, are sins, certainly if salvation depended upon the condition of keeping the law, altogether no one would be saved according to their opinion.

As much as Chemnitz turns his back on Luther, and lies, he is compelled to confess, unless he means to become a Papist, that Christians are not obliged to preserve the law to the extent that their salvation depends upon its observance. Moreover, this is the very thing which the Council condemns and anathematizes. Now we come to the second utterance of Chemnitz, that the teaching of the Council is that the grace of Baptism depends upon the condition of preserving the law, which is a lie. The Council does not say this, nor insinuate it in any word, but asserted the contrary in clear words in countless places, especially in sess. 6, ch. 8, where it says *no merit*

Chapter XV: Baptized are not Free From God's Law 393

of ours is before the grace of justification. In that very canon 7 on Baptism, the Council clearly says the debt to preserve the law of Christ is born from Baptism itself, from which it is manifestly gathered that the condition to keep the law is not required to obtain the grace of Baptism, rather it is only proposed *to keep it after Baptism*. The second Council of Arausicanus taught the same thing much earlier in can. 25.

Now I respond to the conjecture of Chemnitz that the Council took up the phrase from Galatians. *Firstly*, the Council of Trent did not cite, nor name the epistle to the Galatians. *Secondly*, I say, in the epistle to the Galatians, Paul either speaks from his own mind, or according to the mind of others, that before Circumcision one was not held to keep the law, but *after* Circumcision. These words express it, "I testify to every man circumcising himself, that he is a debtor to do the whole law" (5:3). Add thirdly, that Chemnitz says Paul spoke from the abuse of the Pseudo-Apostles, which Calvin also holds in his *Antidote* on this canon 7, but it is a manifest perversion of Scripture. Paul witnesses in earnest it is so, as he says, "I testify to every man, etc." Therefore, if it was false, as Calvin and Chemnitz would have it, the Apostle Paul was a false witness.

Moreover, those two sophisms, which Chemnitz objects to himself in the name of the Council, are mad dreams. If he were awake and sane, at least he would have made up some things which had at least some appearance of an argument. However, they have altogether no appearance of it. From the fact that we renounce Satan in Baptism and promise hereafter that we will serve God, it can in no way be gathered that the grace of Baptism depends upon the condition of *fulfilling* the law, since on the contrary, we profess by that renunciation and that promise, that before Baptism we served Satan and not God. The Council, however, carefully named the *law* of Christ, not the Gospel, to condemn the error of the Lutherans, who would have it the Gospel is the only promise of grace, not also the *promulgation* of the new law, although Christ himself said in Matt. 28:19, "Teach all nations, baptizing them in the name of the Father, and of the Son, and of the Holy Spirit, teaching them to preserve everything which I have entrusted to you." From where even Paul calls it the law of Christ, "Whereas I was not without the law of God, but was in the law of Christ" (1 Cor. 9:21) and "I myself mindfully serve the law of God" (Rom. 7:25).

3) Note thirdly, the error which is condemned by the Council of Trent in canon 7. Namely, that Christians are not under obligation to the law in such a way that salvation does not depend upon their obedience is going to be refuted in the disputation on justification, which is its proper place. Meanwhile, very clear testimonies of the Scriptures may be advanced. In Matt. 19:17 it is said, "If you wish to enter into life, keep the commandments." Rom. 8:12, "We are not debtors to the flesh, that we would live according to the flesh. For, if you will live according to the flesh, you will die; but if you mortify the deeds of the flesh by the Spirit, you shall live." 2 Cor.

5:10, "We must all be manifested before the judgment seat of Christ, that every one may receive the proper things of the body, according as he has done, whether it be good or evil." Gal. 6:7-8, "Do not err, God will not be mocked; that which a man has sown, this also he shall reap." Lastly, Scripture proclaims nothing more often than that God is going to reward each man according to *his works*.

Yet, Luther's response to these and similar passages is altogether characteristic, "When they ensnare you with arguments taken from the Scriptures for the defense of good works, you must simply answer: Here Christ is with me, there with you are the testimonies of Scripture on behalf of works. But Christ is the Lord of Scripture and good works. Likewise, simply answer: You insist the slave, that is Scripture, which I leave to you; I insist on the Lord, who is the king of Scripture." A truly remarkable solution, as if Christ and Scripture were contrary and Christ does not rather address us through Scripture. That I might pass over that this is the Luther who, in his book *On the Abrogation of Mass* and in nearly all his writings, says that *relying on Scripture alone, he scorns all the Fathers, all Councils, and every custom of the Church and the whole world.* Namely, he wanted to obtain the position that he would be held as the one not only in place of all the Fathers and Councils, but even in place of all the Divine Letters.

CHAPTER XVI

Through Baptism Men Are Not Freed from Obligation to Ecclesiastical Law

THE *third* proposition: *Baptism does not free men from the oblation of Ecclesiastical law.* This is held in Trent's seventh session, canon 8, and it was posited against Luther, who in his book *On the Babylonian Captivity* and in other works, teaches that neither the Pope nor any man can decree one syllable which obliges the consciences of baptized men.

Here we must make the observation that our adversaries use one method to free the faithful from obedience to divine law and another to free them from the obedience to human law. They affirm divine laws oblige in conscience, so that it would be a sin to violate them; nevertheless, they add that the faithful are forgiven from transgressing laws of this sort, or they are not imputed, and by this it is the same thing as if they were free from the observance of these laws. But human laws, whether Ecclesiastical or civil, they affirm do not oblige in conscience except by reason of scandal or contempt for the things that are forbidden by divine law. Consequently, our adversaries hold that to transgress human law, even intentionally, is not only not imputed to sin, but is no sin at all. This is why both Chemnitz (*Examination of the Council of Trent*) and Calvin (*Antidote to the Council of Trent*) simply reject canon 8 and openly defend Luther's opinion.

Now, because we painstakingly refuted this error in the disputation *On the Roman Pontiff* and briefly in *On the Sacraments in General* (2, 31, on Ceremonies), in this place it will be sufficient to show that the obligation of human law is not opposed with Baptism. We will do that by answering their objection, which is of this sort:

By Baptism we are added to the divine service, therefore we are freed from all other bonds. This is what Scripture everywhere teaches. In Matt. 28:19-20, "Baptizing them in the name of the Father, and of the Son, and of the Holy Spirit, teaching them to preserve everything whatsoever I have entrusted to you." 1 Cor. 7:23, "You are bought with a great price, do not become servants of men." Col. 2:20-22, "If you have died with Christ by the elements of this world, why do you yet decide upon living as though you were in the world? Do not touch, do not taste, do not handle, which are all unto destruction by the very use, according to the precepts and doctrines of men." Ezech. 20:18, "Do not waLk. in the precepts of your fathers." Matt. 15:9, "Without cause they worship me, teaching doctrines and commandments of men." Chemnitz certainly advances this, and he adds the one thing which by itself was sufficient for Calvin, from Jas 4:12, "And there is one lawgiver, who can destroy and save." Calvin says, "Let them show where this is false, then we will not refuse to be bound by their laws."

Yet, it is not necessary to show that what James says is false, since it is very true. Rather, Calvin badly gathers from that verse *not rightly understood* that something is false, pernicious, and opposed to the word of God. James speaks about the supreme legislator, who imposes laws on others in such a way that he would receive nothing from any other who can destroy and save in that way, to condemn some and to absolve, that he would need the help of none, and could not be impeded by any other. Such a legislator, however, we affirm is not the Pope, nor the Emperor, but the one and only *God*. Thence, it is not rightly gathered that there are also not certain men who are truly legislators, although they are constituted under God, the supreme Legislator, so that just as they give laws to inferiors, so they also receive them from a superior, i.e., from God.

Moreover, the sense of James is clear. *Firstly*, from the very context. James meant to show that men should not disparage other men. He shows it because the law of God forbids it, "Who disparages the law, judges the law; but if you judge the law, you are not a doer of the law, but the judge" (Jas 4:12). He proves that no one should judge the divine law, because "there is one lawgiver," i.e., only one who gives law to all, and altogether everyone without exception is subject to the law. Rightly understood, this argument of St. James proves nothing other than apart from God there is no such legislator who does not receive the law from another. *Secondly*, the same thing is clear because the Scriptures, which certainly do not contradict themselves, often attribute the word legislator and judge to men, such as in Prov. 8:15, "Kings rule through me, and lawgivers decree just things." Psalm 2:10, "Be instructed so that you may judge the earth." It is confirmed from similar things. Matt. 23:9, "Your Father is one, who is in heaven." Likewise, in verse 8, "Your teacher is one." And nevertheless, the Apostle calls himself a father in 1 Cor. 4:15, and a teacher in 2 Tim. 1:11.

Now I respond to the others, which are of Chemnitz alone. Through Baptism we are attached to God in servitude, and hence freed from *a contrary* servitude. The contrary service, however, is not obedience and service which is furnished to men, but *the service of the devil and sin*, for latter alone impedes us from serving God, the former rather help us than impede us. This is why in Rom. 6:18, it is said, "You are freed from sin," not from men, "you have become servants of justice." The same Apostle everywhere commands, after Baptism, slaves to serve their masters, sons their parents, citizens magistrates and civil officials, and even ecclesiastical ministers (Ephes. 6:1, Col. 3:20, Rom. 13:5, Heb. 13:7, and other places).

To the first passage from Matt. 28:19-20: If Chemnitz knew how to construct arguments, he would argue this way, "The Lord commands

Chapter XVI: Not Free From Ecclesiastical Law

that the baptized be taught to preserve all his precepts." Yet, one of those precepts is that we observe the laws of prelates, "he that hears you hears me" (Lk. 10:16), therefore he opposes the word of the Lord, and with the profession of Baptism, refuses to be obliged to observe Ecclesiastical laws. Although the Lord in that passage of Matthew does not expressly and by name command the laws of the Church to be kept, nevertheless, he *generally and implicitly* commanded it.

To the *second* from 1 Cor. 7:23: The Apostle does not forbid human service absolutely; in the same place he approves it as useful for humility, but he only forbids it insofar as *it would be contrary to divine service*, which would happen if someone would serve a man in those things which are against God, or if he would serve a man especially *on account of man*, since we should be prepared to serve man on account of God, whose particular servants we are. The Apostle expressed such a sense more clearly in Col. 3:24, where he commands slaves to serve their masters as Christ, so that in man, whom they serve, they do not so much consider a man as they do Christ, on account of whom they are gladly subjected to a man.

We already answered the other passages in the last chapter of the *Sacraments in General*.

CHAPTER XVII

All Vows Are Not Invalidated by Baptism

THE *fourth* proposition: *All vows are not invalidated by Baptism.* This is held in the Council of Trent's seventh session, can. 9, and it is against Luther in his book *On the Babylonian Captivity*, as well as in his book *On Monastic Vows*. Still, it is also against Calvin (*Antidote*) and Chemnitz (*Examination*) on this canon 9, who teach through Baptism men are freed from all vows, not only those which were made before, but even those made afterward, with the exception of that one which is made in Baptism, when we promise that we are going to keep the law of God.

These are their foundations. *Firstly*, that God, in the Old Testament, laid down in regard to vows: how they were to be made, and when, and on what matters. Now in the New Testament, Christ and the Apostles prescribed nothing except one promise, which is made in Baptism (Matt. 28:20). *Secondly*, because we either wish to make a vow over things commanded by God, or things not commanded. If they were commanded, we do it in vain, since we vowed all precepts in Baptism. If they are not commanded, then we oppose ourselves with Baptism, which freed us from all human inventions. *Thirdly*, in Baptism we vow more than we can fulfill, therefore it is stupid for a man to vow something else, and he does injury to Baptism, as if the vow we made during that Sacrament was not sufficient.

These foundations are weak. To respond to the *first*, even if Christ and the Apostles commanded nothing regarding vows, it would be a wonder since vows are *from natural law*, as is clear from the vow of the Patriarch Jacob (Gen. 28:20). Nevertheless, it is false that the Apostles handed down nothing concerning vows, since in 1 Tim. 5:12, St. Paul speaks on the consensus of all interpreters on the vow of continence, where he says certain widows, if they marry, have condemnation because they made void the first faith.

I respond to the *second*: A vow can be made not only on the things commanded by God, but even for things not commanded, provided they are *good*. One does not make a vow over things commanded in vain, both because through a vow a man is more bound and rendered more certain to fulfill it, and also because what is from a precept, and from a vow, is an act of two virtues, and hence more excellent than that which is from a precept alone. To vow a thing which has not been commanded, however, is not against the profession of Baptism, because, as we said above, Baptism frees from sin, not from other matters which help one to avoid sin and subject

Chapter XVII: Baptism Does Not Invalidate Vows

himself more to God as well as bind himself to him, such as vows do. Nor can vows be called human inventions, since they are commended in Scripture. Psalm. 75:11, "Vow, and fulfill." Eccl. 5:3, "If you vowed anything to God, do not delay fulfilling it." Nor can one answer that vows belong to the Old Testament, for the book of Psalms and Ecclesiastes hand down moral documents, which are suitable for all. Lastly, the violation of vows is more opposed with Baptism, for we profess in Baptism that we will keep all the commands of God; one of these commands of God, however, is to fulfill vows, which is clear from the passages that have been cited.

To the *third*, I answer: what our adversaries assume, that in Baptism we promise more than we can fulfill, is false and blasphemous, for that is also opposed to the words of Christ, who in Matt. 11:30 calls his law the sweet yoke and his burden light. Furthermore, it is opposed to the words of Paul, who says in Rom. 8:4 that Christ died that the justification of the law would be fulfilled in us. It is also opposed to the second Council of Arausicanus (can. 25), where it is defined that a baptized man can preserve all the commands of God, and to Basil, in his *Oration,* on the verse *attend to yourself,* and to the other Fathers who say it is a blasphemy to assert the commands of God are impossible. Nor do we suppose a promise made in Baptism is insufficient. For it is sufficient to its end, namely, to save men, although something can be added to it so that someone will be saved more easily or more excellently. It is in the same way in which Baptism is not insufficient, although it is better to be baptized and receive the Eucharist—even by the testimony of our adversaries—than to be baptized alone; nor is the word of God insufficient, although it is better to hear the word of God and receive the Sacraments than to hear the word of God alone. Lastly, if the Jews in Circumcision promised that they would keep the law of God, and still apart from these they could vow many other things, as Chemnitz upholds, then it could not be said that the promise of Circumcision was insufficient. So, why could Christians not vow something, even if they promised in Baptism that they will keep the law of God? Or why should the promise of Baptism be said to be insufficient? That suffices for this place, for we explicitly treated on vows in the disputation *On Monks*.

CHAPTER XVIII

Sins Which Are Committed after Baptism Cannot Be Forgiven by the Sole Memory of Baptism

THE *fifth* proposition: *The sins which are committed after Baptism cannot be forgiven by the sole memory and faith of the Baptism that has been received, rather the Sacrament of Penance is necessary*. This is found in the Council of Trent, sess. 6, can. 10, and it is against Luther in his work *On the Babylonian Captivity* (c. On Baptism), Calvin in the *Institutes* (4, 10 §3&4) as well as in *The Antidote*, along with Chemnitz in their censure of canon 10.

1) Moreover, we must note the difference between what our adversaries teach and what the Church teaches on this matter. *Firstly*, they teach that Baptism does not justify other than by subjecting the promise before the eyes, and in that way arousing the faith which alone justifies. *Secondly*, they gather from this, that when someone sins after Baptism, by the memory of Baptism he can again return to the very grace of Baptism. Just as Baptism itself exposes before the eyes the promise, so also the memory and thought of Baptism causes it; hence, even the memory itself arouses faith, and justifies in that way. We also see this in other matters, since, were anyone to be moved to the love of Christ crucified after seeing the image of a crucifix, certainly later when he is not looking at it, if he will recall it mentally and remember the image, he will be moved. *Thirdly*, from there they again gather that the Sacrament of Penance is nothing other than the repetition of Baptism itself in memory and faith, and just as after Baptism no satisfaction remains, neither are indulgences necessary, nor Purgatory after this life. They suppose in this way: that after penance, i.e., after the memory of Baptism, no satisfaction remains, etc. *Fourthly*, they gather from there that Jerome did not rightly say in regard to Penance that it is the second plank after the shipwreck (*On Isaiah* 3, and *Epist. ad Demetriadem*, and before him Tertullian in *de Poenitentia*). For the ship of Baptism is never broken, but those who sin fall off of it, which is why, when they come back to their senses, there is no need to look for a plank, since they can return to the boat itself, which is whole and intact, waiting for them. This is the teaching of the heretics, and it is certainly foppish and soft enough that it could not even displease Epicurus.

On the other hand, Catholics teach otherwise by far. *First*, they affirm in Baptism sins are remitted *ex opere operato*, i.e., by the force of the Sacrament, as we have already shown. *Secondly*, from there they gather that the efficacy of Baptism does not extend itself to the future, but only

Chapter XVIII: Memory of Baptism doesn't Forgive 401

to the *past*; it remits sins already committed which have not yet been forgiven, i.e., those which it finds in a man when he really receives the Sacrament. The memory of Baptism is certainly useful to give thanks to God, and to serve as a restraint so as not to sin, but in no way does it suffice for justification. *Thirdly*, from there they gather that grace once lost cannot again be recovered through Baptism; rather, another remedy must be sought that is more arduous and difficult, namely the Sacrament of Penance. After that, one must suffer temporal punishment to make satisfaction, and thence follows the advantage of Indulgences, and the place of Purgatory, etc. *Fourthly*, they gather from there that the Fathers were most correct when they said Penance after Baptism is the second plank after the shipwreck, because those who are repentant do not return to the ship of Baptism, but sail with great labor clutching the plank which carries them after the shipwreck.

2) Note *secondly*, that Chemnitz (*Examination*) badly explains canon 10, as well as the teaching of Catholics. On page 229, he says Catholics assert a man cannot, even through true penance, return to the grace of Baptism and the covenant which God made with us in Baptism. Catholics, however, do not say this; we affirm that a man can return to grace and the covenant begun with us in Baptism by true repentance, i.e., that we again are sons of God through grace; but we deny it can be done *through the same instruments of the covenant, that is through Baptism or memory of it*, rather, through another Sacrament. Even if for the most part sins are not so blotted out through the Sacrament of Penance so that some temporal punishment to suffer would not remain, nevertheless, there can be such repentance that would plainly blot out all punishment, and so one is returned to grace altogether similar to that which was possessed in Baptism.

Chemnitz says (*ibid.*) that Catholics, when they sin after Baptism, rest upon their own contrition and satisfaction to return to grace. This is also said falsely. We rest upon *the grace of God, the merits of Christ, as well as the virtue and the efficacy of the Sacrament*, not on our own contrition; although we require contrition as the disposition, just as also when we are baptized we require faith and repentance, still, we do not rest upon those things as the causes of justification, rather, upon the grace of God, the merits of Christ, and the efficacy of the Sacraments.

Then, on pp. 235-236, Chemnitz says the Council did not dare to expressly condemn the teaching of Luther because it feared the judgment of pious ears before such a light of the Gospel; therefore, it made a strawman, and in this way condemned the strawman. He shows it to have so misrepresented the case, because the Council says anathema to those who teach that sins which are committed after Baptism are forgiven by the sole memory of the Baptism received; this is, a man who without repentance would persevere and continue in his crimes, for these men, if they will only recall perfunctorily and historically that at some time they were baptized, then sins are forgiven by such a memory. Then Chemnitz adds, this truly Epicurean teaching is condemned by their own sonorous voice. Yet the good Chemnitz, while he means to show that the Council set up a strawman of Luther's teaching, makes a strawman out of the Council's own teaching, and indeed, it is such a manifest lie that it is a marvel. The Council, in canon 10 itself, which Chemnitz cites in the same words, described in his *Examination*, does not say by the sole memory of Baptism, and that perfunctory and historical sins are forgiven among the Lutherans, rather, it says, "By the sole memory and faith of Baptism." There, the Council adds *faith* (which Chemnitz always omits when he attacks this canon), and does not add historical or perfunctorily, which Chemnitz adds on his own. Therefore, Chemnitz partly by disparaging, partly by adding, makes a strawman of this canon of the Council. Moreover, the Council, in a few words, simply understood the teaching of Luther in the manner of other canons and clearly condemned it.

3) Note *thirdly,* the accurate proof of Catholic truth, and the refutation of the error of the Lutherans, is not for this place, but for the disputation on the Sacrament of Penance. Still here, we will briefly prove that those who sin after Baptism cannot return to the ship of Baptism, but need another remedy. *Firstly,* it is proven from Paul in Heb. 6:4, "It is impossible for those who were once illumined, ... again to be renewed to repentance." There, the Apostle does not mean to say the lapsed cannot return to repentance in any way, for that is the error of the followers of Novation, which our adversaries do not approve of; rather, he means to say they cannot *be renewed to penance* in the way those who are baptized are renewed. Ambrose, Chrysostom and other interpreters explain it this way, and Chemnitz admits the same exposition in his examination of the following canon (p. 240). The same thing is clear from the words "illumined and renewed, crucifying the son of God," which are proper to Baptism, in which we are illumined and renewed and in which we imitate the death of Christ.

Perhaps someone will say on Chemnitz's behalf that this passage proves that Baptism cannot be repeated, but it does not prove a man cannot return to reconciliation by the memory of Baptism, nay more, this passage particularly proves it. Now, even if our adversaries deny that the sprinkling of water is repeated, nevertheless, they would have it the *efficacy* of Baptism is repeated, so that sins committed after Baptism are forgiven through it and are remitted by the same facility and perfection, not to mention plenitude, just as before, so that the second reconciliation will in no way be more laborious than the first. This is the very thing which the Apostle denies. In the first place, he refused to say that it is impossible to be baptized again, rather, it is impossible to again be renewed to penance, namely *Baptismal.* Besides, what has been proposed by the Apostle, is to deter baptized men from sins, which would deter them for the very reason that they can no longer be reconciled *with the same facility.*

However, according to Lutherans the facility is the same, indeed greater in the second reconciliation than the first, seeing that it is easier to remember and think about Baptism than to be really baptized.

Secondly, the same thing is proven from the testimonies of the Fathers, who always imposed serious labors upon men who sinned after Baptism before they would reconcile them. This is clear from Cyprian (*de Lapsis*) and others, whom it is not necessary to name seeing that Calvin says nearly all the Fathers, whose books are extant, spoke too bitterly and harshly in regard to the lapsed (*Instit.* 3, 4, §38). There, he clearly confesses the ancient Fathers, and nearly all, did not hold the same teaching as he, that reconciliation is equally easy in Baptism and after Baptism.

Thirdly, the same thing is clear from reason. Justice does not suffer that men who sin before Baptism and men who sin after should have an equally easy road to the grace of God. The former did not know God, while the latter knew him; the former did not have grace, the latter did. Even if Catechumens know God before Baptism through faith, often they also burn with charity; nevertheless, all of these pertain to the grace of Baptism. Even instruction in the Catechism, the disposition to Baptism, as well as that grace and charity, which is sometimes found in Catechumens, proceeds from the desire for Baptism. Now let us also briefly rebut their arguments.

a) The *first* argument of Luther is taken from that promise of Mk. 16:16, "He that will believe and be baptized will be saved." He says this promise always remains and is always true. For this reason, a man who recedes from faith and Baptism by sinning, if he would again believe and embrace the covenant of his Baptism, will certainly be saved. Luther confirms this, because in this way in the Old Testament of the Jews, when they returned to penance so as to be reconciled to God, recalled the memory of the exodus from Egypt.

I respond: This argument concludes nothing, because although the truth of the promise is perpetual, nevertheless it is *conditional*, not absolute. Otherwise, all apostates would be saved, because it is also true of them that they believed and were baptized. Therefore, the condition is understood: *If a man remains in the faith and the Baptismal covenant*, he will be saved, but if he does not remain, he will not be saved by this remedy, but rather must seek another. A man who once departed from the covenant of Baptism by mortal sin cannot again return to it; he does not return to the covenant of Baptism through the sole thought or memory of Baptism. To really be baptized [again], which would truly return to the covenant of Baptism, is in no way lawful. It is clear from the example of faith and other things; a man is not said to return to faith who thinks upon believing at some time, but who begins to believe again *in act*. The confirmation, however, from the exodus from Egypt also proves nothing, for they did not commemorate that exodus as if by that commemoration they were cleansed of their sins, rather, to complain of their ingratitude toward God, and we do not deny that to produce Baptism in this way is suitable for us. Additionally, if Luther's opinion were true, the Jews rather ought to have commemorated Circumcision, which was for them in place of Baptism, than the exodus from Egypt.

b) The second argument is of Chemnitz: When the Scriptures speak about the effect of Baptism, sometimes they describe it in regard to the past, sometimes in regard to the future, and sometimes even in respect to the present; therefore, Baptism has the power to cleanse all sins, past, present, and future. The antecedent of the argument is proven. In Tit. 3:4, it is said about the past, "He saved us by the laver of regeneration." Mk. 16:16 speaks about the future, "He that will have been baptized will be saved." 1 Pet. 3:21 speaks about the present, "Baptism saves you," as well as Eph. 5:26, "Cleansing it in the laver of water." St. Augustine comments on this passage (*de Nuptiis et Concupiscentia*, 1, 33), and speaks in this way, "When Paul says, 'Cleansing it in the laver of water,' we must receive it in the same washing of regeneration and in the word of sanctification, altogether all the evils of regenerated men are cleansed and healed, not only of past sins, all of which are now remitted in Baptism, but even of what will be committed later by human ignorance or weakness; not that Baptism should be repeated as often as a man sins, but that by it, which was once given, it happens that it obtains forgiveness for the faithful of all sins committed not only before, but after." Lastly, Chemnitz adds that the whole thing is clearly explained in Romans 6.

I respond: There is no passage of Scripture whereby it can be proven that future sins are blotted out by Baptism, or even present ones, namely which we commit in the present when we have already been baptized, which with respect to one's Baptism, can be called future. The objection from Mk. 16:16, however, "He will be saved," is received in two ways: One is on salvation *in re*, i.e., on eternal glory itself, and there is no doubt that it is in the future, but it is not the effect, rather *the end* of Baptism. We are treating on the effect, however, for the effect of Baptism is the remission of past sins, but the end is the blessed life in the future, according to that of the Apostle in Romans 6:22, "Now freed from sin, you have been made servants of God, you have your fruit in sanctification, the end in eternal life." The other, is on salvation *in hope*, i.e., on the very grace of justification, and that is certain to follow soon after Baptism, and hence, it is indeed future in respect to Baptism, but *of past* sins, not future ones. Just the same, a man who says if you receive some kind of medicine, you will be cured indicates the cure is going to follow the medicine, but that cure is for a disease already contracted, not contracted after he receives the medicine.

What he objects from 1 Petr. 3:21, "Baptism saves you," does not bear on the matter, for Peter, when he speaks about the present time, does not compare Baptism with sins, but the *time of Christ with the time of Noah*, and he says that just as in the time of the flood of Noah, he saved eight men

Chapter XVIII: Memory of Baptism doesn't Forgive

in the ark, so now in the time of Christ Baptism saves believers, etc.

What he objects from Eph. 5:26, "cleansing it," is easily explained, for that "cleansing" is not related to individual men, but to *many*, who constitute one Church. Christ daily cleanses the Church with the laver of water because daily some are baptized; nevertheless, by being baptized everyone is cleansed from *past* sins, not future ones. If someone were to relate this to individual men, then it must be said that in Baptism future sins are cleaned, but not immediately, rather, *mediately*, because a man that has been baptized, through the grace which he receives in Baptism, obtains forgiveness of venial sins which he commits later, if he seeks it, and besides, through the character of Baptism he has the right to the Sacrament of Penance, whereby mortal sins are cleansed, while those who lack Baptism cannot partake of that Sacrament. This is what Augustine says in the place which Chemnitz cites. Augustine only says that future sins are cleansed by Baptism *in some way*, because without having partaken of Baptism, the other means whereby sins are cleansed, Penance, almsgiving, fasting, etc., profit nothing. He says, "What benefit is the penance before Baptism, except that Baptism follows, or after, except that it preceded?" This is why the same Augustine, when he speaks on the immediate and proper effect of Baptism, clearly writes the contrary, as in *Epistle* 23 *to Boniface*, "A child does not lose the grace of Christ once it has been received, except by his own impiety, if by the onset of age he would go out wicked, for then he will also begin properly to have sins which are not taken away by regeneration, but healed by another cure."

Lastly, what he objects from Romans 6 is of little importance. In that chapter, the Apostle does not teach on the way sins are remitted after Baptism, but the way in which they ought to be *avoided*. He says through Baptism a man dies to sin so that he may live in God; hence, a man once reborn in Christ ought to be on guard with all care, lest he would sin again and die. But what has this to do with the matter we are discussing?

c) The *third* argument is also from Chemnitz. The covenant of God with man is perpetual. Isa 54:8, "With everlasting kindness I have had mercy on you." Rom. 3:3, "Shall their unbelief make the faith of God without effect?" 2 Tim. 2:13, "If we do not believe, he continues to be faithful, he cannot deny himself." Jer. 3:1, "You have been wanton with many lovers, but turn back to me, says the Lord." Therefore, the covenant begun with us in Baptism is never broken in such a way that we could not return to it, and renew it. He confirms it because Paul, in Gal. 3:26 and 1 Cor. 12:13, recalls the lapsed after Baptism to the promise of the grace of Baptism. Lastly, he adds the very nature of that promise shows this. The promise of Baptism is "that being justified in the grace of Christ we are heirs according to hope of eternal life" (Tit. 3:7). This is the general notion of justification after each fall; therefore, we are always justified through Baptism.

I respond: Chemnitz shamelessly plays with the Scriptures, and abuses their testimonies. In Isaiah 54:8, it contains an *absolute* promise, namely on perpetually maintaining the Church; this promise does not depend on any condition. The matrimony between Christ and the Church is clearly indissoluble. The passage of Romans 3:3 similarly contains an *absolute* promise, in regard to sending the Messiah into the world. Now, the promise of Baptism is not absolute, rather *conditional*, which is obvious because it includes the condition of faith, perseverance, etc. The passage of 2 Tim. 2:13, however, favors us. When Paul says "if we do not believe, he remains faithful, he cannot deny himself," he means God is faithful since he does what he promises and at the same time he rewards the just and punishes the impious. This is why he prefaces in verse 12, "If we suffer, we will reign with him; if we deny him, he will deny us." There you see a *conditional* promise. The passage of Jer. 3:1 teaches God receives men if they return to grace, but it does not teach it *in that way and through the same instrument* whereby he received us before. The passage of Gal. 3:26 does not bear on the matter, for Paul does not teach in that passage the way in which the impious that have fallen are justified after Baptism, as Chemnitz pretends, but it teaches men are not justified by Circumcision and other works of the law, but *through the faith of Christ*; it proves that those who are baptized put on Christ. The passage of 1 Cor. 12:13 does not even address the matter at hand. Paul only says we are all one body because we are baptized in one spirit; he adds nothing on the justification of those who fell after Baptism. Lastly, the argument on the nature of the promise of Baptism is an inept sophism. Even if Baptism promises salvation through Christ, and whoever is justified after any fall is justified through Christ, nevertheless, it does not follow that men who fell after Baptism are justified through Baptism. It is obvious men are justified more broadly through Christ than justified in Baptism through Christ, seeing that the Sacrament of Penance, and of the Eucharist, and the others, also promise salvation through Christ.

d) The *fourth* argument is of Calvin from the *Institutes* (4, 15 §3). In Baptism we are sharers in the purity of Christ. Yet, this is always in force, nor is it oppressed by any stains, therefore, the power of Baptism once conferred remains in us, and we can always return to it and be justified by it. He confirms it from the Fathers, who rebuke those who delay Baptism even to death, for once many were deceived by this error, that Baptism does not cleanse any but past sins, so they refused to be baptized except in the end of life, when they were going to sin no more. Since the Fathers convicted an error of this kind, hence if follows that they believed that all sins, even future ones, are cleansed in Baptism.

I respond: The argument of Calvin rests upon a false foundation, namely that we are justified by the very justice of Christ imputed to us. That is truly always in force, nor is it oppressed by any stains, but it is false that we are *formally* justified by it. We are justified by our own justice adhering in us, which plainly is not [always] in force and is ruined and abolished

Chapter XVIII: Memory of Baptism doesn't Forgive

by blemishes when we sin. I respond to the confirmation, that it favors us. If the Fathers believed the thing which Calvin believes, when they were rebuking those who delayed Baptism, they would have given that reason, because Baptism even washes future sins, for nothing more efficacious could be applied. Yet, none of the Fathers gave this reason, rather, other reasons, as is clear from Basil (*Orat.* 13 *On the Exhortation to Baptism*), and Nazianzen (*Orat. On the Holy Laver*), and Chrysostom (*Hom.* 1 in *Acts*), who exhort men not to delay Baptism not only on account of the danger of an uncertain death, but even more on account of the many goods which Baptism brings with it.

e) The *fifth* argument is also of Calvin (*ibid.* §4), that the power of the keys cannot be separated from Baptism; therefore, when men who have fallen after Baptism are reconciled by the power of the keys, they are reconciled by Baptism. The antecedent is proven, for the power of the keys is not exercised without the preaching of the Gospel, whereby we announce that the impious are cleansed in the blood of Christ; the sin, however, and testimony of the shedding of the blood of Christ is Baptism, consequently, the power of the keys is not exercised without Baptism.

I respond: If the argument would avail for something, it would also avail that no one is reconciled except through the Eucharist, or the memory of it, for the Eucharist is also a sign and testimony of the shedding of the blood of Christ. But the argument concludes nothing, both because it is false, the power of the keys is not exercised except by the preaching of the Gospel, and also because the impious are cleansed far more in the blood of Christ than in Baptism. Accordingly, the blood of Christ is that which always cleanses, but it is applied *through different instruments*: sometimes through Baptism, sometimes through other Sacraments, sometimes without the Sacraments through faith and true conversion, sometimes through martyrdom, as we said above.

CHAPTER XIX

The Errors in Regard to the Baptism of John

The eighth controversy follows on the comparison of the Baptism of Christ with the Baptism of John, which constitutes the first Canon of the Council of Trent in sess. 7 on Baptism, "If anyone will say the Baptism of John had the same force with the Baptism of Christ, *anathema sit.*" There are three parts of this controversy. *Firstly*, we will explain the errors and opinions. *Secondly*, we will clarify and confirm the truth. *Thirdly*, we will refute the objections.

Now what pertains to the first: There was an ancient error of Petilian the Donatist, that the Baptism of Christ and John were one. He distinguished three degrees of the same Baptism and says that John baptized with water, Christ with the spirit, and the Paraclete with fire, but these three pertain to one and the same Baptism, as Augustine relates and refutes (*Contra Literas Petiliani*, 2, 32, 34 & 37).

In our times, Luther in the beginning of his preaching clearly distinguished the Baptism of John from the Baptism of Christ. In his disputation *On the Baptism of the Law, John, and Christ* (published in 1520), he posits distinctions between these Baptisms. *First*, that the Baptism of John is not a Sacrament, whereas Christ's is. Second, that the former does not remit sins, the latter does. *Third*, that those baptized by John had to be baptized again, but not those baptized in the Baptism of Christ.

Moreover, this opinion, because it was inconsistent with the rest of the doctrine of the Lutherans on the Sacraments, did not please Luther's disciples. They all taught the contrary namely that the Baptism of John was a Sacrament and remitted sins, and those who were baptized by him were not to be baptized again. Melanchthon teaches in this way in *Loci Communes* (published in 1558, tit. *De Baptismo Joannis*), "Even if there was a difference on this point: John preached in regard to the Christ that was to suffer,; the Apostles on the Christ that had suffered and was raised; nevertheless, it was the same mystery, and the effect has the same things among believers." There, he openly retracts what he had written in *Loci* published in 1522, for there he taught with Luther that the Baptism of John was a sign of mortification, but the Baptism of Christ was a sign of justification, and on that account, those whom John had baptized ought to be baptized again. Melanchthon also, along with the Lutherans Alesius and Lossius, hold the same thing in their commentary on 1 John. Likewise, Martin Bucer; David Chytraeus, on Matt. 3; Brenz, in *Hom.* 21 and 29 in *Luke*. The Centuriators

Chapter XIX: Errors on John's Baptism

hold the same thing (*Centur.* 1, c. 4, col. 146, and c. 10, col. 361). Likewise, Nicholas Selnecker (*Paedagog.* 2, tit. *De Baptismo*), Zwingli (*On True and False Religion*, c. on Baptism), and Calvin in his *Antidote to the Council of Trent* as well as the *Institutes* (4, 15 § 7 & 8). Lastly, Martin Chemnitz his *Examination of the Council of Trent* (2 part. p. 175 *et seqq.*). They all agree that the Baptism of John remitted sins and was the same Sacrament with the Baptism of Christ, which the Apostles administered; nevertheless, he did not dare to define whether there were any baptized by John who were again baptized in the Baptism of Christ. On the proposed question, and the reasons for each side, at length he speaks this way on p. 190, "Thus, we leave the question hanging, as each side has arguments on its behalf." He did so very cautiously and skillfully, for in this manner he does not openly oppose the earlier teaching of Luther and Melanchthon, or the later and common teaching of Lutherans; besides, he freed himself from a difficult question, in which others had labored with much sweat, but still did not make themselves ready to answer how in Acts 19:5, those who were determined to have been baptized by John were commanded to be baptized in the Baptism of Christ.

Among Catholics there were also two opinions on the Baptism of John: one of which is considered erroneous, the other very improbable. *a)* The *first* was of St. Peter Lombard, who in 4, dist. 2, distinguishes two kinds of those baptized by John. One of these who were so baptized by John, that they placed their hope in that Baptism and made no notice of the Holy Spirit; these he affirms needed to be baptized in the Baptism of Christ. The other group of these who were baptized by John, did not place their hope in that Baptism, and had notice of the Holy Spirit; and these, he says, did not need to be baptized in the Baptism of Christ. This opinion, apart from the arguments we will advance later against the heretics, can be refuted from what Lombard himself, and all Catholics concede. In the consensus of all, *the Baptism of Christ obligated all men after its promulgation*, but the Baptism of John was not the Baptism of Christ, as Lombard teaches in the same distinction; consequently, those baptized by John were obliged to receive the Baptism of Christ. This is why St. Thomas (III q. 38, last article) writes this opinion was altogether irrational.

b) The second opinion is that the Baptism of John was a type of Sacrament, such as the Sacraments of the Old Law were. Lombard teaches this way, as well as many Scholastics and even St. Thomas himself (4, dist. 2), but St. Thomas duly taught the contrary in the *Summa* (III, q. 38, art. 1). The Sacraments of the Old Law began with the law itself, and endured for the whole time that the law itself endured. Yet, the Baptism of John began at the end of the law, and did not endure more than a year or so. This is why St. Thomas rightly says that the Baptism of John did not pertain to the Old Law, but rather more to the New, as a type of *preparation for the Baptism of Christ*.

Someone will say that the Baptism of John was not a Sacrament of the Old Law or the New, but a middle between each. That cannot be the case, for there cannot be a middle Sacrament between the Sacraments of the two laws, unless there was also a middle law. There was, however, no middle law between the New and Old; when the one was abrogated, the other immediately succeeded it. This is why if the Baptism of John was a Sacrament, it would altogether be of the Old Law or the New. Nor does it suffice for the notion of a Sacrament (which seems to have deceived the ancients), to signify the Baptism or Christ, or even the grace that was going to be given through Baptism. Even the flood (1 Petr. 3:21) and the Red Sea (1 Cor. 10:2) signified Baptism, and the manna signified the Eucharist, nevertheless, they were not Sacraments, but only *figures* of the Sacraments. Now, passing over these matters, we come to constitute the truth, and prove it against the heretics.

CHAPTER XX

The Baptism of John Was Not the Same Sacrament as the Baptism of Christ

To explain and prove the truth, we are going to constitute three propositions.

The *first* proposition: *The Baptism of John was not the same Sacrament as the Baptism of Christ*. This is against Melanchthon, Calvin, Chemnitz, and the others, who assert the ministry of John and the Apostles was the same. It is proven firstly, that the Baptism of John was instituted by John himself; consequently, it was not a Sacrament, especially of the New Law. The consequent is clear, because no mere man can institute Sacraments, especially of the New Law, as we proved above from testimonies, even those of our adversaries. The antecedent is proven, because in the Scriptures, the Baptism is everywhere called "of John," such as in Matt. 3:7, "John, seeing many of the Pharisees and Sadducees coming to his Baptism," and Matt. 21:25, "The Baptism of John, was it from heaven, or from men?" We read the like in Mk. 11:30, Lk. 20:4, Act. 1:5, 18:25, and 19:3. This wording, however, cannot mean John was a mere minister of that Baptism, but also its *author*, otherwise, the Baptism of Christ could also be called the Baptism of Peter, Paul, Philip, and others. Instead, Scripture is very careful that they do not appear to be the authors of Baptism, as Augustine notes (*On Baptism* 5, 13, and elsewhere).

Someone will say: The Baptism of John seems to have been instituted by God, not by him. He speaks in this way, "He that sent me to baptize in water said to me...." I respond with Augustine (*loc. cit.* 9 & 13) and with Tertullian (*de Baptismo*), where he treats on that question proposed by Christ, whether the Baptism of John was from heaven or from men: The Baptism of John was instituted by God, but *by the medium of John himself.* God only inspired in general, and commanded it by that inspiration, that he would baptize, but the rite *in particular*, whereby he was to baptize, John himself instituted; he did not receive it prescribed by God. This is why the Baptism is truly said to be of John.

Secondly: *In the Baptism of Christ not only water is of the essence of the rite, or Sacrament, but also the invocation of the Trinity.* We proved this above, nor do our adversaries disagree, at least in practice, since they themselves also baptize in this way. Yet, the Baptism of John did not have the invocation of the Trinity; consequently, it is not the same Sacrament with the Baptism of Christ. The assumption is proven because although the Centuriators (*Cent. I*, 2, c. 6, col. 496) affirm John baptized in the name of the Father, and of the Son, and of the Holy Spirit, still neither Scripture, nor any tradition of the Fathers taught this. We cannot, however, in matters of this sort, except very rashly, make up something without the testimony of Scripture or tradition. There were indeed some who supposed John, in his Baptism, had use of a certain form of words, namely in the name of the Messiah to come, on account of these words of Paul in Act. 19:4, "John baptized the people in a Baptism of penance, saying, that they should believe in him who is going to come after him." Ambrose teaches in this way (*On the Holy Spirit*, 1, 3), as well as Jerome (*On Joel* 2) and Hugh of St. Victor (*de Sacramentis* 2, part. 6, cap. 6). These very authors, especially the latter two, warn that John did not baptize in the name of the Father, and of the Son, and of the Holy Spirit, and on that account, it was not a perfect Sacrament. Additionally, it is very probable that John was altogether unaccustomed to use any form of words. The words of Paul do not seem to signify that John baptized in the name of the one to come, but only admonished the people to believe in the coming Messiah. John also baptized Christ in that rite in which he baptized the rest, and certainly it would be ridiculous if Christ baptized in the name of the one to come.

Thirdly: The Baptism of Christ is the Sacrament of the New Testament. As a result, it was instituted by the author of the New Testament, and our adversaries cannot deny this fact. Melanchthon, in *Loci.*, published in 1558 under the title *On the Number of the Sacraments*, says Baptism and the Lord's Supper, as well as Absolution are Sacraments that were instituted in the preaching of Christ, and hence they are Sacraments properly so called. Chemnitz also, in his definition of a Sacrament properly so called, posits as the third condition that it was instituted and commanded in the New Testament. The Baptism of John was not instituted in the preaching of Christ, nor did he command it, rather it began with John before the author of the New Testament began to preach; consequently, it is not a Sacrament of the New Testament, much less the same with Christ's Baptism.

Fourthly: The Baptism of Christ cannot be repeated. All Catholics teach this, as well as the heretics of our day, apart from the Anabaptists. On the other hand, those who were baptized by John were commanded to be baptized again by the Apostles; thus, what John administered was not the Baptism of Christ. Calvin denies the assumption of this argument, as well as others, but it will be proved in the *third proposition*.

Moreover, Chemnitz denies the consequent, after the assumption has been admitted. He supposes, as we said above, that those whom John had baptized could be baptized in the Baptism of Christ, because although the ministry is the same in regard to its substance, nevertheless, it differs in regard to *signification*. Chemnitz distinguished three things which effect the same thing under a different signification, Circumcision, the Baptism of John, and the Baptism of Christ, of which Circumcision means the Messiah to come, the Baptism of John that the Messiah is already on the way and

Chapter XX: John's Baptism and Christ's

coming, the Baptism of Christ that the Messiah has come. From there, he gathers that just as those who came to John should be circumcised so as to be baptized in his Baptism, so they should profess that they believe that the Messiah is now coming, although they would be justified through Circumcision; so even those baptized by John should later be baptized in the Baptism of Christ so as to profess that they believe the Messiah has come, although they were already justified in the Baptism of John.

On the other hand, we object to these sophistries of Chemnitz firstly from Augustine, who in *On Baptism* (5, 9) comes to the same conclusion as we do and which Chemnitz denies, "Paul commanded the men who had previously been baptized in the Baptism of John, as we read in Acts of the Apostles, to be baptized because the Baptism of John was not the Baptism of Christ." Besides, if Chemnitz's reasoning would avail, we would also prove those baptized by the Apostles before Christ's passion and resurrection should be baptized again after the resurrection, for the Baptism of Christ before his passion, signified the future passion of Christ, but later it began to signify the past passion of Christ.

CHAPTER XXI

The Baptism of John Did Not Have the Same Force and Efficacy Which the Baptism of Christ Had

THE *second* proposition: *The Baptism of John did not have the same force and efficacy which the Baptism of Christ had.* Note, the question is not whether the Baptism of John *could* forgive sins from the devotion and faith of those coming to him or even from the contrition which men conceived from the preaching and Baptism of John. That could easily happen, and some of the Fathers receive the words of Mark 1:4 in this way, namely "preaching a Baptism of repentance in remission of sins" (Basil, *de Baptismo* 1, 2; and Gregory of Nyssa, his brother, in the *Oration* on the praises of Basil; as well as the author of *Questions on the New Testament*, quest. 29, in the fourth tome of the works of St. Augustine). Augustine also (*On Baptism* 5, 10), although he supposed those words must be received otherwise, nevertheless, did not suppose that those who teach the Baptism of John remitted sins in *some mode* must contentiously be resisted, provided they affirm there is a distinction between the Baptism of Christ and John. Thus, the whole question is whether the Baptism of John was efficacious, as the Baptism of Christ, so that if the Baptism of Christ remits sins *by its own power*, or *ex opere operato* (as we proved above), the same must be attributed to the Baptism of John.

Besides, our adversaries attribute the same efficacy and effect to both Baptisms. The Council of Trent, however (sess. 7, can. 1 on Baptism), decreed the contrary in these words, "If anyone will say that the Baptism of John had the same power as the Baptism of Christ, *anathema sit.*" This truth is proven *firstly* from Scripture. In Mk. 1:8, John the Baptist distinguished his Baptism from the Baptism of Christ, because he baptized in water, while Christ was going to baptize in the Spirit, "I baptized you in water, but he will baptize you in the Holy Spirit."

Melanchthon, Calvin, and Chemnitz respond (*loci cit.*) that in this passage John meant to distinguish the external ministry, which suited him, from the internal ministry, which is of Christ alone. Therefore, they say that in the Baptism of John remission was given, but by Christ *through the ministry* of John. And Chemnitz adduces a similar passage, from 1 Cor. 3:6, "I planted, Apollo watered, but God gave the increase."

Yet, this answer is easily refuted. John speaks about his ministry in *the past* tense, but on the operation of Christ in *the future* tense, "I baptized you in water, he will baptize you in the Holy Spirit." So, Christ did not

Chapter XXI: John's Baptism and Christ's

give remission through the ministry of John, or else he would have said, "I baptized you with water, but he baptized you in the Holy Spirit"; just as Paul, in the passage cited by Chemnitz, did not say, "I planted, Apollo watered, God will give the increase," rather, "God gave the increase." Hence, among the other Evangelists (Matt. 3:11 and Lk. 3:16), John speaks in the present tense, "I baptize you with water," and on Christ in the future, "He will baptize you in the Holy Spirit, and fire."

Chemnitz tries to oppose our answer in two ways: *Firstly*, he says on p. 191 that through the Baptism of Christ in the Holy Spirit, and fire, the effusion of visible gifts is understood, which took place on the day of Pentecost. He shows it both from the word "fire," and from the testimony of Christ and Peter, who take up this phrase from John. In Act. 1:5, Christ said to the Apostles, "John baptized with water, you, however will be baptized with the Holy Spirit in a few days." And Peter in Act. 11:6, "I recall the word of the Lord, just as he said: John indeed baptized with water, you however will be baptized in the Holy Spirit." Therefore, the Baptism of John is not opposed to the Baptism of Christ, but the Baptism of water, in which the Holy Spirit is not visibly given, is opposed to that visible effusion of gifts, which took place without water in the primitive Church after Baptism, when the Apostles imposed hands.

This first answer is not sufficient. In the first place, the word *fire* does not impede us from understanding the words of John, "He will baptize you in the Holy Spirit, and fire," on the Sacrament of Baptism. Nearly all interpreters understand it in this way, and they say the addition of the word "fire" is because after the Baptism of Christ the fire of tribulation follows, as well as the fire of divine judgment, and the fire of purgatory, and in the primitive Church the Holy Spirit was given after Baptism in the visible form of fire through the laying on of the hands of the Apostles. See Hilary, Jerome, and Chrysostom on Matthew 3, and Ambrose and Bede on Luke 3. In what pertains to the words of Christ and Peter, however, it is not certain that Christ and John the Baptist said those words in the same sense. The Lord could allude to the words of John, and still advance them in another sense, as St. Bernard frequently does in using the words of Scripture, and also as St. Paul cites the words of Epimenidis in Tit. 1:12, in another sense, when he says, "Cretans are always liars, this testimony is true." Moreover, the Fathers, as I said, explain the words of John on the Sacrament of the Baptism of Christ; however, the words of Christ and Peter cannot be explained except on the sending of the Holy Spirit.

Lastly, if we were to admit both John and Christ, along with Peter, advanced these words in the same sense, then we will say three Baptisms are distinguished according to the Scriptures. One in water alone, and this was of John, because in Scripture it is perpetually said to be in water, to distinguish it against the Baptism in the Spirit. The other in the Spirit and in fire alone, i.e., not in water, and this is the visible sending of the

Holy Spirit, which indeed does not only contain that visible appearance of fiery tongues, but also internal charity and grace infused by the Holy Spirit, which is signified by these external symbols, as even Chemnitz admits (p. 192). This is why the Baptism of John in water alone is not only distinguished against the Baptism of fire, i.e., the visible form of fire, but also against the Baptism of the Spirit, i.e., the internal grace infused by the Holy Spirit. The third Baptism is in water, together with the Spirit, and this is the Sacrament of the Baptism of Christ, which in John 3:5 is said to be from water and the Holy Spirit. Therefore, we see the words of John, however they are understood, always distinguish the Baptism of John, as external and merely corporeal, from the Baptism of Christ, which is partly spiritual and partly corporeal, since it is constituted from the Spirit and fire, or from water and the Spirit.

Now, the second answer of Chemnitz, who, when he saw the first was insufficient, returns to the common answer (p. 193) that "he will baptize you in the Holy Spirit, and fire," is related to the internal operation of Christ in the very Baptism of John. Since the future tense (he will baptize you) seems to be opposed to this sense, Chemnitz tries to show the same Scripture speaks on the operation of Christ even in the present, nay more, even in the past tense. Consequently, he cites those passages of John 1:33, "This is the man who baptizes in the Holy Spirit." There it is said in the present tense, "he baptizes," and still then he neither baptized by himself nor through the disciples; therefore, he baptized through John. Likewise, in verse 16, "And of his fullness we have all received." There, "we have received" is said in the past tense, so Christ worked by an internal operation, even before he began to baptize through disciples. Lastly, in Matt. 3:16, that we would understand that there is no ministry without the efficacy of the Baptist, the Holy Spirit appeared in him baptizing in the form of a dove. He also adds the words of the angel in Lk. 1:16, "He converted many of the sons of Israel to the Lord their God," from which he says it is particularly clear that the ministry of John was not inefficacious.

This shall be refuted with hardly any effort. In the first place, Chemnitz never gives the reason why all the Evangelists speak in the future tense, "He will baptize," if Christ worked interiorly in the time in which John worked outwardly.

Then, the passages he has brought forward do not bear on the matter, for "his is the man who baptizes in the Holy Spirit" does not mean that Christ baptized at the moment when John spoke thus; rather, it means that Christ, *when he baptizes*, does so in the Holy Spirit, not in water alone as John did (as Augustine rightly explains (*Tract. in Jo.* 13, and elsewhere). Similarly, when John says in the same place, "Behold the lamb of God, behold he who takes away the sin of the world," he meant Christ was going to take away the sins of the world, since that is the nature of the lamb immolated on the cross; not, however, because he would take them away

Chapter XXI: John's Baptism and Christ's

at the very moment when John spoke. The verse "We have all received of his fullness" means the grace with which John was endowed flowed from Christ, so also the grace of all the other saints. Why did John the Baptist say this? Even if, on account of the merits of Christ, he foresaw grace was given to all the saints, nevertheless, it was not given through the Baptism of John, but *in another way and through other instruments.* Moreover, the dove, which appeared while John baptized, did not witness the efficacy of the ministry of John, as Chemnitz foolishly and rashly writes. Otherwise, it would be fitting to affirm the ministry of John was efficacious in Christ himself, for the dove only appeared when Christ was being baptized. This is impious and blasphemous. The efficacy of John's Baptism did not need an innocent lamb, who takes away the sins of the world, as John witnesses in the same place. Therefore, the dove signified the innocence and purity of Christ himself, and that he was the one who would sanctify, and cleanse the waters, and through the waters and the Spirit, regenerate men.

Lastly, the words of the Angel in Lk. 1:16 are not said in regard to the Baptism, but on the *preaching* of John. No man denies, however, that John efficaciously preached and converted a great many men to God. It is one thing, however, in the preaching of the word to move the hearts of men, and another to cleanse these through Baptism. That is enough for the first argument.

Secondly, it is proven from the testimonies of the Fathers. Origen, on *Romans* 5, explaining chapter 6, teaches and proves with a few arguments that the Baptism of John did not remit sins, and in this it is distinguished from the Baptism of Christ. Other Greek Fathers teach the same thing (Justin *Quaest. 37 ad Orthodoxos*; Gregory Nazianzen *Orat. On the Holy Lights*; John Chrysostom *Homil.* 10 & 12 on Matthew, and *Homil.* 16 on John, and *Homil.* 1 & 40 on Acts). The author of the *Homilies on Mark*, which is found in the second volume of Chrysostom (*Homil.* 1) says the same thing. Cyril of Alexandria on John (2, 57) where he avowedly treats on this and says the Holy Spirit foresaw that in the future some rash men, who did not differentiate between the Baptism of Christ and of John, would overthrow John himself, that he clearly said he only baptized in water. St. John Damascene (*de fide* 4, 10) holds the same thing, as well as Theophylactus on *Luke* 3. Lastly, St. Basil, even if he says in *On Baptism* (book 1) that the Baptism of John gave the remission of sins, nevertheless in the same book he speaks in this way, "As much as the Holy Spirit is more excellent than water, so also the man who baptizes in the Holy Spirit surpasses the man who baptizes in water, and Baptism itself." In *Orat.* 13, which is an exhortation to Baptism, he has, "John preached a Baptism of penance, the Lord, however, announced a Baptism more excellent by far, that of the adoption of sons. Likewise, the Baptism of John was for beginners, that of Christ for the perfect. The former called away from sin, the latter joined with God and rendered men part of his household." From this we understand that Basil did not attribute the same efficacy to the Baptism of Christ and of John, nay more, he did not attribute any power to justify to the Baptism of John, except by reason of penance and contrition. In this way, the words of Gregory of Nyssa should also be understood.

Now from the Latins. Tertullian (*de Baptismo*) says, "John's Baptism supplied nothing heavenly, but he was appointed over heavenly things, namely penance. ... Rather, were it a heavenly Baptism, then he would have given the Holy Spirit and remission of sins." There, Tertullian contends that the Baptism of John was not heavenly, but human, because it did not give the Holy Spirit, nor the remission of sins. Later, he adds, "Now, that Baptism of repentance was dealt with as if it were a candidate for the remission and sanctification shortly about to follow in Christ," from which we understand in what way the words of the same author should be received, "Nor is there any distinction between those whom John baptized in the Jordan and those whom Peter baptized in the Tiber." He does not speak on the whole Baptism, but only on the matter, and he teaches that it is no importance with which water someone is baptized. The other Latin Fathers speak in a similar fashion. Cyprian (*Serm.* On Baptism); Hilary (*on Matt.* 3); Optatus (*Contra Parmenianum* 5); Ambrose (*on Luke* 3); and Ambrose also in his Preface for Psalm 37 calls the Baptism of Christ the *eye of graces*, because it gave grace and the Baptism of John, the *eye of supplicants*, because it was only a Baptism of Penance. Jerome (*Dialogue contra Luciferianos*) holds similar things, and Innocent I (*Epist.* 22, 5), Leo (*Epist.* 4, 6), and Gregory (*Homil supra Evangelia.* 7, 20). Lastly, Augustine in many places (*Epist.* 48 and 163; *Enchirid.* 49; *Contra Literas Petiliani* 2, 37 & 3, 76; *Contra Donatistas* 5, 9-10 & 14; *de Unico Baptismo* 7; *de Unitate Ecclesiae* 18; *Tract. in Joa.* 5).

Calvin does not answer these citations other than scorning them, as he is wont, for he speaks in this way in the *Institutes* (4, 15 §7), "This is why it disturbs no man that the Fathers put effort into distinguishing the one [Baptism] from the other [Baptism]. These should be no more than a pebble to us, that would shake the certitude of Scripture. Who would listen to Chrysostom more than Luke? Nor should Augustine's petty argument be accepted, that sins were forgiven in John's Baptism in hope, but really forgiven in the Baptism of Christ." We, on the other hand, can speak more correctly: Who would listen to Calvin more than Chrysostom, and Augustine, and so many ancient and learned Fathers? The question is not whether we should believe Luke or the Fathers, but *whether Calvin understood Luke better than so many Fathers.*

Next, Chemnitz, in his *Examination* (*loc. cit.*), tries to show in nearly the whole disputation, that question is not necessary and hence does not report on whether they said this or that. On the other hand, the Fathers themselves do not speak in this way. Jerome, in his *Dialogue against the Luciferians*, does not think this matter is so very trifling, since he says the men who confuse these Baptisms have gone out into *perverse doctrine*, and

Chapter XXI: John's Baptism and Christ's

when they attribute more to the Baptism *of a servant* than is right, they destroy the very Baptism of the Lord. Augustine (*Contra Literas Petiliani*, 2, 37), where he had said the Baptism of John is not the Baptism of Christ, also did not unite any part or degree of the contrary opinion, and assails it as an impious and *sacrilegious* opinion. Lastly, Cyril of Alexandria (on *John* 2, 57), calls those temerarious who think the contrary.

After these have been omitted, the truth is proved *thirdly* from the very person and office of John. John was the *precursor* of the Lord and only came for this purpose, that he would prepare the way for him. The Angel foretold this in Lk. 1:17, "He will go before him in the spirit and truth of Elijah, to convert the hearts of fathers to their children. ... To prepare a perfect people for the Lord." His father foretold the same thing, "You will go before the face of the Lord to prepare his ways" (Lk. 1:76). Next, he witnesses the same thing, producing the prophecy of Isaiah in Jn. 1:23, "I am the voice crying out in the wilderness, prepare the way of the Lord." Certainly, to prepare the way for the Savior is not to give salvation and justify, but *to dispose* to receive the savior and salvation; otherwise, he would have been a *Savior*, not a precursor of the Savior. This is why his father Zachariah, in Lk. 1:77, properly designating the office of the Baptist ("to give knowledge of salvation to his people"), did not say to give salvation, but *knowledge of salvation*. John taught how salvation would be found, namely by belief in Christ, since he points him out with his finger and says, "Behold the Lamb of God, behold he who takes away the sin of the world."

CHAPTER XXII

That after the Baptism of John It Was Necessary to Receive the Baptism of Christ

THE *third* proposition: *It became necessary to obtain the Baptism of Christ after the Baptism of John.* This is against Chemnitz, who calls it into doubt, and against Calvin and the rest, who openly deny it. It is proved *firstly*, from the words of John in Matt. 3:11, Lk. 13:16, Mk. 1:8, "I baptize in water, he will baptize you in the Holy Spirit, and fire." If here a comparison were to be made between the Baptism of Christ and of John, we clearly see that the same men whom John baptized are said to need to be baptized again by Christ. Moreover, it happens to be the case that the comparison of the two Baptisms is the common opinion of interpreters, such as Ambrose, and Bede (on *Luke*), Hilary, Jerome, Chrysostom (on Matthew), and of other Fathers whom we have cited.

Secondly, it is proven from the history of the Gospel and Acts. As we read in Mk. 1:5 and Matt. 3:5, as well as Lk. 3:7, all of Jerusalem and Judaea, as well as all the regions near the Jordan, went out to John to be baptized. Nevertheless, after the Lord's Ascension on the very day of Pentecost in Jerusalem, St. Peter began to preach the necessity of Christ's Baptism to all men, "Do penance, and be baptized every one of you in the name of Jesus," and three thousand were baptized, then a little later five thousand, apart from those whom Philip later baptized, and the other disciples in various places of Judaea and Samaria, as we see in Act. 2, 4, 8 and in other places. So it is necessary that many that were baptized by John were again baptized by the Apostles. How believable would it be that among so many thousands whom the Apostles baptized in Jerusalem, there was no one who had before been baptized by John, if it is true what Mk. 1:5 says, that all of Jerusalem was baptized by John?

Thirdly, it is expressly proven from Act. 19:5, where Paul commands twelve men to be baptized in the name of the Lord, who had confessed that they had nothing other than the Baptism of John.

It is incredible that our adversaries devise so many different explanations for this passage; at least ten are numbered among their different opinions. 1) *Firstly*, that in this chapter, Baptism is always received metaphorically, both when it is a question on the Baptism of John, and when it is a question on the Baptism of Christ. In this way, Zwingli (*True and False Religion*, chapter on Baptism) proposes Baptism be received for *doctrine*, so that the sense would be those twelve men, who previously were only instituted in

Chapter XXII: Necessity of Christ's Baptism 421

the *doctrine of John*, later began to be instituted in *the doctrine of Christ*.

2) The *second* is that Baptism is always received metaphorically, but in the first place for doctrine, in the second place for the gifts of the Holy Spirit, which are given through the laying on of hands. Brenz and Lucas Lossius argue for this in their commentary on Acts 19.

These two explanations are refuted by one argument, that these authors twist the clear and historical words without any cause to an improper signification. It is not lawful, especially in histories, to confect a figure of speech at will; otherwise, nothing would be certain in any Scripture.

3) The *third* explanation is that the Baptism of John is received metaphorically for doctrine; the Baptism of Christ properly, and also so those twelve men were only baptized once, and by Paul, not by John. This is of Henry Bullinger (on *Act.* 19).

4) The *fourth* is contrary to those above, that the Baptism of John is received properly, whereas the Baptism of Christ improperly *for doctrine*. Thus claims Chemnitz (*Exam.* pp. 198-199), where he also tries to drag Ambrose into this opinion (*On the Holy Spirit* 1, 3 as well as the *Interlinear Gloss* on Acts 19).

5) The *fifth* is of Calvin (*Insit.* 4, 15 §18), that the Baptism of John is received properly, the Baptism of Christ improperly, not for doctrine, as Chemnitz says, but *for the gifts of the Holy Spirit*.

These three expositions, apart from the fact that they make up figures of speech in a history at will, also admit a foul equivocation in the same chapter within a few lines. What Chemnitz says is not true, that this is the explanation of Ambrose or the *Interlinear Gloss*. Ambrose (in his commentary on Gal. 3 as well as *On the Holy Spirit* 1, 3) clearly says those twelve men were *truly and properly* baptized at Paul's command. Chemnitz also admits this on the following page; so, in two pages he opposes himself in citing Ambrose. The *Interlinear Gloss*, however, only says they were not *rebaptized*, because the words of Paul corresponded with the doctrine of John. There, the *Gloss* does not deny that those men were *truly* baptized at the command of Paul; rather, it denies that it was an *Anabaptism*. Anabaptism is the repetition *of the same Baptism*, for they were not sprinkled twice in the same Baptism, but in two very different ones. The commentators understood from the words of Paul that the Baptism of John was one thing, and of Christ another, and that John also taught this.

6) The *sixth* exposition is that in that very chapter, Baptism is always received properly but it is not done except in regard to the Baptism of John. Accordingly, the authors of this exposition deny they are of Luke's narration, namely, what these men should do after they heard the words of Paul. Rather, they are of the narration of the same Paul, on what the disciples of John customarily did after they heard the words of the same John preaching that Christ was going to come, namely, that they were baptized by the same John in the name of the Christ to come.

Nicholas Selnecker recites this explanation and praises it as elegant and pious (*Paedagogia* 2 part.). Whatever it is, it is hardly pious and probable, rather, a sophism. *Firstly*, Paul says that John baptized the people; *secondly*, he adds the same John in baptizing admonished the people to believe in the Christ to come. So, if the following words (*after they heard this they were baptized*) pertained to the people to whom John spoke, it follows that the people were baptized *twice* by John, or certainly, that Paul did not explain the matter correctly—both of which are absurd. Lastly, either those twelve men were baptized in the Baptism of Christ at Paul's command, or they were not. If they were baptized, it is the very thing which we contend. If they were not baptized, what is the purpose of Paul's narration? Certainly, Paul taught these men who were baptized in John's Baptism alone for no other reason than that they would understand the Baptism of Christ is necessary *besides*.

7) The *seventh* exposition is that the word "Baptism" is received properly in the whole chapter, and those twelve men were baptized twice. Nevertheless, it took place because they did not have the true Baptism of John, but a corrupt and adulterated one in regard to the form, namely, without the name of the Holy Spirit, as the Centuriators teach (*Cent.* 1, 2, 6 col. 496) as well as Bucer (*Commentary* on Matt. 3). Ambrose seems to have favored this opinion not a little. In his commentary on *Galatians* 3, and *On the Holy Spirit* (1, 3), he says those whom Paul commanded to be baptized in Act. 19:5 were not previously baptized in the true Baptism of John, but in a certain Baptism, which was said to be of John, but was not.

This exposition rests upon a false foundation; namely that John baptized in the name of the Trinity, or certainly in the name of the Christ to come, which (as we said above) is not true. Moreover, Ambrose indeed says those twelve men did not have the true Baptism of John, but he does not say that if they had the true one, they would not have been baptized again, which our adversaries contend. Nay more, the contrary is gathered from his testimonies. On Luke 3, he clearly says the Baptism of John was only in water and of penance, not grace, and different from the Baptism of Christ which is constituted from water and the Spirit, and confers grace.

8) The *eighth* exposition is that the Baptism of those twelve men was corrupted not by reason of the form, but by reason of those approaching it, who were not rightly instructed in the doctrine of the Lord when they approached, since they were ignorant of the Holy Spirit and the Baptism of Christ itself. So Otho Brunfels teaches in his annotations on Acts 19.

This exposition is refuted, because ignorance does not violate Baptism. And truly, Calvin did not say it badly when he refuted this exposition, saying, "The waters would not suffice if they needed a new Baptism to correct for ignorance of this sort" (*Instit.* 4, 15 §18).

9) The *ninth* is that those twelve men were really rebaptized, but badly, and through an error, and before Paul came there. So says Musculus (*Loci*

tit. *De Baptismo*).

This exposition corrupts the text; nothing in the text is more clear than that after they heard Paul, they were baptized at his command.

10) The *tenth* is of Chemnitz in his *Examination of the Council of Trent* (2 part. pp. 196 & 202), where he says that passage is very obscure, since it is explained in so many different ways by the doctors, and on that account, each exposition may be true, for nothing could be gathered from it for certain, for doctrines must not be proved from ambiguous passages.

We oppose ourselves to all of these perversions [of the Scripture]. *Firstly*, the text itself, which, if it were explained simply, and properly, and without prejudice to some preconceived opinion, without a doubt offers the sense which we defend. *Secondly*, we supply the unanimous consensus of the Fathers we have cited, and especially Augustine, who constantly teaches those men were baptized again (*loci cit.*), something all the ancient expositors of Acts hold, such as Chrysostom, Bede, and Oecumenius. Nor can the passage be called ambiguous because the heretics do not agree in explaining it; this sort of ambiguity does not arise from the nature of the thing, i.e., from the obscurity of the book, but from *their pertinacity* in defending their errors. Otherwise, even the Fathers would not agree if the passage was truly ambiguous, and if every passage were to be called ambiguous in which some men do not agree, then altogether nothing could be proven from the Scriptures, for there are no passages in which one cannot disagree from another, if he means to act pertinaciously.

CHAPTER XXIII
Objections Are Answered

1) THE *first* argument is of Calvin in his *Antidote to the Council of Trent*, as well as in the *Institutes*, which we cited above. It was the same doctrine, the same rite, the same oblation of grace in the Baptism of John and of Christ; thus, it was the same Baptism and the same efficacy. The antecedent proves it, for what pertains to doctrine, John preached Christ is the holocaust for our sins, when he says in John 1:29, "Behold the lamb of God, behold he who takes away the sin of the world," which certainly is the summary of the whole Christian doctrine. Inasmuch as the rite, he baptized in water and in the name of Christ, as is clear in Act. 19:4. Lastly, inasmuch as the oblation of grace, both baptized in penance and in the remission of sins, as is clear from the Baptism of John in Lk. 3:3 and of Christ in Act. 2:38.

I respond: This argument is the particular foundation of the position of our adversaries and Chemnitz, Melanchthon, and others use it, but it is not difficult to answer. What pertains to doctrine, our adversaries err in two ways, namely in the antecedent and the consequent of the argument. Accordingly, it is not true that the doctrine of John and Christ were the same, except in the sense that John taught *nothing contrary* to Christ. Otherwise, John taught nothing on the resurrection of Christ, nay more, he did not even expressly teach on the passion. The fact that he called him the Lamb of God could be related to his innocence and meekness, even if he were not a victim. Next, doctrine does not make the essence and truth of a Sacrament, otherwise the heretics, who have false doctrine, would have false Sacraments, which is the error of the Donatists and is also rejected by Calvin and the Lutherans. So, just as the diversity of doctrine does not make a different Baptism, so the similitude of doctrine cause Baptisms to be one or similar.

In regard to the rite, we showed above that there was no similitude except in the *matter*.

In regard to the oblation of grace, what Calvin says is false, namely that "both baptized in penance and in the remission of sins." John's Baptism is everywhere called a Baptism of Penance (Matt. 3:11, Mk. 1:4, Lk. 3:3, Act. 13:24 and 19:4). The Baptism of Christ was never called a Baptism of Penance, rather, the laver of regeneration (Tit. 3:5). The objection from Act. 2:38 does not convict the matter. Peter does not say the Baptism of Christ is the Baptism of Penance, i.e., that it calls one to penance, as John's Baptism did. Rather, he says penance is required *as a disposition before Baptism itself.*

Chapter XXIII: Objections Are Answered

He says, "Do penance, and let every one of you be baptized." Consequently, penance stands in the contrary place in the Baptism of Christ to where it was in the Baptism of John. Penance follows the Baptism of John as its *effect*; it precedes the Baptism of Christ as its *disposition*. What pertains to the remission of sins however, is attributed to the Baptism of Christ as its *immediate* effect in Acts 2:38, "Let each one of you be baptized in the name of Jesus Christ in remission of sins." In Ephes. 5:26, "Cleansing it in the laver." Tit. 3:5, "He saved us through the laver ..." In the Baptism of John, the remission of sins is never attributed as an immediate and proximate effect; our adversaries can only advance the words of Mk. 1:4 and Lk. 3:3, "Preaching a Baptism of penance in remission of sins." There, however, the remission of sins is not attributed to Baptism, but *the penance*, which that Baptism called forth.

This is the sense of that passage: John preached a Baptism of penance, i.e., that which incited and invited to penance. Whoever did such a penance, as they should, would obtain the remission of sins. The Fathers who attribute a great many things to the Baptism of John explain it in this way, such as Basil and Gregory of Nyssa (cited above). So others such as Tertullian (*de Baptismo*), Augustine (*Contra Donatistas* 5, 10), Gregory (*Hom. in Evang.* 20), as well as Bede on Luke 3, who relates the words "in remission of sins" to the Baptism of *Christ*, not John, since John baptized in penance and at the same time preached the Baptism of Christ would be in remission of sins.

2) The *second* argument is of Chemnitz (p. 183). In Eph. 4:5, the Apostle shows through the gradation in the New Testament where there is one body, one spirit, one hope of calling, one Lord, one Father, one faith, there also is one Baptism. Just the same, all of these were in the time of John the Baptist's preaching, as a result then, it was the same Baptism.

I respond: If this argument would avail, then the Baptism of Christ also existed in the time of Moses and David. At that time there was the same one body of the Church, the same hope, the same faith, the same God, etc. Besides, this argument would prove among the heretics that the Baptism of Christ is not a true Baptism, since among them there is not one body, one spirit, one faith, etc. As a result, the Apostle does not show Baptism is the same where the God is the same, the faith is the same, etc., rather, he shows that Christians ought to preserve the *unity of the spirit in the bond of peace* with all diligence, because there is one body, one spirit, one God, one faith, one hope, and they have one Baptism.

3) The *third* argument, which Chemnitz in particular advances (*ibid.* p. 183), is of this sort, that it is the sweetest consolation of all Christians, one and the same Baptism with Christ their head. This consolation perishes if the Baptism of John is not the same as that of Christ, for Christ was baptized by John the Baptist, whereas we in the Baptism of Christ.

I respond: It is not a good consolation which either detracts from the glory of Christ or inflicts contumely and injury. The Baptism of Christ itself, however, we can hardly attribute to Christ without injury to him. Since it is the laver of regeneration and adoption of sins, if it were attributed to Christ, it would seem that he needed regeneration and adoption, which certainly is the greatest blasphemy against Christ, since he is the natural son of God, and was always most holy and full of grace from his very conception, so much so that he could not increase in grace.

Perhaps he will say with Luther, his master, in his *Commentary* on Galat. 3 and in his *Homily On Baptism*, that Christ was indeed holy in himself; still, because he received our sins, he was by the notion of those sins *a thief, a robber, a murderer, and indeed, the greatest sinner of the whole world*, and so needed a Baptism in the remission of sins apart from all men, because it was on account of all men. Now, all of these are mere blasphemies against Christ. Even if Christ took upon himself the burden of our sins, nevertheless, he cannot truly be named a thief, a robber, a murderer, a sinner, as Luther impudently calls him without any example of Scripture or of the Fathers, for a thief is not defined as the man who pays the debt which the thief owes, rather, *who steals someone else's property*. For equal reasoning, Christ cleansed our sins by the works of his virtues, not by the force of some Sacrament administered by another man.

Someone will say that Christ could receive his Baptism not to obtain the effect of regeneration and adoption, but for some other reason, in the way that he received Circumcision, which he did not need, and the Baptism of John, which was a Baptism of Penance, when still he did not need to do penance, and lastly, in the way he received the Eucharist, which he simply did not need.

I respond: Whatever about this, certainly it was more glorious for Christ not to receive his Baptism, than to receive it. While he confers Baptism and does not receive it, he shows himself to be the commander and leader of this army, nay more, who imprints his mark upon others. On the other hand, if he were to receive it, it would seem that he was also enrolled in the army. Lastly, it should be a greater consolation to us that we put on Christ through Baptism and are configured to the similitude of his death, than if we are washed together with him.

4) The *fourth* argument (*ibid.*): When Christ was baptized by John, he sanctified the waters by the contact with his flesh, and besides, willed the visible presence of the Holy Spirit in the appearance of a dove and to sound out by voice that God was well pleased, which are invisibly in our Baptism; consequently, John's Baptism and ours are not different.

I respond: The Fathers bring forward different reasons why Christ wanted to be baptized by John. *a)* The first is, for the example of humility, as he himself says in Matt. 3:15, "Suffer it now, in this way it is fitting for us to fulfill all justice." On that reason, see Augustine (*Enchirid.* 49) and Bernard (*Serm.* 4 *on the Epiphany*). *b)* The second is to confirm the Baptism

Chapter XXIII: Objections Are Answered 427

of John as good and pleasing to God, as Jerome teaches (*Matt.* 3). *c)* The third, to show that sinners ought to receive the Baptism of their Lord, seeing that the Lord himself, the just one, received the Baptism of his servant. Augustine argues this way in *Tractates on John* (tr. 4 and 13). *d) Fourthly*, to wash our crimes in the Jordan, as the Church sings on the day of Epiphany, and as Nazianzen writes in his *Oration on the Holy Lights*, as he drowned the old Adam in the waters and caused the new to emerge. What he did, as we said above, was not by the force of the Baptism he received, but rightly because of his humility. *e) Fifthly*, that he would signify our Baptism in his person, as well as the grace which we receive in it, as Augustine teaches (*de Trinitate*, 15, 36).

It was clear, however, that he instituted and consecrated salutary Baptism. He instituted it by sanctifying the waters with his flesh, as we showed above from Ambrose and Bede commenting on Luke 3, from Chrysostom and Jerome commenting on Matthew 3, and from many other fathers, and at the same time, he figuratively showed the effect of his Baptism when he willed the heaven to be opened, and the Holy Spirit to descend, and the voice to be heard, etc., as is clear from Hilary (in Matt. 3). What do these things do for Chemnitz? Nay more, how do they not oppose Chemnitz? Before the Lord was baptized, a dove never appeared, nor was a voice heard from heaven, nor the waters sanctified, and still, he holds the Baptism of John to be the same as that which was later. As a result, the Baptism which the Lord had from John was not the same as ours, for *he received* it, he did not institute it; ours, however, *he instituted*, he did not receive.

5) The *fifth* argument is also of Chemnitz (*ibid.* p. 119). Paul says in 1 Cor. 12:13 that we are made one body through Baptism. Now, we become one body, not only among ourselves, but also with Christ; therefore, we have one Baptism with Christ.

I respond: This is another contumely against Christ, as if he needed Baptism to become a member of the Church; it is a marvel that Chemnitz did not add also that Christ would obtain remission of sins through faith and penance. Thus, I answer that Paul speaks only about *the body*, not the head, for we are members of Christ and hence become one body of Christ through Baptism, because we are regenerated by this Sacrament and joined to Christ. He became our head, not by Baptism, but *by the grace of the hypostatic union*. In the same way also, the sons of Adam became like a body through carnal generation, but Adam did not become the head of the human race through carnal generation, rather through the singular creation and grace of God.

6) The *sixth* argument: We are one body, not only among ourselves, but also with those who were while John preached and baptized before the Lord began to baptize and yet we are still made one body through one Baptism.

I respond: The Church was always one mystical body; still, men were not always joined to this body by the same Sacrament. At one time, through Circumcision, in regard to the Jews; or in another way, in regard to the Gentiles; now, however, after the time of Christ, through Baptism. As a result, in the time of John there were Jews who were one body through Circumcision, but not through the Baptism of John or Christ. Paul, however, speaks *about his own time.*

7) The *seventh* argument is against the preceding answer. Even in the time of Paul, many were the one body of Christ, who still did not have any but the Baptism of John. The Apostles were not baptized, except in the Baptism of John, save for Paul. *Similarly*, a certain Apollo in Acts 18 did not know any but the Baptism of John, and still he was not compelled to be rebaptized. Lastly, the Baptist himself was not baptized by Christ or by his disciples.

I respond: Tertullian (*de Baptismo*) and Augustine (*Epist.* 108 ad Seleucianum, *On the Origin of the Soul* 3, 9) write and prove that the Apostles were baptized in the Baptism of Christ. When in John 3:5 the Lord so clearly pronounced that no man is saved without Baptism, it cannot be doubted that all who lived after those times received the Baptism of Christ, and it is certain they were joined to the Church of Christ, even if it was not written. Otherwise, we will also deny the Romans, Galatians, Ephesians, Philippians, Timothy, Titus, Philemon, and others to whom Paul wrote, were baptized, because we read no writing when and by whom they were baptized. The same thing can be said in regard to Apollo, who was baptized in the Baptism of Christ, as Chrysostom and Oecumenius affirm in their commentary on Acts 18. Lastly, in regard to John the Baptist, just as it was not written that he was baptized by Christ, so also the contrary was not written. It is a weak conjecture that he was baptized by Christ, because Matt. 3:4 says, "I should be baptized by you." Whatever about this matter, it is certain he was at least baptized by Christ *in the Spirit*, as Nazianzen affirms (*Orat. On the Holy Lights*), as well as Jerome, and the author of the incomplete commentary on Matt. 3, which Chrysostom cites. Yet, if John was not baptized by water, it is no wonder, because he died before the law on the Baptism of Christ became obligatory.

CHAPTER XXIV

On the Ceremonies of Baptism

THOMAS WALDENS wrote copiously about the ceremonies of those receiving Baptism (*de Sacramentalibus*, tom. 3, tit. 5, cap. 45) and on the following seven, against John Wycliffe, who rejected nearly all the rites and ceremonies of the Catholic Church in regard to Baptism. The Roman Ordinal profusely hands down and explains these same ceremonies. Also Alcuin (*de Divinis Officiis*, c. *de Sabbato Sancto*), Amalarius (*de Officiis Ecclesiasticis* 1), and Rabanus (*De Institutione Clericorum*, 1). From the Fathers, Cyril (*Catecheses*) and Ambrose (*de Sacramentis*).

The heretics of this time also condemn the same rites, with very few exceptions, especially John Calvin in the *Institutes* (4, 15 §19) and Illyricus (*Cent.* 1, 2,6; *Cent.* 2, c. 6) who still do not advance any argument except that these rites are not in Scripture nor commended by precept or example.

On the other hand, we object two things to them. 1) *Firstly*, they also prescribe something in the administration of Baptism which they do not find in Scripture. In a little book on the formula for the administration of the Sacraments, Calvin prescribes: *Firstly*, that an infant should be brought for Baptism on Sunday, or certainly on another day in which people come together in the Church for a sermon, so that the Baptism would take place in the presence of the people. *Secondly*, those who bring the infants should be asked whether they promise to instruct them in the doctrine of faith and morals, so when they come to adolescence, they will continue in the promise made in Baptism. *Thirdly*, to give a name to the infant being baptized. *Fourthly*, that the form of the Sacrament be pronounced in the language of the country. *Fifthly*, that they recite the Creed, and the Lord's Prayer, and other prayers, but none of these are found in Scripture. The Lutherans also add the renunciation of Satan and his allurements, as is clear from the Saxon ritual and other similar books. This is why Illyricus did not dare to reject the renunciation in the *Centuries* (1, lib. 2, cap. 6, col. 497), and even Chemnitz himself (*Examination of the Council of Trent*, 2 part. p. 219) in his examination of canon 7 on Baptism. There he upholds those to be baptized must display the renunciation. Lastly, Luther, in his *Catechism*, would have it that the sign of the Cross be depicted on the forehead and heart of the one to be baptized. I would like to see some testimony or example of these things in the Scriptures. Scripture recounts the Baptism of many thousands in Acts 2:41 and 4:4. Likewise, the Eunuch of the Queen of Ethiopia in Acts 8:38, St. Paul in Acts 9:18, Cornelius in

Acts 10:47, Lydia and the guard of the jail in Acts 16:33, and the twelve Asiatics in 19:5, but there is no mention in these verses about Sunday, or a Church, or the gathering of the people, or giving a name, or taking up a promise or the Lord's Prayer, the Apostles' Creed, or even the sign of the cross, which even the Centuriators note are not found in Scripture (*Cent.* 1, lib. 2, cap. 6, col. 496 & 497). Nor is it opposed that the Lord's Prayer is in Scripture, as well as the Creed, at least in regard to the sense, for in Scripture, it is not held *that they recite it in Baptism*; nay more, no prayer is read to have been made in so many passages of Scripture where it relates Baptisms. So, either our adversaries altogether reject all ceremonies, and only baptize by sprinkling water and reciting the words, or certainly, they should look for other arguments with which to oppose the rites approved by the Church.

2) The *second* thing that we object to them is the testimony of the Fathers of the Church. All the rites which we use now are very ancient; they either flow from the tradition of the Apostles or they were instituted by very holy Fathers, whose authority, especially confirmed by so many centuries, ought to avail more among us than the din of the innovators, since they cannot prove to us that anything is *against* the Scripture. Consequently, we must furnish this alone, that we would advance the testimonies of antiquity for each rite. That is more easily done if we distribute the ceremonies of Baptism in three classes. Those that precede Baptism, those that accompany it, and those that follow it.

CHAPTER XXV

There are Twelve Ceremonies Before Baptism

1) THE *first* ceremony is that Catechumens who desire to be baptized *would give their name*, and from that time they are called Competents (*Competentes*) or Chosen (*Electi*) and received by the Church to be instructed and prepared for Baptism. Hence, there are two kinds of Catechumens (as Rabanus teaches). One, of those who listen to sermons and will to become Christians, but have not yet sought Baptism; these are called *auditors*, or *those listening*. Others seek Baptism and are called *Competents* or *Chosen*. St. Leo (*Epist.* 4, 5&6) calls them *electi*, as they are also called in the Roman Ordinal, but Augustine ordinarily calls them *Competentes*, for he says (*On the Care for the Dead*, 12), "As Easter was approaching, he gave his name among other Competents." See also *Confess.* 9, 6, *de Fide et Operibus* 6; *Serm. de Tempore* 116, which is to the Competents. Jerome uses the same name in *Epist. ad Pamach. On the errors of John of Jerusalem*.

2) The *second* ceremony is *the scrutiny*, which means a certain proper examination and exploration whether the Competents firmly and sincerely believe; still this term embraces also Catechism, and Exorcism, and all ceremonies which are done from the day on which they give their name, even to the day on which they are baptized. Seven scrutinies are conducted, the principal one of which is the third, and it usually takes place on the Wednesday after the fourth Sunday of Lent. Then, nearly all the ceremonies are done on which we will soon speak, as is clear from the authors cited above. Hence, not only does the Roman Ordinal use this word "scrutiny," but also Alcuin, Amalarius, and Rabanus, and even more ancient authors, such as Augustine (*de Fide et Operibus* 6), and Leo (*Epist.* 4,6 *ad Episcopos Siciliae*).

Other fathers clearly call to mind ceremonies of this sort, such as Cyprian (*de Duplici Martyrio*), Origen (*Hom.* 12 *on Numbers*), Cyril (*Catechesi Myst.* 1), Basil (*de Spiritu Sancto* 11 et 27), Chrysostom (*Hom.* 21 *ad populum*), Ambrose (*de Sacramentis* 1,2; 2,7), Jerome (on *Amos* 6), Augustine (*On the Creed to Catechumens* 1; *On the Merit and Remission of Sins* 1, 34).

4) The *fourth* ceremony is the profession of faith, which they answer as often as they are asked, and later, on the very day of Baptism, they also pronounce it publicly by reciting the Creed. Clement and Dionysius call to mind this ceremony. Likewise, Origen (*Hom.*5 on *Num.*); Cyprian (*Epist.* 1, 12); Cyril (*Catech.* 1); Hilary (on Matt. 15); Jerome, in his *Dialogue against the Luciferians*; Epiphanius (*Anchorato*), and Augustine in *On Faith and*

Works (11; and *Confess.* 8,2) where he relates the history of the Baptism of Vicotrinus. When the priests offered to him that he might recite the symbol of faith privately if he wished, he preferred to pronounce the faith publicly from an elevated place, by his custom [as an orator].

5) The *fifth* is the *sign of the cross on the forehead and the chest*; the sign of the cross is imprinted on each during the scrutinies by priests or by clergy. Dionysius calls this ceremony to mind (*loc. cit.*), as well as Basil (*On the Holy Spirit* 27), who places this ceremony among the Apostolic traditions such as the renunciation and other things which are done in Baptism. Augustine, in *On Catechizing the Unlearned* (20), addressing a catechumen on the first day of instruction, says, "By the sign of the cross on the forehead, today you are going to be signed just as the doorpost." See the same thing in *Epist.* 118, in Ps. 36; *Tract. on John* 3 and 36, and *Serm.* 19 on the saints.

6) The *sixth* ceremony is exorcism, i.e, the adjuration of demons carried out with certain prayers, that they would recede from the baptized man. Calvin singles out this ceremony to mock even more than the rest, calling it inane and fictitious (*Instit.* 4, 19 §24). Now, we can easily show that everything which the Church today retains in regard to Exorcism from the books of nearly all the Fathers.

In the first place, the most ancient Fathers testify that the Church received the power to coerce demons by exorcisms. Justin Martyr (*Dialogue with Trypho*), "They obey us when they are adjured in the name of Jesus Christ." Tertullian holds the same thing in his book *de Corona Militis*; and *Ad Scapulam, Apologeticus* (32); and in his book *de Spectaculis.* Cyprian, (*ad Demetrianum*) says, "O, if you would see and hear them when we adjure and torture them." Minutius Felix holds similar things in *Octavius.* Lactantius (2, 16) also says that when exorcists ask the demons to give their name, they answer by what name they are called. Bede also calls this to mind in his commentary on Luke 8. See also Lactantius (4, 27; 5, 22) and Augustine (*City of God* 10, 22). Lastly (to pass over countless others), Prudentius sings this way in *Apotheosis*, 403-404; 412-413 against the Jews:

> Apollo is tormented,
> Struck in the name of Christ, he cannot bear
> The lightning of the word.
> The Lord's bishop thunders: Away cunning serpent,
> Cast off your limbs, and loose the hidden coils.
> Cyllene burns and shrieks in the midst of these words,
> Let Jove lament the fires he knows so well.

Next, there is in the Church not only a gift of certain holy things, but also the *ordinary* office of exorcism and coercing demons, as the ancient Councils witness: Antioch (can. 10), Carthage IV (can. 7), Laodicea (can.

Chapter XXV: The Ceremonies Before Baptism

29), as well as the ancient Fathers such as Cyprian (*Epist.* 4, 7), Cornelius (*Epist.* ad Fabium the Antiochen, cited by Eusebius, *hist.* 6, 33).

Thirdly, Exorcisms were not any prayers you like said at the will of the Exorcist, rather *certain prayers prescribed by the Church*, which are properly called exorcisms. This is clear from the fourth Council of Carthage (*loc. cit.*) and from John Micrologus in his work *On Ecclesiastical Observances* (ch. 7), where he also teaches that exorcisms are not concluded "through Christ our Lord," as other prayers, but rather, "through he that is coming to judge the world in fire," because the demons especially fear the last judgment.

Fourthly, Exorcisms *precede Baptism*, as Dionysius witnesses (*loc. cit.*), as well as Nazianzen (*Orat. On the Holy Laver*), "Do not fail to have care of exorcism, for it is itself of natural sincerity. ..." Cyril in *Catech.* 1 says, "Take from the heavenly treasury, and zealously labor in exorcisms." He repeats the same thing in many places in his preface to the *Mystical Catechesis*. See also Cyprian (*Epist.* 4, 7), Ambrose (*de Sacramentis* 1, 5), Optatus (*contra Parmenianum* 4), and Augustine (*de Fide et Operibus* 6; *On Marriage and Concupiscence* 2, 18), who says this is itself the custom of the whole Church, and Celestine I (*Epist.* 1, 12). Lastly, Leo I (*Epist.* 4, 7), where he says that *according to the Apostolic rule*, Catechumens are to be scrutinized with exorcisms.

7) The *seventh* ceremony is the *exsufflation* (act of blowing), which is connected to the exorcisms. By the words of the exorcisms demons are expelled, and the ceremony of the exsufflation signifies their expulsion, and at the same time the breathing in of a good Spirit, which men receive when the evil spirit recedes.

Augustine (*Contra Julianum* 6, 5) says, "The Church would not exorcize the sons of the faithful, nor blow upon them if they would not deliver them from the from the power of darkness and the prince of death. ... You were afraid to mention it, as though you yourself would be exsufflated by the whole world, if you were to contradict this exsufflation whereby even from infants the prince of this world is cast out." He repeats similar things in *On Original Sin* (2, 40) and *On Marriage and Concupiscence* (2, 17, 18), and *Hypognosticus* (5).

8) The *eighth* ceremony is the *taste of salt*. Catechumens are given to taste salt, as is clear from Origen (*Homil.* 6 on *Ezechiel*), and the third Council of Carthage (can. 5); and perhaps Augustine alludes to this salt, when he speaks about his childhood in *Confessions* (1, 11), "I was already signed in the sign of the cross and seasoned by its salt." Blessed bread was given in place of the Eucharist, as Augustine witnesses in *On the Merit and Remission of Sins* (ch. 26). Although, that this salt was also given in place of the Eucharist is certain from the Council of Carthage (*loc. cit.*).

9) The *ninth* is when their noses and ears are touched with saliva and it is said to them, "*Epheta*, that is, be opened." Calvin marvels exceedingly of this, and spits upon it, but Ambrose proves and explains this in his work

de Sacramentis (1, 1) and in his work *On the Mysteries* (c. 1), where he also asserts the example of the Lord, who in Mk. 7:33 touched the tongue of the mute and the ears of the deaf, and said, "Epheta." Thus, were Calvin to ask why we also touch the noses and ears of Catechumens with spit, we may answer that he should tell us why the Lord touched the tongue and ears of the mute and deaf man with spit (Mk. 7:33) and the eyes of the man born blind (John 9:6). Certainly, the Lord could cure anyone he likes without these ceremonies.

10) The *tenth* ceremony is the *laying on of hands and the priestly blessing*. Dionysius calls this to mind (*loc. cit.*), as well as Clement (*Const.* 7, 39), and the fourth Council of Carthage (can. 85). Likewise, Cyprian, relating the acts of this Council of Carthage in the testimony of Vincent a Thibari, asserts that the laying on of hands with exorcisms should precede Baptismal regeneration. Augustine (*On the Merit and Remission of Sins* 2, 26) says, "I regard the Catechumens are sanctified according to their specific manner, through the sign of Christ and the prayer of laying on of hands." Truly, this ceremony is very frequent in Scripture. Even the Lord imposes hands upon children (Matt. 19:15), and the Apostles almost always add the laying on of hands in their prayer over men, as is clear from Act. 8:18, 9:17, 13:3, and elsewhere.

11) The *eleventh* is *anointing*. Catechumens are anointed with blessed oil before Baptism on their chest and shoulders that are going to be anointed with Chrism after Baptism. Clement calls this anointing to mind (*Recognitionum* 3, where we add that even if this book is unreliable in regard to dogma, nevertheless it is very ancient), "Each of you, while in the perennial waters, in the name of the triune beatitude invoked upon you, were anointed in oil that had first been sanctified through prayer." Chrysostom (*hom.* 6 on Coll. 2) says, "The man about to be baptized is anointed after the fashion of athletes who are preparing to enter the race." Justin (*Quaest.* 107) asks why Christians are anointed twice, once before Baptism, and again after it. Ambrose also calls to mind both anointings, indeed the first in *de Sacramentis* 1, 2, the second in 2, 7. Cyril recalls both anointings; the first in the *Second Mystagogical Catechesis* 2, the second in the *Third Mystagogical Catechesis*. Augustine recalls both in *Serm.* 206 *de Tempore*.

12) The *twelfth* is the *abstinence from wine, meat, and even marital relations*, and other works of penance, not for satisfaction, but to be better prepared to approach the Sacrament of Baptism, as is clear from Cyril (*Cateches.* 1), Nazianzen (*Orat.* 1 *On the Holy Laver*), Augustine (*On Faith and Works* c. 6) and the fourth Council of Carthage (can. 85).

CHAPTER XXVI

On the Ceremonies Which Accompany Baptism

These ceremonies are applied in Baptism itself. 1) *Firstly, a name is given to the baptized.* What Illyricus says in the *Centuries* (Cent. 1, 2, 6 col. 497) is utterly ridiculous, because he makes the case that this ceremony was not in use in the time of the Apostles because the Eunuch of Queen Candace in Act. 8 is always called a Eunuch, both before and after Baptism, as if "Eunuch" were the proper name of a person, and not rather designates a vice of the body which cannot truly be removed by Baptism. It seems this ceremony was taken up from the Old Testament. In Circumcision, a name was given to the child, as is clear from Lk. 1:63 in regard to John, and Lk. 2:21 in regard to Christ. Among Christians, Dionysius the Areopagate (*loc. cit.*) calls to mind the same thing among Christians. The ancients, who because they were baptized either at the end of their life, or certainly when they were already adults, did not change their names in Baptism, as is clear from Saul (Act. 9), Cornelius (Act. 10), as well as Ambrose and Augustine, and others. Nevertheless, when infants were baptized, their fathers customarily gave them names of saints, as we do now. That is clear from Dionysius of Alexandria (cited by Eusebius *hist.* 7, 20, in the version of Christopherson). Dionysius writes that the sons of Christians were often customarily given the names of Peter, Paul, John, etc. The same is clear from many of the names of the Fathers such as Peter of Alexandria, Peter the brother of Basil, John Chrysostom, John Cassian, and others, who had Hebrew names although they were Greeks. Nay more, it is also extant on this matter among the Canons of the Council of Nicaea (can. 30), recently translated from Arabic into Latin and published by Francis Turrianus, in which Christians are commanded to give names to their sons in Baptism, not of the pagans, but of Christians.

2) The *second* ceremony is *that they should have helpers*, by whom they are lifted into the sacred font and after more diligently instructed in the faith. Dionysius the Areopagate calls them *susceptores* (helpers), while Tertullian calls them *sponsores* (sponsors). See Augustine on the same in *Serm.* 116 *de Tempore*, which is the third of Palm Sunday, and *On the Merit and Remission of Sins* 1, 34.

3) The *third* is *the consecration of the water*, which Dionysius calls to mind (c. *de Baptismo*), "The water of regeneration is consecrated first by sacred invocations." Cyprian holds the same thing (*Epist.* 1), as well as Ambrose (*de Sacrament.* 1, 5), and Basil in *On the Holy Spirit* (27), where

he calls this Apostolic tradition. Lastly, Augustine (*in Julianum* 6, 8; *Fifty Homilies*, 27, *Tract. in Joan.* 118).

4) The *fourth* is the *three-fold immersion*, which Clement calls to mind (*Can.* 49 *of the Apostles*), Dionysius (*loc. cit.*), Tertullian (*de Corona Militis*; *Contra Praxeam*), Cyril (*Catech.* 2), Basil (*On the Holy Spirit* 27), Chrysostom (*Homil.* 24 *in John*) and Augustine (*Serm.* 91 & 201). Here we must observe, however, that the Arians began to abuse this ceremony (as Gregory writes in *Epist.* 1, 41 to Leander) to make their error firm. When Catholics performed the threefold immersion to signify the three divine persons and the three days of the burial of Christ, as Gregory says (*ibid.*), the Arians used a threefold immersion to signify the three natures of the three persons. This is why it seemed to Gregory that in Spain they did one immersion; the fourth Council of Toledo confirmed the same a little before him (ch. 25). Now, however, it varies by region, either one or the threefold immersion is applied, for neither regards the essence of the Sacrament, as Gregory and the aforementioned Council witness.

5) The fifth is *Paschal time and Pentecost*. Even if Baptism can be given at any time that necessity demands, nevertheless the Fathers most diligently preserved this ceremony, that ordinarily they would only baptize on the Saturdays of Easter and Pentecost. There are decretal epistles extent on this matter from Pope Syricius (1, 2), Leo I (*Epist.* 4 and 80), and Gelasius (1, 12), where they severely rebuke certain Bishops who dared to confer Baptism on Epiphany or the feasts of the Martyrs outside of a case of necessity, and they command the ancient custom to be preserved so that Baptism would only be given in the Easter season and Pentecost. Likewise, that this is an ancient and universal custom is clear from the *Catecheses* of Cyril, which were given in Lent, because they were preparing to celebrate Baptism on Easter. Likewise, from Jerome (*Epist. ad Pammachium*, against the errors of John of Jerusalem), and from the words of Augustine in *On the Care to Be Had for the Dead*, ch. 12, "As Easter was approaching, he gave his name among the other Competents." Then God was pleased that this ceremony could be gathered from a miracle, which Paschasius the bishop relates in an epistle to St. Leo (*Epist.* 64 of Leo), where he says in Sicily, in his time, there was a sacred font, in a very small Church on a certain mountain, and only on the Easter Vigil (the time in which Baptism is given) the waters flowed at the hour for Baptism, although at no time were channels, waterfalls, or water itself ever seen. Illyricus, however, objects from the Acts of the Apostles, which did not preserve these times in baptizing Paul, Cornelius, and similar men. Ambrose answers this objection in his commentary on *Ephesians* 4, where he says that in the beginning of the Church, that the Christian people would easily be propagated, it was conceded to all to baptize at any time; nevertheless, shortly after the Church was constituted, the order was established that only certain men would baptize, namely priests, and only on certain days.

CHAPTER XXVII

On the Ceremonies Which Follow Baptism

The Ceremonies which follow Baptism are five.

1) The *first* seems to have been the *kiss of peace*, as a sign that the baptized is our brother. Cyprian calls this to mind (*Epist.* 3, 8 *ad Fidum*), for he responds to certain men who thought that newborn infants should not be baptized, and advanced the argument because it is fitting to give the kiss of peace to an infant, but everyone hesitates to kiss a newborn infant. Cyprian responds that there is no reason why a Christian should hesitate to kiss that which God himself created.

2) The *second* is *the anointing of Chrism on the crown*; this seems to have been introduced because the bishop was not always present, who could immediately give the Sacrament of Confirmation after Baptism. Therefore, while the baptized is anointed by the priest, it is not on the forehead, but on the crown with Chrism consecrated by the Bishop. Damasus calls this to mind in the life of Sylvester, as well as Innocent I (*Epist.* 1, 3), Ambrose (*de Sacramentis* 3, 1), and Jerome in his *Dialogue against the Luciferians*, where he says it is not lawful for priests to baptize without chrism. There, he clearly speaks in regard to the anointing of chrism which is given by the priest on the crown, for in the same place he asserted a little earlier that the Sacrament of Confirmation is given by none except a bishop.

3) The *third* ceremony is a lit candle, which is given to the Baptized man as a sign of faith and the grace that he has received, and that he has passed from the power of darkness to the light, and lot of the saints. Gregory Nazianzen recalls this ceremony in his *Oration on the Holy Laver*, as well as Augustine on *Ps. 65*, in the verse "we have passed through fire and water."

4) The *fourth* is *a white garment*, which they usually wear from Holy Saturday even to White Sunday. Dionysius recalls this (*de Eccl. Hier.* c. *de Baptismo*), as well as Ambrose (*On Those Who Are Initiated in the Mysteries* c. 7) and Augustine (*serm. 157* on the first day in the octave of Easter).

5) The *fifth* ceremony was once a sample of miLk. and honey, or wine, which, nevertheless, is not in use today. Tertullian recalls this ceremony (*Contra Marcionem* 1), as well as Jerome in his *Dialogue against the Luciferians*, where he says it was customarily done as a sign of the new infancy in Christ. This is why, even in the Mass of White Sunday, the Church reads from the epistle of Peter, "Desire miLk. as newborn infants" (1 Pet. 2:2). It does not seem that this was general, since Jerome, in his *Commentary* on Isaiah 55 on the verse *Buy wine and milk*, writes that it

only flourished in the West. Therefore, it is no wonder if at length it fell away, just as those which Ambrose calls to mind (*de Sacramentis* 1,3), of washing the feet of Neophytes right after Baptism, was particular to certain Churches and so easily died out.

BOOK II

ON THE SACRAMENT OF CONFIRMATION

There are six controversies on the Sacrament of Confirmation. 1) First, whether it is a true and proper Sacrament. 2) Second, on the matter. 3) Third, on the form. 4) Fourth, on the effect. 5) Fifth, on the minister. 6) Sixth, on the ceremonies. So that we may begin the first, there will be three parts of the first controversy. In the first we will relate the errors in regard to the Sacrament of Confirmation. On the second, we will confirm the truth. In the third, we will answer objections.

CHAPTER I

On the Errors and Lies in Regard to the Sacrament of Confirmation

Nearly all of the heretics of our day remove Confirmation from the number of the Sacraments. Even if in 1548 in the gathering at Leipzig, the Theologians of Leipzig and Wittenberg received seven Sacraments, and namely Confirmation as a Sacrament properly so-called and conferring grace, nevertheless, they did not persist in that confession. Accordingly, nearly all of their doctors, both those before that time, and those who wrote after, reject the Sacrament of Confirmation.

Nevertheless, because they cannot deny there was in the ancient Church some rite which should be called Confirmation, they pretended that rite was not indeed a Sacrament instituted by Christ, but was a type of ceremony profitably introduced by the Church, which Chemnitz distinguishes in six headings in his *Examination of the Council of Trent* (2 part. p. 320). He very accurately describes the order of Lutheran Confirmation. *Firstly*, he says that when children baptized in infancy arrive at the years of discretion, they ought to be instructed in the doctrine of the Catechism, and where they at least learn the principles, should be offered to the bishop, who admonishes the boy in the presence of the Church about his Baptism, which he received and promised, etc. *Secondly*, children should publicly receive the confession of faith and doctrine which they learned. *Thirdly*, they should be questioned about the principle Christian chapters and also respond to them. *Fourthly*, they should be advised to show by this profession of faith that they reject all heathen, heretical, fanatical, and profane opinions. *Fifthly*, they should be admonished with a grave exhortation that they must persevere in the agreement made in Baptism and the profession of faith, and be confirmed in that profession. *Sixthly*, public prayer should be made for those children, that God would deign to govern and confirm them in his Holy Spirit in this profession of faith, and at the same time the laying on of hands should be given.

Luther briefly traced out this opinion in his book *On the Babylonian Captivity* (c. On Confirmation), for, he both denies it is a true Sacrament and adds that it can be received for an Ecclesiastical ceremony, such as the consecration of water, and other things, but Luther does not call to mind a Catechism, or an examination in the rite of Confirmation. Zwingli (*On True and False Religion*, c. On the other Sacraments) denies that Confirmation is a Sacrament, and adds it was a rite instituted in the Church for the examination of children who were baptized in infancy. Melanchthon taught the same thing (*Loci*, c. On Confirmation), as well as Calvin in the *Institutes* (4, 19 §4) and Brenz in the *Wittenberg Confess.*, c. On Confirmation, as well as others.

Now, they are not the first who rejected this Sacrament. Wycliffe (*Trialogi* 4, 14) though he did not altogether seem to reject this Sacrament, nevertheless he would not have it that it can be proven from the Scriptures, and clearly rebukes the teaching of Catholics. Nay more, he says that it seemed to certain men that the Confirmation of bishops with all its rites was introduced by the devil; he does not rebuke them, but rather more shows that he prefers a teaching of this sort. In another book, which perhaps is no longer extant, he clearly rejects the anointing of Chrism, as Thomas Waldens testifies (*de Sacramentis*, 2, 113). Before Wycliffe, the Waldensian heretics rejected the same Sacrament, as Aeneas Sylvius testifies in his *Historia Bohemica* (c. 35), and before all these, the Novatianists, about whom Theodoret speaks (*Haeret. Fab.* 3), "The Novatianists from their gathering hinder penance altogether, and do not offer the sacred Chrism to whose they baptize. This is why, when men who came from this heresy are joined to the Church, the blessed fathers command them to be anointed." The reason why the Novatianists rejected this Sacrament seems to be that there was no convincing reason or evident testimony of Scripture, but because

Chapter I: The Errors and Lies about Confirmation

Novatian himself (as Eusebius writes concerning Pope Cornelius, *hist.* 6, 43), reclining on his bed, was baptized without the customary rites of the Church and later he did not take the time to receive the other things which were necessary, nor was he confirmed with the seal of the Holy Spirit. On account of which, since everyone held him in bad repute, he devised this remedy, to deny that it is fitting for men to be anointed with Chrism after Baptism. The Donatists also were contumelious against the holy chrism, as Optatus writes (*Contra Parmenianum* 2), but it is not certain whether the Donatists hated this Sacrament absolutely, or only that it was given by Catholics. Nevertheless, it is probable that they scorned this Sacrament, as even the Arians and many other heretics, since when they came to the Church, they were bidden to be anointed with Sacred Chrism, as we will speak about later.

Now, let us return to the heretics of our time. They weigh down their doctrine with such crass lies and such shameless abuse and blasphemy, that it becomes painfully clear they, who oppose this Sacrament, receive the plenitude of a wicked spirit; just as on the contrary, those who reverently receive it obtain the plenitude of the Holy Spirit.

John Calvin, in his *Antidote to the Council of Trent*, on sess. 7, can. 2, says, "None of the fathers make mention of the oil, nay more, there is nothing from that middle age, which already abounded in many vices." On the other hand, a great many of the Fathers call to mind the oil, even the most ancient. Tertullian, in the first book of his work *Against Marcion*, speaking about the Sacraments of Christ, says, "He neither rejects the water of the creator, whereby he washes his own creation, nor the oil, in which he anoints it." And Augustine (*Contra Donatistas* 5, 20), "If what is said in the Gospel, 'God does not hear sinners' (John 9:31), extends as far as the notion that the Sacraments cannot be celebrated by a sinner, how then does he hear a murderer praying, either over the water of Baptism, or over the oil, or over the Eucharist, or over the heads of those on whom his hand is laid?" Next, Tertullian, Cyprian, and Cyril recall chrism so clearly and frequently that Chemnitz rejects these Fathers by name, and calls the Sacrament the Chrism of Cyril from contempt.

Calvin also (*ibid.* can. 3) calls the Fathers of Trent asses and pigs, although he would have it that he is being rather restrained. Moreover, in the *Institutes* (4, 19 §8) he says, "The word of the anointers says that they received no promise in Baptism to equip them for the contest." On the other hand, no Catholic teaches this. What Calvin cites from the epistle of St. Melchiadis, "In Baptism we are regenerated unto life, in Confirmation we are armed for the fight," is related to the proper effects of these Sacraments. Baptism properly regenerates unto life, although that grace of regeneration also avails to avoid sins; Confirmation, however, is properly given for an increase of strength, and to fight for the faith.

Again (*ibid.* §10) he advances another lie when he says, "Do they not betray themselves as Donatists, who affirm the Sacrament on the basis of the dignity of the minister?" This is because we say the Sacrament of Confirmation cannot ordinarily be conferred except by a Bishop. Now, Calvin is not unaware that the Donatists customarily spoke in regard to another dignity, namely on the dignity of *uprightness and innocence*, not on the dignity of an Ecclesiastical minister. Otherwise, Calvin would also be a Donatist, since he would have it that Baptism cannot be conferred by a layman, nor even a woman, but only by a public minister of the Church. Consequently, he spoke against his own mind and conscience, and in this way lied.

After Calvin had cited the words of St. Melchiadis, Pope and Martyr (*ibid.*), he speaks in this way, "O Sacrilegious mouth! Dare you oppose oil merely polluted with your fetid breath and charmed by your muttered words, to the Sacrament of Christ and compare it with water sanctified by the word of God? But even this was not enough for your shamelessness, but you would also prefer it. Such are the responses of the Holy See, such the oracles of the Apostolic Tripod." Could Calvin more shamefully blaspheme against this most holy man? Could he not more clearly show that there is nothing in common between him and the ancient Church? Accordingly, every Church which existed then communicated with St. Melchiadis, and Augustine speaks about him this way (*Epist.* 162), "What sort of man was St. Melchiadis, that the last thing said of him was, how innocent, how wholesome, how prophetic, and peaceful? ... O best of men, O son of Christian peace, O Father of the Christian people."

Lastly (*ibid.* §11), Calvin advances another lie, "Behold, passing over the water, and holding it of no account, they place a great value on oil alone in Baptism." He creates this lie by seizing upon the opportunity given by a bad explanation of the words of Peter Lombard. Now Lombard, in 4 dist. 7, c. 2, says the Sacrament of Confirmation is more noble than the Sacrament of Baptism in some way, namely by reason of the minister by whom it is given and by reason of the member in which it is perfected, for Confirmation cannot be completed except on the forehead, the most noble of all the members. Calvin received these words as if Lombard compared the anointing of Confirmation, which is done on the forehead, with the anointing of Baptism, which is done on the crown, and hence did not constitute the Sacrament of Baptism in water, but in oil alone. Yet, Calvin did not wish to understand the words of Lombard, for he compares the anointing of Confirmation, not with the anointing of Baptism, but *with Baptism itself*, which is confected from water, not oil. He discusses the Sacraments among themselves, but not the Sacrament of anointing in Baptism, rather the sprinkling of water. But Calvin says the sprinkling of water is also done on the forehead. *I respond:* This is the difference between Baptism and Confirmation, that Confirmation is not carried out except on the forehead, but the sprinkling of water of Baptism can be done on the forehead, but can also be done outside the forehead, nay more, now ordinarily when infants are baptized, water is only poured on the crown of their heads. Just as Confirmation is given by a bishop alone, Baptism can be given by a Bishop, but can also be given by a priest, and for that reason, by the notion of the minister, as by reason of the subject, Confirmation excels Baptism, as Lombard rightly says. This is why Calvin lies for no reason when he says that Catholics hold the water of Baptism of no account.

Calvin says (*ibid.*) that he does not even give a heap of dung about the oil, whether in Baptism or in Confirmation. All the saints and ancient Fathers, on the other hand, always spoke in a most respectful way about the oil in both Sacraments, as we showed above in the disputation on the ceremonies of Baptism and as we will below when we argue on the matter of Confirmation.

Now, Martin Chemnitz holds many similar lies and abusive things, but I will be content with one citation. In the *Examination of the Council of Trent* (2 part. p. 298), he devises three lies at once. First, that the anointing of Chrism is from the school of the Montanists. Second, that Tertullian and Cyprian were Montanists in this matter. Third, that Jerome refutes their assertion in the *Dialogue against the Luciferians*.

Now, no author ever asserted that this was the heresy of Montanus. Tertullian wrote about the errors of Montanus in *de Praescriptionibus*, Epiphanius in the *Panarion* (haeres. 48), Eusebius (*hist.* 4, 14), Clement of Alexandria (*Strom.* 4), Philastrius (*Catalogus*), Jerome (*Epist.* ad Marcellam on the errors of Montanus), Augustine (*haeres.* 26), Theodoret (*On the Fables of the Heretic* 3), and Damascene (*On One Hundred Heresies*). In none of these authors is there any word on the matter, but the ingenious Chemnitz gathers that this was an error of Montanus (although no man ever wrote that), simply because Tertullian was a Montanist, and he is the one who writes that the Holy Spirit is given to the Baptized through the anointing of Chrism. Yet, not everything which Tertullian wrote pertains to the errors of Montanus, although in the last part of his life he became a Montanist; otherwise, that Christ is the son of God, Baptism must be celebrated in water, the Eucharist in bread and wine, and many other things of this sort which Tertullian wrote would be heresies of the Montanists.

Lastly, how shameful is it to make St. Cyprian, a most celebrated martyr, a Montanist heretic? Why is what Chemnitz himself wrote on this matter not certain for him? On p. 317, he says this error was fabricated by the most ancient fathers: Tertullian, Cornelius, and Cyprian. But if they made it up, then they did not receive it from Montanus.

Lastly, the idea that Jerome refutes it in his *Dialogue against the Luciferians* is an absurd lie. In that *Dialogue*, St. Jerome only explains how the Holy Spirit is said to be given through the laying on of hands, when he was also given in Baptism. But he does not name Montanus, nor Tertullian, nor the holy bishops Cornelius and Cyprian; the lie of Chemnitz, that

Jerome refutes them, is absent from there. Nor does it follow from what Jerome says, that in Baptism the Holy Spirit is given, that the assertion of Tertullian and Cyprian is refuted, who say the Holy Spirit is given in Confirmation; otherwise, Jerome would have also refuted Luke, who says in Act. 8:16, "For he was not as yet come upon any of them; but they were only baptized in the name of the Lord Jesus. Then they laid their hands upon them, and they received the Holy Spirit." Jerome refutes none of them, for they do not deny Luke, and others, that in Baptism the Holy Spirit is given, except in that plenitude in which he is given in Confirmation.

CHAPTER II

The Sacrament of Confirmation is Proven from Scripture

WE must prove with five arguments that Confirmation is truly a Sacrament, properly speaking, as the Council of Trent teaches in session 7, can. 1 on Confirmation. *Firstly*, from Scripture. *Secondly*, from tradition and the testimonies of the Supreme Pontiffs. *Thirdly*, from the testimonies of Councils. *Fourthly*, from the testimonies of the Greek Fathers. *Fifthly*, from the testimonies of the Latin Fathers.

What pertains to the first: Three things are required unto the essence of a Christian Sacrament properly so called. *Firstly*, the promise of grace; *secondly*, a sensible sign with the word, which is the medium or organ whereby the promise is applied; *thirdly*, the divine command whereby it is bidden to be administered. Calvin demands these three things be shown to him on the question of Confirmation from the Scriptures (*Instit.* 4, 19 §5), as well as Chemnitz (*Examination of the Council of Trent*, 2 part. p. 276). "In this question," Chemnitz says, "what are the means through which they would have us believe the Holy Spirit is efficacious, we seek above all from the word of God that the command and divine promise be shown unto us, for when we have those things, then we know by those means, namely it was of divine institution, to be used reverently; we also know why it must be attributed to them." So, they require nothing else, and duly, for all things are recalled to this by unanimous consensus, it is a Sacrament properly so called where these three things are found.

Now the *promise* is certainly found most fully in Jo. 14:26, where the Lord promises the Paraclete, the Spirit, who consoles in all adversity. Likewise, in 15:26, where he promises the same Holy Spirit, who shall make the disciples strong and fearless in the witness of truth. In 16:8, to convict the world for sin, justice, and judgment, i.e., who would give strength to the Apostles to convict the infidelity of men, and witness the justice of Christ, as well as to announce the prince of this world has already been judged. Likewise, in Lk. 24:48, "You will sit in the city, until you are clothed with power from on high." Then in Act. 1:8, "You will receive the power of the Holy spirit coming upon you, and you will be my witnesses, ..." This is certainly a divine promise, and found in the Scriptures, and it can in no way be denied that a fuller grace of the Holy Spirit is promised by it to just men that have already been baptized, whereby they become strong in the confession of faith.

Now the laying on of hands with prayer was the *means*, or *organ*, or the sensible sign constituted of things and words whereby that promise is applied, for the Apostles, by a singular miracle and favor, received that promised grace on the day of Pentecost without any means, or Sacrament, as is known from Act. 2:4. But truly, the rest received that same grace by the ministry of the Apostles through that means, as is clear in Act. 8;17, "then they laid their hands upon them, and they received the Holy Spirit," and before he said they came to pray. The same is found in Act. 19:6. This medium was the means whereby the promise made about sending the Holy Spirit is applied, and it is clear from the effect. The Apostles gave the laying on of hands to every baptized man, and the Holy Spirit came upon them. Lastly, the fact that this very gift, which was given at that time by the imposition of hands, was that very thing which was promised to the Apostles, is clear from the testimony of St. Peter in Act. 2:17. There, he preached to the people and promised the same gift which he had received if they would believe and be baptized, and he laid before them Joel, who foretold that the gift would be poured *upon all flesh*, not only on the Apostles (Joel 2:28). Peter testifies of the same thing in Act. 11:17, that Cornelius and his companions received the same gift which the Apostles received on Pentecost. Then, in Acts 15:9 he says, "He placed no difference between us and them," and still Scripture never recalls another means or sensible sign in which that gift would be given, except the laying on of hands and prayer.

Only the *command* remains. In place of the command we give him *the execution* of the command. The Apostles would never have so ordinarily and securely laid hands upon all baptized men so that the Holy Spirit would come upon them, unless the Lord would have commanded them to do this. In the same way, even here on earth when a servant does something which he could not otherwise do except by the command of his master, and is not a fool, everyone understands that he has a command, even if he does not say that he was commanded, just as if lictors take some great man in the middle of the marketplace or if travelers announce to assemblymen on such a day an assembly must be held, etc. The fact that this rite was, however, ordinary and common to all the baptized is clear from Act. 8:17, 19:6, and from Hebrews 6:2. Consequently, even Calvin himself, when he demanded a command be shown to him (*Inst.* 4, 19 §6), answers in the name of Catholics (§6), "They do defend themselves by the example of the Apostles, whom they think did nothing rashly," and admitting that answer, says, "and they do rightly; nor would we rebuke them if they would show themselves to be imitators of the Apostles."

Now we must see how our adversaries answer this argument. The first answer is of Calvin (*loc. cit.*), that the laying on of hands was not a Sacrament, but a certain offering of the baptized to God, for they customarily offer to God those whom they had baptized.

Yet, this answer is easily refuted. In the first place, Calvin merely says

Chapter II: Confirmation Proven from Scripture

it, but does not prove, nor can prove it by any testimony except that it be taken on his own authority. He speaks in this way, "I think there was no deeper mystery under this laying on of hands, but I interpret that this kind of ceremony was used by them to intimate, by that very act, that they commended to God and, as it were, offered the man upon on whom they laid hands." Then, Scripture says that the effusion of a wondrous gift followed immediately after that imposition of hands, nay more, Scripture even asserts that the Holy Spirit was given through that imposition of hands (Acts 8:17), just as Titus 3:5 says we became saved by the laver of regeneration. Consequently, as the laver is not a simple oblation, but *a mystery conferring grace*, so also the laying on of hands. Besides, to offer the baptized to God is not something greater than to baptize, especially according to Calvin, who says there is no deep mystery in this ceremony; as a result, those who baptize could make the offering to him.

But Scripture teaches the contrary. In Act. 8:12, Philip baptizes, and still, he cannot impose hands; rather, Peter and John come to do this. In Act. 19:5, twelve men were baptized while Paul was present, though it does not say by whom, because anyone could do that, but Paul himself imposes hands upon the baptized. Lastly, why would a new offering be needed, since by the very fact that a man is baptized, he offers himself to God and subjects himself to his laws and service?

The *second* answer is also of Calvin (*ibid.*) and Brenz (*Wittenberg Confession*, on Confirmation), who say God, in the beginning of the nascent Church, through the hands of the Apostles gave certain visible gifts of the Holy Spirit to the faithful, such as the gift of tongues, miracles and similar things, from which it follows that the imposition of hands was not a Sacrament, because it did not give the grace of justification. They strengthen the argument from similar things, that men were cured by Peter's shadow (Act. 5:15) and by the sweat of Paul (Act. 19:12), and still we do not make Sacraments of these.

This answer can also be easily rejected. What they say, that the laying on of hands did not give anything except certain gifts of speaking in tongues and miracles, is false. In the first place, those gifts were given gratuitously, and Scripture does not simply say they are of the Holy Spirit, nor does it say the Holy Spirit dwells in the man who possesses only these gifts; on the contrary, the Holy Spirit rather more will flee one who pretends, and will not dwell in a body subject to sin (Wisdom 1:4). Those gifts, however, were sometimes found to have also been gratuitously given to sinners, as is clear from Matt. 7:22. But through the laying on of hands by the Apostles the Holy Spirit himself was given (Act. 8:17, 19:6), not only those gratuitous gifts. Secondly, it is given through the laying on of hands, which the Lord promised in Jo. 14:26, 15:26, 16:8, and Lk. 24:49, as we showed above. What the Lord promised, however, was not the gift of tongues, nor healing (that was something additional), but a grace *fortifying* and *strengthening* in faith.

Thirdly, those gifts were not common to all, as is clear from Rom. 12:6 and 1 Cor. 12:29, "Do all prophesy? ... do all speak in tongues?" Now, the Holy Spirit is given *to all* by the laying on of hands, as is clearly gathered from the Act. 8:17 and 19:6. *Fourthly*, in Heb. 6:2, the Apostle numbers the laying on of hands with Baptism, with faith, with Penance, with other things which pertain to salvation, nay more, even to the *foundations* of religion, as the Apostle says in the same place. Certainly, to speak in tongues and to prophesy, do not pertain to salvation, much less to the foundations of religion. *Fifthly*, if the Holy Spirit being given conferred nothing else by the laying on of hands than these gifts of miracles, certainly the primary Apostles James and John would not have come down to Samaria from Jerusalem to impose hands. Philip worked enough many miracles in Samaria so that it would not be necessary for other men to be there to work miracles. *Sixthly*, the examples which our adversaries proffer, namely on the shadow of Peter and the sweat of Paul, show the same thing. We never read that the Holy Spirit was given through these instruments, but only temporal healing.

The *third* answer is something which Calvin touches upon (*loc. cit.*), but which Chemnitz follows up more broadly (p. 290). To give the Holy Spirit through the laying on of hands was a singular privilege among the Apostles. This is because the command and promise on this matter was peculiar to them. We, on the other hand, do not have a command of this sort, and a promise; consequently, we rashly try to imitate them. The argument is confirmed from the event. The effects followed their imposition of hands, but nothing follows ours, even if someone would impose hands thousands of times, fiery tongues do not descend. Therefore, that gift ceased, and hence that ceremony remains idle and inane.

We can also easily reject this answer. In the first place, our adversaries do not show where the Lord commanded the Apostle to impose hands to receive the Holy Spirit. We read in Mk. 16:18 that "They shall lay their hands upon the sick, and they shall recover." However, that is said *to all* the faithful, not to the Apostles alone, "These signs shall follow them that believe," and on that account, that laying on of hands *to cure illnesses*, is not a calling down of the Spirit. Likewise, we read Ananias (Act. 9:12) received the command to lay hands upon Paul. Calvin badly explains this passage in regard to the laying on of hands which we do now, in his *Antidote* (sess. 7 can. 3, on Confirmation) and in the *Institutes* (4, 19 §10). Nevertheless, that passage does not bear on the matter, for that laying on of hands was *curative*, to repel corporeal blindness, not to give the Holy Spirit; this is why it is also done before Baptism. *Secondly*, they do not show a promise was ever made to the Apostles that the Holy Spirit would be given to men upon whom they lay hands. The Lord promised the Holy Spirit to the Apostles, whom they received on the day of Pentecost, but we do not read that they ever themselves gave it to others, and still they gave it, and *ordinarily*. As

Chapter II: Confirmation Proven from Scripture

a result, a peculiar promise was not required. *Thirdly*, the general promise was not only made to the Apostles, but to the whole Church; consequently, the ceremonies also, whereby the promise is applied, should be general and perpetual. The antecedent is proven: even if the Lord addressed the Apostles when he was promising the Holy Spirit, still, he addressed the whole Church in them, as St. Leo says (*Serm.* 9 on Lent), "The whole Church universally received its salvation in those who were there." The Lord also said in Matt. 28:20, "I will be with you in all days, even to the consummation of the world." There, everyone he addressed was going to die within a hundred years, and still, he says that he will be with them always, because without a doubt, even they will always exist in their posterity. Likewise, from what Lk. 22:19 says, "Do this in my commemoration," which certainly also pertains to those who were not Apostles. This is why St. Peter, who most rightly understood those promises, promised the Holy Spirit in Act. 2:38 to everyone if they would believe and be baptized, and he laid before them the prophecy of Joel, "I will pour out my spirit upon all flesh." We can add clear reason. The cause why God promised and gave the Holy Spirit is not less important in us than in the Apostle, accordingly the faithful in every time need the power of the Holy Spirit to resist in persecution and confess the faith. The Lord could not provide, or will for his Church for only ten or twenty years, and not perpetually, when it requires that help.

But Chemnitz answers that, though the promise is indeed general, still the organ whereby it is applied is not now the laying on of hands, but other instruments, namely Baptism and the Eucharist. On the contrary, this is to confect organs whereby the divine promises are applied rashly and by one's own authority, nay more, even against the word of God. If Baptism and the Eucharist apply the aforesaid promise, why do the Apostles use the laying on of hands? Perhaps they were in want of Baptism and the Eucharist? Next, the Apostles, were baptized and received the Eucharist before the Passion of Christ, and still after all those the Holy Spirit was promised to them. So, they didn't receive this gift, namely in that plenitude, which was given in the Sacrament of Confirmation, through Baptism and the Eucharist. Besides, in Act. 8:16, the Samaritans were baptized, and still Luke very clearly says the Spirit did not come upon any of them until after the laying on of hands of the Apostles. Lastly, when Scripture itself so clearly teaches the medium to receive this gift is the laying on of hands, what kind of temerity is it to reject this means and make up another one?

Yet, they say, the effect ceased, which followed the imposition of hands.

I respond: It ceased in regard to visible symbols, not in regard *to invisible grace*. The fact that the Holy Spirit can also be given invisibly is clear from what the Lord did in Jn 20:22, where he breathed on them and said, "Receive the Holy Spirit"; that he ought to be given at least invisibly, we proved a little while ago. The reasonable cause, however, why at that time it was given visibly, but now only invisibly, is that in the beginning of the Church, miracles of this sort were necessary to plant and nourish the faith. This is why Augustine (*de Baptismo* 3, 16) says, "The Holy Spirit is not only given by the laying on of hands amid the testimony of temporal sensible miracles, as he was given in former days to entrust the faith to the unlearned and for the extension of the first beginnings of the Church. Who expects in these days that those on whom hands are laid to receive the Holy Spirit should immediately begin to speak with tongues? But it is understood that invisibly and imperceptibly, on account of the bond of peace, divine love is breathed into their hearts." Those who believed at the beginning of the Church worked miracles according to that of Mk. 16:17-18, "These signs shall follow those who believe ... they shall lay their hands upon the sick, and they shall recover." Now that effect of faith has ceased. Nevertheless, faith is not idle and inane, since its *principal* effect is to give life, "For the just man lives by faith," (Heb. 10:38). See Gregory in his *Homilies* on the Gospel of the Ascension. For equal reasoning, in the beginning of the Church, sinners were punished with visible penalties, as is clear from Ananias and Sapphira in Act. 5:5, on Elymas the magician (Act. 13:11), and those who received communion unworthily (1 Cor. 11:30). Yet, since these sins are not punished with visible punishments today, will they remain unpunished and not receive at least an invisible punishment either here or in the next life? Consequently, so also even among the good.

The *fourth* answer is of Chemnitz (*Exam.* 2 part., p. 291). He argues that the whole passage of Act. 8:17 and 19:6 does not favor us, since we reject the laying on of hands and in its place substitute the anointing of Chrism.

This answer is nothing, for, that I might pass over what is said about the chrism, it is false that we reject the laying on of hands. The bishop gives the laying on of hands to those who are to be confirmed, just as it can be understood from the *Roman Pontifical*, once when he extends his hands over them and prays and again when he signs them on the forehead and anoints them, for that anointing and signing, when it is done by hand, is rightly called a laying on of hands, as Hugh of St. Victor teaches (*de Sacramentis* 2, part. 7, c. 2). Wherefore, even Mk. 7:33, when a certain man demanded that the Lord would give the laying on of hands to a lunatic, he did it, for he touched his tongue and ears with his finger.

CHAPTER III

The Truth Is Proven from the Testimonies of the Supreme Pontiffs

Now, the truth will be proved secondly from the responses of the ancient and holy Pontiffs. We do not, however, advance testimonies which affirm in clear words that Confirmation is a Sacrament, since that is not necessary and could easily be twisted to the signification of a Sacrament received in the broad sense. Rather, we advance testimonies which demonstrate the very fact, i.e., a ceremony giving grace, and distinct from Baptism.

1) The *first* is St. Clement of Rome. See the *Constitutions* (3, c. 10, 16 & 17, as well as 7, 44).

2) The *second* is St. Urban in his decretal, "All the faithful through the laying on of hands of bishops, should receive the Holy Spirit after Baptism, to be found full Christians."

3) The *third* is St. Cornelius, Pope and Martyr (*Epist. ad Fabium Antiochenum*, cited by Eusebius, *hist.* 6, 33), "He was not completed by the seal of chrism, so he could not obtain the Holy Spirit."

4) The *fourth* is St. Melchiades, Pope and Martyr, in his *Epistle to the Bishops of Spain*, asking whether Baptism or Confirmation is a greater Sacrament, and he answers in these words, "Know that both are great Sacraments," and he adds that Confirmation excels Baptism inasmuch as it alone is conferred by supreme priests, namely Bishops. There, he clearly teaches that Confirmation is a Sacrament *truly and properly speaking*, because it confers, with Baptism, and in some matter even excels Baptism; everyone upholds Baptism, however, as a Sacrament truly and properly speaking.

5) The *fifth* is Pope St. Eusebius, who says in his third epistle, "The Sacrament of the laying on of hands must be held in great veneration, because it cannot be carried out by any other than the supreme priests." He proves it from Acts of the Apostles.

6) The *sixth* is Innocent I (*Epist. ad Decentium*, 1, 3) who says, "It is lawful for priests to anoint the baptized with chrism, but because it was consecrated by the Bishop; still, it is not lawful for them to sign the forehead with the same oil, because it was given to Bishops alone when they give the Holy Spirit, the Paraclete." He also brings in the example of the Apostles in Act. 8, where Innocent clearly distinguishes the Episcopal Confirmation, whereby he says the Holy Spirit is given, and hence it is a Sacrament distinct from the anointing which is done in Baptism, which is

not a Sacrament, but some Sacramental, and besides, this comes down from the doctrine *of the Apostles*.

7) The *seventh* is from Pope St. Damasus in *Epist.* 4.

8) The *eighth* is St. Leo in *Epist.* 86 (also numbered 88).

9) The *ninth* is Pope John III, in his *Epistle to the bishops of Germany*. These three Popes declare that not choir-bishops, but only Bishops give the Holy Spirit through the laying on of hands and the anointing of chrism on the forehead. Furthermore, John III cites Popes Damasus and Leo, and gives the reason why both he and they gave decrees on this matter: because in Act. 8, the Apostles alone gave the Holy Spirit through the laying on of hands, where we see they speak on those ceremonies *which were in use among the Apostles*.

10) The *tenth* is Pope St. Gregory I, who in his *Epistles* (3, 9) warns priests lest they would dare to sign the baptized with chrism on the forehead, since this pertains to the office of a bishop. On *Cantic.* 1:13, on the verse, *in the vineyards of Engaddi*, he says, "Balsam arises, which when it has been blessed by a bishop with oil, it becomes chrism whereby the gifts of the Holy Spirit are expressed." Add also Innocent III, c. *Cum Venisset, extra, de Sacra Unctione.*

CHAPTER IV

The Truth Is Proven from the Testimonies of Councils

1) The *first* is the very ancient Council of Elvira, in can. 38. After it said a layman may baptize in necessity, it adds, "If he will live, bring him to the bishop, so that he can be completed through the laying on of hands." It commands a deacon to do the same thing in can. 77 if he baptized someone.

2) The *second* is the first Council of Arles, celebrated in the time of St. Sylvester, which commands heretics returning to the Church, if they were baptized in the name of the Father, and of the Son, and of the Holy Spirit, to not be baptized again, but to have a Bishop lay hands upon him so that they would receive the Holy Spirit, because without a doubt those heretics customarily give Baptism, but not Confirmation.

3) The *third* is the second Council of Arles, celebrated under the same Sylvester, which decreed the same thing in can. 17, except that it pronounces chrism be applied by the laying on of hands.

4) The *fourth* is Laodicea, also an ancient Council, where in can. 7 the followers of Novatian are commanded to be anointed in the holy Chrism; and in can. 48 it says, "The baptized must partake of the most holy chrism, and become partakers of the heavenly kingdom."

5) The *fifth* is the Council of Aurelian, cited by Gratian (*de Consecrate.* dist. 5, can. *Ut Jejuni*), which says, "Let those who are the proper age who come to Confirmation first be taught to make a confession, so that they might avail, while clean, to receive the gift of the Holy Spirit.

6) The *sixth* is the Council of Meldense, also cited by Gratian (*ibid.* dist. Can. *Ut Episcopi*), which says, "That Bishops would not give the Holy Spirit through the laying on of hands except while fasting."

7) The *seventh* is the second Council of *Hispalense*, can. 7, where the same thing is found which we cited above from Leo I.

8) The *eighth* is a Council which St. Boniface, bishop and martyr, celebrated, which is extant in his life in the tome of Surius (tom. 3) where it was decreed that Bishops should travel their diocese to give Confirmation.

9) We can add to these the general Councils of Constantinople III, can. 7, Florence, in its *Instruction of the Armenians*, and the Council of Trent, sess. 7, can. 1, *On Confirmation*.[19]

---

[19] *Recognitio V:* I cited III Constantinople, can. 7. It must be known that this canon is one from those nine which is ascribed to the sixth General Council, which was the third held at Constantinople, and found in a certain Codex in the Monastery of St. Bavonis, with Gandavus, as is annotated in the second tome of

CHAPTER V

The Truth Is Proven from the Testimonies of the Greek Fathers

1) The *first* from the Greek Fathers is Dionysius the Areopagate. In his *Ecclesiastical Hierarchy* (c. 2, part. 2) he so holds, "When he has been baptized and clothed in a white vestment they lead him to the Bishop; he signs the man with the divine, and altogether deific anointing." In part. 3, "That perfecting anointing completes him." In part. 3 c. 4, "But even for these who are consecrated by the most holy mystery of regeneration, the anointing consummating the arrival of the Holy Spirit is celebrated." Here you see the ceremony and its effect, and hence the notion of a Sacrament properly speaking.

2) In the *second* place issues Clement of Alexandria, who by Eusebius' witness (*Hist.* 3, 17, according to Christopherson's version), relates the history of a certain young man commended to the care of St. John the Evangelist, and for his diligence was recently created a bishop. Among other things he spoke in this way, "Who (a bishop) illuminated a man with the Sacrament of Baptism, then has sealed him with the Lord's seal as a safeguard of his soul perfected." There, he clearly speaks about the Sacrament of Confirmation, which is the Lord's seal impressed on the forehead, and offering custody through grace, which it confers.

3) The *third* is Justin (*Quaest.* 137 *Orthodoxorum*), who writes that after the mysteries of Baptism are carried out, the faithful are sealed with the sacred anointing.

4) The *fourth* is Origen, who in his eighth *Homily on Leviticus*, says, "So after they have been converted, a certain purification from sin is given through all those which we spoke of earlier; the gift of grace of the Spirit through the image of oil, however, is designated, so that a man can not only attain purgation, who is converted from sin, but is completed with the Holy Spirit," and in *Homil.* 9, "Everyone at all anointed by the anointing of the sacred Chrism becomes a priest, just as even Peter says to all the Church: You are a chosen race, a royal priesthood."

5) The *fifth* is Cyril of Jerusalem from the five *Mystagogical Catheceses*. He wrote 1 and 2 on Baptism, 3 on the Sacrament of Confirmation, 4 and 5 on the Eucharist, which are the three Sacraments which are received by Neophytes on the same day. From where it appears that Cyril did not Councils. I wished to mention this, lest anyone would think I cited canons from the Council of Trullo.

Chapter V: Confirmation Proven from the Greeks 455

only hold Confirmation for a Sacrament, but also for a Sacrament *most properly speaking*, seeing that he placed it with Baptism and the Eucharist. Besides, in Catechesis 3, already cited, he speaks in this way, "Just as the bread of the Eucharist, after the invocation of the Holy Spirit, is no longer common bread but the body of Christ, so also this holy anointing, after it has been consecrated, is no longer a mere anointing. Rather, it is the chrism of Christ, which by the arrival of the Holy Spirit has divine energy through his divinity; whereby the forehead, and your other senses are anointed by that unction, but the soul is sanctified by the holy and lifegiving spirit." Note this citation, *firstly* compares the chrism with the Eucharist, which is an argument that both are equally and properly a Sacrament. *Secondly*, note the consecrated anointing has the power to sanctify, which is proper to true Sacraments, which are instruments of sanctification. *Thirdly*, not only does it have the power to sanctify, but the soul is also *really* and truly sanctified when the forehead is anointed with chrism. *Fourthly*, this author speaks cautiously when he says the bread of the Eucharist after consecration is the body of Christ, while he does not say the anointing after the consecration is the Holy Spirit. This is so we would not suppose that Cyril makes transubstantiation similar to anointing, in the way it takes place in the bread, rather he says it is not a mere anointing, but the chrism of Christ having the energy to sanctify by the Holy Spirit.

Cyril also teaches (*ibid.*) that just as Christ first received Baptism, secondly the dove descended upon him, thirdly temptation followed him, so with us; it also happens when we are first baptized, then we receive the Holy Spirit through chrism, and so at length, we descend to battle with the devil. He also says that a Christian properly obtains this name from chrism. Since a Christian is called as if *anointed*, he does not seem worthy of this name who has not been anointed with this unction, whereby Christians are perfected. Lastly, in the same place, when he also says that John (1 Jo. 2:27), "And as for you, let the anointing which you have received from him, abide in you.... Just as his anointing teaches you all things," alludes to this holy chrism, through which the Holy Spirit is given, who teaches us all things.

6) The *sixth* is Gregory Nazianzen, in his *Orat. On the Holy Laver*, where he says, "But if you would fortify yourself through Baptism, secure yourself with the best and strongest of all aids, being sealed both in body and in soul with the anointing, as Israel once was with the blood and anointing of the firstborn at night that guarded him, what then can happen to you, and what has been wrought for you? Listen to Solomon, 'If you sit, you will be without fear, and if you sleep, your sleep shall be sweet' (Prov. 3:24)."

7) The *seventh* is Amphilochius, in his life of St. Basil (if he is the true author of this book), "Maximinus the bishop baptized Basil and Eubulus, and clothed them in white, and also anointing them with the holy chrism, gave to them life-giving communion."

8) The *eighth* is Theodoret (*Commentary on Cant.* 1), "Those who

are initiated in Baptism, after they have renounced Satan and made the confession of faith, they are anointed with the chrism of spiritual unction just as in a sign and a royal mark, and they partake of the grace of the most Holy Spirit by the invisible species of that visible anointing."

9) The *ninth* is John Damascene (*de Fide* 4, 9) who says, "Oil is employed in Baptism, signifying the anointing and making us Christs, and announcing the mercy of God toward us through the Holy Spirit." There he very clearly speaks about the Sacrament of Confirmation, which is given after Baptism. A little before, he said the Holy Spirit was given to the Apostles in the form of fire, and then added that he is given to us through oil. Certainly, however, the Confirmation of the Apostles on the day of Pentecost does not correspond with Baptism, but *Confirmation* through chrism. Later, the same author says that just as the dove brought the olive branch after the flood, the Holy Spirit arrives through the oil, whose figure the dove with the olive branch was. Lastly, the Greek words τὸ ἔλαιον Βαπτίσματι παραλαμβάνεται are rightly translated as "The oil follows in Baptism," rather than "the oil in Baptism employed," as Oecolampadius translates it. In Greek, it is not "in Baptism," and the word παραλαμβάνεται is properly said in regard to a thing which is taken up so another would succeed it.

CHAPTER VI

The Truth Is Proven from the Testimonies of the Latin Fathers

1) Tertullian seems to have briefly reviewed the whole rite in his work *On the Resurrection of the Flesh*, namely the anointing, the sign of the cross, and the laying on of hands, "The flesh is anointed so that the soul is consecrated; the flesh is sealed, so that the soul would be fortified; the flesh is overshadowed by the laying on of hands, so that the soul would be illuminated." He also joins this Sacrament with Baptism and the Eucharist, for just before he said, "The soul is washed so that it is without stain," and after these things he adds, "The flesh feeds upon the body of Christ, so that God may lavishly feed the soul." Likewise, in *Contra Marcion* (1) he again joins the anointing of oil with the water of Baptism and the bread of the Eucharist; and in a similar fashion, in his work *de Praesciptione haereticorum*. Lastly, in his work *On Baptism*, he says, "When we go out from the laver, we are anointed with blessed oil.... The anointing runs down us carnally, but it takes its effect spiritually. ... From here the laying on of hands is given, calling down the blessing and inviting the Holy Spirit."

2) The *second* is St. Cyprian (*Epist.* lib. 1, last epistle), "It is necessary for a man who has been baptized to be anointed, so that after he has received the Chrism he is the anointed of God and can have the grace of Christ in himself." In *Epistle* 2, 1, he says, "then at length they can be fully sanctified and sons of God, if they are born from each Sacrament." You see, the Sacrament is called Confirmation and is conferred with Baptism. Likewise, in his *Epistle* to Jubajanus, "Now also among us it is borne that those who are baptized in the Church are offered by the bishops of the Church, and through our prayer and the laying on of hands, obtain the Holy Spirit, and are completed in the Lord's seal." If someone were to object, that Cyprian argues the cause of Anabaptism in all these places, we will respond: It is true, but not on account of that is what he says on the rite and effect of sacred chrism false. The Catholic Church always noted the error of Cyprian on Anabaptism; it never marked down as an error what he writes on Confirmation. St. Augustine (*On Baptism*, book 5) refuted the arguments of Cyprian for Anabaptism, still, he never condemned the slightest vowel which Cyprian so magnificently wrote on this Sacrament.

3) *Thirdly*, the author of the *Sermons on the Cardinal Works of Christ*, which are held among the works of Cyprian, although Cyprian did not write them, nevertheless that ancient and learned author clearly attributes

to Chrism that has been consecrated the force to sanctify in the way in which we heard Cyril speaking. He speaks in this way in his sermon on the anointing of chrism, "Today in the Church, sacred chrism is confected, in which royal balsam is mixed with oil, expressing the unity of sacerdotal glory; after such dignities the divine anointing was instituted, so as to sanctify the people of acquisition in the participation of dignity and the name." Then speaking on the Chrism, "Now that the elements have been sanctified, they do not supply the effect of their own nature, rather the divine power works all the more powerfully, and the truth is present in the sign and Sacrament of the Spirit. ... By the benefit of this anointing divine wisdom and understanding is given us; heavenly counsel and fortitude will flow; knowledge, piety, and fear is infused by inspirations from on high. We are anointed by this oil so that we may contend with spiritual wickedness."

4) *Fourthly*, Eusebius of Emesa, or whoever was the author of the sermon on Pentecost (without doubt he was a Latin, and famous), "Now, what is attributed individually when we confirm the Neophytes with the laying on of hands, in former times this was the very thing that the descent of the Holy Spirit in the people of believers gave to all. ... Therefore, the Holy Spirit, who descended upon the waters in salutary Baptism, by the flow on the forehead gave plenitude to innocence, and in Confirmation furnished an increase of grace."

5) *Fifthly*, Prudentius in ψυχομαχία, when he describes the battle of lust and sobriety:

> After the seals of the forehead were inscribed with oil, through which
> The royal anointing was given, and the perpetual chrism.

And in his hymn before sleep:

> Worshiper of God be mindful,
> You from the dew of the
> Font and laver became holy,
> You were enrolled in Chrism.

6) The *sixth* is Pacianus of Barcelona (*de Baptismo*), "In the laver, sins are cleansed, in Chrism the Holy Spirit is poured out, but we obtain each of these from the hand and mouth of a bishop." Likewise, in his first *Epistle* to Symproniaus Novatianus, "If, then, the power of both Baptism and Confirmation, which are far greater than charisms, is passed on in this way to the bishops (from the form of the Apostles), then too, the right of binding and loosing was with them." There you see that Chrism is not only joined with the Sacrament of Baptism and Penance, but even excels the Sacrament of Penance, for he says the power of greater charisms can

Chapter VI: Confirmation Proven from the Latins 459

anoint with chrism than to bind or loose, because he can baptize and sign in Chrism, which are greater offices. He says the same thing in *Epist.* 2, "How does the priest that has been anointed by the Spirit not fix a seal upon your people?"

7) *Seventhly*, Ambrose (*de Sacramentis* 3,2) says, "The spiritual seal follows, because after the forehead it follows that completion comes about, when by the invocation of the priest the Holy Spirit is poured forth." In his book *On Those Who Are Initiated in the Mysteries*, cap. 7, "Return, because you have received the spiritual seal. ... Preserve what you have received; God the Father sealed you, Christ the Lord confirmed you."

8) The *eighth* is Jerome, in his *Dialogue against the Luciferians*, after he had said that bishops, by the laying on of hands upon the baptized, give the Holy Spirit, he adds, "You ask where it has been written? In the Acts of the Apostles. But even if the authority of Scripture did not give a basis for it, the precept would be obtained by the nature of the consensus of the whole world in its favor."

9) The *ninth* is Augustine. In *de Trinitate* (15, 26), he says the Church still preserves what the Apostles did in Act. 8, that they give the laying on of hands to receive the Holy Spirit at his command. He also calls to mind chrism (*ibid.*). Likewise, in his preface to his second sermon on Psalm 26, he says men are completed spiritually by this anointing. Likewise, in *de Baptismo* (3, 16) and *Tract. in Epist. Joan.* He says now those upon whom the laying on of hands is given after Baptism do not speak in tongues; nevertheless, they really receive the Holy Spirit, and charity is invisibly infused, and in a hidden manner. The particular passage is in his *Against the Letters of Petilian* (2, 104), "You would have it that the Sacrament of Chrism is interpreted among the class of visible signs, like Baptism itself, but yet can exist even among the worst of men. ... Separate the visible holy Sacrament, which can exist both in the good and in the bad; in the former for their reward, in the latter for judgment; separate it from the invisible anointing of charity, which is the peculiar property of the good."

10) The *tenth* is Bede (*in Luke* 6), who in explaining the words of Lk. 22:39, *And going out, he went, according to his custom, to the mount of Olives*, says, "On the mount of Olives, he led out the disciples to denote that all who had been baptized in his death, must be confirmed by the lofty chrism of the Holy Spirit."

Those who treat on this Sacrament in earnest are added to these fathers.

11) The *eleventh* is Rabanus (*De Instit. Cler.* 1, 30).

12) The *twelfth* is Amalarius (*de Officiis Ecclesiasticis* 1).

13) The *thirteenth* is Hugh of St. Victor (*de Sacr.* 2, part, 7, etc.).

14) The *fourteenth* is St. Peter Lombard, together with all the Scholastics in *Sent.* 4, dist. 7.

Here we can add three miracles which God showed in confirmation of this Sacrament. The *first* is extant in Optatus (lib. 2), where he relates the bottle of holy chrism was thrown out the window by the Arians, but could not hit the ground as it was held up by the hand of an Angel. The other is extant in the life of St. Rembert, the Bishop of Bremen (with Surius, tom. 1 *in mense Februario*, which was written around 900 A.D.). There, we read St. Rembert restored sight to a blind man who was among those to be confirmed. The *third* is extant in the life of St. Malachi, written by St. Bernard. There he says, "There was a boy seized in mind, like those whom they call 'lunatics,' who was among those to be confirmed, and Malchus cured the boy with sacred anointing." He speaks there about Bishop Malchus, the teacher of St. Malachi.

CHAPTER VII

The Answers Which Our Adversaries Give to the Testimonies of the Fathers Are Rebutted, Which Are Also Their Arguments against the Truth

Now let us see what our adversaries have to say in response to so many testimonies of the Fathers and what they object to us.

1) Calvin, at first simply rejects the Fathers. In the *Institutes* (4, 19 §4) he says Jerome was hallucinating because the supposed rite of Confirmation was of Apostolic observance. In § 8 and 10, he forcefully inveighs against St. Melchiadis, as we noted above in chapter 1. Then, in §12, he speaks this way, "When they see that the word of God, and everything like plausible argument fail them, they pretend, as they are wont, that the observance is of the highest antiquity and is confirmed by the consent of many ages. Even were this true, they gain nothing by it. A Sacrament is not of earth, but heaven; not of men, but the one God." As if we would advance the Fathers to teach they instituted the Sacrament! We affirm Sacraments are from heaven, not earth, but still, we apply men as *witnesses* of the Sacraments. Nevertheless, this testimony should not be said to be of earth, but of heaven, for they do not confect this testimony from their own head, but from *the doctrine and tradition of the Apostles*. Add the fact that we do not admit that the word of God has failed us, as we showed above in chapter 2.

2) *Secondly:* Calvin (*ibid.*) denies the Fathers recognized this Sacrament, "Why throw in antiquity, since the ancients, whenever they speak properly, nowhere mention more than two sacraments? Were the bulwark of our faith to be sought from men, we have an impregnable citadel in this, that the fictitious Sacraments of these men were never recognized as Sacraments by the ancients. They speak of the laying on of hands, but do they call it a Sacrament? Augustine (*De Baptismo* 3, 16) distinctly affirms it is nothing but a prayer." Chemnitz adds (*Exam.* p. 319) the authority of Gratian, who in can. *Arianos*, 1, q. 1, gathers from this passage of St. Augustine, the laying on of hands is not a Sacrament, because it can be repeated, whence it is nothing other than a type of prayer.

This second answer is constituted from two very clear lies. What Calvin says, that the Fathers do not acknowledge any but two Sacraments properly so-called, is a certain lie from the testimonies that have been cited, and we refuted the same lie when we argued on the number of the Sacraments. The fact that Calvin denies the ancients called the rite of Confirmation a

Sacrament is clear from the testimonies of Melchiadis, Eusebius, Cyprian, and also Augustine (cited above). I answer the citation from Augustine, that he spoke on the *simple* laying on of hands, which was usually done in the reconciliation of penitents, not on the laying on of hands with chrism, which is properly the Sacrament of Confirmation.

Calvin doubles down, however, and says, "Let them not here yelp one of their pedantic distinctions, that the laying on of hands to which Augustine referred was not in regard to Confirmation, but curative or reconciliatory. His book is extant and in men's hands. ..." He shows it is a question of both at once, because Augustine speaks about heretics who return to the Church, who are not rebaptized, but they receive the laying on of hands in the way the Holy Spirit is given to them. He offers as confirmation from *de Baptismo* 5, 23.

I respond: If all this would prove anything, it would only prove Confirmation is a *repeatable* Sacrament, but it would not show that it is not a Sacrament properly speaking, which is what Calvin meant to show, for Augustine speaks in this way, "The laying on of hands, however, not like Baptism, which cannot be repeated, for what else is it but a prayer over men?" There, Augustine does not gather from the fact that the laying on of hands is a prayer, that it is not a Sacrament, but it is not such a Sacrament that *it could not be repeated*. Otherwise, it is manifestly shown to be a Sacrament, for here is the sensible matter, the laying on of hands, there is a form, namely prayer, there is an effect, the grace of the Holy Spirit, as Calvin himself contends. So why is it not a Sacrament? It also cannot be proven from this that Confirmation is a repeatable Sacrament, for (as I said) this is not a question on Confirmation, but on *the reconciliation of penitents*. I will show it from these arguments.

a) Firstly, Augustine teaches everywhere that Confirmation is done with chrism, as is clear from the passages we have already brought forward. In this place, however, not only does he fail to mention chrism, but clearly indicates he speaks about a laying on of hands without chrism; otherwise, he would not have said, "What else is it but a prayer?" It could be answered that the consecration and sealing through anointing, through the anointing of chrism.

b) Secondly, the Sacrament of Confirmation cannot be repeated once it has been given, as is clear from the Council of Tarraco, and from the rescript of Gregory II, as Gratian witnesses (*de Consecrat.* Dist. 5, can. *Dictum est*, & can. *De homine*). And besides, it is clearly gathered from Augustine (*Contra Literas Petiliani* 2, 104) where he says the Sacrament of Confirmation, just as also Baptism, remains in the very worst men, even to judgment. If it also remains in the worst, it may and must not also be given when they are reconciled, because they already have it, nor do they lose it. But in this place he says the laying on of hands can be repeated; therefore, he does not speak about the laying on of hands in Confirmation.

Chapter VII: Heretical Arguments are Refuted

c) Thirdly, Augustine speaks about the reconciliation of heretics, as Calvin affirms, and that is clear from each citation. Now, the reconciliatory laying on of hands was distinct, especially in the western Church, from the laying on of hands in Confirmation. The assumption is proven from Pope Vigilius (*Epist.* 1, 3) where he expressly witnesses this, as well as from Gregory (*Epist.* 9, 61) where he says the Arians in the eastern Church were customarily received by the anointing of chrism, but in the western Church only through the laying on of hands. The reason for such a diversity is usually assigned because the eastern Arians were not confirmed by chrism in their sects. The western ones, however, were confirmed, and therefore, in the East it was necessary to anoint them when they returned to the Church because they lacked this. This is why even in the Council of Nicaea (from the Arabic translation can. 31), the Arians were commanded to be anointed when they came to the Church. Or certainly if the Arians in the western Church also rejected Confirmation, still when they returned to the Church they were not immediately anointed with chrism, but later at an opportune moment, in the way we do with Lutherans. Lastly, that anointing in the eastern Church was not a Sacrament, but a certain *rite*. Whatever it is, Gregory says expressly they are not anointed in the west, but simply reconciled by the laying on of hands. This is why Augustine, who was in the western Church, when he speaks about the reconciliation of heretics through the laying on of hands, is not addressing Confirmation, which is not done without anointing, but only simple reconciliation.

Two things would seem to stand in the way of our explanation. *One*, that Augustine in *de Baptismo* (3, 16), in that very chapter where he says the laying on of hands is nothing but a prayer, also says it is not expected through this laying on of hands that men should speak in tongues as they did in the times of the Apostles, but it is enough if the Holy Spirit is poured out invisibly; we cited that passage above in favor of the Sacrament of Confirmation. Consequently, Augustine speaks in regard to the laying on of hands in Confirmation, or certainly he receives the laying on of hands equivocally in one and the same chapter, which seems absurd. The *second* is that he also (*ibid.* 5, 23) says through the reconciliatory laying on of hands the Holy Spirit is given. This is an effect of Confirmation for us; therefore, the laying on of hands in Confirmation and reconciliation of penitents was the same in Augustine.

I respond to the first: Augustine receives the laying on of hands in that chapter in a different way but without any vice. He had set out to answer the argument of St. Cyprian, who gathered from the fact that in the Catholic Church alone the Holy Spirit can be given and received that the Sacraments of the heretics are not true and valid. To refute that argument in the beginning of the chapter, Augustine explains what should be understood by the Holy Spirit when it is said to be given or received except in the Catholic Church through the laying on of hands. He says the gift of charity is understood, for this cannot be possessed except by the good, and therefore, it is not in any but the Catholic Church because outside of it there are no good men. In this place Augustine receives the laying on of hands in general, whether it is confirmatory, reconciliatory, or (if I may speak in this way) ordinary, for grace is always given through it, as well as charity, provided an obstacle has not been placed in the way. Next, Augustine means to show that by the laying on of hands the gift of charity is really given, and declares by the example of a confirmatory laying on of hands when he says it is not to be expected that men would speak in tongues, on whom the laying on of hands was given, rather charity is infused in them in a hidden way. Therefore, there he receives the laying on of hands more strictly (i.e., only confirmatory); still, it is not a vicious equivocation because it is suitable for the whole class rightly declared by the example of one species. Later, he returns to the argument of Cyprian and distinguishes three things: the Sacrament; the gratuitous gift of the Holy Spirit (such as prophecy); the gift *gratum faciens*, i.e., charity. He says that outside the Church, or in wicked men, the first two can exist, but not the third. Thus, he should return to the Church so that through the reconciliatory laying on of hands, he would receive it. Because someone could suspect that this laying on of hands cannot be repeated, just as neither Baptism, nor Confirmation, nor Order can be repeated; therefore, Augustine added that the laying on of hands that is reconciliatory may be repeated, because it is nothing other than a prayer upon men, i.e., it is not some consecration which remains and impresses a character, and whence it could not be repeated, but only a ceremony profitable for prayer.

I respond to the second argument: As I have already said, the Holy Spirit is given through every laying on of hands, but for different effects. Through the confirmatory laying on of hands it is given to strengthen a soul in the confession of faith; through the reconciliatory it is given for the remission of sins; through the ordinary it is given for the power to administer the Sacraments.

To the citation of Gratian added by Chemnitz, *I respond:* Gratian means to say the laying on of hands about which Augustine speaks is not the Sacrament of Order, or even Confirmation; he says that rightly, and duly proves it from the fact that it cannot be repeated. He does not, however, deny it is the Sacrament of reconciliation, for otherwise the Eucharist could not be repeated, and still it is the truest Sacrament.

3) The *third* answer is that among the Fathers, Confirmation was only a Catechesis of children, who were baptized in infancy. Thus, Calvin (*ibid.* §4, and 13), who cites Leo I (*Epist.* 35 & 77) and Jerome (*Dialogue against the Luciferians*), and all others embrace the same answer. But it is very vain: *Firstly*, neither Scripture nor any of the Fathers call to mind this catechesis. Scripture, in Act. 8 & 19, says the Apostles prayed and gave the laying on of hands, and in that way gave the Holy Spirit: they make no mention

CHAPTER VII: HERETICAL ARGUMENTS ARE REFUTED   465

of the examination of children. Similarly, the Fathers speak as we spoke above. Hence, even St. Leo (*Epist.* 35 & 77) says nothing on the matter; he speaks on the reconciliation of heretics, not on the examination of children. Jerome also does not name an examination. Besides, this answer is not only out of conformity with the doctrine of the Fathers but is also opposed to them, for the Fathers gave Confirmation through anointing and the laying on of hands, even to infants, as Innocent I expressly teaches (*Epist.* 1; *de Ecclesiasticis dogmatibus*, c. 52), not to mention the *Roman Ordinal*. Besides, it is very certain that they once gave the Eucharist to infants also, as is clear from Cyprian in his sermon *de Lapsis*, and still they did not give the Eucharist until after Confirmation, as is clear from Dionysius, Ambrose, and others. Certainly, infants do not have the capacity for an examination, nor Catechism, nor would our adversaries mean to say that there was also an examination of infants, rather only boys in adulthood. As a result, it is clear that all the Fathers do not speak on the rite of Confirmation in the way the heretics of our time have made up for themselves. Lastly, nearly all the Fathers call to mind chrism and the seal of the cross on the forehead, and in this they place the essence of this Sacrament, as is clear from their testimonies.

Now, Chemnitz (*Exam.* 2 part., p. 297) thereupon makes a dissertation on the teaching of the Fathers and recalls all of their answers to five headings. *a) Firstly*, he says many authors who are cited in favor of the Sacrament of Confirmation are apocryphal and spurious. But this is nothing, for the cited epistles of Melchiadis, Eusebius, and Urban, or still the book of Dionysius the Areopagate, the homilies of Eusebius of Emesa, and the sermons of Cyprian on the *Cardinal Works of Christ*, if some of those writings were in doubt or suspected of being spurious, still many others are held to be certain and the authors most true; they are also very ancient, and the best, although it is not certain whether they are the authors of the works which bear their name.

b) Secondly, Chemnitz adds other authors who argue on the chrism, and certainly existed, but issued from the school of Montanus, such as Tertullian and Cyprian. We already demonstrated that this is an impudent lie in chapter 1.

c) Thirdly, he says some authors are certain, and approved, who mention anointing, but call it a Sacrament improperly and broadly, because it is a certain human ceremony customarily applied in Baptism; so he explains those passages of Augustine that we cited from *de Trinitate* 15, 26, and *Contra Literas Petiliani* 2, 104. Now here Chemnitz is wide of the mark! We showed above that nearly all the Fathers distinguish Confirmation from Baptism and attribute to it a spiritual effect which does not suit anything but the Sacraments truly and properly speaking. That much is also manifestly clear from the passages of Augustine (*loc. cit.*), which Chemnitz abridged, as is his custom, and imperfectly cited. In the first passage, he says the Bishops of the Church give the laying on of hands, and anoint with chrism so that the Holy Spirit would be given, as the Apostles formerly did (Act. 8:17). Certainly, the action of the Apostles was not a human ceremony joined to Baptism, but another thing, and indeed, *divine* and most efficacious. In the second place of Augustine, he labors much to show that true Confirmation may be given and received by the wicked, as even Baptism itself. But why would it be necessary to prove this in regard to a human and sterile ceremony, for who could be uncertain about that? Next, (*ibid.*), Augustine says the wicked receive the visible Sacrament of Confirmation without the invisible grace of the Holy Spirit, and therefore judgment. Certainly, he would not distinguish a visible Sacrament from invisible grace in the wicked unless he believed that in the good these are joined, and one is given through the other; nor are human ceremonies received unto judgment, even if the wicked receive them. Lastly (*ibid.*), Augustine says the Sacrament of Chrism is sacrosanct, just as even Baptism itself. But how great a blasphemy would it be to equate a human ceremony with the Sacrament of Baptism?

d) Fourthly, Chemnitz says, that even if the fathers spoke in different ways on this matter, still there is no o Father in the first part of antiquity who takes its effects from Baptism so that he would attribute them to Chrism, as the Papists do now. Because Cyril of Jerusalem seems to stand very much in his way, he calls into doubt whether they are his *Catecheses*, and whether or not he wandered from the faith at some time; at length, he rejects what Cyril says as false. But these are mere trifles, for we do not say that we take the effects from Baptism, rather, we attribute to each Sacrament its own effects. Yet no man ever had any doubts about the *Catecheses* of Cyril, nor does Chemnitz advance any reason or conjecture as to why there should be a doubt. On the faith and uprightness of Cyril, there is an outstanding testimony from the Council of Constantinople to Damasus (cited by Theodoret 5, 9) where that whole Ecumenical Council strongly commends Cyril because of the many struggles he waged with the Arians for the sake of the Catholic faith.

e) Fifthly, Chemnitz says that the Fathers speak very differently from more recent authors, for the Fathers inculcate the laying on of hands, although now it has been abolished; likewise, the Fathers name oil, but no esteemed author added the mixture with balsam, as all more recent authors do. The ancients attribute those effects to Baptism which more recent writers attribute to Confirmation, such as to give grace, to give the Holy Spirit, to perfect, to arm against the devil, etc. Lastly, the Fathers connect anointing with Baptism; more recent authors separate them as if they were two Sacraments. But here, Chemnitz also hallucinates very much. In the first place, it is false that the laying on of hands was abolished, as we showed above in ch. 2. Next, Pope Gregory I explicitly mentions the mixing of balsam with oil (*Cant.* 1), who certainly is a most upright author, but we

Chapter VII: Heretical Arguments are Refuted

will address this matter later. Besides, it is false that the Fathers attributed the same effects to Baptism which we attribute to Confirmation, even if the names of the effects are often the same. Baptism gives grace and the Holy Spirit, but for other effects than Confirmation. This is why the Lord gave the Holy Spirit to the Apostles through breathing in Jo. 20:22, and still at the same time he promised the Holy Spirit to them in Act. 1:8 and he gave it in Act. 2:4; so also Baptism arms, because it gives grace to do well, but Confirmation adds a peculiar strength to profess the faith. This is why in Luke 24:49 it is said to the Apostles, though they were already baptized, "Remain in the city, until you are clothed with power from on high." Lastly, Baptism perfects in its genus because it truly and wholly causes men to be just and sons of God; nevertheless, Confirmation still perfects but in another genus, in the way an infant is a complete human in everything that regards its essence, and still it has not been completed in regard to the mass of difficulties of life. Therefore, the same Fathers who speak splendidly on Baptism, also speak splendidly about Confirmation (*loc. cit.*).

What Chemnitz objects, however, on the joining of anointing with Baptism, shows his ignorance. For the Fathers usually also join the Eucharist with Baptism, whether they would baptize adults or infants, and still no man denies they are distinct Sacraments, Baptism and the Eucharist. In this time, when adults are baptized, Baptism, Confirmation, and the Eucharist are given on the same day, just as the Fathers did; but when infants are baptized, the other two Sacraments are delayed until those who are going to receive them would obtain the use of reason, because these Sacraments are not necessary for infants and are received with greater fruit and reverence by adults. Nor do the Lutherans disagree with us in this matter.

CHAPTER VIII

On the Matter of the Sacrament of Confirmation

A SECOND question follows on the matter of this Sacrament. Even if we have already said certain things on that in the previous question, still we must explain the matter more accurately. Therefore, Catholics teach in a common consensus that the remote matter of this Sacrament is *oil mixed with balsam and consecrated by a bishop;* the proximate matter which is properly the second part of the Sacrament, is *the anointing from the aforesaid oil, applied on the forehead in the form or figure of a cross.* The heretics not only reject the whole, but also mock it, as can be understood from their citations in the previous question, where they call it oiliness by a contumely, and Chemnitz (*Exam.* p. 324) does not think a man impious who would rub his shoes with the sacred chrism when they have been dried out from a journey. In France, the Calvinists are said to oil their greaves with chrism. However, to be able to prove this truth more suitably, I will establish the following propositions.

1) *Chrism, or anointing, is the matter of the Sacrament of Confirmation.* This is absolutely certain for Catholics, from the Council of Florence (Instruction of the Armenians) and the Council of Trent (sess. 7 can. 2 on Confirmation). It is proven *firstly,* from two passages of Scripture where either this anointing is expressly mentioned, or is certainly alluded to. The first is 2 Cor. 1:21, "Now God is the one that confirms us with you in Christ, and has anointed us; and it is he that has sealed us, and given the pledge of the Spirit in our hearts." St. Ambrose explains this in regard to the Sacrament of Confirmation (*On the Mysteries,* c. 7), as well as Anselm and Theodoret in their *Commentary,* and the words signify this clearly enough. Firstly, the words *he confirms* is proper for this Sacrament, whereby strength is given. Then *he anointed us* is either referred to that outward anointing, or if it is referred to the internal, it is an allusion to the external; therefore, that internal illustration and operation of the Holy Spirit is called anointing, because through the external anointing he is customarily given and signified. The verse, however, *he has sealed us* can be referred to the internal sealing through the character and to the external sign of the cross, which is impressed on the forehead in this Sacrament. Lastly, *he has given the pledge of the Spirit in our hearts* very clearly describes the principal effect of this Sacrament, which is the gift of charity. Now, the second passage is 1 John 2:27, "As for you, let the anointing which you have received from him abide in you, ..." Cyril explains this passage in regard to

Chapter VIII: The Matter of Confirmation

the Sacrament (*Catech. Mystagog.* 3), as well as Augustine (*Tract. in Epist. Joannis* 3), where he says it is a certain Sacrament of Anointing, whose power is only invisible.

Secondly, it is proven and indeed more efficacious from the common consensus of the Popes, Councils, and the Fathers, both Greek and Latin, whom we have already cited. Even if the testimonies of Scripture hold first place when they are clear, nevertheless when they are not so obvious, the authority of the Church, which Scripture itself clearly commends, is of greater importance.

2) The second proposition: *The matter of Confirmation is not simple oil, but oil mixed with balsam.* It is proven *firstly* from the tradition of the ancients. Dionysius the Areopagate, even if he does not name balsam, sill clearly describes it from the effect, or propriety; accordingly, in *The Ecclesiastical Hierarchy*, (4, part. 3) he says chrism is composed from different things and is fragrant, "We say the composition for the anointing is a gathering of sweet breathing material." *Secondly*, Clement (*Constit. Apostol.* 7, 44), in the blessing of Chrism, mentions the fragrance of the odor. *Thirdly*, Fabian, Pope and Martyr, in his second *Epistle ad Orientales* clearly says Christ himself established that chrism would be consecrated from oil mixed with balsam. *Fourthly*, Cyprian, or whoever is the author, in the sermon *On the Anointing of Chrism*, says, "Today in the Church the sacred chrism is confected wherein balsam that has been mixed with oil expresses the unity of the sacerdotal and royal glory." *Fifthly*, Gregory of Tours (*de Gloria Martyrum*, 40), relating the great miracle which is extant even in Prudentius (*contra Judaeos*) for the fact that Prudentius had said "washed and anointed" (for so the notion of the song requires), says, "Washed in Baptism, anointed in balsam." There, we see Gregory's interpretation that in the time of Prudentius balsam was in chrism, even for a long time before Prudentius, for he relates the history which took place in the time of a pagan emperor. When this emperor went to inspect the innards of the sacrifices, and seek a response by the arts of the demons, he could do nothing because the demons feared the presence of a youth who was present with the Emperor, who had been washed in Baptism and anointed on the forehead with chrism. *Sixthly*, Pope Gregory the Great, as we cited above (*Cant.* 1), asserts in clear words that chrism is confected from oil and balsam, and he did not institute something new, but only related what was in the use of the Church. *Seventhly*, the second Council of Braga (can. 4) was celebrated a little after the death of Gregory, and it also expressly mentions balsam, as even the Council of Florence in the *Instruct. To the Armenians*, and all the Scholastics, as well as more recent authors.

The rest of the ancient Fathers, even if they do not expressly name balsam, nevertheless seem to signify the same thing clearly enough, since they do not call the anointing oil, but chrism, which is given in the Sacrament of Confirmation; for chrism, in the use of the Church, does not signify simple oil, but *anointing confected from many things*. It is clear from Innocent III (c. *Pastoralis,* extra, *de Sacramentis non iterandis*), who, relating that a certain man that had been anointed in the Sacrament of Confirmation with simple oil by mistake, not with oil and balsam, as is the custom; he writes the man was anointed with simple blessed oil, not chrism, where he distinguishes chrism from oil on account of the mixture of another liquid. So also the second Council of Carthage (can. 3) and the third Council of Carthage (can. 36) say that a priest is not permitted to confect chrism. What is it to confect chrism, except to make an anointing from many liquids?

Secondly, we add the figures of the Old Testament. Anointing, which God commanded to be done in Exodus 30:25 to anoint the tabernacle as well as priests, was a figure of Chrism whereby the Church, which is the true tabernacle of God, is anointed, as Cyprian teaches in a sermon on the Anointing of Chrism, and Peter Damian in his first sermon on the dedication. That, however, was from olive oil mixed with fragrant juices, one of which was בֶּשֶׂם (*besschem*), which is the oil of myrrh, and was also called balsam.

Lastly, we add also a congruency which Chemnitz, in his attempt to ridicule it, simply ridicules himself. The argument of Theologians, and even St. Thomas himself (III q. 72, art. 2) is that the matter of a Sacrament ought to signify the effect of the Sacrament. Hence, the effect of this Sacrament is particularly *strengthening in faith*, which requires two things: purity and ardor for the faith in heart, and a constant confession in mouth. The first is very clearly signified in oil, because it is a very pure and delicate liquid, lucid and clear; the second is no less suitably signified by balsam, which pours forth out a good smell to others.

Besides, the effects of this Sacrament were signified in the fiery tongues, which appeared over the Apostles on the day of Pentecost. Even if the Apostles were confirmed immediately by God without the Sacrament on that day, still not without the visible symbol signifying the invisible effect. Therefore, to these two symbols, fire and tongues, or rather, one constituted from the two parts, i.e., fiery tongues, the oil and balsam in our Sacrament, or chrism constituted from oil and balsam, correspond in the best possible way.

Chemnitz mocks this notion in these words, "Raise your ears, dear reader, for you will hear great and characteristic acumen! ... You will marvel, I know, when you hear: Oil in the papist Confirmation corresponds to the fire in Pentecost. By what reason? Because oil feeds the fire. But an oak stave that has been hardened by smoke does the same thing. Balsam corresponds to the appearance of tongues because it puts out a fragrance. But what do tongues and smells have in common? Do we smell with a tongue?"

It is no marvel if an absurd man absurdly understood what learned

Chapter VIII: The Matter of Confirmation

men have written well, for we do not say oil corresponds to fire because it nourishes fire, but because, just as in the Scriptures through fire wisdom and charity are signified, and the Holy Spirit himself, illuminating and warming hearts, just as fire gives light and enkindles corporeal things; so also in the Scriptures, oil or anointing signifies the same charity and wisdom as the Holy Spirit himself. Oil makes things bright and clear, and at the same time warms, softens, penetrates, etc. Therefore, we read in regard to fire in Lk. 12:49, "I came to send fire upon the earth"; and Hebr. 12:29, "God is our consuming fire,"; and similarly we read about anointing in Act. 10:38, "He anointed with the Holy Spirit, and power"; and 1 Jn. 2:27, "[His] anointing will teach you about all things." Chemnitz, however, will not find where in the Scriptures the Holy Spirit is compared to an oak stave. What pertains to tongues and balsam, the similitude was placed in the fact that just as a word is communicated by a tongue, and in that way the confession of faith goes abroad, so through balsam the odor is shared, and in the same way the outward protestation of the true faith. Now, that is enough for the petty trifling of Chemnitz.

3) The third proposition: *Chrism, which is the matter for the Sacrament of Confirmation, should first be consecrated and blessed.* All Catholics also agree on this point. On the other hand, Calvin, and Chemnitz call this blessing superstitious and magical, to such an extent that Calvin in the *Institutes* (4, 19 §8) calls consecrated chrism the oil of the devil polluted by a lie, and Chemnitz (p. 287) says it should be called bewitched. This truth must be proven by the testimonies of ancient holy Popes, of Councils, and the Fathers.

It is proved firstly from the Ecclesiastical tradition of the Holy Popes. Clement the Roman treats profusely enough on this consecration, which he also attributes to the Apostles (*Apostol. Constitut.* 7, 42 & 44). Pope Fabian, who was also a martyr, teaches the same thing (*loc. cit.*), who also adds that each year on Maundy Thursday new chrism is consecrated. Damasus I (*Epist.* 4), Innocent I (*Epist.* 1, 3), Leo I (*Epist.* 88), Gelasius I (*Epist.* 1) and John III (*Epist.*), Gregory I (*loc. cit.*), as well as Innocent III (cap. *Cum venisset*, extra *de sacra unction*) all clearly teach chrism must be consecrated and by the Bishop alone.

Secondly, it is proven from Councils. The Council of Nicaea (can. 69 according to the Arabic codex), expressly mentions a threefold consecration, which is in force in the Church today, i.e., the oil of the Catechumens, the oil of the Sick, and Chrism. The Council of Laodicea (can. 48) calls chrism most holy, a description they would not have used unless it were consecrated. The Roman Council under Sylvester (can. 5) forbids priests from making chrism, because it pertains to the office of a Bishop. Hence, to make chrism is not only to mix oil with balsam, but also to consecrate it at the same time, for otherwise, any druggist could make chrism. The second and third Councils of Carthage (*loci cit.*) a little later forbade the same thing. The fourth Council of Carthage bid parish priests every year during Easter to ask for chrism from their own bishop, and that not by younger clergy, but themselves, or through the one who is in charge of the sanctuary. There we see in this Council, which is held in the greatest authority by all, the same thing is held in regard to renewing chrism each year, which is found in the Epistle of Fabian, although some would hold it as apocryphal. We see besides what reverence the Council showed to this holy oil, since it forbade younger clergy from conveying it, rather, it expressly commanded that the priest himself, who is in charge of a parish, or certainly who is in charge of the sanctuary, to receive it from the Bishop. The Council of Vasense holds the same thing (can. 3) where it also says it is not fitting for the greatest things to be committed to the lowest, and therefore no cleric should deliver the chrism unless he was at least a Subdeacon. The first Council of Toledo (can. 20) again declares that it is lawful for a bishop alone to consecrate chrism, and each year it is to be sought from him a little before Easter. The second Council of Hispalense (can. 7) and the first Council of Braga (can. 37), the Council of St. Boniface the Martyr, which is extant in his life, and the Council of Worms, can. 2 & 8, and lastly the Council of Florence (*Inst. to the Armenians*) all teach the same thing.

Moreover, we must remark that these Councils, apart from Florence, are not only ancient, but were celebrated in different places: Nicaea and Laodicea in Greece, Rome and Florence in Italy, Carthage in Africa, Toledo and Hispalense in Spain, Braga in Portugal, Vasense in France, the Council of St. Boniface as well as Worms in Germany. From this it can altogether be gathered that the heretics of this time, who detest the consecration of chrism as a magical thing, despise the whole ancient Church.

Thirdly, it is proven from the Fathers. Dionysius the Areopagate (*Ecclesiastical Hierarchy* c. 4) treats on this consecration, which he also affirms that he learned from the Apostles. Theophilus, the sixth bishop of Antioch after the Apostle Peter (*Ad Autolycum* lib. 1, which is held in the fifth volume of the *Bibliotheca Sanctorum Patrum*) calls sacred chrism the divine oil, where he also says Christians are given their name by this anointing. This must be remarked upon against Chemnitz, who on p. 305 convicts Cyril of a lie against the word of God because he had said those who were not anointed with Chrism are unworthy of the name of Christian. "Since still it is certain," Chemnitz says, "the Christian name arose at Antioch, as Luke witnesses (Act. 11:26)." As if this name could not have first been imposed at Antioch, and nevertheless be derived from chrism. Certainly, Theophilus, the Bishop of Antioch, knew Antiochene affairs better and was nearer in time to Apostolic affairs than Chemnitz the German, who was only born yesterday.

Tertullian, in his book *On Baptism*, "After this, when we have issued from the laver, we are thoroughly anointed with a blessed anointing." Cyprian (*Epist.* 1, 12), says, "Oil is sanctified on the altar; but one could not

Chapter VIII: The Matter of Confirmation

sanctify the creature of oil, who had neither an altar nor Church. This is why there cannot be a spiritual anointing among the heretics, when it is certain the oil cannot be sanctified and the Eucharist made among them." The author of the sermon *On the anointing of Chrism*, found in the works of Cyprian, "Today (i.e., Maundy Thursday) the anointing is prepared to sanctification." Basil (*On the Holy Spirit*, 27), "We bless water in Baptism, and oil in Unction." Cyril (*Catech. Mystagog.* 3), "The holy anointing is no mere anointing after it has been consecrated, but the chrism of Christ." Optatus (lib. 2), "So that your bishops would violate everything that is most holy, they command the Eucharist to be given to dogs, and the vessels of chrism thrown out the window to break them." But certainly, Chrism would not be called most holy, nor could it be compared to the Eucharist, unless it had been consecrated. Augustine (*On Baptism* 5, 19 & 20) answers the argument of Cyprian, in which he would have it that heretics do not have true Sacraments because they cannot consecrate the oil to anoint the baptized so they would receive the Holy Spirit. There, he does not say (but certainly should have according to Calvin and Chemnitz) it is not necessary to consecrate oil, nay more the consecration of oil is a superstition and a magic spell; rather, he answers that the heretics can consecrate oil, because without a doubt the power of consecration is not in them from heresy, but from *ordination*, which they received that is true and holy. He proves it from a similitude, for if priests can be murderers and adulterers in the Church, even Cyprian agreed they could consecrate oil; so why not heretics, provided they were truly ordained? "Why," he asks, "by the words which proceed from the mouth of a murderer, could God sanctify oil, and not be able to on the altar which heretics laid down, I do not know." See also *Tract. In Joan.* 118, near the end.

We can add to these Bede (*on Act. 8*) and Rupert (*de Divin. Offic.* 5, 17 & 18); Isidore (*de Divin. Office.* 1, 28); Alcuin (*de Divin. Offic.* cap. *de feria V in Coena Domini*), and Amalarius (*de office. Eccl.* 1, c. *de feria V in Coena Domini*) and St. Peter Damian in his first sermon on the *Dedication of a Church*.

4) The fourth proposition: *The anointing of chrism in the form of a cross on the forehead of a baptized man should be done so that it is the true and proximate matter of the Sacrament.* This is clear from what we have already cited. The Popes Damasus, Innocent, Leo, John III, and Gregory I expressly name the seal on the forehead. From Councils: II Hispalense as well as Florence. From the Fathers: Tertullian (*de Praescriptione*) says, "He signs his solders on the forehead"; Cyril (*Cateches. Mystagogic.* 3); Prudentius in ψθχομαχία; Augustine on *Ps. 141*, on the words, *In this way upon which I was walking, they have hidden the snare of pride for me*, where he says the different Sacraments are received in different parts, certain ones in the whole body, such as Baptism, and in the mouth such as the Eucharist, or the sign of the cross on the forehead in Confirmation. His reason is that the

forehead is the place of shame; this seal is given, however, so that we will not be ashamed to confess the Lord, even in the presence of our persecutors. Rabanus, Peter Damian, and all the others hold the same thing.

CHAPTER IX

The Objections against the Matter of Confirmation Are Answered

1) THE *first* objection is of Brenz in the Wittenberg Confession (cap. *de Baptismo*). The use of chrism pertains to the elements of this world and to Jewish ceremonies, from which Paul recalls us in Coloss. 2:20, "If you are dead with Christ, from the elements of this world, why are you still resolved to live as in the world?"

I respond: If the argument were to avail, it would prove that not even water is to be used in Baptism nor bread in the Eucharist, because the Jews also used these things when they had the water of expiation and the bread of proposition; this is why, just as water and bread could be of service to a shadow and the truth, so also can oil. Paul, however, recalls us from *Jewish* ceremonies, which were truly elements, and needy, as he says elsewhere, since they could not justify, not about *Christian* Sacraments, however, although they consist in the same matter.

2) The *second* objection: Dionysius the Areopagate does not obscurely signify the Rite of Chrism was taken from the athletic anointings of the pagans and partly from the Mosaic Law, but Moses, in Deut. 12:30, says, "Beware, lest you imitate the Gentiles, and seek after their ceremonies ..."

I respond: Dionysius attributes Chrism to a doctrine of the *Apostles of Christ*, not the pagans or the Jews, as we showed above. What he says in regard to the Jews pertains to the figure of this Sacrament, not to its essence and truth. What he says in regard to athletes does not pertain to a ceremony and cult, as Brenz dreams up, but to the effect of the Sacrament that must be explained through a similitude: as athletes were anointed to win a physical battle, so we are anointed in holy chrism so that we may win in the spiritual battle. Many Fathers use that similitude, such as Chrysostom, Ambrose, Augustine, and others. Now, the testimony of Deuteronomy does not bear on the matter, since athletes are not anointed to worship God by that ceremony.

3) The *third* objection: The Acts of Councils witness that Chrism was instituted by Sylvester; therefore, it could not have been in use among the Apostles, as Fabian writes.

I respond: The Acts of Councils, or rather Damasus in the *Life of Sylvester*, only witnesses that Sylvester commanded priests to touch the crown of the baptized man with chrism. That is an anointing distinct from the Sacrament of Confirmation, which is given on the forehead by a bishop. Chrism, however, could not have been instituted by Sylvester, as is abundantly clear from Tertullian, Theophilus of Antioch, Cyprian, Cornelius, and others cited above, who lived before Pope Sylvester, and expressly mentioned Chrism.

4) Chemnitz's first argument is to object against the first proposition which we laid down in the last chapter and was taken from the Scriptures, for in Act. 2:4 and 10:44, the Holy Spirit is given without any chrism. Likewise, in Act. 8:17 and 19:6, while it mentions the laying on of hands, it does not mention chrism.

I respond: What pertains to Act. 2 and 10, in these passages the Holy Spirit was not given by the ministry of the Sacraments, rather, the *effect* of the Sacrament was given by God in a singular privilege, without the Sacrament.

In what pertains to the other two passages, two answers are customarily given. The *first* is of some Scholastics, who say the Apostles administered this Sacrament in a different way. In the earliest times, since the Holy Spirit visibly descended, they did not use any anointing but the simple laying on of hands. Accordingly, the outward fire, which appeared from heaven, sufficiently witnessed the internal effect. Later, when these visible forms ceased, then they began to apply anointing, so that they would signify through it what was signified by the appearance of the visible species from heaven. If someone would object that the Apostles could not institute the matter of the Sacrament, they respond, that the Apostles did not institute it, but received that command from Christ, but first used only the laying on of hands, and later chrism precisely as they judged it to be opportune. This answer is not altogether improbable, and St. Thomas is not adverse to it (III q. 72 art. 2), and perhaps the testimonies of the Council of Florence and Innocent III (cap. *Cum Venisset,* extra., *de Sacra Unctione*) who say the Sacrament of Confirmation is given in the Church in place of the Apostolic laying on of hands.

Nevertheless, there is another solution, which seems to me more probable by far, of Thomas Waldens (*de Saramentis* 2, 113) and Hugh of St. Victor (*de Sacramentis* 2, p. 7, cap. 2) who say the anointing of chrism, and the laying on of hands is the same thing, since the one who anoints gives the laying on of hands. Both are shown, even if only the second seems to be expressed. This answer is more probable, for it is certain that the Apostles, in Confirmation, used chrism, since Dionysius and Clement assert the fact; besides, very ancient authors call it to mind, such as Theophilus of Antioch, Tertullian, Cyprian, Cornelius, Origen, and others, before whom there was no Ecumenical Council, in which it could be instituted. It is also certain that it would be desirable that it could be defended that the Apostles always used the same matter, not one now and another later, for that is safer and more expedient. But why, I ask, can that not be defended? They say, "Because Luke mentions the laying on of hands, but not chrism." But

Chapter IX: Objections Answered 477

neither Luke, nor any other Scripture, nor even any of the Fathers, ever said the Apostles ministered this Sacrament in a different way. Besides, in the words of Luke chrism can also be understood and we can prove it in many ways. That the Apostles changed the matter, however, I do not know whether it can be proven in any way except from the authority of more recent authors.

a) Firstly, I so prove the Apostles always, by giving the laying on of hands, sealed with chrism, and hence Luke touched upon that rite in a compendium and understood the whole matter from one side, for the Fathers say in one place that the Holy Spirit is given by the laying on of hands, the same in another place say it is given through the anointing of chrism, and sometimes join both together at the same time, from which it appears that both pertain to this rite, and so it is for them, whether they express one or the other. Tertullian in *de Resurrectione*, treating on this rite, says the flesh is anointed, sealed, and overshadowed by the laying on of hands. Still, in *de Praescriptionibus* he only expresses that the sign is made on the forehead, in *Contra Marcionem* (lib. 1) he only expresses anointing, and in *de Baptismo*, he expresses anointing and the laying on of hands. So we see one author here express one part, there two, another three of the same rite, and still he always signified the same thing. Cyprian in the first book of his *Epistles*, the final epistle, only calls to mind anointing; in the second book, *epistle* 1, he only mentions the laying on of hands, although he speaks on one and the same thing. Then in his *Epistle to Jubajanus*, he adds the Lord's seal by the laying on of hands, on which he had spoken in the first two epistles. So also, the first Council of Arles (can. 8) only names the laying on of hands, and still in the second Council of Arles, celebrated a little later, treating on the same manner in can. 17, names the anointing of chrism. Damasus and Leo (*loc. cit.*) say it is not lawful for Choir-bishops to anoint the forehead of the baptized with Chrism, and still John III, citing this very decree and bringing forward Damasus and Leo by name, does not even once mention chrism or the forehead, but always calls this rite the laying on of hands; a great many examples of this sort can be advanced. Why would it be surprising if Luke signified the whole rite from one part?

b) Secondly, I prove the same for another reason. The Fathers, when they say the Bishops alone give the Holy Spirit through the anointing of Chrism, they always bring forward the words of Luke in Act. 8:17. (Pope Innocent I, *Epist.* 1; Damasus, *Epist.* 4; Leo, *Epist.* 88; Cyprian, *ad Jubajanum*, Augustine *de Trinitate* 15, 26) and from others cited above. Therefore, either the Apostles in Act. 8:17, by giving the laying on of hands anointed with chrism, or all these Fathers argued badly. Now, someone will say: They argued well, because although in Act. 8:17 the Apostles did not use chrism, still chrism succeeded in place of the laying on of hands, which they used. On the contrary, for if it were so, at least some of the Fathers at some time would have showed it, so that we would understand the force of their argument.

c) Thirdly, I prove the same thing from similar passages of Scripture, where something is dealt with very briefly and still it is necessary to understand more things. For example, what Paul says in his epistles to Timothy and Titus always calls ordination *the laying on of hands*. Augustine advances an example in his book *on Faith and Works* (ch. 9) from Act. 8:37, where we read the Eunuch was baptized by Philip when he said, "I believe Jesus is the son of God." Augustine, however, rightly notes that Luke touched on the matter as through a compendium. In point of fact, we should altogether believe that the Eunuch was asked about many other matters, and many other ceremonies would have been applied in that Baptism. Another example can be that which Luke says, that the Apostles baptized in the name of Christ (Act. 8:12, 19:5, and elsewhere). As we said above, Luke preferred to speak in a compendium, knowing the matter was already widely known. Another can be in the fact that Paul says to Titus (Tit. 3:5) that we are saved by the laver of regeneration, where he said nothing about the word and still understood without any doubt the laver with the *word*, as he expressed the same thing elsewhere (Eph. 5:26). There are many things of this sort, which would be very long to review here.

c) There is one difficulty, that this, our answer, seems to be opposed to Innocent III (cap. *Cum Venisset*, extra, *de Sacra Unctione*) and the Council of Florence (*Instruct. Armenorum*). Innocent says through the chrismation of the font the laying on of hands of the Apostles is signified; the Council, however, says Confirmation is now given in the Church in place of that laying on of hands.

I respond: In the first place, not everything which is found in decrees or Councils pertain to faith, but only those things which *are defined*. This, however, on which we are treating, was not defined, but only said in passing to explain the matter.

Nevertheless, I would say it is safer and better that Innocent and the Council did not mean to say chrism is in place of the laying on of hands, as if the Apostles did not use chrism and we do not use the laying on of hands; rather, they meant to say it is the very thing which the Apostles did, since they were saying to give the laying on of hands, bishops do now when they are said to confirm or chrismate. In these places rite is not distinguished from rite, rather *a manner of speaking from a manner of speaking*, and *persons from persons*, and then that particular laying on of hands, from this which is now. Accordingly, at that time this Sacrament was commonly called *the laying on of hands*, now it is commonly called *Confirmation*. Besides, the Apostles gave the former, the bishops the latter; lastly, it was more efficacious, because with the internal effect it also gave an external one, and with *gratia gratum faciens*, it was also giving the gratuitous gifts of tongues and miracles, etc. So by this reasoning, it can be said that what is done now is in place of that which was done

Chapter IX: Objections Answered

then, although it is the same thing in regard to *substance*. That this is the sense of those citations is proven in two ways. *Firstly*, because the Council and Innocent III do not say chrism is in place of the laying on of hands, but the Sacrament of Confirmation is in place of the laying on of hands. Certainly, the Apostles, by the consensus of all, were giving the Sacrament of Confirmation, whether they applied chrism or not. *Secondly*, because the Council of Florence and Innocent say in the same place that bishops in the Church are *in place of*, or *in succession to*, the Apostles. Now certainly, the Apostles were true bishops, even if being an Apostle was something more.

5) The *second* objection of Chemnitz is against the same proposition taken from the Fathers. He says, that Tertullian (*de Baptismo*) says this anointing is taken from ancient discipline, i.e., from the Old Testament, and hence was not instituted by Christ. Cyprian, in his *Sermon on the Washing of Feet*, says these ceremonies are not from Christ, but were instituted by men, and in his *Sermon on Chrism*, says this anointing was left behind from the Old Testament. Basil says a λόγον γεγραμμένον (written word) does not exist on the anointing of chrism. Consequently, Chemnitz says the life of Fabian, Pope and Martyr has been refuted sufficiently enough, namely that this anointing was handed down by Christ himself to the Apostles.

I respond: Tertullian only asserts the fact that *figures* of this Sacrament preceded in the Old Testament, from which it does not follow that it was not instituted by Christ. He asserts (*ibid.*) that the flood was a figure of Baptism, and still Chemnitz would affirm that Tertullian does not deny Baptism was instituted by Christ. Cyprian, in his *Sermon on the Washing of Feet*, does not speak about the Sacrament of Confirmation when he says the ceremonies of the Sacraments were instituted by men, but understands *other* rites which we apply. Nay more, the contrary of what Chemnitz says is gathered from this author, for in that sermon (*ibid.*) he says Christ is the author of this Sacrament, and in the following sermon, which is on Chrism, he says this anointing was divinely instituted and is a Sacrament, from which it is certainly gathered that it was instituted by Christ. Nor is it opposed that he asserts that it remains from the Old Testament, because he understands it by the notion *of figures*, as we said about Tertullian. Next, Basil upholds nothing against us or St. Fabian. Neither St. Fabian nor we say that the institution of Chrism was written in Scripture, rather we say it is held *from the unwritten tradition, and still is very certain*, and to which faith must be applied, just as to the written word, as Basil writes in the same place, and clearly in his book *On the Holy Spirit* (c. 27). Nor is it opposed to those things which were said in the beginning of the previous chapter, there is a *mention* in the epistles of Paul and John, but not the institution of Chrism.

3) The *third* objection of Chemnitz is against the second proposition. Native balsam, together with its trees, certainly perished long ago. Pliny writes (12, 25) that true balsam customarily arose in two gardens of Judaea,

but these gardens were devastated long ago. "Therefore," Chemnitz says, "the matter of Confirmation perished, if it necessarily requires balsam; nor can natural balsam be supplied by unnatural and artificial balsam; just as artificial water cannot be supplied for the water of Baptism, nor the wine of the Eucharist by some artificial wine." Certain Catholics add to this that it is not probable that Christ willed to institute some Sacrament in a matter so uncertain, rare and precious, which can scarcely be obtained with great labor and consumed.

I respond: There is a question among Theologians, as to whether balsam is required in chrism by the necessity of the Sacrament, or only by the necessity of precept. All the old Theologians commenting on the *Sentences* (4, dist. 7), as well as *Jureconsultis* (cap. *Pastoralis*, extra, *de Sacramentis non iterandis*), teach balsam is required by the necessity of the Sacrament, so that the Sacrament would be invalid if it were given without balsam. Nevertheless, certain more recent theologians suppose balsam is not required for the essence of the Sacrament, but must necessarily be applied by *divine* precept (Cajetan in 3 part. q. 72, art. 2; Domingo del Soto *Sent.* 4, dist. 7 q. 1 art. 2; Francis Victoria *Summa de Sacramento Confirmationis*). Both opinions rest upon a certain text of Canon Law, in the chapter *Pastoralis*, extravagantes, *On the Sacraments That Are Not Repeated*, and each opinion brings that text to itself. Neither opinion is *de fide*, or against the faith, and Chemnitz is deceived on p. 309, where he teaches the Council of Florence defined against the Scholastics that balsam is required in chrism, for the Council did not express in what way it was required, but said the matter is oil with balsam, just as even in the Eucharist it had said the matter is wine with water, and still all affirm water is not so required of its essence, that without it the Sacrament would be invalid.

Now, as far as Chemnitz's argument, I deny that true and native balsam perished. Even if in some opinion of Pliny balsam originated in two gardens of Judaea, nevertheless it is found in the Indies, and is still conveyed hence. Nor does Pliny relate if he is unaware of it, for he could not know everything. The balsam which is brought from the Indies should not be called unnatural and artificial, although it is perhaps not the same species as that which is native to Palestine. There can be different species of balsam, just as there are different species of wine, and each are suitable to confect the Sacrament. Add that what Pliny relates about the two gardens refers to *antiquity;* for in his time he affirmed there were many balsam trees in Palestine. Jerome, who lived three hundred years after Pliny, in his *Commentary on Ezechiel* (ch. 27) and Gregory (*Cantic.* 1), who lived two hundred years after Jerome and five hundred after Pliny, both affirm in their time balsam was normally grown in the vineyards of Engaddi. Thus, it is false that native balsam perished. The practice of the Church responds to the confirmation. Although balsam is rare and precious, still the Church was never without it, nor on account of scarcity of balsam did it

Chapter IX: Objections Answered

at sometimes go without Confirmation. But if God has provided for nearly 1600 years, certainly it will not be without it hereafter.

6) The *fourth* objection of Chemnitz is against the third proposition, because the rite of consecrating chrism seems to be a certain species of magic and spells. We already spoke about this argument above on the matter of the Sacraments in General, and we will speak also later, when we argue on the ceremonies of this Sacrament.

7) The *fifth* objection is against the fourth proposition, which Chemnitz takes from Cyril and Ambrose. In *Cateches. Mystagog.* 3, Cyril says nearly every sense of the body is anointed with chrism; Ambrose, however, in *de Mysteriis* (ch. 6) says the head is anointed, and thence the anointing flows down to the beard. Therefore, it is not certain what we say, that chrism must be applied on the forehead.

I respond: Cyril (*loc. cit.*) expressly says the forehead *in particular* is anointed, then the other senses, which is not against us; accordingly, we merely assert that unless chrism is applied on the forehead, the Sacrament is null, but we do not deny that then some other parts of the body can be anointed according to the customs of different Churches. Moreover, Ambrose (*loc. cit.*) does not argue about Confirmation, but the anointing which is done in Baptism, which even we affirm must be done on the crown of the head; Ambrose does, however, argue about Confirmation in the following chapter of *de Mysteriis*.

CHAPTER X

On the Form of the Sacrament of Confirmation

The form of this Sacrament are these words, "I seal [*consigno*] you with the sign of the cross, and I confirm you with the chrism of salvation, in the name of the Father, and of the Son, and of the Holy Spirit." There cannot be any doubt whether this form is suitable, since it clearly explains both the principal cause, which is the Holy Trinity, and the ministerial cause, which is the man who says the words, and then the effect of the Sacrament, which is to make one a soldier of Christ by sealing him with the cross, and to strengthen as well as to arm by confirming with chrism. This form is found in clear words in the Council of Florence in the Roman Pontifical, and they are cited by St. Thomas (III q. 72 art. 4).[20]

Not all of these words are found among the more ancient authors, and in this order; nevertheless, the same sense is found, and that is enough. The force of the sacramental form is posited in *the sense*, not in the sound or number of letters; otherwise, if someone were to advance these words in Greek, or Hebrew, or in another language, it would effect nothing. Thus, the Roman Ordinal, which is a most ancient book, seeing that it is cited by both Alcuin and Amalarius, who lived around the year 800, in *The Office of Holy Saturday*, describing the rite of Confirmation, it says the Bishop pronounces these words in the manner of a prayer, "Seal them, O Lord, with the sign of the cross." Thereupon, when he touches the forehead with his thumb, he says, "I confirm you in the name of the Father, and of the Son, and of the Holy Spirit," where we see clearly the same sense of the words. It is of no importance that it is said there, "Seal him," and we say, "I seal you," for we always signify that it is God who principally seals and man who ministerially seals. This is why, even with the form of Baptism which the Greeks use, "Let the servant of Christ be baptized" is regarded as legitimate by everyone, although it is said in another way. It is also does not seem to be of much importance that in the Roman Ordinal "chrism of salvation" is not found, for it is included in the word "I confirm," and is sufficiently shown in the action itself that one is confirmed with chrism in the way in

---

20 *Recognitio* n. VI: In chapter 10, I said, "The form of the Sacrament of Confirmation is: I seal you with the sign of the cross, etc." The word *consigno* is certainly found in St. Thomas (III q. 72 art. 4), still in the Council of Florence and the Roman Pontifical, *consigno* is not found, but *signo*. Although the sense is the same, nevertheless, *signo* must be retained because it is also held in the most ancient Roman Ordinal and is cited by Ambrose (*de Mysteriis*, ch. 7) and by the Apostle in 2 Cor. 1:22.

Chapter X: The Form of Confirmation 483

which it would be the same thing if anyone were to say, "I baptize you," or, "I baptize you with water." This is why it does not seem to be an essential particle, although it should not be omitted because the Church prescribes that it be said; in the same way, in the form of Baptism: *Ego te baptizo*, ... the pronoun *ego* is not of the essence, and in the form of the Eucharist, *Hoc est enim corpus meum*, *enim* and in the form of the chalice *mysterium fidei*, and certain others do not regard the essence [of the form].

From the foregoing we understand two specific things. *Firstly*, Alcuin in *De Divinis Officiis*, cap. *de Sabbato sancto*, where he says the Bishop of Rome, when he confirms, customarily anoints the forehead and says, "In the name of the Father, and of the Son, and of the Holy Spirit"; he does not relate the whole form, but only part of it, for he cites the Roman Ordinal, in which many more things are expressly found, as I have already said. *Secondly*, we understand that certain men are deceived who suppose Ambrose placed the form of Confirmation when he said, "You came to the priest, what did he say to you? God the almighty Father, who regenerated you from water and the Holy Spirit, pardoned your sins, he anointed you in eternal life" (*de Sacramentis* 2, 7). These words which Ambrose lays down, are said in the Roman Ordinal by the priest when he seals the crown of the head of the baptized; after that ceremony, the Episcopal Confirmation follows later. This is why, even Amalarius (*de Officiis Ecclesiasticis* 2, 27) says these words are of the priest, who alone uses the deprecatory form. The Bishop does not only say deprecatorily, but even from his own power, which he received from God, "I confirm you." Moreover, from the Fathers, Ambrose mentions this form clearly enough when he speaks in *de Mysteriis* (ch. 7), "Preserve what you have received, God the Father sealed you, Christ the Lord confirmed you." Nor is it a wonder that he omitted certain things, for in that place he does not relate the form itself, but only recalls in the memory of the confirmands the very rite whereby they were confirmed. It was enough for his purpose if he called to mind the *principal* words.

Nor should it seem marvelous if the Fathers do not expressly posit this form; for they do not describe the forms of the Sacrament. This was not only because these matters were known to all Christians on account of daily use, and even more lest mysteries of this sort would be betrayed to the pagans who saw our books without necessity. Consequently, there is hardly any among the Fathers who clearly wrote the form of Baptism, "I baptize you in the name of the Father, and of the Son, and of the Holy Spirit." They only say Baptism is given with the invocation of the Trinity. Nay more, Dionysius (*Ecclesiastical Hierarchy*) says it is not lawful to commit to letter what the Church uses in the administration of the Sacraments. Innocent I (*Epist.* 1, 3), speaking on Confirmation, says, "I cannot say the words lest I would appear more to betray than answer a question." Lastly, Peter Lombard himself (4, dist. 7) refuses to lay down the words of the form of this Sacrament; he merely says the form is manifest, namely the words which the Bishops use everywhere when they administer this Sacrament.

Now let us see the objections of the heretics.

1) The *first* objection is of Calvin (*Instit.* 4, 19 §5). After he recited the form, "I seal you with the sign of the cross ...," he says, "How now! Beautiful and charming, but where is the word of God?"

I respond: The written word of God does not attest to it, rather the custom of the universal Church *that has been handed down* attests to it clearly enough. The form of the other Sacraments is not expressly found in Scripture; in no place was it written that in Baptism "I baptize you" must be said. Besides, Calvin affirms that the Ordination of ministers is a Sacrament (*ibid.*, §31), and still, he will discover no word in Scripture which would make the Sacrament with the element, as he requires for Confirmation. Besides, I add that *in general*, we have a word in Act. 8:16, where the Apostles are said to have prayed when they gave the laying on of hands. For the Fathers always call the form of the Sacraments *mystical prayers*, although meanwhile they are advanced through the word of indication, for the principal operation in the Sacraments is hoped for and sought from God. Lastly, in 2 Cor. 1:21, when Paul is alluding to the form of this Sacrament, he expresses the principal words when he says, "God is the one who confirms us and sealed us ..."

2) The *Second* objection of Calvin (*ibid.* §7), "How is it that they call it the oil of salvation? Who taught them to look for their salvation in oil? ... I boldly declare this, not of myself, but from the Lord. Those who call oil 'the oil of salvation' abjure the salvation which is in Christ, deny Christ, and have no part in the kingdom of God. Oil is for the belly, and the belly for oil, but the Lord will destroy both."

I respond: This whole argument rests upon the authority of Calvin. He did not advance the word of God, however much he lies about speaking in the name of God, where those who call the oil of Confirmation salutary are said to abjure salvation, which is in Christ. If we were to seek salvation in oil without Christ, then Calvin would have something to say. Yet, since we make oil an *instrument* merely to apply the grace of Christ, one marvels at how Calvin could suspect that those who call oil salutary deny Christ. Add, that phrases of this sort appear very frequently in the Scriptures, such as in 4 Kg. 13:17, "the arrow of salvation," and in 2 Cor. 6:2, "the day of salvation," Act. 13:26 "the word of salvation," Lk. 1:77, "the knowledge of salvation." Add also, that the argument of Calvin avails no less against the water of Baptism and the bread of the Eucharist, than against the oil of Confirmation, for these are called the laver of regeneration and renewal (Tit. 3:5), and the bread of the Eucharist is called the bread of life (Jo. 6:35). Calvin answers (*ibid.*) that two things are considered in the Sacraments, the nature of elements, that they are given to corruption and so cannot confer salvation, and the spiritual power impressed upon them by the word of God. By that notion, the water in Baptism as well as the bread and wine

Chapter X: The Form of Confirmation

in the Eucharist confer salvation. But why, I ask, can we not say the same thing in regard to the oil?

3) The *third* objection is of Chemnitz (*Examination of the Council of Trent*, 2 part., p. 288). The form of this Sacrament, *I seal you with the sign of the cross* ..., is not found in ancient writers nor in Canon law, etc. *I respond:* We already gave the reason for this matter.

4) The *fourth* objection is also of Chemnitz. The form is not the same among the papists themselves. Gabriel Biel recites certain words in place of *Chrism of salvation* to say *Chrism of Sanctification*, and Gerson holds the form *I strengthen you with the sign of the cross and the Chrism of salvation*.

I respond: All of these coincide with our form. The sense is always the same whether you were to say *of salvation*, or *of sanctification*, or *I confirm*, or *I strengthen*, etc., although it behooves one to use the prescribed words and change nothing; anyone who would do this would sin. Nevertheless (as we have often said), while the same sense remains, the Sacrament is always confected, and it can easily happen that in different Churches there would be some variety in terms, provided the same teaching would remain, as is clear in the form of Baptism among the Latins and the Greeks.

CHAPTER XI

On the Effect of This Sacrament

The effect of this Sacrament is two-fold. 1) One, that it confers *gratia gratum faciens*, and greater than Baptism itself, in the manner of fortifying the soul against the assault of the devil, but lesser in the manner of the remission of sin; it does not remit all sin, as the grace of Baptism does. Nor is it necessary to add something here, when it was copiously proven above in the first Controversy; from there we proved that Confirmation is a Sacrament, properly speaking, because the Scriptures and all the Fathers affirm the most copious grace is given by this ceremony, and what is more, the Holy Spirit himself.

2) The second effect is the character, whereby we are enrolled in the army of Christ, just as through Baptism in the household of Christ. This character of Confirmation, however, is proven in the way in which the character of Baptism was proven, from the fact that Confirmation cannot be repeated. We showed above the reason why certain Sacraments are unrepeatable, no sufficient argument can be given apart from the character. For that reason, the character is evidently shown from the effect when we show some Sacrament is unrepeatable.

The fact that Confirmation is unrepeatable is expressly proven by the Apostle in Heb. 6:1-2, "Not laying again the foundation of penance from dead works, and of faith towards God, of the doctrine of baptisms and the laying on of hands, ... ," where by the witness of Chrysostom, Theodoret, Theophylactus, and others, the Apostle understands by the laying on of hands *Confirmation*, which was given immediately after Baptism, and he teaches it is not lawful for a man who falls after Baptism and Confirmation to again return to Baptism and Confirmation. These are the foundations which are laid but once. *Secondly*, the same is clear from the eighth Council of Toledo (can. 7) where it is clearly said that chrism, once conferred, cannot be repeated, just as Holy Orders. Likewise, the Council of Tarragona, and from a decree of Gregory II cited by Gratian (dist. 5 *de consecration*, can. *Dictum est* and can. *De homine*). Add to that the Council of Florence (*Instruct. Arm.*) and the Council of Trent, sess. 7 can. 9. *Thirdly*, the same thing is clear from the Fathers. Cyprian, or whoever was the author of the sermon *On the Washing of Feet*, says, "The rules of the Church forbid Baptism to be repeated; no man renews Holy Orders once they have been given; no man anoints or consecrates again what has been anointed with sacred oil; no man repeals the laying on of hands or the ministry of priests, because

Chapter XI: The Effect of Confirmation

it would be a contumely against the Holy Spirit if what he sanctified were made void, or he would improve another sanctification which he once set in place and confirms." Augustine (*Contra Petil.* 2, 104) clearly teaches the Sacrament of Chrism once given even remains in the wicked and is never destroyed. It manifestly follows from this that it cannot be repeated. Rabanus teaches similar things (*de Instit. Clericorum* 1, 30) Amalarius (*de officiis Ecclesiasticis* 1, 7) and other more recent authors.

CHAPTER XII

On the Minister of this Sacrament

THE *fifth* controversy follows: Whether the minister of the Sacrament of Confirmation is the Bishop alone. The heretics, although they remove this rite from the number of the Sacraments, still, even if it were a Sacrament by any of their opinions, they deny its ministry pertains in any way to Bishops alone. John Wycliffe (*Trialogi* 4, 14) clearly denies it is the proper office of Bishops to confirm. Calvin holds the same thing (*Instit.* 4, 19 §10) as well as Chemnitz (*Exam.* 2 part. p. 324) and perhaps all others, especially since they scarcely acknowledge a difference between a Bishop and a priest, as we showed in the book *On Clergy*.

From Catholics, only Richard FitzRalph, the Bishop of Armagh (*Armenicarum Quaest.* 11, 4) supposed the office of Confirmation is common to Bishops and priests, and Thomas Waldens (*de Sacramentis* 2, 114) supposed that Wycliffe drew his heresy from FitzRalph, since he was a little older than Wycliffe, although they lived in the same time. All the rest teach in a common consensus, that the Bishop alone is the proper minister of this Sacrament.

Now there is a question among Catholics, whether a priest could at least confer this Sacrament by a dispensation. St. Bonaventure, Durandus, and Adrian (4, dist. 7) contend that it can in no way be consigned to priests, but St. Thomas (III q. 72, art. 11) and all of his disciples, as well as many other theologians commenting on 4, dist. 7, such as Richardus, Paludanus, Marsilius, and others, and all Canonists on can. 1, dist. 95, teach the contrary. What the later authors affirm is truer by far. Ambrose (in *Ephes.* 4) witnesses that in Egypt, priests confirm in the absence of Bishops, nor did he rebuke the use. Gregory (*Epist.* 3, 36) clearly permitted the priests of Sardinia to confirm in the absence of Bishops. Now, it seems that this citation of Gregory has been corrupted, perhaps by those who favor the contrary opinion, for he says he permits "... to anoint those who are going to be baptized," when he ought to say, "to anoint those who have been baptized." When this passage is compared with *Epistle* 9 from book 3, then the corruption will manifestly appear. Accordingly, in *Epistle* 26, he says he permitted what in *Epistle*. 9 he had forbidden. However, he had forbidden priests from anointing the baptized on the forehead. This is why even Gratian and St. Thomas cite this passage as it should be, not as it is now read in printed codices. Besides, the first Council of Arausicanus (can. 1 & 2) and Toledo (can. 20), as well as Martin of Braga (*Graecarum*

Chapter XII: The Minister of Confirmation

Synodorum, ch. 52) and Florence (*Instruct. Arm.*), hold the same thing. Lastly, the Council of Trent (sess. 7, can. 3 on Confirmation). Therefore, he says the *ordinary* minister is the Bishop, to show the same thing can be done *by extraordinary* power by a priest. Thus, the error of Chemnitz appears, who in his *Examination* (part. 2 p. 224) says the Council defined against St. Thomas and certain other doctors, nay more even against St. Gregory himself, that the Bishop alone is the minister of Confirmation.

But let us pass over all these things and prove Catholic truth from the clear testimony of Scripture. In Act. 8:14, Peter and John were sent to give the Holy Spirit by the laying on of hands to those whom Philip had baptized in Samaria. In Act. 19:6, the Apostle Paul himself gave the laying on of hands to those whom others had baptized. Certainly, it seems no reason can be given as to why the Apostles alone gave the laying on of hands; nay more, why they came for this purpose from one place to another except because this office properly pertains to the first Ecclesiastical degree, which is without controversy, Episcopal.

Wycliffe answers this that those whom Philip baptized perhaps were not legitimately baptized and therefore needed to be baptized again by the Apostles so as to receive the Holy Spirit.

But this answer is completely inept. Who would believe that Philip the deacon, after he had received the Holy Spirit, did not rightly baptize, and then, if they needed to be rebaptized, it was necessary for the Apostles to come from Jerusalem? Could they not show by letters, or send another man who would baptize them correctly? Lastly, why did only the Apostles give the laying on of hands, and not also baptize, if they were not duly baptized? Nor is it opposed that they were said to be baptized in the name of the Lord Jesus, and not in the name of the Trinity, for (as we showed above) Luke briefly described the rite of Baptism, meaning for the whole to be understood from a part.

Calvin responds (*loc. cit.*) that what the Apostles did cannot be attributed to Bishops, or certainly not to Bishops alone, for Bishops are not Apostles, but if they hold the place of the Apostles in regard to something, priests also hold the same place. Otherwise, it would not be lawful for priests, but only Bishops, to give communion under either species; for the Apostles alone did it in the Lord's Supper.

I respond: Bishops alone simply and absolutely succeed the Apostles. We must observe that all Ecclesiastical power is contained in Apostolic authority. First, the Apostles were Christians and members of the Church. *Secondly*, they were priests. *Thirdly*, the supreme priests. *Fourthly*, they were supreme not in one place, but in the whole world; for everywhere they could preach, baptize, ordain, impose laws, punish, etc. This last office was ordinary in Peter alone; in the others it was extraordinary and delegated, and for that reason, we see Peter alone succeeded in that supreme power over the whole world, not any other Apostle. The other three things were ordinary to all. This is why all Christians succeed the Apostles in some way, insofar as they were first Christians; and all priests succeed the Apostles in the same, insofar as they were first priests; and all Bishops succeed them insofar as they were first supreme priests. Nevertheless, they only succeed them simply, because they succeed in *their whole ordinary authority*, in which they alone can succeed. That is also clear from the praxis and testimony of the Saints, for if anyone would ask who succeeded James the Apostle everyone would answer the Bishop of Jerusalem. Who succeeded the Apostle John? The Bishop of Ephesus. This is why the Council of Neocaesarea (can. 13), Damasus (*Epist.* 4 *de Chorepiscopis*), Jerome (*Epist.* 88), Augustine (Ps. 44, on the verse *Your sons were born to you in place of their fathers*), and other Fathers affirm that Bishops succeed the Apostles.

Now, someone will say, "How do we know the Apostles gave the laying on of hands in Act. 8:14, as Bishops, and not as priests, or as Apostles through extraordinary power?" I answer, that it is certain not as priests, because Scripture never attributed this office to anyone but the Apostles themselves, although it attributes other offices such as preaching and baptizing to inferior ministers; that it was not as Apostles by extraordinary power is gathered from the fact that in Heb. 6:2 this laying on of hands is numbered with the rest of the ordinary rites of the Church; lastly, from the fact that this usage that Bishops give the laying on of hands to men that have been baptized always remained in the Church.

Secondly, the same truth is shown from Ecclesiastical tradition. Councils, Popes, and the Fathers cited in the first controversy teach in a common consensus that Bishops alone are properly ministers of this Sacrament, and they prove it from Acts chapter 8.

Thirdly, it is also proven by reason, for Confirmation is *completion and perfection of Baptism*; hence, it is fitting that it should be given by the primary minister, so in all other things the last form is impressed by the first agent. Besides, in Confirmation we are enrolled in the army of Christ, but it is proper for a general and commander to enroll a man in the army.

The arguments of Calvin and Chemnitz are answered without much difficulty. 1) The *first* argument of Calvin is that it is an error of the Donatists that the Sacrament depends upon the dignity of the minister. *I respond*: If it is a question of the *moral* dignity, it is true; if it is about *Ecclesiastical* dignity, it is very false. Otherwise, it would also be an error of the Donatists that priests alone administer the Lord's body, and according to Calvin, even Baptism.

2) Calvin's *second* argument: Priests succeed the Apostles, as is clear from the ministry of the Eucharist, which was consigned to the Apostles alone. *I respond*: The Apostles, in the Last Supper, were created priests, but not Bishops, for they became Bishops after the resurrection when it was said to them in John 20:21, "Behold I send you, ..." Therefore, priests succeed the Apostles in some way, but not in all, nor absolutely, as we said.

Chapter XII: The Minister of Confirmation

3) Calvin's *third* argument is that in 1 Tim. 4:14. Paul says, "Do not neglect the grace that is in you, which was given to you by prophecy, with the laying on of the hands of the priesthood." Ananias, in Act. 9:17, gave the laying on of hands to Paul, and still he was not a Bishop.

I respond: This is the same argument of Richard FitzRalph. In this passage of Scripture Paul does not treat on Confirmation, but on the *Ordination* of Timothy, and besides, by that term *presbyteri*, an assembly of priests is understood, i.e., *of Bishops*, as Chrysostom explains; many other bishops ordain one bishop, but only one confirms.

Now the argument from Ananias Calvin borrows from Wycliffe, just as he borrowed it from FitzRalph. I say Ananias gave the laying on of hands to Paul for this purpose, that he would receive a sign, as we read in the same place. For this reason, that laying on of hands was not confirmatory, but *curative*. This is why it was done *before* Baptism, not after when Confirmation should be done; nor did the Holy Spirit descend visibly at that time, rather they fell from his eyes like scales. Now, they will say, "Laying his hands upon him, he said, 'Brother Saul, the Lord Jesus has sent me, he that appeared to you in the way as you came; so you would receive your sight, and be filled with the Holy Spirit'." *I respond:* Ananias explained *the proximate and remote* end of his arrival at the same time, for the proximate end was the cure from blindness, the remote end perfect justification and the infusion of the Holy Spirit, which Paul obtained a little later through Baptism. This is why the vision of Paul was described first, whereby he foresaw what was going to happen, "And he saw a man approaching him, Ananias by name, and giving him the laying on of hands, so he would receive sight," and in Act. 22:13, where Paul himself relates this whole history, he says that he received nothing from Ananias except the warding off of his blindness and later Baptism. It is very probable that Paul received Confirmation immediately from God, like the rest of the Apostles, without a human laying on of hands.

4) The *fourth* argument: If it is by divine law that it is proper for Bishops to confirm, why is Gregory recorded to have conceded it to priests also? *I respond:* It is divine law that Bishops alone are the ordinary ministers of this Sacrament, but it does not follow from there that it could not also be fitting for priests *by an extraordinary concession*, just as also by divine law it is proper for Bishops to preach, and still priests also preach by their concession, and sometimes even deacons.

Certain Catholics urge: To confirm is either suited to a Bishop by the notion of order or by the notion of jurisdiction. If by the notion of order, it can in no way be conceded to those who do not have that order, as is clear from similar things, for no dispensation can be given so that a deacon would consecrate the Eucharist. If by the notion of jurisdiction, then a Bishop that has not been consecrated cannot confirm, because he has priestly ordination and Episcopal jurisdiction.

I respond: To confirm is an act of order, and that order is also in the priesthood, at least inchoate and imperfect. We must observe that the Episcopal character, whether it is something other than the priestly character or it is the same thing but more extensive and greater, is an *absolute, perfect, and independent* power to confer the Sacraments of Confirmation and Order, and therefore, not only can a Bishop, without any other dispensation, confirm and ordain, but he also cannot be impeded by any higher power, so that he really would confer these Sacraments if he willed, although he would sin if he did it while the Supreme Pontiff forbade. The priestly character, however, is certainly an absolute, perfect, and independent power, whereby he confers the Sacrament of Baptism and the Eucharist; however, it is an inchoate, imperfect power, dependent upon the will of a superior *in regard to the Sacrament of Confirmation*. This is why, unless that power were perfected by the dispensation of a superior, a priest does nothing in giving Confirmation, but if it were to be perfected, then he will confirm by his own character. That will seem no less marvelous if we will reflect upon the fact that the character is not some physical potency which works something physical (then it would be difficult to understand how it could be perfected through a Pontifical dispensation), rather it is a sign of a certain divine arrangement whereby God engages to produce the sacramental effect with the one who has the character, and not with others; one character is easily understood to be a sign of an absolute arrangement, another is a sign of a conditional arrangement. Now, that is enough on these matters.

5) The *fifth* argument is of Chemnitz (*loc. cit.*): Scripture does not know of a difference between a Bishop and a priest. *I respond:* Scripture does indeed know, but Chemnitz does not know the Scripture. In 1 Tim. 5:19, when it is said, "Do not receive an accusation against a priest unless it has two or three witnesses," very clearly it places a distinction between Bishop and priest as great as there is between a prince and his subject. For this reason, the followers of Aërius were called heretics, because they denied this distinction (Epiphanius, *Panarion*, haer. 75, and Augustine *hares.* 53).

6) The *sixth* argument is of the same Chemnitz. Jerome, in his *Dialogue against the Luciferians*, says it is because of the honor shown to the priesthood that Bishops alone would impose hands, not because of the necessity of law.

I respond: This passage especially works in our favor. Jerome does not deny that it is lawful for Bishops alone to give Confirmation after Baptism. He also affirms this, and later proves this very thing, from the example of the Apostles, who were sent into Samaria so that they would confirm those whom Philip baptized. Besides, he gives the reasoning why the Lord willed it that this be proper to Bishops, because the honor of the priesthood required it. A little later he explains the same thing more, that it is necessary in each Church that there be one Bishop, so that there will not

Chapter XII: The Minister of Confirmation

be many equals and great schisms will not come about. So, the Lord willed that certain things would be proper to Bishops, and from there, it appears they are more eminent than the rest. That, however, (*not on account of the necessity of law*) is not related to a law to administer Confirmation, but to the law *to obtain salvation*, for Jerome shows it is not necessary for salvation absolutely for someone to be confirmed by a Bishop, since one can also be saved by Baptism alone without Confirmation. Wherefore, he immediately adds, explaining what he had said, "It is not on account of the necessity of law, otherwise those who die in their bonds, being baptized only by priests or deacons, and not visited by Bishops, would have to weep." If this isn't satisfactory, it can also be said that Jerome spoke about a law which is taken *from the nature of the thing*, so the sense would be that it is attributed to Bishops alone, not on account of the necessity of law, i.e., not because the nature of the thing necessarily requires it, as if it could not be done otherwise, but because the Lord willed in this matter to honor the Episcopal dignity.

7) The *seventh* argument. Many years ago, almost no Bishops in Germany gave Confirmation, but certain suffragans who were counterfeit bishops, and rather more mannequins of Bishops than Bishops.

I respond: Suffragans are true Bishops because they have both ordination and jurisdiction, although they lack the possession of their own Church. This is why they are not able to confirm outside their Church on their own authority; nevertheless, they can if they are invited by the Bishop of a place.

CHAPTER XIII

On the Ceremonies of Confirmation

THE ceremonies in this Sacrament are twofold. First, many ceremonies are applied in the consecration of Chrism on Maundy Thursday. Then, certain ones are also applied in the very conferral of this Sacrament.

Firstly, to begin with the first class, all the authors who write on the divine offices for Maundy Thursday treat on the rite of consecration, namely Alcuin, Amalarius, Rabanus, Rupert, and others.

Four ceremonies are done. Firstly, the blessings of the oil and balsam through prayers; this cannot be rebuked, since the Apostle, in 1 Tim. 4:5, says everything is sanctified by the word of God, and prayer.

Secondly, the blessings of oil and balsam are also done by the sign of the cross, and not even this can be rebuked, since without this sign nothing can be consecrated, as nearly all the Fathers witness, and especially Chrysostom (*Homil.* 55 *in Matt.*, and in his book *That Christ is God*), as well as Augustine in *Tractates on John* (tr. 118) and *Sermon* 181 (*de Tempore*, ch. 3).

Thirdly, the bishop breathes [on it] as often as he opens the vessel of chrism. This seems ridiculous and magical to the heretics, for Chemnitz clearly writes it (*loc. cit.* p. 285) and Calvin looks to this ceremony when he says, "oil merely polluted with your fetid breath" (*Instit.* 4, 19 §10). Nevertheless, it is very ancient, and the cited authors, such as Amalarius and others, mention it; besides, it is taken from the example of the Lord, who breathed upon the Apostles in John 20:22 to show by that ceremony that the Holy Spirit descends upon them. Rightly, when the Church means to show the descent of the Holy Spirit to sanctify something, what better sign could it use than that which Christ himself willed to use to signify the same thing? Now, if this ceremony is magical, we will make Christ a teacher of magic, which is impious and blasphemous. No ceremony can be called magical unless a miraculous effect from the devil were hoped for, with whom magicians enter into contract. We, however, do not look to any effect from the devil, rather from *God* alone, from whom we seek it through prayer, as we said above.

The *fourth* ceremony is that chrism that has already been consecrated is greeted by the Bishop and priests in these words, "Hail O holy Chrism." Our adversaries call this ceremony idolatrous, such as Tilman Hesch (*The Errors of the Papists*, tit. 22 n. 26). "Chrism," he says, "must not be adored; accordingly they command these words to be said: Hail Holy Chrism." Chemnitz (p. 289) and Calvin (*loc. cit.* §21) also find fault with this ceremony.

Chapter XIII: The Ceremonies of Confirmation

Yet, they ineptly compare this to idolatry, since it is one thing to greet, and another to worship; otherwise, the Lord also, in Matt. 28:9, when he said to the women, "Hail!" would be said to have worshiped them. Reverence is shown to consecrated chrism because it is a sacred thing and has the power to be an instrument of God to sanctify, but it is not worshipped as God; otherwise, even the Jews would have been idolatrous who adored the wooden ark of the Lord and were advised to do so by the prophet, "Adore his footstool, because it is holy" (Ps. 98 [99]:5). Someone will say that it seems ridiculous to greet an inanimate thing. *I respond:* It is a very customary behavior to greet even inanimate things as a sign of congratulations, as if they were alive and thought. Nazianzen (*Orat. to 150 Fathers*) acted in this way when he abdicated from the Episcopate; he says goodbye to his seat, the Church, the psalmody, and other things of this kind. Jerome, in his *Epistle on the Death of Paula*, describes the salutation which Bl. Paula gave to Bethlehem when she first saw it. Aeneas, in Virgil in book 7, greeted Italy when he first saw it. There are almost infinite examples of this kind.

Moreover, in Confirmation itself, apart from the essential ceremony of anointing and making the sign of the cross on the forehead, eight other ceremonies are applied. The *first* is a sponsor is present, just as in Baptism, who offers the confirmand to the Bishop. This ceremony is very ancient, as is clear from the decrees of ancient Popes and Councils, which are cited by Gratian (30 qu. 1, can. *Si quis* and can. *De His*; as well as q. 4, can. *Si Quis ex Uno* and *de consec.* dist. 4, can. *In Catechismo*).

The *second* is that different prayers are said over the confirmands, and indeed with the laying on of hands; our adversaries do not find fault with that rite alone.

The *third*, that peace be given to the man who is confirmed by the Bishop, in a sign of the reception of the grace of the Holy Spirit, whose effect is peace.

Fourth, that the Bishop would gently strike the confirmed man with his hand, so he would understand he must stand against ignominy and blows that he receives for Christ, and to be armed especially with patience.

Fifth, a fascia is bound on his forehead, but so the chrism would not easily run down, and to signify that the grace he has received must be diligently preserved, according to that of 1 John 2:27, "The anointing which you have received from him shall remain in you." In this matter the custom of the Church must be preserved; in some places the fascia is preserved for seven days, others for three, others it is immediately washed off and the chrism is dried by the priests, so that they do not need the fascia.

Sixth, that they would not wash their head or forehead for seven days. Hugh calls this ceremony to mind (*de Sacramentis*, 2, p. 7, c. 6). Tertullian (*de Baptismo*) writes that from the day of Baptism for the whole week Christians customarily do not bathe, which they not only did on account of Baptism, but also, perhaps especially, on account of the Chrism, which was usually given on the same day.

The *seventh*, that Confirmation was given on the Saturday of Easter and Pentecost because clearly Baptism should be given on those days, as we said above. Still, in this time, because it often happens that these Sacraments are not given together, it is a praiseworthy custom of many Bishops that on the feasts of Pentecost they would confirm in particular, because namely, in that feast the first Confirmation was given by God upon the holy Apostles.

The *eighth*, that those who are to give and receive Confirmation would be fasting. There are canons of Councils extant on this matter, cited by Gratian (*de consecrate.* dist. 5, can. *Ut Jejuni*, and can. *Ut Episcopi*).

Chemnitz adds to all these (p. 323) that it is a marvel why the Papists prefer these ceremonies to the examination of boys, the profession of faith, and the exhortation, and asks why we have tragically rejected all of these things, nor can we suffer any wish for betterment. However, all these are idle words, for we reject none of these, but would have it that all are done *in the proper place and time*; nor do we suffer a Sacrament instituted by Christ and ceremonies handed down to us by the Fathers to be ripped away from us under the pretext of an examination of youths. Now, we have said enough on the Sacrament of Confirmation.

END OF THE BOOKS ON BAPTISM AND CONFIRMATION

AD HONOREM DEI

The De Controversiis of

St. Robert Bellarmine

Tomus I: On the Word of God, & On Christ

Tomus II: On the Roman Pontiff*

Tomus III: On the Church vol. 1: On Councils, the Church Militant, and the Marks fo the Church*

Tomus IV On the Church vol. 2: On Clergy, Monks and Laity

Tomus V: On the Church Suffering, and Triumphant*

Tomus VI: On the Sacraments in General, Baptism, and Confirmation*

Tomus VII: On the Holy Eucharist and the Holy Sacrifice of the Mass

Tomus VIII: On Penance and Indulgences

Tomus IX: On Extreme Unction, Order, and Matrimony

Tomus X: On Original Sin and Grace

Tomus XI: On Justification, and On Good Works

*= Currently available from Mediatrix Press

www.ingramcontent.com/pod-product-compliance
Lightning Source LLC
Chambersburg PA
CBHW021147230426
43667CB00006B/292